D1732151

Sex and the Ancient City

Trends in Classics – Supplementary Volumes

Edited by
Franco Montanari and Antonios Rengakos

Volume 126

Sex and the Ancient City

Sex and Sexual Practices in Greco-Roman Antiquity

Edited by
Andreas Serafim, George Kazantzidis and
Kyriakos Demetriou

DE GRUYTER

ISBN 978-3-11-069577-9
e-ISBN (PDF) 978-3-11-069579-3
e-ISBN (EPUB) 978-3-11-069588-5
ISSN 1868-4785

Library of Congress Control Number: 2022932188

Bibliographic information published by the Deutsche Nationalbibliothek
The Deutsche Nationalbibliothek lists this publication in the Deutsche Nationalbibliografie;
detailed bibliographic data are available on the Internet at http://dnb.dnb.de.

© 2022 Walter de Gruyter GmbH, Berlin/Boston
Editorial Office: Alessia Ferreccio and Katerina Zianna
Logo: Christopher Schneider, Laufen
Printing and binding: CPI books GmbH, Leck

www.degruyter.com

Acknowledgements

The editors would like to acknowledge a number of individuals and institutions whose help and support have been invaluable in the conception and completion of this volume. We would like to thank the two editors of Trends in Classics at De Gruyter, Professors Antonios Rengakos (Aristotle University of Thessaloniki/ Member of the Academy of Athens) and Franco Montanari (University of Genova), for having believed in the significance of this volume and supported its preparation and publication wholeheartedly.

Andreas Serafim would like to thank the Research Centre for Greek and Latin Literature of the Academy of Athens for providing excellent research facilities that make the completion of this volume possible; and Millie Gall for reading and commenting on the Introduction and other chapters within the volume. The Department of Social and Political Science at the University of Cyprus is also to be thanked for generously covering the expenses of the conference "Sex and the Ancient City: Aspects of Sexual Intercourse in Greco-Roman Antiquity" (11–13 June 2019), which allowed the idea of this volume to germinate and grow.

Above all, the editors would like to thank the contributors: we have been fortunate to work alongside, share the knowledge and admire the professionalism of the contributors from the initial exchange of ideas to the preparation of the final full manuscript of the volume. We are sure that they will forgive us for having bombarded them with countless questions and requests which placed a huge demand on their time. The publication of the volume at hand reimburses us all for our labours.

Abbreviations throughout this volume follow those in *L'Année philologique* or the *Oxford Classical Dictionary*. A certain level of formatting standardisation has been imposed to ensure consistency across the volume, but individual stylistic distinctiveness has been respected. The volume is intended for the specialist scholars and graduate students of gender/sex studies both within the confines of Classics and beyond. All long quotations of Greek and Latin are accompanied by English translation.

Andreas Serafim, George Kazantzidis and Kyriakos Demetriou
Athens, Patras and Nicosia, February 2022

https://doi.org/10.1515/9783110695793-202

Contents

Part I: Aspects of Homoeroticism

Part II: Sex and Medicine

Part III: The Use and Abuse of Sex Objects

Part IV: Sexual Liminality

Part V: Sex and Disgust

Part VI: The Scripts of Sexuality: Drama, Novel, Papyri and Later Texts

List of Figures

https://doi.org/10.1515/9783110695793-204

Andreas Serafim, George Kazantzidis and Kyriakos Demetriou
Sex, Sexuality, Sexual Intercourse and Gender: The Terms and Contexts of the Volume

1 What this volume is about: Terms, contexts and topics

Much time has passed since scholars were afraid that their papers and lectures about, or pedagogical discussions of, aspects of ancient Greek and Roman sexuality could be seen as inappropriate or even offensive. Nowadays, a Cambridge Dean, unlike the one mentioned in E.M. Forster's novel, *Maurice*, would never ask a student to omit "a reference to the unspeakable vice of the Greeks", i.e. pederasty.[1] Despite the study of gender and sexuality in the classical world being a relatively new field of enquiry, which has really only developed over the last thirty-five years, there is a booming interdisciplinary bibliography discussing as many as possible of the myriad particulars of ancient Greek and Roman sexuality and gender. What is still relatively understudied in classical scholarship, a battleground where many claims are still contested, is sex and sexual practices themselves. This volume aims to revisit, further explore and, through updated interdisciplinary approaches, shed more light on the textual and non-textual sources that help us reconstruct a clearer, more coherent and precise overarching picture of sex and all the practices related to it in Greco-Roman antiquity.

Let us start with an attempt to explain the use, in this volume, of terminology. There is a term in the subtitle of the volume which is of fundamental importance for marking the purposes and (the limits of) the content of the present book, which should be given a semantic clarification: *sexuality*. Sexuality remains a contested notion that cannot be unanimously defined. M. Foucault, D. Halperin and J. Butler, among other cultural constructionists, point out that it is a modern concept, being the product of acculturation that differs from time to time and from culture to culture, and that any theory about its application in the ancient world is permeated by modern sensibilities.[2] For Halperin, sexuality is a cultural construction and an object of cultural interpretation that is attached to specific

---

1 See also: Halperin 1990, 1.
2 Foucault 1978; Halperin 1990, 5; Butler 1999, 2004.

https://doi.org/10.1515/9783110695793-001

cultural institutions and contexts — this is what he calls *cultural poetics*: "the process whereby the society and its subgroups construct widely shared meanings — behavioural conventions, social distinctions, conceptual schemes, aesthetic values, religious attitudes, moral codes, gender roles and paradigms of sexual excitement. These meanings are jointly produced, distributed, enforced and subverted by human communities".[3] A similar idea appears in M. Foucault's study, *History of Sexuality*: sexuality is seen as a cultural construction, which is covered by multiple layers of historical and cultural specificity that are generated by the conventions, the rules and practices of specific communities in human history.[4] This specificity reminds us of the principles of the theory of New Institutionalism: different institutions have different *logics of appropriateness*. This means that "there are structures of meaning, embedded in identities and belongings: common purposes and accounts that give direction and meaning to behaviour, and explain, justify and legitimate behavioural codes".[5] The meaning of sexuality, in other words, is different from one time or cultural context to another.

Despite this profound cultural relativism, and perhaps also anachronism, in defining notions that relate to sexuality and its complex interrelation with two other notions, *sex* and *gender*,[6] the insights that the chapters of this volume bring to the fore allow us to define *sexuality* as an individual's *habitus*: both the physical (i.e. biological, bodily and erogenous) and cognitive/emotional traits or behaviours, which are exercised within, and are influenced by, a well-defined sociopolitical, legal, religious and moral — in broader terms, cultural — context. Sexuality as *habitus* is a performative act: it is not something one *is*, but rather something one *does* through sexual actions, desires, fantasies, fetishes and other cognitive behaviours (i.e. both verbal and non-verbal means of communicating what people, or groups of people, believe, think of or desire about sexual practices) in particular cultural contexts.

---

3 Halperin 1990, 4. On arguments for the opposite position, i.e. that the use of the terms *sex*, *sexuality* and *gender* to understand and theorise about the Greek and Roman worlds is not anachronistic: Holmes 2012, 6–11; Foxhall 2013, 3–4; Masterson, Rabinowitz and Robson 2015, 1–2.
4 Foucault 1985.
5 March and Olsen 2005, 4. Further on New Institutionalism: Merton 1938, 672–682; Simon 1965; Pitkin 1967; Meyer and Rowan 1977; Kratochwil 1984, 695–708; Apter 1991, 463–481; Weaver and Rockman 1993; March and Olsen 1995; Egeberg 2003.
6 Selected readings on sex, sexuality and gender include: de Beauvoir 1973; Manniche 1987; Dover 1989; Butler 1990, 1993; Laqueur 1990; Cohen 1991; Zeitlin 1996; Fausto-Sterling 2000; Brisson 2002; Skinner 2005; Johnson and Ryan 2005; Graves-Brown 2008; Blanshard 2010, xii; Holmes 2012; Hubbard 2014; Masterson, Rabinowitz and Robson 2015, 1–12.

This approach to sexuality points to the theories of S. de Beauvoir and J. Butler. The former "rejects the 'mute facticity' of bodies and, in *The Second Sex*, argues that a woman (and, by extension, any gender) is the result of culturally enforced actions and not of biological status ('one is not born, but, rather, *becomes a woman*'). The latter, likewise, rejects the idea that body pre-exists or is outside the gendered self. A central concept of Butler's theory is that specific aspects of self are constructed through repetitive performance acts".[7] Seen from this angle, sexuality is an overarching term that includes both *sex* and *gender*. These two notions, protean in meaning and complicated historically, have left the scholarly community unable to provide a unanimous definition or factual description. The traditional perspective is that *sex* refers to "the erogenous capacities and genital functions of the human body", as Halperin, Winkler and Zeitlin define *sex* in their volume *Before Sexuality*,[8] while *gender* is labelled as being the cultural construction of sexes, self and identity.[9] Sexuality, as used in this volume, has an overarching semantic breadth, since it encompasses the dimensions of both sex and gender. To put it in a different way, sexuality in this volume is seen as being made of both sexually existentialist views, i.e. those about the (sexual) existence of individuals,[10] and the corporeality of *sexual practices*, the physical acts of sexual intercourse.

The chapters of this volume aim to examine a variety of topics that have to do with that dual semantic meaning of sexuality, paying attention, in other words, both to the acts and practices of sexual intercourse and to the context that affects, determines, relates and gives meaning to them, i.e. legal, social, political, religious, medical, cultural/moral and interdisciplinary (e.g. emotional, performative, anthropological, psychological). Sexual practices and the contexts in which they appear are examined, as they are manifested in Greco-Roman *textual*

---

7 Serafim 2017, 4. See de Beauvoir 1973, 301; Butler 1986, 35–49; 1990, 129. Also: West and Zimmerman 1987, 126. For Beauvoir and Butler, there are actually three notions: *sex* as a biological factor of determining human self and identity; *sex category*, which is all the markers that denote biology; and *gender*, which refers to the variety of culturally constructed activities that are carried out or performed by individuals.

8 Halperin, Winkler and Zeitlin 1990, 3.

9 On the traditional distinction between sex and gender: Comfort 1963; Oakley 1972.

10 The existential character that we suggest sexuality has is also evident in the succinct description by Halperin, Winkler and Zeitlin 1990, 5–6: "sexuality represents the most intimate feature of an individual, that dimension of the personality which it takes longest to fathom and which, when finally known, reveals the truth about much of the rest... Sexuality is thought to provide a key to unlocking the mysteries of the self, even for *my* self: that is, I can explore and discover what my sexuality is".

and *non-textual* sources (i.e. iconography, epigraphy, cultural artefacts etc.). The combination of the two enables us to better understand the all-inclusive notion of sexuality, as examined in this volume.

A caveat is necessary at this point: the chapters included in this volume are primarily concerned with sexuality, not with issues of gender, though gender is touched upon in several chapters where possible, as when the authors have to discuss the difference between (the theories of) naturally-given biological sexes and the cultural construction of gender roles. Another methodological remark is useful: Greece and Rome are not dealt with separately. Rather, each of the thematic units of this volume includes chapters that cover both cultures, as far as the subject matter allows, aiming at delineating continuities and differences and thereby offering valuable opportunities for comparison between Greek and Roman perspectives, though the space given to Greece and Rome respectively is unequal: only six chapters are devoted to the exploration of the sexual practices of Romans.

The value of this volume lies in two distinctive features. The first is the interdisciplinary approach to topics that are (largely) understudied in classical scholarship on ancient Greek and Roman sexualities. A synergy between the classical scholarship on sexuality in antiquity and modern interdisciplinary fields of research, ranging from psychology and cognitive sciences to performance studies, modern sex/gender theories and neuroscience is used as a methodological tool for shedding light on sexual practices in antiquity. Some of the chapters of this volume draw on and use a range of interdisciplinary perspectives and theories to approach ancient sexual practices. The chapter of Andreas Serafim, "Making the Body Speak: The (Homo)Sexual Dimensions of Sneezing in Ancient Greek Literature", for example, explores how sneezing is presented in ancient texts as denoting an individual's *kinaidic*, pathetic homosexual nature and effeminacy — a topic that draws on a variety of interdisciplinary theories, such as performance and non-verbal communication, social psychology and cognitive neurophysiology. The second distinctive feature of this volume is that it draws both on textual and non-textual sources to reconstruct a more accurate picture of the bodily sexual practices in ancient Greece and Rome. Chapters such as the one by Bartłomiej Bednarek, entitled "The Iconography of Soft Pornography: Allusions to Erotic Foreplay in Greek Vase Painting", focus on the examination of non-textual sources, such as Greek vase paintings, to enhance our knowledge and understanding of intriguing and largely under-studied topics, as the sexual dimension of the use of chairs and stool is.

This updated approach to sexuality and sexual practices in the ancient Greek and Roman world has the potential to enhance our knowledge and understanding not only of matters that are related to sex *per se*, but also of the cultural workings in antiquity, i.e. how the beliefs of the ancients about sexuality connect with, and are being interpreted through the lens of, life within the civic and cultural communities of the past. Just as an individual's behaviour used to be judged in the light of civic ideals, arguments, thoughts and actions, as they are described in texts, so too was his/her sexual behaviour. The sexual use (or even abuse) of one's body is considered an expression of nature, infallible as it is, in the sense that it cannot be (fully or for long) manipulated to become a means of moral and behavioural disguise and deception (cf. *Book of Physiognomy* 74 B38).[11] This is crucial in determining the qualities, virtues and personality traits of the ideal citizen, which are perfectly encapsulated in the ideal of καλὸς κἀγαθός, "the beautiful and good" man (or, generally, individual). It has been argued, for example, that the references, in Demosthenes 18.259–260, to the Dionysian/ Bacchic ecstatic dancing moves of Aeschines, point not only to his sexual (im)morality, but also prominently to his low economic status (as he was notoriously accused of carrying out menial jobs) and his foreign roots.[12]

In elucidating the features, the functions and the cultural importance of sexuality and sexual practices in the intercultural context of ancient Greek and Roman worlds, this volume aspires to establish a framework within which the ancient textual and non-textual sources might be further explored. The insights taken from the contributions to this volume will attract the attention and research interest not only of classicists, but also of scholars in the disciplines of psychology, anthropology, sociology, communication, performance, sex/gender studies and body culture studies, contributing to the purpose of these disciplines to understand the world, including that of the past. The intercultural dimension of this (and any) discussion about sexuality and sexual practices in past textual or non-textual sources is a challenging research inquiry that should be undertaken be-

---

11 In the *Book of Physiognomy* 74 (B38), two types of movements of movements are mention, the *natural* and the *affected* (i.e. the movements or mannerisms that people use to fulfill specific purposes). One of these purposes is disguise; for, there are "those who are certainly deviants, but who try to remove suspicion from themselves by striving to assume a manly appearance; for they imitate the gait of a young man and strengthen themselves with a certain stiffness and strain their eyes and voice and straighten their whole body, but they are easily detected when their true nature wins through and exposes them; for they often lower their neck and voice and relax their hands [...] Often they are detected when yawning too".

12 See Serafim 2019, 233–253.

cause it significantly enhances our knowledge and understanding of cultural systems. This volume does not aim, and cannot credibly pretend, to be the last word in the ever-growing field of sex/gender studies in the classical Greek and Roman world. It does not even aspire to provide a comprehensive survey of every bodily and biological aspect of sexual practices. It can only display some new sketches of topics which have the potential to enhance our knowledge and understanding of sexuality in antiquity, and which may ignite interest for further research.

2 Current scholarly perspectives and approaches

Continuing research, (non-)textual interpretations and a broad analytical focus emphasising socio-political, interpersonal and cultural approaches have shed welcome light on sexuality and sexual practices in the ancient Greco-Roman world. Two memorable books started the trend: *Sexual Life in Ancient Greece* (1932) by Paul Brandt (hidden behind the pseudonym "Hans Licht"), which, examining literary, historical and artistic evidence, presents the first full picture of several matters of sexuality and gender in ancient Greece (including details about prostitution, homosexuality and the sexual position of women in Greek life); and Michel Foucault's *The Use of Pleasure: The History of Sexuality*, which delineated the approaches to (ancient) sexuality in the mid-1980s. Since then issues revolving around, and relating to, (broadly defined) sexuality in antiquity have been among the most widely discussed topics in classical scholarship.[13] Much work has been done on homosexuality (e.g. Kenneth Dover: *Greek Homosexuality*; David Halperin: *One Hundred Years of Homosexuality*; James Davidson: *The Greeks and Greek Love*);[14] pederasty (Thomas K. Hubbard: *Greek Love Reconsidered*; Anthony Lear and Eva Cantarella: *Images of Ancient Greek Pederasty*);[15] male and female physiques, bodies and garbs (Mireille M. Lee: *Body, Dress and Identity*; Lloyd Llewellyn-Jones and Glenys Davies: *Greek and Roman Dress from A to Z*); Eros and the erotic in myth and literature, with emphasis on the erotic as an emotion (Ed

---

13 On a comprehensive survey of classical scholarship on sexuality, starting from the works of Fredrich-Karl Forberg on Latin erotic poets and the hermaphrodites and discussing scholarship until the time of Jeffrey Henderson, Kenneth Dover and Claude Calame: Halperin, Winkler and Zeitlin 1990, 7–20.
14 Also: Sergent 1986, 1986a; Dover 1989; Davidson 1997, 2001, 2007; Hubbard 1998, 2000; Rabinowitz and Auanger 2002; Cantarella 2002; Verstraete and Provencal 2005.
15 Also: Shapiro 1981, 2000; Percy 1996; Dodd 2000; Cartledge 2001; Konstan 2002; Scanlon 2005; Laes 2010; Lear 2011, 2014, 2015; Lear and Cantarella 2008; Shapiro 2015.

Sanders, Chiara Thumiger, Chris Carey and Nick Lowe: *Erōs in Ancient Greece*); adultery (Edward Cohen: *Law, Sexuality and Society*), pornography (Amy Richlin: *Pornography and Representation in Greece and Rome*); and prostitution (Christopher Faraone and Laura McClure: *Prostitutes and Courtesans in the Ancient World*; Konstantinos Kapparis: *Prostitution in the Ancient Greek World*), to name a few, among other important studies.

Scholarly works on the history of sexuality in the diversified cultural contexts of antiquity, such as Halperin's *Before Sexuality*, James Robson's *Sex and Sexuality in Classical Athens*, the *Companion to Greek and Roman Sexualities* edited by Hubbard, and *Sex in Antiquity: Exploring Gender and Sexuality in the Ancient World* edited by Mark Masterson, Nancy Sorkin Rabinowitz and James Robson, also offer insights on sexuality and gender. Works that explore the cultural context in which ancient sexualities were manifested are also important in shedding light not only on the sexual life of the ancients, but also on the social organisation and the cultural patterns of ancient communities. Some insights can be taken from the few mentions we can make here: on women (Sarah Pomeroy: *Goddesses, Whores, Wives, and Slaves: Women in Classical Antiquity*; Helene Foley: *Reflections of Women in Antiquity*; Nancy Sorkin Rabinowitz and Amy Richlin: *Feminist Theory and the Classics*); on power and identity construction (Lin Foxhall and John Salmon: *When Men Were Men: Masculinity, Power and Identity in Classical Antiquity*; and more recently, "Rhetorical Masculinity in *Stasis*: Hyper-andreia and Patriotism in Thucydides' *Histories* and Plato's *Gorgias*" by Jessica Evans, in Sophia Papaioannou, Andreas Serafim and Kyriakos Demetriou: *The Ancient Art of Persuasion across Genres and Topics*).

Paul Chrystal in his book, *In Bed with the Romans: A Brief History of Sex in Ancient Rome*, offers invaluable information about sexual practices such as cross-dressing, transsexualism, same-sex marriage, orgies, rape and bad language. But, as this extremely selective and condensed overview of the most fundamental trends in the study of ancient sexuality (and gender) indicates, there remains scope for further research on sexual practices. The time has come for a comprehensive study of this subject throughout Greek and Roman texts, contexts and visual evidence, which synthesises the work that has been done, teases out seminal topics which relate to sexuality and which have remained (largely or vastly) under-researched, and outlines promising new directions for future scholarship.

3 The composition of the volume

This volume's parts are six in number, either revisiting topics that are still contentious and discussing them from an interdisciplinary perspective, or presenting new ideas and perspectives on sexual practices. The titles of the sections are the following: Part I. Aspects of Homoeroticism; Part II. Sex and Medicine; Part III. The Use and Abuse of Sex Objects; Part IV. Sexual Liminality; Part V. Sex and Disgust; and finally, Part VI. The Scripts of Sexuality: Drama, Novel, Papyri and Later Texts. Given the nature of this and any other multi-authored volume, consisting of several chapters from varied literary traditions (here ancient Greek and Latin), historical and cultural phases in human history, and a large pool of topics, the analysis of sexuality is unavoidably fragmentary. We hope, however, that taken as a whole both within the immediate context of each one of the six sections and within the wider context of the volume itself, these chapters carry out the three aims which are described in the last paragraph of the previous section: to synthesise current scholarly perspectives, to enhance scholarly knowledge by discussing understudied topics and, finally, to open up new directions in the scholarly discussion about (broadly defined) sexuality.

Part I, *Aspects of Homoeroticism*, consists of five chapters, the first of which, "Dover's 'Pseudo-sexuality' and the Athenian Laws on Male Prostitutes in Politics", by Konstantinos Kapparis, discusses the context and rationale behind the introduction of the *hetairēsis* and *dokimasia rhētorōn* (or *epangelia*) laws, as cited by Demosthenes and Aeschines. Kapparis focuses his attention on two laws, which, according to contemporary sources, were introduced to safeguard the democratic constitution. He compares the commentary on these laws in contemporary authors with their modern interpretations, as expressions of a moralistic attempt to rein in the desires of Athenian men towards each other, and he suggests that the wild speculation about these laws and their astounding misinterpretation in modern literature are not simply due to misunderstanding, but are a deliberate distortion of the historical truth for reasons and objectives which have to do with modern sexual identity politics. Kapparis argues that these laws were introduced as an exaggerated reaction to fears that low-life politicians, eloquent but shameless and corrupt, who had not hesitated to sell their own bodies for profit, would infect the institutions of democracy, damage public life, function as a bad influence on the people, and ultimately undermine and destroy the democratic constitution from within.

The second chapter, entitled "Group Sex, Exhibitionism/Voyeurism and Male Homosociality", is authored by Thomas K. Hubbard. One of the striking features of Greek erotic vase painting is its tendency to show intimate love-making, whether of a same-sex or heterosexual nature, occurring in public spaces in full view of others who are engaged in similar acts or have some interest in what is happening. Recreational sex, aimed only at pleasure, not reproduction or pedagogy, is represented as a pre-eminently social activity which men and youths enjoyed in the company of other men and youths. Whether two men are enjoying a single woman together or one is just watching, the common thread through all the representations studied here is the centrality of masculine spectatorship and performance to the erotic imagination of a culture familiar with athletic display of nude bodies. The female prostitutes involved are of low status and no importance to the men, whose valued relationship is "homosociality" with each other.

In the third chapter of the first part of the volume, "Making the Body Speak: The (Homo)Sexual Dimensions of Sneezing in Ancient Greek Literature", Andreas Serafim, using ancient treatises, especially those on physiognomy where information about bodily stature and physical mannerisms is given, and modern interdisciplinary theories that mostly draw on social psychology, cognitive neurophysiology and performance, with a particular interest in non-verbal communication, aims to show how and why sneezing is presented as denoting the homosexual nature of individuals, even if they try to hide it behind a strong physique or specific patterns of behaviour. It is argued that the non-verbal performance, i.e. the sound produced by sneezing and involuntary movements that may have accompanied it, seems to be the reason for the physiognomist's recognition of a *kinaidos*.

In the fourth chapter, "Fell in Love with an Anus: Sexual Fantasies for Young Male Bodies and the Pederastic Gaze in Rhianus' *Epigrams*", Manolis Spanakis aims to give a fresh reconsideration of Rhianus' epigrams, examining fantasy for young male bodies. The narrator's eternal pursuit for sexual desire invites us to think about the existence of unfulfilled *pathos* in the Cretan poet's narrative. The thematic focus of this chapter is on two motifs in Rhianus' homoerotic epigrams: that the Graces bestow divine beauty and *charis* upon pubescent male bodies and adorn them with flowers; and that the allegorical use of hunting is demonstrated as an amatory game between the *erastēs* and the *erōmenos*.

The fifth and last chapter of Part I, "Silencing Female Intimacies: Sexual Practices, Silence and Cultural Assumptions in Lucian, *Dial. Meretr.* 5", by Andreas Fountoulakis, aims to explore the ways female homosexuality is thematically integrated in Lucian's fifth *Dialogue of the Courtesans*, a text that focuses on the sexual adventures of a hetaera called Leaina with another woman called Megilla and her female partner Demonassa. Despite its theme, the relevant details are not fully revealed as the narrative is articulated through an interplay of speech and silence. Drawing on texts such as Herondas' mimiambs or the *Dream Analysis* of Artemidorus, this chapter seeks to specify the sexual practices alluded to by Leaina and the reasons why she avoids getting more specific about them. Her references and the reasons for her silence are related to broader assumptions and moral standards concerning gender and sexuality which were prevalent in Greek society and culture. This interplay of speech and silence is one of Lucian's narrative strategies to evoke cultural assumptions of a Greek past, and yet undermines by means of insinuation the values upon which that past was based. Issues of gender and sexuality thus become parts of a wider discourse focused on a process of cultural formation and change prevalent in Lucian's cultural milieu.

Part II focuses on the examination of aspects of sexuality that relate to ancient medicine — thus the title *Sex and Medicine*. The first of the two chapters this part consists of, "Clitoridectomy in Ancient Greco-Roman Medicine and the Definition of Sexual Intercourse", by Chiara Thumiger, discusses the definition of sexual intercourse (and violence) from a historical perspective. She begins with the testimonies about clitoridectomy left by a handful of ancient medical authors, and places them in dialogue with a broad selection of interventions on the female body by figures of power or authority of various kinds from ancient literature and the modern era. Thumiger argues that these appear to reveal a common script in which control, violence and sex are central and intertwined. She illustrates the point through a number of figurative, as well as poetic images. Despite variations in details and register, what is usually meant by "sexual interaction" in literature or artistic figurations is the interaction between two bodies that involves the genitals of one or both — or some Ersatz or sex toy — for the purpose of the pleasure or gratification of one or both, and that sometimes raises concerns about procreation. Thumiger extends the definition of the English expression "sexual intercourse" to include intercourse as intrusion and action of one body, cast in a position of power and/or authority or seniority, on another body (typically female) by means of *some instrument* — whether an object or a part of one's body. The sexual pleasure, or sexualised satisfaction, is distributed in a way different from what is expected, eluding the body at the centre to only benefit the external actors and the attending audience.

The second chapter, "Sex and Epilepsy: Seizures and Fluids in Greek Medical Imagination", by George Kazantzidis, aims to examine the pathologisation of sexual intercourse by looking at ancient Greek medical sources which, either implicitly or explicitly, assimilate sex and orgasm to an epileptic fit. The case is made that the Hippocratic author of *De morbo sacro* includes hints that guide the reader's imagination in this direction. The association between sex and epilepsy is then examined in the writings of Aretaeus of Cappadocia, who makes the striking claim that sexual intercourse "bears the symbols of the disease". While the metaphorical and literal connections between desire and "madness" have been thoroughly discussed in scholarship, relatively little attention has been paid to the morbid associations of sex itself. Through an investigation of a common vocabulary of spasms and fluids, involuntary bodily movements and induced shame, Kazantzidis' chapter seeks to fill this gap by proposing epilepsy as an appropriate disease to think with when we are trying to approach the pathological dimensions of sex.

Part III, *The Use and Abuse of Sex Objects*, includes four chapters, all of which examine how inanimate objects are used in sexual intercourse or practices. In the first chapter of this part, "Some Dirty Thoughts about Chairs and Stools: Iconography of Erotic Foreplay", Bartłomiej Bednarek presents the motif of clothes deposited on a chair or a stool, which pervaded vase painting from the late archaic period onwards. It was, arguably, recognised by ancient viewers as an allusion to undressing. Chairs and stools with clothes deposited on them were humble witnesses to the sexual practices of ancient men and women, and became somewhat marginal components of outwardly erotic scenes. More interestingly, seats without clothes on them also gradually became more and more a conventional sign of undressing. Such an iconographic marker set in a context that may be evocative of eroticism (ranging from kisses and gift-giving to something that could be taken as an innocent conversation), should, in many cases, be taken as a clear allusion to the intentions of the figures represented on vases, which may have triggered viewers' fantasies about the aftermath of the scene they were looking at.

In the second chapter, "Olive Oil, Dildos and Sandals: Greek Sex Toys Reassessed", Emma Stafford aims to reassess our limited evidence, considering the extent to which a class of "sex toy" can be identified, and the range of contexts in which such aids might have been used, in real life and/or as the stuff of erotic fantasy. Discussing the scene on an Attic red-figure pelike attributed to Euphronios, Alan Shapiro speculates whether the sandal might have been "known as Leagros' favourite sex-toy" (in Thomas K. Hubbard, ed., *Greek Love Reconsidered*, New York, 29). The term appears anachronistic, but modern definitions frequently cite, as an example of the sex toy, the dildo — the object most often discussed as a sexual aid in scholarship on ancient Greek sexuality. Martin Kilmer's *Greek Erotica on Attic Red-Figure Vases* (London 1993) provides the most systematic assessment of the subject, categorising olive oil and dildos as "sexual accessories" (the slipper comes under the heading "sexual violence"). Whilst useful as a collection of evidence, however, Kilmer does not always give sufficient weight to the problematic nature of his material, and he begs many questions especially concerning female sexuality. More recent studies have provided more nuanced readings of individual images and texts, but no one since Kilmer has attempted a systematic treatment of the use of sexual aids in ancient Greece.

The third and fourth chapters deal with the use of statues in sexual intercourse. In the third chapter, "Statues as Sex Objects", Regina Höschele examines how ancient literature presents the sexual interaction between humans and statues. While ancient texts mostly show us men filled with desire for images of beautiful boys or women (in some cases actually engaging in sexual activities with them), there are also some references to women yearning to satisfy their lust with the help of sculptures. In several tales, their desire appears frustrated by the immobility and coldness of the stone, even as the unresponsiveness of the image may further fuel erotic longing. Höschele contemplates these textual accounts against the backdrop of ancient sexual discourses, determines underlying narrative patterns and investigates what tales of agalmatophilia may tell us about ancient conceptions of art and beauty.

The fourth and last chapter of Part III, "Having Sex with Statues: Some Cases of Agalmatophilia in Latin Poetry", by Charilaos N. Michalopoulos, examines stories of agalmatophilia in Latin literature, which seems to have had a particular taste for this kind of aberration. The theme is persistent across time and genres (epic, elegy, epigram), offering thus a wide range of tones which vary from profound sophistication to playful aesthetic delight. The Ovidian version of Pygmalion's romantic involvement with his statue (*Met.* 10.243–297) serves as a starting point, since it offers a set of motifs with high frequency in agalmatophilia narratives. Laodamia's infatuation with the wax effigy of her dead husband (Ovid, *Heroides* 13) and a selection of epigrams from the *Priapea* are used as case studies. In most instances agalmatophilia motifs help to establish the erotic character of the liaison between the human and the statue. In the *Priapea*, however, the human-centred approach is replaced by the perspective of the statue. The motifs of agalmatophilia are still present, but only to cause laughter and derision. Moreover, as it turns out, their (mis)application is not meant to undo them, but rather to reaffirm their (structural and thematic) importance as indispensable components in agalmatophilia narratives.

Part IV, *Sexual Liminality*, consists of three chapters that examine sexuality in contexts of liminality, a term that refers, in this volume, to the sexually ambiguous or ambivalent (mythical or textual) figures, contexts and binary situations. There is *human-animal liminality*, exemplified in the figure of the Satyr, which is the topic of the first chapter by Jeremy McInerney, and in human-animal sex, which is examined in the second chapter, that of José Malheiro Magalhães. In more detail, the first chapter, "Hephaistos Among the Satyrs: Semen, Ejaculation and Autochthony in Greek Culture", argues that the Satyr figure provides a model for understanding the role of Hephaistos, a god whose physical shortcomings mark him out as distinctly unOlympian. In common with the Satyrs, Hephaistos is a comic figure connected to sexual incompetence. These shortcomings, however, take on more significance than simple parody in the episode of Hephaistos' attempted rape of Athena. This is a fundamental part of the Athenians' autochthony narrative, which is shown to be deeply ambiguous. Exploring the paradox of pollution and procreation, this chapter finds that the foundation myth of the Athenians included parodic and transgressive elements as a way of giving expression to a subversive narrative that undercut a simple glorification of autochthonous Athenians.

Bestiality is the topic under examination in the chapter "Human-animal Sex in Ancient Greece", which explores examples of human-animal sex in different ancient sources, aiming to ascertain if any of these literary accounts convey the cultural and social views on sex between humans and animals. The author, José Malheiro Magalhães, starts by approaching the mythological traditions of three female figures — Leda, Europa and Pasiphae — explaining the differences between these myths and breaking down the information they provide regarding human-animal sex in ancient Greece. He then explores references and allusions to human-animal sex in the works of several ancient authors, including Herodotus, Theocritus, Plutarch and Artemidorus Daldianus, analysing their context and ascertaining if the information they provide conveys the social perception of this sexual act.

Another kind of liminality, the *male-female liminality*, is discussed by Catalina Popescu in her chapter, the third in Part IV of the volume, which is entitled "The Womb Inside the Male Member: A Lucianic Twist". The deconstruction of gender boundaries and polarities in Lucian's *Verae Historiae* has been discussed in scholarship: it has been argued that, with the aim of ridiculing the ancient fear of feminine power and sexuality (which permeates the episode of sex between Greek sailors and Vine-women), Lucian creates an all-male society on the Moon. His Moonites practice sex in the back of their knees and scholars notice that much of their alien anatomy is altered as to avoid the feminine biology or to render it invisible in androgynous forms. Popescu argues that the feminine principle is not lost to the Moonites, and that Lucian playfully rediscovers it in their faulty gestational physiology, their difficulty to give birth and their post-partum nursing (dis)abilities. In other words, although the Moonites are male and carry enhanced masculine appendages, they essentially operate as cryptic and (at times) dysfunctional females.

In Part V, *Sex and Disgust*, the chapter of Gabriel Evangelou, entitled "Sex and Disgust in Martial's *Epigrams*", examines Martial's notorious invective against lascivious old women who engage in sexual relations with other women, freeborn men who allow themselves to be anally penetrated, and anyone who performs oral sex on a man or a woman. Martial repeatedly and emphatically expresses the repulsion and disgust that he experiences at the sight or the thought of such people, whom he condemns for indulging in their sexual proclivities openly or behind closed doors. While his continuous attacks on these groups of people have received considerable attention in scholarship, the central role that the arousal of disgust and repulsion plays in his epigrams has not been adequately explored. Hence, this chapter examines the possibility that his harsh reproaches are not only used to criticise many of his fellow citizens who fail to control their sexual urges, but primarily to provoke laughter through the exaggerated depiction of anyone who deviates from the strict mores of society.

Part VI, the last of the volume, consists of six chapters that discuss aspects of sexuality in dramatic, papyrological, and other texts and contexts of ancient literature — hence the title *The Scripts of Sexuality: Drama, Novel, Papyri and Later Texts*. In the first chapter of this part, "To Voice the Physical: Sex and the Soil in Aeschylus", Nikos Manousakis discusses the display of sexual activity in Aeschylus, focusing on how sex is constantly presented in terms (imagery) of agricultural living, bringing to the fore the — rather neglected — sensuality of Aeschylean poetry. In the rather short Aeschylean corpus of plays and fragments one finds several vivid implied references to sexual encounters voiced through the language of agriculture and fertility. Both heterosexual and homosexual activity is discussed with the aim of exploring aspects of sensuality in Aeschylus' poetry.

The second chapter, "Seminal Figures: Aristophanes and the Tradition of Sexual Imagery", by Dimitrios Kanellakis, outlines the history of farming and sailing imagery pertinent to sex and politics up to Aristophanes' time, and discusses how the comic dramatist builds on that tradition. It is argued that in *Peace* he pursues a connection between the sexual and the political uses of agricultural imagery, both carrying negative connotations since Hesiod, thus promoting a so-far-overlooked ironic interpretation: more than just a cheerful call for ending the Peloponnesian War, the play hints at the risks for securing peace. Its pornographic content is a celebratory effect *prima facie*, but a political warning on a second level. Naval metaphors, on the other hand, are traditionally used independently for sex or politics, and so they are in Aristophanes. At any rate, comedy's capability to bring such metaphors on stage challenges the boundaries between mental visualisation and optical perception.

The third chapter, "The Maiden who Knew Nothing about Sex: A Scabrous Theme in Novella and Comedy", by Ioannis M. Konstantakos, examines the literary history of a recurrent figure in the ancient Greek humorous tradition: the ingenuous personage who has no idea of sex and cannot understand what the sexual act means. It is usually female characters who appear in this role. In an old Ionian novella, which subsequently survives as an inserted tale in the *Vita Aesopi* (131) and in the corpus of Aesopic fables (386 Perry), an imbecile girl is deceived by a rustic, who satisfies his lust upon her. In a coarser and more grotesque variation of the story, also included in a later collection of fables (410 Perry), the young girl is replaced by an ignorant old woman unwittingly raped by a youngster. The Archaic Ionian tradition also offers a male counterpart, Margites, the fool who did not know what to do with his wife on their wedding night. An analogous Hittite *Schwank*, the *Story of Appu*, suggests that the theme may have passed into Ionian narrative lore from Anatolian sources. The same pattern was dramatised in the Attic theatre, in a mythological comedy by Amphis burlesquing the myth of Callisto. The old Ionian tale was perhaps known to Boccaccio and inspired the story of Rustico and Alibech in *Decameron* 3.10.

Two of the chapters of the last section of the volume focus on papyrological sources. In their joint chapter, "Sex and Abuse in Unhappy Marriages in Late Antique Oxyrhynchus: The Case of Two Women's Narratives Preserved on Papyrus", Amphilochios Papathomas and Aikaterini Koroli examine aspects of sexuality in unhappy or abusive marriages and their connection to the exercise of physical and psychological violence against women, as it is attested in documentary papyri from Greco-Roman Egypt. The chapter focuses on two well-preserved narratives from late antique Oxyrhynchus, namely P.Oxy. VI 903 (4th cent. AD), and P.Oxy. L 3581 (4th–5th cent. AD), both written by women. These emotionally charged texts, serving as institutional means of defence for the victimised women, abound in information concerning sex in relation to forced marriages and domestic violence. Papathomas and Koroli offer an analysis of the two papyri, having three aims: first, to locate the implications of the problems in their sexual life, i.e. either non-consensual sex and/or sexual deceit; second, to sketch the portrait of the abused woman and the man-abuser; and third, to compare the texts that are under study with other texts, mostly documentary papyri, falling into the same thematic area, and to place them in their historical and philological context.

The other chapter that discusses texts in papyri is authored by Rosalia Hatzilambrou and has the title "'Asexuality' in the Greek Papyrus Letters". This chapter explores the scarcity of love letters among the Greek letters written on papyrus and similar materials. In the first part of her chapter Hatzilambrou briefly presents the extant specimens of Greek love correspondence in post-pharaonic Egypt, while also commenting on points in them that are relevant to her argument. In the second part, Hatzilambrou argues that the small number of papyrus love letters is striking, when compared to the emphasis placed on love and sexual desire in other texts of the same period, for instance in the magical papyri. The chapter puts forward the argument that the reason for the observed "asexuality" in the corpus of the Greek papyrus letters lies in a range of factors, which have nothing to do with the sexuality of the Greek speaking inhabitants of Egypt in the Imperial and Byzantine periods.

The last chapter of the volume is jointly authored by Stephanos Efthymiadis and Charis Messis and has the title "From Plato's *Symposium* to Methodius' and Late Antique Hagiography: 'Female' Readings of Male Sexuality". This chapter examines a cluster of texts of late Roman antiquity, in order to see through and define what has been regarded as the womanly-female perspective of eroticism and sexuality. The figure of Diotima as in Plato's *Symposium* is the starting point of this discussion, which chiefly dwells on the ten philosophising women as they appear in the Christianised version of *Symposium* attributed to Methodius of Olympus, an author of the third-fourth centuries AD. Attention is also paid to the way women are portrayed in the *Pseudo-Clementines*, an apocryphal text of the New Testament written in the first half of the third century. The chapter ends with a presentation of a new theory of gender and sexuality as launched in the *Christian Martyrdom of Sts Nereus and Achilles* (*BHG* 1317), a hagiographical text that brings out the rejection of marriage and sexuality. In all these texts *women*'s voices become a powerful instrument in the service of male writers.

Bibliography

Apter, D.A. (1991), 'Institutionalism revisited', in: *International Social Science Journal* 43, 463–481.

Beauvoir, S. (1973), *The Second Sex*, New York.

Blanshard, A. (2010), *Sex: Vice and Love from Antiquity to Modernity*, Chichester/Malden, MA.

Brisson, L. (2002), *Sexual Ambivalence: Androgyny and Hermaphroditism in Graeco-Roman Antiquity*, Berkeley.

Butler, J. (1986), 'Sex and Gender in Simone de Beauvoir's Second Sex', in: *Yale French Studies* 72, 35–49.

Butler, J. (1990), *Gender Trouble: Feminism and the Subversion of Identity*, New York/London.

Butler, J. (1993), 'Critically Queer', in: *GLQ. A Journal of Lesbian and Gay Studies* 1, 17–32.

Butler, J. (1999), *Gender Trouble: Feminism and the Subversion of Identity*, New York.

Butler, J. (2004), *Undoing Gender*, New York.

Chrystal, P. (2016), *In Bed with the Romans: A Brief History of Sex in Ancient Rome*, Stroud.

Cohen, D. (1991), *Law, Sexuality, and Society: The Enforcement of Morals in Classical Athens*, Cambridge.

Comfort, A. (1963), *Sex in Society*, London.

Davidson, J. (2007), *The Greeks and Greek Love: A Radical Reappraisal of Homosexuality in Ancient Greece*, London.

Dover, K.J. (1989), *Greek Homosexuality*, Cambridge, MA.

Egeberg, M. (2003), 'How Bureaucratic Structure Matters: An Organizational Perspective', in: B.G. Peters/J. Pierre (eds.), *Handbook of Public Administration*, London, 116–126.

Evans, J. (2019), 'Rhetorical Masculinity in *Stasis*: Hyper-andreia and Patriotism inThucydides' *Histories* and Plato's *Gorgias*', in: S. Papaioannou/A. Serafim/K. Demetriou (eds.), *The Ancient Art of Persuasion across Genres and Topics*, Leiden, 209–224.

Faraone, C./McClure, L. (2006), *Prostitutes and Courtesans in the Ancient World*, Madison.

Fausto-Sterling, A. (2000), *Sexing the Body: Gender Politics and the Construction of Sexuality*, New York.

Foley, H. (1992), *Reflections of Women in Antiquity*, London/New York.

Foucault, M. (1978), *Foucault, The History of Sexuality*, Translated by Robert Hurley, New York.

Foucault, M. (1985), *The Use of Pleasure, Vol. 2: History of Sexuality*, Translated by R. Hurley, New York.

Foxhall, L. (2013), *Studying Gender in Classical Antiquity*, Cambridge.

Foxhall, L./Salmon, J. (2005), *When Men Were Men: Masculinity, Power and Identity in Classical Antiquity*, Berkeley/Los Angeles/London.

Graves-Brown, C. (2008), *Sex and Gender in Ancient Egypt. Don Your Wig for a Joyful Hour*, Swansea.

Halperin, D.M. (1990), *One Hundred Years of Homosexuality: And Other Essays on Greek Love*, New York/London.

Halperin, D.M./Winkler, J.J./Zeitlin, F. (1990), *Before Sexuality, The Construction of Erotic Experience in the Ancient Greek World*, Princeton, NJ.

Holmes, B. (2012), *Gender Antiquity and its Legacy*, Oxford.

Hubbard, T.K. (2000), *Greek Love Reconsidered*, New York.

Hubbard, T.K. (ed.) (2014), *A Companion to Greek and Roman Sexualities*, Malden, MA/Oxford/Chichester.

Johnson, M./Ryan, T. (2005), *Sexuality in Greek and Roman Society and Literature: A Sourcebook*, London/New York.

Kapparis, K. (2017), *Prostitution in the Ancient Greek World*, Edinburgh.

Kratochwil, F. (1984), 'The force of prescription', in: *International Organization* 38, 685–708.

Laqueur, T. (1990), *Making Sex: Body and Gender from the Greeks to Freud*, Cambridge, MA.

Lear, A./Cantarella, E. (2008), *Images of Ancient Greek Pederasty*, New York.

Lee, M.M. (2015), *Body, Dress and Identity*, Cambridge.

Licht, H. (1932), *Sexual Life in Ancient Greece*, London.

Manniche, L. (1987), *Sexual life in ancient Egypt*, New York.

Llewellyn-Jones, L./ Davies, G. (2007), *Greek and Roman Dress from A to Z*, Cambridge.

March, J.G./Olsen, J.P. (1995), *Democratic Governance*, New York.

March, J.G./Olsen, J.P. (2005), 'Elaborating the New Institutionalism', in: *ARENA Centre for European Studies*, Online publication: http://unesco.amu.edu.pl/pdf/olsen2.pdf

Masterson, M./Rabinowitz, N./Robson, J. (2015), *Sex in Antiquity. Exploring Gender and Sexuality in the Ancient World*, London/New York.

Merton, R.K. (1938), 'Social Structure and Anomie', in: *American Sociological Review* 3, 672–682.

Meyer, J./Rowan, B. (1977), 'Institutionalized Organizations: Formal Structure as Myth and Ceremony', in: *American Journal of Sociology* 83, 340–363.

Oakley, A. (1972), *Sex, Gender and Society*, Farnham.

Pitkin, H. (1967), *The Concept of Representation*, Berkeley.

Pomeroy, S.B. (1976), *Goddesses, Whores, Wives, and Slaves: Women in Classical Antiquity*, New York.

Rabinowitz, N.S./Richlin, A. (1993), *Feminist Theory and the Classics*, London.

Richlin, A. (1992), *Pornography and Representation in Greece and Rome*, Oxford.

Robson, J. (2013), *Sex and Sexuality in Classical Athens*, Edinburgh.

Sanders, E./Thumiger, C./Carey, C./Lowe, N. (2013), *Erōs in Ancient Greece*, Oxford.

Serafim, A. (2017), *Attic Oratory and Performance*, London/New York.

Serafim, A. (2019), 'Constructing Identities: Religious Argumentation, Sexuality and Social Identity in Attic Forensic Oratory', in: *Annals of the Faculty of Law in Belgrade* 67, 233–253.

Simon, H.A. (1965), *Administrative Behavior*, New York.

Skinner, M.B. (2005), *Sexuality in Greek and Roman Culture*, Maiden, MA/Oxford.

Weaver, R.K./Rockman, B.A. (1993), *Do Institutions Matter? Government Capabilities in the United States and Abroad*, Washington, DC.

West, C./Zimmerman, D.H. (1987), 'Doing Gender', in: J. Lorber/S.A. Farrell (eds.), *The Social Construction of Gender*, Stanford, 13–37.

Zeitlin, F.I. (1996), *Playing the Other: Gender and Society in Classical Greek Literature*, Chicago/London.

Part I: **Aspects of Homoeroticism**

Konstantinos Kapparis

Dover's "Pseudo-sexuality" and the Athenian Laws on Male Prostitutes in Politics

Abstract: This chapter challenges the widespread view that the laws on *hetairēsis* and *dokimasia rhētorōn* were intended to curb the sexual desires of Athenian men for other men, and that they had a normative effect on perceptions of same sex relations. It is argued that such views are based upon modern prejudices and sexual identity politics, while contemporary ancient sources offer a different interpretation of these laws. Contemporary sources commenting on the purpose of these laws always raise concerns about public life, and the impact that low-life politicians who had not hesitated to hire their bodies for money would have on the political life of the city, if they were allowed to gain power. Male prostitutes are demonised and presented as a much greater threat to the Athenian democracy than the few, socially marginalised men of a poor background, who had practiced prostitution, could ever be.

1 Introduction

Athenian orators frequently expressed fear about the state of the Athenian democracy, its fragility and the numerous enemies surrounding it from all directions.[1] They highlighted the dangers from populist politicians, for whom they even created a new word in the later 5th century: they called them demagogues (δημαγωγοί), those who were leading the demos astray.[2] The Athenians had every reason to believe, especially in the 5th century, that sympathisers of the

---

1 E.g. Andoc. 1.95–97, 3.1; Isoc. 4.6, 19.319; Dem. 15.14, 20.48, 24.144 et al. See also Carey 2017, and especially 33–36 and 141–150; Ober 1989; Atack 2017, 576–588; Lehmann 2019, 643–670; Sebastiani 2018, 490–515.

2 The verb ἄγω never means "to lead" in a positive sense, like "ἄρχω" or "προΐσταμαι"; along with its compound παράγω it always means "to deceive, to lead astray, or to force someone down a path where they do not wish to go", and this is why the term δημαγωγός had an inherently negative meaning since its inception. The first confirmed reference is found in Thucydides (4.21.3, 8.65.2), and the dubious honour of embodying the first and quintessential demagogue of the Athenian democracy was given by Thucydides to Kleon, a man he hated with a vengeance.

https://doi.org/10.1515/9783110695793-002

old aristocracy were still fostering deep hostility for everything democratic, not least because political pamphlets and philosophical works of the time expressed such sentiments openly and fearlessly.[3] Twice in the late 5th century (in 411 and 404) the enemies of the Athenian democracy succeeded in their efforts to overturn it, taking advantage of the woes which war, instability and famine had inflicted upon the city, and twice the Athenian democracy was brought back from the precipice some months later. This could be interpreted as a strength or a weakness of the Athenian democracy, but either way we can understand why its defenders and supporters frequently expressed their anxiety about the fragility of democracy, and the need to protect it from its enemies with specific and firm legislation.[4]

It is the contention of this chapter that such anxieties were behind the introduction of two heavily discussed laws regulating the level of participation in public life for citizen men who had practiced prostitution. Such an interpretation of these legal documents is not new. All ancient sources which discuss these documents strongly emphasise their political background as well as their importance for the defence of the democratic constitution from dangers such as populism, corruption, deep and lasting damage to the fabric of the democracy and its institutions, including state religion, and the infection of the citizen body with foul ideas and unpatriotic practices. However, modern scholars almost unanimously have ignored the commentary on these statutes by contemporary authors and interpreted them as a moralising attempt to reign in the desires of Athenian men towards each other, as a conservative turn in Athenian views to sexuality, and as an effort to legislate on appropriate practices of courtship, forms of sexual contact, acceptable sexual positions (if any at all), and even the permissible emotions among Athenian males. I argue that these laws did none of these things, and that, just as their contemporary commentators repeatedly state, the rationale behind the introduction of these laws was firmly embedded in anxieties concerning the public life of the city, the protection of the Athenian democracy and its institutions, and the prevention of public corruption and malfeasance. Moreover, I suggest that the wild speculation, sys-

---

3 See for example the ferocious critique of the Athenian Democracy in pseudo-Xenophon's *The old Oligarch* and Plato's *Republic*, and also Cooper 1997, 455–482; Finley 1962; Henderson 2003, 155–179; Paionidis-Giannakopoulos 2018; Rhodes 2016, 243–264; Jordović 2018, 183–208; Kastely 2015; Sorensen 2016.

4 An excellent example of such precautionary legislation is ostracism, where a very distinguished, influential and powerful citizen was exiled for 10 years (but allowed to keep his property), so as not to become a danger to democracy. See Beneker 2004, 3–10; Forsdyke 2005; and 2000, 232–263; Kosmin 2015, 121–161; Phillips 1982, 21–43.

tematic misinformation and stunning misinterpretation of these laws in modern literature is not simply a misunderstanding but a deliberate distortion of the historical truth for reasons and objectives which have to do with modern gender identity politics.

While these laws have nothing to do with same-sex relations, since they were only concerned with male prostitution, they have played a disproportionately weighty part in discussions on Greek same-sex relations as a whole. This kind of mix up is neither naïve nor innocent, since homophobic narratives in the second half of the 20th century frequently and intentionally confused consensual same-sex relations based on love, affection and mutual attraction with all kinds of unsavoury, illegal and socially unacceptable practices, such as paedophilia, prostitution or sex trafficking. We do need to clear the rubble and restore the historical truth about these laws and their context. In order to be able to explain how and why modern research has systematically and purposefully misinterpreted these laws, after a brief presentation of the laws themselves, it is necessary to give a brief outline of attitudes to Greek same-sex relations since the publication of Dover's pioneering work *Greek Homosexuality*, in the 1970's, and its reception in later years.

2 The laws

2.1 The law on *hetairēsis*

Aeschin. 1.19–20: ἄν τις Ἀθηναίων, φησίν, ἑταιρήσῃ, μὴ ἐξέστω αὐτῷ τῶν ἐννέα ἀρχόντων γενέσθαι, ὅτι οἶμαι στεφανηφόρος ἡ ἀρχή, μηδ' ἱερωσύνην ἱεράσασθαι, ὡς οὐδὲ καθαρῷ τῷ σώματι, μηδὲ συνδικησάτω, φησί, τῷ δημοσίῳ, μηδὲ ἀρξάτω ἀρχὴν μηδεμίαν μηδέποτε, μήτ' ἔνδημον μήτε ὑπερόριον, μήτε κληρωτὴν μήτε χειροτονητήν· μηδὲ κηρυκευσάτω, μηδὲ πρεσβευσάτω, μηδὲ τοὺς πρεσβεύσαντας κρινέτω, μηδὲ συκοφαντείτω μισθωθείς, μηδὲ γνώμην εἰπάτω μηδέποτε μήτε ἐν τῇ βουλῇ μήτε ἐν τῷ δήμῳ, μηδ' ἂν δεινότατος ᾖ λέγειν. Ἐὰν δέ τις παρὰ ταῦτα πράττῃ, γραφὰς ἑταιρήσεως πεποίηκε καὶ τὰ μέγιστα ἐπιτίμια ἐπέθηκεν.

If any Athenian, he says, works as a prostitute, he cannot be appointed as one of the nine archons (I believe because this is a crowned office), nor assume any priesthood (because his body is not clean), nor become a public advocate, nor serve as a magistrate either at home or abroad, appointed by lot or elected; he is not to serve as a herald or an ambassador (and he is not to judge those who have served as ambassadors, or engage in sycophantic activities for money), nor can he voice his opinion either in the Council or in the Assembly, not even if he is a highly accomplished speaker. If someone disobeys these laws, the lawgiver has established a *graphe* for prostitution and the most severe penalties.

This law was introduced in the late 5th or early 4th century. The earliest certain reference to it is in the speech of Dem. *Against Androtion* (see no. 3 below). K.J. Dover suggested that a passage in the *Knights* of Aristophanes should be interpreted as a reference to this law, which would set 424, when the *Knights* was produced, as a *terminus ante quem*. Several scholars have agreed with Dover.[5] However, MacDowell, an exceptionally learned scholar in both Athenian law and Attic comedy, clearly did not consider this passage to be a reference to the law of *hetairēsis*, since he makes no mention of it in his discussion of the law.[6] I also think that it is highly unlikely that this is a reference to the *hetairēsis* law once we take a closer look at the language of this passage, and also take into account that the term *hetairēsis* was a neologism which had been barely into existence in 425, and one wonders whether such a new word would have been used in the conservative language of a legal document shortly after its inception.[7] Another passage from the speech of Andoc. *On the Mysteries*, which has been interpreted as a potential reference to this law, can be explained in different ways, not necessarily as a reference to the *hetairēsis* law.[8] On balance, it would be safe to assume that the law of *hetairēsis* was introduced at some point in the late 5th or early 4th century. Even this rather extended range is helpful because this was the era of the demagogues, populist politicians who often came from the lower strata of Athenian society, and in their pursuit of a speedy ascendancy and short-term political gain would not hesitate to propose measures damaging to the fabric of the Athenian democracy. Not surprisingly the democratic constitution was overturned twice in a decade (in 411 and 404), and the deep traumas caused by these upheavals would live in the collective memory of the Athenians for much of the 4th century. This was the sociopolitical context, and, as I argue, the primary motive for the introduction of this law. It is noteworthy that, as far as we can tell, no Athenian was ever prosecuted under this statute; the force of this law appears to have been a bogeyman used by politicians to threaten their opponents.

---

5 Ar. *Eq.* 876–880; Dover 1978, 34; See also Lanni 2010, 56.
6 MacDowell 2000, 13–27.
7 It would be not unlike using the verb "to google" in a legal document introduced in 2010. For a more detailed discussion of this point see my previous account in Kapparis 2018, 151–152.
8 And. 1.95 and 100, with MacDowell 1962, com. *ad loc.*

2.2 The law on *epangelia*

Aeschin. 1.28–30: Τίνας δ' οὐκ ᾤετο δεῖν λέγειν; τοὺς αἰσχρῶς βεβιωκότας· τούτους οὐκ ἐᾷ δημηγορεῖν. Καὶ ποῦ τοῦτο δηλοῖ; «δοκιμασία», φησί, «ῥητόρων· ἐάν τις λέγῃ ἐν τῷ δήμῳ τὸν πατέρα τύπτων ἢ τὴν μητέρα, ἢ μὴ τρέφων, ἢ μὴ παρέχων οἴκησιν·» τοῦτον οὐκ ἐᾷ λέγειν. Νὴ Δία καλῶς γε, ὡς ἔγωγέ φημι. ... Καὶ τίσι δεύτερον ἀπεῖπε μὴ λέγειν; «ἢ τὰς στρατείας», φησί, «μὴ ἐστρατευμένος, ὅσαι ἂν αὐτῷπροσταχθῶσιν, ἢ τὴν ἀσπίδα ἀποβεβληκώς», δίκαια λέγων... Τρίτον τίσι διαλέγεται; «ἢ πεπορνευμένος», φησίν, «ἢ ἡταιρηκώς»· τὸν γὰρ τὸ σῶμα τὸ ἑαυτοῦ ἐφ' ὕβρει πεπρακότα, καὶ τὰ κοινὰ τῆς πόλεως ῥαδίως ἡγήσατο ἀποδώσεσθαι. Τέταρτον τίσι διαλέγεται; «ἢ τὰ πατρῷα», φησί, «κατεδηδοκώς, ἢ ὧν ἂν κληρονόμος γένηται»· τὸν γὰρ τὴν ἰδίαν οἰκίαν κακῶς οἰκήσαντα, καὶ τὰ κοινὰ τῆς πόλεως παραπλησίως ἡγήσατο διαθήσειν, καὶ οὐκ ἐδόκει οἷόν τ' εἶναι τῷ νομοθέτῃ τὸν αὐτὸν ἄνθρωπον ἰδίᾳ μὲν εἶναι πονηρόν, δημοσίᾳ δὲ χρηστόν, οὐδ' ᾤετο δεῖν τὸν ῥήτορα ἥκειν ἐπὶ τὸ βῆμα τῶν λόγων ἐπιμεληθέντα πρότερον, ἀλλ' οὐ τοῦ βίου.

Who did he consider unsuitable for speaking? Those who have lived inappropriately; he does not allow these men to address the assembly. Where does he say so? "scrutiny", he says, "of the Speakers: If someone is addressing the Assembly, while he is beating his father or mother, or he does not provide for them or offer them accommodation", he does not allow this man to speak, by Zeus, rightly so in my opinion. ... After this whom did he bar from speaking? "The man", he says, "who has not taken part in the military campaigns assigned to him, or has dropped his shield", correctly so. ... Then, whom does he address after that? "A man who has been a male prostitute", he says, "or has sold his body", because he believed that a man who has sold his own body to be abused, he would easily sell the common affairs of the city. Then whom does he mention? "If he has squandered his parental estate", he says, "or his inheritance", because he believed that a man who has mismanaged his own estate, would dispose of the goods of the state in a similar fashion. The lawgiver did not believe that it was possible for the same man to be bad in his private life, but good in public. Moreover, the lawgiver did not think that a man should step on the roster, having taken care of his speech, but not his own life.

This law was introduced in the first half of the 4th century as part of a broader effort to enact greater scrutiny of all magistrates of the Athenian state.[9] Not surprisingly the influential speakers in the Assembly, who were responsible for proposing most domestic and foreign policy, were included in this greater effort to scrutinise the magistrate of the Athenian democracy. However, unlike other state officials entering into specific offices for a fixed period of time, the speakers in the Assembly were not fixed. Any citizen could respond to the call of the herald in the Assembly when he asked τίς ἀγορεύειν βούλεται; ("who wishes to speak?"), so how could this person be impromptu scrutinised? The solution was

---

9 The first confirmed reference for the *hetairēsis* and the *dokimasia* laws is in Dem. 22, *Against Androtion* 31–32 (c. 355 BC).

to place a number of existing legal provisions under the umbrella of a new law and require all citizens who were prepared to stand up and advise the Assembly to be complying with these legal provisions. They needed to be citizens in good standing, who had been looking after their parents and their patrimony (thus, men who were looking after their *oikos* in its entirety), meeting their military obligations, and not engaging in prostitution. The last of these provisions partially incorporates in the new law on the scrutiny of the speakers in the Assembly, the law on *hetairēsis*. The pre-existence of the *hetairēsis* law may be offering a partial answer to the difficult question why of all kinds of behaviours which could be considered as incompatible with the lifestyle of an upstanding citizen, well-qualified to advise his fellow citizens, prostitution was singled out and explicitly included in the new law. The *hetairēsis* law was an obvious source, since it discouraged an activity which anyone would consider to be visibly incompatible with the lifestyle of someone worthy to advise the city. However, I do not believe that this is the whole story; there is certainly more to it which is discussed in section 5. As far as we know, only one person has ever been prosecuted under this law, the politician Timarchos, in a stunning and unorthodox case at the centre of an acrimonious and consequential political contest, which ultimately would decide the fate of Athens as an independent and sovereign city-state.[10]

2.3 The laws as interpreted by Demosthenes

Dem. 22.31–32: ἀλλὰ ταῦτ' ἀπεῖπεν ὑπὲρ ὑμῶν καὶ τῆς πολιτείας. ᾔδει γάρ, ᾔδει τοῖς αἰσχρῶς βεβιωκόσιν ἁπασῶν οὖσαν ἐναντιωτάτην πολιτείαν ἐν ᾗ πᾶσιν ἔξεστι λέγειν τἀκείνων ὀνείδη. ἔστι δ' αὕτη τίς; δημοκρατία. οὔκουν ἐνόμιζεν ἀσφαλές, εἴ ποτε συμβήσεται γενέσθαι συχνοὺς ἀνθρώπους κατὰ τοὺς αὐτοὺς χρόνους εἰπεῖν μὲν δεινοὺς καὶ θρασεῖς, τοιούτων δ' ὀνειδῶν καὶ κακῶν μεστούς· πολλὰ γὰρ ἂν τὸν δῆμον ὑπ' αὐτῶν ὑπαχθέντ' ἐξαμαρτεῖν, κἀκείνους ἤτοι καταλῦσαί γ' ἂν πειρᾶσθαι τὸ παράπαν τὸν δῆμον (ἐν γὰρ ταῖς ὀλιγαρχίαις, οὐδ' ἂν ὦσιν ἔτ' Ἀνδροτίωνός τινες αἴσχιον βεβιωκότες, οὐκ ἔστι λέγειν κακῶς τοὺς ἄρχοντας), ἢ προάγειν ἂν ὡς πονηροτάτους εἶναι, ἵν' ὡς ὁμοιότατοι σφίσιν ὦσι. τὴν οὖν ἀρχὴν τοῖς τοιούτοις ἀπεῖπε μὴ μετέχειν τοῦ συμβουλεύειν, ἵνα μὴ φενακισθεὶς ὁ δῆμος ἐξαμάρτοι μηδέν. ὧν ὀλιγωρήσας ὁ καλὸς κἀγαθὸς οὗτος οὐ μόνον ᾤετο δεῖν λέγειν καὶ γράφειν οὐκ ἐξόν, ἀλλὰ καὶ παρὰ τοὺς νόμους ταῦτα ποιεῖν.

---

10 Late antiquity grammarians and rhetoricians were as obsessed with the case against Timarchos, as modern scholars are, and if they knew of another case that went to court under the *dokimasia rhētorōn law* (or *epangelia*) chances are that we would know about it too.

He imposed this disability in the interests of you and of the State, for he knew — I say, he knew that of all states the most antagonistic men of infamous habits is that in which every man is at liberty to publish their shame. And what state is that? A democracy. He thought it would be dangerous if there ever happened to coexist a considerable number of men who were bold and clever speakers, but tainted with such disgraceful wickedness. For the people may be led astray by them to make many mistakes, and such men may attempt either to overthrow the democracy completely, — for in an oligarchy, even if there are viler livers than Androtion, no one may speak evil of dignities — or to debauch the people, so that they may be as nearly as possible like themselves. He therefore absolutely forbade such men to take any share in the counsels of the State, lest the people should be deluded into some error. Disregarding all this, our honourable gentleman here thought fit not only to make speeches and proposals, though not entitled to do so, but even ventured to make illegal ones.

The presentation of the *hetairēsis* and *dokimasia* laws by Demosthenes is the oldest certain reference to these laws, and proceeds the account of Aeschines by a decade. Demosthenes focuses on the beneficial effects of these laws in public life and provides valuable commentary about the rationale behind their introduction. His interpretation is firmly affixed in public life and lacks moralistic tones and high-pitched rhetoric which marked the sensational commentary of Aeschines on the same statutes about 10 years later, in 346. As I argue, it is precisely this dry and utilitarian rationale which Demosthenes provides that makes his account easier to trust than the Aeschinean banalities, misinterpretations and alleged scandals.

3 Deveraux, Dover and Foucault on penetration, active and passive lovers

Dover's book on homosexuality has dominated perceptions of Greek sexuality since the late 70's. It has advanced views which, although very often and very obviously wrong in a very pronounced way, still dictate the narrative. How we discuss Greek views of sexuality and what we teach our students in the 21st century have been profoundly influenced by Dover's account. Why this is happening, and what was the reason behind the enduring success of such a demonstrably flawed, and to modern sensibilities patently offensive book, is one of the questions which I hope that I answer convincingly in this chapter.

The employment of the term "homosexuality" in the title of Dover's book is charged. It implies a different, distinct form of sexuality, "antithetical to heterosexuality", in the author's own words.[11] However, he confesses that he finds the terms homosexual and heterosexual unsatisfactory: "but if I followed my inclination to replace 'heterosexual' by 'sexual' and treat what is called 'homosexuality' as a subdivision of the 'quasi-sexual' (or 'pseudo-sexual'; not 'parasexual')".[12] This stunning admission that only heterosexuality is the genuine form of human sexuality, and everything else is pseudo-sexual, some form of fake or imitation, sets the tone for what is to follow and should have alarmed readers. And yet, it seems to have done the exact opposite, it has reassured many of his readers that in reality when the Athenians touted relations between members of the same sex they understood such relations as primarily intellectual and educational. Some readers were in fact so profoundly reassured that they reached the conclusion that Athenian men could not have penetrative sex with other youths or citizen men because this would debase the penetrated partner and put him in a position not unlike that of a slave.[13] J. Davidson has discussed in an article how Dover's views on the topic were based on an article by G. Deveraux, a profoundly homophobic pseudo-scientist from the École des Hautes Études, and further crystallised through their communications.[14] Upon such ill-constructed foundations Dover proceeded to build his edifice. He recognises as sources Aristophanes, Plato, Aeschines' *Against Timarchos*, Hellenistic poetry and Attic vase iconography. Of these Aristophanes and Hellenistic poetry only served as casual references. The other three served as the main sources. Among these vase iconography posed the most serious challenge for the traditional classical scholar accustomed to reading literature rather than interpreting images. Major methodological errors have been committed in this part of the work. Suffice to say, the interpretation of images on vase paintings, made exclusively for the Etruscan market, and undoubtedly adapted to the tastes of that alien audience on the basis of texts written two centuries later, like Plato and Aeschines, is very unsafe. Dover was aware of this major discrepancy, but chose to ignore it. As M. Kilmer puts it, it would be like trying to employ Victorian texts to interpret pornographic images from our times.[15] With the inexperienced eye of a traditional classical scholar with no background in art history, he treated the images of these vases as historical reality, and placed them

---

11 Dover 1978, p. vii.
12 Dover 1978, pp. vii–viii.
13 E.g. Patzer 1982; Golden 1984, 308–324; Cohen 1987, 3–21; Lanni 2016 and 2010, 45–67; on the other hand Bartolomiej Bednarek has rightly expressed well-founded skepticism about the presence of homophobia in classical Athens, and such scepticism is pervasive in James Davidson's substantial volume on Greek same sex relations (2007).
14 Davidson 2001, 9–10.
15 Kilmer 1993, 4–5.

in the sociocultural context of the fourth century, even though they had been painted one or two centuries in the past.

Equally reckless was Dover's handling of literary sources. While the bulk of the evidence outside Plato and the speech *Against Timarchos* was ignored,[16] the eccentricities of Plato or the high-pitched and purposefully misleading rhetoric of Aeschines have been treated as accurate reflections of historical realities. Both of these flaws proved fatal. By ignoring the bulk of the evidence, Dover intentionally excluded a large number of sources which suggest a complex variety of patterns governing same sex relations within the spectrum of human sexuality, as one would expect. Instead, there was a tight focus upon relationships of older men with youths because these unequal relations could be explained as educational, something which would have been impossible in relationships among peers or indeed older adults.[17] On the other hand, by focusing excessively on Plato and taking the philosopher's intellectual pursuits as the reflections of historical reality, Dover has developed some imbalanced and irrational views on eroticism and sexual pursuit which can be easily summed up by the joke of the comic poet Amphis that someone who claims to desire only the soul of a beautiful boy would resemble a poor man who pursues rich people but does not want their money.[18]

By establishing a framework for what are good and acceptable forms of "homosexuality", which positions are permitted during sexual encounters, how

---

[16] Specifically, there are 2855 references to the term ἐραστής, 1008 references to the term ἐρώμενος, 741 references to παιδικά, plus 27 more terms referring to persons who engaged in same sex relationships in the body of Greek literature. Although not all this evidence is relevant or confined to classical Athens, much of it is, and shifting through it to synthesise a more accurate and comprehensive account would be a Herculean task. Even Davidson in his large 2007 volume, and Hubbard in his most useful collection of primary sources, in 2003, only partially explore the wealth of the available evidence.

[17] On the subject of peer relationships see Hubbard 2014, 128–149; Bremmer 1989, 1–14. Davidson 2007, 3–115 offers a highly articulate and severe critique of the conceptualisation of "pederasty", as understood by Dover and many of his followers. It may be noteworthy that in the vast majority of real-life same-sex couples known by name, both partners were over 18, just as Davidson has pointed out, amid fierce criticism.

[18] Amphis *Dithyrambos* fr. 15:

What are you saying? Are you really trying to tell me
That someone in love with a pretty boy
Is enamoured with his personality, and not his looks?
He must be really stupid. And I don't believe it.
It would be like a poor man who keeps pestering
rich people but does not want their money.

and when the good citizen boy could accept a lover, for how long he should pretend that he was not interested, why and how he should be playing hard to get, and most important of all, how he should avoid showing signs of sexual gratification during the encounter, Dover introduced a level of absurdity into the entire discussion which defies common sense and would fail to pass even the most elementary reality check. The obsession with the simple biological function of penetration, which Dover astoundingly considers to be a form of domination which reduces and compromises the penetrated partner, influenced Foucault and much of the discussion not only concerning sexual positions but also wider political and social issues in classical Athens. Davidson in his thoroughly justified critique of these views points out that paradoxically Dover oversexed the Greeks and put undue emphasis on penetration. At the same time Dover's account depended heavily on Platonic attempts to sanction nonphysical aspects of such relations.[19]

Dover's approach to the excesses of Aeschinean rhetoric was even less guarded. Aeschines won a stunning victory with a familiar recipe, which even in our times we have seen in action turning around an unwinnable vote. As I argue in a forthcoming study, the main ingredients were bold lies and misinformation, misdirection, agitation of fears and anxieties, and a promise to disrupt the corrupt political establishment represented by Demosthenes and his allies. The powerful deployment of these ingredients assisted by a favourable political climate at the time of the trial allowed Aeschines to win a victory so unexpected that when Demosthenes commented on it a few years later he compared it with the paradox of rivers running upstream.[20] And yet, Dover and many of his followers have treated the speech as a reliable source for our understanding of the milieu of 4th century Athenian morality, and have swallowed the crafty rhetoric and misdirection of a brutally effective orator and populist politician whole and unfiltered. While the speech remains an important source of 4th century Athenian history, it is imperative to see through the rhetoric, to put the orator's statements through some heavy filters and to carefully extract what is valuable and important information.

This confused blending of Platonic philosophical ideas with high-pitched and supremely crafty rhetoric, fortified by the misreading of Attic vase paintings, which do not belong to the same area as these literary sources, has created a lethal combination of misinformation. The *hetairēsis* and *dokimasia* laws have

---

19 Davidson 2007, 119–204; 2001, 3–51.
20 Dem. 19.287: ἀλλὰ δῆτ' ἄνω ποταμῶν ἐκείνῃ τῇ ἡμέρᾳ πάντες οἱ περὶ πορνείας ἐρρύησαν λόγοι. But in truth, on that day all this talk about prostitution was like the rivers running upstream.

been particularly savaged by these distortions. First, they have been treated as centrally important statutes regulating homosexual relations among males in Athens, when in reality these laws had nothing to say about same-sex relations. These laws were meant to deter male prostitutes from seeking high office and advising the Assembly. While within the context of homophobia which dominated the 1970s it might have been an easy conceptual leap from homosexual relations to male prostitution, the distinction was crystal clear in a society which was not plagued by the same taboos.[21] While same-sex relations, based on charis, physical attraction, emotional bonding and sometimes deep, true love, are attested in our sources as a reality across the boundaries of social class, wealth, privilege, political affiliation or citizen status, male prostitution among citizens is only attested at the lowest strata of Athenian society and seems to have been a practice confined to economically depressed youths and men from broken families. The difference could not be clearer at many levels; these laws were not intended to interfere in any way with the private lives and relationships of men who consented to relations with other men or youths. They only targeted men[22] who had sold sexual favours for money, for reasons which we are in danger of missing if we allow ourselves to be carried away by the torrent of Aeschinean rhetoric.

---

21 See for example, Ar. *Plu.* 153–156; Ant. Test. 3, D-K = X. *Mem.* 1.6.13: ᵀΩ Ἀντιφῶν, παρ' ἡμῖν νομίζεται τὴν ὥραν καὶ τὴν σοφίαν ὁμοίως μὲν καλόν, ὁμοίως δὲ αἰσχρὸν διατίθεσθαι εἶναι. τήν τε γὰρ ὥραν ἐὰν μέν τις ἀργυρίου πωλῆι τῶι βουλομένωι, πόρνον αὐτὸν ἀποκαλοῦσιν, ἐὰν δέ τις, ὃν ἂν γνῶι καλόν τε κἀγαθὸν ἐραστὴν ὄντα, τοῦτον φίλον ἑαυτῶι ποιῆται, σώφρονα νομίζομεν·"Antiphon, it is considered to be equally possible to treat one's physical and mental peak well or badly. If someone sells his physical peak for money to anyone willing to pay, they call him a whore; however, if one offers his affections to someone whom he knows to be attractive and of good character, we consider this person to be wise".
22 Aeschin. 1.13–14, 39 makes clear that these laws did not affect under age boys, since they might have been forced into prostitution by relatives or guardians. In fact the law sternly prohibited (διαρρήδην ... οὐκ ἐᾶ) prosecutions on the basis of these laws against boys forced into prostitution by their families. Only men who had chosen to practice prostitution in adulthood were subject to the disabilities of these laws. This legal provision invalidates the argument of Lanni 2010, 45–67 that these laws had an "expressive effect" and might discourage boys from engaging in same-sex relations, because later on they might be prosecuted for prostitution under these laws.

4 The rationale behind the introduction of the *hetairēsis* and *dokimasia* laws

Contemporary sources provide ample comments on the rationale behind these two laws. These comments have been completely side-lined by modern studies in favour of moralising explanations about the improprieties of prostitution or even same-sex relations altogether. Such explanations reflect the cultural bias of their authors, not the jurisprudence of the Athenian democracy. One of the few things on which Demosthenes and Aeschines agree is that a bad person cannot possibly give good advice to the city, and that a man who has mistreated his own body, family and property will also mistreat the city and its affairs. Ultimately, they both agree that the prevailing philosophy behind the introduction of these laws was to protect the Athenian democracy, its institutions and the people themselves from the bad influence of an unworthy public servant, be it a speaker in the Assembly, a magistrate, a priest, a herald on an ambassador.[23] For both Demosthenes and Aeschines, these laws have very practical objectives; they are not vague moralising principles. These objectives in both cases have to do with public, not private life, and the ultimate goal is the protection of the city and the democracy. When it comes to the specifics each orator emphasises different aspects of these goals, and while they seem to diverge beyond a certain point, even through the torrent of Aeschinean rhetoric, which has fuelled many of Dover's misinterpretations, the defence of the *polis* seems to be the ultimate objective.

A good example is the Aeschinean narrative on the excesses of Timarchos. At first sight it appears to be a critique, the chastisement of immoral behaviour, where a citizen man was willing to offer his body for the sexual pleasure of others because he loved luxury.[24] Aeschines ultimately will link this fondness of Timarchos for luxury and excess to allegations of corruption in public life, and to his unsuitability for public office on account of these allegations. Even sensational allegations such as these must be seen in a political context. Aeschines at this point reflects the commonly held view that men and women who entered into prostitution did so because they loved luxury. This was a profoundly an un-

---

23 See Dem. 22.31–32 and Aeschin. 1.30.
24 Aeschin. 1.42–3, 42, 53, 75, 115. See also Dem. 19.229, where Demosthenes is accusing Aeschines that he sold out the affairs of the city, for money, which he used to buy luxuries, like prostitutes and fish.

Greek behavioural pattern, characteristic of oriental cultures.[25] In reality, citizen prostitutes that we know about, male or female, came from poor backgrounds, and often from fatherless homes, where in the absence of the head and provider of the *oikos* women and children were left to fend for themselves in a world which provided limited opportunities for them.[26] Modern research confirms this pattern suggesting that the prevailing reason why people take up prostitution without coercion is not an excessive love for luxury but simply hope for a better life away from poverty and destitution.[27]

The most persistent problem for authors who argue that prostitutes are unsuitable for public life is the lack of boundaries. Demosthenes and Aeschines imply that a man who did not hesitate to sell his own body would not hesitate to sell out the city. Plato argues that such a man would do anything in the service of the person who was paying his wages.

Pl. *Symp.* 185a: εἰ γάρ τις ἐραστῇ ὡς πλουσίῳ πλούτου ἕνεκα χαρισάμενος ἐξαπατηθείη καὶ μὴ λάβοι χρήματα, ἀναφανέντος τοῦ ἐραστοῦ πένητος, οὐδὲν ἧττον αἰσχρόν· δοκεῖ γὰρ ὁ τοιοῦτος τό γε αὐτοῦ ἐπιδεῖξαι, ὅτι ἕνεκα χρημάτων ὁτιοῦν ἂν ὁτῳοῦν ὑπηρετοῖ, τοῦτο δὲ οὐ καλόν.

If someone offers himself to a lover under the assumption that he was rich, but is deceived and does not receive any money, because it turns out that the lover was poor, this is not any less improper, because such a man seems to have proven for himself that he will do anything to anyone for money, and this is not good.

---

25 E.g. Pl. *Alc.* I. 122b: εἰ δ' αὖ ἐθέλεις εἰς πλούτους ἀποβλέψαι καὶ τρυφὰς καὶ ἐσθῆτας ἱματίων θ' ἕλξεις καὶ μύρων ἀλοιφὰς καὶ θεραπόντων πλήθους ἀκολουθίας τήν τε ἄλλην ἁβρότητα τὴν Περσῶν, "Then again, if you want to look up to wealth and luxuries and the fancy clothes and dresses with long coats and perfume ointments and a large retinue of servants and the rest of the softness of the Persians". On the subject see my previous discussion in Kapparis 2018, 73–98, 302–312; see also Davidson 1997 for thorough discussions on the perceptions of luxury and excess in Athenian literature.
26 For example, the hetaira Timadra and her sister were orphaned from a young age (Hyp. Fr. 164 Jensen), Mania (aka Melitta) had no family (Machon 13.174–15.257), Diophantos was an orphan (Aeschin. 1.58), while the paternity of Mnesitheos and Molon was doubtful, according to Aeschin. 1.158. Lucian reflects these realities of classical Athens in the famous *DMeretr.* 6, where the desperate widow Krobyle is pushing her young daughter Korinna to become a hetaira, with a view to a better life for the two of them. We hear that the two women had experienced severe financial hardship after the death of Korinna's father and main breadwinner of the household, who was a blacksmith. Timarchos does not fit into this pattern, since he came from an affluent household, but then again it is highly unlikely that Timarchos was ever a male prostitute.
27 See Khan et al. 2010, 365–383.

This perception is also reflected in Aeschines, who uses the term δουλεύων (to work as a slave) to describe the submission of Timarchos to Misgolas in exchange for luxurious meals, parties, female prostitute entertainers and gambling.[28] Likewise, Apollodoros, when discussing Neaira's career as a prostitute in a dramatic climax asks the question "what do you think a woman under the power of others and following the one who was providing for her would do? Would she not serve every lustful desire of the men who were using her"?[29] Aeschines makes a clear connection between the inability of someone to manage well his own private life, and his inability to manage the affairs of the city:

> Aeschin. 1.30: τὸν γὰρ τὴν ἰδίαν οἰκίαν κακῶς οἰκήσαντα, καὶ τὰ κοινὰ τῆς πόλεως παραπλησίως ἡγήσατο διαθήσειν, καὶ οὐκ ἐδόκει οἷόν τ᾽ εἶναι τῷ νομοθέτῃ τὸν αὐτὸν ἄνθρωπον ἰδίᾳ μὲν εἶναι πονηρόν, δημοσίᾳ δὲ χρηστόν.

> He (sc. Solon) believed that a man who has mismanaged his own estate, would dispose of the goods of the state in a similar fashion. The lawgiver did not believe that it was possible for the same man to be bad in his private life, but good in public.

The underlying argument is that someone who lacks boundaries and cannot manage his own private life would be open to all kinds of corruption.

In extension, Demosthenes argues that men who have no boundaries to the point of being prepared to sell their own body also have no shame. Arrogant and insolent as they are (δεινοὺς καὶ θρασεῖς), they would not hesitate to cross the boundaries and speak openly about the shameful things in which they are engaged (πᾶσιν ἔξεστι λέγειν τἀκείνων ὀνείδη). Aeschines frequently refers to the lack of shame which Timarchos often exhibited in public places, including meetings of the Assembly (26). In one particular meeting of the Assembly his shamelessness was such that, according to Aeschines, some members were covering their faces embarrassed on behalf of the city by the kind of men that they were using as advisors to the people (τούς γε εὖ φρονοῦντας ἐγκαλύψασθαι, αἰσχυνθέντας ὑπὲρ τῆς πόλεως, εἰ τοιούτοις συμβούλοις χρώμεθα). He also repeatedly says that Timarchos felt no shame about his actions or what he was inflicting upon his own body.[30] He concludes that there is no point

---

28 Aeschin. 1.42. No Greek would bat an eyelid when told that a man who offered his body to other men for money was also spending lavishly on female prostitutes. All this would be considered to be part of the improper lifestyle of extravagance and excess, of which Aeschines is accusing Timarchos.

29 Dem. 59.108: τὴν δὴ ὑφ᾽ ἑτέροις οὖσαν καὶ ἀκολουθοῦσαν τῷ διδόντι τί οἴεσθε ποιεῖν; ἆρ᾽ οὐχ ὑπηρετεῖν τοῖς χρωμένοις εἰς ἁπάσας ἡδονάς;

30 Aeschin. 1.40, 42, 54, 55.

trying to eject this type of men from the roster with cries of disapproval because they have no shame.[31] They show contempt to the gods, they have no regard for the laws, and do not care about any form of shame.[32] This is powerful rhetoric because Aeschines does not exactly define what αἰσχύνη is, and which acts should bring shame to someone, but nonetheless uses this broad term to make all kinds of innuendos, and essentially allow his readers to fill in the dots and imagine what they care to imagine, while at the same time he promotes himself as a defender of decency and appropriateness in public life.

Especially in the account of Demosthenes, but also to some extent in the account of Aeschines, this lack of boundaries and shame is going hand-in-hand with the ability to speak persuasively (εἰπεῖν μὲν δεινοὺς καὶ θρασεῖς). It is a stereotype which we easily recognise from comedy, Plato and certainly the orators. In 424 Aristophanes won first prize with the *Knights*, a play where he satirised men of low birth and the tall ambition to lead the Assembly, and profit greatly from it. Greek even created a special term for it, δημαγωγός, which ever since has made its way into many modern languages to describe one particular type of populist politician with the ability to generate a large following without having any scruples. As far as we can tell, the term came into existence in the last quarter of the 5th century when under the pressures of the war, and in the vacuum of power that the death of Pericles had left this new type of politician came to prominence.[33] In the *Knights* the embodiment of this kind of politician is the Paphlagonian, a thin disguise for Kleon, only to be outmatched and outmanoeuvred by an even more vile and unscrupulous demagogue, the Sausage-seller. Several Platonic works, especially *Phaedrus* and *Gorgias,* also issue stern condemnations of those demagogues and their skill of rhetoric altogether.

The topic of low class men, who are capable with words and dangerous for that, because their ability was not accompanied by the moral character necessary to lead the Assembly and the *polis*, is also a frequent topic in the Attic orators.[34] To give a couple of examples, Aeschines paints the portrait of a corrupt demagogue for Demosthenes, while Deinarchos in the speech *Against Demosthenes* opens the speech with the words ὁ μὲν δημαγωγός and makes this theme

---

31 Aeschin. 1.34.
32 Aeschin. 1.67: καταφρονοῦντας μὲν τῶν θεῶν, ὑπερορῶντας δὲ τοὺς νόμους, ὀλιγώρως δὲ ἔχοντας πρὸς ἅπασαν αἰσχύνην.
33 See also p. 1 and n. 2.
34 See also Kamen 2020 and the Introduction, in particular n. 1–3, for relevant sources and bibliography.

a central point of his prosecution by portraying Demosthenes as the quintessential demagogue.[35]

The anxieties which seemingly urged the introduction of these laws, as these are expressed by both Demosthenes and Aeschines, are familiar. They are the anxieties which we find in Old Comedy about lowlife demagogues taking over, damaging the city and spreading corruption everywhere; in Thucydides, where populist politicians like Kleon, Alcibiades and Hyperbolos bring defeat and the final downfall of Athens; in the traumatic memories of the tyranny of the Thirty,[36] where unworthy men had brought about the suspension of the democratic constitution, and caused untold suffering in the citizen and metic population of the city; and also in the political dialogue which the Athenian democracy continued to have with itself about impending dangers from within and from outside. However, a closer look suggests that there was a certain amount of paranoia and exaggerated reaction behind the introduction of these laws. First, the number of politically active citizen men who had been prostitutes at some point in their adult lives must have been small.[37] We only have evidence of five citizen men who had been prostitutes:[38] Diophantos the orphan, Kephisodoros the so-called (καλούμενον) son of Molon, Mnesitheos the so-called son of the cook (τὸν τοῦ μαγείρου καλούμενον), Aristion the son of Aristoboulos, the pharmacist from Plataia, and Theodotos of Plataia.[39] All five were men from the lowest socioeconomic strata of Athenian society, and some were

---

35 See especially Aeschin. 3.77–78 and Deinarchos 1, *passim*. Deinarchos in fact opens his speech with the term "demagogue", Ὁ μὲν δημαγωγὸς ὑμῖν ὦ Ἀθηναῖοι καὶ θανάτου τετιμημένος ἑαυτῷ...

36 See Wolpert 2001.

37 Among female hetairai, where we are much better informed, only a tiny fraction were Athenian (like for example the quick-witted Mania, aka Melitta, Lamia the flute-player, the mistress of Demetrios Poliorcetes, or Thais, who allegedly started the fire at the palace of Persepolis); see the catalogue in Kapparis 2018, 384–442. Things may have been different among men, but we have no good reason to think that this percentage was much higher if one considers that male citizen prostitutes had more to lose than female citizen prostitutes.

38 Aeschines claims that the list was much longer, but he would rather willingly forget their names. This feigned embarrassment is not convincing; it is a standard rhetorical trick for *amplificatio*. Aeschines wants to present this rather short list as much longer, but since he lacks evidence to support this claim, he pretends that he needs to cut his narrative short, out of moral outrage.

39 Aeschin. 1.158; Lys. 3. Since the Plataians and their descendants had been offered Athenian citizenship in 427 ([Dem.] 59.104–106), I consider the two Plataian men in this list to be citizens and subject to the force of the *hetairēsis* and *dokimasia* laws, if they ever decided to pursue public office, or they were appointed to it through sortation like most magistrates.

orphaned, or men of questionable paternity (a rather important shortcoming for the establishment of citizen identity). These five fit well the profile of men or women, who took up prostitution for a living pushed by poverty, as outlined in numerous other sources.[40] In the light of this discussion we need to ask the question whether any of these men actually had the ambition to lead the city and pursue public office. One would think that such ambitious goals would seem remote to men who had found themselves in this predicament. The small number of men we know about who were citizen prostitutes, as well as the low likelihood that they would seek to lead the Assembly and occupy magistracies, raise the question why the Athenian state was so alarmed by this possibility that it introduced two different laws in a row so as to discourage them. In order to be able to answer this question we need first to understand that the introduction of a new law does not always have to be a reasonable and measured response to an existing problem; it can simply be an exaggerated and paranoid reaction to a perceived threat.

Aeschines makes clear that religious considerations played a major role in the introduction of the *hetairēsis* law (and indirectly the *dokimasia* law). He says that a male prostitute should not be appointed to any priesthood because his body is unclean. An inscription from Asia Minor indicates that one needed to wash themselves or abstain from entering the temple for a number of days after certain activities, while a hetaira was allowed to enter after three days of purification. Another inscription from Rhodes ordains that a man may enter the temple on the same day after intercourse once he purifies himself with a bath, but after thirty days of purifications if he has intercourse with a common woman. Another inscription requires three days of purification after intercourse with a hetaira.[41] Of course, such restrictions were localised and relatively inconsistent,

---

40 See also n. 26 above.

41 *Lois Sacr. de l'Asie Mineure* 18.6–15, *Lois Sacr. des cités gr. Supp.* 91.16–17; see also *LSAM* 12, where married men and women may enter the temple after intercourse on the same day, once they purify themselves. Men and women may purify themselves and enter on the second day after intercourse with someone else, and also after coming in contact with a funeral or a woman who has given birth. *LSAM* 29 states that someone may enter two days after intercourse with his wife, and three days after intercourse with a hetaira (ἀπὸ/ [γυν]αικὸς τῆς [ἰδία]ς ἡμέρας δύ[ο], [ἀπὸ ἑ]ταίρας τρεῖς). *LS* 154 A 22 requires that the priestess must abstain from all intercourse with anyone (ἀγνεύεσθαι τὰν ἱέρην τῶνδε ν μυσαρῶι μ[ὴ συμμείγνυσθαι μηδενὶ μηδαμῶς]). There are more examples of this suggesting a broad variety of rules and regulations, and affirming that impurity from intercourse with a prostitute was only mildly more severe than intercourse within marriage, and demanded maybe an additional day or two of purification.

and, to my knowledge, we do not have specific examples from Attica, but the need for purifications after intercourse and a funeral, or after a woman had given birth seems to have been transcending local boundaries. It is noteworthy that in these examples prostitutes were treated differently, and intercourse with them required a somewhat longer period of purification. Although this limited evidence does not allow us to get specific about the details and rationale behind such cultic restrictions, it still sheds some light to the comment of Aeschines that a male prostitute carries a certain impurity which would prevent him from serving as a priest (ὡς οὐδὲ καθαρῷ τῷ σώματι). The other comment of Aeschines, that a male prostitute should never exercise one of the offices of the nine archons because of their extended religious duties, part of which was to wear a crown (ὅτι οἶμαι στεφανηφόρος ἡ ἀρχή), also makes sense in this context.[42] It seems that the lawgiver considered male prostitutes to be physically unclean and, therefore, unfit to exercise religious offices, and banned them altogether. In this instance the numbers or realistic chances of a male prostitute occupying a priesthood were irrelevant. Even if one unsuitable person ever came to exercise this office it would be sufficient to offend the gods. Religious scruples do not deal in numbers; they deal in principles, and in black and white terms.

A touch of paranoia maybe adding another piece to the puzzle. The literature of the classical period contains an abundant number of references to sycophantic activities, suspicions, conspiracies, plans and real or perceived threats and attempts against the democratic constitution.[43] Isocrates (3.10) eloquently summarises these anxieties in the early 4th century:

> Αὐτοὶ γὰρ ἡμεῖς δὶς ἤδη τὴν δημοκρατίαν ἐπείδομεν καταλυθεῖσαν καὶ δὶς τῆς ἐλευθερίας ἀπεστερήθημεν οὐχ ὑπὸ τῶν ταῖς ἄλλαις πονηρίαις ἐνόχων ὄντων ἀλλὰ διὰ τοὺς καταφρονοῦντας τῶν νόμων καὶ βουλομένους τοῖς μὲν πολεμίοις δουλεύειν, τοὺς δὲ πολίτας ὑβρίζειν.

> Ourselves saw democracy abolished twice, and twice we were deprived of freedom not by men guilty of other crimes, but because of men who were contemptuous of the laws, and willing to serve the enemy and abuse the citizens.

Especially in the literature of the early 4th century, when most likely these laws were introduced, the memory of the loss of democracy and freedom was particu-

---

42 Lys. 24.13 attests that disabled persons could not serve as one of the nine archons, either, for a similar reason as male prostitutes, because the divine would not be fond of physical imperfection, in this case caused not by someone's actions, but by his condition.

43 See for example, Th. 1.107.7, 6.27.3; Isoc. 17.64; Ar. *Ec.* 453; And. 1 *passim*; Lys. 13.12, 15, and many more.

larly traumatic, as A. Wolpert has demonstrated in his excellent monograph on the subject.[44] So the question should not be whether there were anxieties, justified or not, about the future and well-being of the Athenian democracy, and the threats against it by unsuitable advisors, corrupt magistrates or unwholesome priests. The real question is why male prostitutes were singled out through the *hetairēsis* law, and were viewed as a serious threat to democracy and the institutions of the *polis*, when in reality their numbers were small and most of them had no political ambitions. D. Kamen suggested to me an answer which I find convincing.[45] She argued that male prostitutes were singled out because they were a clearly defined, more visible, and easier to target group than other perceived threats. Many of them would have been inscribed on lists of sex-workers who paid the prostitution tax (πορνικὸν τέλος) every year, and could be easily identified.[46] In fact, Aeschines anticipated the question whether Timarchos, whom he accuses of prostitution, was ever inscribed in one of those lists, and since he certainly was not, he tries to provide some explanation why he was not.[47]

Male prostitutes became a symbol, a *pars pro toto*, and were turned into a scapegoat for an entire class of the citizen body, the poor, low-born, squalid rubble of the marketplace, vilified in conservative literature like the *Old Oligarch*, ridiculed in Aristophanic plays and often viewed with disdain by the literary elite of Athens.[48] All things considered, it is reasonable to suggest that the *hetairēsis* and *dokimasia* laws were introduced as an exaggerated reaction to fears that low-life politicians, eloquent but shameless and infinitely corrupt, who had not even hesitated to sell their own body for profit, would infect the institutions of the democracy, damage public life, function as a bad influence on the people, and ultimately could undermine and destroy the democratic constitution in its entirety.

---

44 Wolpert 2001.
45 Kamen made this suggestion providing feedback to a paper on the topic delivered at the 2021 Conference of the Society for Classical Studies. I am grateful to her for this ingenious solution to a challenging problem.
46 See Kapparis 2018, 271–275.
47 Aesch. 1.119–120.
48 See for example, Ar. *Pax* 570; X. *Cyr.* 1.2.3, *Vect.* 3.13; Pl. *Prt.* 347c; Arist. *EN* 1391 a 26–30; Alcid. 16.27 Radermacher, and also Kamen 2020; Rhodes 2009, 8–13; Rosivach 1991, 189–198; Vartsos 1978, 226–244; Pipili 2000, 153–179; Patriquin 2015; Carey 2000.

5 Conclusions

The enduring success of Dover's model for Greek same-sex relations is largely owed to the fact that it was acceptable to the moral majority of his time, and addressed some of their deepest anxieties. Modern prejudices provided an influential interpretative model for ancient laws, a shining monument of 1970's homophobia with the seal of approval of a preeminent classical scholar. Dover succeeded in his efforts to whitewash the Greeks, present their constant talk and artworks about same-sex relations as more palatable and less dangerous, and reassure many of his morally upstanding and abundantly homophobic readers that the Athenians did not really enjoy homosexual relations. They were as properly (hetero)sexual as they should be, and what we find in their literature and art were simply peculiar manifestations of "quasi-sexual" educational activities. So, his readers could continue to love the Athenians free of anxieties about corrupting influences on their morals.

Modern sexual identity politics have often led scholars to project their own anxieties and prejudices upon the *hetairēsis* and *dokimasia* laws, ignoring the discussion in contemporary sources. These sources are telling us that the rationale behind their introduction, whether we consider it reasonable and justified or paranoid and distorted, was firmly rooted in the public life of the city. These statutes were the legacy of traumatic memories and ubiquitous anxieties about the dangers which the democratic constitution was facing not from outside enemies but from within, from individuals who were disregarding the law and treating contemptuously their fellow citizens, as Isocrates puts it. The fact that citizen men who had practiced prostitution were treated as the scapegoats for an entire social class, which is routinely berated in our sources and considered responsible for many of the failings of the Athenian democracy, should not surprise us. Many prostitutes and other vulnerable social groups were unreasonably and unjustly held responsible for all the ills and dysfunctions of society. To consider the small number of poor citizen, men who were pushed by unusual and extreme personal circumstances to prostitution, as the cause for the suspension of the democratic constitution twice in the late 5th century, and as an enduring existential threat for the Athenian democracy, its institutions and the entire citizen body was an outlandish exaggeration. However, history has demonstrated many times and beyond reasonable doubt that pogroms and persecutions against an entire class of citizens invariably is an irrational reaction, motivated by fear, anger or deep-seated insecurities. These documents were not a measured and calculated response to a specific need for regulation in certain areas of public life, but rather an obfuscated expression of the anxieties, traumatic memories and guilt of the dominant class in Athenian society at a point in history when the wounds of war and successive defeats were still fresh, and the memory of the assault on the democracy by the populist demagogues in the latter years of the Peloponnesian war was exacerbated by ubiquitous concerns about corruption and mismanagement in public life.

Bibliography

Atack, C. (2017), 'The History of Athenian Democracy now: Review Article', in: *History of Political Thought* 38, 576–588.

Bednarek, B. (2017), 'Ancient Homophobia: Prejudices against Homosexuality in Classical Athens', in: *Humanitas: Revista do Instituto de Estudos Clássicos* 69, 47–62.

Beneker, J. (2004), 'The Theory and Practice of Ostracism in Plutarch's *Lives*', in: *Ploutarchos: Scholarly Journal of the International Plutarch Society N.S.* 2, 3–10.

Bremmer, J.N. (1989), 'Greek Pederasty and Modern Homosexuality', in: J.N. Bremmer (ed.), *From Sappho to de Sade: Moments in the History of Sexuality*, London, 1–14.

Carey, C. (2017), *Democracy in Classical Athens*, 2nd edition, London.

Cohen, D. (1987), 'Law, Society and Homosexuality in Classical Athens', in: *Past & Present* 117, 3–21.

Cooper, C. (1997), 'Idomeneus of Lampsacus on the Athenian Demagogues', in: *Échos du monde classique = Classical views, N. S.* 16, 455–482.

Davidson, J. (2001), 'Dover, Foucault and Greek Homosexuality: Penetration and the Truth of Sex', *Past & Present* 170, 3–51.

Davidson, J.N. (1997), *Courtesans & Fishcakes: The Consuming Passions of Classical Athens*, London.

Dover, K. (1978), *Greek Homosexuality*, Cambridge, MA.

Finley, M.I. (1962), 'Athenian Demagogues. *Past and Present*', in: *A Journal of Historical Studies* 21, 3–24.

Forsdyke, S. (2000), 'Exile, Ostracism, and Athenian Democracy', in: *Classical Antiquity* 19, 232–263.

Forsdyke, S.L. (2005), *Exile, Ostracism, and Democracy: The Politics of Expulsion in Ancient Greece*, Princeton.

Golden, M. (1984), 'Slavery and Homosexuality in Athens', in: *Phoenix: Journal of the Classical Association of Canada = Revue de la Société Canadienne des Études Classiques* 38, 308–324.

Henderson, J. (2003), 'Demos, Demagogue, Tyrant in Attic Old Comedy', in: K.A. Morgan (ed.), *Popular Tyranny: Sovereignty and its Discontents in Ancient Greece*, Austin, 155–179.

Hubbard, T.K. (2003), *Homosexuality in Greece and Rome: A Sourcebook of Basic Documents*, Berkeley/Los Angeles/London.

Hubbard, T.K. (2014), 'Peer Homosexuality', in: T.K. Hubbard (ed.), *A Companion to Greek and Roman Sexualities*, Oxford, 128–149.

Jordovic, I. (2010), 'Herodotus and the Emergence of the Demagogue Tyrant Concept', in: *Göttinger Forum für Altertumswissenschaft* 13, 1–15.

Kamen, D. (2020), *Insults in Classical Athens*, Madison.

Kapparis, K. (2018), *Prostitution in the Ancient Greek World*, Berlin.

Kastely, J.L. (2015), *The Rhetoric of Plato's Republic: Democracy and the Philosophical Problem of Persuasion*, Chicago.

Khan, M.S./Johansson, E./Zaman, S./Unemo, M./Rahat, N.I./Stålsby Lundborg, C. (2010), 'Poverty of Opportunity Forcing Women into Prostitution— A Qualitative Study in Pakistan', in: *Health care for women international* 31, 365–383.

Kilmer, M.F. (1993), *Greek Erotica on Attic Red-Figure Vases*, London.

Kosmin, P.J. (2015), 'A Phenomenology of Democracy: Ostracism as Political Ritual', in: *Classical Antiquity* 34, 121–161.

Lanni, A. (2010), 'The Expressive Effect of the Athenian Prostitution Laws', in: *Classical Antiquity* 29, 45–67.

Lehmann, H.J.C. (2019), 'The Rhetoric of Home and Homeland in Demosthenes 19, *On the false embassy*', in: *American Journal of Philology* 140, 643–670.

MacDowell, D.M. (ed.) (1962), *On the Mysteries*, Oxford.

MacDowell, D.M. (2000), 'Athenian Laws about Homosexuality', in: *Revue Internationale des Droits de l'Antiquité* 42, 13–27.

Ober, J. (2001), 'The Debate over Civic Education in Classical Athens', in: Y.L. Too (ed.), *Education in Greek and Roman Antiquity*, Leiden/Boston, 175–207.

Paionidis, F./Giannakopoulos, N. (2018), *Αθηναίοι Δημαγωγοί: Ανασκευάζοντας ένα Αντιδημοκρατικό Στερεότυπο*, Athina.

Patriquin, L. (2015), *Economic Equality and Direct Democracy in Ancient Athens*, New York.

Patzer, H. (1982), *Die Griechische Knabenliebe*, Wiesbaden.

Phillips, D.J. (1982), 'Athenian Ostracism', in: G.H.R. Horsley (ed.), *Hellenika. Essays on Greek History and Politics*, North Ryde, 21–43.

Pipili, M. (2000), 'Wearing an Other Hat: Workmen in Town and Country', in: B. Cohen (ed.), *Not the Classical Ideal: Athens and the Construction of the Other in Greek Art*, Leiden, 153–179.

Rhodes, P.J. (2009), 'How Seriously Should We Take the Old Oligarch?', in: *Pegasus: The Journal of the Department of Classics and Ancient History in the University of Exeter* 52, 8–13.

Rhodes, P.J. (2016), 'Demagogues and Demos in Athens', in: *Polis: The Journal for Ancient Greek Political Thought* 33, 243–264.

Rosivach, V.J. (1991), 'Some Athenian Presuppositions about the Poor', in: *Greece and Rome: Journal of the Classical Association* 38, 189–198.

Sebastiani, B.B. (2018), 'The Coups of 411 and 404 in Athens: Thucydides and Xenophon on Conservative Turns', in: *Greek, Roman and Byzantine Studies* 58, 490–515.

Sørensen, A.D. (2016), *Plato on Democracy and Political Technē*, Leiden/Boston.

Vartsos, J.A. (1978), 'Class Divisions in Fifth Century Athens', in: *Platon: Deltion tis Etaireias Ellinon Filologon* 30, 226–244.

Wolpert, A. (2001), *Remembering Defeat: Civil War and Civic Memory in Ancient Athens*, Baltimore.

Thomas K. Hubbard
Group Sex, Exhibitionism/Voyeurism and Male Homosociality

Abstract: This chapter examines several scenes in which we see either group sex or a male figure watching others having sex. These scenes typically involve both a bearded and unbearded male figure with a nude female between them, suggesting that sex with a prostitute or flute girl could be a social activity enjoyed together by *erastēs* and *erōmenos*. These scenes should not be interpreted as satirical depictions of debauchery and excess, but as titillating conversation pieces inviting the viewers' hermeneutics. Whether sexual pedagogy or unabashed hedonism, the common thread through all the representations we study here is the centrality of masculine spectatorship and performance to the erotic imagination of a culture familiar with athletic display of nude bodies. The females in these scenes are of little interest, mere vehicles for cementing bonds of male homosociality.

One of the striking features of Greek erotic vase painting is its tendency to show intimate love-making, whether of a same-sex or heterosexual nature, occurring in public spaces in full view of others who are engaged in similar acts or have some interest in what is happening. These public spaces may be marked as gymnastic or symposiastic, drunken revels in the street, or even open orgy rooms within brothels. In only a few scenes (for examples, see Johns 1982, fig. 105–106; Dierichs 1993, 88–91) do we see the accoutrements we would expect in a private bedroom. We should not make the mistake of assuming this meant that most ancient Greek sex was public. Of course wives and concubines were shrouded in privacy, and the consequences of exhibiting one's wife inappropriately were illustrated too well by Candaules' downfall (Hdt. 1.8–10). But recreational sex, aimed only at pleasure, not reproduction or pedagogy, appears to have been a preeminently social activity that men enjoyed in the company of other men.

What we see on sympotic tableware was often deliberately provocative and even pornographic, designed to titillate inebriated men by allowing them to become voyeurs[1] into a realm of uninhibited sex and fantasy, and possibly aspirational participants. The serious academic study of pornography by contemporary

---

1 Throughout this chapter I use the term "voyeur" not in the narrow sense of a "peeping Tom" who spies on others' intimacy without their consent, but in the sense more appropriate to the

https://doi.org/10.1515/9783110695793-003

media scholars[2] highlights the appeal of such images not as confirmations of normative everyday protocols, but as exaggerated projections of the transgressive and *outré*. What these images tell us is not necessarily what most or even very many Greek men did, but what turned them on, what appealed to their innermost fantasies, what they might like to do if given the opportunity. What I wish to argue is that the kind of men who bought and used these vessels were especially stimulated by the fantasy (and in some cases reality) of having sex with women in front of or in collaboration with other men.[3]

In exploring or at least fantasising about the pleasures of watching and being watched, Greek erotic vase painting exhibits an affective pattern familiar to us from the contemporary Western digital media that have proliferated online mechanisms of voyeurism and exhibitionism, whether in teen sexting, amateur porn, webcamming, posting intimate photos on hook-up apps, or gay men using electronic devices to watch each other masturbate during periods of social isolation. Anonymous (or sometimes not anonymous) erotic subjects derive a special *frisson* and *jouissance* from unveiling to the world what should be private, or being invited safely and consensually into the intimate space of others' private interactions. In this environment, the visual replaces the tactile as the primary modality of sensual transcendence and release from our ever-narrowing boundaries of acceptable social conduct. The digital self becomes both performer and audience in a communal release of the Dionysian id. Even as the last three decades have provided our contemporaries with new technologies of unveiling the erotic self, the rapid development of more naturalistic red-figure vase painting around the turn of the century 2500 years ago produced a similar visual re-imagining of erotic space and community.

The symposiastic milieu in which these vessels were utilised is itself a male homosocial space. Even if it were one of the more sober parties, like Plato's and Xenophon's symposia, the presence of such tableware would provide occasion for sexualised and witty conversation among men. As the host provided one of these provocative kylixes to be passed around among dinner guests, would he be

---

less repressed Greek mores, namely "one who enjoys watching others with their implied consent or at least indifference". It was only with application to the former that Licht 2000, 438–439 declared voyeurism and exhibitionism absent in Greek art; Sánchez 2013, 145–150 thinks them more characteristic of Roman art.

2 The academic journal *Porn Studies* has been published by Routledge since 2014. For groundbreaking collections of essays, see Williams 2004, Coleman/Held 2014, Waugh/Arroyo 2019.

3 In favor of the group sex scenes being fantasy, see Stafford 2011, 355. On the other hand, Johns 1982, 127 and Reinsberg 1989, 103–104 think these scenes are realistic depictions of what sometimes happened.

gazing at them to assess their reactions as they examined the XXX scenes depicted on the sides of the cup? Would they quietly smile, would they laugh and then stifle their reaction, would they frown in disgust, or would they say something elegant and apropos? Would they boldly engage in intellectual hermeneutics of the interactions, as we shall do in the following analyses? What would the reclining bearded man and his younger, attractive couch companion say to each other about what they saw? Would they look at each other, giggle, kiss, or appear awkward and surprised? How would it affect their aspirational intimacy? How would guests react to the kylix tondo, once the cup was tipped to their lips and its image became gradually more visible to their eyes only inches away? The dinner guests would themselves become exhibits to the host's voyeurism, as he examines and tests their sexuality. As the gay film studies scholar Thomas Waugh put it, in discussing the all-male social environment for screenings of mid-20th century stag films in a union hall or Elks Lodge basement, "the specularization of homosocial desire is in place, in the screening room, on the screen: men getting hard pretending not to watch men getting hard watching images of men getting hard watching or fucking women".[4] Only in the Greek case, they might not need to pretend as much.

The viewing subject or audience of symposiastic pornography thereby becomes an object or spectacle in the eyes of the host who exposes them. But the viewing host/subject also submits to the risk of turning himself into an objective spectacle for his guests by revealing to them the kind of object he likes to collect. Presenting such an object at a party is tantamount to a confessional gesture, as he shares with his friends an aspect of his own erotic fantasies and predilections. How will they judge him? A gay blade? A dirty old man? Degenerate with dignity? Or just degenerate? Does his dinnerware show he likes boys or girls or both? Oral, anal, vaginal or intercrural? Group action or solo? Vanilla or rough sex? Rape fantasy or gentle persuasion? Will he be offering such entertainment to his guests later in the evening, or is he just teasing them with the suggestion of group action? Every piece we shall examine in this chapter needs to be interrogated in these terms, as an intimate act of sexual deconcealment involving both host and guest. Socially circulated pornography becomes a medium of intersubjective exposure to the Lacanian gaze of the Other, but the gaze is undermined and attenuated by a shared vulnerability to that most human of all instincts. When the pornography itself focalises scenes of mutual viewing and display of complex sexual performances, the dialectic of erotic subject and object becomes all the more powerfully deconstructed on the aesthetic as well as the social plane.

---

4 Waugh 2001, 280.

* * * * * * *

My approach is, therefore, different from the school that follows Otto Brendel's influential essay in regarding these scenes as satirical depictions of drunkenness and excess, intended to disgust rather than titillate a proper symposiast.[5] I do not think prudish moralists like Pericles[6] would have been the primary market for purchasing such unusual commodities or displaying them at their parties; they could find plenty of less risqué alternatives in the potters' quarter. I fear that scholars' tendency to dismiss these pieces as laughable cartoons of acts no one in their right mind would ever want to attempt may project our own discomfort with the queerness of the images, which sometimes fail the test of egalitarian collaboration that is at the heart of modern sexual ethics. No respectable scholar would want to confess to finding these mingled bodies and acts erotically exciting. This is to say that we would be bad guests at classical Greek symposia, where mutual exposure of both host's and guests' sexuality was part of the game, as Plato, Xenophon and Athenaeus all understood well in their sympotic works.

Scholars are wont to project modern standards of privacy onto Greek men by arguing that sex in front of others is behaviour the Greeks attribute only to a few barbarians at the outer limits of civilisation, like the Anatolian tribe encountered by Xenophon (*Anab*. 5.4.34).[7] However, the casualness of public nudity by Greek men and boys tells us that their standards of public decency were very different from ours, and a private party of drunk friends or their nude and lewd komastic revels in the street are hardly equivalent to the customs of barbarians who openly

---

5 Brendel 1970, 26–27, who called **Figure 1** "an early example of erotic art that is intended as social criticism… a protest against social manners or, more generally, impatience with human nature as such". He compares such representations to the art of Rembrandt or George Grosz. Also taking this approach are more recent critics, including Sutton 2000, 184; Neer 2002, 22–23; Topper 2012, 108–121; Parker 2015, 80–93; and with reference to homosexual orgies specifically, Blanshard 2015. It is interesting that this approach did not find favor in the abundant critical literature from the 1970s to the 1990s.

6 Pericles was well-known for his sobriety and dislike of symposia (Plutarch, *Pericles* 5.1–4, 7.4–5). As I have argued, in Hubbard 2015a, 384–385, this extended to conservative sexual morality that foregrounded family-life and depreciated male homosociality, given his policy of encouraging native-Athenian population growth to rule an expanding empire.

7 See Dover 1974, 206, and Parker 2015, 80, relying mostly on philosophical texts that advise ideal behaviour, rather than describing universal practice. *Dissoi Logoi* 2.4 refers only to avoiding husband-wife intimacy outdoors, and Herodotus 2.64 merely pertains to avoiding sex in temples and sacred precincts, as if it were permissible in some other outdoor spaces. That it did sometimes occur outdoors is implied by the anecdote about a boy stealing Sophocles' cloak when they lay together outside the city walls (Athenaeus 13.604D–E, citing Hieronymus of Rhodes).

copulate *en plein air*. Even if some behaviours like non-dyadic or semi-public sex might be shunned by the vast majority of Athenian citizens, transgression of conservative sexual norms in itself often appeals to the young and/or adventurous. Severe prohibitions against adultery did not prevent it from occuring in ancient Greece.

I would propose that we reconsider the matter by comparing a number of group sex scenes involving men and women. I find it significant that we have no available examples of Greek vases showing two or more women gratifying a single man (a common staple of modern pornography),[8] but many examples of two men with a single woman or men watching other men with women. This suggests to me that semi-public sex (whether actual or imagined) was a social performance in which much of the stimulus was in being seen and perhaps even envied by one's fellow men as an accomplished *magister amandi*. Aristophanes (*Frogs* 524–528) implies that intercourse with a sex worker in the presence of one's own slave was normal as a manifestation of the master's privilege.

Outside of comedy, we do not have many literary sources from classical Greece that discuss sex acts in detail, but there are a few. Most relevant for our purpose is the oration *Against Neaera* ([Dem.] 59.33–35), which tells us that Phrynion, one of the erotic star's early patrons, was so proud of having her as his possession that he enjoyed performing sex with her at parties in front of other men, thereby attaching distinction (*philotimia*) to himself in the eyes of the onlookers. However, one night, when both of them were wasted with drink, the onlookers, including even some of their host's slaves, helped themselves to a share of that distinction by having intercourse with her. Humiliated by being treated as a common prostitute, Neaera absconded to Megara with her own possessions and many of Phrynion's.

Aeschines tells us that Timarchus' lovers purchased the services of flute-girls and expensive *hetairai* for him (1.75), as well as treating him to extravagant meals and gambling. Are we to imagine that he went off to a private room and enjoyed these female companions on his own, or is it not more likely that the lovers who paid his bills enjoyed them with him? Clearly, facilitating his intimacy with the women was part and parcel of his wealthy lovers' sexual intimacy with Timarchus himself. Prior to Phrynion, Neaera was owned by two young friends, Eucrates and Timanoridas ([Dem.] 59.29–30), both of whom wanted to get her out of Corinth when it came time for them both to marry. That they acted together in such concord suggests a *menage à trois* in which the relationship of the two men to each other was more important than Neaera.

---

8 Kilmer 1993, 58; Sánchez 2013, 130; Robson 2013, 133–134.

To illustrate the possibilities of such homoerotic involvement through the medium of a purchased woman, let us view some suggestive images, such as the familiar cup of the Pedieus Painter **(Figure 1)**. A bearded man penetrates a woman from the rear, while an unbearded youth shoves his penis into her mouth. This is one of several acts of copulation around the sides of the kylix, but this is the only one that completely preserves both of the male figures on each side of the woman such that we can estimate their relative ages. All of the women appear flabby and unattractive, with short hairstyles typical of slaves;[9] although some have interpreted the lines around their mouths as marks of unnatural distention caused by the oral sex,[10] that is not what oral sex actually looks like and the lines are more likely wrinkles, complementing their double chins and denoting that these are older *pornai* who submit to humiliating treatment out of desperation.[11] Indeed, toothless old women would doubtless be the best at oral sex.[12] Three of the women on both sides of the cup crouch down uncomfortably on all fours like animals; the woman on the table has her body twisted around in an impossible posture, with her legs widely splayed as the bearded man impales her with his thrusting member.[13] The unusually long and thick member of the youth on the right also seems to emphasise the discomfort of the woman whose mouth is stretched wide to receive it; he has to support her head with his left arm to tilt it at the correct angle for his comfort.

I find it revealing that the bearded man in this threesome does not even look down at the woman, but looks straight ahead toward the face of the youth, whose pleasure seems to interest him more than anything in the woman's body. The youth in turn looks at the bearded man's act of penetration at the other end of the action. That the older man holds a sandal need not necessarily mean that the sex is coerced against the woman's will so much as that he is the one in control of the situation, giving orders to his partners.[14] He is likely the one who paid for this entertainment.

---

9 Sutton 2000, 196–197.

10 Reinsberg 1989, 117; Kilmer 1997, 116; Kurke 1997, 137; Sutton 2000, 196–197; Robson 2013, 134.

11 That these are older women was recognised by Keuls 1985, 184; Pfisterer-Haas 1989, 197. See Brendel 1970, 27, on the women's "haggard, avid, worn-out features".

12 As recognised in Nicarchus' epigram (*AP* 5.38). See Henderson 1991, 183–85; Sutton 2000, 191.

13 Reinsberg 1989, 117.

14 Note that the woman's right elbow is raised in a blocking move. I would interpret the sandal in this case as symbolic of control rather than strictly necessary for that purpose. It is not aimed at the buttocks or any sensitive part of the body. Presumably, these experienced slave prostitutes

Most of these threesomes reveal a similar composition **(Figure 2a)**: a confident and fully naked bearded man approaches the woman for genital penetration, in this case assertively laying hold of her butt cheeks, while a beardless youth holds her head for oral gratification. This youth does a high kick with one of his legs, as if to betray his animated excitement (or inexperienced clumsiness) as he struggles to disrobe himself. The youth's visibly eager penis contrasts with the man's tightly infibulated member, suggesting the adult's calmness and superior self-control. The parallel scene on the other side of the same cup **(Figure 2b)** again shows the bearded man claiming access to the woman's genitals, his authority reinforced by the presence of a sandal hidden behind his back. The woman's raised leg appears to open herself up to his advance, so the hidden sandal is probably not a mark of direct coercion; Kilmer has argued that its function in these scenes is stimulus.[15] Again, the excited boy does an awkward dance as he untangles himself from his cloak to join the action.[16] Although his penis is partially obscured by the hanging drape of his cloak, the part we do see is visibly thicker and tumescent in contrast to the man's complete self-control. Or could the unaroused state of the two men suggest they needed more foreplay than their horny, but inexperienced adolescent companion? The scenes beg for hermeneutic intervention by the symposiasts as they pass the cup around.

---

knew what their job was; as unattractive older women, they were not in a strong position to negotiate the terms of their engagement, but might agree to a little light spanking for an extra drachma. On the other hand, Keuls 1985, 180–181 speaks of "forcible coercion of resisting hetaerai". Other than the woman's right elbow getting in the way of any use of the sandal, I do not see gestures of resistance to sexual penetration, such as pushing the men away. See also Kurke 1997, 137, on what she interprets as "repeated scenes of violence and sexual abuse of female participants". At the other extreme of interpretation is Kilmer 1993, 114–118, who constructs a fantastic scenario in which the man is mischievously about to give the woman, who is close to orgasm, a stimulating slap which will enhance her vaginal contractions, but simultaneously cause her to bite down on the youth's penis. This assumes rivalry rather than collaboration.

15 Kilmer 1993, 110–112. Far from seeing it as a sign of phallic domination, Kilmer suggests the man on side B is impotent, and is perhaps going to present the sandal "as a shy prelude to asking her to do it to him". In contrast, Keuls 1985, 180 thinks the man is pretending "to caress the girl" before he sadistically slaps her with the hidden sandal.

16 The awkward posture of the boy on Side A might be explained by both of his hands being occupied, as if he had not thought that he needed to get his garment off before grabbing the woman's head. However, the boy on Side B has both hands free and still seems to struggle with rapid removal of his clothing. Both boys appear to be excited latecomers to the action, not quite assured in their technique. Dierichs 1993, 85–86 speaks of the youths' *Anfeuerungsbewegungen* in this piece.

In **Figure 3**, a column krater once owned by the famous gay connoisseur E.P. Warren,[17] we see a komastic scene in which a fully nude bearded man faces the woman frontally, extending his hand toward her pelvic area and pointing straight at it with a phallic staff. Far more excited is the youth on the other side of the woman, who rushes to grab her shoulder while he holds a wineskin with the other hand, as if eager to pour another drink of unmixed wine into the cup she is holding. It is unclear whether the man and youth are companions or rivals, but their presence in the same processional komos makes the former more likely. There are no signs that they are about to come to blows over the woman. The man's demeanour is calm and controlled; note that he has no erection, compared to the more urgent member of the youth. Indeed, the woman is moving away from the enamored youth who grabbed her, looking back at his erection with a facial expression of some alarm. The gesture of the man's hand could be meant as a sign to the youth to stop his advance upon her, as if to warn him that she belongs to another or that she is already drunk enough to be socially lubricated or that they should wait until they arrive at their destination before becoming too eager to consummate. The man's gaze appears to focus in the direction of either the woman's private parts or the wineskin held by the youth. Again, the ambiguous action invites hermeneutic insertion of the viewer into the scene.[18]

A somewhat different and less ambiguous scenario involving three men is at work in **Figure 4**. A bearded man on one side and a smiling youth on the other together lower a fair-haired woman, legs spread wide apart and vulva prominently displayed, onto the partially erased penis of another youth lying on a table. Again, the man is not erect, but the two youths are, and the man's gaze appears to fix not on the woman, but on the male partner opposite him, who gazes at the woman's face, as she in turn gazes down at his erect member. This is clearly a scene of collaboration, not competition.[19] The woman gives no sign of struggle, but extends her arms outward as a way of balancing herself during the sexual acrobatics.

---

17 On whom, see Hubbard 2015b.

18 Keuls 1985, 174 says the man's staff suggests "that he will soon brutalise the hetaera and force her to practice *fellatio* on him". I do not think the man's exact intentions are so easily legible.

19 However, La Rocca 1978, 122 interprets the youth's expression as "almost funereal" and likens the whole scene to a "torture chamber." Keuls 1985, 84 refers to the piece as "distasteful obscenity... by a coarse hand". Von Bothmer 1967, 818–819 declared the piece to be a 19th century forgery; his doubts are echoed by Kilmer 1993, 169. As we have seen before, such negative judgments may reflect the critic's discomfort rather than the evidence of the illustration.

So far, we have been examining scenes involving the interaction of two or three men, one bearded (signifying "fully mature") and the others unbearded (signifying "younger"). Both use the woman as a mere tool for their mutual pleasure and typically delight in sharing her body between them.[20] What is their relationship to each other? *Erastēs* and *erōmenos*? Older and younger brother going out for a night on the town? Uncle and nephew? Gasp, father and son? Before we dismiss the latter possibilities out of our incest aversion, let us consider the hydria in **Figure 5**. This is not a sexually explicit scene: Eva Keuls even supposed it was a father and his sons bringing money home to his wife. Others have associated the moneybag with its more typical use in such scenes, which is to denote prostitution, which may also be implied by the mirror this seated woman holds and the alabastron hanging on the wall.[21] But Keuls' intuition of a familial connection between the man who leans forward to talk, and the stiff, tightly wrapped, bashful looking youth behind him may not be far from the mark.[22]

---

20 A variant of this type is the lost kylix by the Antiphon Painter (*ARV²* 339.55, depicted as R490 in Kilmer 1993). Side A gives us a typical scene of an aggressive man, in this case with a neatly trimmed goatee and mustache, fully nude and aroused, pulling up a woman's legs and about to hit her with a sandal, while a half-naked youth on the other side dances or gesticulates. It is unclear whether he is objecting to his partner's violence (so Keuls 1985, 183), but the flaccidity of his penis suggests his motives are not sexual (so Kilmer 1993, 112, who suggests he is a mere voyeur). More striking is the other side of the same piece, where the figure on the far right again establishes his control by threatening the woman with a sandal. Since his lower face is mostly obscured by his shoulder, we cannot tell whether he is bearded or unbearded, but he does appear larger and more muscular than the adolescent on the other side. The incipient action is watched by a woman being penetrated from the rear by a smaller adolescent, who wraps his hands around her thighs and back. We may be meant to see the difference between a more violent and more cooperative interaction. A timid adolescent is less likely to need or want force, perhaps content with plain vanilla dorsal sex.

21 Keuls 1983, 228–229, and 1985, 260–262, saying the woman's stern affect would win her few customers if she were a prostitute; Keuls is followed by Bundrick 2012, who admits some ambiguity, however. For the view that she is a prostitute, see Murray 1985, 26, and Neils 2000, 211–213. Dyfri Williams 1993, 97 proposed that the smaller boy was the prostitute's son (or slave), and the man might be "a father paying for his shy son's first adventure". On the other hand, Fischer 2007 thinks he is an *erastēs* paying for his *erōmenos* to receive sex education from the courtesan, and that the gym equipment is meant to suggest their association in the homoerotic world of the palaestra. She sees a visual contrast of the aryballos between the two men (representing gymnastic homoeroticism) and the alabastron hanging in front of the woman (representing feminine allure).

22 As both Fischer 2007 and Bundrick 2012, 17–18 note, the sponge and strigil suspended midair in front of the youth should not be interpreted as literally hanging on an otherwise invisible wall, but serve a symbolic function, identifying him as a youth of good class who attends the palaestra. He is certainly not a slave.

While most critics have thought the smaller boy inside the house is the prostitute's son or tout, who has brought her customers, one wonders why a boy luring customers into a brothel would be so modestly dressed. He could also be a slave belonging to the man,[23] but we then have to question why he would be the first to present himself to her, unless perhaps his childish voyeurism brought him such pleasure that he was eager to facilitate the transaction. It is notable that his posture and dress make him look exactly like a smaller version of the tall youth walking behind the man, suggesting he is a younger brother.[24] Could his relative forwardness reveal that he is an even younger son the man is bringing to her for his sexual initiation? If so, does his older brother approve or disapprove? Could the initiation be witnessing the father's technique with a prostitute? Could this be a scenario behind some of the other scenes we have seen? The Hebrew injunction not to "uncover the father's nakedness" hardly applied in a culture where male nudity was routine and sex was frankly acknowledged. As in other scenes, the picture seems to pose a hermeneutic challenge to its audience, raising more questions than answers.

Sometimes group sex involves youths of the same age interacting with a prostitute. For example, in **Figure 6a**, a lively kantharos by the Nikosthenes Painter, and also one of E.P. Warren's favourites, we see four youths at play, as a woman prepares to fellate a reclining youth, while another youth is about to penetrate her from the rear with an artificial phallus (from among others hanging on the wall of the brothel),[25] perhaps not yet ready with his own erection or perhaps wanting to dilate her anus in preparation for anal sex. Note that the fellated youth does not look down to the woman, who is overweight and unattractive, but across her back to his friends at the other end, as if watching their enjoyment is his primary source of pleasure. Although he holds a sandal in his right hand, his arm is in a relaxed posture behind his head, such that the sandal is more symbolic than necessary. What I find especially interesting in this piece are the two youths on the left, who on the same long couch are about to have intercourse with each other, again suggesting that homoerotic and heteroerotic couplings could be at work in the same space and even act as a stimulant to each other. Martin Kilmer believed that the second figure is a woman with an "androgynous figure", but the

---

23 As suggested by Murray 1985, 26.
24 Bundrick 2012, 14.
25 Lear/Cantarella 2008, 120 suggest he was inserting into her rectum the nipple of a wineskin, perhaps with the goal of making her drunk.

breast shape and hairstyle are more consistent with the male youths on the other side of the vase, **Figure 6b**.[26]

It is interesting that we find youths about to have anal intercourse with each other, but we do not on any of these vases find youths about to have intercourse with women, other than oral; instead they probe with sex toys or a tentative finger, as we see the skinny boy on Orvieto 585 (= ARV^2 339.51, Beazley Archive #203485) does, although he seems a bit uncertain in finding the right spot, as if deliberating whether to explore her anus or less accessible vagina.[27] Actual intercourse with women is the privilege of the adult men in these group scenes, although we clearly see youths learning their way around women's bodies and even sometimes appropriating the tools of command, like the almost ubiquitous sandal. Although curious about the heterosexual events around them, some of the boys feel more comfortable having sex with each other. Others want to have the reassurance of a more experienced friend or older male companion with them as they sample the other sex. Group sex may well have been thought to have a pedagogic function within the social environment of the late sixth and early fifth centuries, to which all of these pieces belong. At the very least it appealed to the imagination as an opportunity for men and youths to interact with one another intimately, or of youthful friends to visit a brothel together, like sailors or "fratbros" out for a night at the local whorehouse.

There is also a class of depictions in which we see one of the parties merely as an interested onlooker to a sex act or its prelude. For example on one side of a fine kylix by the Brygos Painter (**Figure 7**), we see a bearded man on a sympotic

---

26 Kilmer 1993, 116–117, 182, who believes the vase painter made an error in depicting the breast. For a similar view, see Peschel 1987, 66–68; Rabinowitz 2002, 142–145; Parker 2015, 62–63. That the figure is male was correctly understood by Dover 1978, 86–87; Reinsberg 1989, 99–100; Dierichs 1993, 85; Lear & Cantarella 2008, 119. A similar element of homoerotic mingling in the absence of enough women is evident in **Figure 6b**, where the eager youth in the center rubs his groin against the buttocks of the youth to his right, who grabs a fleeing woman's breasts, as does the youth on his left, whom he turns around to watch.

27 For a line drawing of both sides of this piece, see Kilmer 1993, R486. He believes (in 1993, 46–47) that the two sides illustrate the same characters at different stages, with the two youths standing by as the woman drains a huge amphora on one side and drawing closer as she crouches "doggy-style" in preparation for (but not yet consummation of) penetration from both ends: "exploratory rather than copulatory" in Kilmer's phrase, as appropriate for adolescents (1993, 112–113). However, the woman's hairstyle appears to be different on the two sides, so I do not think we need to conceive of these as two panels in a sequential cartoon. Still, the association between female inebriation and sexual availability is clear. It is interesting that the interior of this piece features a mostly undraped boy holding a lyre and skyphos and turning around to gaze, as if he has just seen something interesting.

couch, who is clearly the central and dominant figure in this carefully composed scene, balanced by two other males of different ages on the extremes and two women in between each of the three males.[28] To the left, in front of his couch, are a blond flute girl seated on on a stool and a naked serving boy leaning on the pillar in a seductive contrapposto, his buttocks turned toward the banqueters as if begging attention that he does not receive. The bearded man pays them no attention, but instead twists his body around to watch the action on the right, on another couch beside his: a younger man and woman tentatively caress each other, while he encourages them by offering a skyphos of wine as a social lubricant. The young man has his lips parted as if he is speaking to the girl,[29] into whose eyes he directly gazes, as she coyly lowers her own gaze. The girl appears not quite certain of her reaction to the young man, her legs partly on the couch and partly off,[30] her lower body facing forward, but her torso twisted in the other direction as the young man engages her. The young man holds her left forearm with his left hand, and grasps her left shoulder with his right hand; she in turn wraps her right hand around his right forearm,[31] such that their arms create an intimate criss-cross pattern. Her downcast gaze directs our attention to the young

---

28 Note the same general composition in the banquet scene on the other side of this kylix, where we again have three males of different ages separated by two females. Again, we have a skinny boy leaning against a column on the far left (this one fully clothed and holding a lyre; Filser 2017, 238 wrongly supposes him a mature youth, but his proportions are clearly smaller), a seated woman doing her own thing (in this case drinking), and men on two separate couches, but in this case the younger man, his head wrapped in a long fillet characteristic of victorious athletes (although Filser 2017, 238 wrongly thinks it is a mitra), is the dominant figure on the central couch, and he turns around to talk to the bearded man on the far right. Kilmer 1993, 119 believes that they are both looking at the standing flute-girl between them, but their line of vision is directly into each other's eyes: all the youth could see of the flute girl is her backside, and neither of them have their heads raised to be looking at her face, which is on a higher level. As in many other scenes we have discussed, the primary social relationship is between the older and younger man, with the women being no more than intermediaries in mutual pleasure.

29 Kilmer 1993, 119 believes the younger man has a light beard, but closer examination of the piece using modern digital technology reveals that he does not have one, but merely an elongated chin, perhaps meant to emphasise his open mouth.

30 Kilmer 1993, 119 believes the position of the legs suggest she has just climbed up onto the couch, but is "not yet completely committed". However, she does not sit on the end of the couch in a defensive posture facing opposite the young man, but with her feet forward like his, as if she were getting ready to lean back in his arms.

31 Kilmer 1993, 119 interprets this as a gesture of resistance, but it could also be reciprocation for his holding her left arm. Given the woman's awkward twisted torso, she could also be using his right arm to support herself.

man's bare chest, below which his left hip is exposed, leaving his as yet una-roused genitals hanging just above the coverlet.[32] His right foot is visible against her right thigh, as if stroking it. Watching this young couple's cautious first steps in love-making is of far more fascination to the central figure than either of the available sex partners directly in front of him. We should note that the pubescent wine-server at the extreme right mirrors the bearded man (and the young woman on the couch) by twisting his torso around to gaze at the scene of the two young lovers, perhaps with developing interest for active sports that may be in his own future.[33]

On a later stamnos by Polygnotus (Paris CP9682 = *ARV²* 1029.16, Beazley Ar-chive #213398) we see a youthful (unbearded) lyre player as an onlooker, while two naked, ithyphallic men carry off a naked woman between them, with the clear intention of using her sexually, perhaps with simultaneous vaginal and anal penetration. The lyre player is certainly not a participant in the action, as he is fully clothed, but his forward gaze beholds it. He raises his cloak with one arm as if to conceal any erection that he might have. At this moment, he is holding his lyre rather than playing it, as only one hand is available, the other doing who knows what underneath his cloak.[34]

Several other vases show voyeurs watching others perform acts of varying levels of intimacy. These can range from single men comfortably facing or con-

---

32 Filser 2017, 671 n. 461 takes note of the girl's sandal in an upright position, leaning against the footstool and pointing vertically to the youth's flaccid penis. He sees its implications as erotic, as in other scenes of a hetaera unbinding her sandal. That she removed it and positioned it so carefully against the footstool on which she may have previously been sitting suggests a level of deliberate intentionality in climbing up onto the couch. Note also the prominence of her bare foot dangling off the couch.

33 It is a matter of controversy whether these naked serving boys were pretty slaves or boys of free status who were given this role as an initiation into the ways of the symposium. For a survey of the question, see Topper 2012, 53–62. Their mythological forebears, Ganymede, Pelops, and Dionysus' son Oenopion, were boys of the highest status, and the historian Kleidemos (*FGrH* 323F5) reports that it was a role performed by Athenian heralds. Even if the boy on this vase is merely a slave, he is clearly male and curious, like any boy of his age.

34 Marcadé 1965, 143; also Kilmer 1993, 168–169 notes that the pair of men holding the woman aloft are coded as older (full beard) and younger (developing chin hair), with the younger man gazing at his companion. Reinsberg 1989, 133–135 regards it as a highly collaborative and even "romantic" scene in which even the woman displays her enthusiasm by masturbating the younger man with one hand, stroking his hair with the other, and gazing up at the heavens with an expression of rapture.

versing with an intimate couple to servants or dancers watching full-blown intercourse.[35] On the shoulder of an interesting hydria by the Kleophrades Painter (Munich 2427 = ARV^2 189.72, Beazley Archive #201720), we see as the central figure in a five-person composition a tiny, barely pubescent serving girl with a fruit basket balanced on her head and an alabastron in her hand, who turns around to watch a long-haired young woman attempting to seduce a seated ephebe by placing her hand on his shoulder, as if to push his cloak down further. This clearly interests the girl more than the couple on her other side, who reverse the order of standing and seated as a bearded man more confidently presents a gift to a seated woman.[36] The scene is clearly meant to be a brothel,[37] but we can hardly imagine the young woman is purchasing the services of the youth. This may be his first visit to such an establishment, accompanying the older man on the right side, who is either his father or *erastēs*. That he would sit down in one of the chairs meant for the prostitutes suggests inexperience, which may be why this attractive young *hetaera* takes the initiative with him. Although she looks down at his face, he shows little interest and looks straight ahead, meeting the gaze of the young girl with the basket as she sees him watch the actions of the older man and *hetaera* behind her. The young girl may be envisioning her own future as she watches the young woman's technique of seduction, much like the serving boy on the far left of **Figure 7**. She obviously prefers to envision that future in the eyes of the rather unsure male teenager who looks back at her, not the older man in front of her. This scene is like **Figure 7** in showing the specularisation of desire

---

35 For the former type, see Villa Giulia 50458 (=ARV^2 173.5, Beazley Archive #201569). A lost piece once in Corneto (for a reproduced photo, see Reinsberg 1989, Fig. 112) shows a banqueter turning around to watch a man and youth on the next couch actively converse. For the latter type, see London W39 (= ABV 297.16, Beazley Archive #320395), where an excited male dancer watches a man and youth having intercrural intercourse, or Getty 82.AE.27, where an ithyphallic boy runs to join in the active intercourse in front of him, but for now has to be satisfied with spectatorship (see Dierichs 1993, 87; Kilmer 1993, 35; Parker 2015, 88) is wrong to dismiss him merely as a hired dancer, as the erection indicates he is aroused by what he is watching). Also of interest is the komastic scene on a cup by the Brygos Painter (Würzburg L479 = ARV^2 372.32, Beazley Archive #203930), where a youth turns around to speak to the couple behind him, pointing to the two men in front of them, who are about to come to blows over one of the *hetaerai*. At the tail end of the procession is a neglected serving boy who turns away from the whole scene in disgust or disinterest (or disappointment?). Note also the seated women at each flank of New York 07.286.47 (=ARV^2 175, Beazley Archive #201603), who watch, apparently with more amusement than disapproval, the man on the banqueting couch diddling the pubescent penis of the serving boy.

36 This woman also has a slim figure, but shorter hair. Hoesch 1990, 233 thinks she looks older.

37 Reinsberg 1989, 125–126; Hoesch 1990, 233.

in three different age groups (pubescent, late adolescent and fully adult), but distinctive in its specularisation of budding female desire.

Figure 8 is heavily damaged, but also quite extraordinary in its articulation of active female desire. The outside of this kylix by the Thalia Painter depicts an orgy of no fewer than 17 characters, but it is the interior I find most fascinating. Here the tables are turned as a woman on top uses the sandal to subdue a bearded man underneath her. This should cause us to agree with Kilmer in questioning narrow interpretations of the sandal as merely a tool of rape or sexual coercion: the man, who has most likely been the one to pay for the encounter, finds sexual stimulus in adopting a masochistic position. The sight so excites the youth sitting next to them that he masturbates and appears ready to join in, although it is not yet clear whom he will penetrate.[38] The man in turn focuses his gaze on the masturbating woman underneath the couch, who faces the ground and whose eyes are shut.[39] Her pleasure is not visual, like that of the two males, but aural, focused on fantasies derived from the sound of what is going on above her. The whole composition of the piece emphasises the unity of the four participants, with interlaced limbs (one can never be sure exactly whose), similar hairstyles on both male and female figures, and everyone appearing to take pleasure in this sexual romp. This piece is unique and challenging in its depiction of female dominance, male masochism and female pleasure, but it does at least suggest that these were possibilities of which a Greek audience was aware. The kylix depicts women as active and willing participants who seem to be having a good time: some on the sides of the cup perform lewd dances, another leads a man by his erection, and another receives cunnilingus from a man sitting on the floor.[40]

---

38 Brendel 1970, 23–24 thinks this youth is merely a slave shouting to encourage his master, but his involvement in the scene seems much closer than that. He also thinks the woman is punishing the man for losing interest in her and paying too much attention to the other woman on the ground.
39 Some scholars think the woman on the floor is asleep and merely resting her hand over her private parts. See Johns 1982, 149–150, and Dierichs 1993, 86–87. La Rocca 1978, 91 has it both ways by saying that she is masturbating, but sleepy. In favor of conscious masturbation, see von Bothmer 1964, 409; Boardman 1975, 61; Peschel 1987, 52; Kilmer 1993, 65; Kurke 1997, 134; Parisinou 2000, 25.
40 See the remarks of Peschel 1987, 50–55; Reinsberg 1989, 115–117; Kurke 1997, 134–135; Stewart 1997, 165; Hedreen 2015, 267–271.

Figure 9 shows multiple acts of oral gratification and intercourse by women who appear stout and older, like those of **Figure 1**.[41] It is the non-participant figure who is most interesting, in this case a clothed man on the far right holding a lamp in one hand and his staff with the other arm.[42] Sutton believes the man is shocked and attempting to interfere with what he sees going on, as if he were scandalised, but I think it more likely that the room he has entered is an open brothel that is rather dark.[43] As his staff and attire indicate, he has just entered from outside and is beholding the kind of pleasures on offer here; note that his lips are parted as if he is speaking. Seeing is one step closer to participating.[44] Although some of the scenes we have viewed are clearly symposiastic or komastic, in most of them wine and drinking vessels play little role and we may be safe in concluding that they are, like this one, action that goes on inside a brothel.

---

41 See Pfisterer-Haas 1989, 198. However, Keuls 1985, 181–182 notes that the "girl" being lifted up for copulation is slimmer, more supple, and younger than the others.

42 LaRocca 1978, 95 and Parisinou 2000, 25 believe the man is intentionally holding the flaming lamp beneath the buttocks of the girl held aloft directly in front of him, but if that were the case, he would be looking down at it. If he were already that involved in the action of this scene, one would expect him to be naked like all the other men. Compare the boy (perhaps a slave, but ithyphallic) who holds a lamp on Side B of the orgy scene in **Figure 1** and the lampstand in his other hand, suggesting both his voyeuristic pleasure in seeing the action and that it may be transpiring in a rather dark room. However, Parisinou also reads this scene as meant to coerce a woman into submission. These are the only two cases she can posit for lamps being used sadistically; all of the many other cases she examines (2000, 24–28) are about illumination, especially in sexual spaces. Kilmer 1993, 44 n. 34 thinks the proximity of the lamp to her buttocks is an illusion created by the lack of three-dimensional perspective.

43 Sutton 1997, 12. Specifically, he thinks the man is looking beyond the couple directly in front of him, with his line of vision focused on the flute the long-bearded, hairy-chested man is holding to threaten the kneeling woman into oral sex. This sadistic interpretation is also favored by Keuls 1985, 181–182, and admitted as a possibility by Kilmer 1993, 124–125. Although she does reach out with her hands toward the flute, the compulsion she fears may not be that she is about to be struck with it, but that it is her flute (often a symbol of oral sex) that the man has taken. The visual pun may be that he wants something else in her skilled mouth other than her flute. Hers are not gestures of supplication toward the man, but more the motions of someone reaching out to grab it back. The man, for his part, is not holding it up as one holds a sandal if about to use it, but is teasing the girl's by holding it back just beyond her reach. I do not think he needs it to compel oral sex, as the woman is already naked, kneeling, opening her mouth, and even sexually excited, as one can see from her erect nipple; also noted by Kilmer 1993, 125. In favour of this room being a brothel, where no Greek man would be shocked to find such action, see Wrenhaven 2009, 375–378.

44 Sánchez 2013, 130–132 thinks the man is too old to be anything but a voyeur, but I see no obvious signs of age. If anything, some of the other men have longer beards.

Finally, let us look at the all-male orgy scene of **Figure 10a**. Blanshard suggests that this tableau is not meant to be erotically attractive because only one youth appears to be receiving penile stimulation.[45] However, the four dancing youths on each side of the middle threesome are all looking at the action intently, even when they need to twist their heads to do so. The spectating youth to the left of the threesome displays a prominent erection (**Figure 10b**), as if he is ready to take his turn in these naked frolics, just like the voyeuristic youths we have seen on other pieces. Although more difficult to see because of damage to the paint on this part, the two youths on the flanks of the composition appear to have turned away to attend to their own members, but peer over their shoulders for voyeuristic stimulus.[46] This is hardly a scene of scandalous drunken excess, as there is not a wine cup in sight on this side of the kylix. We do see similar youths drinking on the other side, but no sign of sexual excitement. Perhaps the point is to illustrate two different and distinct types of youthful pleasures on the respective sides.

I have elsewhere explained this scene as an example of "sexual experimentation" by youths, which can sometimes take non-standard forms of play.[47] Holt Parker is without a clue about the scene, declaring it "not evidence of anything".[48] But the point is not to produce evidence of what people actually did, but what they found interesting to imagine. Here, what is imagined is a milieu of free and open sexual play among teenage boys without a hint of shame or any inhibition by normative sexual scripts or "protocols". Upon receiving this cup in their hands, mature symposiasts would be tempted to recite nostalgic elegiac verses like those of Mimnermus (fr. 1 W) or Theognis (1063–1070). This image's transgressive and non-normative sexual scenario "queer" it, such that critics intent on discerning only their own personal versions of "normative" either pass it over in silent *aporia*, like the otherwise loquacious Dover, or dismiss it as some kind of

---

45 Blanshard 2015, 105–107. Reinsberg 1988, 206 finds the scene disgusting for a different reason because she thinks all seven boys are either male prostitutes or boys of good class behaving sluttishly like male prostitutes. But there is no older man present to buy their favors or anything else to suggest these are anything but boys just wanting to have wholesome safe sex and non-penetrative fun with each other. They are all age equal, and there is nothing to suggest any hierarchy among them.

46 This painter does pay attention to the pelvic regions of the two youths with a wineskin between them on the other side of the kylix, where the fine lines are better preserved. Unfortunately the fine lines on this side have eroded away with time, making it difficult to determine exactly what the two flanking youths are doing with their hands.

47 Hubbard 2003, 20, and 2014, 131. See Kilmer 1993, 57: "adolescents were expected to be more experimental, less governed by taboo and social constraint".

48 Parker 2015, 50.

bad joke. Queer criticism can read such a piece with more sensitivity to its implications.

What does any of this reveal about the contemporary reality of group sex in late archaic and early classical Greece? Even if the majority of Greek men did not practice it, and it is not, therefore, a "normative protocol" some queer men of relatively elite status (or young men with an elite lover) almost certainly did enjoy it. Other more modest men might not have done it, but heard about it or saw one of these cups and then fantasised about it. The most straight-laced types, like Pericles, would not attend any but the most sober symposia and would never purchase such ceramics, much less show them to guests. Even if we find only one clear mention in a literary source, that should not surprise us.

If in our own era plague, nuclear war or rapid climate change were to wipe out all but a few scattered and remote human settlements, and all that remained to record our civilisation for people 2500 years later were a few hundred of the most important books and popular DVDs, and of those DVDs more than a few were pornographic, and a certain percentage of those featured group sex, later archaeologists would be surprised by the inconsistency between what these pornographic movies showed of group sex and its virtual absence in the serious literary, historical and scientific texts, where almost all sexual discussions are based on the dyadic norm. They might conclude that this variant of pornography was meant to disgust rather than titillate because there is so little written record of such activity going on. They would also conclude that no one actually performed sex this way except actors in a film. They would be wrong, as group sex (if we define it as any act with more than two participants) is in fact quite common today in the gay male and swinger communities, and has even been tried on one or more occasions by many non-swinger heterosexual couples. Some activities are merely diversions and fail to leave a mark in the serious literary record.

* * * * * * *

In a culture that routinely trained boys from an early age to shed their clothes in athletics and display their budding citizen bodies[49] to the public without any sense of shame or inhibition, the phenomenon or fantasy of semi-public sex in front of other consenting males should not surprise us. T. Scanlon has argued

---

49 Exercising in the public gymnasium was a citizen privilege denied to slaves, a defining principle going back to the time of Solon; see Kyle 1984 and Fisher 1998. In that sense, public nudity was a class privilege and responsibility, demonstrating to the citizen body one's transparency. A free citizen should have nothing to hide. See Miller 2000.

that athletic nudity was itself meant as an erotic spectacle.[50] The plain and sometimes mature women in these group sex encounters are seldom the focus of much interest or concern; they are rather vehicles for solidifying affective and even sexualised bonds between men, what E. Kosofsky Sedgwick has called "male homosociality". In the context of the early modern and 19th century English narratives she analyzes, this takes the form of erotic rivalry between men whose emotional relation to each other is more important than the woman in question. In the Greek context, where openly homosexual associations are less repressed, these bonds are collaborative and usually intergenerational; pederasty functioned as a kind of sex education for the young from the dawning of adolescence, hence the fetishistic gesture of pederastic lovers in exciting boys' genitals, whose developing capacity for arousal betokened emerging sexual maturity, as seen on the interior of the famous Brygos Painter cup in the Ashmolean Museum (Oxford 1967.304 = ARV^2 378.137, Beazley Archive #204034).[51] Vase paintings showing women shared between men and youths must be interpreted as a more advanced stage of participatory sex education, not with respectable women, but appropriately compensated *pornai* and boys who are growing into ephebes.

However, not all images are scenes of sexual pedagogy. Sometimes boys enjoy watching each other or performing in front of each other, and we also find depictions of adult men who enjoy watching their younger companion. The common thread through all the representations we have studied here is the centrality of masculine spectatorship and performance to the Greeks' erotic imagination.[52]

Bibliography

Blanshard, A. (2015), 'Fantasy and the Homosexual Orgy: Unearthing the Sexual Scripts of Ancient Athens', in: M. Masterson/N.S. Rabinowitz/J. Robson (eds.), *Sex in Antiquity: Exploring Gender and Sexuality in the Ancient World*, London, 99–114.

Boardman, J. (1975), *Athenian Red Figure Vases: The Archaic Period*, London.

---

50 Scanlon 2002, especially 64–97, 199–273. See also Larmour 1999, 139–144.

51 The motif was common to both black-figure and red-figure representations. For other examples, see Vatican 352 = *ABV* 134.30, Beazley Archive #301064; Würzburg 241 = *ABV* 169.5; Munich 1468 = *ABV* 315.3; Boston 08.292 = Beazley Archive #1408; Berlin F2279 = ARV^2 115.2, Beazley Archive #200977; New York 07.286.47 = ARV^2 175, Beazley Archive #201603. Note also the enthusiastic aestheticisation of boys' sex organs by the Greater Logos in Aristophanes, *Clouds* 973–980.

52 For my previous treatment of the erotic dynamics of vision in literary, philosophical and iconographical contexts, see Hubbard 2002.

Bundrick, S.D. (2012), 'Housewives, *Hetairai*, and the Ambiguity of Genre in Attic Vase Painting', in: *Phoenix* 66, 11–35.

Brendel, O.J. (1970), 'The Scope and Temperament of Erotic Art in the Greco-Roman World', in: T. Bowie/C.V. Christensen (eds.), *Studies in Erotic Art*, New York, 3–107.

Coleman, L./Held, J.M. (eds.) (2014), *The Philosophy of Pornography: Contemporary Perspectives*, Lanham, MD.

Dierichs, A. (1993), *Erotik in der Kunst Griechenlands*, Mainz.

Dover, K.J. (1974), *Greek Popular Morality in the Time of Plato and Aristotle*, Berkeley.

Dover, K.J. (1978), *Greek Homosexuality*, Cambridge, MA.

Filser, W. (2017), *Die Elite Athens auf der attischen Luxuskeramik*, Berlin.

Fischer, M. (2007), 'Sport Objects and Homosexuality in Ancient Greek Vase-Painting: The New Reading of Tampa Museum Vase 86.70', in: *Nikephoros* 20, 153–175.

Fisher, N. (1998), 'Gymnasia and the Democratic Values of Leisure', in: P. Cartledge/P. Millet/ S. von Reden (eds.), *Kosmos: Essays in Order, Conflict and Community in Classical Athens*, Cambridge, 84–104.

Hedreen, G. (2015), *The Image of the Artist in Archaic and Classical Greece*, Cambridge.

Henderson, J. (1991) [1975], *The Maculate Muse: Obscene Language in Attic Comedy*, Oxford.

Hoesch, N. (1990), 'Hetären', in: K. Vierneisel/B. Kaeser (eds.), *Kunst der Schale, Kultur des Trinkens*, Munich, 228–234.

Hubbard, T.K. (2002), 'Pindar, Theoxenus, and the Homoerotic Eye', in: *Arethusa* 35, 255–296.

Hubbard, T.K. (2015a), 'Diachronic Parameters of Athenian Pederasty', in: J.M. González (ed.), *Diachrony: Diachronic Studies of Ancient Greek Literature and Culture*, Berlin, 363–389.

Hubbard, T.K. (2015b), 'Ned Warren's Passion: The Life and Work of a Uranian Connoisseur', in: *Arion* 22.3, 145–170.

Johns, C. (1982), *Sex or Symbol: Erotic Images of Greece and Rome*, Austin.

Keuls, E.C. (1983), 'Attic Vase Painting and the Home Textile Industry', in: W.G. Moon (ed.), *Ancient Greek Art and Iconography*, Madison, 209–230.

Keuls, E.C. (1985), *The Reign of the Phallus: Sexual Politics in Ancient Athens*, New York.

Kilmer, M.F. (1993), *Greek Erotica on Attic Red-Figure Vases*, London.

Kilmer, M.F. (1997), 'Rape in Early Red-Figure Pottery: Violence and Threat in Homo-erotic and Hetero-erotic Contexts', in: S. Deacy/K.F. Pierce (eds.), *Rape in Antiquity*, London, 123–141.

Kurke, L. (1997), 'Inventing the *Hetaira*: Sex, Politics, and Discursive Conflict in Archaic Greece', in: *Classical Antiquity* 16, 106–150.

Kyle, D.G. (1984), 'Solon and Athletics', in: *Ancient World* 9.3–4, 91–105.

Larmour, D.H.J. (1998), *Stage and Stadium: Drama and Athletics in Ancient Greece*, Hildesheim.

La Rocca, E. (1978), 'The Erotic Art of Greece: A Critical Analysis', in: J. Boardman/E. La Rocca (eds.), *Eros in Greece*, London, 69–167.

Lear, A./Cantarella, E. (2008), *Images of Ancient Greek Pederasty: Boys were their Gods*, London.

Licht, H. (2000) [1932], *Sexual Life in Ancient Greece*, Transl. by J.H. Freese, London.

Marcadé, J. (1965), *Eros Kalos: Essay on the Erotic Elements in Greek Art*, Geneva.

Miller, S.G. (2000), 'Naked Democracy', in: P. Flensted-Jensen/T.H. Nielsen/L. Rubenstein (eds.), *Polis and Politics: Studies in Ancient Greek History*, Copenhagen, 277–296.

Murray, S.P. (1985), *Collecting the Classical Past: Antiquities from the Joseph Veach Noble Collection*, Tampa.

Neer, R. (2002), *Style and Politics in Athenian Vase-Painting: The Craft of Democracy, ca. 530-460 B.C.E.*, Cambridge.

Neils, J. (2000), 'Others within the Other: An Intimate Look at Hetairai and Maenads', in: B. Cohen (ed.), *Not the Classical Ideal: Athens and the Construction of the Other in Greek Art*, Leiden, 203–226.

Parisinou, E. (2000), '"Lighting" the World of Women: Lamps and Torches in the Hands of Women in the Late Archaic and Classical Periods', in: *Greece & Rome 47*, 19–43.

Parker, H. (2015), 'Vaseworld: Description and Depiction of Sex at Athens', in: R. Blondell/ K. Ormand (eds.), *Ancient Sex: New Essays*, Columbus, 23–142.

Peschel, I. (1987), *Die Hetäre bei Symposion und Komos in der attisch-rotfigurigen Vasenmalerei des 6.-4. Jahr. v. Chr.*, Frankfurt a.M.

Pfisterer-Haas, S. (1989), *Darstellungen alter Frauen in der griechischen Kunst*, Frankfurt a.M.

Rabinowitz, N.S. (2002), 'Excavating Women's Homoeroticism in Ancient Greece', in: N.S. Rabinowitz/L. Auanger (eds.), *Among Women: From the Homosocial to the Homoerotic in Ancient Greece*, Austin, 106–166.

Reinsberg, C. (1989), *Ehe, Hetärentum und Knabenliebe im antiken Griechenland*, Munich.

Robson, J. (2013), *Sex and Sexuality in Classical Athens*, Edinburgh.

Sánchez, C. (2013), *Kunst & Erotik in der Antike*, Berlin.

Scanlon, T.F. (2002), *Eros and Greek Athletics*, New York/Oxford.

Sedgwick, E.K. (1985), *Between Men: English Literature and Male Homosocial Desire*, New York.

Stafford, E. (2011), 'Clutching the Chickpea: Private Pleasures of the Bad Boyfriend', in: S.D. Lambert (ed.), *Sociable Man: Essays on Ancient Greek Social Behaviour in Honour of N. R. E. Fisher*, Swansea, 337–363.

Stewart, A. (1997), *Art, Desire, and the Body in Ancient Greece*, Cambridge.

Sutton, R.F. (1992), 'Pornography and Persuasion on Attic Pottery', in: A. Richlin (ed.), *Pornography and Representation in Greece and Rome*, New York/Oxford, 3–35.

Sutton, R.F. (2000), 'The Good, the Base, and the Ugly: The Drunken Orgy in Attic Vase Painting and the Athenian Self', in: B. Cohen (ed.), *Not the Classical Ideal: Athens and the Construction of the Other in Greek Art*, Leiden, 180–202.

Topper, K. (2012), *The Imagery of the Athenian Symposium*, Cambridge.

von Bothmer, D. (1964), Review of A. Greifenhagen, *CVA Germany 21: Berlin Antiquarium 2.3*, in: *Gnomon 36*, 407–409.

von Bothmer, D. (1967), Review of B. Philippaki, *The Attic Stamnos*, in: *Gnomon 39*, 813–819.

Waugh, T. (2001), 'Homosociality in the Classical American Stag Film: Off-Screen, On-Screen', in: *Sexualities 4.3*, 275–291.

Waugh, T./Arroyo, B. (eds.) (2019), *I Confess! Constructing the Sexual Self in the Internet Age*, Montreal.

Williams, D. (1993), 'Women on Athenian Vases: Problems of Interpretation', in: A. Cameron/ A. Kuhrt (eds.), *Images of Women in Antiquity*, London, 92–106.

Williams, L. (ed.) (2004), *Porn Studies*, Durham, NC.

Wrenhaven, K.L. (2009), 'The Identity of the "Wool-Workers" in the Attic Manumissions', in: *Hesperia 78*, 367–386.

Figures

Fig. 1: Pedieus Painter (c. 510 BC), Paris G13 = *ARV²* 86 = Beazley Archive #200694. © RMN-Grand Palais / Art Resource, NY.

Fig. 2a and b: Onesimus (c. 490 BC), Basel BS440 = *ARV²* 326.86 bis = Beazley Archive #203338. © Antikenmuseum Basel und Sammlung Ludwig.

Fig. 3: Pig Painter (c. 470 BC), Harvard 1960.346 = *ARV*² 563.8 = Beazley Archive #206433. Harvard Art Museums / Arthur M. Sackler Museum, Bequest of David M. Robinson. © President and Fellows of Harvard College.

Fig. 4: Unknown painter (c. 440 BC), Athens A2579 = Beazley Archive #15807. By courtesy of National Archaeological Museum, Athens.

Fig. 5: Red-figure Hydria attributed to the Harrow Painter (c. 475 BC), Tampa 1986.070 = Beazley Archive #202666. By permission of the Tampa Museum of Art, Joseph Veach Noble Collection, purchased in part with funds donated by Mr. and Mrs. James L. Ferman, Jr.

Fig. 6 a and b: Nikosthenes Painter (c. 510 BC), Boston 95.61 = *ARV*^{2} 132 = Beazley Archive #201063. Photograph ©2021 Museum of Fine Arts, Boston.

Fig. 7: Brygos Painter (c. 475 BC), London E68 = *ARV²* 371.24 = Beazley Archive #203923. By courtesy of British Museum Images.

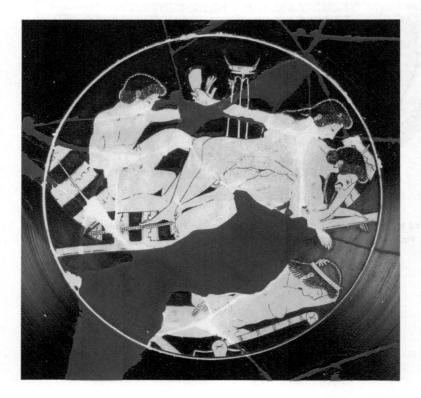

Fig. 8: Thalia Painter (c. 510 BC), Berlin 3251 = *ARV²* 113.7 = Beazley Archive #200964. Photo Credit: bpk Bildagentur / Berlin, Antikensammlung / Johannes Laurentius / Art Resource, NY.

Fig. 9: Brygos Painter (c. 475 BC), Florence 3921 = *ARV²* 372.31 = Beazley Archive #203929.
Photo Credit: Scala / Art Resource, NY.

Fig. 10: Manner of the Epileios Painter (c. 500 BC), Torino 4117 = *ARV*² 150 = Beazley Archive #201359. © MiBACT – Musei Reali, Museo di Antichità.

Andreas Serafim

Making the Body Speak: The (Homo)Sexual Dimensions of Sneezing in Ancient Greek Literature

Abstract: This chapter examines the ways in which sneezing indicates male (homo)sexuality. Ancient sources (e.g. Diogenes Laertius 7.173 and Dio Chrysostom's *First Tarsian Oration* 39 and 53–54) say that even if men try to hide homosexuality behind a strong physique and behavioural mannerisms, physiognomists are able to find it out when they hear them sneezing. Using both ancient treatises (e.g. the *Book of Physiognomy*, a work that probably dates back to the end of the 4th century AD and offers information about the physical features of the masculine and feminine bodies, together with the ways in which the ancients practised physiognomy) and modern interdisciplinary research theories, this chapter sheds some light on the potential of voice, sound and involuntary bodily movements to reveal sexuality.

Scholars have identified and briefly discussed the references, in ancient sources, to sneezing (or sternutation, i.e. the semi-voluntary convulsive expulsion of air and mucus from the lungs through the nose and mouth) as pointing to and revealing the sexual orientation of individuals — particularly their pathetic homosexual, or *kinaidic*, nature.[1] This chapter proceeds a step further: by using ancient

I owe the idea to investigate the sexual dimensions of sneezing in Greek literature to Peter Höschele: his perceptive observation about Diogenes Laertius' reference to sneezing as a means of indicating homosexuality (7.173) ignited my interest in this intriguing topic. The insightful feedback that I received from the audience at the international conference "Sex and the Ancient City" (University of Cyprus, 11–13 June 2019), which allowed the idea for this chapter and the whole volume to germinate and grow, was also important for the completion of this paper. I owe particular thanks to Thomas K. Hubbard, Lesley Dean-Jones, Marcel Lysgaard Lech and Maria Pavlou for the references to sneezing that they shared with me, and for their encouragement to proceed with the investigation of what proves to be a stimulating research paper. I decided to humbly dedicate this paper to the memory of Zak Kostopoulos, a tireless queer activist and human rights defender in Greece, who died on 21 September 2018, following a violent attack; and to Sam Albatros, a persona of a queer poet and translator, whose work, personal input and life experiences help hundreds of people to understand and respect themselves.

1 See, for example, Halperin 1990, 407; Gleason 1995, 77; Boys-Stones 2007, 78.

https://doi.org/10.1515/9783110695793-004

treatises, especially those on physiognomy where information about bodily stature is given, and modern interdisciplinary theories, i.e. cognitive neurophysiology, performance and non-verbal communication, it aims to show how sneezing is presented as denoting the homosexual nature of individuals, even if they try to hide it behind a strong physique or specific behavioural mannerisms. The discussion starts with a survey of Greek textual sources (extended, whenever possible and useful, to modern intercultural information) about sneezing and its use within a variety of ancient texts and contexts, proceeds to a general discussion about the sexual dimensions of sneezing and ends with a discussion of the ways in which sneezing is presented as specifically indicating homosexuality.

1 Intercultural sneezing: Folklore and ancient literature

Nowadays, sneezing neither concerns people nor worries them to the point of thinking further and more seriously about it, its causes or its implications for serious medical conditions. But there are still some cultural patterns, mostly based on folklore beliefs or superstitions, which point to the ancient roots of the perception about sneezing being a complicated and important physiological condition. In certain parts of Eastern Asia (e.g. Japan) and Europe (e.g. Greece and Cyprus), for example, a sneeze without an obvious cause is generally perceived as a sign that someone is talking about the sneezer. In English-speaking countries, such as the United Kingdom and the United States, it is customary to accompany sneezing with a wish, like "bless you", which is thought to be more than an act of courtesy (cf. Petronius, *Satyricon* 98: "Eumolpus turned toward the commotion and said dryly, 'Bless you, Giton'").[2] In a similar vein, there is an Indian cultural pattern, especially in northern parts of India, based on a common superstition that a sneeze taking place before the start of any work was a sign of an impending negative interruption. A custom was to pause an activity to drink water and then resuming it, with the aim of preventing any misfortune from happening. This practice was usually based on Islamic sacred passages, where it is mentioned that "when one of you sneezes, let him say, 'Al-hamdu-Lillah' ('Praise be to Allah'), and let his brother or companion

---

2 Transl. Hubbard 2003, 421.

say to him, 'Yarhamuk Allah' ('May Allah have mercy on you'). If he says, 'Yarhamuk-Allah', then let [the sneezer] say, 'Yahdeekum Allah wa yuslihu baalakum' ('May Allah guide you and rectify your condition')".[3]

In ancient Greece, there are superstitious beliefs and folklore about sneezing. Indicated by the verbs πταίρω, πτείρω and πτάρνυμαι, sneezing, for the ancient Greeks, was a sign of the Gods revealing the future (not necessarily impending doom). There is a passage in Homer's *Odyssey* which points to this nature and function of sneezing. In 17.541–542, we are told that Penelope and Eumaeus talk privately about Odysseus, and the suitors feast in the halls of the palace, when Telemachus sneezes, provoking laughter to Penelope (ὣς φάτο, Τηλέμαχος δὲ μέγ' ἔπταρεν, ἀμφὶ δὲ δῶμα σμερδαλέον κονάβησε γέλασσε δὲ Πηνελόπεια). Penelope laughs because she takes the sneezing as a god-sent indication that Odysseus will return to overcome the suitors. "Did you not see how my son sneezed as I finished then? So death for the suitors may still not be unachieved" (*Odyssey* 17.544–545). The Homeric narrator does not explicitly say that sneezing is a god-driven omen, but, using information from other sources (e.g. Homer's *Hymn to Hermes* 293–303,[4] Aristophanes' *Birds* 719–721,[5]

---

3 Khan 2018, 133–134.
4 Transl. Evelyn-White 1914: ὣς ἄρ' ἔφη καὶ παῖδα λαβὼν φέρε Φοῖβος Ἀπόλλων./ σὺν δ' ἄρα φρασσάμενος τότε δὴ κρατὺς Ἀργειφόντης/ οἰωνὸν προέηκεν ἀειρόμενος μετὰ χερσί,/ τλήμονα γαστρὸς ἔριθον, ἀτάσθαλον ἀγγελιώτην./ ἐσσυμένως δὲ **μετ' αὐτὸν ἐπέπταρε**: τοῖο δ' Ἀπόλλων/ ἔκλυεν, ἐκ χειρῶν δὲ χαμαὶ βάλε κύδιμον Ἑρμῆν./ ἕζετο δὲ προπάροιθε καὶ ἐσσύμενός περ ὁδοῖο/ Ἑρμῆν κερτομέων καί μιν πρὸς μῦθον ἔειπε:/ θάρσει, σπαργανιῶτα, Διὸς καὶ Μαιάδος υἱέ:/ εὑρήσω καὶ ἔπειτα βοῶν ἴφθιμα κάρηνα/ τούτοις οἰωνοῖσι: σὺ δ' αὖθ' ὁδὸν ἡγεμονεύσεις. "So said Phoebus Apollo, and took the child and began to carry him. But at that moment the strong Slayer of Argus had his plan, and, while Apollo held him in his hands, sent forth an omen, a hard-worked belly-serf, a rude messenger, and **sneezed directly after**. And when Apollo heard it, he dropped glorious Hermes out of his hands on the ground. Then sitting down before him, though he was eager to go on his way, he spoke mockingly to Hermes: 'fear not, little swaddling baby, son of Zeus and Maia. I shall find the strong cattle presently by these omens, and you shall lead the way'".
5 Transl. van der Horst 2014, 241: ὄρνιν τε νομίζετε πάνθ' ὅσαπερ περὶ μαντείας διακρίνει:/ φήμη γ' ὑμῖν ὄρνις ἐστί, **πταρμόν** τ' ὄρνιθα καλεῖτε, / ξύμβολον ὄρνιν, φωνὴν ὄρνιν, θεράποντ' ὄρνιν, ὄνον ὄρνιν. "You even use the word bird for anything that brings good luck or bad luck, whether it is a chance remark, **a sneeze**, an unexpected meeting, a noise, a servant or a donkey, you call it a bird!".

Theocritus' *Idyll* 18.16–17,[6] Plutarch's *Life of Themistocles* 13.2;[7] Menander's fr. 534.9;[8] also in Latin sources: Pliny the Elder's *Naturalis Historia* 2.5),[9] this is what we can reasonably surmise.[10] The idea of sneezing being taken as an omen also appears in Herodotus 6.107.[11]

Plutarch, in Περὶ τοῦ Σωκράτους δαιμονίου 581b, says that the "Socrates' daemon was nothing else but the sneezing either of himself or others; for if another sneezed, either before, behind him, or on his right hand, then he pursued his design and went on to action; but if on the left hand, he desisted. One sort of sneezing confirmed him whilst deliberating and not fully resolved; another stopped him when already upon action". If Socrates himself sneezed when he was indecisive about whether or not he should have undertaken any action, this was considered a positive sign; but if he sneezed after he had undertaken an action, he immediately stopped it. Catullus, in a similar vein, points out, in *Carmina 45: Acme and Septimius*, that sneezing to the right was considered fortunate and to the left unlucky ("Love stood listening with delight/ and sneezed his auspice on the right").[12]

---

6 Transl. van der Horst 2014, 242: ὄλβιε γάμβρ᾽, ἀγαθός τις **ἐπέπταρεν** ἐρχομένῳ τοι/ ἐς Σπάρταν, ἅπερ ὥλλοι ἀριστέες, ὡς ἀνύσαιο. "Happy groom! Some man of good omen **sneezed** upon you as you went to Sparta with other heroes, that you might win your quest".

7 Transl. van der Horst 2014, 242–243: τούτους ἰδὼν Εὐφραντίδης ὁ μάντις, ὡς ἅμα μὲν ἀνέλαμψεν ἐκ τῶν ἱερῶν μέγα καὶ περιφανὲς πῦρ, ἅμα δὲ **παρμὸς ἐκ δεξιῶν ἐσήμηνε**, τὸν Θεμιστοκλέα δεξιωσάμενος ἐκέλευσε τῶν νεανίσκων κατάρξασθαι καὶ καθιερεῦσαι πάντας ὠμηστῇ Διονύσῳ προσευξάμενον· οὕτω γὰρ ἅμα σωτηρίαν τε καὶ νίκην ἔσεσθαι τοῖς Ἕλλησιν. "When Euphrantides the seer caught sight of them, at one and the same moment a great and glaring flame shot up from the sacrificial victims and **a sneeze from the right gave forth its good omen**; then he clasped Themistocles by the hand and bade him consecrate the young men and sacrifice them all to Dionysus Carnivorous, with prayers of supplication, for in this way the Greeks would have a saving victory".

8 Menander's fr. 534.9: "let someone sneeze and we are perturbed".

9 *Naturalis Historia* 2.5: "witness the warnings drawn from lightning, the forecasts made by oracles, the prophecies of augurs, and even inconsiderable trifles counted as omens — a sneeze or a stumble".

10 On sneezing as omen: van der Horst 2014, 241–247.

11 Herodotus 6.107.3: καί οἱ ταῦτα διέποντι **ἐπῆλθε πταρεῖν** τε καὶ βῆξαι μεζόνως ἢ ὡς ἐώθεε: οἷα δέ οἱ πρεσβυτέρῳ ἐόντι τῶν ὀδόντων οἱ πλεῦνες ἐσείοντο: τούτων ὦν ἕνα τῶν ὀδόντων ἐκβάλλει ὑπὸ βίης βήξας: ἐκπεσόντος δὲ ἐς τὴν ψάμμον αὐτοῦ ἐποιέετο σπουδὴν πολλὴν ἐξευρεῖν. "As he was tending to this, **he happened to sneeze** and cough more violently than usual. Since he was an elderly man, most of his teeth were loose, and he lost one of them by the force of his cough. It fell into the sand and he expended much effort in looking for it, but the tooth could not be found".

12 In ancient Greek thought, there are descriptions of contrasted symbolic associations between right and left, with the first thought to be the lucky side and the latter the ominous one (cf. *Iliad*

It is also related that just before the battle of Salamis (480 BC), and while Themistocles, the Athenian commander, was offering a sacrifice to the gods on the deck of his galley, a sneeze was heard on the right hand, which was hailed as a fortunate omen by Euphrantides, the soothsayer (Plutarch, *Life of Themistocles* 13.2). In Xenophon's *Anabasis* 3.2.9, there is another sign pointing to the belief that sneeze can be seen as a divine omen. Xenophon, an Athenian general, delivered an exhortation in 410 BC to his soldiers to motivate them to follow him in a fight against the Persians. He tried to assure them of a safe return to Athens; then, a soldier sneezed. "As he was saying this, a man sneezed (πτάρνυται), and when the soldiers heard it, they all with one impulse made obeisance to the god; and Xenophon said, 'I move, gentlemen, since at the moment when we were talking about deliverance, an omen from Zeus the Saviour was revealed to us'".[13] Taking this sneeze as a favourable divine sign, the soldiers were supported morally and followed the commands of Xenophon.[14] Sneezing was something that could not be *fully* controlled by an individual and so it was understood (by Xenophon and the ancients in general) as a supernatural cause or influence.

Sneezing can, of course, be caused by individuals themselves, as is the case of the comic poet Aristophanes, who, in Plato's *Symposium* 189a, claimed that, advised by Eryximachus the physician, he provoked sneezing to cure his hiccough.[15] This description of the hiccough being cured by a sneeze serves to satirise Aristophanes by having him, a comic poet who uses words to lampoon politicians and citizens alike, not being able to say a single word because he was

---

24.315–321, *Odyssey* 2.146–154). On the difference between right and left hand in ancient literature: Lloyd 1962, 58–59; Sonin 1999, 75–79. The use of the right hand also has a ritualised dimension, as it is used when swearing an oath (cf. *Iliad* 4.159) or when carrying out sacred rituals, such as the ritual of purification after homicide (cf. Euripides' *Hercules* 926–927, 928–929 where it is said that a torch is carried in the right hand to dip into water).

13 Xenophon's *Anabasis* 3.2.9: τοῦτο δὲ λέγοντος αὐτοῦ πτάρνυταί τις· ἀκούσαντες δ' οἱ στρατιῶται πάντες μιᾷ ὁρμῇ προσεκύνησαν τὸν θεόν, καὶ ὁ Ξενοφῶν εἶπε· Δοκεῖ μοι, ὦ ἄνδρες, ἐπεὶ περὶ σωτηρίας ἡμῶν λεγόντων οἰωνὸς τοῦ Διὸς τοῦ σωτῆρος ἐφάνη.

14 Pease 1911, 429, 437; van der Horst 2013, 213–221. A dated but still useful survey of the consideration that sneezing was an omen of divine significance for the ancient Greeks and Roman can be found in Pease 1911, 429–443.

15 Plato, *Symposium* 189a: ἐκδεξάμενον οὖν ἔφη εἰπεῖν τὸν Ἀριστοφάνη ὅτι Καὶ μάλ' ἐπαύσατο, οὐ μέντοι πρίν γε τὸν πταρμὸν προσενεχθῆναι αὐτῇ, ὥστε με θαυμάζειν εἰ τὸ κόσμιον τοῦ σώματος ἐπιθυμεῖ τοιούτων ψόφων καὶ γαργαλισμῶν, οἷον καὶ ὁ πταρμός ἐστιν· πάνυ γὰρ εὐθὺς ἐπαύσατο, ἐπειδὴ αὐτῷ τὸν πταρμὸν προσήνεγκα, "then, as my friend related, Aristophanes took up the word and said: 'Yes, it has stopped, though not until it was treated with a course of sneezing, such as leaves me wondering that the orderly principle of the body should call for the noises and titillations involved in sneezing; you see, it stopped the very moment I applied the sneeze to it'".

blighted by an uncontrolled bodily reaction. The comic effect of this exaggerat-
edly awkward moment, enhanced by the description of a well-known physician
of the time advising Aristophanes about how to overcome a physiological problem (i.e. by gargling water, holding breadth and provoking sneezing), is based on
ancient medical knowledge (cf. Hippocrates, *Aphorisms* 6.13: "sneezing coming
on, in the case of a person afflicted with hiccup, removes the hiccup"; pseudo-
Aristotle, *Problems* 961b20–26: "why do sneezing and holding breath and vinegar
stops hiccups?", 963a17: "why does sneezing stop hiccupping?"), and points to
the thought that sneezing is correlated with medical conditions that needed to be
cured. In Hippocrates' *The Book of Prognostics* 14, for example, sneezing is presented as being dangerous, if it precedes or follows affections of the lungs.[16] Hippocrates, in *Aphorisms* 5.35, also points out that "sneezing occurring to a woman
affected with hysterics, and in difficult labour, is a good symptom", while
pseudo-Aristotle observes that one sneezes more after one has looked at the sun
(*Problems* 961b4). This is known today as "photic sneeze reflex" (or "sun sneezing"): a reflex condition that causes sneezing in response to light stimuli. Furthermore, Askenasy, who offers a useful (though condensed) historical overview
of sneezing across times and cultures, points out that "during the Middle Ages
the history of [the] sneeze received the well-known mystic aura of the period. Its
ominous threat located the sneeze as being close to evil. The negative aspect of
the sneeze gained strong momentum by the Bubonic plague which afflicted Rome
in the period 590–610. In this epidemic, people suddenly died while sneezing".[17]

2 The (homo)sexual dimensions of sneezing

Sneezing was, and still is, considered as being connected with an individual's
sexual orientation. Nowadays, sneezing is used in folk expressions, such as "you
sneeze glitter", to point to the sexual status of individuals with allusions to homosexuality. There are also stories about people who sneeze uncontrollably after
sex, or sometimes, even by thinking of it.[18] Research and bibliography on medicine recognise the connection between sneezing and sexual thoughts, ideation,
arousal, intercourse or orgasm. In the 19th century, scholars recognised that

---

16 In *Problems* 961b16–20 sneezing is presented as being caused by hot lungs.
17 Askenasy 1990, 549.
18 Bhutta/Maxwell 2008, 587–591.

there is a close association between the human nose and the genitals.[19] Fliess developed the (unsuccessful and failed) theory of "nasal reflex neurosis", according to which the nasal mucous membranes are connected with erectile tissues in the genital area, and that dysmenorrhoea was due to a nasal disorder.[20] Everett and an Anonymous report published in the *Journal of the American Medical Association* propounds the theory of Fliess that sneezing is connected with sexual ideation.[21] Another report, one in the *Journal of the Royal Society of Medicine*, points out that the linkage between the nose and the genitals can be threefold: first, sneezing is a psychological means of discharging sexual tension (without this being an effective way of approaching the issue since sneezing is not always volitional); second, sneezing is thought to be occurring after sexual orgasm; and third, the nervous system gets automatically its wires crossed and sends signals to both the nose and the genitals during sexual intercourse or fantasies.[22]

This connection between the nose, the genitals and masculinity is also known in ancient Greek texts and inscriptions. In Aristophanes' *Clouds* 344, it is mentioned that the chorus has noses that indicate that its members are men (εἴξασιν γοῦν ἐρίοισιν πεπταμένοισιν, κοὐχὶ γυναιξίν, μὰ Δί', οὐδ' ὁτιοῦν: αὗται δὲ ῥῖνας ἔχουσιν "at any rate they resemble spread-out fleeces, and not women, by Jupiter! Not a bit; for these have noses"). As Davies points out, the chorus-men would have worn masks with big and grotesque, comic-oriented noses that may be phallic in shape.[23] In an inscription in the so-called "Memnon pieta", with Eos lifting up the body of her son Memnon (Attic red-figure cup, c. 490–480 BC, from Capua, Italy) there is also a reference to the nose that may be an allegory for the genitals, pointing to love between Douris and Hermogenes ("if he tickles my nose, Hermogenes is handsome").

The clearest indication that sneezing has a sexual dimension, particularly one that is connected with homosexuality, can be found in a passage from Diogenes Laertius 7.173. The passage suggests that, even when a *kinaidos* has a strong body, he cannot hide his sexuality: sneezing can reveal it.

λέγεται δέ, φάσκοντος αὐτοῦ κατὰ Ζήνωνα καταληπτὸν εἶναι τὸ ἦθος ἐξ εἴδους, νεανίσκους τινὰς εὐτραπέλους ἀγαγεῖν πρὸς αὐτὸν κίναιδον ἐσκληραγωγημένον ἐν ἀγρῷ, καὶ ἀξιοῦν

---

19 Watson 1875; Mackenzie 1884, 360–365; 1898, 109–123.
20 Young 2002, 992–995; Jones 1974.
21 Everett 1964, 483–490 — in this work, there is also an interesting reference to sneezing as a result of looking at sunlight; Anonymous 1972, 1350–1351.
22 Bhutta/Maxwell 2008, 587–591.
23 Davies 1982, 117.

ἀποφαίνεσθαι περὶ τοῦ ἤθους τὸν δὲ διαπορούμενον κελεῦσαι ἀπιέναι τὸν ἄνθρωπον. **ὡς δὲ ἀπιὼν ἐκεῖνος ἔπταρεν "ἔχω", εἶπεν, "αὐτόν", ὁ Κλεάνθης, "μαλακός ἐστιν".**

And it is reported that, after he asserted that according to Zeno the character may be appre-hended from appearance, some young men playing a trick led to him a *kinaidos* who had been brought up hardy in the field, and they demanded that he give an account concerning the man's character, and Cleanthes, who was at a loss, bid the man go away. **But when, after going away, that fellow sneezed, Cleanthes said, "I have him. He is effeminate".**

It is not clear from the text itself what makes a *kinaidos* be recognised as such when sneezing. The *Book of Physiognomy*, a work of an unknown author (falsely attributed to Loxus, Aristotle, Polemon or Apuleius), which (probably) dates back to the end of the 4th century AD, offers specific clues that it was the sound that enabled Cleanthes, the physiognomist,[24] to find out the homosexual identity of the strong man whose physicality is described in Diogenes Laertius' passage. The *Book of Physiognomy* gives detailed accounts of the physical features of the mas-culine and feminine bodies, together with the ways in which the ancients prac-tised physiognomy. One of those ways was that "they observed that whatever ex-pression or posture of body a man had through the particular movements of his mind that was the expression of an angry man, of a thinking man, of a fearful man, of a man prone to desire and of a man who was mad. And so whomever the physiognomist saw to have an expression like one who was mad, even though there was no cause for his madness, or like one who was angry, even though there was no anger, or like one who was thinking, even though there was no obvious thought, they pronounced mad or angry or a thinker respectively".[25]

The *Book of Physiognomy* describes what seems to be the ideal masculine body: "the neck should be of moderate thickness, somewhat extended, the top of the head rather upright, the shoulder-blades huge, the shoulders and upper parts of the body to the navel rather broad, the lower parts rather drawn in with de-creasing width. He should be muscular, with big bones, the knuckles and joints

---

24 Barton 1994, 101 claims that "third-century BC Stoic physiognomist Cleanthes makes it his business to unmask charlatans, effeminates and adulterers". A telling passage about the work of a physiognomist is in Demosthenes 25.98: ἐν δ' εἰπὼν ἔτι παύσασθαι βούλομαι. ἔξιτ' αὐτίκα δὴ μάλ' ἐκ τοῦ δικαστηρίου, θεωρήσουσι δ' ὑμᾶς οἱ περιεστηκότες καὶ ξένοι καὶ πολῖται, καὶ κατ' ἄνδρ' εἰς ἕκαστον τὸν παριόντα βλέψονται καὶ **φυσιογνωμονήσουσι** τοὺς ἀπεψηφισμένους, "you will soon be leaving this court-house, and you will be watched by the bystanders, both aliens and citizens; they will scan each one as he appears, and **detect by their looks** those who have voted for acquittal". This passage seems to indicate, according to Sonin 1999, 15, that there was a popular practice of discovering an individual's character, actions or emotions through fa-cial expressions or bodily stature, a practice that is still being exercised by people.
25 Translation: Repath 2007, 561.

at the ends of the feet and hands solid, yet not stiff, but just right apart and separate near the end, with a high and prominent chest, detached collar-bones, a
broach stomach pressed slightly inwards [...] Also the masculine body is strong
and tolerant of hard work, has a strong voice which is rather hoarse and occasionally deep, as if echoing from somewhere deep and hollow, like that of li-
ons".[26] This description of the ideal male body coincides with archaeological
data, e.g. the discus-thrower man, a statue that was made by the Greek sculptor
Myron (in the middle of the 5th century BC), an exemplification of male athletic
musculature and beauty in sculpture. Despite the *kinaidos* being that strong in
body, however, and despite his effort to conceal sexual identity beyond deceptive
physical tendencies and behavioural mannerisms, "it was the sound of his voice,
without any speech being made, that uncovered one man at the baths as a slave
of lust, and another man confessed that he was no man by a sudden sneeze".[27]

Voice, sound and body language, aspects of performance that can be described by the notion of *non-verbal communication*, "a useful umbrella, or covering term for all human acts and responses capable of communication — conscious, intentional, voluntary, or otherwise — and including gesture, posture,
body-talk, paralinguistics, chronemics and proxemics, ... somatic, vocal, dermal,
thermal, and olfactory messages and experiences",[28] have the potential to reveal
the ethical character and the sexual nature of individuals. As mentioned in the
Book of Physiognomy 74 (B38), there are two types of movements, the *natural* and
the *affected* (i.e. the movements or mannerisms that people use to fulfill specific
purposes). One of these purposes is disguise; for, there are "those who are certainly deviants, but who try to remove suspicion from themselves by striving to
assume a manly appearance; for they imitate the gait of a young man and
strengthen themselves with a certain stiffness and strain their eyes and voice and
straighten their whole body, but they are easily detected when their true nature
wins through and exposes them; for they often lower their neck and voice and

---

26 Translation: Repath 2007, 559.
27 Translation: Repath 2007, 563.
28 Lateiner 1995, xix; also: Boegehold 1999, 12–28; Serafim 2020, 114–143 with a specific focus
on oratory. An aspect of non-verbal communication that has specifically to do with vocalics, and
is useful in identifying the *kinaidic* sexual nature and behaviour of individuals, is *paralinguistics*;
for Lateiner 1995, xix, this is "any... communicative event produced by the vocal apparatus except for the very words themselves. For example, tone, volume, pitch and pace; nasalization,
hoarseness, whistling and accents; pauses and breathing accompaniments, such as panting and
wheezing". On paralinguistics: Abercrombie 1968, 55–59; Crystal 1963, 25–29; 1966, 93–108;
1974, 265–295; Pennycook 1985, 259–282.

relax their hands [...] Often they are detected when yawning too".[29] At a different point, in paragraph 78 (B42), we read that "those who have a sharp and soft voice are effeminate" (*effeminati*). The passage does not use a term for *kinaidos* (or *cinaedus* in Latin), but, since effeminacy is a quality of a *kinaidos*, as ancient sources indicate, it is fair to assume that this is what the text means. In paragraph 115, however, the Greek term *kinaidoi* is explicitly used when a description of these people is provided,[30] once again with a reference to vocality: "they have a voice that sounds as if it had been broken" (cf. Aristotle, *Physiognomics* 806b26ff.: "high and slack voice means cowardice"; *Book of Physiognomy* 132, 2.144F and 52, 75–76F where tremor of voice is, specifically, mentioned together with hands physicality).[31]

The potential of voice, sound and involuntary bodily movements to reveal the sexual identity of a person is also discussed in modern interdisciplinary scholarship. "People categorise individuals as gay or heterosexual on the basis of indirect cues, including their physical appearance, their body language and their vocal characteristics".[32] It is a widespread belief that individuals are able to detect other people's sexual orientation from *involuntary* vocal information, i.e. information that comes through the pitch and the tone of an individual's voice, qualities that are given by nature and are largely uncontrolled by the individuals themselves. Several modern studies indicate, for example, that involuntary human vocality, such as the pronunciation of /s/ with a longer duration, points to homosexuality.[33] Other aspects of non-verbal communication that indicate one's sexuality include attire and clothing style,[34] jewellery, facial expressions, pos-

---

29 Translation: Repath 2007, 603.
30 On *kinaidos*: Dover 1978, 75–76; Winkler 1990, 178–186; Gleason 1995, 63–64; Davidson 2001, 23; Halperin 2002, 32–38; Hubbard 2003, 7; Skinner 2013, 155.
31 Cf. Gleason 1990, 407–408.
32 Fasoli, Maass, Paladino and Sulpizio 2017, 1261–1277. See also: Lakoff 1975 and McConnell-Ginet 1983, 69–88 who argue that homosexual men's intonation is more dynamic and pitch is higher than that of heterosexuals; Dunkle and Francis 1990, 157–167; Gaudio 1994, 30–57; Flipsen, Shrilberg, Weismer, Karlsson and McSweeny 1999, 663–677; Shelp 2002, 1–14; Munson, McDonald, DeBoe and White 2006, 202–240; Munson 2007, 125–142; Rieger et al. 2010, 124–140; Barton 2015, 1615–1637; Rule 2017, 129–139; Ambady/Weisbuch 2017, 616–628; Fasoli/Hegarty/Maass/Antonio 2018, 59–64; Fasoli/Hegarty 2019, 1–22.
33 Linville 1998, 35–48; Smyth, Jacobs/Rogers 2003, 329–350; Fuchs/Toda 2010, 281–302; Zimman 2013, 1–39.
34 Scholars have long ago theorised about the use of attire as a means of constructing and demonstrating a variety of identities, individual and community, "gendered", "sexualised" and "socio-politicised". Bibliography on the impact that attire has upon the demonstration or construction of

ture, body type, walk or gait, and both the type and frequency of gestures. According to modern cognitive research on non-verbal communication, gay men can even be identified from photos presenting facial characteristics and expressions.[35] Voice and sound, especially during non-volitional physical reactions, as sneezing is, are considered uncontrollable by people — so also effectively indicating the sexual status of an individual, the so-called "auditory gaydar". Studies also show that there is a high level of accuracy behind people's predictions of the sexual — either heterosexual or homosexual — status of people, after evaluating non-verbal, vocal or gestural, behaviour.[36]

Theorists, like Butler, Beauvoir, Wittig and Foucault, examine how sex/gender identity is moulded by performativity. As I argued elsewhere, "Beauvoir rejects the 'mute facticity' of bodies: in *The Second Sex*, she argues that a woman (and, by extension, any gender) is the result of culturally enforced actions and not of biological status ('one is not born, but, rather, *becomes* a woman'). Butler likewise rejects the idea that body pre-exists or is outside the gendered self. A central concept of Butler's theory is that specific aspects of self, such as gender, are constructed through repetitive performance acts. Wittig and Foucault also argue against the formation of a stable identity and for the cultural construction of gendered identity that is signified through activity and conduct. To say that self is 'performanceful' is to argue that 'it is real only to the extent that it is performed': self/gender is not something one *is*, but something that one *does* through corporeal performance (action, dress and manner, including the production of sounds) and through language. This correlates Butler's performativity with Austin's speech-acts and Searle's illocutionary speech-acts: language *does* something rather than merely represents something".[37] Sneezing can be seen, through this theoretical angle, as an act of performativity: the sound sneezing produces is an (involuntary) action that *does* something, and this *doing* has the potential to reveal the sexual orientation of an individual. The involuntary and humanly uncontrollable nature of the action helps people to understand the inner and real (sexual) self that an individual cannot successfully hide.

---

identity: Holman 1981; Lurie 1981; Tseelon 1989, 1995; Davis 1992; Entwistle 2000; Arvani-tidou/Gasouka 2013, 111–115.

35 Rule/Ambady 2008, 1100–1105; Zebrowitz 2017, 62–88.

36 Gaudio 1994, 30–57; Ambady/Hallahan/Conner 1999, 538–547; Rule/Ambrady/Adams/Macrae 2008, 1019–1028; Rieger et al. 2010, 124–140; Ambady/Hallahan 2012, 320–332.

37 Serafim 2017, 4. See, further, Beauvoir 1973, 301; Butler 1986, 35–49; 1988, 527; 1990, 129, 145; Salih 2007, 55. For a comprehensive overview of the gender theories of Beauvoir, Wittig, and Foucault: Butler 1986, 505–516; 1990, 1–35, 93–106. On speech act theory: Austin 1962; Searle 1969; 1975, 59–82; 1976, 1–24; Risselada 1993, 26–29.

A story similar to that in Diogenes Laertius 7.173 is discussed in Dio Chrysostom's *First Tarsian Oration* (33). Dio is candidly and openly critical towards homosexual relationships, losing no opportunity, in his second speech to Tarsus, to refer scathingly to the men who engaged in promiscuous sexual intercourse and those who breathe heavily. Dio denigrates men's "voice, glance, posture, hairstyle, gait, inverting the eye, bending the neck (which are also indications of *kinaidia* in early Greek sources, e.g. in Aristotle's *Nicomachean Ethics* 1148b15–1149a20 and the pseudo-Aristotelian *Physiognomics* 806b26ff., 808a), and conversing with palms turned upward" (33.52).[38] In paragraphs 53–54, Dio tells the story of Cleanthes and how he recognised the homosexual identity of a man from a sneeze:

> προσάγουσιν αὐτῷ σκληρόν τινα τὸ σῶμα καὶσύνοφρυν ἄνθρωπον, αὐχμῶντα καὶ φαύλως διακείμενον καὶ ἐν ταῖς χερσὶ τύλους ἔχοντα, φαιόν τι καὶ τραχὺ περιβεβλημένον ἱμάτιον, δασὺν ἕως τῶν σφυρῶν καὶ φαύλως κεκαρμένον· καὶ τοῦτον ἠξίουν εἰπεῖν ὅστις ἦν. ὁ δὲ ὡς πολὺν χρόνον ἑώρα, τελευταῖον ὀκνῶν μοι δοκεῖ τὸ παριστάμενον λέγειν οὐκ ἔφη ξυνιέναι, καὶ βαδίζειν αὐτὸν ἐκέλευσεν. **ἤδη δὲ ἀποχωρῶν πτάρνυται· κἀκεῖνος εὐθὺς ἀνεβόησεν ὡς εἴη κίναιδος.**

> The people brought before him a person of rugged frame and knitted brows, squalid and in sorry state and with callouses on his hands, wrapped in a sort of coarse, grey mantle, his body shaggy as far as the ankles and his locks wretchedly shingled; and our friend was asked to tell what this man was. But after he had observed the man for a long while, the expert finally, with seeming reluctance to say what was in his mind, professed that he did not understand the case and bade the man move along. **But just as the fellow was leaving, he sneezed, whereupon our friend immediately cried out that the man was a *kinaidos*.**

Again, the non-verbal performance, i.e. the sound produced by sneezing and the involuntary movements that may have accompanied that physical expiratory reflex, seems to be the reason for the physiognomist's recognition of the *kinaidos*. Humans do not fully control their body, which often reflexively communicate messages that can be evaluated by a physiognomist as indicating sexuality or gender identity. People may try, of course, to manipulate their bodies and bodily behaviours or mannerisms, in order to hide their true nature, but a keen observer has the ability to see what is intended to be hidden. This assumption is corroborated by Dio's reference, a few paragraphs earlier, in 33.39, to sound as indicating

---

38 Translation: Swain 2007, 190. A parallel to Dio Chrysostom's description of men in 33.52 can be found in Aristotle, *Physiognomics* 808a14ff.: "the character of *kinaidos* is shown by being weak-eyed and knock-kneed; his head is inclined to the right; he carries his hands palm upward and slack, and he has two gaits — he either waggles his hips or holds them stiffly; he casts his eyes around him like Dionysius the sophist".

the identity of *androgynoi*, "the men who are between a man and a woman",[39] as the *Book of Physiognomy* 98 (B52) defines the term. It is also good to bear in mind that Demosthenes is called, in Aeschines 2.127, *androgynos* because of the effeminate physique that is frequently attributed to him in ancient sources.[40]

This short study of the physiognomic and sexual dimensions of sneezing — what I call "mute language" in a forthcoming publication on non-verbal communication, which proposes to examine several references, in ancient literature, to the handshake as denoting fake reconciliation, reciprocity and friendship — has the potential to reveal a lot about ancient thinking, technical (e.g. medical) knowledge, literary strategy and the set of values that determine people's (inter)personal life and forge their identity. In an "extraordinarily performanceful" society, to use a phrase of Taplin,[41] where the use of body and voice was of paramount importance for the art of public speaking, communication and persuasion, "mute language" can tell us as much about institutional workings and the ancient societies themselves as the language *per se* can. References to sneezing are certainly not a hackneyed feature of the texts and contexts in which they appear: this bodily reaction is presented as having important functions from presenting a divine omen to giving a means to opponents to satirise people, and from being considered a serious medical incident to be seen as a feature of individuals which defines their sexual, ethical and personal identity, and the ways in which they are seen by others. It is for these reasons that more work on "mute language" as a means of reconstructing a clearer and deeper understanding of ancient societies is compelling.

---

39 In comic sources, the figure of *androgynos* is connected with soldiering, draft evasion and the lack of martial manliness. Eupolis, a comic poet contemporary of Aristophanes, wrote a comedy entitled Ἀνδρόγυνοι ("The Womanly Men") or Ἀστράτευτοι ("The Draft-Dodgers"). Theopompus, in addition, wrote another comic play, Στρατιωτίδες ("The Lady Soldiers"), in which women take over the male duty of soldiering.

40 The nickname Βάταλος despite being of unknown origin seems to be associated with Demosthenes' effeminate and defective physique and with his moral vices and cowardliness (as in Plutarch, *Demosthenes* 4.3–4; *Scholia in Aeschines* 2, 218a).

41 Taplin 1999, 33.

Bibliography

Abercrombie, D. (1968), 'Paralanguage', in: *International Journal of Language & Communication Disorders* 3, 55–59.

Ambady, N./Hallahan, M./Conner, B. (1999), 'Accuracy of Judgments of Sexual Orientation from Thin Slices of Behavior', in: *Journal of Personality and Social Psychology* 77, 538–547.

Ambady, N./Hallahan, M. (2002), 'Using Nonverbal Representations of Behavior: Perceiving Sexual Orientation', in: A.M. Galaburda/S.M. Kosslyn/C. Yves (eds.), *The Languages of the Brain*, Cambridge, MA, 320–332.

Ambady, N./Weisbuch, M. (2017), 'Facial Expressions: Culture and Context', in: A.J. Calder/G. Rhodes/J.V. Haxby/M.H. Johnson (eds.), *The Handbook of Face Perception*, Oxford, 616–628.

Anonymous (1972), 'Paroxysmal Sneeze Following Orgasm', in: *JAMA* 219, 1350–1351.

Arvanitidou, Z./Gasouka, M. (2013), 'Construction of Gender through Fashion and Dressing', in: *Mediterranean Journal of Social Sciences* 4, 111–115.

Askenasy, J.J.M. (1990), 'The History of Sneezing', in: *Postgrad Med J* 66, 549–550.

Austin, J.L. (1962), *How to Do Things with Words*, Cambridge, MA.

Barton, B. (2015), 'How Like Perceives Like: Gay People on "Gaydar"', in: *Journal of Homosexuality* 62, 1615–1637.

Barton, T.S. (1994), *Power and Knowledge: Astrology, Physiognomics, and Medicine under the Roman Empire*, Michigan.

Beauvoir, S.de. (1973), *The Second Sex*, New York.

Bhutta, M.F./Maxwell, H. (2008). 'Sneezing Induced by Sexual Ideation or Orgasm: Anunderreported phenomenon', in: *Journal of the Royal Society of Medicine* 101, 587–591.

Boegehold, A.L. (1999), *When a Gesture was Expected: A Selection of Examples from Archaic and Classical Greek Literature*, New Jersey.

Boys-Stones, G. (2007), 'Physiognomy and Ancient Psychological Theory', in: S. Swain/G. Boys-Stones/J. Elsner/A. Ghersetti/R. Hoyland/I. Repath (eds.), *Seeing the Face, Seeing the Soul: Polemon's Physiognomy from Classical Antiquity to Medieval Islam*, Oxford, 19–124.

Brand, J. (1813), *Observations on Popular Antiquities: Chiefly Illustrating the Origin of Our Vulgar Customs, Ceremonies and Superstitions*, London.

Brand, J. (1986), 'Variations on Sex and Gender: Beauvoir, Wittig and Foucault', in: *Praxis International* 4, 505–516.

Brand, J. (1988), 'Performative Acts and Gender Constitution: An Essay in Phenomenology and Feminist Theory', in: *Theatre Journal* 40, 519–531.

Brand, J. (1990), *Gender Trouble: Feminism and the Subversion of Identity*, New York/London.

Crystal, D. (1963), 'A Perspective for Paralanguage', in: *Le Maître Phonétique* 120, 25–29.

Crystal, D. (1966), 'The Linguistic Status of Prosodic and Paralinguistic Features', in: *Proceedings of the University of Newcastle-upon Tyne Philosophical Society* 1, 93–108.

Crystal, D. (1974), 'Paralinguistics', in: T. Sebeok (ed.). *Current Trends in Linguistics*, vol. 12, The Hague, 265–295.

Davidson, J. (2001), *The Greeks and Greek Love: A Radical Reappraisal of Homosexuality in Ancient Greece*, London.

Davies, M. (1982), 'The Tickle and Sneeze of Love', in: *American Journal of Archaeology* 86, 115–118.

Davis, F. (1988), 'Clothing, Fashion and the Dialectic of Identity', in: D. Maines/J. Couch (eds.), *Communication and Social Structure*, Springfield, 23–38.

Davis, F. (1992), *Fashion, Culture and Identity*, Chicago.

Dover, K. (1978), *Greek Homosexuality*, London.

Dunkle, J.H./Francis, P.L. (1990), 'The Role of Facial Masculinity Femininity in the Attribution of Homosexuality', in: *Sex Roles* 23, 157–167.

Entwistle, J. (2000), *The Fashioned Body: Fashion, Dress and Modern Social Theory*, Cambridge.

Evelyn-White, H.G. (1914), *The Homeric Hymns and Homerica*, Cambridge, MA/London.

Everett, H.C. (1964), 'Sneezing in Response to Light', in: *Neurology* 14, 483–490.

Fasoli, F./Hegarty, P. (2019), 'A Leader Doesn't Sound Lesbian! The Impact of Sexual Orientation Vocal Cues on Heterosexual Persons' First Impression and Hiring Decision', in: *Psychology of Women Quarterly* 20, 1–22.

Fasoli, F./Hegarty, P./Maass, A./Antonio, P. (2018), 'Who Wants to Sound Straight? Sexual Majority and Minority Stereotypes, Beliefs and Desires about Auditory Gaydar', in: *Personality and Individual Differences* 130, 59–64.

Fasoli, F./Maass, A./Paladino, M.P./Sulpizio, S. (2017), 'Gay- and Lesbian-Sounding Auditory Cues Elicit Stereotyping and Discrimination', in: *Archives of Sexual Behavior* 46, 1261–1277.

Flipsen, P.Jr./Shrilberg, L./Weismer, G./Karlsson, H./McSweeny, J. (1999), 'Acoustic Characteristics of /s/ in Adolescents', in: *Journal of Speech, Language and Hearing Research* 42, 663–677.

Fuchs, S./Toda, M. (2010), 'Do Differences in Male versus Female /s/ Reflect Biological or Sociophonetic Factors?', in: F. Susanne/T. Martine/M. Zygis (eds.), *An Interdisciplinary Guide to Turbulent Sounds*, Berlin, 281–302.

Gaudio, R.P. (1994), 'Sounding Gay: Pitch Properties in the Speech of Gay and Straight Men', in: *American Speech* 69, 30–57.

Gleason, M.W. (1990), 'The Semiotics of Gender: Physiognomy and Self-Fashioning in the Second Century C.E.', in: D. Halperin/J. Winkler/F. Zeitlin (eds.), *Before Sexuality*, Princeton, 389–415.

Gleason, M.W. (1995), *Making Men: Sophists and Self-Presentation in Ancient Rome*, Princeton, NJ.

Halperin, D.M. (2002), *How to Do the History of Homosexuality*, Chicago.

Halperin, D.M./Winkler, J.J./Zeitlin, F.I. (eds.) (1990), *Before Sexuality: The Construction of Erotic Experience in the Ancient Greek World*, Princeton.

Holman, H. (1981), 'Product Use as Communication Source', in: B. Enis/K. Roering (eds.), *Review of Marketing*, Chicago.

Hubbard, T.K. (2003), *Homosexuality in Greece and Rome. A Sourcebook of Basic Documents*, Berkeley/Los Angeles/London.

Jones, E. (1974), *The Life and Work of Sigmund Freud*, London.

Khan, I. (2018), 'Sneezing, Science Behind the Veil', in: *International Journal of Complementary & Alternative Medicine* 11, 133–134.

King, M.B. (1990), 'Sneezing as a Fetishistic Stimulus', in: *Sexual and Marital Therapy* 5, 69–72.

Kock, T. (1880–1888), *Comicorum Atticorum Fragmenta*, 3 vols., Leipzig.

Lakoff, R. (1975), *Language and Woman's Place*, New York.

Lateiner, D. (1995), *Sardonic Smile: Nonverbal Behaviour in Homeric Epic*, Michigan.

Linville, S.E. (1998), 'Acoustic Correlates of Perceived Versus Actual Sexual Orientation in Men's Speech', in: *Folia Phoniatrica et Logopaedica* 50, 35–48.

Lloyd, G. (1962), 'Right and Left in Greek Philosophy', in: *Journal of Hellenic Studies* 82, 56–66.

Lurie, A. (1981), *The Language of Clothes*, London.

Mackenzie, J.N. (1884), 'Irritation of the Sexual Apparatus as an Etiological Factor in the Production of Nasal Disease', in: *American Journal of Medical Science* 87, 360–365.

Mackenzie, J.N. (1898), 'The Physiological and Pathological Relations Between the Nose and Sexual Apparatus of Man', in: *Journal of Laryngology, Rhinology and Otology* 13, 109–123.

McConnell-Ginet, S. (1983), 'Intonation in a Man's World', in: B. Thorne/C. Kramarae/N. Henley (eds.), *Language, Gender and Society*, Rowley, MA, 69–88.

Munson, B. (2007), 'The Acoustic Correlates of Perceived Masculinity, Perceived Femininity, and Perceived Sexual Orientation', in: *Language and Speech* 50, 125–142.

Munson, B./McDonald, E.C./DeBoe, N.L./White, A.R. (2006), 'The Acoustic and Perceptual Bases of Judgments of Women and Men's Sexual Orientation from Read Speech', in: *Journal of Phonetics* 34, 202–240.

Pease, A.S. (1911), 'The Omen of Sneezing', in: *Classical Philology* 6, 429–443.

Pennycook, A. (1985), 'Actions Speak Louder Than Words: Paralanguage, Communication and Education', in: *Tesol Quarterly* 19, 259–282.

Repath, I. (2007), 'Anonymus Latinus, *Book of Physiognomy*', in: S. Swain (ed.), *Seeing the Face, Seeing the Soul: Polemon's Physiognomy from Classical Antiquity to Medieval Islam*, Oxford, 549–635.

Rieger, G./Linsenmeier, J.A./Gygax, L./Garcia, S./Bailey, J.M. (2010), 'Dissecting "Gaydar": Accuracy and the Role of Masculinity–Femininity', in: *Archives of Sexual Behavior* 39, 124–140.

Risselada, R. (1993), *Imperatives and Other Directive Expressions in Latin: A Study in the Pragmatics of a Dead Language*, Amsterdam.

Rule, N.O. (2017), 'Perceptions of Sexual Orientation from Minimal Cues', in: *Archives of Sexual Behavior* 46, 129–139.

Rule, N.O./Ambady, N. (2008), 'Brief Exposures: Male Sexual Orientation is Accurately Perceiving at 50ms', in: *Journal of Experimental Social Psychology* 44, 1100–1105.

Rule, N.O./Ambrady, N./Adams, R.B./Macrae, C.N. (2008), 'Accuracy and Awareness in the Perception and Categorization of Male Sexual Orientation', in: *Journal of Personality and Social Psychology* 95, 1019–1028.

Salih, S. (2007), 'On Judith Butler and Performativity', in: K. Lovaas/M.M. Jenkins (eds.), *Sexuality and Communication in Everyday Life: A Reader*, 1st ed., Thousand Oaks, 55–67.

Searle, J.R. (1969), *Speech Acts*, Cambridge.

Searle, J.R. (1975), 'Indirect Speech Acts', in: P. Cole/J.L. Morgan (eds.), *Speech Acts*, New York, 59–82.

Searle, J.R. (1976), 'The Classification of Illocutionary acts', in: *Language in Society* 5, 1–24.

Serafim, A. (2017), *Attic Oratory and Performance*, New York/London.

Serafim, A. (2020), 'Paralinguistics, Community and the Rhetoric of Division in Attic Oratory', in: *Roda da Fortuna. Electronic Journal about Antiquity and Middle Ages* 22, 114–143.

Shelp, S.G. (2002), 'Gaydar: Visual Detection of Sexual Orientation Among Gay and Straight Men', in: *Journal of Homosexuality* 44, 1–14.

Skinner, M.B. (2013), *Sexuality in Greek and Roman Culture*, Oxford.

Smyth, R./Jacobs, G./Rogers, H. (2003), 'Male Voices and Perceived Sexual Orientation: An Experimental and Theoretical Approach', in: *Language in Society* 32, 329–350.

Sonin, J. (1999), *The Verbalisation of Non-verbal Communication in Classical Greek Texts*, Ph.D. Thesis, Cambridge.

Swain, S. (2007), 'Polemon's *Physiognomy*', in: S. Swain (ed.), *Seeing the Face, Seeing the Soul: Polemon's Physiognomy from Classical Antiquity to Medieval Islam*, Oxford, 125–201.

Taplin, O. (1999), 'Spreading the Word Through Performance', in: S. Goldhill/R. Osborne (eds.), *Performance Culture and Athenian Democracy*, Cambridge, 33–57.

Tseelon, E. (1989), 'Communicating via Clothes', Unpublished paper, Oxford.

Tseelon, E. (1995), '*The Masque of Femininity*', London.

van der Horst, P.W. (2013), 'The Omen of Sneezing in Pagan Antiquity', in: *Ancient Society* 43, 213–221.

van der Horst, P.W. (2014), *Studies in Ancient Judaism and Early Christianity*, Leiden/Boston.

Watson, W.C. (1875), *Diseases of the Nose and its Accessory Cavities*, London.

Winkler, J.J. (1990), 'Laying Down the Law: The Oversight of Men's Sexual Behaviour in Classical Athens', in: D.M. Halperin/J.J. Winkler/F.I. Zeitlin (eds.), *Before Sexuality*, Princeton, 171–209.

Young, A.R. (2002), 'Freud's Friend Fliess', in: *The Journal of Laryngology & Otology* 116, 992–995.

Zebrowitz, L.A. (2017), 'Ecological and Social Approaches to Face Perception', in: A.J. Calder/G. Rhodes/J.V. Haxby/M.H. Johnson (eds.), *The Handbook of Face Perception*, Oxford, 62–88.

Zimman, L. (2013), 'Hegemonic Masculinity and the Variability of Gay-sounding Speech. The Perceived Sexuality of Transgender Men', in: *Journal of Language and Sexuality* 2, 1–39.

Manolis Spanakis

"Fell in Love with an Anus": Sexual Fantasies for Young Male Bodies and the Pederastic Gaze in Rhianus' *Epigrams*

To my best friend,
Renos P.

Abstract: In this chapter, Spanakis examines the fantasy for young male bodies and the pederastic gaze in Rhianus' epigrams. First, he considers the limited biographical data about Rhianus as a *palaestrophylax* and his relationship with the gymnasium and the athletes. Second, he presents the current approaches and arguments of scholarship about Greek homosexuality and especially the erotic gaze of older men for young male boys. Third, he examines two main motifs traced in Rhianus' short poems, which are the Graces that bestow beauty upon young ephebes and hunting as an amatory game between the *erastēs* and the *erōmenoi*. He concludes that Rhianus' description of the erotic gaze is perceived in the context of his social status as an older male, an *erastēs*, who admires pubescent male beauty and uses his poetry to vividly convey this beauty as an object of desire and an unfulfilled pathos.

According to the editors, the volume at hand aims to explore "a variety of topics that have to do with that dual semantic meaning of sexuality, paying attention, in other words, both to the acts and practices of sexual intercourse and to the context that affects, determines, relates and gives meaning to them, i.e. legal, social, political, religious, medical, cultural/moral and interdisciplinary (e.g. emotional, performative, anthropological, psychological)".[1] My contribution to exploring these themes aims to shed further light on aspects of *paederastia*, the love affairs between adult men and adolescent boys. The subject of Greek homosexuality is well-trodden ground for modern scholars, who have discussed the theme

I am deeply thankful to the editors of this volume for inviting me to present my research on Rhianus' homoerotic intercourse and fantasies. I would more specifically like to thank Andreas Serafim, George Kazantzidis, Jonathan Griffiths and Manolis Pagkalos for reading earlier drafts of this chapter. I am also grateful to the anonymous readers for their useful comments and suggestions. All remaining errors are my own.

1 Introduction, p. 3.

https://doi.org/10.1515/9783110695793-005

from various perspectives, including its origins, its level of social acceptability, its popularity in Greece and its links to the *palaestra*.[2] I offer an overview of the current approaches and arguments in the subject of Greek homosexuality by examining the portrayal of a fantasy for young male bodies in Rhianus' epigrams. The narrator's eternal pursuit of sexual desire invites us to consider the question of an unfulfilled *pathos* in the Cretan poet's narrative accounts. References to a physiology of desire ("with certain symptoms and certain modes of action which operate in a network of social relations") emphasise similarities among the short poems of Rhianus.[3] The narrative voice is often equated with the voices of men who express their desire while gazing at their potential lovers' bodies. Especially in the epigrams of the *Musa puerilis* the older men's gaze is, in fact, a "male pederastic gaze" — a subcategory of the male gaze evidenced in ancient Greece and associated with the erotic fantasies of older men for post-pubescent boys.[4]

The thematic focus of this chapter is on two main motifs in Rhianus' homoerotic epigrams: first, that the Graces bestow divine beauty and *charis* on pubescent male bodies and adorn them with flowers; and second, that hunting is used as allegory for the amatory game between the *erastēs* and the *erōmenos*. The erotic epigrams of Rhianus[5] (and other epigrammatists as well) are short and consist of elegiac distichs that bring to mind the verses of Theognis due to their form (in elegiacs) and their thematic similarities (cf. *AP* 12.146 and Thgn. 949–974 on νεβρόν). Gutzwiller rightly points out that variation among the epigrams in question should not be viewed as "an effet product of degenerate Hellenic culture, but as aesthetically satisfying response to historical circumstance with ties to other forms of poetry, to rhetoric, and to art".[6] With this in mind, my reading of Rhianus' epigrams focuses on intertextuality and their relationship to other literary texts and the textual codes within which the poet worked.

---

2 Cf. Barringer 2001, 125–127.

3 Calame 1999, 56.

4 Fountoulakis 2012, 293–296.

5 For Rhianus' *floruit*, cf. Rigsby 1986, 351f., Castelli 1994, 75f., and Cameron 1995, 298f. A relationship between Rhianus and the Peloponnese is attested by an epigram on the children of Troezen (cf. *AP* 12.58); see e.g. Leonidas *AP*. 6.188; cf. also Celotto 2015, 479–487, for evidence of similar relations between Crete and the Peloponnese, especially Arcadia, in Leonidas' dedicatory epigram.

6 Cf. Gutzwiller 1998, 235, on the art of variation in Hellenistic epigrams.

1 Rhianus, the *palaestrophylax* and the gymnasium

Among the limited biographical testimonies we have about Rhianus, the Suda (*Sud.* p 158, IV.293.27 Adler) tells us that:

παλαίστρας πρότερον φύλαξ καὶ δοῦλος, ὕστερον δὲ παιδευθεὶς ἐγένετο γραμματικός.

First, he was a guard of the *palaestra* and a slave, and after he was educated, he became a grammarian.

This fragmentary biography does not allow us to trace the poet's transition from slavery to education and fame as a grammarian. Furthermore, we do not know where he received his education; Meineke claims that Rhianus received a proper education in Alexandria as a Homeric editor, while Jacoby and Fraser do not find any adequate reason to connect the Cretan poet with the Alexandrian grammarians.[7] The case of the Cretan Rhianus follows a literary motif of the ancient biographies about poets. The presence of this biographical pattern (of slave origins) lessens the need to speculate about the poet's liberation or the way he moved from the status of slavery to education and grammatical knowledge.[8]

According to biographical accounts, Rhianus' status as a slave preceded his position as a grammarian. The available sources we have about Cretan society and ethnography were mostly written by non-Cretans and vary in date: Plato and Aristotle wrote in the fourth century BC, Polybius in the second century BC and Strabo wrote during the reign of Augustus. Unfortunately, our knowledge about the Cretan historiographers, Dosiadas and Pyrgion, who are mentioned by Athenaeus (6.84) in the second century BC, is also limited; we suppose, however, that they probably flourished in the Hellenistic period. The writers mentioned above tend to derive evidence from inscriptions, especially from the legal codex of Gortyn in the fifth century BC, in order to present a homogenous picture of Cretan

---

7 See Meineke 1843, 174; *FGrHist* IIIb, 91; Fraser 1972, vol. 1: 625, vol. 2: 650 n. 22. Rhianus could be a slave and familiar with the Homeric poems, recalling the lyric poet Archilochus the Parian, about whom it is known that his father, Telesicles, had an aristocratic origin, although his mother, Enipo, was a slave. See also Rankin 1977, ch. 2, who argues that aristocratic origin was not a necessary condition for Homeric knowledge, although Archilochus' example strengthens even further the argument that slavery was a motif in the ancient biographies, especially in Rhianus' case, where biographical evidence is poor and inconsistent.

8 See Lefkowitz 2012, 118–136; Kivilo 2010, 201–223, on patterns and literary motifs in the ancient biographies (especially those of the Hellenistic poets).

society.[9] Consequently, Rhianus' status as slave, along with his duty as a guard of the *palaestra*, is contrasted with Aristotle's *Politics*, 1264a.21–22:

> ἐκεῖνοι γὰρ τἆλλα ταῦτα τοῖς δούλοις ἐφέντες μόνον ἀπειρήκασι τὰ γυμνάσια καὶ τὴν τῶν ὅπλων κτῆσιν.

> Because they (the Cretans) entrusted everything else to slaves and only refused them entry to the gymnasia and the possession of weapons.

We can assume that the term γυμνάσια refers not to the buildings, but to the training of the young men, which was a duty of teachers and pediatricians (παιδονόμοι or ἀγελάτας, according to the Cretans). However, the word *palaestrophylax*, referred to Rhianus by the Suda (ρ 158 Adler), is probably interpreted as guarding the place of the *palaestra*, if that was actually Rhianus' duty. Cretan slaves were not related to the gymnasium, as Aristotle mentions.[10]

Furthermore, Rhianus' duties as a *palaestrophylax* are ambiguous, depending on his status as a slave or a free citizen. However, they seem to be important in understanding the amatory context of Rhianus' epigrams and his desire for young males. A general distinction needs to be made between, on the one hand, the *palaestrophylax*, who was a slave and, on the other hand, the duties of the guard shared by free citizens.[11] According to Golden, established rules in the Greek world forbade slaves from exercising in the *gymnasia* or the *palaestra*; such rules were already known in Athens, Crete, Cyzicus, Sparta and Nisyrus, with some exceptions during the Hellenistic and Roman periods.[12] Bonfante argues that these rules did not exclude slaves from duties, such as the guarding of the building.[13] Besides, Archaic and Classical Attic vessels depict small male figures standing next to, or helping a boxer: some of them may have been slaves, although they may also have been free boys.[14] In Sparta, where the political and social system resembles the Cretan one, guards were "selected" to perform various duties and were free citizens. In Arcadia, they were probably *ephēboi* with

---

9 Westgate 2007, 424.
10 Mayhoff 1870, 9.
11 See LSJ *s.v.* παλαιστροφύλαξ, where the word is interpreted as "inspector of a wrestling school", although later an interpretation of "the attendant in a wrestling school" is supplemented. In Rhianus' case, it is important to point out the distinction between the slave keeper of the *palaestra* and the free citizen who is responsible for the duty of inspecting a *palaestra*.
12 Golden 2008, 40–41.
13 Bonfante 1989, 556.
14 Golden 2008, 59.

special responsibilities or distinctions.[15] From the arguments discussed above, we may conclude that Rhianus was a citizen who probably had the duty of the *theōrodokos* (*SEG* 26.624, coll. III. 111, Delphi — II BC), and, if he ever was a *palaestrophylax*, he may have belonged to the free guards of the *palaestra*, who used to preserve bonds with the athletes and the athletic ideal of the *gymnasium*.[16]

The discussion above refers to the environment of a *gymnasium*, which does not contradict Rhianus' later status as an epic poet, an epigrammatist, and above all as a scholarly editor of Homer.[17] Meleager included Rhianus in his garland and remarks (*AP* IV 1.11); τῇ δ' ἅμα καὶ σάμψυχον ἀφ' ἡδυπνόοιο Ῥιανοῦ ("along with marjoram from Rhianus with the sweet breath"), and praised his poetic talents. The epithet ἡδύπνοος is a recurrent epithet of the Muses and is probably connected with pleasant and peaceful rhythm. At the same time, σάμψυχον alludes to the aromatic nature of a song.[18] Consequently, Rhianus' affiliations with the *gymnasium* and the exercise of young *ephēboi* could motivate him to express his feelings for these boys and may well reflect the amatory gaze of older males to young boys in his epigrams.

2 The male gaze theory and *paederastia*

This section explores the brief period of young male beauty before a man becomes fully mature. Acosta-Hughes argues that shorter poetic passages, such as in epigrammatic poetry, represent "the ideal artistic medium for such portrayals: as the moment of perfection is a brief one, so too the poetry that encapsulates it is more often shorter, self-contained descriptive frame".[19] Archaic and classical Greek literature and art do not retreat from celebration of the male form. There is a development in a new direction in the Hellenistic period, which particularly arises from the focused gaze on male beauty and what the gaze perceives.

---

15 *IG* 2² 1011.21, Athens, 107/106 BC; See also *AthMitt* 32 (1907) 273, Pergamus (?), first century BC.

16 See Golden 2008, 64–65, who discusses the important legal distinctions between slaves and free citizens in Greece, which were however ignored in daily life. Besides, slaves who took part in the athletic activities of the gymnasium prepared the way for the development of a term for a duty performed only by citizens, including prominent ones. This is further clarified in Peloponnesian inscriptions for the festival–game of Spartan *Leonideia*, an Arcadian testimony about a headmaster, and other inscriptions that reflect the life of the gymnasium.

17 See p. 92 n. 8 above.

18 Saal 1831, 14–15.

19 Cf. Acosta-Hughes 2016, 1, on male bodies as erotic objects in the epyllion tradition.

At the beginning of the twentieth century, the notion of gaze and its role in homoerotic experience became a subject of serious scholarly interest and inquiry. Beazley published several articles on Attic vases with (homo)erotic paintings and inscriptions, providing thereby the first systematic analysis of pederasty in the visual arts.[20] Dover and Foucault claimed that domination was what defined the relationship between the *erastēs*, who assumed the active role (meaning that the *erastēs* could "help" the *erōmenos* ejaculate in order to to be relieved from sexual *pathos*), and the *erōmenos*, who assumed the receptive role and was thus ever at risk of denigration.[21] Hubbard also argues that the emotional bond between the *erastēs* and the *erōmenos* continued to attract increasing attention, and in more contemporary interpretation, the supposedly frigid and unwilling behaviour of the youthful lover is being carefully revised based on sources such as archaic poetry, in which the active participation and passions of the youthful lover are articulated.[22]

Goldhill noted "the erotics of the gaze" as a topic of broad interest and argued further that the passionate inspection of the youthful body and its beauty have indeed been variously explored within classical studies.[23] However, research into the amorous (male) gaze is mostly conducted in relation to heterosexual expressions in both literature and art.[24] Commentators often stress that the male gaze was also present when speaking of the male body as the object of the gaze, with Richlin claiming that a boy rather than a woman was the object of the gaze, but often without delving deeper into the ancient meaning and manifestations of this expression.[25]

Bartsch stressed that in ancient thought the eyes were seen as both the most powerful of our senses and the most vulnerable of our "bodily inroads" and, referring to Plato's views on the sublimated erotic power of the gaze, connects the Roman rejection of this conception with their fear of "ocular penetration", which was regarded as a violation of the integrity of bodily boundaries.[26] Fountoulakis explored the perceptions and representations of *erōs* in the epigrammatic *Musa*

---

20 Beazley 1935, 475–488.
21 Foucault 1976–1984; Dover 1978.
22 Hubbard 2000, 12–13.
23 See Goldhill 2002, 154.
24 This does not mean, though, that the existence of a homosexual perspective has not been acknowledged, as indeed it commonly has. For example, it has been pointed out that artistic objects were primarily centered on male reception. It was initially the male body that provided an eroticised display and as such became objectified; see also Barrow 2018, 9.
25 See Richlin 2015, 360.
26 Bartsch 2006, 57–114.

Puerilis of Strato of Sardis[27] (in which Rhianus' pederastic epigrams were also included) by using the theory of male gaze in combination with pederasty.[28] He effectively demonstrates that in the epigrammatic poems a critical impetus for establishing an emotional connection between the desiring man and the desired boy was often expressed by the act of the former looking upon the latter's body.[29]

As we shall see below, the gazes of both the author and reader are directed towards the narrated bodies and their beautiful qualities, such as their plumpness or captivating eyes, which instill a fire of longing in the poetic self.[30] This chapter focuses on Hellenistic epigrammatic poetry as the basis for inquiring into how the gaze and inspection played a role in the evolution of Hellenistic pederastic culture in the second half of the third century BC. In particular, it is discussed how the gaze influenced literary depictions of young male characters and their bodies in the humorous and sexual manner of the epigrammatic style. For example, in *AP* 12.38 the narrator indicates his love for the handsome and graceful buttock of young Menecrates, who attracts older men. The recipient of this epigram is later revealed with references to the buttock's responses. Furthermore, in *AP* 12.121.6 the narrator humorously compares himself to an αὐηρήν ἀνθερίκην, "a dry reed", moving away from the smoldering Cleonicus. In *AP* 12.146 Rhianus cleverly plays with the motif of hunting which changes into a game of love because (v. 4) the poet later reveals that his competitors stole his prey — his *erōmenos* — and curses them to have a heavy Love.

---

27 This is due to the title Στράτωνος τοῦ Σαρδιανοῦ *Παιδικὴ Μοῦσα* given to Book 12 in the Palatine codex. Despite this title, the book includes not only the pederastic poems of Strato, which most probably date to the end of the first and beginning of the second century AD, but also poems on pederastic themes by earlier authors such as Callimachus, Meleager, and, of course, Rhianus of Crete. These were added to the collection of Strato's poems by later anthologists so as to form the collection found in Book 12. See Cameron 1993, 39–42, 121–159; Gutzwiller 1998, 281–301, esp. 282 n. 111; Fountoulakis 2013, 687 n. 1; 2013, 293 n. 1–2, for further bibliography.
28 See Fountoulakis 2013, 293–311.
29 Fountoulakis 2013, 295–298.
30 Fountoulakis 2013, 297.

3 Graces and a dialogue with the anus (*AP* 12.38)

In this section, I examine fundamental patterns and motifs of Rhianus' homoe-rotic epigrammatic poetry concerning the Graces and the imagery of *Horae* (Sea-sons) that bestow natural beauty upon young male bodies. I shall prove that these motifs' liturgical role is to divinise the image of pubescent boys in front of the eyes of the older *erastēs* — the narrator. As a special case, I explore the descrip-tion of a young *pygē* in its ultimate beauty and brightness, which reveals the poet's desire and admiration for the *ephēboi*. The imagery of the *Horae* (Seasons) and the Graces bestowing natural beauty was frequently attested in Greek litera-ture, although the Horae usually pour dew, rain and water from the spring.[31] The *Horae* also indicate that the inelegant and immature elements of puberty are mixed in a harmonic ensemble. Moreover, in this appropriate period, a young boy (or a girl) is attracted by a potential lover.[32] The *Horae* are thus presented as being powers of nature, seasons that lead to fruition.[33]

Young men such as Menecrates in Rhianus (*AP* 12.38) have reached their ma-ture time for love, and, as we frequently observe in the poet's epigrams, they are pictured as either adorned with or collecting flowers.[34] In this context, Rhianus describes graces such as those of young Cleonicus (cf. *AP* 12.121.4: πεποίησαι δ' ἡλίκος ἐσσὶ χάρις "you have so grown up, as your grace"). Grace conveys the charm of puberty and disappears when this time passes, like the fading of the elegant spring flowers.[35] Grace is also connected with the freshness of youth

---

31 Gow 1952, 150; for example, in Archaic lyric poetry, Pindar describes a handsome boy in a state of mature manhood, comparing him to Zeus' Ganymedes (*Ol.* 10.103–4).

32 Similarly, in Hes. *Op.* 75 Pandora received her charming powers from the Graces and Peitho, while the *Horae* adorned her with flowers of the Spring; cf. also Plat. *Symp.* 188, on the im-portance of the right mixture of elements in the boys' puberty.

33 MacLachlan 1993, 56–57.

34 Cf. in *Cypria* (frr. 5–7 West) the imagery of Aphrodite dressed with ornaments which the Graces and the *Horae* made for her. Sourvinou-Inwood 1987, 137 also notes the role of flowers in the iconography of abduction scenes found on Greek vessels. Sappho also describes the image of a sweet young girl gathering flowers (fr. 122 Voigt) and frequently connects flowers and girls' amorous experiences (cf. frr. 81, 94, 96, 98, 105).

35 MacLachlan 1993, 58–59. Cf. also Pi. *Pyth.* 6.48, on the fading of puberty, where Pindar be-gins his song about Theoxenus with a piece of advice on his feelings of passion for respecting this little moment of freshness and flourishing youth. See also Gutzwiller (2014, 58–59), who compares Rhianus' epigram *AP* 12.121 with the introductory poem of the *Anacreontea*; the scholar mentions that Rhianus' epigram closes "with a wish to be kept far from the boy for fear of the power of his attraction, just as the introductory poem in the *Anacreontea* ends with a regretful confession to foolish acceptance of the erotically binding garland offered by the dream version

which expires in older age.[36] Irwin comments that this "grace" of flourishing flowers lasts for a short period before it fades.[37] Flowers, even within their time of beauty, appear to be vulnerable; the moment of their perfection passes, they die. The same also happens to youth and puberty.

Furthermore, in *AP* 12.93 Rhianus concludes his epigram with praise of beautiful young boys (vv. 11–12):

χαίρετε, καλοὶ παῖδες, ἐς ἀκμαίην δὲ μόλοιτε ἥβην

Farewell, handsome boys, may you come to your prime youth

He adds puberty (ἥβην) as a distinct element of these young boys. One cannot help but think of Pindar and his contribution to this Rhianic epigram. This praise may recall Pindar's (fr. 123.11–12 Maehler):

εὖτ' ἂν ἴδω / παίδων νεόγυιον ἐς ἥβαν

Every time I look on the flourishing youth of the boys

Theoxenus was a young man with whom the poet was probably in love, and the boy's time of puberty was irresistible to him. Puberty belongs to the authority of the Graces and Peitho.[38] Following a similar pattern on pubescence, already visible in Pindar, Theodorus, Philocles and Leptines in Rhianus present an irresistible attraction for the *erastēs*. Rhianus' wish for the boys implies that each has reached their highest youth, and thus, the point when youth becomes attractive to lovers. Pindar also mentions later in the text the pubile parts of Theoxenus' body. Rhianus, similarly, describes the rich flesh of youth (*AP* 12.93.3–4 πίονα σαρκὸς ἀκμήν); the untouchable flower of Theodorus' limbs (*AP* 12.93.3–4 γυίων ἄνθος ἀκηράσιον); the golden face and the heavenly grace of Philocles (*AP* 12.93.5–6 χρύσεον ῥέθος οὐρανίη δ' ἀμφιτέθηλε χάρις); and the bright eyes of Leptines (*AP* 12.93.9–10 σέλας ὄμμασιν αἴθει). This splendid description of young male bodies is conveyed under the aspect of the pederastic gaze. These young

---

of Anacreon". Clearly, the two poems present a strong similarity, although with the difference that in Rhianus the gift of the Graces makes a boy into an object of desire, whereas in the Anacreon's poem the garland presented by the old poet accompanied by *Eros* infuses a force of desire that turns the "I" speaker into a lover and, so necessarily, a poet.

36 Cf. also Pi. *Pyth.* 6.48, on the fading of puberty.
37 Irwin 1984, 152.
38 Other distinct elements of the highest moment of youth include the first fluff of the face, cf. Plat. *Prot.* 309a; Dover 1978, 85–86.

ephēboi are the object of desire and the reason for attraction by the older male — *erastēs*, such as the poet and narrator. Rhianus' focus upon the three bodies is turned into an extra-diegetic gaze directed towards the poem's audience, which is treated as a community of lovers, invited to turn its gaze towards the desired bodies through the narrator's eyes (pederastic vision).

A special case worthy of discussion is Rhianus' poem *AP* 12.38 in the context of the twelfth book's numerous pederastic epigrams. It contains implicit homosexual references to young *ephēboi* who are athletes in the *palaestra*. These epigrammatic lines could allude to the pleasures of anal intercourse in the context of pederastic sexual relationships. The vision could be that of an older *erastēs*, here perhaps Rhianus himself as a *palaestrophylax*:

> Ὡραί σοι Χάριτές τε κατὰ γλυκὺ χεῦαν ἔλαιον,
> ὦ πυγά· κνώσσειν δ' οὐδὲ γέροντας ἐᾷς.
> λέξον μοι, τίνος ἐσσὶ μάκαιρα τὺ καὶ τίνα παίδων
> κοσμεῖς; ἁ πυγὰ δ' εἶπε· "Μενεκράτεος".   4

> The Hours and Graces shed sweet oil on you,
> *pygē*, and you let not even old men sleep.
> Tell me whose you are and which of the boys
> you adorn. And the answer of the pygē was, "Menecrates".

The epigram may be taken to suggest, as a variation on the *pygē* theme, a sexual fantasy about the intercourse that a boy can offer to an older man.[39] This suggestion draws attention to the epigram's potential association with socially constructed concepts, and highlights the *Anthology*'s poems within their literary culture. Yet, social concepts fail to show the epigram's deeper roots in its social and cultural context. Readers, especially those acquainted with the domain of pederastic experience and the vocabulary developed therein, were likely ready to discern in these lines a far more nuanced nexus of semantics. Throughout the twelfth book, whenever reference is made to a boy's buttock and related anatomical parts, this is either through a more elevated vocabulary using medical terminology, such as σφιγκτήρ or ὄπιθεν, through words such as πυγή (buttock) and its cognates, or through metaphors and innuendoes.[40] For example, either in Dioscorides' *AP* 12.37 or Rhianus' *AP* 12.38 πυγή is used to describe the buttock of boys.

---

39 See Richlin 1992², 36; Fountoulakis 2013, 303–304.
40 Cf. Richlin 1992², 37, 129–130. Similar non-literal references to the penises of boys occur in Strato's *AP*. 12.3; cf. Clarke 1994, 466–472.

In *AP* 12.38.1, Rhianus mentions the graceful buttock of young Menecrates. In the introductory verse six divinities are mentioned, the Horae and the Graces, who pour sweet oil onto the young boy:

Ὧραί σοι Χάριτές τε κατὰ γλυκὺ χεῦαν ἔλαιον

The Horae and the Graces poured upon you their sweet oil

This imagery implies that the young boy mentioned later, whose nature and status have already been elevated because he is accompanied by the female deities, is further adorned with freshness, perfume and softness.[41] The Horae and the Graces are usually depicted as pouring dew, rain or spring water,[42] although the oil here further alludes to Callimachus, where the poet asks the Graces to wipe the oil dripping from their hair on his elegies (*Aet.* fr. 7.13–14 Harder):[43]

ἔλλατε νῦν,] ἐ|λέ]γοισι [δ]' ἐνιψήσασθ[ε] λιπώσ|ας|χεῖρ|ας ἐμ|οῖς, ἵνα μο|ι πουλὺ μένως[ι]ν ἔτος,

be gracious now, and wipe your shining hands upon my elegies, so that they will remain for many years (transl. by Harder 2012)

Rhianus intelligently adopts this idea of the oily hair of the Graces to describe the rubbing oil, which improves the boy's charm.

The invocation ὦ πυγά (v. 2) indicates that Rhianus is not addressing a person, but the buttock of a boy. Tarán considers that he probably parodies here the motif of a dialogue between a passer-by and a figure at a grave or statue.[44] In my view, however, the poet-lover talks to an actual buttock here, not to an artistic representation of it. The epigram *AP* 12.37 of Dioscorides was probably Rhianus' model, since both poets praise beautiful youth and the soft buttock that attracts divine attention. The buttocks are so attractive that they invite the old men's gaze. Murgatroyd discerns the exorbitance and parody of the old men's sleepless nights due to the wonderful buttock.[45] Moreover, a divine character is given to the buttock in a literal sense with the anointing of the oil by the Graces, an allusion to

---

41 Cf. Ibyc. *PMGF* 288, Meleag. *AP.* 5.140, 196.
42 Cf. Pi. *Nem.* 8.1, Ap. Rh. *On Found. Naucr.* fr. 7 Powell, Hermipp. the comic poet fr. 5 K.–A.
43 Cameron 1995, 299.
44 Tarán 1979, 43.
45 Tarán 1979, 44. The motif of the senior lover also occurs in other epigrammatists and poets, cf. *AP.* 5.46, 101, 242, 250, 267, 12.8, 101, 155, Ibyc. *PMGF* 287, Tibul. 1–2.89–90. For the lack of sleep due to love, cf. *AP.* 5.119, 166, 237, 12.22, Ap. Rh. *Arg.* 3.751, Verg. *Aen.* 4. It is also a literary *topos* in Latin love elegy e.g. Catullus (22, 50 etc.) and his description of sleepless nights. The

the oil used in the athletic practice of young boys, and in a metaphorical sense through the emphasis on their brightness.[46]

Rhianus' fantasy presents the youthful buttock in its greatest athletic beauty, relating it to the *Horae* and the Graces, and attributing to it the good fortune of belonging to Menecrates, changing the adjective μάκαρ into a pompous compliment. The verb κοσμεῖς (adorn) is emphasised by its metrical position — an inaugural spondee — the name of the boy (Μενεκράτεος) is mentioned only at the end, as a revelation of the owner.[47] The recurrent invocation *pygē* in v. 4 and the buttock's response to the poet-lover make this epigram more amusing and unpredictable. The form of this short dialogue also strengthens its lively and playful style.[48] However, it is unknown whether the narrator's fantasy changed into reality with sexual intercourse between the youth and the older man. We could generally claim that this is a simple fantasy — an imaginary dialogue between the *erastēs* and the buttock — where the poet expresses his admiration for young male bodies. This admiration for a *pygē* leads to a tortured gaze for older males and reveals a weakness of vision. Here, in a playful style, the narrator elevates the ephebic body to a divine level by considering it graceful and exotic.

4 The *erastēs* as hunter, the *erōmenos* as prey (*AP* 12.142)

In many other cases Rhianus considers the suggestive role of hunting in the homoerotic game of love, both literally and metaphorically. Hunting in literature often acquires an erotic dimension; it is often used as a metaphor to describe a game of love between the lover and his *erōmenos*. For example, in *AP* 12.146, we

---

torturing of vision and general weakness of the senses recall Archilochus fr. 26d West (ἐσμυρισμένας κόμας | καὶ στῆθος, ὡς ἂν καὶ γέρων ἠράσσατο), and Latin elegy (cf. Ov. *Am.* 3.7). The second verse probably corresponds to what Dioscorides calls βροτολοιγός love. "Homicide" in love here assumes a symbolic meaning and implies that the beautiful buttock makes humans fall in love with it. The adjective μάκαρ (v. 3) "blessed", "happy" frequently defines gods and goddesses, and here again suggests divine honours for the buttock; cf. also *AP* 7.61, 9.518, 6.339, 6.354.4, 12.52.3, 12.95.9, 12.160. See also Murgatroyd 1989, 309.

46 Cf. Diodor. *AP* 5.122; Tarán 1979, 44.

47 Murgatroyd 1989, 308.

48 The motif of the buttock is a recurrent subject, cf. *AP* 5.35, 54, 55, 60, 132, 12.6, 7.15, 37 (see Henderson 1991[2], 51, 109). For the invocation of the buttock, cf. Aristoph. *Ran.* 238, Sen. *Apocol.* 4.3 (see also Maxwell-Stuart 1972, 307–326; Giangrande 1975, 31–44).

meet a different kind of hunting, which concerns pederastic love, expressed through the form of metaphor:[49]

Ἀγρεύσας τὸν νεβρὸν ἀπώλεσα, χὠ μὲν ἀνατλάς
μυρία καὶ στήσας δίκτυα καὶ στάλικας
σὺν κενεαῖς χείρεσσιν
ἀπέρχομαι· οἱ δ᾽ ἀμογητί
τὰ μὰ φέρουσιν, Ἔρως, οἷς σὺ γένοιο βαρύς

After I caught the fawn, I lost it, I who suffered
from enumerable passions, I set up nets and stakes
go away empty-handed, And they effortlessly
took my prey with them, *Erōs*, may you become heavy to them

The Cretan poet first refers to a fawn, which he loses. However, at the end of the epigram, Rhianus reveals that the fawn was actually the young boy captured by his rival hunters — lovers.[50] In the first verses, Rhianus presents an actual image of hunting, in which the reader learns how the unfortunate hunter lost the fawn which he had caught after many efforts, setting up nets and stakes. In the following verses, the imagery is reversed and assumes a metaphorical sense. Here, the curse of the poet-narrator against the deceit of his opponents is revealed; he wishes that love be heavy for them. In other words, hunter-lovers deceitfully stole the fawn-*erōmenos*, whom the poet tried to seduce and catch with great effort.

The animals that are usually chosen as erotic gifts, such as the rooster, the hare, the deer and the young cat, are critical to our understanding of the negotiation. These gifts signify the metaphor of pederasty through the language of

---

49 Barringer 2001, 70.
50 Homoerotic love and hunting were a crucial subject of late archaic and early classical Athenian masculinity which was bound to the social policy of the aristocracy. Pederasty was included in the ceremonies of the *ephēboi* and demonstrated their sexual and social maturity. Participation in pederastic love was both important and acceptable in the aristocratic world (Plat. *Symp.* 178c), while the exchange of gifts between lovers and their *erōmenoi* involved dynamics of power, control, and social status. Scholars argue that the hunter in the game of love is always the lover, while the prey (or victim) of this game is the *erōmenos*. The former has the power, while the latter is the victim. However, their relationship is usually more complex and vague and can include an exchange of power among old lovers, who acquire social status, and the *erōmenoi*, who also have power due to the passion they inspire in lovers. See Dover 1964, 37; Koch–Harnack 1983; Sergent 1993, 154. Cf. also See Koch-Harnack 1983, 27–28, on social status; Detienne 1979, 34; Dover 1989, 87–88; Cohen 1991, 186; See also Csapo 1993, 22, who mentions this bipolar relationship of lover and *erōmenos*, as well as Schnap 1997, 254–55, 331 and 345.

hunting.[51] It is worth mentioning that deer (ἔλαφοι) or fawns (νεβροί) are occasionally offered as gifts in pederastic iconography. They appear to be especially small and young, and the hunters hold them upon their shoulders like small dogs, or they appear standing on the ground.[52] Heroes, such as Heracles and Theseus, or mortal hunters occasionally hunt deer, as they hunt wild boar, even if deer-hunting was not as famous as boar-hunting. In literature, the *erōmenoi* are frequently compared with small captive fawns. However, the hunter-lovers can also be similar to deer, as they easily attract the *erōmenoi*, like deer attract snakes, according to Plutarch (cf. *Mor. Quest.* 976d *elaphoi*, for their power of attracting snakes) and Aelian (*On Anim. Nat.* 8.6).[53]

Finally, it is worth explaining the importance of captivity in erotic hunting, as described in *AP* 12.146.2: στήσας δίκτυα καὶ στάλικας ("I set up nets and stakes"). The roles of the lover and the *erōmenos* are fluid: they could change in different literary contexts because the animals as gifts express the idea of pederastic love as a form of hunting either for the lover or for the *erōmenos*. In these cases, it becomes unclear who the victim is. The literary references to pederasty mention nets and stakes to express the idea of the erotic pursuit, as was the case

---

51 Barringer 2001, 89 considers that the choice of these animals was not random as only certain animals were offered as gifts and this choice was specific to the context of pederasty. Elements in the iconography of hunting create a metaphor of pederasty as a hunting activity and the chosen animals may be considered metaphorical expressions of characteristics of either the *erōmenos* or the lover. Less frequently among the gifts were also birds; see Bremmer 1990, 142, who claims that gifts usually demonstrate the honourable traits of the *erōmenos*.

52 Barringer 2001, 98.

53 The deer is famous for being satisfied with its prey without looking for more than it has (Ael. *On Anim. Nat.* 6.13) and, like the hare, it is smart, but cowardly (Arist. *On anim. Hist.* 1.1.488b15). The metaphor of animals as gifts in pederastic love provides us with important information about the relationship of power among the participants and the characteristics of both sides, the lover and the *erōmenos*. In literature, as far as the treatment of pederasty through the metaphor of hunting is concerned, the oscillation of power between the lover and the *erōmenos* persists because both are men. See Koch-Harnack 1983, 220. Latin poetry also presents this reversion of sexes and sexual roles, albeit only in heterosexual relationships; see also Miller 1998, 181–184, 198–199. In accepting this metaphor of pederasty as hunting, we may notice that the captive animals, here the fawn (*AP* 12.146) and the blackbird (12.142), are metaphors of the trapped *erōmenos* and the lover respectively. This idea was rejected by Plato, *Laws* 823b–824b, where the philosopher distinguishes suitable from unsuitable hunting.

with hunting already from c. 530 BC.[54] In some cases, the roles of hunter and victim are reversed; the lover becomes the victim of passion or love.[55] In Rhianus' epigram (*AP* 12.146), nets and stakes indicate the hunter-lover's efforts to catch the *erōmenos*, and are contrasted with the deceitful trap set by other lovers to steal his prey, as seen in *AP* 12.146.3–4: οἱ δ' ἀμογητί | τἀμὰ φέρουσιν ("and they effortlessly take my prey with them").

The epigram *AP* 12.142 is also attributed to Rhianus. Its similarity with Rhianus' *AP* 12.146 and the amatory hunting theme make this attribution plausible.[56] The poem is distinguished by its complex style, its quips, elegance, allusions and its artful refinement:

Ἰξῷ Δεξιόνικος ὑπὸ χλωρῇ πλατανίστῳ
κόσσυφον ἀγρεύσας, εἷλε κατὰ πτερύγων·
χὠ μὲν ἀναστενάχων ἀπεκώκυεν ἱερὸς ὄρνις.
Ἀλλ' ἐγώ, ὦ φίλ' Ἔρως, καὶ θαλεραὶ Χάριτες,
εἴην καὶ κίχλη καὶ κόσσυφος, ὡς ἂν ἐκείνου   5
ἐν χερὶ καὶ φθογγὴν καὶ γλυκὺ δάκρυ βάλω.

Dexionicus, having caught a blackbird with lime
 under a green plane-tree, held it by the wings,
and it, the holy bird, * screamed complaining.
But I, dear *Erōs*, and you blooming Graces,
would wish to be even a thrush or a blackbird,
so that in his hand I might pour forth my voice and sweet tears.

In the first distich, the context seems to concern the hunting of birds. In line 3, the poet reveals the erotic element in his narrative, since the narrator is jealous of the bird being captured by young Dexionicus. Rhianus closes his erotic epigram with a wish to the divinity Love and the Graces to transform him into a

---

54 In one of our earliest references Ibycus speaks about Love, who throws him into Aphrodite's nets; see Ibyc. *PMGF* fr. 287 Davies Ἔρως αὖτέ με κυανέοισιν ὑπὸ βλεφάροις τὰ κερά, ὄμμασι δερκόμενος κηλήμασι παντοδαποῖς, εἰς ἄπειρα δίκτυα Κύπριδος βάλλει· "Love, once again looking at me meltingly from beneath dark eyelids with his eyes throws me into the boundless net of Cypris, with all sorts of charms;" Similar images describe captivity through nets and stakes (see Ibyc. 287), a kind of hunting which is already familiar to us from tragedy, lyric poetry, Plato (*Phdr.* 241d, *Lys.* 206a), Xenophon (*Memor.* 1.2.24), and epigrams (Strato *AP.* 12.92).
55 For example, Sophocles describes a woman, who is usually the receiver of passion, and who is hurt by a natural desire, as she was caught in the nets, in fr. 932.3–4 Radt ἐντοῖσιν αὐτοῖς δικτύοις ἁλίσκεται | πρὸς τοῦ παρόντος ἱμέρου νικωμένη "in these nets she was caught, defeated by the present passion".
56 Cf. Gow-Page 1965, 443, on the prescription Ῥιανοῦ.

blackbird at the hands of young Dexionicus.[57] I suggest that this poem might belong to the corpus of dedicatory epigrams where the hunter dedicates his prey to a deity. In a similar dedicatory epigram, the hunter's success is described before the actual dedication.[58] The noun κόσσυφον is the well-known blackbird (or *Turdus merula*), otherwise also known as a κόψιχος.[59] Dexionicus holds the blackbird by its wings, and the preposition κατά is used to describe a hostile deed against the bird.[60]

However, the narrative of the following lines contains a different shift that suggests the change of the poet into the captured bird. Firstly, Dexionicus is misleadingly characterised by the epithet ἱερός, and the narrative emphasises the bird's mourning through the participle ἀναστενάχων and the verb ἀπεκώκυεν.[61] The invocation to Eros and the Graces (l. 4) reveals the first erotic element of the epigram, which may surprise the readers, who would expect a dedicatory scene or a common hunting act. The reason for this is not immediately clear, and the puzzling question is answered only at the end of the last distich.[62] Rhianus addresses Love and the Graces since they are responsible for his wish in line 5; thus, this poetic allusion here shows the narrator's gratitude to their divine influence.

---

57 Cf. *AP* 6.11–16, 75, 109, 152, 179–187, 296, 7.171.
58 Cf. *AP* 6.110, 111 and 168, see also Gow 1952, 359; the scenery includes a green plane tree where Dexionicus holds the bird in his hands. The early form πλατάνιστος is attested in *Iliad* 2. 307, 310 as a Homeric δὶς λεγόμενον, and appears again in Theocritus 18.44, 22.76 and 25.20. This plant was widely known in antiquity.
59 Cf. Aristoph. *Bir.* 305, 806, 1081, Antip. *AP* 9.76, Arch. *AP* 9.343; see also Gow-Page 1965, 508.
60 See Gow-Page 1965, 508.
61 See further Murgatroyd 1989, 303. The active voice of the verb ἀναστενάχω is elsewhere attested only in *Iliad* 23.211 τὸν πάντες ἀναστενάχουσιν Ἀχαιοί (cf. *Il.* 18.315 and 355 for the middle voice of the verb). The compound verb ἀπεκώκυεν is translated "lamented loudly" and is also attested in Aesch. *Ag.* 1544 ἄνδρα τὸν αὐτῆς ἀποκωκῦσαι, although with the preposition ἀπό similar verbs occur, such as θρηνέω, ὀδύρομαι and οἰμώζω. The tragic ring to this verb ascribes a profound seriousness to the poem's style. Furthermore, the phrase ἱερὸς ὄρνις recalls Alcman *PMGF* fr. 26.4 ἁλιπόρφυρος ἱαρὸς ὄρνις, in which the old poet wants to be a cyrril and uses this phrase to describe the bird. What is more, this phrase also recalls Mnasalces *AP* 7.171.1–2 = *HE* 8 ἀμπαύσει καὶ τῇ δε θοὸν πτερὸν ἱερὸς ὄρνις | …ἑζόμενος πλατάνου, who was almost a contemporary of Rhianus (cf. Gow–Page 1965, 400). Murgatroyd (1989, 304) considers Alcman's fragment as the possible model for the common detail of the poet's wish to transform into an ἱερὸν ὄρνιν, although in Rhianus the birds are not standing and do not fly above the sea with νηδεὲς ἦτορ (cf. also Q.S. 13.107–8 ἀνατρίζουσι φοβεύμεναι ἱερὸν ὄρνιν· | …Τρωιάδες μέγ᾽ ἐκώκυον, where ἱερὸς ὄρνις is an eagle). Furthermore, in Antip. Thess. *AP* 9.76 = *GPh* 80 the blackbird is called ἱερόν, in *AP* 9.343.5 = *GPh* 24 Archias narrates ἱρὸν οιδοπόλων ἔτυμον γένος and in Paul. Sil. *AP* 9.396 the blackbird's song focuses on the explanation of his escape.
62 Murgatroyd 1989, 303.

The adjective θαλεραὶ defines the Graces and indicates their influence on young Dexionicus. The poet wishes to be transformed into a thrush (κίχλη) or a blackbird and to have physical contact with young Dexionicus, who is portrayed as famous and gifted; the poet simply wishes to be one of his bird victims.[63] Thus, Rhianus skillfully changes this event with the bird into a compliment and expresses the lover's wish to be transformed. Murgatroyd claims that the poet does not see this transformation as possible, and Love would hardly change him into a bird.[64] He comments that the speaking voice would not have great success in approaching the young boy and, thus, expresses the wish to come closer to him, preserving his human features (see the tear in v. 6).[65]

The speaking voice laments and screeches like the blackbird, although pleasure and joy will reduce the tears since he will be a captive in the hands of Dexionicus. But the poet does not mourn because he is not captured; he contrasts himself with the bird. It would be strange to complain that he was caught since his capture is actually his physical contact with the young boy. Hence, a reasonable assumption is that the narrator takes the chance to mourn his rejection by the boy and that this chance to touch him would constitute the sweet and pleasant (γλυκύ) tear. The narrator thereby mourns as a blackbird, although his complaints are, in contrast, full of joy and happiness that he has been caught by his lover.[66]

Thus, we may generally conclude that Rhianus creates an interplay of the eyes and the ears for the narrator — the *erastēs* (who may be Rhianus himself) — and his readers who are present for an imaginary transformation. The bold antithesis of both "eye" (i.e. the transformation of the narrator into the bird) and "ear" (i.e. the antithesis of the bird's crying with the narrator's tears) changes an actual gaze upon a hunting scene into an imaginary gaze upon an erotic scene, as if it were real event, and not an illusion. The feeling that words have a natural

---

63 See *AP* 9.76, 9.343, 9.396; cf. Thompson 1936, 149; Arnott 2007, 140–141; blackbirds and thrushes are frequently mentioned together, although thrushes, in contrast to blackbirds, are usually mentioned as a kind of food, not as singers, and normally they do not flourish in Greece, except for the Mistle Thrush (which has pale spots on its chest).

64 Murgatroyd 1989, 303–304.

65 The transformation of the poet recalls Ovid's transformation into a ring, *Am.* 2.15.25–26 *tenuda mea membra libidine surgent,* | *et peragam parte sanulus ille viri*; cf. also Anacr. *PMG* 22.5, *Conv. trag. PMG* 900, 901, Theocr. 3.12, AP. 5.83, 84, 174, 7.669, 12.52, 190, Logg. *Daph. and Chl.* 2.2, 4.16; see also van Buren 1959, 380–382; Hiltbrunner 1970, 283; Murgatroyd 1984, 51; On the typical Hellenistic variation of the transformation motif, see Giangrande 1967, 85 and 1970, 46; Ludwig 1968, 299; Tarán 1979.

66 See Murgatroyd 1989, 304.

aptitude for what they express is particularly intense in the narration of the disappointed lover and the blackbird's desperate crying because the awakening of this feeling is thematised and staged as an attunement to the sounds of an imaginary poetic world. Hearing a human and avian language properly is one and the same experience in the poet's fantasy. Thus, the readers are engaged with passionate fantasy that turns into a reality in front of their eyes.

5 Conclusion

The amatory epigrams of the Hellenistic period are all short poems, comprising elegiac distichs similar to the verses of Theognis, and they all constitute poetic manifestations of an "I" grappling with the torments of love. Typically, they are addressed to an implied addressee in a situation that is made highly specific, even if it is probably fictitious.[67] Furthermore, they all seem to describe either attempts at seduction or poetic substitutes for it in situations of unreciprocated and unfulfilled love. All the references emphasise the similarity that these poems make to a physiology of desire, a tradition first introduced by archaic poetry.

Rhianus seems especially interested in the literary side of the love-affair. His handling of models, forms, themes and imagery is often imaginative and is characterised by combinations, variation and innovation. Murgatroyd notes appropriately that Rhianus is a "meticulous craftsman", carefully ordering his material and frequently manipulating his readers. For example, Rhianus' audience is captured by the unique description of the graceful young bodies and feels both amused and astonished by the divine description of the Graces bestowing natural beauty on a buttock. The audience is also invited to attend a "dream" that could be changed into reality in front of their eyes; the readers can see the transformation of a bird into the poet-*erastēs* who is captured by his hunter — the *erōmenos*. However, this is only a dream, an erotic fantasy which, although vividly conveyed in front of the readers as an actual event, it remains in the narrator's poetic sphere.

The Cretan poet's language and expression are often plain and direct, but are also "versatile and sensitive" and generally economical, with very few real redundancies.[68] It seems useful to remember that the poet in archaic Greece and beyond was a performer; Rhianus might have been a peripatetic poet, visible at

---

67 Calame 1999, 56.
68 Cf. Murgatroyd 1989, 312–313 on Rhianus' epigrammatic art and practice.

Panhellenic festivals and dependent on commissions (as was Simonides), who took part in festivals such as the Delphic *Soteria*, as is alluded to in his poem *Pheme*.[69] Audience, patronage, social position and the changing of political atmosphere in Greece must all have affected such poetry's nature and context. If something was worth remembering and passing on, it would be better remembered in poetic form, providing erotic desire with vivid images and language to both the subject and the poet respectively.

Readers may ask the question "is Rhianus parodying epigrams on human body parts or praising the *pygē* sincerely?" I cannot give a full answer to this question; readers observe an actual praise of a part of the human male body and, more specifically, a buttock. This actual applause reveals Rhianus' admiration for male ephebes. At the same time, the personification of the male buttock gives a sense of parody and lightness that is further bolstered by the humorous style of the epigram within the context of a short dialogue. It may also be possible that Rhianus reveals the social and political environment of his day with a shift in the relationship between the lover and the *erōmenos*, since he presents cases where the *erōmenos* is the predator, while *erastēs* is the victim. Hence, I identify Rhianus as a citizen *palaestrophylax* with apparent affiliations with the gymnasium and the young *ephēboi*. His erotic gaze is perceived in the context of his social status as an older male, an *erastēs*, who admires pubescent male beauty and uses his poetry to vividly convey this beauty as an object of desire and an unfulfilled *pathos*.

Bibliography

Acosta-Hughes, B. (2016), 'The Breast of Antinous. The Male Body as Erotic Object in Hellenistic Image and Text', in: *Aitia. Regards sur la culture hellénistique au XXIe siècle* 6.

Arnott, W.G. (2007), *Birds in the Ancient World from A to Z*, London.

Barringer, J.M. (2001), *The Hunt in Ancient Greece*, Baltimore, MD.

Barrow, R. (2018), *Gender, Identity and the Body in Greek and Roman Sculpture*, Cambridge.

Bartsch, S. (2006), *The Mirror of the Self: Sexuality, Self-Knowledge, and the Gaze in the Early Roman Empire*, Chicago.

Beazley, J.D. (1935), 'Some inscriptions on vases. III', in: *American Journal of Archaeology* 39, 475–488.

Bonfante, L. (1989), 'Nudity as a Costume in Classical Art', in: *American Journal of Archaeology* 93, 543–570.

Bremmer, J. (1990), 'Adolescents, Symposion, and Pederasty', in: O. Murray (ed.), *Sympotica: A Symposium on the Symposion*, Oxford, 135–148.

---

69 Cf. Rutherford 2009, 240; Petrovic 2009, 215–216.

Calame, C. (1999), *The Poetics of Eros in Ancient Greece*, Princeton.

Calame, C. (2016), 'The Amorous Gaze: A Poetic and Pragmatic Koine for Erotic Melos?', in: V. Cazzato/A.P. Lardinois (eds.), *The Look of Lyric. Greek Song and the Visual*, Leiden, 288–306.

Cameron, A. (1993), *The Greek Anthology from Meleager to Planudes*, Oxford.

Cameron, A. (1995), *Callimachus and his Critics*, Princeton.

Cantarella, E./Lear, A. (2008), *Images of Ancient Greek Pederasty*, London.

Castelli, C. (1994), 'Riano di Creta: Ipotesi Cronologiche e Biografiche', in: *Rendiconti. Classe di lettere e scienze morali e storiche (RIL)* 128, 73–87.

Celotto, G. (2015), 'Leonidas *AP* 6.188 (= 4 *HE*)', in: *Mnemosyne* 68, 479–487.

Clarke, W.M. (1994), 'Phallic Vocabulary in Straton', in: *Mnemosyne* 47, 466–472.

Cohen, D. (1991), *Law, Sexuality, and Society: The Enforcement of Morals in Classical Athens*, Cambridge.

Csapo, E. (1993), 'Deep Ambivalence: Notes on a Greek Cockfight (Part I)', in: *Phoenix* 47, 1–28.

Detienne, M. (1979), *Dionysos Slain*, transl. M. Muellner/L. Muellner, Baltimore.

Dover, K.J. (1964), 'Eros and Nomos (Plato, *Symposium* 182A–185C)', in: *Bulletin of Classical Studies* 11, 31–42.

Dover, K.J. (1989), *Greek Homosexuality*, updated edition, Cambridge, MA.

Foucault, M. (1976), *Histoire de la Sexualité*, Paris.

Foucault, M. (1985), *The Use of Pleasure. Vol. 2, The History of Sexuality* (transl. R. Hurley), New York.

Foucault, M. (1986), *The Care of the Self. Vol. 3, The History of Sexuality* (transl. R. Hurley), New York.

Fountoulakis, A. (2012), 'Male Bodies, Male Gazes: Exploring Eros in the Twelfth Book of the Greek Anthology', in: E. Sanders/C. Thumiger (eds.), *Eros in Ancient Greece*, Oxford, 293–312.

Fountoulakis, A. (2013), 'On the Nature of Strato's Humour: Another Look at *Anth.Pal.* 12.6', in: *Greek Roman and Byzantine Studies* 53, 687–707.

Fraser, P.M. (1972), *Ptolemaic Alexandria* (Vol. 2), Oxford.

Giangrande, G. (1967), 'Arte Allusiva and Alexandrian Epic Poetry', in: *Classical Quarterly* 17, 85–97.

Giangrande, G. (1975), 'Fifteen Hellenistic Epigrams', in: *Journal of Hellenic Studies* 95, 31–44.

Golden, M. (2008), *Greek Sport and Social Status*, Austin.

Goldhill, S. (2002), 'The Erotic Experience of Looking: Cultural Conflict and the Gaze in Empire Culture', in: M.C. Nussbaum/J. Sihvola (eds.), *The Sleep of Reason: Erotic Experience and Sexual Ethics in Ancient Greece and Rome*, Chicago, 374–399.

Gow, A.S.F. (1952), *Theocritus* (Vol. 2), Cambridge.

Gow, A.S.F./Page, D.L. (1965), *The Greek Anthology: Hellenistic Epigrams*, Cambridge.

Gutzwiller, K.J. (1998), *Poetic Garlands: Hellenistic Epigrams in Context*, Berkeley.

Hiltbrunner, O. (1970), 'Ovid's Gedicht vom Siegelring und ein anonymes Epigramm aus Pompei', in: *Gymnasium* 77, 283–300.

Houston, G.W. (2008), 'Tiberius and the Libraries: Public Book Collections and Library Buildings in the Early Roman Empire', in: *Libraries & the Cultural Record* 44, 247–269.

Hubbard, T.K. (2000), 'Pederasty and Democracy: The Marginalization of a Social Practice', in: T.K. Hubbard (ed.), *Greek Love Reconsidered*, New York, 1–11.

Irwin, E. (1984), 'The Crocus and the Rose', in: D.E. Gerber (ed.), *Greek Poetry and Philosophy: Studies in Honour of Leonard Woodbury*, Chico, CA, 147–168.

Kivilo, M. (2010), *Early Greek Poets' lives*, Leiden.

Koch-Harnack, G. (1983), *Knabenliebe und Tiergeschenke: Ihre Bedeutung in Päderastischen Erziehungssystem Athens*, Berlin.

Lefkowitz, M.R. (2012), *The Lives of the Greek Poets*, London.

Ludwig, W. (1968), 'Die Kunst der Variation im hellenistichen Liebesepigram', in: A.E. Raubitschek/B. Gentili/G. Giangrande/L. Robert/W. Ludwig/J. Labarde/A. Dihle/G. Pfoh (eds.), *L'Epigramme Grecque*, Entretiens sur l'Antiquite Classique 14, Geneve.

MacLachlan, B. (2014), *The Age of Grace: Charis in Early Greek Poetry*, Princeton.

Maxwell-Stuart, P.G. (1972), 'Strato and the Musa puerilis', in: *Hermes* 100, 215–240.

Mayhoff, K.F.T. (1870), *De Rhiani Cretensis studiis Homericis*, Leipzig.

Meineke, A. (1843), *Analecta Alexandrina: Sive, Commentationes de Euphorione Chalcidensi, Rhiano Cretensi, Alexandro Aetolo, Parthenio Nicaeno*, Berlin.

Miller, P.A. (1998), 'Catullan Consciousness, the 'Care of the Self,' and the Force of the Negative in History', in: D.H.J. Larmour/P.A. Miller/C. Platter (eds.), *Rethinking Sexuality: Foucault and Classical Antiquity*, Princeton, 171–203.

Murgatroyd, P. (1984), 'Amatory Hunting, Fishing and Fowling', in: *Latomus* 43, 362–368.

Murgatroyd, P. (1989), 'The Amatory Epigrams of Rhianus', in: *Echos du monde classique: Classical Views* 33, 301–313.

Payne, M. (2013), 'The Understanding Ear: Synaesthesia, Paraesthesia and Talking Animals', in: S. Butler/A.C. Purves (eds.), *Synaesthesia and the Ancient Senses*, London, 43–52.

Rankin, H.D. (1977), *Archilochus of Paros*, Park Ridge, NJ.

Rigsby, K.J. (1986), "Notes sur la Crète hellénistique", in: *Revue des Études Grecques* 99, 350–360.

Richlin, A. (1992), *The Garden of Priapus: Sexuality and Aggression in Roman Humor*, Oxford.

Richlin, A. (2015), 'Reading Boy-Love and Child-Love in the Greco-Roman World', in: M. Masterson/N. Sorkin Rabinowitz/J. Robson (eds.), *Sex in Antiquity: Exploring Gender and Sexuality in the Ancient World*, London, 352–373.

Rutledge, S.H. (2008), 'Tiberius' Philhellenism', in: *Classical World* 101, 453–467.

Saal, N. (1831), *Rhiani quae supersunt*, Bonn.

Schnapp, A. (1989), 'Eros the Hunter', in: C. Bérard/C. Bropon/D. Lyons (eds.), *A City of Images: Iconography and Society in Ancient Greece*, Princeton, 71–87.

Sergent, B. (1993), 'Paederasty and Political Life in Archaic Greek Cities', in: *Journal of Homosexuality* 25, 147–164.

Skinner, M.B. (1997), 'Ego mulier: The Construction of Male Sexuality in Catullus', in: J.P. Hallett/M.B. Skinner (eds.), *Roman Sexualities*, Princeton, 129–150.

Sourvinou-Inwood, C. (1987), 'A Series of Erotic Pursuits: Images and Meanings', in: *The Journal of Hellenic Studies* 107, 131–153.

Tarán, S.L. (1979), *The Art of Variation in the Hellenistic Epigram*, Leiden.

Thompson, D.A. (1936), *A Glossary of Greek Birds*, Oxford.

van Buren, A.W. (1959), 'A Pompeian Distich', in: *American Journal of Philology* 80, 380–382.

Vidal-Naquet, P. (1986), *The Black Hunter: Forms of Thought and Forms of Society in the Greek World*, transl. A. Szegedy-Maszak, Baltimore, MD.

Westgate, R. (2007), 'House and Society in Classical and Hellenistic Crete: A Case Study in Regional Variation', in: *American Journal of Archaeology* 111, 423–457.

Andreas Fountoulakis

Silencing Female Intimacies: Sexual Practices, Silence and Cultural Assumptions in Lucian, *Dial. Meretr.* 5

Abstract: This chapter aims to explore aspects of female homosexuality in Lucian's fifth *Dialogue of the Courtesans*, where a narrative focusing on sexual intercourse among three women is articulated through an interplay of speech and silence. Fountoulakis seeks to specify the sexual practices alluded to in that text and the reasons why they are not explicitly mentioned. The relevant references and the reasons of the subsequent silencing are related to broader assumptions and moral standards concerning gender and sexuality, which were prevalent in Greek society and culture. It is argued that this interplay of speech and silence forms part of Lucian's narrative strategies which evoke long-standing Greek cultural assumptions and yet undermine traditional Greek values by means of insinuation. Issues of gender and sexuality thus become parts of a wider discourse focused on a process of cultural formation and change prevalent in Lucian's cultural milieu.

1 Introduction

When, in April 1895, Oscar Wilde was brought to court charged with gross indecency, the prosecutor asked him about the meaning of the phrase "I am the Love that dare not speak its name". The phrase appeared in a poem by Lord Alfred Douglas, which had the title "Two Loves" and was printed the previous year in *The Chameleon*. In his famous response Wilde declared that it suggested the affection of an older man for a younger one in a noble form which could hardly be understood by the world. This lack of understanding was apparently due to the prevalent morality of late Victorian England and determined what someone could talk about or leave in silence, what was considered as decent or shameful, and, subsequently, what was regarded as beneficial or harmful to society.

Douglas' perception of homosexual desire in terms of speech and silence as well as in terms of decency and shame are also found in Lucian's fifth *Dialogue of the Courtesans*: an important text focusing on female homosexuality, which has

https://doi.org/10.1515/9783110695793-006

attracted only in recent years the scholarly attention it deserves.[1] Considering that the rest of the fifteen texts included in the *Dialogues of the Courtesans* refer to the affairs of hetaerae with men, such a topic is quite unusual. In this text a hetaera called Leaina talks to a fellow-hetaera called Clonarium about her sexual adventures with another woman called Megilla and her female partner Demonassa, but hesitates to name the exact acts into which she has been involved. The account of Leaina's sexual encounter is placed within a narrative framework determined by eagerness to talk about something extraordinary and reluctance to refer to something shameful in which she has been involved. Speech and silence emerge interwoven with a discourse of shame, and form main features of the dialogue's narrative strategies. Such a silencing of female homosexuality appears to echo relevant Greek moral standards, but manage in fact to draw the attention of the dialogue's addressees to the details of Leaina's sexual adventure which are provided by her either explicitly or implicitly.

The aim of this chapter is to shed light on the potential types of Leaina's sexual encounter as well as on the reasons why she avoids being more specific about them. This may explain the narrative device of revelation and concealment employed in the dialogue. It may also shed some light on the morality and the relevant cultural assumptions evoked throughout the dialogue as well as on the ways these may be undermined. It will be argued that the interplay between what may be done in one's bed and what not, what may be said about it and what not, and what may stand as a moral standard pertaining to it and what not, form important elements of the fifth *Dialogue of the Courtesans*, which are closely related to some of the aims of Lucian's prose within the wider cultural context of the Second Sophistic.

2 Between speech and silence

Although female homosexuality is an important thematic strand of Sappho's poetry, Amphis' *Callisto* and Plato's *Symposium* and *Laws*,[2] in antiquity it must have been a subject not to be spoken of mainly on moral grounds. Kenneth Dover notes that even the comic poets, who often refer for comic purposes to male homosexuality, do not mention female homosexuality, and takes this to reflect a kind of

---

1 See Haley 2002; Gilhuly 2006; Boehringer 2007, 349–356; Blondell/Boehringer 2014; Boehringer 2015.
2 Sappho, frr. 1.13–24, 16, 31, 49, 81, 82 Voigt; Amphis, fr. 46 K.–A.; Plato, *Symp.* 191e, *Laws* 636c.

male anxiety towards the subject.[3] Bernadette Brooten has shown that in the Roman period female homosexuality was perceived by Greek and Latin authors as a sign of masculinity endorsed by women and this was regarded by those authors as unnatural, repulsive, unlawful and monstrous.[4] In an important study on female homosexuality in ancient Greece and Rome, Sandra Boehringer notes the reluctance of classical authors — with the exception of Plato — to refer to sexual relations between women, and attributes it not so much to the nature of such relations, but to the fact that those involved in them were women.[5] This silence or even aversion to female homosexuality may also suggest a male fear about this blatant female incontinence and indifference towards male authority as expressed in male sexual domination. Such an exchange of roles between males and females[6] would threaten a system of values and hierarchies that regulated the proper function of ancient societies. Especially in the classical period such a blight on social order might well be seen as directed against the *oikos* and consequently against the *polis*.[7]

This socially produced inhibition is partially reproduced in Lucian's dialogue where it serves the employment of a narrative strategy of revelation and concealment. The embedding of the account of Leaina's adventures in her dialogue with Clonarium enables the adoption of this narrative strategy and the development of their comments on Leaina's confession.[8] Speech and silence thus emerge connected with a discourse of shame in the opening lines of the dialogue and appear again in its closing lines. This provides the text with a circular structure that highlights the significance attached to the elements of speech, silence and shame

---

3 Dover 1978, 172–173. Cf. Boehringer 2007, 160–162.

4 Brooten 1996, 29, 42–57. Cf. Williams 2010², 8–9, 233–239, 274–276.

5 Boehringer 2007, 157–174. In Plato, *Laws* 636b–d, for instance, the Athenian's comments on homosexuality are almost entirely devoted to male homosexuality, whereas there is only a passing reference to female homosexuality.

6 It is highly unlikely that the female homosexual was in antiquity perceived as a separate social category beyond the binary perception of male and female. For this reason, the action, the attitude and the mentality of Megilla in *Dial. Meretr.* 5 are described as male. Cf. Boehringer 2014, 150, 160–161.

7 In the less powerful *poleis* of the Roman period, in which citizenship was not as important as it used to be in the classical *polis*, factors contributing to the construction of citizen identity were no longer particularly important. It is for this reason that distinctions between masculine and feminine roles in the *oikos* and beyond were not as important as they used to be in the past and this is reflected in the construction of masculine and feminine sexual roles in genres such as the novel. Cf. Konstan 1994, 230.

8 Boehringer 2007, 355 sees in Leaina a persona of the author and in Clonarium that of his readers.

since Clonarium's curiosity and persistent questions, and Leaina's reluctance to provide answers form main features of the narrative process. Clonarium represents a wider community[9] before which Leaina's sense of shame is being developed.

When Clonarium begins her conversation with Leaina with a reference to the latter's alleged sexual relations with Megilla from Lesbos, who is supposed to love her like a man, she wonders if the rumours heard are true and asks for more details, noting that her interlocutor is blushing full of shame: Καινὰ περὶ σοῦ ἀκούομεν, ὦ Λέαινα, τὴν Λεσβίαν Μέγιλλαν τὴν πλουσίαν ἐρᾶν σου ὥσπερ ἄνδρα καὶ συνεῖναι ὑμᾶς οὐκ οἶδ' ὅ τι ποιούσας μετ' ἀλλήλων. τί τοῦτο; ἠρυθρίασας; ἀλλ' εἰπὲ εἰ ἀληθῆ ταῦτά ἐστιν "We've been hearing strange things about you, Leaina. They say that Megilla, the rich Lesbian woman, is in love with you just like a man, that you live with each other, and do goodness knows what together. Hullo! Blushing? Tell me if it's true".[10] Leaina admits that the rumours are true and says that she feels ashamed because of the "unusual nature"[11] of the affair: Ἀληθῆ, ὦ Κλωνάριον· αἰσχύνομαι δέ, ἀλλόκοτον γάρ τί ἐστι "Quite true, Clonarium. But I'm ashamed, for it is unnatural".[12] The words καινὰ and ἀλλόκοτον introduce this discourse of homosexuality in paradoxographical terms which raise the curiosity of the text's addressees. The word ἀλλόκοτον, in particular, invests female homosexuality with an otherness which underlines its non-conformity to the socially dominant standards of heteronormativity.[13] It is due to Clonarium's persistence and her successive questions that Leaina decides to talk to her: Πρὸς τῆς κουροτρόφου τί τὸ πρᾶγμα, ἢ τί βούλεται ἡ γυνή; τί δὲ καὶ πράττετε, ὅταν συνῆτε; ὁρᾷς; οὐ φιλεῖς με· οὐ γὰρ ἂν ἀπεκρύπτου τὰ τοιαῦτα "In the name of Mother Aphrodite, what's it all about? What does the woman want? What do you do when you are together? You see, you don't love me, or you wouldn't hide such things from me".[14]

---

9 Boehringer 2007, 351–352 thinks that Clonarium represents a community of courtesans, but, in fact, gathering from what she says, she represents fifth-century Athenian society and its morality.

10 Lucian, *Dial. Meretr.* 5.1. Both the text and the translation of Lucian's *Dialogues of the Courtesans*, which appear in this paper, come from Macleod 1961.

11 For the meaning of ἀλλόκοτος as something or somebody "of unusual nature", see LSJ⁹, s.v. ἀλλοκοτία.

12 Lucian, *Dial. Meretr.* 5.1.

13 Libanius, *Or.* 54.73 refers to the love of Pasiphae for the bull as ἀλλόκοτον ἔρωτα. This is another instance where the word ἀλλόκοτος is again used in order to describe sexual conduct which was considered as unthinkable and socially unacceptable.

14 Lucian, *Dial. Meretr.* 5.1.

The fact that Clonarium asks for details about something which in Greek culture was a taboo topic in combination with Leaina's hesitation to talk about it sparks interest among the dialogue's addressees and directs their attention to Leaina's reply. Such a manipulation of their expectations is reinforced by the shame Leaina says that she feels (αἰσχύνομαι), which is also noted by Clonarium observing her blushing (ἠρυθρίασας;). Considering that a woman of her social status would not easily feel shame about many things, one is bound to think that her adventures might include actions that are extremely shameful and distressing.[15] Leaina's sense of shame evokes fundamental values of a culture of honour and shame inextricably linked with a Greek cultural past. These values are based on culturally determined assumptions pertinent to what may be regarded as shameful and what not with respect to male and female identities, and sexuality. This is not surprising if it is born in mind that the action of Lucian's *Dialogues of the Courtesans* is set in classical Athens. Leaina appropriates a set of cultural assumptions pertinent to the ideal of the chaste wife, sister and daughter who acted as passive agents before male authority and domination. Those assumptions were prevalent in the *polis*[16] and are vividly recalled so as to provide the dialogue with an established cultural framework which is evoked and yet challenged by the two interlocutors.[17] At the same time, the morality that her sense of shame presupposes is contrasted with her status along with her activities,[18] and ironically creates a particularly humorous effect peculiar to Lucian's satire.

Leaina's hesitation to talk about her sexual adventures with Megilla and her female partner disappears soon after Clonarium's entreaties and appears again

---

15 In addition to her references to the shame she felt at both the beginning and the end of the dialogue, Leaina says at 5.3 that she felt distress (ἐταράχθην ἰδοῦσα) when she saw Megilla taking her wig off and showing a shaven head as if she were a terribly masculine male athlete.

16 As may be inferred from Artemidorus of Daldis, many of those assumptions, such as those concerning roles of male dominance and female subordination in patriarchal societies, were still current in Lucian's times. Cf. Winkler 1990, 17–44. Yet, as this chapter aspires to show, those assumptions did not remain unchallenged or unchanged, and Lucian's text reflects, is part of and contributes to such cultural changes.

17 In epic poetry and tragedy women exhibit a profound sense of shame with respect to matters of sexual morality. Loyalty and propriety are values which determine their sexuality and are safeguarded by their *aidōs*. See further Cairns 1993, 120–126, 305–340. It is reasonable to suppose that such a link between shame and sexuality was socially informed. At the same time, it may well have shaped feminine identities in social contexts.

18 It should nevertheless be noted that a hetaera was supposed to be much different from a common prostitute since she was expected to have received some kind of education. This might have entailed moral education not much different from the education offered in philosophical schools. See Kapparis 2018, 47–63.

only when it comes to the description of the type of intercourse she had with her female lover. Thus Leaina says that as a guitar player she had met Megilla during a symposium organised by the latter and her female partner Demonassa from Corinth. Demonassa's name and place of origin[19] may imply that she is an ex-prostitute or a woman of similar moral standards capable of being involved in shameful acts, and it is this latter feature that is exploited in Lucian's narrative. This would explain the ease with which she enters into a relationship with Megilla and has sex simultaneously with more than one partners. Leaina considers her acts as shameful not only because they are homosexual, but also because they entail the participation of three persons. The context of the symposium points towards a common context of Platonic dialogue and hence towards the quasi-philosophical overtones of Lucian's dialogue. As a sphere of male activity, it also highlights the delineation of Megilla's assumed masculinity. As the only women who normally took part in a symposium in addition to female slaves were hetaerae or common prostitutes, it underlines Leaina's actual status and prepares her intratextual and extratextual addressees for the description of licentious acts taking place in an ambience encouraging immorality and debauchery.

After the end of the symposium the two women asked her to sleep with them. In extant Greek literature this is an unprecedented instance of a description of a female homosexual threesome. As soon as the three women were in bed, Megilla and Demonassa started kissing Leaina passionately, biting her lips and pressing her breast: ἐφίλουν με τὸ πρῶτον ὥσπερ οἱ ἄνδρες, οὐκ αὐτὸ μόνον προσαρμόζουσαι τὰ χείλη, ἀλλ' ὑπανοίγουσαι τὸ στόμα, καὶ περιέβαλλον καὶ τοὺς μαστοὺς ἔθλιβον· ἡ Δημώνασσα δὲ καὶ ἔδακνε μεταξὺ καταφιλοῦσα "at first they kissed me like men, not simply bringing their lips to mine, but opening their mouths a little, embracing me, and squeezing my breasts. Demonassa even bit me as she kissed".[20] Both Megilla and Demonassa play thus an active role. Megilla took then her wig off revealing her shaven head and assuming a manly appearance: χρόνῳ δὲ ἡ Μέγιλλα ὑπόθερμος ἤδη οὖσα τὴν μὲν πηνήκην ἀφείλετο τῆς κεφαλῆς ... καὶ ἐν χρῷ ὤφθη αὐτὴ καθάπερ οἱ σφόδρα ἀνδρώδεις τῶν ἀθλητῶν ἀποκεκαρμένη "eventually Megilla, being now rather heated, pulled off her wig... and revealed the skin of her head which was shaved close, just as on the most energetic of the

---

19 Her name, which derives from the words δῆμος and ἄνασσα, and literally means "Queen of the people", may point to her popularity among her male clients and be related to Aphrodite *pandēmos*. Moreover, Corinth, her place of origin, was notorious for its prostitutes. Cf. Haley 2002, 296; Boehringer 2007, 352; Gilhuly 2017, 11–42; Kapparis 2018, 266–269. For other possibilities concerning the origins of Demonassa's name, see Gilhuly 2017, 112.
20 Lucian, *Dial. Meretr.* 5.3.

athletes".[21] Then Megilla had sex with Leaina saying that, although she did not have a penis, she had her own far more pleasant way of approaching her erotically: καὶ τὸ ἀνδρεῖον ἐκεῖνο ἔχεις καὶ ποιεῖς τὴν Δημώνασσαν ἅπερ οἱ ἄνδρες; ἐκεῖνο μέν, ἔφη, ὦ Λέαινα, οὐκ ἔχω· δέομαι δὲ οὐδὲ πάνυ αὐτοῦ· ἴδιον δέ τινα τρόπον ἡδίω παρὰ πολὺ ὁμιλοῦντα ὄψει με "and you have everything that a man has, and can play the part of a man to Demonassa?" "I haven't got what you mean", said she, "I don't need it at all. You'll find I've a much pleasanter method of my own".[22] Later on she becomes even more specific saying that she has a penile substitute: πάρεχε γοῦν, ὦ Λέαινα, εἰ ἀπιστεῖς, ἔφη, καὶ γνώσῃ οὐδὲν ἐνδέ-ουσάν με τῶν ἀνδρῶν· ἔχω γάρ τι ἀντὶ τοῦ ἀνδρείου "If you don't believe me Leaina", said she, "just give me a chance, and you'll find I'm as good as any man; I have a substitute of my own".[23] Although the description is already revealing, when Leaina is asked about Megilla's substitute and its function, she refuses to provide further details.[24] It appears that it is not homosexuality *per se*, but the dissociation of active and passive roles from biological sex as well as the fact that such roles can be assumed by both men and women that undermine cultural assumptions pertinent to gender roles and cause Leaina's anxiety and shame.

At this crucial point, the dialogue is already near the end. In its closing lines, when Clonarium asks about the way Megilla has had sex with Leaina as if she were a man, Leaina refuses to answer stating that she cannot tell because such things are shameful: Μὴ ἀνάκρινε ἀκριβῶς, αἰσχρὰ γάρ· ὥστε μὰ τὴν οὐρανίαν οὐκ ἂν εἴποιμι "Don't enquire too closely into the details; they're not very nice; so, by Aphrodite in heaven, I won't tell you".[25] Clonarium's invocation of Aphrodite at 5.1 is here repeated by Leaina who attributes her hesitation to provide further details to her sense of shame and the consideration of the acts in which she has been involved as shameful (αἰσχρὰ) as if what she has already said was not shameful. The invocation of Aphrodite *Ourania*, in particular, who is also mentioned with respect to *erōs* in Plato, *Symposium* 180e–181d, appears to comply with the expression of her sense of shame and invests Lucian's dialogue with philosophical overtones.[26] Despite the irony generated by the contrast between her supposed dignity and her actions and social status, this enables her to put an end to her recitation, set in motion the imagination of the dialogue's addressees,

---

21 Lucian, *Dial. Meretr.* 5.3.
22 Lucian, *Dial. Meretr.* 5.3.
23 Lucian, *Dial. Meretr.* 5.4.
24 Lucian, *Dial. Meretr.* 5.3–4.
25 Lucian, *Dial. Meretr.* 5.4.
26 Cf. Gilhuly 2017, 112.

intrigue them and prompt their curiosity. In an ironical manner, her status and actions are again contrasted with the values and the morality of Greek cultural past.

The narrative is based upon a constant succession of revelation and concealment. The internal moral conflicts experienced by Leaina are mirrored in the development of her narrative voice in two separate directions as if this is divided in two separate and competing voices. The first one puts forward a discourse of female homosexuality. The second evokes moral codes firmly rooted in Greek cultural past. Such an evocation results in Leaina's self-censorship which counterbalances the account of her sexual adventures. In fact, this narrative conflict sheds even more light on the implications of the expression of the feminine and the homosexual within a social and cultural ambience based on values and power relations with a very different orientation.

3 Female pleasures

One may wonder what kind of action would have been considered as shameful in Leaina's social milieu and by a woman who had the status of a hetaera. Considering what is said in the context of Lucian's text as well as in the wider context of Greek culture, both that of fifth-century Athens and that of Lucian's times, two kinds of sexual acts appropriate for the culmination of female homoerotic encounter would justify Leaina's embarrassment: her penetration by Megilla and cunnilingus.

To begin with a potential penetration by Megilla, such an act would comply with her portrayal and her appropriation of features pertinent to males and not to females. Kate Gilhuly, in an important article on Lucian's fifth *Dialogue of the Courtesans*, perceptively underlines the manly features of Megilla and the development of her character in terms of a phallic and penetration-centred conception of sexual relations in ancient Greece. The phallus could accordingly turn a man into an active, dominant and powerful agent, and a woman into a passive, submissive and weak one in sexual and, subsequently, social relationships that lacked symmetry.[27]

---

27 See Gilhuly 2006, 281–283. Cf. Dover 1978, 183; Cantarella 2002², 93; Boehringer 2007, 353; Boehringer 2015, 259–260, 270. For this type of sexual power relations, see Dover 1978, 84–91, 100–109; Foucault 1992, 187–225; Halperin 1990, 15–40; Winkler 1990, 45–70.

It is nevertheless worth bearing in mind that the pattern of active and passive agents in penetration-centred relationships was not a rule governing the perceptions of all sexual relations in antiquity.[28] It is also worth bearing in mind that female pleasure, in particular, may be achieved through acts of stimulation of the clitoris, the urethra and the anterior vagina not necessarily involving penetration.[29] The word τριβάς, which denotes in Greek "the female homosexual", is etymologically linked with the verb τρίβειν meaning "to rub"[30] and suggests that in antiquity homosexual practices between women were mainly thought to involve not penetration, but rubbing of the female genitals.

Yet it is reasonable to assume that a text such as *Dial. Meretr.* 5, which is written by a male author and addressed to male readership, would adopt a phallocentric viewpoint that would associate masculine sexuality with an active role in penetrative sexual relations, and this is what, in fact, happens.[31] Even female poetic voices such as that of Sappho appear to endorse such a viewpoint which was dominant in their cultural ambience. The melancholic overtones of Sappho, fr. 31 Voigt, for instance, may thus be linked to her inability to fully adopt a masculine role and offer pleasure through penetration to her female object of desire.[32]

As if she were a socially autonomous man, Megilla, being rich, is capable of organising a symposium, a field of male activity, together with Demonassa, as well as offering gifts in order to seduce her potential lovers.[33] This "masculine" attitude is echoed in her appearance as a young male athlete with a shaven head, when she takes her wig off and culminates in the adoption of a male social identity which becomes apparent when she claims that she is a young man (νεανίσκος) called Megillos and married to Demonassa who is her/his wedded wife: ἡ δέ, Ὦ Λέαινα, φησίν, ἑώρακας ἤδη οὕτω καλὸν νεανίσκον; Ἀλλ' οὐχ' ὁρῶ, ἔφην, ἐνταῦθα νεανίσκον, ὦ Μέγιλλα. Μή καταθήλυνέ με, ἔφη, Μέγιλλος γὰρ ἐγὼ λέγομαι καὶ γεγάμηκα πρόπαλαι ταύτην τὴν Δημώνασσαν, καὶ ἔστιν ἐμὴ γυνή "but she said, "Leaena, have you ever seen such a good-looking young fellow?" "I don't see one here, Megilla", said I. "Don't make a woman out of me", said she. "My name is Megillus, and I've been married to Demonassa here for ever so long;

---

28 Cf. Davidson 2001, 3–51.
29 Cf. Jannini/Buisson/Rubio-Casillas 2014, 531–538; Pauls 2015, 376–384.
30 See Chantraine 1999², 1137, *s.v.* τρίβω. Cf. Boehringer 2007, 261.
31 Cf. Brooten 1996, 154; Hallett 1997, 226–227; Haley 2002, 299–300. For the *Dialogues of the Courtesans* as a group of texts considering the persona of the hetaera from a Greek elite male point of view, see Gilhuly 2007.
32 See Devereux 1970, 17–31.
33 Lucian, *Dial. Meretr.* 5.2 and 4.

she's my wife".[34] It is nevertheless likely that when she says that γεγάμηκα πρό-παλαι ταύτην τὴν Δημώνασσαν,[35] she does not refer to proper marriage, but to the sexual intercourse she has with her. In this sexual relationship Megilla holds an active role.[36] That role is suggested by the active γεγάμηκα, which underlines the asymmetrical character of their relationship and the essentially masculine role she rehearses. Demonassa's passive role in their relationship becomes discernible when she finds herself in bed with Megilla and Leaina, where she only kisses Leaina.[37] The gender role Megilla performs is permeated by a phallic mentality associated with her sexual and social dominance.[38]

Megilla's disturbing image reveals the shifting boundaries of gender identities, a reversal of the conventional manifestations of gender and a subsequent subversion of social norms concerning the formation of the *oikos*. This image is nevertheless not entirely alien to Lucian's educated readers. In the world of ritually generated reversals and liminalities of Aristophanic comedy, one of Lucian's probable sources,[39] female characters appear performing male roles, as happens with Praxagora and the Athenian women in the *Ecclesiazusae*, where gender-determined social roles are strongly associated with appearance and, more specifically, with attire.[40] The discrepancy between social perceptions of gender roles and the unexpected ways these roles may be performed may have been the cause of anxiety among Aristophanes' male spectators. At the same time, it would have generated a particularly comic effect enhanced by the comic ambience of Aristophanes' plays. In the context of Lucian's *Dialogues of the Courtesans* the comic overtones of Megilla's appearance as a distant echo of Aristophanic comedy may set the tone of Lucianic satire in a mixture of serious and comic elements.

---

34 Lucian, *Dial. Meretr.* 5.3.
35 Lucian, *Dial. Meretr.* 5.3.
36 Cf. Cameron 1998, 142–144; Haley 2002, 297–298. Boehringer 2015, 261 thinks that Megilla refers to "a permanent bond as much as a sexual relationship". For the use of Greek and Latin terms relating to marriage in contexts pertinent to sexual union, see Adams 1982, 159–161; Boehringer 2007, 353, n. 10.
37 Lucian, *Dial. Meretr.* 5.3.
38 Cf. Butler 1993, 28–57.
39 Cf. Rosen 2015, 141–162.
40 The sexually ambiguous Dionysus of the *Frogs* and the disguise of the Kinsman and Agathon in the *Thesmophoriazusae* reflect an interest of earlier Aristophanic plays in the comic exploitation of the possibilities of gender subversion and reversal. Such an exploitation relies on the construction of gender through mask and costume, and the unexpected handling of gender related stereotypes and role components. Cf. Stone 1980, 410–411; Taaffe 1993, 103–133; Compton-Engle 2015, 74–82, 94–102, 104–107; Medda 2017, 137–151.

It is within this serio-comic context that Leaina appears frustrated and wonders if Megilla is transvestite, hermaphrodite or transsexual. Achilles, Hermaphroditus and Teiresias form in her thought relevant mythical paradigms which point to the existence of relevant social and sexual categories in the collective consciousness of Lucian's addressees.[41] They suggest a socially current perception of gender as a human feature closely related to clothing, which may at times combine both the masculine and the feminine, and change easily from the masculine to the feminine and vice versa.[42] Yet Megilla stresses that she/he is a man in every respect (τὸ πᾶν ἀνήρ εἰμι).[43] She also draws a sharp distinction between her biological sex and her gender stating that even though she was born a woman having all the features women have, her way of thinking (γνώμη) as well as her desires (ἐπιθυμία) are male: ἐγεννήθην μὲν ὁμοία ταῖς ἄλλαις ὑμῖν, ἡ γνώμη δὲ καὶ ἡ ἐπιθυμία καὶ τἆλλα πάντα ἀνδρός ἐστί μοι "I was born a woman like the rest of you, but I have the mind and the desires and everything else of a man".[44] She thus dissociates both mentality and sexuality from her inborn physical features. Leaina herself had earlier described her as "terribly manly" (δεινῶς ἀνδρική).[45] This suggests a perception of gender as a social and cultural construct pertinent to roles which are performed by an individual and involve one's body, appearance, social position, mentality, emotions, attitude and identity.[46] The use of the adverb δεινῶς has moral overtones and suggests her amazement as well as her anxiety before the contrast between Megilla's biological sex and gender. In the Hippocratic corpus the difference between men and women is linked with specific biological features as well as with body temperature and this means that one's sex may be modified according to the changes of one's temperature.[47]

---

41 Although those three categories, and especially those of the hermaphrodites and the transsexuals, were not always distinguished from each other, as they are distinguished in Lucian's text, they were recognised as such in Greek mythology as well as in the fields of Greek comedy, medicine and paradoxography. See Delcourt 1961, *passim*; Dreger 1998, 32; Brisson 2002, *passim*; Androutsos 2006, 214–217; Carlà-Uhink 2017, 3–37; Doroszewska 2019, 123–134; Costello 2020, 201.
42 See Lee 2015, 28, 37–46, 51, 68–78, 182.
43 Lucian, *Dial. Meretr.* 5.4.
44 Lucian, *Dial. Meretr.* 5.4. Cf. Haley 2002, 295–298, who sees in Megilla's male appearance and attitude indications of transgenderism.
45 Lucian, *Dial. Meretr.* 5.1.
46 In Lucian's text all these fields contribute to the construction of Megilla's gender which is not "a temporary state or a behaviour", as Boehringer 2015, 273 believes with respect to Megilla's virility.
47 See King 1998, 21–39.

Although Lucian's dialogue is one of the few ancient texts that refer in such an explicit manner to the associations between sexuality and gender roles, it must reflect views current in his social ambience. In a work entitled *On Chronic Diseases*, Caelius Aurelianus, a fifth-century AD medical author, considers homosexual women (*tribades*) as women who behave like men, considering this masculinity as a broader social — and not as an exclusively sexual — category. Sex between women is considered only the symptom of a mental disorder consisting of the adoption of a social role which is not linked by society to biological features either male or female.[48] Sexuality becomes thus a state of mind dissociated from biological sex. Considering that Caelius Aurelianus is believed by historians of medicine to draw heavily from the second-century AD medical author Soranus of Ephesus, it is reasonable to suppose that the perception and distinction of social gender and biological sex which appears in Lucian's text reflects a socially recognised perception of female homosexuality in terms of a distinction between masculine and feminine social roles as well as of a link between such roles and sexuality.

In a culture where masculine and feminine attitudes and identities were linked to a phallocentric perception of human sexuality and the subsequent ability of a male to penetrate a female, it is not surprising that Leaina asks Megilla whether she also has a penis.[49] This suggests her adoption of a phallocentric viewpoint ready to conceive sexual relationships in terms involving penetration as well as active and passive agents. As her question would appear reasonable to Lucian's male readership, such a viewpoint must have been a component of the readers' horizon of expectations. The fact that Megilla does not have a penis does not mean that she could not adopt a sexual identity analogous with her adopted social role, and this is what happens when she says that she has a substitute. This is the manifestation of the conceptual phallus she has developed. Such a phallus dominates her mentality and directs her action towards the construction of the unconventional sexual and social role she performs.[50] She first states that she has a far more effective way of giving pleasure to a woman than a penis (ἴδιον δέ τινα τρόπον ἡδίω παρὰ πολὺ ὁμιλοῦντα ὄψει με "you'll find I've a much pleasanter method of my own")[51] and then she says that she has something that may be used instead of the male organ (ἔχω γάρ τι ἀντὶ τοῦ ἀνδρείου "I have a substitute of my

---

48 Caelius Aurelianus, *On Chronic Diseases* 4.9.132–133 Drabkin. See Boehringer 2007, 339–341.
49 Lucian, *Dial. Meretr.* 5.3.
50 Cf. Butler 1993, 28–57.
51 Lucian, *Dial. Meretr.* 5.3.

own").[52] This may be specified as an object or as another bodily part or organ. Clonarium admits that this could happen provided that Megilla is an ἑταιρίστρια. The term is defined by her as referring to some women from Lesbos who are manly (ἀρρενωπούς), do not want to be penetrated by men and come close to other women as if they themselves were men.[53] This explains her earlier statement that Megilla loves Leaina like a man.[54] Leaina admits that this is the case.

The ability of a woman to penetrate another woman is acknowledged by Artemidorus of Daldis in his *Interpretation of Dreams* 1.80 (p. 97 Pack), where he uses the terms περαίνειν and περαίνεσθαι to refer to such acts: Γυνὴ δὲ γυναῖκα ἐὰν περαίνῃ, τὰ ἑαυτῆς μυστήρια τῇ περαινομένῃ κοινώσεται. ἐὰν δὲ ἀγνοῇ τὴν περαινομένην, ματαίοις ἐπιχειρήσει πράγμασιν. ἐὰν δὲ γυνὴ ὑπὸ γυναικὸς περαίνηται, χωρισθήσεται τοῦ ἀνδρὸς ἢ χηρεύσει "if a woman penetrates a woman, she will share her secrets with her. If she does not know the woman she penetrates, she will undertake useless projects. If a woman is penetrated by a woman, she will be separated from her husband or will be widowed" (transl. J.J. Winkler). This type of sexual intercourse is described by Artemidorus as unnatural (παρὰ φύσιν) as happens with intercourse with gods, animals, corpses and oneself. The principles used by Artemidorus for his analysis of dreams stem not only from earlier books of dream interpretation, but also from actual observation of the results of dreams and people's consideration of them. Dream interpretation thus becomes a way of deciphering people's values, beliefs, fears, hopes and mentalities. It is, therefore, likely that the moral values, beliefs and codes evoked in his *Interpretation of Dreams* reflect the morality which prevails in his social and cultural ambience.[55] If seen from the phallocentric perspective, according to which this is an act that reverses the socially acceptable schema of a male active agent who penetrates a socially inferior such as a female passive agent,[56] one may understand the reasons why Artemidorus considers the penetration of a female by another female unnatural. One may also understand the reasons why Leaina, feeling ashamed, wishes to remain silent.[57]

The phallocentric perspective which determines such a consideration of sexual relationships among women also determines the ways sexual roles within

---

52 Lucian, *Dial. Meretr.* 5.4.
53 Lucian, *Dial. Meretr.* 5.2.
54 Lucian, *Dial. Meretr.* 5.1.
55 See Winkler 1990, 23–41; Harris-McCoy 2012, 13–18.
56 Cf. Winkler 1990, 39–40, 86; Boehringer 2007, 337.
57 In Lucian's *Philopseudes* 15 a woman referred to as ἐραστὴς γυνή, as a woman that is who assumes the sexual and social role of an older male in a pederastic relationship, is described as having a very bad reputation.

such relationships are shaped. Although penetrative sex between women is invested with negative overtones with respect to both partners, it is the passive partner who is supposed to find herself in the worst position. According to Artemidorus, the one who penetrates only shares her secrets with her partner or is engaged in something useless, whereas the one who is penetrated is separated from her husband or becomes a widow and this suggests her degradation and isolation from the world of male society. Having assumed a passive role in such a type of sexual contact, this is another reason why Leaina feels shame and prefers silence.

Gilhuly believes that Megilla's reluctance to specify the kind of penile substitute she has makes problematic any assumption concerning the potential use of an overdeveloped clitoris or an ὄλισβος and leads us to interpret it on a symbolic level.[58] Similarly, Brooten regards Megilla's substitute as a mental one.[59] Yet Megilla's silence may result from the fact that sexual pleasure is not always associated with penetration or from the culturally determined negative semantic nuances attached to this kind of penetration. Scholars such as Anderson and Winkler believe that what Megilla has in mind is a dildo.[60]

Herondas' *Mimiamb* 6, a text which may give us some hints about the practical aspects of such a penile substitute, betrays a similar hesitation to refer explicitly to a kind of act that could be considered shameful or unnatural. In that text a woman called Coritto is the owner of a red βαυβών (l. 19): a leather dildo like an ὄλισβος that passes from woman to woman in a way that suggests a solitary use. Such objects are mentioned by comic poets and mimographers and are depicted in the form of penises in vase-paintings.[61] Yet the way the βαυβών is described in Herondas suggests that it was specially designed for encounters similar to that alluded to in Lucian. Thus Coritto says that her βαυβών has the ability to stand upwards as straight as a man's erect penis and that it is as smooth as sleep (ll. 69–71): τὰ βαλλί' οὕτως ἄνδρες οὐχὶ ποιεῦσι / – αὐταὶ γάρ εἰμεν · ὀρθά· κοὐ μόνον τοῦτο, / ἀλλ' ἡ μαλακότης ὕπνος "men can't make their pricks stand as straight — it's all right, we're on our own. And not only that, their smoothness is sleep itself" (transl. G. Zanker). Her references emerge from a mixture of speech and silence. The privacy of her conversation with her friend Metro enables Coritto and Metro

---

58 Gilhuly 2006, 82. For such misgivings, cf. Boehringer 2015, 271–273.
59 Brooten 1996, 52–154.
60 Anderson 1976, 95–96; Winkler 1990, 39–40.
61 See Aristophanes, *Thesm.* 478–501, *Lys.* 108–110, *Peace* 978–986, fr. 592.15–27 K.–A.; Cratinus, fr. 354 K.–A.; Epicharmus, fr. 226 K.–A.; Sophron, fr. 23 K.–A.; Σ Aristophanes, *Lys.* 107, 109, 110; Keuls 1985, 82–86, 116–117; Lissarrague 1990, 59, 63, 79; Olender 1990, 84; Boehringer 2007, 146–150; Zanker 2009, 197; Stafford in this volume.

to talk about a topic which should otherwise be left in silence. Moreover, Coritto says that her βαυβών has small straps that feel as if they were made of wool and not leather (ll. 71–72): οἱ δ᾽ ἱμαντίσκοι / ἔρι᾽, οὐχ ἱμάντες "and their dear little straps are wool, not leather" (transl. G. Zanker). Considering that such straps are absent from the depiction of similar objects in vase-paintings, it is reasonable to assume that those straps had some special function since they would be useless if the object was employed only for masturbation. This function could be nothing other than the adjustment of the object on a woman's body so that she could penetrate another human body. That is why the fact that they feel smooth is thought to be important. The object would thus resemble an erect penis and could be used for the penetration of another woman in cases of homosexual encounters during which the woman wearing it would assume a role similar to that of a man.[62]

Herondas' red βαυβών may well be no other than a dildo functioning as a strap-on in female homosexual encounters as this is described in the pseudo-Lucianic *Affairs of the Heart* 28: χάρισαι τὴν ἴσην ἐξουσίαν καὶ γυναιξίν, καὶ ἀλλήλαις ὁμιλησάτωσαν ὡς ἄνδρες· ἀσελγῶν δὲ ὀργάνων ὑποζυγωσάμεναι τέχνασμα, ἀσπόρων τεράστιον αἴνιγμα, κοιμάσθωσαν γυνὴ μετὰ γυναικὸς ὡς ἀνήρ· τὸ δὲ εἰς ἀκοὴν σπανίως ἧκον ὄνομα — αἰσχύνομαι καὶ λέγειν — τῆς τριβακῆς ἀσελγείας ἀνέδην πομπευέτω. πᾶσα δ᾽ ἡμῶν ἡ γυναικωνῖτις ἔστω Φιλαινὶς ἀνδρογύνους ἔρωτας ἀσχημονοῦσα "but bestow the same privilege upon women, and let them have intercourse with each other just as men do. Let them strap to themselves cunningly contrived instruments of lechery, those mysterious monstrosities devoid of seed, and let woman lie with woman as does a man. Let wanton Lesbianism — that word seldom heard, which I feel ashamed even to utter — freely parade itself, and let our women's chambers emulate Philaenis, disgracing themselves with Sapphic amours" (transl. M.D. Macleod). The *Affairs of the Heart* focuses on a rhetorical debate concerning the merits of the love for boys and those of the love for women. Although those references form part of a rhetorical argument aiming at the defence of the love for boys and providing a female parallel,[63] they may well be based on actual practice. The development of a simple dildo into a strap-on complies with perception of female homosexuality in terms of penetration-centred relationships, involving active and passive agents as well as the homosexual

---

62 If such an object is seen from a metapoetic point of view, it may represent the allegedly infertile pleasure produced by female poets and the criticism exercised against them in Herondas 6. See further Warwick 2020, 333–353.

63 Cf. Boehringer 2014, 159–160.

woman as a man.[64] This is stressed three times in the pseudo-Lucianic text,[65] where it is obvious that homosexuality is not considered a separate type of sexual identity.[66] It is rather the distinction between natural impulse and culture as expressed in philosophical reasoning that is drawn in that text and homosexuality stands on the part of culture as an allomorph of philosophical discourse.[67] The perception of female homosexuality through a penetration-centred lens and of the female homosexual as a man emerges also in Lucian's fifth *Dialogue of the Courtesans* with respect to the delineation of Megilla's masculine traits and the declaration of her intention of having sex with Leaina like a man. Such a sexual stance may be due both to the use of a strap-on and the development of male mentality. Significantly enough, in both texts even talking about such matters is thought to be shameful.

Although the fact that Leaina might have been penetrated with the use of a strap-on would comply with the description of Megilla's manly appearance, attitude and mentality, cunnilingus is another probable option for the kind of action Leaina's description alludes to. Even if it is considered from the perspective of Megilla's masculine presence, cunnilingus, in antiquity, was another type of sexual contact a man might have had with a woman. The mythographer Phaedrus notes that Prometheus had created the female tongue out of the male organ's moulding: *formavit recens / a fictione veretri linguam mulieris. / adfinitatem traxit inde obscenitas* "Lately he formed the tongue of woman from the moulding of the male organ. From this source obscenity has attracted a bond of kinship by marriage" (transl. J.P. Hallett).[68] In a context concerned with an *aition* relating to the *tribades*, "the masculine homosexual women",[69] this suggests a perception of fe-

---

64 Cf. Stafford in this volume.

65 See, in particular, the phrases ἀλλήλαις ὁμιλησάτωσαν ὡς ἄνδρες, κοιμάσθωσαν γυνὴ μετὰ γυναικὸς ὡς ἀνήρ and Φιλαινὶς ἀνδρογύνους ἔρωτας ἀσχημονοῦσα in Ps.-Lucian, *Affairs of the Heart* 28.

66 Cf. Halperin 1992, 255–256. Note, however, that placing homosexual females in the same group as Philainis, who becomes in this passage a paradigmatic homosexual woman, implies their perception as a separate category. Despite the silence that is meant to be imposed on the topic of female homosexuality as well as the negative overtones with which it is invested, the narrative strategy of revelation and concealment brings the topic to the foreground of the *Affairs of the Heart*. The use of the term ἀνδρογύνους may suggest an understanding of sexuality in terms of the distinction between male and female, but implies also that these two categories may be mixed in order to produce a third one. Cf. Boehringer 2007, 298–300, 304, 306–314.

67 Cf. Goldhill 1995, 102–110.

68 Phaedrus, *Fable* 4.15.

69 Phaedrus, *Fable* 4.16.

male homosexuality not as a separate social, psychological or biological category, but in terms of a dichotomy associated with the masculine and the feminine. The homosexual woman's deviation from an ideal femininity appears to bring her close to the adoption of a male sexual identity which is also placed in a distant Greek past.[70] It also suggests a consideration of the female tongue in particular as, among other things, a penile substitute.[71] Although a tongue is substantially smaller than a penis, its use in cunnilingus might involve not only licking the external female genitals, but also vaginal penetration. Licking and penetration of the female genitals with the use of one's tongue may well be accompanied by a similar rubbing and penetration with the use of one's fingers. Seen from such a perspective, cunnilingus is not incompatible with a penetration-centred pattern of sexual conduct.

From the beginning of the dialogue it is stated that Megilla is from the island of Lesbos. It may be easily inferred by a modern reader that this is an implicit acknowledgment of the fact that she is a lesbian in the modern sense of a word, implying that she is a homosexual woman. Such an interpretation is enhanced by Clonarium's reference to a rumour concerning the existence of such women in Lesbos (*Dial Meretr.* 5.2). Although this may be a kind of cultural stereotype related to the articulation of female homoerotic speech by authoritative poetic voices like that of Sappho,[72] it should be born in mind that λεσβιάζειν in antiquity was associated with various forms of sexual debauchery. In authors such as Aristophanes, Pherecrates and Theopompus the verb λεσβιάζειν and its cognates are used in order to refer to sexual vices with no particular reference to any sort of specific action.[73] In a summary of Suetonius, *On Blasphemies*, preserved in cod. Paris. Bibl. Nat. suppl. gr. 1164 as well as in Eustathius' commentary on the *Iliad* (P.741.19–24 Stallbaum), the verb λεσβιάζειν is thought to suggest τὸ αἰσχρο-ποιεῖν, to perform shameful acts. Harry Jocelyn in his discussion of these texts has noted that the verb may point towards various sexual vices, but must also

---

70 Cf. Hallett 1997, 256–258; Parker 1997, 57; Boehringer, 2007, 261–267; Williams 2010², 125–159, 211–212.

71 See Haley 2002, 299, who on these grounds sees the description of Megilla's "kissing like a man" as an allusion to female penetration.

72 It was after the first century AD that female homosexual practices were associated with Sappho and the island of Lesbos. See further Boehringer 2007, 211–215, 352 with n. 6. Cf. Boehringer 2015, 263, who aptly notes that the fifth *Dialogue* is one of the earliest texts in which the connection between lesbianism and Lesbos is made; Gilhuly 2017, 91–116.

73 See Aristophanes, *Wasps* 1345–1350, *Frogs* 1301–1308, *Eccl.* 918–923; Pherecrates, *Cheiron* fr. 159 K.–A.; Theopompus, fr. 35 *FrHistGr*; Jocelyn 1980, 31–33; Haley 2002, 296; Cantarella 2002², 87.

refer to oral sex which in antiquity was thought to be a particularly shameful sexual practice.[74] This is suggested by Pherecrates, *Cheiron* fr. 159 K.–A., who states that seven Lesbian women amount to seven λαικαστρίας: [A.] δώσει δέ σοι γυναῖκας ἐπτὰ Λεσβίδας. / [B.] καλόν γε δῶρον, ἔπτ' ἔχειν λαικαστρίας "[A.] He will give you seven women from Lesbos. / [B.] nice gift, to have seven *laikastrias*". Although the word was often used as a derogatory reference to a woman with low moral standards not much different from those of a common prostitute, the verb λαικάζειν and its cognates were used with reference to the act of fellatio.[75] It is perhaps for this reason that many later grammarians associated the Lesbians with the performance of oral sex placing the link between λεσβίζειν and λαικάζειν in the existence of the initial λάβδα these words have in common.[76]

When Clonarium refers to the potential sexual activities of the ἑταιρίστριαι from Lesbos, she notes that such women are masculine and do not want to be penetrated by men, but approach other women as if they were men: οὐ μανθάνω ὅ τι καὶ λέγεις, εἰ μή τις ἑταιρίστρια τυγχάνει οὖσα τοιαύτας γὰρ ἐν Λέσβῳ λέγουσι γυναῖκας ἀρρενωπούς, ὑπ' ἀνδρῶν μὲν οὐκ ἐθελούσας αὐτὸ πάσχειν, γυναιξὶ δὲ αὐτὰς πλησιαζούσας ὥσπερ ἄνδρας "I do not understand what you mean, unless she's a sort of woman for the ladies. They say there are women like that in Lesbos, with faces like men, and unwilling to consort with men, but only with women, as though they themselves were men" (transl. M.D. MacLeod).[77] The word πλησιαζούσας, meaning "those who approach", as opposed to the more specific αὐτὸ πάσχειν, refers to the penetration of women by men, may point not specifically to penetration, but also — and perhaps mainly — to other forms of sexual encounter, and oral sex was one of them even though it might involve a form of small-scale penetration.

In the erotic spells attested in the Greek magical papyri a demonic agent is often asked to bring torture to a woman and bind her so that she may not be able to have vaginal intercourse, anal intercourse, fellate or do anything for the pleasure of any man other than the one who casts the spell.[78] Considering the fact that

---

74 Jocelyn 1980, 18.

75 Jocelyn 1980.

76 For those sources, see Jocelyn 1980, 33–34.

77 Lucian, *Dial. Meretr.* 5.2.

78 In *Suppl. Mag.* I 46.8ff., for instance, a love charm from Egypt used by a certain Poseidonius in order to attract Heronous these three types of sexual congress are clearly distinguished when he asks the demonic agent he invokes to bind her ὅπως μὴ βεινηθῇ, μὴ πυγισθῇ, μὴ λεικάσῃ, μηδὲν πρὸς ἡδονὴν ποιήσῃ ἄλλῳ ἀνδρὶ εἰ μὴ ἐμοὶ μόνῳ Ποσιδωνίῳ "so that she will not have vaginal intercourse, anal intercourse, fellate and do anything for the pleasure of any man other

only the third major type of sexual encounter is less penetration-centred in the sense that it may only involve licking one's genitals, it becomes likely that the acts that are described by the πλησιαζούσας may be associated with oral sex. According to Galen, various Pompeian graffiti and many of Martial's epigrams, oral sex was thought, in antiquity, to be a particularly perverse form of sexual action, and this may explain Lucian's vagueness.[79] Artemidorus, *Interpretation of Dreams* 1.79 (pp. 95–96 Pack) classifies oral sex among unconventional sexual acts,[80] which violate the norms of the conventional vaginal contact between man and woman, and the equally conventional reception of semen on the part of the woman, and warns of something bad if seen in a dream. Significantly enough, such acts are never named by Artemidorus who uses the verb ἀρρητοποιεῖσθαι, literally meaning "to perform the unspeakable", and its cognates to refer to them.[81] As may be inferred from the same passage of Artemidorus, such a conception of oral sex may not be associated only with the violation of conventions related to procreation, penetration and relevant social power relations, but rather to an abusive treatment of the human mouth. In classical Athens fellatio was one of the repulsive acts a male passive homosexual (*kinaidos*) might have been engaged into, and this resulted in the pollution of his mouth and speech that rendered him totally unsuitable for public speech and active involvement in the affairs of the city.[82] Scholars such as Parker and Davidson rightly associate this socially determined conception of oral sex with a kind of pollution that stems from it and violates the sanctity and purity of the human head whose mouth was regarded as intended for uttering prayers, receiving food and giving kisses capable of bringing together the souls of two persons.[83]

---

than myself Posidonius". For this and other similar instances in the Greek magical papyri, see Jocelyn 1980, 20–21; Winkler 1990, 94–95; Fountoulakis 1999, 199.

79 See Galen vol. 5, p. 30 Kühn with the observations of Winkler 1990, 223, n. 20, who refers to this passage. See also *CIL* 4.2360, 4.2400, 4.8230, 4.8380; Martial 2.28, 2.50, 4.43, 11.61, 11.95; Williams 2010², 177–179, 218–224, 292–295.

80 These are referred to in Artemidorus, *Interpretation of Dreams* 1.78 (p. 89 Pack) as παράνομος συνουσία.

81 Cf. Winkler 1990, 38, 215.

82 See Worman 2008, 255–256.

83 See Parker, 99–100, with n. 101; Davidson 2007, 120.

4 Narrative strategies and cultural assumptions

It is tempting to see Lucian's text as a pornographic experiment aiming at the mental exposure of the female body to the male gaze and the fulfillment of the voyeuristic desires of some of its male addressees.[84] It is perhaps the same voyeuristic desires that explain female nudity as well as the depiction of sexual acts involving women in vase paintings from the classical period onwards.[85] A special interest in the depiction of female penetration either by men and satyrs or by dildos suggests a male perception of female sexuality as built around the male organ or its artificial imitations, and dependent on penetration.[86] Such a perception may emerge even in a homosexual context as in Lucian's text. In one of Alciphron's *Letters of the Courtesans*,[87] a contemporary body of texts which share many of the thematic interests of Lucian's *Dialogues of the Courtesans*, the account of a party among hetaerae is permeated by eroticised references to their bodies and bodily contacts. This work's intradiegetic gaze might lead the voluptuous gaze of the letter's male addressees to the visualisation and fulfilment of male phantasies that involve the expression of female sexuality in a homosocial ambience.[88] Yet in Lucian's text specific reference is made to sexual contact between females even though not every detail is revealed. Far from seeing a presentation of sex acts *per se*, this reference associates sexuality with socially significant gender roles. Moreover, the way in which that text evokes established moral standards reveals a far more nuanced and complex association with a cultural past as well as with its social and cultural ambience.

Clonarium's use of the term ἑταιρίστρια to refer to a homosexual woman points towards the unique use of this word in Plato, *Symposium* 191e–192a, where it is employed in Aristophanes' famous speech with reference to the existence of female spherical beings composed of women who are attracted to other women and are described as such.[89] Although the scarcity of references to this term in Greek authors may be due to the fact that female homosexuality was a taboo topic

---

84 For the relations of this voyeurism with misogynistic or homophobic aspects of earlier Greek literature, see Haley 2002, 298.

85 For reservations concerning the presentation of female homoeroticism on Greek vases, see Rabinowitz 2002, 106–166. Cf. Boehringer 2007, 150–157; Boehringer 2014, 154.

86 See Keuls 1985, 82–86; Shapiro 1992, 54–55, 60–61; Petersen 1997, 35–74; Rabinowitz 2002, 106–166.

87 Alciphron, *Let.* 4.14.

88 Cf. Brooten 1996, 53–54.

89 Cf. Halperin 1990, 180.

in antiquity inasmuch as male passive homosexuality was a damnable kind of sexuality,[90] its use in Lucian, which occurs for the first time after Plato, turns Megilla into a unique representative of the species described in the *Symposium*. Such a representative is capable of speaking about herself and those of her kind, and promotes a discourse on female homosexuality.[91] Yet while Plato's theorising focuses on the power and diversity of *erōs*, Megilla's attitude and behaviour draws attention to the importance of the body as a physical and social entity in the construction of sexual identity.[92]

In a similar manner, the use of the name Megilla/Megillos points towards Megillos from Plato, *Laws* 636b and 836b, and a discourse of homosexuality as opposed to natural impulse and the encouragement of virtue, which is found there. The Spartan Megillos is supposed to represent Sparta's encouragement of homosexual ethics and practices as well as a strand of pro-homosexual moral reasoning which in the *Laws* is clearly opposed to by the Athenians. The Lucianic figure of Megilla appears as a transmutation of the Platonic Megillos and carries with her the discourse of homosexuality found in the *Laws*.[93] As this discourse involves a silencing imposed on homosexuality, the intertext of the *Laws* emerges as a philosophical paradigm promoting heteronormativity within a system of patriarchal morality.[94]

Such allusions constitute narrative strategies reinforced by the dialogical form of Lucian's *Dialogues of the Courtesans*. They thus betray those *Dialogues'* generic affiliations with Platonic dialogue and the promotion of philosophical discourse found there.[95] Yet Plato's *Symposium* is different from his *Laws* in that the former offers an aetiological conceptualisation of homosexuality, either male or female, in the light of the power of *erōs*, while the latter suggests its exclusion from the civic space.[96] The allusions, in the fifth *Dialogue of the Courtesans*, to

---

90 Cf. Dover 1978, 20, 172–173. The rare use of the term ἑταιρίστρια, whose literal meaning falls within the semantic fields of "companion" and "hetaera", in connection with the fact that the word τριβάς, which denotes "the female homosexual", is attested in Greek after the second century AD, may also suggest that the Greeks of the classical and the Hellenistic periods were not familiar with the notion of female homosexuality, at least in its modern sense. Cf. Boehringer 2014, 154, 156; Boehringer 2015, 263–264; Gilhuly 2017, 112–113.
91 Cf. Gilhuly 2006, 284–287; Blondell/Boehringer 2014, 253–257 and *passim*.
92 Cf. Boehringer 2007, 91–119.
93 Cf. Gilhuly 2006, 279–282.
94 For the negative stance of Greek philosophy towards female homosexuality, see also Aristotle, *Politics* 5.1311a.
95 See further Anderson 1976, 6–7; Branham 1989, 67–123; Whitmarsh 2001, 258–263; Boehringer 2015, 269–270.
96 Cf. Boehringer 2007, 134–139.

both the *Symposium* and the *Laws* result in an antiphonal reference to female homosexuality which is manifested through the interplay of speech and silence or of revelation and concealment. This narrative strategy is thus a fundamental feature of a discourse that eventually sheds light on female homosexuality. The fifth *Dialogue of the Courtesans* is placed within a tradition of philosophical discourse which imposes a silencing on female homosexuality,[97] and exhibits an appropriation of, and at the same time a differentiation from, that tradition through the interplay of speech and silence about that topic. Yet it eventually turns that interplay into a further narrative strategy which, in an implicit and subversive manner, manages to place female homosexuality at the centre of philosophical discourse.

In Lucian the promotion of such a discourse occurs in a very different manner from that of Plato and is designed to surprise the readers and draw their attention to the significant differences of the fifth *Dialogue*. Unlike the condemnation of pederasty in the *Laws*, Lucian's text invests homosexuality with a positive light by presenting it as a possible biological and social alternative to heterosexuality. Moreover, its reference to homosexuality evolves around an extreme form of it, as female homosexuality was considered in antiquity, and focuses on the practicalities of sex between women far beyond the relevant Platonic theorising and the implications of *erōs* between women. This happens in a way which is paradoxically enough far more revealing than expected considering Leaina's declared inhibitions and final silence. It puts into question established cultural assumptions that relate to the power of shame, the social roles of male and female and the socially constructed associations between biological sex and gender in terms of active and passive agents. Such a questioning undermines long-standing moral standards and subverts traditional Greek roles and hierarchies that have to do with the position of male and female in the *oikos* and the *polis*.

While either penetration or cunnilingus may well be hinted at in Lucian's text, they are never explicitly mentioned. Such an inexplicit reference may be due to Lucian's intentions of reproducing a relevant socially and culturally determined inhibition concerning female homosexuality. This happens despite the fact that in the works of Greek and Latin authors of the same period homosexual males are projected as attractive or even engaging characters to such an extent that they are likely to reflect a relevant homosexual subculture and its interests.[98]

---

97 On philosophy's silence, see Boehringer 2007, 162–168.
98 See, for instance, Catullus 16, 25; Petronius 23.3; Strato, *Anth. Pal.* 12.1–11, 175–229, 234–255, 258; Lucian, *Paid Companions*; Fountoulakis 2013, 293–294; Richlin 2017, 127–129.

Lucian's approach should nevertheless not be taken as part of a moralising tendency of authors such as Plutarch.[99] It is rather related to the hesitation of authors to represent sex acts between people of the same sex and, more specifically, between women. Even in the coarse world reflected in the Greek magical papyri one may discern a similar inhibition which is nevertheless not so often attested in heterosexual magical spells.[100] Yet, despite Leaina's declared shame and the consideration of her acts as shameful,[101] she does not appear particularly concerned with her *aidōs* as happens, for instance, with Phaedra in Euripides' *Hippolytus*, a dramatic character providing a paradigmatic fifth-century ideal of female *aidōs* that was due to mark ideal femininities of the centuries to follow.[102] Displaying "double consciousness",[103] she takes part in the acts she is supposed to consider shameful and proceeds into detailed descriptions, which allude even to acts she ostensibly refuses to mention. In spite of a superficial attempt to reproduce traditional moral standards, Lucian's dialogue exposes thus the fragility of major Greek ethical norms such as those of honour and shame, and undermines the culture which endorsed them.

Leaina's references to her sexual adventures are part of a gradual process of revelation and concealment, which provides her with the opportunity to talk about sexuality and, at the same time, evoke moral codes aiming at its control and suppression. The silencing of female homoeroticism should nevertheless not be seen as the result of the adoption of such codes. By contrast, as Michel Foucault has perceptively observed, it may be considered as part of a wider discourse of suppression, silencing, expression, knowledge and power, which is associated with sexuality. He notes in particular:

> Silence itself — the things one declines to say, or is forbidden to name, the discretion that is required between different speakers — is less the absolute limit of discourse, the other

---

99 Cf. Duff 1999, 94–95; Xenophontos 2016, 108–125.

100 In *PGM* XXXII 1–19 and *Suppl. Mag.* I 42, for instance, two of the few lesbian spells that happen to survive, the desire aimed at by the spell may be as intense as that which is aimed at by heterosexual spells. The paucity, however, of lesbian spells and the lack in them of any explicit reference to specific sexual acts, as opposed to the explicitness of the heterosexual spells, may suggest an anxiety felt towards sexual acts between women, which transgress moral values and codes endorsed within the boundaries of Greek culture, as well as a concern about related social restrictions. Cf. Montserrat 1996, 158–159; Brooten 1996, 77–90; Faraone 1999, 147–149.

101 Lucian, *Dial. Meretr.* 5.1, 4.

102 Cf. Cairns 1993, 314–340.

103 For a "double consciousness" relating to Sappho's appropriation of a male-oriented cultural framework and her own homoerotic sensibility, see Winkler 1990, 162–187.

side from which it is separated by a strict boundary, than an element that functions along-side the things said, with them and in relation to them within over-all strategies. There is no binary division to be made between what one says and what one does not say; we must try to determine the different ways of not saying such things, how those who can and those who cannot speak of them are distributed, which type of discourse is authorised, or which form of discretion is required in either case. There is not one but many silences, and they are an integral part of the strategies that underlie and permeate discourses.[104]

Leaina's silence may accordingly be an eloquent way of casting a marginalised form of sexual expression into the centre of the conversation inasmuch as her discourse concerning sexuality is cast into the centre of a broader discourse involving values and moral standards of a Greek cultural past. The dialectics of revelation and concealment produces a discourse of sexuality which undermines certainties and assumptions of the dialogue's addressees in a constant process of cultural formation and change.

Such a narrative strategy would certainly not be related only to Lucian's hypothetical intentions of challenging predominant assumptions concerning gender and sexuality, as Haley seems to believe.[105] The portrayal of persons who reproduce moral codes prevalent in Greek culture from the classical period onwards and the adoption of allusive narrative strategies which subvert these codes may appear contradictory, but they constitute, in fact, part of a wider discourse pertinent to the transmutation of major cultural assumptions and norms. What thus emerges is a perception of Greek culture through the filter of Lucian's satire and the potential expectations of its addressees. In the programmatic statements found in his *Double Indictment* 33 Lucian identifies philosophical dialogue as the starting point of his work. Yet the serious moral concerns of that dialogue are thought to be undermined by the insertion in his work of elements coming from the taunting spirit of iambic poetry, comedy and satyr play. The subversive power of this awkward mixture of serious and comic elements is regarded as being enhanced by the subsequent insertion in his work of the prickly irony of the cynic philosopher Menippus, whose point of view provides many of Lucian's works with a carnivalesque overturning of traditional Greek values, often crystallised in the realms of religion and philosophy.[106]

---

104 Foucault 1978, 27.
105 Haley 2002, 298–301. Cf. Boehringer 2007, 355.
106 Cf. Jones 1986, 24–32; Branham 1989, 67–123.

The author also identifies his persona as a barbarian, despite his Greek cultural identity.[107] Considering the fact that his work makes extensive use of a diverse Greek literary and cultural heritage placing thus itself in the core of Greek culture, it is at first sight surprising that its author is being identified as an outsider. Yet this is only another manifestation of his authorial strategies. His voice is the subversive voice of an outsider inasmuch as the voices of Leaina and Clonarium are the subversive voices of the oppressed.[108] As happens with the perception of traditional values through the subversive humour of comedy, iamb and Menippean cynicism, the author appears thus capable of portraying the decomposition of the constituents of Greek culture in the face of new cultural formulations from the viewpoint of the marginal or the outcast.[109] It is this "double consciousness" which enables him to put forward a discourse of cultural change and diversity inasmuch as Leaina's "double consciousness" enables her to talk about new ethical norms, forms of sexual expression, gender roles and social power relations.[110] His narrative strategies thus produce a discourse which promotes, and at the same time is part of, a wider process of change and cultural formation taking place in his cultural milieu.

5 Conclusion

Although the *Dialogues of the Courtesans* are far more dependent on New Comedy than they are on Menippean cynicism,[111] they are differentiated from their comic predecessor with respect to their sense of decorum, the handling of the comic character of the *bona meretrix* and their deviation from the conventional comic plot pattern that ends with marriage. The fifth *Dialogue*, in particular, addresses

---

107 See e.g. Luc. *Double Indictment* 27 and 34; *Fisherman* 19; *The False Critic* 1, 11; *On the Syrian Goddess* 1; Swain 1996, 299, 304; Elsner 2001, 126–128, 133–153; Gilhuly 2006, 276, 289.

108 Unlike their comic predecessors, Lucian's hetaerae are not integrated in the city and the citizen body. See Gilhuly 2007, 67.

109 When, for example, reference is made to the deceitful practices of Alexander of Abonouteichos in his *Alexander or the False Prophet*, Lucian sheds light on a decadent and perverse aspect of ancient religious practices in a distant manner that undermines traditional religion, civic formation and cultural identity.

110 For Lucian's reference to female homosexuality as a conscious subversive reference to earlier discourses and the cultural norms they reflect, see Gilhuly 2006, 284–289; Boehringer 2015, 276–280; Gilhuly 2017, 112–113.

111 On the affinities between Lucian's *Dialogues of the Courtesans* and comedy, see Legrand, 1907; Legrand, 1908.

the taboo topic of female homosexuality,[112] focuses on the practical aspects of lesbian group sex and presents isolated lovers such as Leaina or unconventional quasi-marriages such as that of Megilla and Demonassa. Allusion to female penetration or cunnilingus is made through narrative strategies pertinent to the antithetical use of speech and silence or morality and sexual expression. These strategies form part of a discourse on gender and sexuality, which is developed under the shadow of Plato's *Symposium* and *Laws*. At the same time, the same discourse puts forward ethical norms and gender roles which subvert related norms and roles of a Greek past. Cultural assumptions of the classical Greek world about masculine and feminine identities, sexual power relations or a set of moral norms regulating sexual behaviour are put into question. The silencing of female homosexuality, in particular, is turned into a way of projecting new or unconventional views about it through a filter of ethical codes, which echo the past and, at the same time, are in a state of constant change.

By tackling the taboo topic of sexual relations between women, the fifth *Dialogue* brings to the foreground traditional Greek moral values concerning gender and sexuality. Despite an ostensible, and as a result pretentious, compliance with such values, the allusive manner in which reference is eventually made to attitudes and practices which are never named suggests an innovative perception of gender and sexuality. Yet it provides the dialogue with a way of promoting a discourse not only of gender and sexuality, but also of cultural change and formation which is typical of Lucian's satire. By decomposing and recomposing major Greek cultural norms in the shadow of the Roman Empire, the fifth *Dialogue* reflects challenges and anxieties felt in a world that was heading beyond norms and values pertinent to the social and cultural formation of Greek past.[113]

Bibliography

Adams, J.N. (1982), *The Latin Sexual Vocabulary*, London.
Anderson, G. (1976), *Lucian: Theme and Variation in the Second Sophistic*, Leiden.
Androutsos, G. (2006), 'Hermaphroditism in Greek and Roman Antiquity', in: *Hormones* 5, 214–217.

---

112 New Comedy, in particular, unlike Old Comedy, does not make substantial references to homosexuality. Cf. Lilja 1983, 33; Fountoulakis 2020, 87 with n. 8.
113 Cf. Branham 1989, 220; Swain 1996, 312–329; Whitmarsh 2001, 248–253. Thanks are due to the editors of the volume for their valuable observations and suggestions on an earlier version of this chapter. Of course, I alone am responsible for imperfections that may remain.

Blondell, R./Boehringer, S. (2014), 'Revenge of the *Hetairistria*: The Reception of Plato's *Symposium* in Lucian's Fifth *Dialogue of the Courtesans*', in: *Arethusa* 47, 231–264.

Boehringer, S. (2007), *L'homosexualité feminine dans l'antiquité grecque et romaine*, Paris.

Boehringer, S. (2014), 'Female Homoeroticism', in: T.K. Hubbard (ed.), *A Companion to Greek and Roman Sexualities*, Malden, MA/Oxford/Chichester, 150–163.

Boehringer, S. (2015), 'The Illusion of Sexual Identity in Lucian's *Dialogues of the Courtesans* 5', in: R. Blondell/K. Ormand (eds.), *Ancient Sex: New Essays*, Columbus, 253–284.

Branham, R.B. (1989), *Unruly Eloquence: Lucian and the Comedy of Traditions*, Cambridge, MA.

Brisson, L. (2002), *Sexual Ambivalence: Androgyny and Hermaphroditism in Graeco-Roman Antiquity*, transl. by J. Lloyd of *Le sexe incertain: androgynie et hermaphrodisme dans l'antiquité gréco-romaine*, Berkeley/Los Angeles/London.

Brooten, B.J. (1996), *Love Between Women: Early Christian Responses to Female Homoeroticism*, Chicago/London.

Butler, J. (1993), *Bodies That Matter: On the Discursive Limits of "Sex"*, London/New York.

Cairns, D.L. (1993), *Aidōs: The Psychology and Ethics of Honour and Shame in Ancient Greek Literature*, Oxford.

Cameron, A. (1998), 'Love (and Marriage) between Women', in: *Greek, Roman, and Byzantine Studies* 39, 137–156.

Cantarella, E. (2002²), *Bisexuality in the Ancient World*, transl. by C. Ó Cuilleanáin of *Secondo natura*, New Haven/London.

Carlà-Uhink, F. (2017), 'Between the Human and the Divine': Cross-dressing and Transgender Dynamics in the Graeco-Roman World", in: D. Campanile/F. Carlà-Uhink/M. Facella (eds.), *TransAntiquity: Cross-dressing and Transgender Dynamics in the Ancient World*, Abingdon/New York, 3–37.

Chantraine, P. (1999²), *Dictionnaire étymologique de la langue grecque. Histoire des mots*, Paris.

Compton-Engle, G. (2015), *Costume in the Comedies of Aristophanes*, Cambridge.

Costello, C.G. (2020), 'Beyond Binary Sex and Gender Ideology', in: N. Boero/K. Mason (eds.), *The Oxford Handbook of the Sociology of Body and Embodiment*, Oxford, 199–220.

Davidson, J. (2001), 'Dover, Foucault and Greek Homosexuality: Penetration and the Truth of Sex', in: *Past & Present* 170, 3–51.

Davidson, J. (2007), *The Greeks and Greek Love: A Radical Reappraisal of Homosexuality in Ancient Greece*, London.

Delcourt, M. (1961), *Hermaphrodite: Myths and Rites of the Bisexual Figure in Classical Antiquity*, transl. by J. Nicholson of *Hermaphrodite*, London.

Devereux, G. (1970), 'The Nature of Sappho's Seizure in fr. 31 LP as Evidence of Her Inversion', in: *Classical Quarterly* 20, 17–31.

Doroszewska, J. (2019), 'Beyond the Limits of the Human Body: Phlegon of Tralles' Medical Curiosities', in: G. Kazantzidis (ed.), *Medicine and Paradoxography in the Ancient World*, Berlin/Boston, 117–140.

Dover, K.J. (1978), *Greek Homosexuality*, London.

Dreger, A.D. (1998), *Hermaphrodites and the Medical Invention of Sex*, Cambridge, MA/London.

Duff, T.E. (1999), *Plutarch's Lives: Exploring Virtue and Vice*, Oxford.

Elsner, J. (2001), 'Describing Self in the Language of the Other: Pseudo (?) Lucian at the Temple of Hierapolis', in: S. Goldhill (ed.), *Being Greek Under Rome: Cultural Identity, the Second Sophistic and the Development of Empire*, Cambridge, 123–153.

Faraone, C.A. (1999), *Ancient Greek Love Magic*, Cambridge, MA/London.

Foucault, M. (1978), *The History of Sexuality. Volume 1: An Introduction*, transl. R. Hurley of *La Volonté de savoir*, New York.

Foucault, M. (1992), *The Use of Pleasure: The History of Sexuality. Volume 2*, transl. R. Hurley of *L'Usage des plaisirs*, London.

Fountoulakis, A. (1999), 'Οὐσία in Euripides, *Hippolytus* 514 and the Greek Magical Papyri', in: *Maia* 51, 193–204.

Fountoulakis, A. (2013), 'Male Bodies, Male Gazes: Exploring *Erôs* in the Twelfth Book of the *Greek Anthology*', in: E. Sanders/C. Thumiger/C. Carey/N.J. Lowe (eds.), *Erôs in Ancient Greece*, Oxford, 293–311.

Fountoulakis, A. (2020), 'Glimpses of a Male World: Performing Masculinities in Menander', in: A. Fries/D. Kanellakis (eds.), *Ancient Greek Comedy: Genre – Texts – Reception. Essays in Honour of Angus M. Bowie*, Berlin/Boston, 85–107.

Gilhuly, K. (2006), 'The Phallic Lesbian: Philosophy, Comedy, and Social Inversion in Lucian's *Dialogues of the Courtesans*', in: C.A. Faraone/L.K. McClure (eds.), *Prostitutes and Courtesans in the Ancient World*, Madison, 274–291.

Gilhuly, K. (2007), 'Bronze for Gold: Subjectivity in Lucian's *Dialogues of the Courtesans*', in: *American Journal of Philology* 128, 59–94.

Gilhuly, K. (2017), *Erotic Geographies in Ancient Greek Literature and Culture*, Abingdon, Oxon/New York.

Goldhill, S. (1995), *Foucault's Virginity: Ancient Erotic Fiction and the History of Sexuality*, Cambridge.

Haley, S.P. (2002), 'Lucian's 'Leaena and Clonarium': Voyerism or a Challenge to Assumptions?', in: N.S. Rabinowitz/L. Auanger (eds.), *Among Women: From the Homosocial to the Homoerotic in the Ancient World*, Austin, 286–303.

Hallett, J.P. (1997), 'Female Homoeroticism and the Denial of Roman Reality in Latin Literature', in: J.P. Hallett/M.B. Skinner (eds.), *Roman Sexualities*, Princeton, 255–273.

Halperin, D.M. (1990), *One Hundred Years of Homosexuality and Other Essays on Greek Love*, New York/London.

Halperin, D.M. (1992), 'Historicising the Subject of Desire: Sexual Preferences and Erotic Identities in the Pseudo-Lucianic *Erotes*', in: D.C. Stanton (ed.), *Discourses of Sexuality: From Aristotle to AIDS*, Ann Arbor, 236–261.

Harris-McCoy, D.E. (2012), *Artemidorus' Oneirocritica: Text, Translation and Commentary*, Oxford.

Jannini, E.A./Buisson, O./Rubio-Casillas, A. (2014), 'Beyond the G-spot: Clitourethrovaginal Complex Anatomy in Female Orgasm', in: *Nature Reviews Urology* 11, 531–538.

Jocelyn, H.D. (1980), 'A Greek Indecency and Its Students: ΛΑΙΚΑΖΕΙΝ', in: *Proceedings of the Cambridge Philological Society* 26, 12–66.

Jones, C.P. (1986), *Culture and Society in Lucian*, Cambridge, MA/London.

Kapparis, K. (2018), *Prostitution in the Ancient Greek World*, Berlin/Boston.

Keuls, E.C. (1985), *The Reign of the Phallus: Sexual Politics in Ancient Athens*, Berkeley/Los Angeles/London.

King, H. (1998), *Hippocrates' Woman: Reading the Female Body in Ancient Greece*, London/New York.

Konstan, D. (1994), *Sexual Symmetry: Love in the Ancient Novel and Related Genres*, Princeton.

Lee, M.M. (2015), *Body, Dress, and Identity in Ancient Greece*, Cambridge.

Legrand, P.E. (1907), 'Les « Dialogues des courtisanes » comparés avec la Comédie', in: *Revue des Études Grecques* 20, 39–79.

Legrand, P.E. (1908), 'Les « Dialogues des courtisanes » comparés avec la Comédie (suite)', in: *Revue des Études Grecques* 21, 176–231.

Lilja, S. (1983), *Homosexuality in Republican and Augustan Rome*, Helsinki.

Lissarrague, F. (1990), 'The Sexual Life of Satyrs', in: D.M. Halperin/J.J. Winkler/F.I. Zeitlin (eds.), *Before Sexuality: The Construction of Erotic Experience in the Ancient Greek World*, Princeton, 53–81.

Macleod, M.D. (1961), *Lucian, Vol. VII*, London/Cambridge, MA.

Medda, E. (2017), '"O Saffron Robe, to What Pass Have You Brought Me": Cross-dressing and Theatrical Illusion in Aristophanes' *Thesmophoriazusae*', in: D. Campanile/F. Carlà-Uhink/ M. Facella (eds.), *TransAntiquity: Cross-dressing and Transgender Dynamics in the Ancient World*, Abingdon/New York, 137–151.

Montserrat, D. (1996), *Sex and Society in Graeco-Roman Egypt*, London/New York.

Olender, M. (1990), 'Aspects of Baubo: Ancient Texts and Contexts', in: D.M. Halperin/J.J. Winkler/F.I. Zeitlin (eds.), *Before Sexuality: The Construction of Erotic Experience in the Ancient Greek World*, Princeton, 83–113.

Parker, H.N. (1997), 'The Teratogenic Grid', in: J.P. Hallett/M.B. Skinner (eds.), *Roman Sexualities*, Princeton, 47–65.

Parker, R. (1983), *Miasma: Pollution and Purification in Early Greek Religion*, Oxford.

Pauls, R.N. (2015), 'Anatomy of the Clitoris and the Female Sexual Response', in: *Clinical Anatomy* 28, 376–384.

Petersen, L. (1997), 'Divided Consciousness and Female Companionship: Reconstructing Female Subjectivity on Greek Vases', in: *Arethusa* 30, 35–74.

Rabinowitz, N.S. (2002), 'Excavating Women's Homoeroticism in Ancient Greece: The Evidence from Attic Vase Painting', in: N.S. Rabinowitz/L. Auanger (eds.), *Among Women: From the Homosocial to the Homoerotic in the Ancient World*, Austin, 106–166.

Richlin, A. (2017), 'Retrosexuality: Sex in the Second Sophistic', in: D.S. Richter/W.A. Johnson (eds.), *The Oxford Handbook of the Second Sophistic*, Oxford, 115–135.

Rosen, R.M. (2015), 'Lucian's Aristophanes: On Understanding Old Comedy in the Roman Imperial Period', in: C.W. Marshall/T. Hawkins (eds.), *Athenian Comedy in the Roman Empire*, London, 141–162.

Shapiro, H.A. (1992), 'Eros in Love: Pederasty and Pornography in Greece', in: A. Richlin (ed.), *Pornography and Representation in Greece and Rome*, New York/Oxford, 53–72.

Stone, L. (1980), *Costume in Aristophanic Comedy*, Salem, NH.

Swain, S. (1996), *Hellenism and Empire: Language, Classicism, and Power in the Greek World AD 50-250*, Oxford.

Taaffe, L.K. (1993), *Aristophanes and Women*, London/New York.

Warwick, C. (2020), 'Nossis' Dildo: A Metapoetic Attack on Female Poetry in Herodas's Sixth Mime', in: *TAPA* 150, 333–356.

Whitmarsh, T. (2001), *Greek Literature and the Roman Empire: The Politics of Imitation*, Oxford.

Williams, C.A. (2010[2]), *Roman Homosexuality*, New York/Oxford.

Winkler, J.J. (1990), *The Constraints of Desire: The Anthropology of Sex and Gender in Ancient Greece*, New York/London.

Worman, N. (2008), *Abusive Mouths in Classical Athens*, Cambridge.

Xenophontos, S. (2016), *Ethical Education in Plutarch: Moralising Agents and Contexts*, Berlin/ Boston.

Zanker, G. (ed.) (2009), *Herodas: Mimiambs*, Oxford.

Part II: **Sex and Medicine**

Chiara Thumiger
Clitoridectomy in Ancient Greco-Roman Medicine and the Definition of Sexual Intercourse

Abstract: What could female genital mutilation surgery, sexual penetration, poeticised forms of human sacrifice and medical examinations have in common? This chapter offers a discussion of sexual intercourse in a historical perspective by analysing a number of narratives and images of violent intervention on a female, or "feminised" body, in order to argue for an extension of the definition of "sexual intercourse" parallel to, and part and parcel of, the rewriting of the concepts of "gender" and "sex" in recent and contemporary philosophical reflections. The romantic representation of the default of "sexual intercourse" as mostly cis-gender and heterosexual, with its matrimonial and reproductive validation and its ideologies, deserves to be made the object of a critical analysis of "gender" and "sex" as products and experiences rather than substances. This analysis is carried out through examples from ancient gynaecology, tragedy and epic poetry, and arguing for the relevance of ancient "images" to the development of the modern ideas of sexual "norm" and "health" with reference to the female body.

1 Introduction

This chapter, like others in this volume, offers a discussion of sexual intercourse in a historical perspective. Before I begin this, however, I would like to place our starting point and even our basic vocabulary under discussion. Despite variations in details and register, what most scholars in this volume and elsewhere mean by "sexual intercourse" in literature or artistic figurations is interaction between two

---

I would like to thank George Kazantzidis and Andreas Serafim for their work as editors. I have benefitted greatly from the suggestions and criticism offered by various readers, George Kazantzidis and Sean Coughlin especially, whom I thank. I am also grateful to the audience at the conference in Cyprus, especially to Lesley Dean-Jones, for the useful feedback, and to Douglas Olson for revising the English, as well as providing important comments and offering needed corrections. This work has been generously supported by the Wellcome Trust and, in its final revision stages, by the Excellence Cluster Roots at Kiel University.

https://doi.org/10.1515/9783110695793-007

bodies involving the genitals of one or both — or some ersatz object or sex toy — for the purpose of pleasure or the gratification of one or both partners, sometimes raising concerns about procreation. This basic definition holds also from a medical viewpoint, although pleasure and gratification are in that case a means to the reproductive and hygienic end rather than the main objective or aspect of the experience.

In what follows, I begin with medical sources and extend the definition of the English expression "sexual intercourse" to one that may be unexpected: intercourse as intrusion and as the action of one body, cast in a position of power and/or authority or seniority, on another body — typically female — by means of an instrument, whether an object or a body part. The resulting sexual pleasure, or sexualised satisfaction, is distributed in a way different from the expected, eluding the body at the centre to benefit only the external actors and the attending audience. The purpose of this action is in some form corrective of a perceived flaw, and it blatantly exposes an asymmetric power structure. This extension of the definition of "sexual intercourse" is parallel to, and part and parcel of the rewriting of the concepts of "gender" and "sex" in recent and contemporary philosophy — with which I cannot deal here in detail, but to which I return at the end.[1] The romantic representation of the default of "sexual intercourse" as mostly cis-gender and heterosexual, with its matrimonial and reproductive validation and its ideologies,[2] also deserves to be made the object of a critical analysis of "gender" and "sex" as products and experiences rather than substances.

In this chapter, I focus on the practice of clitoridectomy in medical texts. By means of my rephrasing of the definition of sexual intercourse, I hope to contribute to advancing our understanding of these surgical practices, by framing them more forcefully within the network of cultural, political and psychological aspects surrounding the image of the immobilised female (or feminised) body. The act of anatomical correction, with its politics and normative purposes, emerges — in the light of a number of visual parallels — as resembling or being functionally equivalent to a condensed form of sexual intercourse. In this way, I wish to both elaborate on current reflections on the ontology of sex, and to reinforce the importance of images and imaging in sustaining ideologies.[3]

---

1 See Butler 1990 for the seminal discussion; Bernini 2020 for *inter alia* an overview of the main lines of thinking about these topics in 20th-century and contemporary philosophy.
2 See Thumiger 2020, 1–46 on holism and sex in our culture, and its critics.
3 See Matt 2020 for updated methodological reflections and caveats on the use of visual sources to recover cultural data — in that case emotions — which apply to the present study as well.

As in popular understandings of sexual intercourse, so too with clitoridetomy, the topics of pleasure, control, sexual/gender individuation and moral policing are at the centre. The same is true, of course, although implicitly, in regard to reproduction as a natural outcome of the socialised sexual intercourse that is central to marriage. Identity and self-image are also involved: how a woman perceives her body to be "adequate" and how it is seen by a male other are co-implicated issues, as is the narrated encounter of these spheres in the act of medical correction.

These themes and tropes, according to which the female body has been constructed in our medical history, from its Greco-Roman beginnings to today, have been well explored.[4] Two additional specific features, however, make the sources on clitoridectomy I explore here remarkable. The first is that these themes and tropes are concretely, *physically inscribed* on the (female) human body, carved in its flesh in a permanent way by the knife and the (male) human hand.[5] Second, as already mentioned, the language, moves and actions performed during the process of clitoridectomy can be seen as mimicking sexual intercourse in a visually overt way. This reading will likely appear provocative. I, nonetheless, hope to show that the way ancient medical thinkers (and ancient culture at large) looked at the female body and its sexual life, on the one hand, and the practice of clitoridectomy, on the other, are aligned with the relationship between doctor and female body offering a parallel to the sexual possession of the husband or male of the wife as sexual commodity.

2 On the practice of clitoridectomy, ancient and modern

We have no evidence to suggest that clitoridectomy was carried out routinely in Classical Greece, as Victorian supporters of the practice contended.[6] In ancient

---

4 Beginning with the work of Helen King 1998 and Lesley Dean-John 1992, 1995, 1996, 2003; on ancient gynecology, especially clitoridectomy, see Groff (forthcoming) on the scalpel as instrument to shape and control female "gender and sexuality"; Calà (forthcoming 2021).
5 I react here to Osborne's proposal 2011 to look at visual evidence from ancient Greece as "texts" on which history is written.
6 Helen King, at the beginning of her *Hippocrates Woman* 1998, 15–17, reconstructs the story of the appropriation of antiquity in this case, and in particular the role of the infamous Isaac Baker Brown (1812–1873), an English gynaecologist and president of the Medical Society of London, who believed that "unnatural irritation" of the clitoris could cause epilepsy, *hysteria* and *mania*.

medicine, testimony to the practice from Hippocrates' time is almost entirely lacking; the information we have comes from the medical treatises of Caelius Aurelianus and Mustio (5th/6th–century AD), which go back to Soranus' gynecology (1st/2nd century AD);[7] Aetius (6th century AD), who quotes a 2nd-century source, Philoumenos (2nd/3rd century AD); and finally Paul of Aegina, another encyclopedic author, from the 7th century AD. The medical evidence is thus entirely late-antique; but while it reflects imperial and late-antique medical concerns, the practice is nonetheless premised on an understanding of the female body which falls in line with what we know from classical gynecological texts. The following points can be regarded as key in this sphere of ancient medicine:[8]

1. Sexual intercourse is a hygienic necessity for women of reproductive age, bringing danger if not practiced in a timely way.
2. As such, it is advised for women by male doctors.
3. Female pleasure during intercourse is not a meaningless corollary, but is relevant to the reproductive function. In fact, it signals successful intercourse, according to *On Generation*, since female satisfaction is believed to be achieved when the male ejaculates; it is thus functionally important.[9]
4. There is a fundamental difference between the female and the male body, not only in anatomy and appearance, but also in texture and physiology, and consequently in behaviour and desires/drives. This differentiation is an aspect of human health and should accordingly be safeguarded.[10]

Before looking at the ancient texts to see how these key ideas are reflected in the practice and discussion of clitoridectomy, I offer a brief excursus on the practice itself. The WHO defines clitoridectomy as follows: "female genital mutilation

---

Brown prided himself in having "re-introduced" the ancient practice to the benefit of British women. Mentions of clitoridectomy in ancient literature associate it with Egypt (intriguingly, the most extensive story of female aversion to sexual contact is that of the Danaids, who flee from Egypt to Greece to seek refuge from an unwanted marriage); the earliest instance is Herodotus (2.35, on the enlarged clitoris of Egyptian women, 2.36.3 on excision by the Egyptians); cf. Xanthos FGrH 765 F 4, which is preserved at Ath. 12.515e on the practice by the Lydians; Diod. Sic. 3.32.4–3.33.1; Strabo, *Geographica* 17.2.5 (cf. 16.4.9, 16.4.17; 17.2.5); Philo, *Questions and Answers on Genesis* 3.47; Julius Pollux *Onomasticon* 2.174. Medically, apart from the passages in Aetius and Paul of Aegina I discuss below, see Soranus, *Gynaecorum*, Περὶ ὑπερμεγέθους νύμφης (Book 4.9), with a Latin translation in Mustio; Pseudo-Galen, *Introduction*, 14.706 Kühn = 28,94 Petit. Matthews 2015, 491 also mentions a papyrological source, *UPZ* I 2.9–15.

7 On these texts, see Urso 2003, 2008.
8 See King 1998; Dean Jones 1996; Hanson 1990.
9 On this topic, see Hanson 1985, 1990; Manuli 1980; Dean-Jones 1992; Thumiger 2017, 246–251.
10 See King 2013, correcting Laqueur 1990.

(FGM) comprises all procedures that involve partial or total removal of the external female genitalia, or other injury to the female genital organs for non-medical reasons". (This final specification obviously makes sense only in a world where non-medical and medical are neatly defined and distinguished from each other).[11] The same source states that "more than 200 million girls and women alive today have been cut in 30 countries in Africa, the Middle East and Asia where FGM is concentrated (1)"; one estimate is 3 million a year, every year.

In more concrete terms, the WHO describes four different major types of female genital mutilation (I paraphrase):

Type 1: Often referred to as **clitoridectomy,** this is the partial or total removal of the clitoris (a small, sensitive, erectile part of the female genitals) or in very rare cases only the prepuce (the fold of skin surrounding the clitoris).

Type 2: Often referred to as **excision,** this is the partial or total removal of the clitoris and the labia minora (the inner folds of the vulva), with or without excision of the labia majora (the outer folds of skin of the vulva).

Type 3: Often referred to as **infibulation,** this is the narrowing of the vaginal opening through the creation of a covering seal. The seal is formed by cutting and repositioning the labia minora, or labia majora, sometimes through stitching, with or without removal of the clitoris (clitoridectomy).

Type 4: This includes all other harmful procedures to the female genitalia for non-medical purposes, e.g. pricking, piercing, incising, scraping or cauterising the genital area.

In the sources discussed below, mutilation types 1 and 2 seem to be most relevant. In terms of function and cultural purpose, Helen King also distinguished between clitoridectomy seen as "cure" (as per Victorian doctrines) and the "initiating" practice for girls' coming of age still practiced in various areas of Africa.[12] This distinction is also of value in our material. I would, nonetheless, argue that the distinction between a medical domain and the domain of ritual would make more sense if we applied it to contexts where the categories of "cultural", "religious",

---

11 https://www.who.int/en/news-room/fact-sheets/detail/female-genital-mutilation, accessed 1.11.2020; see also Arnold-Forster 2014.
12 See King 1998, 253 n. 24 on the difference between clitoridectomy for female initiation and as cure, as in Victorian England.

"ritual" and "hygienic" were neatly separated. The political and morally charged idea of health vis-à-vis being a socialised woman has multiple religious and mythological overtones in ancient medical writings, as is also the case with FGM practices in Victorian culture, but also in rural contexts in some parts of Africa today.[13] They all, moreover, reflect a concern with women's perceived "femininity", experience of pleasure, and overall social worth.[14] The cultural framing of the practice of clitoridectomy is emphasised by the WHO in more general terms:

> FGM is often motivated by beliefs about what is considered *acceptable sexual behaviour*. It aims to ensure *premarital virginity and marital fidelity*. FGM is in many communities *believed to reduce a woman's libido* and therefore believed to help her resist extramarital sexual acts. When a vaginal opening is covered or narrowed (type 3), the fear of the pain of opening it, and the fear that this will be found out, is expected to further discourage extramarital sexual intercourse among women with this type of FGM.

> Where it is believed that being cut increases marriageability, FGM is more likely to be carried out.

> FGM *is associated with cultural ideals of femininity and modesty*, which include the notion that girls are clean and beautiful after removal of body parts that are considered *unclean, unfeminine or male* (my emphasis).

3 Ancient medical sources on clitoridectomy

Let us move on to the ancient sources, starting with Caelius Aurelianus' discussion of the "hypertrophic/enlarged clitoris" (87–88 Burguière-Gourevitch-Malinas = II, 112, p. 113 Drabkin):

> *De immodica landica*
> *Quibusdam landicis horrida comitatur magnitudo et feminas partium feditate confundit et, ut plerique memorant, adfecte tentigine uirorum similem appetentiam sumunt et in uenerem coacte ueniunt.*

> On the enlarged/immodest clitoris
> Some clitorises reach a *horrifying size* and fill women with confusion due to the *ugliness/awfulness* of these parts; and according to most authors, these women attain *erections* and *feel*

---

13 See King 2004, 154; 1998, 14–19.
14 For an interpretation of the text as focusing on a concern for female fertility, see Knight 2001.

a desire similar to that of men and agree to engage in a sexual act only if forced/under pressing compulsion (transl. Drabkin with modifications).

It is notable that doctors, as they present the condition motivating surgery on these women, repeatedly foreground the idea of anatomical *deformity*, ugliness or repulsiveness, openly referring to an internalised shame. These women feel "confusion" (*feminas...confundit*), it is said, facing as they do such "ugliness". This aesthetic hideousness is accompanied by a sexual drive that is equally perverted: the women's desire "resembles that of men" (presumably in terms of its intensity), on the one hand, while on the other hand they are *coacte*, they refuse intercourse (or, perhaps, should we interpret it they seek intercourse compulsively/all too quickly?).[15] Caelius continues by reporting the procedure of clitoridectomy, highlighting the severity of the wound and the abundant bleeding it causes:

> *Supina denique mulier locanda est conductis femoribus, ne febre feminini sinus distantiam sumant. Tunc in midio est tenenda superflua atque pro modo alienitatis sue scalpello precidenda. Si enim plurimum extenditur porrecta longitudine sequitur atque ita immodice decissionis largo fluore afficit patientem*

> And so the woman is to be placed lying on her back with her thighs closed, lest the flesh of the feminine fold become distended. Then the superfluous part must be grasped with a small forceps and cut off with one's scalpel like a foreign body; for if the extended portion is stretched further in length, in this way the result is that it affects the patient with an immoderately large loss of blood [...].

The 5th/6th-century gynaecological author Mustio preserves a *locus paralellus* in a section of his *Gynaecia* entitled "On the hypertrophic/enlarged clitoris, which the Greeks call *yos nymfin*" (II, 76 = 87–88 Burguière–Gourevitch–Malinas = 190 Rad). As is the case with Caelius, Mustio mentions indecency along with the female's pathological capacity for erection:

> *Turpitudinis symptoma est grandis yos nymfe. Quidam uero ad seuerant pulpam ipsam erigi ipse similiter ut uiris et quasi usum coitus quaerere.*

> A large *yos nymphe* is a symptom/an instance of *wickedness/foulness* (*turpitudo*). Some maintain, to be sure, that that fleshy part can even experience *erection in the same way as in men* and as it were *yearning for* the act of coitus.

And the treatment:

---

15 I thank Douglas Olson for suggesting this alternative possibility.

Curabis autem eam sic: supinam iactantes pedibus clusi, myzo quod foris est et amplius esse uidetur tenere oportet et scalpello praecidere, deinde competenti diligentia ulnus ipsum curare.

You will *cure* her thus, however. Placing the woman on her back with feet close to one another, one ought to grasp with the forceps what is outside and appears to be too large, and to cut it off with a scalpel, then to treat the lesion itself with the appropriate care (*competenti diligentia*) (my translation).

Here too, moralising and evaluative elements are evident in the approach to the body of the patient: the *turpitudo*, the possible erection, and the scandalous search for coitus.

In sum, what is noteworthy about these two sources is, first of all, the reference to "some cases" — in Caelius, *quibusdam landicis* — which seems to maintain a rhetoric of exception and deformity. Second, there is the casting of a body-part as a seat of shame, and its consideration as foreign, as it were, or even antagonistic to its female owner: the woman is "confused" by it, and the clitoris is seen as *superflua*, an *alienitas*, something located outside, *foris*. These considerations, in combination with the surgical details regarding the correct size of a clitoris, reveal a highly normative conception of the female body as a project set *a priori*. In addition, strong emotions are implicated: the shame and confusion attached to this part for the woman and the world around her; the ugliness and dreadfulness (*foeditas, turpitudo*).

In terms of sexual behaviour, these individuals are described as actively displaying desire. Most significant, their sexual tendencies resemble the drive typical of males, causing special concern, as we have seen. "Women becoming like man", female erection, heightened sensibility of the part in question: all these mean the unacceptable arrogation of volition, initiative, or choice on the part of the female.[16] At the same time, Caelius describes them as taking part in sexual intercourse *coactae* — *in venerem coacte veniunt*. This could mean, surprisingly, that these women must be forced to have sex; or, on the contrary, *coacte* might here indicate an excessive eagerness, "as if obeying a strong impulse". If the first were correct, then the issue would be not excessive sexuality, but, the other way around, a lack of libido. The question would then arise: are these women sexually too proactive, is their *appetentia* too strong in general, like those who suffer satyriasis elsewhere?[17] Or is this man-like *appetentia* a sexual desire for others of an

---

16 See Thumiger 2018, 280–283 on sexual diseases of men and women; Gourevitch 1995.
17 Or for the *tribades* described by Caelius Aurelianus: see Thumiger 2018 on the topic, and on "female" and "male" sexual diseases.

actively penetrative kind? Or should we assume that what Caelius is insinuating is that the excessive sexual desire displayed by these female patients is directed towards women only?

Compare the second most extensive text preserved for us, that of Paul of Aegina, which points more clearly in the second of the two directions. Women who have a large clitoris exhibit an excessive desire for sex, the problem being that they ὁρμῶσιν towards intercourse, are strongly driven to it (Paul of Aegina 112.21–30 Heiberg):

> Περὶ νυμφοτομίας καὶ κερκώσεως.
> Ὑπερμεγέθης ἐνίαις γίνεται νύμφη καὶ εἰς ἀπρέπειαν αἰσχύνης ἀπαντᾷ· καθὼς δέ τινες ἱστοροῦσιν, ἔνιαι διὰ τοῦ μέρους καὶ ὀρθιάζουσιν ἀνδράσιν ὁμοίως καὶ πρὸς συνουσίαν ὁρμῶσιν. διόπερ ὑπτίας ἐσχηματισμένης τῆς γυναικὸς μυδίῳ κατασχόντες τὸ περιττὸν τῆς νύμφης ἐκτέμωμεν σμίλῃ φυλαττόμενοι τὸ ἐκ βάθους αὐτὴν ἐκτέμνειν, ἵνα μὴ ῥυαδικὸν ἐκ τούτου γένηται πάθος. καὶ τὴν κέρκωσιν δὲ σαρκώδη ἔκφυσιν οὖσαν ἀπὸ τοῦ στομίου τῆς μήτρας ἀναπληροῦσαν τὸ γυναικεῖον αἰδοῖον, ποτὲ δὲ καὶ εἰς τὰ ἔξω δίκην κέρκου προπίπτουσαν, παραπλησίως ἀφαιρετέον τῇ νύμφῃ.

> On removal of the clitoris and *cauda*.
> In certain women the *nympha* is excessively large and presents a shameful deformity; as some authorities report, some women have erections in this part in the way men do, and have a drive towards intercourse.

> Wherefore, after the woman has been placed in a supine posture, we seize the redundant portion of the clitoris with a small forceps and cut it off with a scalpel, taking care not to cut it off too low, so that the complaint called *rhoeas* not result. The *cauda*, which is a fleshy excrescence arising from the mouth of the womb and filling the female pudendum, sometimes even projecting externally like a tail, is to be removed in the same manner as the clitoris.

Key here are again the exceptional nature of this deformity, which afflicts "certain women" only; the shame and indecency (εἰς ἀπρέπειαν αἰσχύνης) it causes; the "manly sexuality"; and the casting of a part of a person's body as "residual", "vestigial", "superfluous", τὸ περιττόν — a negative term.[18]

The longest and richest text on the excision of the clitoris, and the most explicit preserved for us, is transmitted by Aetius and attributed to Philoumenos. This passage is of central importance for our discussion, since it is the one which

---

18 τὸ περιττόν is an important topic in ancient medicine and biology, more often employed to indicate physiological substances which are "residual": excrements, but also excessive humours or physiological by-products which need to be expelled, hence the derogatory force of the term here.

describes most vividly the scene of the operation. In addition, Aetius models his description of the excision on a scene of intercourse, strikingly in my view: the way the practical process is carried out, the *celebration* of the act, are here almost as meaningful as its sought-after anatomical-surgical result (whatever that might be).

Aetius, *Libri Medicinales* 16, 95.[19]
Περὶ νυμφοτομίας, Φιλουμένου.
Ἡ λεγομένη νύμφη οἶον μυῶδες ἢ δερματῶδες ἐστὶ συγκριμάτιον κείμενον κατὰ τὴν ἄνωθεν τῶν πτερυγωμάτων συμβολήν, καθ᾽ ὃν τόπον ἡ οὐρήθρα τέτακται· μεγεθύνεται δέ τισιν ἐπὶ πλέον τῶν γυναικῶν αὔξησιν λαμβάνον, καὶ εἰς ἀπρέπειαν καὶ αἰσχύνην γίνεται. ἀλλὰ καὶ παρατριβόμενον συνεχῶς ὑπὸ τῶν ἱματίων ἐρεθίζει, καὶ τὴν πρὸς συνουσίαν ὁρμὴν ἐπεγείρει, διόπερ πρὸ τῆς μεγεθοποιήσεως ἔδοξε τοῖς Αἰγυπτίοις ἀφαιρεῖν αὐτὸ τότε μάλιστα, ὁπότε πρὸς γάμον ἄγεσθαι μέλλοιεν αἱ παρθένοι. ἐπιτελεῖται δὲ ἡ χειρουργία τὸν τρόπον τοῦτον.

On clitoridectomy, from Philomenos.
The so-called *nympha* (clitoris) is a muscle- or skin-like compound structure situated above the point where the wings (of the female genitals) meet, in the place where the urinary meatus is located. *In some individuals* (τισιν), it grows larger than is appropriate for women and tends towards *unseemliness* and *shame*. And furthermore, it is *irritated* when it is constantly rubbed by clothing, and it stimulates the *impulse towards sexual intercourse*. On that account, it seemed reasonable to the Egyptians to amputate the *nympha* before it became too large, especially at the point when their girls were about to be married. The surgery is carried out in the following manner.

In "some women", we read again, this body part is enlarged (αὔξησιν), causing ugliness and shame (εἰς ἀπρέπειαν καὶ αἰσχύνην), as well as sexual stimulation (τὴν πρὸς συνουσίαν ὁρμὴν ἐπεγείρει) inappropriate for a young woman in need of being married.

Reference is made here to the Egyptians — an attribution which is immediately suggestive not only of the "otherness" the land represents and of a distancing move, but also of the well-known connection between Egypt and pharmacological knowledge.[20] Transgression, inversion or perversion of gender- and sexual

---

19 *Aetius Sermo sextidecimus et ultimus erstens aus Handschriften veröffentlicht mit Abbildungen Bemerkungen und Erklärungen*, von Skevos Zervos 1901, 152.
20 On Egypt and female circumcision in antiquity and modern times, see also Knight 2001. The belief in a deep link between alchemic art and Egypt was an old and lasting one in antiquity (see Martelli 2017 on the 3rd/4th-century Zosimos of Panopolis), although its history is wrapped in mythological narratives; on the exchange of pharmacological knowledge between Egypt and Greece in archaic and even pre-Homeric times, see Totelin 2009, 153–158; in Homer, *Od.* 4.219–234, the drug Helen offers to soothe her guests' spirits had been given to her by "Polydamna wife of Thon, a woman of Egypt, where grow all sorts of herbs, some good to put into the mixing-

relations between men and women are part of the bundle of extraordinariness associated with perception of this land. (All these are present, in a different but obvious way, in the story of the Greek Danaids and their flight to escape marriage with their Egyptian cousins; Aeschylus' *Suppliants* emphasises the themes of forced sexual intercourse and female resistance.) These cultural suggestions and stereotypes certainly persisted throughout classical and later antiquity. When we consider the construction of Egyptian women as especially powerful and man-like, or as different from men (Herodotus 2.35 says that in Egypt women do what men are supposed to do and *vice versa*) alongside clitoridectomy as an "Egyptian" way of exercising male control over the female, "taming" and "correcting" her sex, this adds to the well-known history of Greek projection of internal insecurities, flaws, and extremes onto a "barbarian" other.[21]

A parallel is offered by the reference, relevant to our topic, to the barbarian land of the Lydians, comparable for its constructedness as a land of *tyrphē*, "luxury" and royal despotism to Greek audiences.[22] Here clitoridectomy was first practiced, according to Xanthos in Athenaeus: the Lydian king Adramytes was the first to *eunuchise, castrate* his women in order to enjoy them in place of male eunuchs (Xanthos, *FGrH* 765 F 3: Ἀδραμύτην φησὶ τὸν Λυδῶν βασιλέα πρῶτον γυναῖκας εὐνουχίσαντα χρῆσθαι αὐταῖς ἀντὶ ἀνδρῶν εὐνούχων). The paradoxical vocabulary (εὐνουχίζω applied to women) betrays, first of all, the sexual inversion whereby the female body is theoretically *masculinised* in order to be aptly and desirably *feminised* in turn through intervention. Second, in place of a medical motivation there is a sexual one: the king will enjoy them, make use of them (χρῆσθαι αὐταῖς) "in place of men". What this would mean is difficult to fathom; the other relevant source on this information from Xanthos (through the Suda and Hesychius) refers to the practice by the Lydian king (this time Gyges) as aimed at keeping women youthful and more attractive as sexual objects.[23] The credibility of this story is debatable;[24] objection to the historicity of the practice

---

bowl, and others poisonous". Herodotus' Egyptian *logos* is the most extensive illustration of the Greeks' cultural construction of this region as foreign but also familiar and rich with intellectual and material treasures.

21 With Hall 1991; cf. Thomas 2000, 112 on Herodotus' anthropology and his exceptional emphasis on the uniqueness of Egypt.

22 See Matthew 2015, 444–499.

23 Hsch. fr. 7.758–761 = *Suda* ξ 9 Ξάνθος, Λυδὸς ἱστορικὸς, ἐν τῇ δευτέρᾳ τῶν Λυδιακῶν ἱστοριῶν φησὶν ὅτι πρῶτος Γύγης ὁ Λυδῶν βασιλεὺς γυναῖκας εὐνούχισεν, ὅπως αὐταῖς χρῷτο ἀεὶ νεαζούσαις.

24 Against the historicity of the episode, see Matthews 2015, with strong arguments; previously Hübner 2009 hypothesising instead for εὐνουχίζω a form of genital mutilation.

in Lydia, however, does not change our point — the existence, in Greek classical antiquity and its afterlife, of a narrative of female genital mutilation, with orientalising or "barbarising" overtones.

So much about the Egyptian, non-Greek origin of the practice. In the text, Aetius moves on to describe the procedure. I would like to focus more closely on the passage from a pictorial point of view, especially because Aetius' text appears to dwell on the figural qualities of the scene:

> Ἑδραζέτω μὲν ἡ παρθένος ἐπὶ δίφρου, παρεστὼς δὲ ὄπισθεν νεανίσκος εὔτονος ὑποβάλλων τοὺς ἰδίους πήχεις ταῖς ἐκείνης ἰγνύαις, διακρατείτω τὰ σκέλη καὶ τὸ ὅλον σῶμα· ἑστὼς δὲ ἐναντίον ὁ ἐνεργῶν καὶ μυδίῳ πλατυστόμῳ συλλαβὼν τὴν νύμφην διὰ τῆς εὐωνύμου χειρὸς ἀποτεινέτω, τῇ δὲ δεξιᾷ ἀποτεμνέτω παρὰ τοὺς ὀδόντας τοῦ μυδίου.

> The girl should be placed in a chair, and a robust young man (νεανίσκος εὔτονος), standing behind her and placing his arms under the backs of her thighs, should hold her legs and her entire body. Standing opposite her and grasping the clitoris with wide-mouthed forceps, let the surgeon stretch it with his left hand, and cut it off with the right hand just along the teeth of the forceps.

Little doubt is left by Aetius about the potential risks of the procedure, or about the invasiveness of the wounding. As we read later in the text:

> Μετὰ δὲ τὴν χειρουργίαν οἴνῳ προσήκει στύφειν τὴν ἕλκωσιν ἢ ψυχρῷ ὕδατι, καὶ ἀπομάξαντας σπόγγῳ μάνναν ἐπιπάττειν, καὶ μοτὸν ὀξυκράτῳ βρέχοντας ἐπιτιθέναι, καὶ ἄνωθεν σπόγγον ὀξυκράτῳ βεβρεγμένον πάλιν ἐπιτιθέναι· μετὰ δὲ τὴν ἑβδόμην καδμίαν λειοτάτην ἐπιπάσσειν, ἢ σὺν αὐτῇ ῥόδων ἄνθος, ἢ τὸ διὰ διφρυοῦς λίθου ξηρὸν αἰδοῖικόν. καλὸν δὲ καὶ τοῦτο· ὀστᾶ φοινίκων καύσας καὶ λεάνας ἐπίπασσε τὴν σποδόν, ποιεῖ καὶ πρὸς τὰ ἐν αἰδοίοις ἕλκη.

> After the surgery, it is fitting to close up the wound with wine or cold water, and having wiped it clean with a sponge, to sprinkle powder on it, cover it with lint that has been soaked in vinegar water, and place on top a sponge that has been soaked again in vinegar water; and after the seventh day, to sprinkle extremely fine calamine, or rose flowers combined with this, or a dry powder for the genitals prepared from twice-baked clay/tufa stone. This is also good: having burnt and ground up date pits, sprinkle the ash and do [what one does] to wounds of the genitals.

Once more, reference is made to a problematic subgroup – "in *some* women". At the same time, however, we also find a generalisation associating the growth of the clitoris with an age and an ethnic group, the Egyptians. All these categorising choices appear to be strategies that serve to turn this clinical operation into a flexible tool for the individual, the male who finds himself in an authorised position of control: the clitoris is a natural part of the body, but *some women*, in certain regions of the world, at a *certain* age, need treatment when this part becomes somehow alienated, foreign to standard physiology. One person — a doctor, a husband — can decide case by case what is "natural" and "the right size", and what is not; what is essential to a being and what is residual; and so on.

Second, what we witness in Aetius' text is the complete medicalisation of the event, in the most pragmatic sense of the expression: operation, aftercare, excision, complete silencing of the woman as passive patient, with diligence and competence emphasised; all these notions have been discussed above. This medicalisation is coupled with more "plastic" topics centered on the idea of female "virtues": shame, modesty, *decorum*, marriageability. The woman's subjective experience is also medicalised, not only her sensorial abilities: the oversensitivity to stimulation of the enlarged clitoris as it rubs against her clothing, with self-styled realism, is seen as a dangerous aggravation which can make invasive intervention necessary.

4 Intercourses

Dynamics of subjection, passivity and objectification are known topics for those familiar with Greek gynecology.[25] What I promised to draw attention to, however, is the surgery scene in its vividness and materiality, the operation going on, the *intercourse* which enacts the physiological and socio-psychological worlds sketched above.

In the remarkable scene depicted by these authors, and especially by Aetius, we have two male operators acting on a female body which is presented as inert, almost not alive.[26] The operational language obliterates any concern for the patient, so much so that she appears to be most of all a problem in need of fixing, not a patient. The emphasis on immobilisation, the position she is placed in, make this a distinctively pictorial piece. Most of all, the composition of the scene, with a robust young man immobilising the woman and the (older male) operating doctor on the other side of her, produces a classic image of action on female bodies that is worth exploring further.[27] Even if we can easily understand that a strong

---

25 See above, p. 146.

26 Incidentally, this case is different from the operations described in contemporary Africa, where the entire process seems to be a female business, practiced by women on women in secluded contexts.

27 Compare the reports of the surgical procedure for imperforate hymen in Ibn-Sina's *Canon*, quoted by Ostovar et al. 2019, 119. The preparation of the patient is similar: "A chair is prepared for the woman next to the light, and she sits there, leaning backwards slightly. When she is

person would be needed to keep a patient motionless (and here, indirectly, we are given a glimpse into the experience of over-powering and subjugation), the vignette is, nonetheless, culturally loaded. It openly casts two male figures operating in total violence and with consent unknown, a form of penetrative intrusion and mutilation on the body of a woman of marriageable age, and doing so in oboedience to some form of perceived necessity. Pain, bleeding, possibly death can result. Her genitals, her ability to feel pleasure, her sexual drives, perhaps her fertility and marriageability are at stake.

What is missing here to fit a definition of "sexual intercourse"? Condensed in these surgical passages are the medical features of female sexuality mentioned at the beginning: its necessity, its unilateral presentation as something that is a product of domination, recommended from one end (male: doctor, partner) to another (female), its combination of an active intruder and a passive receiver. Let us remind ourselves of the words of the Hippocratic doctor as he offers recommendations about the health of virgins: "I prescribe that virgins should, as soon as possible, when they suffer this ill (*sc.* the madness and fears that typically befall them) go and live' with a man" (κελεύω δ' ἔγωγε τὰς παρθένους, ὁκόταν τὸ τοιοῦτον πάσχωσιν, ὡς τάχιστα ξυνοικῆσαι ἀνδράσιν).[28] Symmetrically and analogously, in the case of clitoridectomy as well we find that combined elements of an intrusive action which aimed at opening, penetration and sexual intercourse, are a cure to return a female body to its state of health.

In figurative terms, this scene also evokes and mimicks dynamics of sexual intercourse in the more literally genital sense. The young assistant who immobilises the woman in Aetius is a νεανίσκος εὔτονος, an expression which invites sexual innuendo; εὐτονία σκελῶν is used in strictly medical contexts to indicate robustness and suitability for a task. But this is also a standard phrase to describe the coupling of bodies in a dance. The dancer's body is "well strung", "vigorous": the use of *eutonos* for the medical assistant shows an aesthetic appreciation of the *schema,* the visual *tableau* offered, as well as of the young man as a dancing and sexual partner, with a touch of complacency.

Even more graphically sexual, finally, is the parallel offered by a famous vase from the Louvre, whereby the female is held down and exposed for all to see. This

---

seated, bind her calves to her spread-out thighs, and all these to her abdomen. Put her hands under her knees. Tighten her in this position with straps". If this is a sensible position for a patient undergoing an exploration of and operation on her genitals, the strong impression (which would need comparative exploration) is that the level of detail about immobilisation and positioning are unparalleled in procedures involving male patients.

28 *Verg.* 1 (8.468 L. = 24 Lami), my translation.

figurative evidence, the threesome pattern with two men and a prostrate woman in the middle — admittedly not a common topic for vase painting — invites our attention to focus on an interaction, and an asymmetry among various actors which are comparable (fig. 11):[29]

Fig. 11: Attic red-figure kylix, c. 510 BC, Louvre Museum (Department of Greek, Etruscan, and Roman Antiquities).

Two strong men (a youth and a bearded adult) hold a woman in place, as she receives their penises into her body at her two ends, mouth and vagina/anus. She has her legs open and is firmly held to perform the acrobatics of double sexual service. The picture evoked is very similar in composition to our surgical scene, an analogy which is hard to miss. This is not to discount the fundamental change in context from pornographic to medical, but to confirm the elements of overpowering manipulation (of a willing part — with qualification of the term "willing", as we will see next), as well as the emphatic nature of frontally displayed genitals

---

29 I thank George Kazantzidis for this suggestion about figurative parallels.

(here perhaps seen from the rear; the restraining of the parted legs, however, delivers the same evidence, either to the drinker or, as an entertaining fantasy, to his drinking companion sitting opposite).

As Barrow notes, the frontal and/or foreground vision of the female genitalia is relatively rare in Greek art, and appears always to be emphatic, as are its function and effect intensified in Greek culture generally — whether grotesque, apotropaic, or even promoting fertility.[30] In conclusion, this is a loaded posture, particular and potentially awkward to Greek eyes. As we read Aetius' texts, we should react to all these points of emphasis, which render the description of the procedure ekphrastic and, in my view, undoubtedly sexualised.

5 On the benefit of cutting women: Images and actions

Our search for images continues now with poetic evidence and with an example that has much to say about women's bodies, the actions they receive and the problem of willingness. With the image depicted by Aetius in mind, and in search of the familiarity and "Greekness" of what the practice described by Aetius represents, we should first turn to a well-known classical story of a gory "surgical" act performed by males on a young woman, one of the instances of virgin sacrifice of which Euripides appeared to be fond from *Iphigenia in Aulis*.[31] It is important to bear in mind that in this example (and other, similar narratives, which have been much analysed and discussed from a variety of perspectives) the victim is cast as somehow willing, the perpetrators as family and/or well-intentioned, or at least not hostile (Agamemnon, Achilleus, the priest), and what is carried out as necessitated by external conditions. A comedy of benignity and necessity, so to speak, surrounds the event.[32]

The passage opens with a crowd of armed men, an audience of male onlookers for a performance carried out by an older actor, Chalcas, and the young

---

30 See Barrow 2018, 41, who quotes the examples of "female breasts or genitals in divine iconography signif[ying] fertility and power"; that of Baubo, the woman who made grieving Demeter laugh by exposing her vagina to her (cf. for example Orph. fr. 50 Kern, quoted by Barrow 41 n. 32), a popular subject in Hellenistic and Roman terracottas; cf. also 72–73.
31 See here too King 1998, 27–28, especially on blood and sacrifice; 283; Foley 1982.
32 See Thumiger 2017, 251–254 on women and death in classical medicine and literature.

Achilleus, to whom Iphigenia believes she is engaged. She has just spoken and has bravely accepted her destiny (*IA* 1561–1579):

τοσαῦτ' ἔλεξε· πᾶς δ' ἐθάμβησεν κλυὼν
εὐψυχίαν τε κἀρετὴν τῆς παρθένου.
στὰς δ' ἐν μέσωι Ταλθύβιος, ὧι τόδ' ἦν μέλον,
εὐφημίαν ἀνεῖπε καὶ σιγὴν στρατῶι·
Κάλχας δ' ὁ μάντις ἐς κανοῦν χρυσήλατον   1565
ἔθηκεν ὀξὺ χειρὶ φάσγανον σπάσας
κολεῶν ἔσωθεν κρᾶτά τ' ἔστειψεν κόρης.
ὁ παῖς δ' ὁ Πηλέως ἐν κύκλωι βωμοῦ θεᾶς
λαβὼν κανοῦν ἔθρεξε χέρνιβάς θ' ὁμοῦ,
ἔλεξε δ'· Ὦ παῖ Ζηνός, ὦ θηροκτόνε,   1570
τὸ λαμπρὸν εἱλίσσουσ' ἐν εὐφρόνηι φάος,
δέξαι τὸ θῦμα τόδ' ὅ γέ σοι δωρούμεθα
στρατός τ' Ἀχαιῶν Ἀγαμέμνων ἄναξ θ' ὁμοῦ,
ἄχραντον αἷμα καλλιπαρθένου δέρης,
καὶ δὸς γενέσθαι πλοῦν νεῶν ἀπήμονα   1575
Τροίας τε πέργαμ' ἐξελεῖν ἡμᾶς δορί.
ἐς γῆν δ' Ἀτρεῖδαι πᾶς στρατός τ' ἔστη βλέπων.
[ἱερεὺς δὲ φάσγανον λαβὼν ἐπεύξατο
λαιμόν τ' ἐπεσκοπεῖθ', ἵνα πλήξειεν ἄν.

She spoke; and each man marveled, as he heard the maiden's brave speech. But in the midst Talthybius stood up, for this was his duty, and bade the army refrain from word or deed; and Calchas, the seer, drawing a sharp sword from its scabbard laid it in a basket of beaten gold, and crowned the maiden's head. *Then the son of Peleus, taking the basket and with it lustral water in his hand, ran round the altar of the goddess uttering these words: "O Artemis, you child of Zeus, slayer of wild beasts, that wheel your dazzling light amid the gloom, accept this sacrifice which we, the army of the Achaeans and Agamemnon with us, offer to you, pure blood from a beautiful maiden's neck; and grant us safe sailing for our ships and the sack of Troy's towers by our spears."* Meanwhile the sons of Atreus and all the army stood looking on the ground. [But the priest, seizing his knife, offered up a prayer and was *closely scanning the maiden's throat* to see where he should strike].[33]

As is well known, in this play Iphigenia suddenly disappears from the altar and is saved from slaughter. The scene of sacrifice, however, its figurative structure, the body parts involved, the apparent friendliness of the operators, the competent *episkopein*, the scanning of the throat in search of the point to cut — all these take us back to the same image, a young woman, sexualised as a partner in marriage and possessor of a virgin body, at the centre of a male-performed scrutiny and intrusive action.

---

33 Transl. Coleridge 1891.

A sacrifice actually carried out is that of Polyxena in Euripides' *Hecuba* — another innocent girl, here sacrificed to the ghost of Achilleus. The sexualisation of her surgical death and slaughtered body, again cut by a man, Neoptolemus, and in the name of duty in front of an audience of men, is even more overt, if less famous than that of Iphigenia. Here is the narrative the messenger delivers to Polyxena's mother, Hekabe:

In full force the Greeks gathered at the tomb for your girl's death. Achilleus' son led your daughter by the hand to the top of the mound. I was standing nearby. A designated corps of young guards followed, on hand to restrain any rearing or bolting of your calf. Neoptolemus took a gold cup, filled it with wine, and lifted it in honour of his dead father. He nodded to me, and on that cue, I raised my voice over the chatter gusting around me and said, "Silence in the ranks. All soldiers hereby stand at attention until further orders." Thus I becalmed the entire army. They stood hushed and breathless as Neoptolemus prayed, "*O Achilleus, father and warrior, accept this cup that the army and I offer you as a gift. Let this libation entice your ghost to appear and drink the maiden's blood, dark and pure* (ὁ δ' εἶπεν· Ὦ παῖ Πηλέως, πατὴρ δ' ἐμός, / δέξαι χοάς μοι τάσδε κηλητηρίους, / νεκρῶν ἀγωγούς· ἐλθὲ δ', ὡς πίῃς μέλαν / κόρης ἀκραιφνὲς αἷμ' ὅ σοι δωρούμεθα / στρατός τε κἀγώ). In return, grant us winds, strong and favourable. Free the prows and bridling ropes of our ships, and fill our sails for safe passage home." Then, *seizing his double-gilt sword by the hilt, he drew it from its sheath and motioned to the guards to seize Polyxena* (εἶτ' ἀμφίχρυσον φάσγανον κώπης λαβὼν / ἐξεῖλκε κολεοῦ, λογάσι δ' Ἀργείων στρατοῦ). Your daughter, when she saw this, gave this proud speech: "O Greeks who sacked my city, *know that I die willingly. Let no man touch me. I will bare the nape of my own neck to the sword.* For the gods' sakes, let me be free of fetters when you kill me so that I may die free, and among the dead I won't have to be ashamed, being a queen, to be called a slave." The troops roared their approval, and, when Agamemnon ordered the guards to release the maiden, they did so immediately. And *immediately Polyxena grabbed the fabric at her neckline with both hands and ripped her dress open, exposing her breasts, her torso smooth and perfect as a statue's* (λαβοῦσα πέπλους ἐξ ἄκρας ἐπωμίδος / ἔρρηξε λαγόνας ἐς μέσας παρ' ὀμφαλὸν / μαστούς τ' ἔδειξε στέρνα θ' ὡς ἀγάλματος / κάλλιστα). Nude to the waist, she dropped on one knee before her executioner and said, "Behold, young man—*if it's my breast you want to strike, strike here; if here beneath the neck, my throat is ready.*" Neoptolemus both unwillingly and willingly cut her throat at the windpipe. *His steel sword sliced deep, and her blood gushed out.* (ὁ δ' οὐ θέλων τε καὶ θέλων οἴκτωι κόρης / τέμνει σιδήρωι πνεύματος διαρροάς· / κρουνοὶ δ' ἐχώρουν). Even as she died, your courageous daughter took care to *fall decently, modestly covering* what must be hid from men's eyes' (ἡ δὲ καὶ θνήσκουσ' ὅμως / πολλὴν πρόνοιαν εἶχεν εὐσχήμων πεσεῖν, / κρύπτουσ' ἃ κρύπτειν ὄμματ' ἀρσένων χρεών).

Here too, we find the passivity — transformed into a fictional, paroxyic voluntariness — of the victim; one man operating — here, the young Neoptolemus — and others aiding him or looking on intently; the patently sexualised, if statuesque beauty of the bare breasts; the modesty of the woman, as she even takes care to cover her private parts as she falls to the ground with a slit throat; and the flowing of the precious, dark blood.[34] The key difference in these tragic scenes from the medical accounts of clitoridectomy is the explicit vocality of the victims, as they insist they are dying willingly, whereas the patient is left in silence. The script is otherwise very much the same.

Finally, let us look at a third ancient testimony, another mythological scene of sexual violence and bodily intrusion. Here the medical parallel is close to the surface, as is an open hostility: the gruesome attack on Philomela by her rapist (and the husband of her sister Procne), the tyrant Tereus, as she challenges him and threatens to reveal his crime, recounted in Ovid's *Metamorphoses* 6.549–562. The aggressor does not merely use a knife for his "operation", but precisely a surgical instrument:[35]

> *Talibus ira feri postquam commota tyranni*
> *nec minor hac metus est, causa stimulatus utraque*   550
> *quo fuit accinctus, vagina liberat ensem*
> *arreptamque coma flexis post terga lacertis*
> *vincla pati cogit. Iugulum Philomela parabat*
> *spemque suae mortis viso conceperat ense :*
> *ille indignantem et nomen patris usque vocantem*   555
> *luctantemque loqui comprensam forcipe linguam*
> *abstulit ense fero. Radix micat ultima linguae,*
> *ipsa iacet terraeque tremens inmurmurat atrae;*
> *utque salire solet mutilatae cauda colubrae,*
> *palpitat et moriens dominae vestigia quaerit.*   560
> *Hoc quoque post facinus (vix ausim credere) fertur*
> *saepe sua lacerum repetisse libidine corpus.*

The savage tyrant's wrath was aroused by these words, and his fear no less. Pricked on by both these spurs, he drew his sword which was hanging by his side in its sheath, caught her

---

34 Sacrificial blood and menstrual blood are often compared in ancient science, by the Hippocratics (e.g. *Mul.* 1.6 (8.30 L.) and repeatedly by Aristotle, for whom a young girl's menstrual blood is οἷον νεόσφακτον, "like that of a freshly-slaughtered beast" (*HA* 581^{b}1–2).

35 Shakespeare's *Titus Andronicus* also elaborates on the topos of the mutilation of the raped victim as a way to secure her silence: Aaron rapes Lavinia and then cuts off her tongue and hands (I thank S. Coughlin for this parallel), a meaningful connection between physical violence and severe abuse; cf. Gildenhard and Zissos 2007 on this episode, although they miss the connection we are underlying: "the severed tongue would be at home on the Homeric battlefield, but is utterly inappropriate in an erotic context. …the grotesque image of the dislocated tongue, twitching helplessly on the ground and murmuring into the black earth (*terraeque tremens immurmurat atrae*) thus emerges as a perverse substitute for the erotic ideal". See Benthien 2001, 110–114 on the symbolism of the tongue, and on the various overtones, sexual among them, of Philomela's tongue in Ovid; on Philomela's rape and silencing, see Richlin 1992.

by the hair, and twisting her arms behind her back, he bound them fast. At sight of the sword Philomela gladly offered her throat to the stroke, filled with the eager hope of death. But he seized her tongue with pincers, as it protested against the outrage, calling ever on the name of her father and struggling to speak, and cut it off with his merciless blade. The mangled root quivers, while the severed tongue lies palpitating on the dark earth, faintly murmuring; and, as the severed tail of a mangled snake is wont to writhe, it twitches convulsively, and with its last dying movement it seeks its mistress' feet. Even after this horrid deed — one would scarce believe it — the monarch is said to have worked his lustful will again and again upon the poor mangled form.

This woman too offers a bodily opening — her throat and mouth — to the knife in the hope of dying. Instead, Tereus, holding her head by her hair, grasps her tongue with a *forceps* and severs it with his sword. The analogy with a clitoridean operation is clear:[36] the two canals and openings, the throat/mouth and the vagina, at either of the body, are connected in important ways and mirror each other in ancient gynecology.[37] Ovid insists on the spasms of the mutilated root (the mangled root quivers, *radix micat ultima linguae*), and on the grotesque liveliness of the cut-off part. The incongruous independent life of this part — a small but fundamental one, insofar as it allows speech — after amputation closely resembles the behaviour of the erectile clitoris in "deformed" women who need to have it removed.[38]

The technicality of the *forceps*, moreover, further alerts us to the medicalisation of the scene. The instrument used for clitoridectomy in Aetius is called a μύδιον: Calà notes that the "surgical instrument called μύδιον… is a 'forceps' with a large opening (πλατύστομον) and teeth (τοὺς ὀδόντας): this instrument occurs in medical literature only few times and never in Galen's treatises".[39] The surgical silencing of the victim thus evokes clitoridectomy, as well as being crowned by the particularly loathsome sexual assault on the maimed victim that follows. Where does sexual intercourse begin, in this scene, and where does it end?

If we look at all this evidence from a distance, I suggest, we can see an ever-repeating scene of overpowering, although in different forms, in which a weaker individual (a young woman) is immobilised, penetrated and cut, made to bleed, by a male often aided by other males. Sometimes the male appears to be well-intentioned, even considerate; and the woman appears variously to accept the

---

36 See in this sense the remarks in Richlin 1992, 164–165; also 175.
37 See King 1998, 28.
38 On the meaning and tradition of the word *nymphe*, see Netz 2014, 2020, 361 n. 28; Totelin 2020, 23 n. 38. For the disturbing aliveness of this part, compare Orpheus' severed tongue, still muttering after the *sparagmos* (*flebile lingua* / *murmurat examinis)* at *Met.* XI, 52–53.
39 Calà 2021.

procedure, or even to welcome and approve of it emphatically, but nonetheless she also needs to be held still. Her precious blood flows visibly; her composure, modesty and dignity are all part of the effectiveness and positive achievement of the operation.

The idea that "sexual intercourse" — in Ovid, "rape" — should be expanded as a concept far beyond genital penetration is not new, of course.[40] It is in the spirit of such an extension that a trend in feminist discourse in the last generation, of a more radical persuasion, vowed specifically to regard any contact with males as a compromise with what they considered to be a diffuse, long-standing aggression against the body perpetrated on women, and in particular to give up penetration as its most symbolic enactment and intrinsically defiling act.[41] In question here is not the soundness of this project but the value of the extension: it is, in my view, appropriate to interpret these ancient instances of clitoridectomy, conveniently orientalised by the Greeks as "Lydian" or "Egyptian", as an expression of a script deeply seated in the sexual relations between women and men in our culture, their sociology, ethics, and familial economy, whether dryly reported by a medical writer, embellished by Euripides, or pushed to a stylistic extreme by Ovid.

Or even, centuries later, soberly painted by a 19th-century artist as an image of a psychiatrist at work. Consider the famous painting by Brouillet, *A Clinical Lesson at the Salpêtrière* (fig. 12). Despite the bloodless context, it is difficult not to notice a pictorial parallel with our script (the mise en évidence of the vulnerable body part, the arena-like setting) in the image of Charcot, aided by a young colleague, dealing with a hysterical woman for the benefit of a male audience. These "demonstrations" too have been critiqued many times as a form of voyeuristic display with sexual overtones. In this image in particular, the exposed neck

---

40 The male actors' counterpart for this extension of the meaning of "intercourse" (which is, of course, not always and not necessarily abusive) is familiar for having been well explored through the rich representation of pederastic love and sexual relations in ancient Greece, in whose images no equivalent is to be found to the exposing frontality of the body with displayed genitals we have discussed for the female examples. On iconography, see the material in Lear and Cantarella 2008, 192–193, and their emphasis on the "dignity [of the *erōmenos,* which] is emphasised not only in the literature but also in vase iconography", as an individual who "participates actively in the exchange which is at the foundation of the erotic relationship"; Davidson's extensive discussion of Greek "love" (2007), which also notably emphasises symmetry and dignity in homosexual relationships; Barrow 2018, 31–34, building on these suggestions, on the possible fluidity between the *erastēs-erōmenos* figures.
41 Most notably Dworkin 1974 and especially 1987.

and chest point again to the weakness (and sexual availability, accessibility) of the (young, attractive, helpless, supposedly sexually frustrated) patient-victim.

Fig. 12: Jean-Martin Charcot demonstrating hysteria in a hypnotised patient at the Salpêtrière. Etching by A. Lurat, 1888, after P.A.A. Brouillet, 1887. Wellcome Collection. Attribution 4.0 International (CC BY 4.0).

6 "Deformed sexes": Images and actions

As the painted image above shows, we are dealing with an enduring script. I conclude with another image to reinforce the transhistorical point: that of a woman in an 1849 patient case published by the *Medical Times* (Oct. 14th 1848 to June 30th 1849) and authored by a certain Charles Waddler, M.D., Obstetric Physician to St. Thomas Hospital.[42] I hope this final image will show the deep and possibly irreducible interconnections between sex as normative (behavioural, what sex one has; reproductive, the offspring one produces; categorical, to be male or female) and violence.

In his paper, Waddler briefly discusses various cases of "hermaphroditism", and then moves to one of his own, that of Mrs. Margaret M., from North Wales. The patient may have been an individual one would today classify as intersex;[43]

---

42 Waller 1849, 37–38.
43 Cf. the definition by the UNFE (Free & Equal, https://www.unfe.org/wp-content/uploads/2017/05/UNFE-Intersex.pdf, accessed 11.11.2020), which I find satisfactory: "Intersex people are

her "pathology", signalled by "anomalous pains in the chest and stomach", gravitates around the look of her genitals, although her general appearances — "stoutness", lack of feminine grace ("except in the eyes"), coarse voice and hairiness — seem to confirm her incongruity as a whole. We cannot, of course, focus here on the details of this inspection; the article is re-printed below. What is important for me, however, is to draw attention to the *images* here: to begin with, the two representations of her "non-conformant" genitals (fig. 13b). Here too, a nominally female individual is reduced to passive specimen and carrier of a curious feature. It is with these before us that we should read the report of the detailed scene: the author describes artificially separating Mrs. M.'s private parts to ease inspection: the graphics clearly represent her as lying down with parted legs. He is "separating with the fingers", an act repeated many times; he is "inserting the finger with ease" into the canal "resembling" a vagina, and seemingly pushing to the point of ascertaining its "being, however, only about two inches in length" and "terminating in a *cul de sac*"; he is "widely" separating the two sides and stretching the prepuce "back to its fullest extent" (fig. 13b). He also reports that "there has yet been no sexual desires" in her — indirect information, as the woman could only speak Welsh, it is said, making communication with her impossible.

Many things can be said here in comment and conclusion. Once again, the ordeal of a female individual — a real one, Margaret M. — is narrated in a way which resembles in many crucial senses that of the clitoridectomy patients in regard to imagery and actions. The female individual is (more or less explicitly) immobilised, her legs parted and her genitals exposed. The "abnormal" genitals of the ancient clitoridectomy patients presented aesthetic, psychological, and moral issues: they were large, could undergo penis-like erection, receive excessive stimulus, and propagate excessive pleasure. The Victorian patient is instead categorised as having no sexual drive, is "modest and gentle", but "curiously constructed" and in gender "I doubt not... masculine". Suggestively, her pencilled portrait can still channel to observers the experience of hopelessness and seclusion which must be at the receiving end of this examination and verdict (fig. 13a). We are also made to wonder, incidentally: how many cases of enlarged

born with sex characteristics (including genitals, gonads and chromosome patterns) that do not fit typical binary notions of male or female bodies. Intersex is an umbrella term used to describe a wide range of natural bodily variations. In some cases, intersex traits are visible at birth while in others, they are not apparent until puberty. Some chromosomal intersex variations may not be physically apparent at all. According to experts, between 0.05% and 1.7% of the population is born with intersex traits — the upper estimate is similar to the number of red-haired people". See below on the same document for a due emphasis on body "integrity".

clitoris for which amputation of the kind discussed was recommended were such intersex occurrences? Where does one draw the line between intersex and endowment with an enlarged clitoris, if the decision is entirely for an individual doctor or agent to make? And, to return to our initial statement: would it not make sense to qualify the operations of the doctor on Margaret M., accompanied by exposure, examination and appreciation of her breasts and body, her "femininity" as a whole, as sexual intercourse? When, in the relation with the outside world, does sexual intercourse for her begin or end?

7 Conclusions

I am aware of the potential pitfalls of the project I have proposed: we began with the ancient world and touched episodically on modern examples to make a universal statement about the ontology of sex and the violence intrinsic in any hint at norms as far as sex, gender identity and sexual activities are concerned. The point was not, of course, to contribute comprehensively to the history of gynecology in our tradition or to originally advance current theoretical or political debates. Instead, it was to expose the ways in which a practice today seen by Euro-American audiences as "tribal" and foreign is actually nested close to the roots of our own, in some cases recent, medical history, with its views of the female body and gender, and of what legitimate and natural, even medically sound sexual intercourse between sexes should look like.[44]

Sex has been arguably at the centre of our history of philosophy and anthropology for a long time — as Bernini shows, a history that unfurls through oblivion and denial as much as open engagement and thematisation.[45] The definition of sexual intercourse in use among historians of medicine cannot ignore the extent to which this intercourse takes place between individuals whose boundaries are physical and bodily, but also social, political, and involved in power in concrete and tangible ways. A more plastic concept of sexual intercourse, apart from being simply truer to human experience, allows us to appreciate in new ways the extent to which sex is central to human culture and society, and more often than not to questions of power and violence (although, and here I differ fundamentally from

---

44 Anachronism and an overcompensating desire to impose at all costs an image of female passivity and oppression of females in medical contexts should of course be avoided: see in this regard King 2011, who demystifies the anachronistic use in modern reception of mis-read ancient sources to find therapeutic masturbation of women by male figures in ancient medicine.
45 Bernini 2020.

the radical style of analysis I mentioned before, it is not the case that the opposite is true — i.e., that power and violence must be central to heterosexual sex). The fundamental contribution offered by Freud, today easily dismissed as hyperbolic, maintains its evident truthfulness; merely witness the plethora of aggressively moralistic and normative positions, in legislation and in society at large, on display in various countries in the "first", as much as in the "third" world as we write.

Regarding this centrality of sex, Euripides' sacrificial virgins offering their throats and bare breasts, the gruesome attack on Philomela's body narrated by Ovid and the hysterical female patients lying abandoned in the arms of Charcot are more enlightening than many words, and provide the necessary undertext to the surgical clitoridectomy coldly reported by our ancient medical sources. A history of "sexual intercourse" must account for the biological, the familial, the comic, the pleasurable, the light, the playful, the erotic, and the sentimental. But it must also find a place for the exercise of sheer power over another which finds in sexual intercourses a key mode of expressing itself.

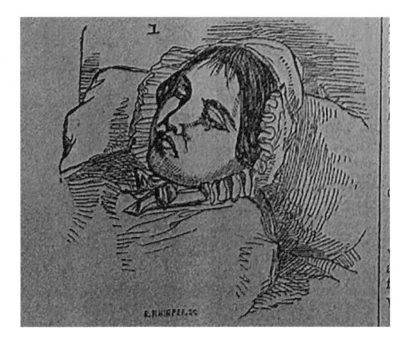

Fig. 13a: Detail of 3b.

Fig. 13b: Waddler, C. 'Case of Hermaphroditism', in: *Medical Times* (Oct. 14th 1848 to June 30th 1849).

Bibliography

Arnold-Forster, A. (2014), 'Clitoridectomies: Female Genital Mutilation c. 1860–2014', online available at https://notchesblog.com/category/medicine-and-the-body/ (accessed 11.11.2020).

Barrow, R.J. (2018), *Gender, Identity and the Body in Greek and Roman Sculpture*, (Prepared for publication by M.S. Silk), Cambridge.

Benthien, C. (2001), 'Zweispältige Zungen. Der Kampf um Lust und Macht im oralen Raum', in: C. Benthien/Ch. Wulf (eds.), *Körperteile. Eine kulturelle Anatomie*, Reinbek, 104–132 (Rowohlts Enzyklopädie 642).

Bernini, L. (2020), *Il sessuale politico. Freud con Marx, Fanon, Foucault*, Pisa.

Bremmer, J. (2013), 'Human Sacrifice in Euripides' Iphigeneia in Tauris: Greek and Barbarian', in: P. Bonnechere/R. Gagné (eds.), *Sacrifices humains / Human sacrifices*, Liège, 87–100.

Butler, J. (1990), *Gender Trouble: Feminism and the Subversion of Identity*, London.

Calà, I. (2021, forthcoming), 'A short remark on Aetius Amidenus book 16th: the case of the clitoridectomy', in: L. Lemhaus (ed.), *Female Bodies and Female Practitioners. Women in Medical Traditions from the Ancient to the Medieval Mediterranean World*, Tübingen.

Dean-Jones, L. (1992), 'The Politics of Pleasure: Female Sexual Appetite in the Hippocratic Corpus', in: *Helios* 19, 72–91.

Dean-Jones, L. (1995), 'Autopsia, historia and what women know: the authority of women in Hippocratic gynaecology', in: D. Bates (ed.), *Knowledge and the Scholarly Medical Traditions: A comparative Study*, Cambridge, 41–58.

Dean-Jones, L. (1996), *Women's Bodies in Classical Greek Science*, Oxford.

Dean-Jones, L. (2003), 'The Cultural Construct of the Female Body in Classical Greek Science', in: M. Golden/P. Toohey (eds.), *Sex and Difference in Ancient Greece and Rome*, Edinburgh.

Dworkin, A. (1974), *Woman Hating: A Radical Look at Sexuality*, New York.

Dworkin, A. (1987), *Intercourse*, New York.

Foley, H.P. (1982), 'Marriage and sacrifice in Euripides' Iphigeneia in Aulis', in: *Arethusa* 15 (1/2), American Classical Studies in Honor of J.-P. Vernant, 159–180.

Gildenhard, I./Zissos, A. (2007), 'Barbarian variations: Tereus, Procne and Philomela in Ovid (*Met.* 6.412–674) and Beyond', in: *Dyctinna* 4, online available at https://doi.org/10.4000/dictynna.150 (accessed: 11/03/2021).

Gourevitch, D. (1995), '"Women who Suffer From a Man's Disease". The Example of Satyriasis and the Debate on Affections Specific to the Sexes', in: R. Hawley/B. Levick, (eds.), *Women in Antiquity*, London, 149–165

Groff, E. (forthcoming), 'Negotiating Women's Sexual Identity with a Scalpel: Ancient and Contemporary Views on Clitoridectomy', in: G. Chesi/M. Gerolemou (eds.), *Body Technologies in the Greco-Roman World: Technosoma, Gender and Sex*.

Hall, E. (1991), *Inventing the Barbarian: Greek Self-Definition through Tragedy*, Oxford.

Hübner, S. (2009), 'Female Circumcision as a Rite de Passage in Egypt—Continuity Through the Millennia?', in: *Journal of Egyptian History* 2, 149–171.

Hanson, A. (1985), 'The Women of the Hippocratic Corpus', in: *Bulletin of the Institute of Ancient Medicine* 13, 5–7.

Hanson, A. (1990), 'The Medical Writers' Woman', in: D. Halperin/J. Winkler/F. Zeitlin (eds.), *Before Sexuality: the Construction of Erotic Experience in the Ancient Greek World*, Princeton, 309–337.

King, H. (1998), *Hippocrates' Woman*, London.

King, H. (2004), *The Disease of Virgins. Greek Sickness, Chlorosis and the Problems of Puberty*, London.

King, H. (2011), 'Galen and the Widow: Towards a History of Therapeutic Masturbation in Ancient Gynaecology', in: *EuGeStA* 1, 205–235.

King, H. (2013), *The One-Sex Body on Trial: The Ancient and Early Modern Evidence*, London.

Knight, M. (2001), 'Curing Cut or Ritual Mutilation? Some Remarks on the Practice of Female and Male Circumcision in Graeco-Roman Egypt', in: *Isis* 92, 317–338.

Laqueur, Th. (1990), *Making Sex: Body and Gender from the Greeks to Freud*, Cambridge.

Lear, A./Cantarella, E. (2008), *Images of Pederasty: Boys Were Their Gods*, London/New York.

Manuli, P. (1980), 'Fisiologia e Patologia del Femminile negli Scritti Ippocratici dell'antica Ginecologia Greca', in: M. Grmek (ed.), *Hippocratica. Actes du colloque hippocratique de Paris*, Paris, 393–408.

Martelli, M. (2017), 'Alchemy, Medicine and Religion: Zosimus of Panopolis and the Egyptian Priests', in: *Religion in the Roman Empire* 3, 202–220.

Matthews, L. (2015), "Xanthus of Lydia and the Invention of Female Eunuchs", in: *The Classical Quarterly* 65, 489–499.

Netz, R. (2014), 'A Possible Etymology for the Greek Anatomical term kleitorís', in: *Studi Italiani di Filologia Classica* 1, 99–105.

Netz, R. (2020), *Scale, Space and Canon in Ancient Literary Culture*, Cambridge.

Osborne, R. (2011), *The History Written on the Classical Greek Body*, Cambridge.

Ostovar, M./Mosavat, S.H./Starr, P.J./Quintern, D./Heydari, M. (2019), 'Female Genital Tract Anomalies Treatment through Surgery in Avicenna's Canon of Medicine (980–1037 CE)', in: *Journal of Research on History of Medicine* 8, 115–122.

Richlin, A. (1992), *Pornography and Representation in Greece and Rome*, Oxford.

Scodel, R. (1996), 'Δόμων ἄγαλμα: Virgin sacrifice and Aesthetic Object', in: *Transactions of the American Philological Association* 126, 111–128.

Thomas, R. (2000), *Herodotus in Context: Ethnography, Science and the Art of Persuasion*, Cambridge.

Thumiger, C. (2017), *The Life and Health of The Mind in Early Greek Medical Thought*, Cambridge.

Thumiger, C. (2018), 'A most acute, disgusting and indecent disease': Satyriasis in ancient medicine', in: C. Thumiger/P. Singer (eds.), *Mental Illness in Ancient Medicine. From Celsus to Paul of Aegina*, Leiden, 269–284.

Totelin, L.M.V. (2009), *Hippocratic Recipes: Oral and Written Transmission of Pharmacological Knowledge in Fifth- and Fourth-Century Greece*, Leiden.

Urso, A.M. (2003) 'Riscritture di Sorano nel mondo latino tardoantico: il caso dei Gynaecia'. In *Galenismo e medicina tardoantica: fonti greche, latine, arabe. Atti del Seminario Internazionale di Siena (Certosa di Pontignano, 9-10 settembre 2002)*, a cura di I. Garofalo e A. Roselli, con l'editio princeps di Galeni qui fertur ad Glauconem liber tertius ad fidem codicis Vindocinensis 109, editionem curavit K.-D. Fischer (Quaderni di A.I.O.N. 71), Napoli, 161–202.

Urso, A.M. (2008), 'Quando l'esegesi cambia il testo: traduzione e riscrittura nei Gynaecia di Celio Aureliano', in: *Femmes en médecine. Journée d'étude organisée en l'honneur de Danielle Gourevitch (Paris, 17 mars 2006)*, éd. par V. Boudon, V. Dasen, B. Maire, Paris, 205–222.

Vitanza, V. (ed.) (2011), *Sexual Violence in Western Thought and Writing: Chaste Rape*, Berlin.

Websites

World Health Organisation – https://www.who.int/en/news-room/fact-sheets/detail/female-genital-mutilation. (Accessed 11.03.2021)

UNFE https://www.unfe.org/wp-content/uploads/2017/05/UNFE-Intersex.pdf. (Accessed 11.03.2021)

Texts and translations used

Aetius Sermo sextidecimus et ultimus erstens aus Handschriften veröffentlicht mit Abbildungen Bemerkungen und Erklärungen, von Skevos Zervos (Leipzig: Verlag von Anton. Mangkos, 1901), 152, 13–153,10.

Euripides. *The Plays of Euripides*, translated by E. P. Coleridge, Volume II, London, 1891.

[Hippocrates] Girls (Virg.), edited and translated by A. Lami (2007) 'Lo scritto ippocratico sui disturbi virginali', in: *Galenos* 1, 15–59.

Drabkin, M.F./Drabkin, I.E. (eds.) (1951), *Gynaecia: Fragments of a Latin Version of Soranus's Gynaecia from a Thirteenth Century Manuscript*, Baltimore.

Soranos d'Éphèse, *Maladies des femmes, Livre IV, texte établi*, traduit et commenté par P. Burguière, D. Gourevitch et Y. Malinas, Paris, 2003.

Bernabé, A. (ed.), *Poetae Epici Graeci. Testimonia et fragmenta*. Pars II. *Orphicorum et Orphicis similium testimonia et fragmenta*. Fasc. 1, 2 (Bibliotheca Teubneriana), München/Leipzig (2004–2005).

George Kazantzidis
Sex and Epilepsy: Seizures and Fluids in Greek Medical Imagination

Abstract: This chapter investigates the connections between sex and epilepsy in ancient medical texts, from the Hippocratic Corpus down to Aretaeus of Cappadocia. I start by considering evidence from classical Greek medicine, and I argue that some sort of implicit association is already present there and is drawn along the lines of a common "symptomatology" including: intense bodily movements, convulsions, moaning, rolling of the eyes and an involuntary release of fluids. I then move to the evidence provided by Aretaeus of Cappadocia, where sex is explicitly said to "bear the symbols" of the disease. Interestingly, while Aretaeus invites us to picture an epileptic body and a body that is having sex as being disconcertingly similar to each other, he also warns us that epilepsy is an envious disease: it leaves the bodies of young people permanently scarred; it takes away their beauty; it makes them feel ashamed about the way they look (especially at the moment that they have a fit); ultimately, it makes them feel *less desirable*. The disease, I conclude, helps to bring out the peculiar, and not always comfortable, relationship between sex and desire in antiquity: a body that is the object of desire can suddenly turn itself into something disgusting when it becomes entangled with another body during sex, descending, as it were, into a messy world of fluids, incomprehensible sounds and uncontainable movements.

> It has been found impossible to maintain that "epilepsy" is a single clinical entity ... It is as though a mechanism for abnormal instinctual discharge had been laid down organically, which could be made use of in quite different circumstances ... This mechanism [cannot] stand remote from the sexual processes, which are fundamentally of toxic origin.

> Sigmund Freud, *Dostoevsky and Parricide* (1928)

Falling prey to erotic desire can be unbearably painful; it can even drive us "mad"[1] with feelings of frustration, wearing excitement, anticipation and unfulfilled longing. But what happens when someone finally gets what s/he wants? Does the pain stop or does it persist in other, perhaps equally excruciating, forms, mental and physical? And a more specific question: what happens at the actual

---

[1] The bibliography on love and madness in ancient Greek and Roman sources is vast; for a recent discussion (with plenty of references to secondary literature), see Thumiger 2013.

https://doi.org/10.1515/9783110695793-008

moment when desire is being consummated by means of sexual intercourse? Is this much anticipated blending of bodies one of pure pleasure? Or does it open the door for new varieties of pain and suffering to creep in? And what about the final climax, orgasm itself? Is this a moment of relief, or does it hurt?

Sexual intercourse presents a complicated conceptual domain for the ancient Greek and Roman imagination. Aristotle famously states that losing semen is the same as losing a quantity of healthy blood (*GA* 726b12–13).[2] Another writer, close to Aristotle's thought, maintains that having sex looks the same as dying: for if you observe someone — he tells us — who is having intercourse (and s/he is enjoying it) and someone whose soul is about to depart from their body, they both cast their eyes upwards.[3] Indeed, a close investigation of philosophical and medical sources reveals that, despite its well-established connections with prime quality pleasure, sex is also a source of deep-seated anxieties which reach to the very core of a person's physical existence. To mention only a few of the side effects of sex as we encounter them in ancient "scientific" texts, we find among others: critical loss of body fat, the drying up of certain parts of the body, loss of moisture and sight, fall of hair, shrinking of the eyes, contraction of the muscles in the groin, and an overall feeling of exhaustion[4] (seminal fluid, it should be remembered, is believed by many medical writers in antiquity to be made up by tiny bits of tissue drawn from all over the body, its hard and soft parts alike).[5] What is at stake in the case of intercourse, in other words, is a critical expenditure

---

2 As Connell 2016, 104 explains, this applies both to men and women.

3 [Arist.] *Problemata Physica* 876a31–32: Διὰ τί ὁ ἀφροδισιάζων καὶ ὁ ἀποθνήσκων ἀναβάλλει τὰ ὄμματα; Significantly, this is the opening question in what then evolves into a fairly extended list of issues concerning sexual intercourse, which are explored throughout the fourth book of the ps.-Aristotelian *Problems* (bearing the title: ΟΣΑ ΠΕΡΙ ΑΦΡΟΔΙΣΙΑ). For a brief discussion, see Laqueur 1990, 46. Cf. *Problemata Physica* 877a24–26: Διὰ τί τοῦ ἀφροδισιάζειν γινομένου διὰ θερμότητα, τοῦ δὲ φόβου ὄντος ψυκτικοῦ καὶ τοῦ ἀποθνήσκειν, ἐνίοις, ὅταν γένωνται ἐν τούτοις τοῖς πάθεσι, σπέρμα προέρχεται; "Why, although having sex occurs because of heat, and being afraid and dying cause cooling, do some people, when they are in these conditions, emit seed?" (transl. in Mayhew 2011, 151).

4 All of the symptoms mentioned here are found in the fourth book of the ps.-Aristotelian *Problemata Physica* (mentioned in the previous footnote).

5 See e.g. [Hipp.] *De genitura* 3 (7.474 L.): Τὴν δὲ γονήν φημι ἀποκρίνεσθαι ἀπὸ παντὸς τοῦ σώματος, καὶ ἀπὸ τῶν στερεῶν καὶ ἀπὸ τῶν μαλθακῶν, καὶ ἀπὸ τοῦ ὑγροῦ παντός, "I assert that seed is secreted from the whole body, from the solid parts and the soft parts, and from all its moisture" (transl. in Potter 2021, 11). For the so-called pangenesis theory, according to which the seed derives from the entire body, see Lonie 1981, 64–67 and Wilberding 2016, 333.

of precious bodily stuff. To put it slightly differently: if "melting" provides a conceptual *metaphor* for erotic desire, sexual intercourse can then *literally* eat you up.[6]

In this chapter I focus my attention on the climax of sexual encounter. The question which I set out to explore is the following: since the long-term effects of sexual intercourse are variously assimilated to those of a wasting disease, what kind of pathology could then be said to underlie and shape the very moment of orgasm? My intention is to bring together and discuss a number of sources which answer this question by proposing, either directly or indirectly, epilepsy as a fitting disease to think with, both about sex and about ejaculation. The association between sex and epilepsy, I argue, is by no means accidental. On the contrary, it is symptomatic of a general tendency to see sex as a profoundly violent thing during which both the male and the female body are subjected to a great deal of suffering.

1 Macrobius' testimony and the Hippocratic Corpus

Let me start with a late antique text which transports us, or so it seeks, to the time and mindset of classical Greek medicine. In *Saturnalia* 2.15–16, Macrobius takes issue with sex and gluttony; and this is what he has to say on the subject:

> Quis igitur habens aliquid humani pudoris voluptatibus istis duabus, coeundi atque comedendi, quae homini cum sue atque asino communes sunt, gratuletur? Socrates quidem dicebat multos homines propterea velle vivere ut ederent et biberent, se bibere atque esse ut viveret. Hippocrates autem, divina vir scientia, de coitu Venerio ita existimabat, partem esse quandam morbi taeterrimi quem nostri comitialem dixerunt. namque ipsius verba haec traduntur: τὴν συνουσίαν εἶναι μικρὰν ἐπιληψίαν.

---

6 For the metaphor of "melting" desire in the ancient sources, see Cairns 2013, 240 with n. 13; cf. Calame 1992, 20. Compare this with a more literal form of melting discussed in [Hipp.] *De morbis* 2.51 (7.78 L.): "Consumption of the back (νωτιὰς φθίσις) arises from the marrow; most frequently it occurs in newly-weds and those fond of venery (λαμβάνει δὲ μάλιστα νεογάμους καὶ φιλολάγνους). They are without fever and eat well, but still they melt away (καὶ τήκονται). If you ask the patient, he will say that starting from his head he feels something crawling down his spine, like ants. When he passes urine or goes to stool, copious moist semen comes forth; he begets no offspring, and he has nocturnal emissions whether he sleeps with a woman or not" (transl. in Potter 1988, 253). For a discussion, see Flemming 2019, 50.

Will anyone with a shred of human decency, then, exult in those two pleasures, of sexual intercourse and gluttony, which human beings share with swine and asses? Indeed, Socrates used to say that many people wish to live so they might eat and drink, whereas he ate and drank so that he might live. Hippocrates, a man of godlike understanding, thought that sexual intercourse has something in common with the utterly repulsive illness we call the "comitial disease": his words, as they've been handed down, are, "Intercourse is a small seizure".[7]

Actually, no such words by Hippocrates have ever been handed down to us. And yet, Macrobius' intriguing testimony cannot be simply dismissed on the assumption that the author is relying here on some false information nor can it be handled with the mere observation that he could be referring to a medical source that is lost to us. The text raises some extremely important issues with regard to sexual intercourse, and its essentially degrading qualities, which have to be tested carefully against the surviving evidence.

Writing in the early 5th century AD, Macrobius lives at a time when the association between sex and epilepsy has evolved, mainly in the context of medical treatises of the Second Sophistic, which will be explored in detail in the following sections. But it is worth our effort to have a look first at what we actually have *in* the Hippocratic Corpus, and see what kind of textual and medical evidence could have led someone to assume that there is a deeper connection there between sex and epilepsy. A first result, speaking in favor of *some kind* of association, is yielded in the context of a short gynaecological treatise (some believe that what survives from the text is only its beginning) entitled *On the diseases of young girls* (*Περὶ παρθενίων* / *De virginum morbis*, 8.466–470 L.).[8] Epilepsy — designated by the author of the treatise as the "so-called sacred disease" (τῆς ἱερῆς νούσου καλεομένης) — heads in that case a list of medical conditions believed to afflict girls who "remain without a husband" (παρανδρούμεναι) even though their time for marriage has come. That they are ready to get married is indicated by the fact that their body has grown, and has collected enough blood in it for menstruation to start happening. According to the author, sudden seizures, apoplexies, unnatural visions and panic attacks occur because the girl's menstrual blood, gathering in her womb in excess, flows downward as if to pass out of the body. Because the "mouth of the exit" (τὸ στόμα τῆς ἐξόδου), however, remains closed, the blood rushes back upwards and floods the area around the heart and the diaphragm,

---

7 Translation in Kaster 2011, 387.
8 For the text, see the useful discussions by Flemming/Hanson 1998 and Lami 2007.

thereby affecting the girl's mental faculties. With the locus of her mental life having been thus compromised,[9] epilepsy ensues and, along with it, fears, terrors, shivering and fever. In order for the patient to be cured, the author suggests that the young girl should marry as soon as possible, have sex and get pregnant (κελεύω δὴ τὰς παρθένους, ὁκόταν τοιοῦτο πάσχωσι, ὡς τάχιστα συνοικῆσαι ἀνδράσιν· ἢν γὰρ κυήσωσιν, ὑγιέες γίνονται). Sex and pregnancy, here as elsewhere in the Hippocratic Corpus, guarantee health;[10] in the meantime, penetration is suggested to help "unblock" and extend the "mouth of the exit", removing whatever kind of impediment might have been in the vagina[11] and allowing the blood which has been trapped inside the body to find its way out.

The medical advice is painfully straightforward and, the way the author is presenting it, it seems to admit of no qualifications or exceptions: when you are about to start menstruating you either have sex (in the formal context of marriage) and save yourself the trouble or you become susceptible to fits of epilepsy and other terrible ills.[12] Obviously, what is being laid out at this point is a far cry from what Macrobius tells us about "Hippocrates": advising sex as a means of avoiding epilepsy is by no means the same with (in fact, it could even be said to be, in a sense, opposite to) claiming that sex resembles epilepsy. The evidence, however, is telling in that it invites us to see the disease as being in some way significant in the context of a person's (a young woman's) sex life. The idea of repression — which the text explores exclusively in physical terms (the female's problem is that of not being able to *let out* menstrual blood), avoiding, that is, to connect it with the affected subject's suppressed desires — is dominant throughout, and pictures the female body as something which, when in need of intercourse in order to release its surplus fluids,[13] becomes all the more likely to experience seizures and convulsions.

---

9 For the cardiocentric theory of sensation in antiquity, see van der Eijk 2005, 125.

10 See e.g. [Hipp.] *De genitura* 4 (on the benefits of sex for women): "The following point is also true for women: if they have intercourse with men they are more likely to be healthy, if not, then less so (ἢν μὲν μίσγωνται ἀνδράσι, μᾶλλον ὑγιαίνουσιν· εἰ δὲ μή, ἧσσον). For first, their uterus becomes moist during intercourse, rather than being in a dry state, and in a dry state it contracts more strongly than it should, and in contracting provokes serious trouble in the body. Second, intercourse makes the menses pass more easily by warming and moistening the blood, whereas if the menses do not pass, women's bodies become prone to disease" (transl. in Potter 2012, 15).

11 It is not at all clear that our author is referring here to the rupturing of the virginal hymen. See the discussion in Sissa 2013, 91–92; cf. Sissa 1990.

12 On the text's "medical terrorism", see Manuli 1980, 404.

13 On the absence of conscious female sexual desire in the Hippocratic Corpus (an idea which implies that women crave for sex only when their bodies feel like it, for a variety of biological reasons), see Dean-Jones 1992.

The *Περί παρθενίων*, essential as it may be for helping us reconstruct the male politics of regulating female sex and desire in antiquity, is not enough by itself to shed light on the type of medical association between sex and epilepsy, which I am pursuing here. One would have thought that such an association could perhaps be recovered from Hippocratic texts which describe sexual intercourse as an intensely physical, overwhelming experience that makes one's body explode and shudder as though it was in the grip of some kind of disease. The answer here is that while we do have in fact some rather thorough medical descriptions of intercourse, which even include details about male and female ejaculation, the medical authors' tone remains always balanced in a way that does not allow for any concretely outlined connections with epilepsy — or any other type of disease, for that matter — to emerge. Take, for instance, the well-known and much discussed passage from *De genitura* 4 (7.474–76 L.),[14] which pays particular attention to a woman's reaction in sex. During intercourse, we are told, the "vagina is rubbed" and the "uterus is moved"; as a result "a kind of tickling sensation" is felt in these parts (ὥσπερ κνησμὸν ἐμπίπτειν), which then "gives rise to pleasure and warmth in the rest of the body" (καὶ τῷ ἄλλῳ σώματι ἡδονὴν καὶ θέρμην παρέχειν). What follows is the ejaculation of female semen, "sometimes into the uterus" and "sometimes externally, if the uterus gapes open more than it should" (μεθίει δὲ καὶ ἡ γυνὴ ἀπὸ τοῦ σώματος ὁτὲ μὲν ἐς τὰς μήτρας ... ὁτὲ δὲ καὶ ἔξω, ἢν χάσκωσιν αἱ μῆτραι μᾶλλον τοῦ καιροῦ). Pleasure and climax are of the essence here, but they are not further explored in terms that could lead to potentially titillating references to e.g. intense convulsions, the thrusting out of arms and legs, moans of satisfaction etc. (after all, this is a medical text and some sense of clinical decorum must be maintained). With men, on the other hand, we seem to be entering a more promising ground: "a woman", we read in the same passage, "feels much less pleasure in intercourse than a man...The reason a man feels more pleasure[15] is that the secretion from his moisture [i.e. ejaculation] occurs suddenly (ἐξαπίνης) as the result of a stronger agitation (ἀπὸ ταραχῆς ἰσχυροτέρης)". The noun ταραχή is fairly suggestive. We typically find it in medical writings as a pathological indication of extreme mental and physical discomfort; it is associated with fevers, trembling, uncontrolled and intense movement of the body,

---

14 See the brief and illuminating discussions in Lonie 1981, 119–121; Hanson 1990, 314–315.
15 Contrast the evidence from myth: when asked who has more pleasure in sex, Tiresias answered that women enjoy it nine times more than men. For a discussion, see Michalopoulos 2012, 229.

screams and pain.[16] Considering the word's semantic range and application, its occurrence in the context of (male) ejaculation in *Gen.* 4 is significant: it could be taken to suggest that some sort of pathologisation of the sexual act is at play. That said, it must be conceded that all this remain allusive at best, since no such point is raised by the medical author in an explicit and straightforward way.

Let us now turn our attention to medical accounts of an epileptic seizure; in these descriptions one could in theory find some kind of sexual imagery, however implicit and indirect, underlying the agony of the patient. The main evidence in this case is provided by *De morbo sacro*, a medical treatise that is entirely devoted to epilepsy. Leaving aside the author's imaginative aetiology of the disease,[17] let us focus on how an epileptic fit is described as shaking and affecting the human body in ch. 7 of the text (6.372 L.). The patient

> ἄφωνος γίνεται καὶ πνίγεται, καὶ ἀφρὸς ἐκ τοῦ στόματος ἐκρεῖ, καὶ οἱ ὀδόντες συνηρείκασι, καὶ αἱ χεῖρες συσπῶνται, καὶ τὰ ὄμματα διαστρέφονται, καὶ οὐδὲν φρονέουσιν, ἐνίοισι δὲ καὶ ὑποχωρεῖ ἡ κόπρος κάτω.

> becomes speechless and chokes; foam flows from the mouth; he gnashes his teeth and twists his hands; the eyes roll and intelligence fails, and in some cases excrement is discharged.[18]

Extreme physical exertion, mental confusion and an involuntary release of fluids (and other substances) appear to provide here the main script for the patient's suffering.[19] What is more, some of the text's details may have borne potentially sexual associations which to us remain more or less invisible. I am thinking here especially of the foam that comes out from the patient's mouth. As a liquid substance, foam (ἀφρός) is intrinsically related to the seminal fluid in classical Greek

---

16 See e.g. [Hipp.] *Epidemiae* 3.3.17(13): ἐξεμάνη· βοή, ταραχὴ, λόγοι πολλοί, *Coa Praesagia* 571: μετὰ ἀγρυπνίης καὶ ταραχῆς, φρενιτικά. For ὄμματα ταραχώδεα see *Epid.* 6.7.6, with Thumiger 2017, 91.

17 For which, see van der Eijk 2005, 131.

18 Translation in Jones 1923, 159.

19 At this point, the patient is described as lying "speechless", but elsewhere in the text attention is drawn to his/her loud groaning and moaning, as if he were an animal. One animal in particular with which the epileptic is associated throughout the text is the goat (ch. 4: καὶ ἢν μὲν γὰρ αἶγα μιμῶνται, καὶ ἢν βρύχωνται...) which is known for its lustful nature. Cf. [Arist.] *Problemata Physica* 879a22–23: Διὰ τί οἱ ἀφροδισιάζοντες ἢ οἱ τοιοῦτοι δυσώδεις, οἱ δὲ παῖδες οὔ; καὶ τοῦ καλουμένου γράσου ὄζουσιν, "Why are those who have sex or such people (as are able to) ill-smelling, but children are not? Indeed they reek of what is called goat-smell" (transl. in Mayhew 2011, 165–167).

medicine and thought.[20] In another Hippocratic text[21] which sets outs to explain why foam *naturally* rises through an epileptic's mouth (ἀφροὶ δὲ διὰ τοῦ στόματος ἀνατρέχουσιν εἰκότως), we are told that a seizure is attributed to an excessive quantity of air that has entered the body's thick, blood-filled veins. Obstructed blood circulation leads to a violent shaking of the body — an external manifestation of the blood's disturbance within. Then, the air, passing through the veins, itself rises and brings up with it the thinnest part of the blood. The moisture (τὸ δὲ ὑγρόν), mixing with the air, becomes white, and this should explain why the foam that comes out eventually has the same colour.

Compare now the account just given with the way semen is said to be produced in *De genitura* 1 (7.470 L.):

φλέβες καὶ νεῦρα ἀπὸ παντὸς τοῦ σώματος τείνουσιν ἐς τὸ αἰδοῖον, οἷσιν ὑποτριβομένοισι καὶ θερμαινομένοισι καὶ πληρευμένοισιν ὥσπερ κνησμὸς ἐμπίπτει καὶ τῷ σώματι παντὶ ἡδονὴ καὶ θέρμη ἐκ τούτου παραγίνεται· τριβομένου δὲ τοῦ αἰδοίου καὶ τοῦ ἀνθρώπου κινευμένου, τὸ ὑγρὸν θερμαίνεται ἐν τῷ σώματι καὶ διαχέεται καὶ κλονέεται ὑπὸ τῆς κινήσιος καὶ ἀφρέει, καθάπερ καὶ τἆλλα ὑγρὰ ξύμπαντα κλονεύμενα ἀφρέει.

Vessels and cords from the whole body lead to the penis, and these, as they are gently rubbed, warmed, and filled, are befallen by a kind of tickling sensation, and from this pleasure and warmth arise in the whole body. As the penis is rubbed and the man moves, the moisture in his body is warmed, turns to liquid, is agitated by his movement, and foams up, just as all other liquids foam when they are agitated.[22]

---

20 Aphrodite, the goddess of desire and sex, derives her name from "foam": περὶ δὲ Ἀφροδίτης οὐκ ἄξιον Ἡσιόδῳ [*Theogony* 196] ἀντιλέγειν, ἀλλὰ ξυγχωρεῖν ὅτι διὰ τὴν ἐκ τοῦ ἀφροῦ γένεσιν Ἀφροδίτη ἐκλήθη (Plato, *Cratylus* 406c). On the link between semen, air and foam, see [Arist.] *Problemata Physica* 953b–954a: "And wine, with respect to its power, contains breath (καὶ ὁ οἶνος δὲ πνευματώδης τὴν δύναμιν) ... And the foam shows that the wine contains breath (δηλοῖ δὲ ὅτι πνευματώδης ὁ οἶνός ἐστιν ὁ ἀφρός)... For this reason wine works as an aphrodisiac, and Dionysus and Aphrodite are correctly said to be with each other (καὶ διὰ τοῦτο ὅ τε οἶνος <u>ἀφροδισιαστικοὺς</u> ἀπεργάζεται, καὶ ὀρθῶς Διόνυσος καὶ <u>Ἀφροδίτη</u> λέγονται μετ' ἀλλήλων εἶναι)... For sexual excitement involves the presence of breath. A sign of this is the penis, in that its expansion is produced quickly from a small size, owing to being inflated. Even before seed is able to be emitted, a certain pleasure occurs in the case of children, when they are near puberty, in rubbing their private parts owing to licentiousness; this becomes clear because of the breath passing through the channels through which the moisture later travels. The outflow of the seed in intercourse and its ejection is obviously due to pushing by the breath" (translation in Mayhew 2011, 283). Cf. Laqueur 1987, 5–7.

21 *De flatibus* 14 (6.110–114 L.).

22 Translation in Potter 2021, 7.

What we should keep from this description is the author's emphasis on intense motion (τοῦ ἀνθρώπου κινευμένου), the warming up of the body (θέρμη) and the final production of foam out of the "moisture" (τὸ ὑγρόν) that resides within. What the author identifies as the "seed" (ἡ γονή) is essentially the fattest and most powerful part of this "foaming moisture" (τοῦ ὑγροῦ ἀφρέοντος τὸ ἰσχυρότατον καὶ τὸ πιότατον) which, once it has been formed, finds its way to the spinal marrow, moves to the kidneys and, through them, reaches the testicles; from the testicles it arrives to the penis, "not running where the urine does, but contained in another passage which exists for it".[23]

It transpires then that people engaged in passionate intercourse subject themselves and their bodies to the same kind of strenuous physical discomfort that an epileptic undergoes during seizure; sex, of course, involves a great deal of pleasure (ἡδονή) — and this makes for an important difference —, however we should not lose sight of the fact that the body is seen in both occasions as behaving and reacting in similar ways: it could even be said that what is principally at stake for both a person who is having sex and an epileptic who is struggling (but failing) to keep themselves controlled is the shared idea that some kind of white, foamy substance will ultimately come out of the body.

But can we really say that foam coming out from an epileptic's *mouth* could have triggered any kind of sexual associations? To answer this, it is important to bear in mind that in Hippocratic medicine the mouth is a sexually loaded part of the body in ways that are not too obvious to us (and which seem to extend far and beyond the mouth's involvement in oral sex). The case here can be better made with reference to the female body[24] for which historians of medicine observe that, according to Hippocratic physicians, there is a passageway connecting directly the aperture of the upper mouth with that of the vagina (it is helpful to be reminded at this point that when the author of *De virginum morbis* is observing that the vagina should be "opened" / "extended" so that menstrual blood flows out freely, he speaks of τὸ στόμα τῆς ἐξόδου, "the mouth of the exit").[25] So, for instance, when a doctor advises that, in order to confirm if a woman will conceive or not, a clove of garlic should be applied into the uterus through a pessary, and the next day it should be checked if the smell of garlic is exhaled from the mouth (*De mulieribus sterilibus* 214, 8.414 L.), he is obviously relying on the assumption

---

23 For this passage, see Laqueur 1990, 35.

24 The best discussion available for women's bodies in classical Greek science is that by Dean-Jones 1994. For a recent discussion of the "Hippocratic body", see Holmes 2018.

25 For the phrase τὸ στόμα τοῦ αἰδοίου, see [Hipp.] *Epidemiae* 2.4.5, *De mulierum affectibus* 1.40, 1.145.

that the mouth and the vagina are intimately connected through some kind of tube that has to remain ideally unblocked.[26] I am not suggesting here that foam being squeezed out of an epileptic's mouth would have been instantly (or necessarily) approximated to other foamy excretions exiting from the body's lower parts (although such possibility should not be excluded either). Be that as it may, when we are discussing the "ancient Greek body", it is crucial to leave some space open for the hypothesis that there may have been erogenous zones and associations which escape our current notions of the modern body's sexual configurations — there may have been, in other words, different kinds of conceptualisation as to what constitutes sexual imagery, and what not. Nancy Worman has brilliantly demonstrated how, in classical Athens, a great deal of (comic) discourse focusing on homosexual appetite revolves precisely around the intrinsic connection between the (male) body's upper and lower orifices: much of this discourse "collapses [the body] on its holes, forging patterns of succinct metonymies that ... most commonly calibrate mouth and anus".[27] The (sensual) association between "up" and "down" need not be part only of comic exaggeration, neither does it exclusively concern homosexual encounters. As we read in [Arist.] HA 10.635b19-24, during intercourse with a man, a woman "becomes moist" (ὑγραίνεσθαι) in her sensitive area; there is some kind of "sweating" down there (ἵδρωμα τοῦ τόπου), "as the mouth is with saliva when we are about to eat" (ὥσπερ καὶ τῷ στόματι σιάλου πολλαχοῦ μὲν καὶ πρὸς τὴν φορὰν τῶν σιτίων). The fact that preorgasmic lubricity is explained in this instance with direct reference to the mouth's salivary glands, triggered into action by the sight of food, is once again indicative of the intimate link between the upper and lower orifices, as well as of their corresponding, and ultimately uncontainable, fluids.

There is also another intriguing detail about the epileptic's body in *De morbo sacro*, and this has to do with the fact that some stuff is actually said to come out from the body's *lower* parts: ἐνίοισι δὲ καὶ ὑποχωρεῖ ἡ κόπρος κάτω (see the cited text above). The reference to excrement is revealing as regards the extent of the loss of control, which the patient is experiencing. Later medical texts delve more extensively on the types of (fluid) substances being involuntarily released from a body in seizure. In one of the most detailed nosological accounts of epilepsy that has survived from antiquity, Aretaeus of Cappadocia informs us that, when the fit is about to come to an end, the patient is discharg-

---

26 For some illuminating discussions of this intriguing passage, see von Staden 1989, 21; Hanson 1991, 86; Jouanna 2012, 5.
27 Worman 2008, 320.

ing urine (οὖρα αὐτόματα), stools (κοιλίης περίπλυσις) *and, in some cases, semen* (μετεξετέροισι δὲ καὶ γονῆς ἀπόκρισις): the latter is explained by the fact that too much "pressure" is being exerted on the vessels where the seminal fluid is stored (τῇ θλίψει καὶ πιέσει τῶν ἀγγείων) or, alternatively, it is attributed to the "tickling sensation" which is produced by the pain, and to the attendant accumulation of excessive "moisture" (γαργαλισμῷ τοῦ πόνου καὶ ὑγρασίης προκλήσει).[28] Galen concurs with this view: in violent attacks of epilepsy, he writes, semen is expelled because the whole body and with it the generative parts are strongly convulsed.[29] Now, the presence of semen — and, along with it, any *clear* suggestion that the disease resembles the sexual act — is not spelled out in the Hippocratic *De morbo sacro*. However, I am tempted to think that, by drawing our attention to the "messy" fluids which are discharged from the epileptic body's lower orifice, the author could be engaging us in thinking towards this direction.

An intimate connection between excrement and semen, though not explicitly present in the Hippocratic Corpus, would not have been at all implausible for the mindset of classical Greek medical thought. Rich evidence is provided especially from the ps.-Aristotelian *Problems*: in *Pr.* 4.7, semen is implicitly linked to the messy stuff which comes out of the body when someone is vomiting or sneezing (all these biological processes, according to the author, require that a person has entered before a "turgid state" (ὀργῶντα).[30] In *Pr.* 4.13, we encounter the surprising (one could even say, disturbing) suggestion that semen and excrement are alike on account of the fact that "life" is created through both of them (why is it — the author asks in this instance — that what is born from our seed we tend to call it our "offspring", ἔκγονον, whereas all those things which emerge from other bodily excretions we treat them as being "foreign" to us (οὐχ ἡμέτερον)? "For many things come to be from what is putrefying as well as from seed", γίνεται γὰρ σηπομένων πολλὰ καὶ ἐκ τοῦ σπέρματος).[31] In another *Problem* (4.26) — this one famous for attempting to provide the first "scientific" explanation of homosexuality in antiquity — we read that the reason why some people desire to be anally penetrated is that their semen, instead of being "naturally" secreted into

---

28 *De causis et signis acutorum morborum* 1.5.6.

29 *De locis affectis* 8.440–41 K.

30 877a35–36: Διὰ τί οὐ δεῖ μὴ ὀργῶντα οὔτε ἀφροδισιάζειν οὔτ' ἐμεῖν οὔτε πτάρνυσθαι οὔτε φῦσαν ἀφιέναι; As Mayhew (2011, *ad loc.*) explains in his note on the text: "The verb translated "is in a turgid state" (ὀργῶντα) can also mean "swells with moisture" and "is excited." In the *History of Animals*, ὀργάω is used to refer to the sexual excitement of both males and females (542a32) and (more specifically) to the excitement of mares and cows in heat (572b1–7, 573a6)".

31 878a2–5.

the testicles and penis, ends up flowing into the anus.[32] A quick look at this evidence yields a messy picture, in the sense that some of these passages ultimately confound the boundaries between precious reproductive matter, on the one hand, and human waste, on the other. There is a feeling here that dirtiness and "impurity" are not categorically (and tidily) fixed to specific substances of the body, but transpire instead to fuse with, and effectively be part of the body's essence as a whole: such impurity seems to be fully disclosed when the human body is engaged in sexual intercourse.[33] What I suggest then is that while semen is not mentioned explicitly in connection with epilepsy in our Hippocratic text (as is in later medical writers such as Aretaeus and Galen), the author's reference to κόπρος directs the reader's attention to the lower parts of the human body, and to an area where the boundaries between the "clean" and the "unclean", between the discharge of dirty matter and the ejection of reproductive fluids become profoundly confounded.[34]

Before I conclude this section, one final comment is due, which relates to the exceptional emphasis placed by *De morbo sacro* on the feeling of *shame* caused by epilepsy. In a well-known passage coming from ch. 12 of the treatise, the author observes that people who become accustomed with lapsing into regular fits of epilepsy (6.382–384 L.),

> have a presentiment when an attack is imminent, and run away from men, to home, if their house be near, if not, to the most deserted spot, where the fewest people will see the fall (ὅπη μέλλουσιν αὐτὸν ἐλάχιστοι ὄψεσθαι πεσόντα), and immediately hide their heads. This is the result of shame at their malady (ὑπ' αἰσχύνης τοῦ πάθεος), and not, as the many hold, of fear of the divine. Young children at first fall anywhere, because they are unfamiliar with the disease; but when they have suffered several attacks, on having the presentiment they run to their mothers or to somebody they know very well, through fear and terror at what they are suffering, since they do not yet know what shame is (τὸ γὰρ αἰσχύνεσθαι οὔπω γινώσκουσιν).[35]

---

32 See the discussion in Dover 1978, 168–170.

33 Substantial work has been done on the notions of "dirt" and the "impure" when it comes to desire and sex in antiquity, especially in connection with women (Carson 1990), whose bodies ancient Greek science tends to treat as being by nature "unclean"; von Staden 1992. The author(s) of Book IV of the ps.-Aristotelian *Problems* seems to adopt a more balance viewpoint: the essential connection between sex and dirt applies both to women and men indiscriminately.

34 For a joke played on the basis of a close association between urine and semen, see Aristophanes, *Frogs* 92–97 (a distinction is drawn in these lines between a "potent" / "reproductive" poet (γόνιμον δὲ ποιητήν) and those failed artists who, after taking a "singles piss against Tragedy" (ἅπαξ προσουρήσαντα τῇ τραγῳδίᾳ), have then been forgotten. The image in the latter case is one of impotence, with "urine" failing to serve as the prime generative matter of a solid creation.

35 Translation in Jones 1923, 171.

This is a wonderful early testimony on the social constructedness of the emotion of shame: little children, not knowing yet what "shame" is, feel "fear" (φόβος) and "terror" (δέος) instead, while they are seeking refuge to their mothers when they know that they are about to have yet another attack. For my purposes here, it should be noted that the passage above yields the clearest textual reference to αἰσχύνη — as a feeling caused by a disease — throughout the Hippocratic Corpus.[36] That αἰσχύνη should appear in this context is by no means surprising, considering the way epilepsy's symptoms have been described by the author — with the patient falling to the ground, rolling his eyes, twisting his arms and legs, foaming at the mouth, groaning and, overall, devolving into the state of an animal. What is striking, however, is that the Hippocratic Corpus discusses many other conditions which could in theory be considered as shame-inducing (think, for instance, of mania or phrenitis), but in none of them "shame" is discussed as being an issue (at least, it is not mentioned explicitly). On the basis of our evidence, it would consequently seem fair to say that, of all terrible diseases explored in early Greek medicine, epilepsy is singled out as the one which brings out, with exceptional force, a deep-seated anxiety about the sick body's *exposure* to the public gaze.[37] What I mean to say is that the idea of a patient's privacy — and the attendant notion that suffering should be contained and kept hidden from indiscreet eyes — is nowhere more insistently fleshed out in our early sources than in the case of epilepsy. I would suggest then that the clear implication of shame in this instance provides yet another potential line of connection between the epileptic's body and the body of a person who has sex: both situations involve a heightened awareness that the body, in the grip of an excruciating disease or operating in the demanding and strenuous context of sexual intercourse, requires a minimum degree of privacy.

---

36 For a detailed discussion of the passage, see Thumiger 2017, 356 and 359ff.

37 The Latin phrase which Macrobius uses for epilepsy, *morbus comitialis*, involves hints of the fear of such exposure. The reason why the illness is called "the comitial disease" is that epileptic seizures were considered bad omens necessitating the cancellation of *comitia*, "public meetings" (Isid. *Etym.* 4.7.7). That the epileptic patient could fall *in front* of so many people and cause the cancellation of the assembly is a scenario which we can easily imagine as being shameful precisely because the patient is *seen* by others.

2 Aretaeus of Cappadocia: Sex, epilepsy and the power of symbols

What is not spelled out by the Hippocratic *De morbo sacro* becomes manifest when we turn our attention to the writings of Aretaeus of Cappadocia (fl. 2nd cent. AD), our next extensive Greek source on epilepsy, which survives from antiquity. Brief reference was made above to Aretaeus' mention of semen as something that comes out of the body — along with urine and stools — when the seizure is reaching towards an end. This is not a random detail; when later on Aretaeus provides a list of the things that help alleviate the condition of an epileptic patient, and conversely a list of things that make their condition worse, sexual intercourse is mentioned explicitly. The relevant passage is worth quoting in full:[38]

> ... περίπατοι· ἐπὶ τοῖσι δὲ θυμηδίη ἄλυπος. ὀργὴ δὲ καὶ λαγνείη κακόν· **καὶ γὰρ τὸ πρῆγμα τῆς νούσου φέρει τὰ ξύμβολα**. ἀπάτη δέ τίς ἐστι μετεξετέροισι ἰητροῖσι ξυνουσίης. ἐπεὶ γὰρ ἡ τῆς φύσιος ἐς ἄνδρα μεταβολὴ ἀγαθόν τι πρήσσει, μετεβιάσαντο τὴν παίδων φύσιν ἀώρῳ ξυνουσίῃ, ὡς θᾶσσον ἀναρρώσοντες· ἀγνοέουσι δὲ τῆς φύσιος τὴν αὐτομάτην προθεσμίην, ἐφ' ᾗ πάντα γίγνεται τὰ ἄκεα. ἥδε γὰρ ἑκάστη ἡλικίῃ ξυντίκτει τὰ οἰκεῖα ἐν χρόνοισι ὡραίοισι· ἐν χρόνῳ γὰρ οἱ πεπασμοὶ σπέρματος, γενείου, πολιῆς. τίς ἂν ἰητρὸς παραλλάξαι <ἂν> τῆς φύσιος, τοῦτο μὲν τὴν ἀρχῆθεν τῶν σπερμάτων μεταβολήν, τοῦτο δὲ τὴν ἐς ἕκαστον προθεσμίην; ἀλλὰ καὶ προσέκοψαν ἐς τὴν φύσιν τοῦ νοσήματος. οὐκέτι γὰρ ἔγκαιροί τινες ἔασι τῇ ἀρχῇ τῆς ξυνουσίης, προσινόμενοι ἀωρίῃ τοῦ πρήγματος.

[It helps the patient to go out for] walks; after these, to recreate himself so that grief is dispelled. Anger is bad, as also is lustfulness; for the sex act itself bears the "symbols"/symptoms of the disease (epilepsy). Certain physicians have fallen into a mistake concerning intercourse; for seeing that the physical change to manhood produces a beneficial effect, they have done violence to the nature of children by [subjecting them to] unseasonable coition, as if thus to bring them sooner to manhood. Such persons are ignorant of the spontaneous law of nature by which all cures are accomplished; for along with every age she produces that which is proper for it in due seasons. At a given time there is the maturity of semen, of the beard, of hoary hairs; for on the one hand what physician could alter Nature's original change in regard to the semen, and, on the other, the appointed time for each? But they also offend against the nature of the disease; for being previously injured by the unseasonableness of the act, they are not possessed of seasonable powers at the proper commencement of the age for coition.[39]

---

38 *De curatione diuturnorum morborum* 1.4.14–15.
39 Translation in Adams 1856, 472–473 (with slight modifications at points).

This is a unique passage: on the one hand, we have the reference to the sexual act which is said to "bear the symbols of the disease" (τῆς νούσου φέρει τὰ ξύμβολα). The word ξύμβολον is used elsewhere by Aretaeus with the meaning of "symptom", as for instance when he is telling us that among the distinctive signs (τῆς νούσου τὰ ξύμβολα) of "vertigo" (σκοτοδινίη) one should count a sense of heaviness in the head, noises in the ears and flashes of light affecting the eyes.[40] But on a different level, ξύμβολον is used also for establishing a figurative association between something that is counted as the original or prototype and something which is conceived as a close imitation of that prototype. In introducing satyriasis, Aretaeus speaks of how the satyrs of Dionysus are depicted in art, in paintings and statues (ἐν τῇσι γραφῇσι καὶ τοῖσι ἀγάλμασι), with their penis erect — "a symbol of the divine thing" (ξύμβολον τοῦ θείου πρήγματος).[41] Verisimilitude in this case establishes a line of connection between the realm of the divine and its representation through art. In light of this usage of the word, we could say that when sex is associated by Aretaeus with epilepsy in a "symbolic sense", the meaning is twofold: taken literally, the medical author could be suggesting that too much sex is bad for an epileptic because it raises the risk of him having an actual seizure during intercourse. At the same time, the assimilation between sex and epilepsy is drawn on the basis of a figural association: if you picture someone having sex — Aretaeus seems to be implying — and if you forget for a moment that he is accompanied by a partner, what you see is a struggling body emitting incomprehensible sounds, ejecting fluids that cannot be contained, moving irregularly and, all in all, entering a symbolic space where the boundaries between pain and pleasure collapse.

Frequent sex is bad for an epileptic, and this leads Aretaeus to criticize those doctors who "prescribe" it, as though it were a good thing, for small children who have the condition on the misguided assumption that a transition to manhood would help them ward off the disease. This is all wrong, Aretaeus remarks: everything has its time, and sexual intercourse has no place whatsoever in the lives of children. What is more, forcing children to have sex and, thus, going against their nature (μετεβιάσαντο τὴν παίδων φύσιν) leaves them scarred physically and emotionally: Aretaeus observes in this context how, having been previously "injured" by the unseasonableness of the act, those children, when they get old enough to have sex, are not fully able to enter a normal sex life (... οὐκέτι γὰρ ἔγκαιροί τινες ἔασι τῇ ἀρχῇ τῆς ξυνουσίης, προσινόμενοι ἀωρίῃ τοῦ πρήγματος). The author's discussion of epilepsy thus yields a reference to what must have

---

40 *De curatione diuturnorum morborum* 1.3.7.
41 *De causis et signis acutorum morborum* 2.12.1.

been a crude practice among doctors during the first and second centuries AD. By doing so it brings to the fore the important issue of how certain models of "clinical treatment" meddled with people's sexuality and with their bodies in extremely violent ways. We can compare this with the Hippocratic writers' assumption that all a young female patient needs to overcome her medical problem is to have sex.[42] With epilepsy we are entering an even more sensitive area because a) the condition is affecting children and b) there is a medical belief that a (forced and untimely) transition to womanhood and manhood can be beneficial.[43] The doctors accused by Aretaeus of essentially ignoring the "nature" of their patients by prescribing "unseasonable sex" are not that different from the author of *De virginum morbis* who, as we have seen above, is adamant that young female patients who have not even started menstruating yet should have sex (and get married) in order to get rid of their epileptic seizures. What we witness here is an environment of "medical terrorism" — to borrow a phrase coined by Paola Manuli —[44] where age, subjectivity, sexual (im)maturity and emotional trauma are all gravely ignored for the sake of imposing an allegedly effective treatment for epilepsy.

But epilepsy, according to Aretaeus, is not only revealed to have a bearing on people's sex identity and lives; crucially, it is also about desire, in a way that is equally disruptive and disturbing. The author introduces the disease by calling it a "strange, evil thing", one that can take "various forms" (ποικίλον ἠδὲ ἀλλόκοτον κακὸν ἡ ἐπιληψίη).[45] Epilepsy can kill (ἔκτεινε γάρ κοτε παροξυσμὸς εἷς), but even when one survives its attacks, the shame s/he has to live with is unbearable (ζῆ μὲν αἴσχεα καὶ ὀνείδεα καὶ ἄλγεα φέρων). The reason for this, as Aretaeus explains, is that epilepsy usually makes its first appearance when someone is at his/her soft age, and at the height of their beauty (ἀλλὰ ἐν ἡλικίῃσί τε τῇσι κρείττοσι ἐνοικέει καὶ ὥρῃ γε τῇ ὡραίῃ, ξυνδιαιτᾶταί τε παισὶ καὶ μειρακίοισι). As the patient is growing older, the disease might leave him/her, "making an exit" just at the time when the "beauty" of adolescence departs as well (ἐξηλάθη δέ κοτε ὑπ' εὐτυχίης, δι' ἄλλης ἡλικίης μέζονος, εὖτε τῷ κάλλεϊ συνέξεισι τῆς ὥρης). This pointed coincidence makes it pretty clear that, for Aretaeus, the disease has the effect of making the patients less "desirable", as it were. The shame caused by it

---

42 For a comprehensive discussion, see Totelin 2007.
43 Cf. Celsus, *De medicina* 3.23.1: "And usually epilepsy persists even until the day of death without danger to life; nevertheless occasionally, whilst still recent, it is fatal to the man. And often if remedies have been ineffectual, in boys the commencement of puberty, in girls of menstruation, has removed it" (*Et saepe eum, si remedia non sustulerunt, in pueris veneris, in puellis menstruorum initium tollit*, transl. in Spencer 1935, 335).
44 Manuli 1980, 404.
45 *De causis et signis diuturnorum morborum* 1.4.

is not of the generic kind which the Hippocratic author has in mind when speaking of the αἰσχύνη τοῦ πάθεος,[46] but rather it is the feeling of shame which people experience when they think of themselves as ugly. That this is so is confirmed by what Aretaeus says next: sometimes, we are told, epilepsy leaves the patient scarred and repulsive, either because one of their hands has been paralyzed, or because there is some permanent distortion left on their face or because one of their senses has been compromised for ever; it is almost as if the disease is doing all this out of "envy" for their beauty (ἀλλὰ καί κοτε μετεξετέρους αἰσχροὺς ἀποδείξασα ἀπόλλυσι τοὺς παῖδας φθόνῳ τοῦ κάλλεος, ἢ χειρὸς ἀκρασίη, ἢ προσώπου διαστροφῇ, ἢ πηρώσει τινὸς αἰσθήσιος).[47] This is a remarkably striking personification, one that falls in line with Aretaeus' tendency to speak of epilepsy as something that acquires a life of its own and develops a "symbiotic" relationship with the patient till s/he dies: ἢν δὲ φωλεύσῃ τὸ κακὸν ἐς ῥίζαν, οὔτε ἰητρῷ οὔτε ἡλικίης μεταβολῇ <ἐς> ἔξοδον πείθεται, ἀλλὰ ξυμβιοῖ μέσφι θανάτου. It is not uncommon for medical or literary writers in antiquity to conceive of a disease as an animate entity that takes residence and feeds on the patient's body;[48] in line with this tradition, Aretaeus explores the idea of disease *qua* lived experience to an (almost oxymorous) extreme: epilepsy literally lives "side by side" (ξυμβιοῖ) with the patient, and ceases to "exist" only when death takes them both (μέσφι θανάτου).[49]

But while deriving its life from the patient, epilepsy is nonetheless envious of him/her, and particularly of the way s/he "looks" (almost as if it were a jealous deity punishing a mortal out of sheer malice), thus creating a disgusting spectacle out of him. Aretaeus returns to the notion of the patient's shame in his section on the therapy of the disease:[50]

Θεραπεία ἐπιληψίης. Ἀκέων ὅτι περ μέγα καὶ δυνατώτατον ἐς ἐπιληψίην χρέεσθαι· φυγὴ γὰρ <οὐ> μοῦνον ἐπιπόνου πάθεος καὶ κινδυνώδεος ἐφ' ἑκάστης ὑπομνήσιος, ἀλλὰ καὶ ἰδέης αἴσχεος καὶ ὀνείδεος τῆς ξυμφορῆς. καί μοι δοκέω, εἴπερ ἐς ἀλλήλους ἐν τοῖσι παροξυσμοῖσι ἐνέβλεπον, ὁκόσα πάσχουσι οἱ νοσεῦντες, οὐκ ἂν ἔτι ζώειν τλαῖεν ἄν. ἀλλὰ γὰρ τὰ δεινὰ ἑκάστῳ καὶ τὰ αἰσχρὰ ἀναισθησίῃ καὶ ἀθεησίῃ κρύπτει.

---

46 See p. 11 above.

47 On shame and disability in the ancient world (with emphasis on the Roman world), see Laes 2018, 62, 69, 116, 164, 181, 183–184. See Gleason 2020 on shame and Aretaeus.

48 See Thumiger 2019, 101 (on Philoctetes' disease in Sophocles' homonymous tragedy).

49 Cf. *De curatione acutorum morborum* 1.5.1: ἡ δὲ νοῦσος ἀπρὶξ ἐμφῦσα ἔχηται, οὐ χρονίη μοῦνον γίγνεται, ἀλλὰ μετεξετέροισι αἰωνίη. ἢν γὰρ ὑπερβάλλῃ τὴν ἀκμὴν τῆς ἡλικίης, ξυγγηρᾷ τε καὶ ξυναποθνήσκει.

50 *De curatione diuturnorum morborum* 1.4.1.

Cure of epilepsy: Of remedies, whatever is great and most powerful is needed for epilepsy, so as to find an escape not only from a painful affection, and one dangerous at each attack, but from the disgust and opprobrium of this calamity. For it appears to me, that if the patients who endure such sufferings were to look at one another in the paroxysms, they would no longer submit to live. But the want of sensibility and seeing conceals from everyone what is dreadful and disgusting in his own case.[51]

This time it is not just about how an epileptic looks to others; Aretaeus moves a step further by imagining what an epileptic's reaction would be, were he able to observe himself while s/he is having a fit: life would become unbearable (οὐκ ἂν ἔτι ζώειν τλαῖεν ἄν). The passage above lingers on the notion of vision:[52] on the one hand, we — as readers — are invited to visualize the sheer brutality and animalisation of a patient in the grip of a seizure; on the other hand, the patient is said to be mercifully unable to watch themselves (ἀθεησίη) because their senses are failing them and keeps the whole thing hidden from them (τὰ δεινὰ ἑκάστῳ καὶ τὰ αἰσχρὰ ἀναισθησίη ... κρύπτει).

3 Conclusion

In the present chapter, I started with Macrobius' testimony according to which "Hippocrates" is reported to have said that "intercourse is a small (epileptic) seizure" (τὴν συνουσίαν εἶναι μικρὰν ἐπιληψίαν). As I have discussed, no such statement survives anywhere in the Hippocratic Corpus, however there are indications (especially in De morbo sacro) that could be pointing in the direction of a possible conceptual blending between epilepsy and sex. As it is, these hints are fully fleshed out in the work of Aretaeus of Cappadocia who explicitly claims that sexual intercourse "bears the symbols" of the disease. But while an epileptic fit for Aretaeus looks disconcertingly similar to a body that is having sex, the long term effects of the condition make that same body less and less desirable, repulsive even. There is an interesting dialectic here between erotic desire and sex: we can think of how desire can be sublimated into a pure, romantic thing that has little to do with the body and is more about a person's feelings and thoughts; and we can then think of how sexual intercourse has a deflating effect by substituting, as it were, that desire with a crudely embodied experience which manifests itself with bites and screams, spasms and fluids. I would be tempted to suggest that

---

51 Translation in Adams 1856, 467–468.
52 On visuality and disease in Aretaeus' medical writings, see Gleason 2020.

Aretaeus' discussion of epilepsy points in the direction of such a contrast: while the epileptic body is the closest we get (in a pathological context) to a body that is having sex, when it comes to its potential to instill desire, it is the least attractive and most repulsive thing one could imagine.

Bibliography

Adams, F. (1856), *The Extant Works of Aretaeus, the Cappadocian*, London.
Cairns, D. (2013), 'The Imagery of *Erôs* in Plato's *Phaedrus*', in: E. Sanders/C. Thumiger/C. Carey/N. Lowe (eds.), *Erōs in Ancient Greece*, Oxford, 233–250.
Calame, C. (1992), *The Poetics of Eros in Ancient Greece* (transl. by J. Lloyd), Princeton.
Carson, A. (1990), 'Putting Her in Her Place: Woman, Dirt and Desire', in: D.M. Halperin/J.J. Winkler/F. Zeitlin (eds.), *Before Sexuality: The Construction of Erotic Experience in the Ancient Greek World,* Princeton, 135–170.
Connell, S. (2016), *Aristotle on Female Animals: A Study of the Generation of Animals*, Cambridge.
Dean-Jones, L. (1992), 'The Politics of Pleasure: Female Sexual Appetite in the Hippocratic Corpus', in: *Helios* 19, 72–91.
Dean-Jones, L. (1994), *Women's Bodies in Classical Greek Science*, Oxford.
Dover, K.J. (1978), *Greek Homosexuality*, Cambridge, MA.
Flemming, R. (2019), '(The Wrong Kind of) Gonorrhea in Antiquity', in: S. Szreter (ed.), *The Hidden Affliction: Sexually Transmitted Infections and Infertility in History*, Rochester, 43–67.
Flemming, R./Hanson, A.E. (1998), 'Hippocrates' *Peri Parthenión ("Diseases of Young Girls")*: Text and Translation', in: *Early Science and Medicine* 3, 241–252.
Gleason, M. (2020), 'Aretaeus and the *Ekphrasis* of Agony', in: *Classical Antiquity* 39, 153–187.
Hanson, A.E. (1990), 'The Medical Writer's Woman', in: D.M. Halperin et al. (eds.), *Before Sexuality: The Construction of Erotic Experience in the Ancient Greek World*, Princeton, 309–338.
Hanson, A.E. (1991), 'Continuity and Change: Three Case Studies in Hippocratic Gynecological Therapy and Theory', in: S.B. Pomeroy (ed.), *Women's History and Ancient History*, Chapel Hill/London, 73–110.
Holmes, B. (2018), 'The Hippocratic Body', in: P.E. Pormann (ed.), *The Cambridge Companion to Hippocrates*, Cambridge, 63–88.
Jones, W.H.S. (1923), *Hippocrates. Vol. II*, Cambridge, MA.
Jouanna, J. (2012), *Greek Medicine from Hippocrates to Galen. Selected Papers* (transl. N. Allies), Brill.
Kaster, R.A. (2011), *Macrobius: Saturnalia 1-2*, Cambridge, MA.
Laes, C. (2018), *Disabilities and the Disabled in the Roman World: A Social and Cultural History*, Cambridge.
Laqueur, T. (1987), 'Orgasm, Generation, and the Politics of Reproductive Biology', in: C. Gallagher/T. Laqueur (eds.), *The Making of the Modern Body: Sexuality and Society in Nineteenth Century*, Berkeley/London, 1–41.
Laqueur, T. (1990), *Making Sex: Body and Gender from the Greeks to Freud*, Cambridge, MA.

Lami, A. (2007), '[Ippocrate], *Sui disturbi virginali*: testo, traduzione e commento', in: *Galenos* 1, 15–59.

Lonie, I.M. (1981), *The Hippocratic Treatises On Generation, On the Nature of the Child, Diseases IV*, Berlin/New York.

Manuli, P. (1980), 'Fisiologia e Patologia del Femminile Negli Scritti Ippocratici dell'antica Ginecologia Greca', in: M.D. Grmek (ed.), *Hippocratica: Actes du Colloque Hippocratique de Paris, 4–9 septembre 1978*, Paris, 393–408.

Mayhew, R. (2011), *Aristotle. Problems, Vol. II*, Cambridge, MA.

Michalopoulos, C. (2012), 'Tiresias between Texts and Sex', in: *EuGeStA* 2, 221–239.

Potter, P. (1988), *Hippocrates. Vol. V*, Cambridge, MA.

Potter, P. (2012), *Hippocrates. Vol. X*, Cambridge, MA.

Sissa, G. (1990), 'Maidenhood without Maidenhead: The Female Body in Ancient Greece', in: D.M. Halperin/J.J. Winkler/F.I. Zeitlin (eds.), *Before Sexuality: The Construction of Erotic Experience in the Ancient Greek World*, Princeton, 339–364.

Sissa, G. (2013), 'The Hymen is a Problem, still. Virginity, Imperforation, and Contraception, from Greece to Rome', in: *EuGeStA* 3, 67–123.

Spencer, W.G. (1935), *Celsus, On Medicine, Vol. I*, Cambridge, MA.

Thumiger, C. (2013), 'Mad *Erōs* and Eroticized Madness in Tragedy', in: E. Sanders/C. Thumiger/C. Carey/N. Lowe (eds.), *Erōs in Ancient Greece*, Oxford, 27–40.

Thumiger, C. (2017), *A History of the Mind and Mental Health in Classical Greek Medical Thought,* Cambridge.

Thumiger, C. (2019), 'Animality, Illness and Dehumanization: The Phenomenology of Illness in Sophocles' Philoctetes', in: G.M. Chesi /F. Spiegel (eds.), *Classical Literature and Posthumanism*, London, 95–102.

Totelin, L.M.V. (2007), 'Sex and Vegetables in the Hippocratic Gynaecological Treatises', in: *Studies in History and Philosophy of Biological and Biomedical Sciences* 38, 531–540.

Van der Eijk, P.J. (2005), *Medicine and Philosophy in Classical Antiquity: Doctors and Philosophers on Nature, Soul, Health and Disease*, Cambridge.

Von Staden, H. (1989), *Herophilus: The Art of Medicine in Early Alexandria*, Cambridge.

Von Staden, H. (1992), 'Women and Dirt', in: *Helios* 19, 7–30.

Wilberding, J. (2016), 'Embryology', in: G.L. Irby (ed.), *A Companion to Science, Technology, and Medicine in Ancient Greece and Rome*, Vol. I, Oxford/New York, 329–342.

Worman, N. (2008), *Abusive Mouths in Classical Athens*, Cambridge.

Part III: **The Use and Abuse of Sex Objects**

Bartłomiej Bednarek
Some Dirty Thoughts about Chairs and Stools: Iconography of Erotic Foreplay

Abstract: In this chapter, Bednarek discusses the iconographic motif of chairs and stools depicted on Attic vases in the context of dressing, undressing, courtship and outwardly erotic scenes. This piece of visual vocabulary to a certain degree reflects the common practice of depositing clothes on seats in a variety of everyday life situations. As an iconographic motif, it became conventional to such a degree that a depiction of a stool or chair in the context of an otherwise seemingly innocent conversation could arguably direct viewers' thoughts towards the idea of undressing, and thus add an erotic dimension to several images.

1 Undressing scenes in literature

This chapter offers a glimpse of the pleasure of undressing female and male lovers alluded to in several Greek vase paintings. As I argue, this allusion was often activated by the iconographic motif of a stool or a chair with clothes on it. Although it is much less conspicuous in literature than in the visual arts, two of its occurrences in extant texts provide a convenient point of departure. Most prominently, this motif appears in the *Homeric Hymn to Aphrodite*, in which Anchises puts his lover's garments and jewellery on "a silver rivetted chair":

> … he [Anchises] took her hand, and smile-loving Aphrodite, casting her lovely eyes down, turned and moved to the well-bedecked bed, where the lord kept it spread with soft blankets, on top of which lay skins of bears and roaring lions that he himself had killed in the high mountains. When they had mounted the sturdy bed, he first removed the shining adornment from her body, the pins and twisted bracelets and ear buds and necklaces; he undid her girdle, and divested her of her gleaming garments and laid them on a silver-riveted chair (ἐπὶ θρόνου ἀργυροήλου). And then Anchises by divine will and destiny lay with the immortal goddess, the mortal, not knowing the truth. At the hour when herdsmen turn

The research presented in this chapter was possible thanks to the generous support of the National Centre of Science in Poland, grant number 2018/31/D/HS3/00128.

https://doi.org/10.1515/9783110695793-009

their cattle and fat sheep back to the steading from the flowery pastures, then she poured a sweet, peaceful sleep upon Anchises, while she dressed herself in her fine garments.[1]

Like in the movies from the 1950s,[2] in which the erotic foreplay is immediately followed by the scene in which the couple smoke in bed, the fifth *Homeric Hymn to Aphrodite* elides the most climactic part of the sexual encounter. This may be quite frustrating if we are interested in reconstructing technical details of the sexual act itself. It is worth emphasising, however, that in this passage, foreplay is described in a way that could have been more stimulating for the ancient Greek imagination than it appears at first glance. It can thus reveal something important about the way in which Greeks experienced and intentionally elicited sexual desire.

The passage does not contain a description of the two, presumably, attractive bodies of the couple, which is not unusual, given that in the archaic Greek poetry men and women are often characterised as beautiful but never described in detail. What the poet offers instead is a brief mention of the animal skins that covered Anchises' bed. They evoke his achievements as a hunter, thus contributing to his characterisation as a brave man. Subsequently the focus shifts towards Aphrodite's undressing, which picks up the motif of her dressing in Cyprus, described in lines 58–67, which, in turn, alludes to the famous scene of the goddess' toilette in the *Cypria* (fr. 4 Bernabé). None of the items she is putting on or taking off in these texts has much practical value. Instead, they are all shiny, glimmering and elaborate. This has to do with a well-recognised feature of the ancient Greek world view: whereas a man's beauty is internal and related to the physical and moral valour (thus, Anchises is characterised as a brave hunter), the female attraction is superficial and results not that much from what a woman actually is but what she puts on. In the *Homeric Hymn*, the poet makes his audience enjoy Aphrodite's charm together with Anchises, who takes each piece of her clothes and jewellery in his hands as if in order to appreciate their quality.

---

1 *HH* 5.155–171; West's translation.
2 I owe this observation to Marek Węcowski. This convention has been parodied e.g. in the *Young Frankenstein*.

The use of the chair in the passage has never attracted much scholarly attention. This is not surprising, given that many readers today take the habit of putting clothes on chairs and stools for granted.[3] Ancient Greeks were equally familiar with this habit, as can be deduced from the references to it in Homer[4] as well as from the famous passage in Herodotus (1.9), in which Candaules instructs Gyges how to peep on his own (Candaules') wife:

> I'll get you to stand behind the open door of our bedroom [...] There's a chair (θρόνος) near the entrance to the room on which she'll lay her clothes one by one as she undresses, so that will make it very easy for you to watch her.[5]

This passage, although much more concise than the one in the *Homeric Hymn to Aphrodite*, seems to evoke the same focus on the experience of male pleasure while gazing at a woman in the process of undressing. We do not know whether the details of the furniture of the royal chamber in Lydia corresponded to its real setting or whether they were a matter of Herodotus' (or his informer's) invention. At any rate, given that in ancient Greece there were various types of furniture, such as chests, shelves and racks, designed specifically for keeping clothes in or on them, depositing garments on a seat was by no means the only possibility. However, Herodotus refers to it in matter-of-fact way, without the elaboration that would be needed unless he expected his audience to take it for granted.

This passage, along with equally laconic references in the *Homeric Hymn to Aphrodite* and in the *Odyssey*, may suggest that ancient Greek authors and their audiences considered putting clothes on seats as being such a natural act that they did not dwell or (probably) reflect on it. It is no surprise then that this cultural practice left relatively few traces in literature. That is why, it is all the more striking how often it is reflected in art. As I argue below, a stool or a chair became one of the conventional signs of undressing and sexual practices. As such, in some contexts, the connotations of an otherwise innocent seat can be similar to those of a bed or a close door, which in ancient vase paintings very often connote the erotic sphere (Fig. 14).

---

3 As far as I can tell, the only philologist who addresses the subject matter is Faulkner 2008, 165 in his commentary on the *Homeric Hymn* to Aphrodite, where he cites some parallel texts from Homer. Otherwise, the habit of putting clothes on chairs and stools seems to be taken for granted.
4 H. *Od*. 17.86; 17.179; 20.249.
5 Translated by Waterfield.

2 A stool as a marker of nakedness

Given that from the geometric period onwards, male figures are usually represented as being without clothing, it is a commonplace that their nudity does not reflect the social practice. Thus, looking at pictures of fighting warriors, men at banquets and religious ceremonies, we can see their naked bodies with all the anatomic details. This does not mean, however, that ancient Greeks would engage in any of these activities in exactly such a way in real life. The nudity of Greek men in art is a matter of convention, and it is reasonable to think that the ancient viewers were as perfectly aware of it as we are. This created a paradoxical situation. Given that nudity in art bore no reference to nakedness in real life, when a painter wanted to stress that the man he painted was actually naked, he could not achieve it by simply showing a body devoid of clothes. An additional indicator was needed to suggest that nudity was at play.

A possible solution to this problem results from a simple consideration that nudity can be thought of as a costume. One puts it on by virtue of taking off another costume, which consists of clothes.[6] Thus, in order to emphasise that a person is "positively nude", one can depict the clothes that are not worn at the moment. This is what the Painter of Boston seems to have done, already in the mid-sixth century BC, in his decoration of a Siana cup (BAPD 1060; Fig. 15) with a group of running athletes. Their bodies are not covered with clothes. A bundle of clothes, however, appears deposited on a stool under the handle of the vessel.[7] The presence of these garments not worn by the runners transforms their (otherwise) conventional nakedness into a markedly athletic nudity.[8] As far as I know, this is the oldest extant specimen of this kind.

A similar motif was adapted by numerous artists during the later period and became widespread by the beginning of the fifth century BC. A particularly fine

---

6 On nudity as a costume, see Bonfante 1989 and Lee 2015, especially 10–32. For the opposition between the *nude* and *naked*, see Clark 1956.

7 Admittedly, the field under vessel's handle does not necessarily belong to the image on the side of it and it is possible that there is no relationship between them. However, the later occurrences of clothes on stools strongly suggest that this juxtaposition was not a matter of coincidence.

8 The history of the "invention" and diffusion of athletic nudity is an intricate issue. For its discussion, see McDonnell 1991; Christesen 2002; 2007, 353–359; 2014, 227; Kyle 2007, 85–90. Most notoriously, Thucydides (1.6) refers to it as a recent development, however, it is not clear what he means by this. At any rate, it seems that when the Painter of Boston decorated his Siana cup, not everyone would take for granted that athletes exercised and competed naked. To a certain degree this may explain why he wanted to emphasise their nudity.

specimen, which allows us to understand how athletes might have used stools, is provided by the red-figure krater attributed by Beazley to Euphronios (BAPD 200063; Fig. 16). On side B of the vessel, there are four youths, two of whom are assisted by younger boys. One of the youths is infibulating, another is exercising with a disc, whereas a draped youth (trainer?) is making a gesture towards his penis. In this way, the most intimate part of the athlete's body becomes the focal point of the composition. Next to them, another youth is folding (or unfolding?) a piece of clothing. On the other side of the krater, there are some other youths,[9] two of whom are standing next to a stool with clothes on it. These clothes clearly belong to a naked athlete who is pouring oil on his palm from an aryballos, ready to anoint himself. The youth on the other side of the stool is holding his clothes on his forearm in a way that suggests that he has just undressed himself and now is folding his garment to put it on the stool and anoint himself as well. The vase is a fine example of a highly idealising depiction of male nudity underlined by an interplay between draped, partially and completely undressed bodies, and garments that have been deposited on a stool and those that are being deposited at the moment when we are seeing the scene. Although it does not contain any outward suggestions of sexual content (infibulation as a means of repression of sexuality might evoke it, but only in an indirect way),[10] there can be little doubt that it had erotic appeal.

It is worth emphasising that, due to its technological limitations and stylistic conventions, unlike photography, vase painting evokes its subject rather than representing it in a realistic way. If attractive bodies depicted on vases were considered sexy, it is because they made viewers think of sexy bodies they had seen in real life. Given that athletes were thought of as beautiful, a picture that conveyed the message "you are looking at an athlete" could also imply "you are looking at something beautiful". This is why markers of role and status of a person shown in a picture become particularly important and why pieces of athletic equipment contributed to the overall eroticism of these images. A stool with clothes on it (or, as we shall see, even one without clothes) could be taken as a sign that evoked the athletic context. Its emotional impact could have been particularly strong, given that it alluded to the thrilling moment in which, by taking his clothes off, a youth would shift from the role of a young citizen to that of an athlete.

---

9 All youths are inscribed with their names, which makes it legitimate to state that those on side A are different from those on side B.
10 On the infibultation, or, more precisely, *kynodesmē*, shown in art as worn not only by athletes, but also komasts, see Zanker 1995, 28–31; Hodges 2001, 381–384.

In the following section, I discuss some of the images that belong to a series of about 20 tondi of red-figure cups in order to illustrate the ways in which ancient painters explored the limits of pictorial language, implicitly inviting their customers to play a conscious and subtle intertextual game.[11] Each of these images contains a stool, sometimes used as a prop[12] by a person represented next to it; sometimes, however, it is added in a way that makes it stand out of the context, which underlines its semiotic function. Having thus illustrated how the motif was used in an athletic context, in the subsequent sections, we will turn to examine its use in images depicting sexual acts and their preliminaries. A systematic analysis of this motif reveals its contextual meaning, which, despite some intriguing nuances, turns out to be quite stable. This allows us to treat it as an item of the "iconographical vocabulary".

3 Athletes and their appetising seats

To begin with the already familiar, unmarked use of the motif,[13] a cup by Douris (BAPD 44039; Fig. 17a)[14] shows a naked athlete with halters in his hands, just about to jump. A stele helps to identify the place as a gymnasium. A sponge and an aryballos suspended behind the youth allude to the washing and anointment. There is also a stool with clothes on it,[15] which, at first glance, does not seem to

---

11 Apart from the tondi, there are some (equally numerous) similar images on the sides of drinking cups and other vessels almost exclusively related to the sympotic context.

12 I owe this point to Ariadne Konstantinou.

13 Following the structural linguistic tradition, I use the term "unmarked" in reference to a sign that is used in the most basic and conventional function, which is not supposed to attract the receiver's attention. By contrast, "marked" is the use of a sign that stands out of its context, attracting the receiver's attention and thus having the potential to become the real subject of the act of verbal or non-verbal communication. This happens when viewers, instead of contemplating the athlete, turn their attention towards a playful transformation of the stool motif, as discussed below.

14 For a similar scene, see BAPD 211461.

15 The identification of the object on which the cloak is deposited is difficult, because a fragment of the picture is missing. What is left may correspond to a leg of a stool, perhaps similar to those painted by Douris under handles of another cup with athletes (BAPD 205079). However, a tondo of a red-figure cup attributed to the Oedipus painter (BAPD 205375) and, according to Beazley 1963, 452, inspired by Douris, provides an alternative interpretation. Thus, according to the description in BAPD, the picture includes: "Athlete, jumping with halters, post, cloak on rock (?), sponge and aryballos suspended". If this is correct, it is possible that the stool was substituted with a block, whose role remains essentially the same.

play any role in the scene, given that the youth is shown at the moment of exercising rather than dressing or undressing. It is thus clear that the presence of garments is meant to be an emblem rather than a prop. It turns the nakedness of the youth into the marked nudity of an athlete and underlines the opposition between two different roles the young man can assume in two different spaces: the civic role characteristic of the world outside vs. that of the athlete he becomes inside the gymnasium.

A playful variation on the theme is provided by a cup attributed to the Byrgos Painter (BAPD 203991; Fig. 17b). It shows a stool with clothes on it. Next to it, there is a naked youth with a strigil in one hand making a gesture with another hand stretched above a cheerful dog. It seems that the youth is either playing with his pet or commanding it to wait for him, presumably outside of the space where the scene is taking place. The setting is further identified as that of a gymnasium by the presence of two javelins shown behind the youth.[16] These elements combined suggest that the young man has just finished his exercise and is washing off the dirt with the strigil. The garments on the stool allude to what is due to happen next — the youth is about to put his clothes on and leave the space reserved for the athletes, entering the world outside to which the dog belongs.

Several other variations on the theme are possible. For example, a cup attributed to the Antiphon Painter (BAPD 200420; Fig. 17c) contains a clear allusion to sport, as a pair of halters are shown suspended behind the naked youth with an aryballos in his hand. There is also a staff, which belongs to the costume worn outside the gymnasium. Finally, there is a stool as well, but there are no clothes on it. If analysed in separation from other images discussed here, the stool in this picture would seem meaningless. However, the parallels provided by other scenes of a similar kind suggest that the meaning of a stool, even when empty, seemed self-evident. A stool set in a context of a naked body of an athlete, juxtaposed with the element belonging to the world *inside* (such as halters or javelins) and that of the *outside* (such as a staff, clothes, or, perhaps, a dog) becomes a marker of a transitional space and time in which a young man switches between two social roles. One of the crucial elements of this transition is constituted by dressing and undressing, which the stool implicitly evokes, even when empty.

As if to allay all doubts regarding the meaning of the stool in this context, there are images that show the other stages of the process of transformation from a "citizen youth" into an athlete and back again. For example, a cup attributed

---

16 It is tempting to think that the dog bears an allusion to the name of the Athenian gymnasium of Kynosarges. On potentially erotic connotations of dogs in gymnasium scenes, see Haworth 2018.

by Beazley to a follower of Douris (BAPD 209929; Fig. 17d) shows a naked youth with a strigil in one hand and a garment hanging from his forearm. A pair of halters is suspended behind him, and an empty stool is in front of him. Another cup attributed to the Triptolemos Painter (BAPD 203883; Fig. 17e) has in its tondo a fully draped youth with a staff in his hand. Next to him, there is an empty stool as well as an aryballos and a strigil suspended. This suggests that the young man has just put his clothes on or is about to undress.

This series of images presents the motif of a stool with clothes on it or without clothes, which in the athletic context can be evocative of the process of dressing and undressing. To put it simply, there are stools with clothes next to naked bodies that underline their nudity. There are also empty stools next to dressed bodies that may evoke the idea of undressing. This item of the "iconographic vocabulary" was often used in a playful way in those scenes that depicted or alluded to sex.

4 Dirty chairs and stools

Turning to something very distant from the subtle eroticism of athletic scenes, clothes on stools are also present in some pictures that explicitly show sexual activity. To begin with the most exceptional specimens, there are only two images that show the use of a stool as a piece of erotic furniture in the narrow sense of this term. Particularly intriguing is a cup by a Little Master (BAPD 350489; Fig. 18) with two men, one of whom bends his buttocks towards the other, while supporting his hands on a stool. The other is hanging or swinging on a pair of straps that are hanging from above. His buttocks touch the buttocks of the man below him, but it is hard to imagine how a genital contact could be achieved in such an awkward position. It is thus clear that the image does not actually show a sexual act. Nevertheless, there can be little doubt regarding the erotic character of the game it depicts.

The other picture with a stool used as a piece of sexual furniture is the famous *hesche hesychos* tondo of a cup attributed to Douris (BAPD 205288; Fig. 19), with a heterosexual couple making love *modo pecudum*. The woman supports her hands on a stool, just like the passive male partner on the previously discussed cup by the Little Master. This time, however, there can be no doubt as to the fact that she is being penetrated by her male partner, perhaps anally, as Kilmer contends.[17] There is also a couch behind the couple, which adds some balance to the composition. Its role, however, does not seem to be purely aesthetic, as it contributes to the characterisation of the space as an interior of a bedroom or a dining hall. It also serves as a playful comment on the rather idiosyncratic taste of the couple, who chose to make love next to the couch rather than on it. The clothes deposited on the stool make us appreciate that the two bodies are completely naked. It can also suggest that one of the partners, or perhaps both, arrived from outside.

A similar narration is evoked by the tondo of a cup attributed by Beazley to the Triptolemos Painter (BAPD 203886; Fig. 20a). It shows a bald man in the act of making love to a young woman. Both are completely naked, if not for a wreath worn by the man. Next to the couch on which the couple is having sex, there is a stool with some textiles on it.[18] Another piece of clothing is hanging from a wall. The artist emphasised that these two garments are different from one another, as the one deposited on the stool has larger folds, which suggests that it is thicker than the other. The hanging piece of textile also has a narrower stripe, which runs further from its rim than in the case of the cloth on the stool. A comparison with other images by the Triptolemos Painter suggests that this may indicate the opposition between an inner and outer piece of clothing respectively.

Given that, as is often underlined,[19] ancient pictures are not just snapshots of reality, it is clear that these items were put in the frame for some reason and not because they simply happened to be in the room where the couple had sex. This situates the clothes that are shown as not being worn at the same level as the bald head of the man and the wreath he is wearing. All of these elements contribute to the meaning of the picture, which seems to evoke a certain situation recognisable to the ancient viewer. Thus, the wreath implies a symposium, however the lack of tableware may suggest that it is already over. The image clearly shows one of the symposiasts, who, certainly under the influence of alcohol,[20] is making love

---

17 Kilmer 1993, 83–84.

18 Unlike in the two images discussed above, this stool is not used for purposes directly related to a sexual act; therefore, it cannot be called a piece of erotic furniture in the narrow sense of this term.

19 See e.g. Green 1994, 23–26.

20 As Dimitrios Kanellakis observed during the conference at the University of Cyprus that allows the idea of this volume to germinate and grow, the clothes suspended behind the man seem to bear an allusion to a satyr's tail. His boldness, his erotic arousal and sympotic connotations of the wreath also belong to the imagery of satyrs. All this suggests that the man is under influence of Dionysus.

with a woman. The difference of age between the two, which is emphasised by the man's baldness, may suggest that she is not his wife. It is a natural guess (although not the only possibility) that she is a prostitute.[21] The two articles of clothing, which clearly represent an inner and outer garment, may both belong to the same person, which suggests that at least one of the partners came from outside. Does it mean that the man is paying a visit to the woman in a brothel? There is no straightforward answer to this question, which does not mean that it is not legitimate to ask it. Indeed, the images on tableware were clearly designed to stimulate viewers' curiosity, as may be deduced from the comparison between this and another, no less well known tondo by the same Triptolemos Painter (BAPD 203885; Fig. 20b).

This image has a very similar composition to the one previously discussed. The couple is making love on a couch in virtually the same position. The man, however, does not wear a crown. The allusion to the sympotic context is nevertheless clear,[22] as the pillow, on which the woman supports her back, has been substituted with a wineskin. There is no stool with clothes on it, nor are there clothes hanging from the wall. Instead, there is a staff leaning against the couch, which is clearly supposed to evoke the same idea as the textiles in the other image — the man has arrived from outside. Thus, the situation alluded to in the two images is virtually the same. The signifiers, however, that contribute to the creation of the meaningful composition on one of the vessels have been substituted by what may be called their "synonyms" on the other cup: a wineskin for a wreath and a staff for clothes.

What is particularly striking is that both images have been always taken as a complementary pair. They have been produced by the same painter and both made their way to Tarquinia, where they are exposed one next to another in the National Archaeological Museum. One may imagine that the member of Etruscan elite who purchased these two cups and subsequently seems to have taken them

---

21 After the period in which almost all women on Greek vases were suspected to be prostitutes, unless there was a clear indicator of their status as goddesses, heroines or "respectable women" (Keuls 1985 is the most often quoted example of this tendency, but Wiliams 1983, 102–105 went even as far as to claim that all females represented at fountain houses must have been prostitutes, because citizen women were not allowed to leave home), a lot of work has been done in order to bring back the balance; see especially Cohen 2015. One of the most precious alterations is that scholars do not think it necessary to label figures on vases as representatives of particular social classes, unless something in the image invites us to do so. See Lewis 2002, 98–128.

22 Pace Lewis 2002, 121, who states that, in both pictures that are discussed here, there is no reference to the symposium.

to his grave must have appreciated their ludic potential.[23] When wine was served in them, the members of his drinking party could play games based on deciphering the meanings encoded in them.[24] They could compare one to another, thus appreciating the painter's wit. The more versatile in the iconographic language they were, the more entertaining such a play could be. This strongly suggests that we should not underestimate Etruscan symposiasts, not to mention Greek painters, who played with the iconography in a very conscious and purposeful way.

5 The courtship and erotic foreplay

The sexually explicit images discussed above allow for a better understanding of the role of a stool in the pictures that show the erotic foreplay rather than sexual intercourse. A perfect example is provided by the already mentioned cup attributed to Douris with a young woman embracing a youth (BAPD 205184; Fig. 14). The affectionate gazes they exchange charge this image with strong erotic tension and there is little doubt as to what is due to happen next thanks to the number of motifs that connote eroticism. There is a closed door behind the couple, which suggests that their intimacy will remain undisturbed. There is a couch and the youth is making a gesture towards it. This is where they will go once they put their clothes off. Quite conveniently, there is also an empty chair on which to deposit the garments. This image is quite exceptional, as it contains a whole catalogue of the motifs that evoke sexual intercourse without actually depicting it.

Less explicit, but still quite eloquent, are images depicting the erotic conquest. A good example is provided by a tondo of a cup attributed to the Painter of Penthesileia (BAPD 211654) with a youth who is just about to put his hand on a young woman's wrist (Fig. 21). This is enough to suggest that he may have erotic intentions.[25] However, as if in order to allay all doubts as to what is happening, the youth is holding a purse, which makes clear that he is willing to pay for the service. It also features an empty stool, which may seem completely innocent. Yet, in the context of the clear, even if not completely straightforward, erotic connotations of the image, it seems natural to conclude that the empty stool juxtaposed with dressed bodies, as in some of the pictures discussed above, was meant

---

23 On the context of finding the two cups, see Boardman, La Rocca 1975, 114; Kilmer 1993, 47.
24 I assume that the pottery found in Etruscan graves was very likely to have been previously used in other context, such as symposium.
25 On the meaning of this, admittedly, ambiguous gesture, see Belfiore 2000, 50–54 with further references.

to suggest that the couple is just about to undress. In this way, the stool does not change the overall meaning of the scene, but it adds some flavour to it by suggesting to the viewer the further development of the events.

On the homoerotic side, a particularly clear example is provided by a tondo of a cup by Douris (BAPD 9024930; Fig. 22), which seems to assemble the whole catalogue of iconographic motifs characteristic for the homoerotic courtship scenes. It features a bearded man in front of a youth. The youth is holding a hare, one of most conventional courtship gifts. There is an inscription *kalos*.[26] Behind the man, there is a folding stool and a set of athletic hygiene items (sponge, aryballos, strigil). This may suggest that they are in a "changing room" of a gymnasium. What is striking, however, is that the man is taking the liberty of touching the piece of boy's garment which covers his head, quite clearly, in order to remove it. Thus, it is not just a scene of a successful courtship, as could be deduced from the fact that it is the boy who holds the hare, which indicates that he accepted the gift. The man, by touching the boy's clothes, makes it clear that he is unwilling to postpone the gratification and the *erōmenos* does not seem to be displeased with it.

An interesting variation of this theme is provided by another Douris' tondo (205077; Fig. 23), in which a bearded man is stretching his hand with a small bag towards a person outside the decorated area of the vase, whose presence is presupposed by this gesture, but whose identity and appearance the viewer is clearly due to imagine himself. Behind the man, there is an empty stool and an athletic hygiene kit, hence, we may assume that the object of desire is male. This is a very similar situation to the one previously described. The main difference is that instead of a traditional courtship gift, the assumed *erōmenos* is receiving a much more ambiguous purse, which, unless it contains some other than money object (e.g. *astragaloi*), it may suggest a contractual character of the exchange taking place in the space of the "changing room".[27]

The role of the stool, however, is not limited to that of indicating the particular space but rather the activity of undressing that is associated with it. This can be deduced from the images that further modify the scheme fully represented in the previously discussed tondi. Thus, for example, a picture attributed to the Euaichme Painter (BAPD 209671; Fig. 24) shows a bearded man offering a rooster to a youth. It is thus one of most typical scenes of the old-fashioned elitist courtship. The *erōmenos* is draped and even his head is partially covered. Yet, an empty

---

26 On the interpretative problems related to these inscriptions, see Lear, Cantarella 2008, 164–173.

27 On the purses in courtship scenes, see Lewis 2002, 194–197; Lear, Cantarella 2008, 80–86.

stool behind the *erastēs* may be taken as an allusion to his erotic intentions and to the idea of undressing. Unlike in the previously discussed images, there are no items related to the athletics, which may suggest that the painter was not interested in characterising the space as that of a gymnasium.

Equally disinterested in the athletic connotations seems to have been a follower of Douris, who decorated the cup in Richmond (BAPD 205359). The tondo shows a man in conversation with a youth, which could seem completely innocent, if not for the string of letters that seems to flow from the man's mouth that indicate the erotic content of the conversation (Fig. 25). Although unparalleled in such a context, the word *apodos* seems to be quite a bold request of sexual gratification.[28] Both, the man and the youth are draped. The latter is also hooded, which makes the image look innocent. Yet, the empty stool behind the man may be taken as an allusion to the otherwise obvious fact that clothes can be removed.

Even more eloquent is the tondo of a cup attributed to the Briseis Painter (BAPD 204415; Fig. 26). The picture is of high artistic quality and its content is far from vulgar. Yet, there can be no doubt as to the strong erotic import of this image of clear mutual desire between a boy and a man, which is skilfully suggested by the exchange of gazes and the ecstatic contortion of the boy's body. Both figures are draped, but there is an empty chair next to them, which can be taken as an allusion to what the couple intends to do next. There is also a column, which evokes an architectural setting. There are no items related to the athletics. What is even more telling is that the piece of furniture is a chair with back rather than a stool, which very strongly suggests that the space was not meant to be understood as that of a gymnasium.[29] It may be a house or a sanctuary.

In all these cases, stools and chairs may contribute to the characterisation of a space in which the courtship and erotic foreplay take place. At the same time, when juxtaposed with dressed bodies they remind the viewer that clothes can be taken off. In this way, the pictures, even though they do not represent naked bodies engaged in intercourse, invite viewers to fantasise about it. Thus, the audience, while identifying themselves with the *erastai*, not only could think of the pleasure of the intercourse, but also of the whole process of flirting with youths, of the subsequent erotic foreplay and of the undressing, which might have been no less pleasurable.

---

28 See Lear, Cantarella 2008, 107–108.

29 Perhaps unexpectedly, in Attic vase paintings, the occurrences of chairs with back are almost exclusively limited to the indoor context, whereas in gymnasia we can see only stools and blocks.

6 The point of arrival

In the tondo of a cup by the Aberdeen Painter (BAPD 211186; Fig. 27), there are two youths in conversation. They are both draped. The smaller of the two seems to be charmingly modest. What can be the subject of their conversation? Perhaps there is no simple answer to this question. Sympotic tableware was used on playful occasions and its iconography was clearly often meant to provide entertainment by letting viewers guess what its meaning was. Thus, a man who thought that the two youths on the cup by the Aberdeen Painter were as innocent, as his thoughts were decent, was probably right enough. However, the stool behind the smaller youth may provide a clue to the opposite effect. Like in the images discussed above, whose erotic content is indicated by some other elements, the stool can be interpreted (and probably was meant to be interpreted) as an allusion to the undressing that might have followed the conversation between the youths. If not for the wreath suspended on the wall, one might think that they are about to undress for a workout in a palaestra. The presence of the wreath, however, evokes a ludic atmosphere of the scene. Hence, the erotic connotations seem justified.

This obviously does not mean that all images with empty stools were meant to evoke sex. In some pictures, an empty stool or chair is clearly meant to be sat upon. In some others, it had another function, for example within the process of textile production. Yet, on many occasions a stool is not just an innocent piece of furniture, and many Greek painters expected their customers to be able to grasp the allusion. According to the saying rightly or not attributed to Freud, sometimes a cigar is just a cigar. However, in a playful context of a symposium, a stool very often is not just a stool.

Bibliography

Belfiore, E.S. (2000), *Murder among Friends: Violation of Philia in Greek Tragedy*, New York.
Boardman, J./La Rocca, E. (1975), *Eros in Grecia*, Milano.
Bonfante, L. (1989), 'Nudity as a Costume in Classical Art', in: *AJA* 93, 543–570.
Christesen, P. (2002), 'On the Meaning of γυμνάζω', in: *Nikephoros* 15, 7–37.
Christesen, P. (2007), *Olympic Victor Lists and Ancient Greek History*, Cambridge/NewYork.
Christesen, P. (2014), 'Sport and Democratization in Ancient Greece (with an Excursus on Athletic Nudity)', in: P. Christesen/D.G. Kyle (eds.), *A Companion to Sport and Spectacle in Greek and Roman Antiquity*, Hoboken/New Jersey, 211–235.
Clark, K. (1956), *The Nude. A Study in Ideal Form*, New York.
Cohen, E.E. (2015), *Athenian Prostitution: The Business of Sex*, New York.

Faulkner, A. (2008), *The Homeric Hymn to Aphrodite: Introduction, Text and Commentary*, Oxford/New York.

Green, J.R. (1994), *Theatre in Ancient Greek society*, London/New York.

Haworth, M. (2018), 'The Wolfish Lover: The Dog as a Comic Metaphor in Homoerotic Symposium Pottery', in: *Archimède* 5, 7–23.

Hodges, F.M. (2001), 'The Ideal Prepuce in Ancient Greece and Rome: Male Genital Aesthetics and Their Relation to Lipodermos, Circumsicion, Foreskin Restoration and the Kynodesme', in: *Bulletin of the History of Medicine* 75.3, 375–405.

Keuls, E. (1985), *The Reign of the Phallus: Sexual Politics in Ancient Athens*, New York.

Kilmer, M.F. (1993), *Greek Erotica on Attic Red-Figure Vases*, London.

Kyle, D.G. (2007), *Sport and Spectacle in the Ancient World*, Malden, MA.

Lear, A./Cantarella, E. (2008), *Images of Ancient Pederasty: Boys Were Their Gods*, London.

Lee, M.M. (2015), *Body, Dress, and Identity in Ancient Greece*, Cambridge.

Lewis, S. (2002), *The Athenian Woman: An Iconographic Handbook*, London.

McDonnell, M. (1991), 'The introduction of athletic nudity: Thucydides, Plato and the vases', in: *JHS* 111, 182–193.

Williams, D. (1983), 'Women on Attic Vases: Problems of Interpretation' in: A. Cameron/A. Kuhrt (eds.), *Images of Women in Antiquity*, London/Sidney, 92–106.

Zanker, P. (1995), *The Mask of Socrates: The Image of the Intellectual in Antiquity*, Berkeley.

Figures

Fig. 14: Red-figure cup attributed to Douris, Canterbury Museum AR 430 (lost), BAPD 205184, drawing by Adam Chmielewski.

Fig. 15: Black-figure Siana cup, attributed to Boston CA Painter, Basel (market), BAPD 1060, drawing by Adam Chmielewski.

Fig. 16: Red-figure calyx crater, attributed to Euphronios, Berlin, Antikensammlung F2180, BAPD 200063, drawing by Adam Chmielewski.

Fig. 17a: Red-figure cup by Douris, New York, private collection, BAPD 44039, drawing by Adam Chmielewski.

Fig. 17b: Red-figure cup attributed to Brygos Painter, Boston, Museum of Fine Arts 01.8038, BAPD 203991, drawing by Adam Chmielewski.

Fig. 17c: Red-figure cup, attributed to Antiphon Painter, Ferrara, Museo Nazionale di Spina T41DVP, BAPD 200420, drawing by Adam Chmielewski.

Fig. 17d: Red-figure cup attributed to a follower of Douris, Cambridge (MA), Arthur M. Sackler Museum 1895.248, BAPD 209929, drawing by Adam Chmielewski.

Fig. 17e: Red-figure cup attributed to Triptolemos Painter, Malibu (CA), J.P. Getty Museum, BAPD 203883, drawing by Adam Chmielewski.

Fig. 18: Black-figure skyphos, Little Master, Riehen, private collection, BAPD 350489, drawing by Adam Chmielewski.

Fig. 19: Red-figure cup attributed to Douris, Boston (MA), Museum of Fine Arts 1970.233, BAPD 205288, drawing by Adam Chmielewski.

Fig. 20 a and b: a) Red-figure cup attributed to Triptolemos Painter, Tarquinia, Museo Nazionale RC2983, BAPD 203886, drawing by Adam Chmielewski. **b)** Red-figure cup attributed to Triptolemos Painter, Tarquinia, Museo Nazionale ARV² 367.93, BAPD 203885, drawing by Adam Chmielewski.

Fig. 21: Red-figure cup attributed to Penthesilea Painter, Copenhagen, Thorvaldsen Museum H614, BAPD 211645, drawing by Adam Chmielewski.

Fig. 22: Red-figure cup attributed to Douris, Tuscania, Museo Archeologico Nazionale, BAPD 9024930, drawing by Adam Chmielewski.

Fig. 23: Red-figure cup by Douris, Dresden, Kunstgewerbemuseum (lost), BAPD 205077, drawing by Adam Chmielewski.

Fig. 24: Red-figure cup attributed to Euaichme Painter, Oxford, Ashmolean Museum V517, BAPD 209671, drawing by Adam Chmielewski.

Fig. 25: Red-figure cup attributed to a follower of Douris, Richmond (VA), Museum of Fine Arts, 56.27.5, BAPD 205359, drawing by Adam Chmielewski.

Fig. 26: Red-figure cup attributed to Briseis Painter, Paris, Louvre G278, BAPD 204415, drawing by Adam Chmielewski.

Fig. 27: Red-figure cup attributed to Aberdeen Painter, Toulouse, Musée St. Raymond 26.156, BAPD 211186, drawing by Adam Chmielewski.

Emma Stafford
Olive Oil, Dildos and Sandals: Greek Sex Toys Reassessed

Abstract: Modern definitions of the term "sex toy" frequently cite as an example the dildo, the object most often discussed as a sexual aid in scholarship on ancient Greek sexuality. Martin Kilmer's *Greek Erotica on Attic Red-Figure Vases* provides a systematic study, categorising olive oil and dildos as "sexual accessories", but does not always give sufficient weight to the problematic nature of the material. Building on more recent, more nuanced readings of individual images and texts, this chapter reassesses the extent to which a class of "sex toy" can be identified in real life and/or as the stuff of erotic fantasy in ancient Greece.

1 Introduction

In discussing an Attic red-figure *pelike* in the Villa Giulia that is attributed to Euphronios, Shapiro speculates whether the sandal might have been "known as Leagros' favourite sex-toy".[1] The term may appear anachronistic, but in fact modern definitions of the sex toy as "an object or device used for sexual stimulation or to enhance sexual pleasure"[2] frequently cite as an example of such a device the dildo — the object most often discussed as a sexual aid in scholarly literature on ancient Greek sexuality. Kilmer's 1993 survey of erotica in Attic red-figure vase-painting provides the most systematic assessment of the subject, categorising olive oil and dildos as "sexual accessories", though considering the slipper under the heading of "sadism and masochism".[3] Whilst useful as a collection of evidence, however, Kilmer's account does not always give sufficient weight to the problematic nature of his material, and he begs many questions especially concerning female sexuality, following in the tradition of Dover's assertion that "there can be no doubt of the women's enjoyment of intercourse" in various examples, so that it is not "surprising that women are shown by the painters as satisfying their sexual cravings artificially by means of *olisboi*".[4] More recent studies of Greek sexuality — notably Stewart 1997, Rabinowitz 2002, Hales 2002, Skinner

---

1 Shapiro 2000, 29, fig. 15.
2 https://en.oxforddictionaries.com/definition/sex_toy
3 Kilmer 1993, 81–102 (sexual accessories), 103–132.
4 Dover 1978, 102.

https://doi.org/10.1515/9783110695793-010

2005, Lear and Cantarella 2008, Stafford 2011, Bissa 2013 and Robson 2013 — have provided more nuanced readings of individual images and texts. Relevant texts have also received attention in the context of literary studies, especially Henderson 1991 [1975] and Robson 2006 on Attic comedy.[5] However, no one since Kilmer has attempted a systematic treatment of the use of sexual aids in ancient Greece. This chapter reassesses our limited evidence, both textual and visual, in the light of scholarship subsequent to Kilmer, considering the extent to which a class of "sex toy" can be identified, and the range of contexts in which such aids might have been used, in real life and/or as the stuff of erotic fantasy. The most abundant material is to be found, unsurprisingly in late archaic Attic vase-painting, from the first 20 years of the fifth century BC and in Old Comedy, some 50 or more years later though at least again from Athens. One or two later texts, particularly on dildos, can cautiously be used to supplement the fifth-century material, though the different contexts present some challenges to interpretation.

2 Olive oil

First, the ubiquitous jar of olive oil, perhaps more of an "accessory" than a "toy", but certainly conducive to the "sexual pleasure" of one or both partners. Kilmer's strongest evidence for the use of oil as a lubricant is the well-known tondo by Douris c. 490 BC (see Bednarek in this volume, Figure 6),[6] on which a mature man penetrates a woman from behind — whether anally or vaginally it is hard to tell, though the former may be indicated by the words coming out of the man's mouth: "Hold still!"[7] Our attention is drawn to an aryballos, a small oil-pot, by its prominent position, balanced on top of the pile of discarded clothes.

The status of the woman in this image is often held to be servile because of her short hair as well as the circumstances, but two passages from Aristophanes strongly suggest that lubrication might be used in the context of marital sex. In *Acharnians* (1058–1066) the bridesmaid to a nervous bride is given an *exaleiptron* of the treaty under discussion, with which "she should rub her husband's cock at night" (τουτῳὶ / νύκτωρ ἀλειφέτω τὸ πέος τοῦ νυμφίου, 1065–1066). The precise shape of vase the term refers to is debated, but its derivation from ἐξαλείφω "to

---

5 Henderson 1991 [1975] has a section on "phallic implements" (120): weapons and other hard elongated objects form an important category of doubles entendres.
6 Boston 1970, 233.
7 Robson 2013, 134–135, fig. 32; Skinner 2005, 101–102, fig. 3.16; Stewart 1997, 163–164, fig. 104; Kilmer 1993, R577; Johns 1982, 129, 134, fig. 111; Dover 1978, R577.

wash over", or "to anoint" in the middle, suggests that it would have held oil, possibly perfumed: the inference is fairly clear that such an anointing of the penis will make its approach less frightening for the woman.[8] The same idea recurs in *Lysistrata*, in the great prick-tease scene where the citizen wife Myrrine has her desperate husband Kinesias apply some scented oil (*myros*). The passage does not actually specify where he is to "rub it in", but it is clear that this item is favoured by the woman, not the man (*Lysistrata* 938–944, transl. Henderson):

ΜΥΡΡΙΝΗ: βούλει μυρίσω σε;
ΚΙΝΗΣΙΑΣ: μὰ τὸν Ἀπόλλω μή μέ γε.
ΜΥΡ: νὴ τὴν Ἀφροδίτην, ἤν τε βούλῃ γ᾽ ἤν τε μή.
ΚΙΝ: εἴθ᾽ ἐκχυθείη τὸ μύρον, ὦ Ζεῦ δέσποτα.
ΜΥΡ: πρότεινε δὴ τὴν χεῖρα κἀλείφου λαβών.
ΚΙΝ: οὐχ ἡδὺ τὸ μύρον μὰ τὸν Ἀπόλλω τουτογί, εἰ μὴ διατριπτικόν γε κοὐκ ὄζον γάμων.
ΜΥΡ: τάλαιν᾽ ἐγώ, τὸ Ῥόδιον ἤνεγκον μύρον.

MYRRHINE: Want some scent?
CINESIAS: Apollo no, none for me.
MYRRHINE: But I will, so help me Aphrodite, whether you like it or not.
CINESIAS: Then let the scent flow! Lord Zeus!
MYRRHINE: Hold out your hand. Take some and rub it in.
CINESIAS: I really dislike this scent; it takes a long time warming up and it doesn't smell conjugal.
MYR: Oh silly me, I brought the Rhodian scent![9]

Representations of male homosexual sex are, of course, much more circumspect, but references to oil are frequent. The proper use of oil may be for rubbing down after exercise, as demonstrated in the gymnasium scene on an Attic red-figure calyx krater by Euphronios, c. 510–500 BC:[10] one youth pours something from an aryballos onto his outstretched hand with an extravagant gesture, presumably before applying it all over his body. Having once identified erotic lubrication as a *possible* use, however, more salacious readings may spring to mind — e.g. that the oil-pouring youth has designs on the youth to the right who has just removed

---

8 Henderson 1991 [1975], 120 n. 71 equates the vessel here with *alabastos* mentioned a few lines earlier, a perfume jar of narrow cylindrical shape susceptible of phallic humour. On this passage see also Lewis 2002, 127–128, and cf. Waite and Gooch 2018, 41–42 on the visual evidence for the alabastron's association with both marital sex and hetairai.
9 See also *Ekklesiazousai* 524–525 for the smell of perfume as a potential indicator of a wife's infidelity. The evidence for perfume in ancient Greece is briefly reviewed by Lee 2015, 62–65. Cf. Montserrat 1996, 68–75 on the evidence for perfume-use in Greco-Roman Egypt, and its erotic symbolism.
10 Berlin F 2180.

his cloak. That this vase is concerned with ideals of male beauty is confirmed by the inclusion, on the reverse, of a youth infibulating — tying up his penis for aesthetic effect as well as the practical demands of exercise.[11]

Euphronios' scene can of course be read without innuendo, as a straightforward gymnasium scene, complete with a discus being thrown on the reverse, but the striking thing is how often references to the gym intrude on homosexual courtship scenes. In the much-discussed scene on an Attic red-figure cup attributed to Peithinos, c. 500 BC (**Figure 1**), of older youths and boys, the courting couples are interspersed with an assemblage of *aryballos*, strigil and sponge — standard gym kit, which the majority of commentators interpret as providing a specifically athletic location for the encounter.[12] This certainly is the most obvious reading, given the literary evidence for the gym as a major site of erotic encounters — but a frisson is added if we take the presence of *aryballoi* to be suggestive of sexual action. It is often remarked that the boy in the central couple seems keener than literature would tell us "nice boys" should, reaching up to pull his taller partner into a kiss. It is not so often noted, though, that he holds an *aryballos* in his left hand — does this signal his eagerness for action? The gym assemblage appears again in the more explicit scene by the Brygos Painter, where a mature man is touching the genitals of a boy, in a state of visible excitement.[13] The boy again indicates willingness in the gesture of his hand behind the man's head, drawing him into an embrace. This time the boy is holding a bag with his other hand, behind his back, probably indicating his acceptance of a gift, in return for which he will be willing to grant favours. That the favour in question is inter-crural sex is suggested by the couple's close face-to-face pose, the man's legs bent in readiness, a supposition strengthened by comparison with Douris' similar scene (**Figure 2**), where the embrace is even closer, and again the gym assemblage can be seen in the background; as Lear and Cantarella note, here the couple are both encompassed by the youth's cloak, which may hint at imminent consummation.[14]

---

11 On the sensuality and potential erotcism of the scenes on this vase, see Osborne 2018, 64–67, figs 1.2 and 3.6 and pl. 5; Lee 2015, 57–58, fig. 3.1.

12 Osborne 2018, 128–130, figs 5.5–6 and pl. 21; Robson 2013, 47–48, 131, fig. 7; Skinner 2005, 92–94, figs 3.8–10; Shapiro 2000, 15, fig. 4; Shapiro 1981, 136, figs 7–10; Stewart 1997, 157–159, figs 95–97; Johns 1982, fig. 82; Dover 1978, 95–96 R196.

13 Oxford 1967, 304. Lear and Cantarella 2008, 54–56, fig. 1.13; Shapiro 2000, 31–32, fig. 16; Shapiro 1981, 135, fig. 6; Johns 1982, fig. 81; Dover 1978, R520. On the "fetishistic gesture" of the older man, see Hubbard in the volume.

14 Lear and Cantarella 2008, 109, fig. 3.3; Kilmer 1993, R573; Dover 1978, R573.

I might, of course, be reading too much into a simple indicator of location —
but if location were the main point, one might expect to see other athletic equipment — a discus, *halteres*, boxing straps — and other people engaged in the location's ostensible activities. Evidence for the gym assemblage having a specifically
erotic connotation is supplied by its unexpected appearance in **Figure 3**, in a heterosexual scene, where a youth and a man proffer purses to women.[15] The setting
is open to debate — the fact that one woman on each side is seated, one with a
mirror hanging behind her, may suggest they are "at home" in a brothel — but it
certainly cannot be the gym. The bathing equipment, then, must be suggesting
something else, and sex is the obvious candidate — especially given the commercial aspect suggested by the handing over of purses.[16]

Cumulatively, then, the vase-paintings are strongly suggestive of the use of
oil as a sexual lubricant. For use in heterosexual sex, we have the evidence of
Aristophanes for comparison, as we have seen.[17] I have not found anything equivalent there for homosexual practices, but this perhaps is not surprising given that
jokes about male-male intercourse tend to present "wide-arsed" passive partners
in an unsympathetic light, and there is a degree of reticence about the love of
boys. The one possible piece of literary evidence comes in a fragment of a much
later poem by the third-century BC Rhianus (fr. 69). He addresses a Bum (*pyx*)
covered with "sweet olive oil" (*glykos elaios*) which is keeping him, an old man,
awake with desire (transl. Kilmer):[18]

Ὡραί σοι Χάριτές τε κατὰ γλυκὺ χεῦαν ἔλαιον,
ὦ πυγά· κνώσσειν δ' οὐδὲ γέροντας ἐᾷς.
Λέξον μοι, τίνος ἐσσὶ μάκαιρα τύ, καὶ τίνα παίδων
κοσμεῖς; ἁ πυγὰ δ' εἶπε· Μενεκράτεος.

"The Hours and Graces covered you with sweet olive oil, O Bum. You don't let even old men
doze. Tell me, whose are you, you divine blessing, which of the young folks do you adorn?"
And the bum said: "I belong to Menekrates".

---

15 Osborne 2018, 131–133 figs 5.7–8 and pl. 22; Kilmer 1993, 84 n. 11 R630.

16 Cf. Fischer 2013 on "spinning *hetaira*" scenes; she alludes to this vase in passing (pp. 227 and
236) as an example of purses being social markers of prostitution. Lee 2015, 169 cites the Foundry
Painter's name-vase (her fig. 2.7b) as another example of the appearance of the gym assemblage
in an unexpected context, possibly alluding to "the homosexual activities of the *symposion*".

17 According to Pliny (*NH* 30.141), olive oil is an ingredient in an antaphrodisiac, taken with
pigeon dung and wine: *inhibent et... fimum columbinum cum oleo et vino potum.* I owe this point to
Andreas Serafim.

18 Kilmer 1993, 81–82. On this poem, and Rhianus' work more generally, see Spanakis in this
volume.

The identity of the Bum's owner — Menekrates — is withheld until the very end, but he is explicitly "one of the boys" (*paides*): *why* the Bum is covered in oil is left to the reader's imagination. Here the back-view is strongly suggestive of anal sex, for which lubrication would be more necessary than the inter-crural sex hinted at by the vase-painters.

3 Dildos

At first sight a more straightforward case can be made for regarding dildos as sex-toys, since they are categorised as such in a modern context. The question, though, is *whose* sexual pleasure is being enhanced. The well-known comic literary sources certainly present dildos as part of the wider characterisation of women as voracious for sex. Lack of a supply of dildos is a problem for the women of Aristophanes' *Lysistrata*, now that Miletos has seceded from the Athenian Empire (107–110):

> ΚΑΛΟΝΙΚΗ: ἀλλ' οὐδὲ μοιχοῦ καταλέλειπται φεψάλυξ.
> ἐξ οὗ γὰρ ἡμᾶς προὔδοσαν Μιλήσιοι,
> οὐκ εἶδον οὐδ' ὄλισβον ὀκτωδάκτυλον,
> ὃς ἦν ἂν ἡμῖν σκυτίνη 'πικουρία.

> KALONIKE: But there isn't the glimmer of a lover left. Since the Milesians betrayed us, I haven't even seen an eight-finger dildo, which we might have had as a leather auxiliary.

Scholia on these lines pick up on the description of the *olisbos* as made of leather, and the particular association with Miletos (Σ *ad Lysistrata* 109–110):

> ὄλισβον: Αἰδοῖον δερμάτινον. καὶ τοῦτο εἰς τὰς Μιλησίας. παίζει δὲ ὡς τοῖς ὀλίσβοις χρωμέναις. σκυτίνη ἐπικουρία: Παρὰ τὴν παροιμίαν, συκίνη ἐπικουρία, ἐπὶ τῶν ἀσθενῶν. ὁ δὲ εἰς τὴν σκυτίνην μετέβαλε. σκύτινοι γὰρ οἱ ὄλισβοι. εἰσὶ δὲ δερμάτινα αἰδοῖα, οἷς χρῶνται αἱ χῆραι γυναῖκες.

> *Olisbos*: Leather genitals. These too are associated with Milesian women. And he is making fun of women who use dildoes. *Skutine epikouria*: Instead of the common phrase "a figwood (*sukine*) helper", for the weak. He has changed it to 'leather' (*skutine*). Because dildoes are made of leather. They are leather genitals used by women bereft of a husband.

The scholia fail to comment, however, on the really interesting feature: this is the only passage to provide any indication of the *size* of the dildo. Modern commentators generally take the "eight-finger" measurement to be one of length, about 6 inches / 15 cm, though it would be possible to think of it as one of diameter.[19] The former seems relatively realistic in terms of modern dildos sold for use by women; the latter is rather bigger even than a modern dildo designed for male use. The "leather thing" beloved of the Milesians is discussed further by two women in a less known passage of Aristophanes, a fragment from the *Second Thesmophorai-zusae* (fr. 592 KA, 15–27):

(A.) τί οὖν γένοιτ' ἄν;
(B.) ἔχ' ἀπ[όκριναί μοι τόδε· τί ἐστι τοῦθ' ὃ λέγουσι τ[ὰς Μιλησίας παίζειν ἐχούσας, ἀντιβολῶ, [τὸ σκύτινον;
(A.) φλυαρία καὶ λῆρος ὕβρεω[ς ἀνάπλεως, κάλλως ὄνειδος καὶ κατ[άγελως δὴ πολύς. το[ύτ]ῳ γὰρ ὥσπερ τοῖσιν [ᾠοῖς χρῶντ' ἀεὶ τ[οῖς] ἀνεμιαίοις...
(B.) κα[ὶ μ]ὴν λέγεταί γ' ὥς ἐσθ[' ὅμοιον ποσθίῳ ἀλη[θ]ινῷ κ[αὶ τ]οῦτο.
νὴ Δ[ί', ὦ τάλαν, ὥσπερ [σ]ελήνη γ' ἡλίῳ· τὴν μὲ[ν χρόαν ἰδεῖν ὅμοιόν ἐστι, θάλπει δ' οὐ[δαμῶς.

A: What would that be?
B: I've got... what's that thing they say Milesian women have to play with — help me out — the leather thing?
A: Tomfoolery and lubricious nonsense, and general disgrace and ridicule... like those wind-eggs...
B: And they say that even this is nothing like a real prick.
A: By god, as the moon is to the sun: the colour is the same to look at, but no way is it as warm.

Although this is in Woman B's possession, she seems to be inexperienced, relying on hearsay for comparison with an actual penis — "they say that even this is nothing like a real prick". Woman A, on the other hand, seems to be speaking from experience when she explains her scathing dismissal of it as "lubricious nonsense": "By god, as the moon is to the sun: the colour is the same to look at, but no way is it as warm".

Aristophanes presents us with the illusion of overhearing a private conversation between two women, which is parallel to the illusion presented by red-figure vase-paintings of a lone woman equipped with one or more dildos. The great majority of these images show the implement as unfeasibly large, making the same sort of joke about women's voracity as Aristophanes — which might support a reading of the *Lysistrata* measurement as one of width. Examples include the tondo of an unpublished kylix of c. 500 BC from Cerveteri in which the woman, naked apart from a headscarf, seems to be running to the left holding in each

---

19 Henderson 1991 [1975], 221–222.

hand a dildo nearly as long as her arm, with a sizeable scrotum.[20] Of a similar design, and only slightly smaller, are the two dildos in a tondo attributed to Epiktetos,[21] which is usually interpreted as showing a woman (again naked apart from a headscarf) about to insert one into each orifice, while stepping over a foot-washing bowl — an action which would be a prodigious feat of balance even if the dildos were not so very large. Even Kilmer concedes that "the subject is more likely to represent male fantasy than actual female practice", interpreting the *podaniptēr* as "add[ing] verisimilitude to a somewhat improbable subject".[22] A slightly less physiologically implausible scene is represented in **Figure 4**, with more modestly-proportioned dildos, one heading for the woman's vagina, the other for her carefully-delineated open mouth.[23] However, this image, like the previous two examples, is in the tondo of a kylix, so very definitely aimed at a sympotic male viewer, to be revealed as he drains his cup of wine: it is his sexual pleasure that is at stake here, rather than that of any real-life woman. The images could be complete fantasy on the part of the vase-painters, but if they are based on any reality at all I would be inclined to side with those scholars who propose that they reflect the live performance of some kind of erotic dance at the symposium.[24] One version of the woman-with-dildo theme which is definitely fantasy is **Figure 5**, where the female — sometimes labelled a nymph or maenad because of the mythological milieu suggested by her companion — holds a very long, double-ended dildo in her left hand, but she seems to have decided to go for the real thing offered up by a satyr.[25] Not only is she in the dominant position here, but she looks directly out at the viewer with a provocative gaze unusual for Greek vase-painting — is she challenging us to comment on her appetite?

Nancy Rabinowitz has made a case for "excavating women's homoeroticism" from vases like these, concluding rather magnificently: "those who dismiss the dildo in these vases as an invasion of male sexuality, or the effect of male fantasy, ignore the difference between the dildo and the penis: there is no man attached to the former".[26] However, I think on balance I tend to a less optimistic view than hers as to how much genuine female sexuality we can read into these images.

---

20 Kilmer 1993, 99 R443.
21 St Petersburgh 14611.
22 Kilmer 1993, 100 R132.
23 Robson 2013, 121 and 135 fig. 28; Kilmer 1993, 100 and 149 R212.
24 John's brisk dismissal of *olisbos* scenes ("this is likely to be for the entertainment of males: there is no need for such equipment between female lovers") is ahead of its time. John 1982, 102; see more recently, Lewis 2002, 127.
25 Lissarrague 1990, 63 fig. 224.
26 Rabinowitz 2002, 146.

I do, though, have briefly to mention one extraordinary element related to the dildo scenes: the so-called "phallus-bird".[27] This is quite literally a bird in terms of its legs, body and wings, but it has an elongated neck which ends with just the sort of eyed penis-head as appears on many dildos. In one example, in the tondo of a cup by Epiktetos, the bird is as big as a large dog, with outstretched wings as though ready to take off, with a naked woman riding on its back.[28] Sparkes calls the phallus-bird "a disembodied expression of female desires as imagined by men" (on the reasonable assumption that the vase-painters concerned are men), while Johns rather nicely suggests that "transforming the phallus into a small independent animal may stress the independent nature of the organ, often very much less under its owner's control than he might wish".[29] The phallus-bird sometimes appears in scenes with several women, as on the exterior of a fragmentary kylix attributed to the Pedieus Painter.[30] Unfortunately, not much of the phallus-bird survives, but it stands between two naked women, one of whom balances a *skyphos* on her arm, while a dildo hangs on the wall between them. The scene on the other side of the vase — which otherwise might be a fairly innocent image of bathing — perhaps acquires erotic overtones from this sort of context, as Kilmer and others have argued — but for my purposes here the fundamental point is that the presence of the phallus-bird confirms that we are firmly in the world of *fantasy* here.

Lastly on dildos and phallus-birds, I have to mention Oikonomides' (1986) theory about the "dildo-loaf". This is based on the very slender evidence of a short entry in Hesychios' lexicon, *sub vide "Olisbokollix"*, which is defined simply as "instead of the real loaf"; the word is a *hapax legomenon* from Old Comedy. Oikonomides' idea is that long thin loaves of bread might have been baked in the form of dildos as a novelty, or that they might simply have acquired the name because of their appearance. He identifies a couple of scenes like **Figure 6** — where a woman reveals a basket full of eyed phalluses — as representing dildo-

---

27 For a survey of this ornithological wonder in Greek art, see Boardman 1992. Lissarrague (1990, 59 figs 11–13) comments on examples involving satyrs.

28 Rome, Villa Giulia 57912. Kilmer 1993, R125.1 (colour plate).

29 Sparkes 1998, 260 (see Plate 15.6 for another example of a woman astride a phallus-bird: white-ground cup, Berlin F 2095); Johns 1982, 68. Cf. Freudian psychoanalysis, in which the bird is considered to be symbolic of the penis on grounds of an equivalence between flight and the erection, though birds may also symbolise the female breast: see e.g. Wormhoudt 1950 for discussion of such symbolism in literature.

30 Paris, Louvre G14. Rabinowitz 2002, 142–143 fig. 5.21; Venit 1998, 128 fig. 4b; Kilmer 1993, 98–99 R152.

loaves, on the grounds that they could not possibly be real dildos, given the expensive and rare nature of these items, according to our literary sources.[31] This proposition is open to challenge anyway, but its concern with verisimilitude completely overlooks the fact that the woman here is holding a diminutive phallus-bird under her left arm. If anything, given the way the eyes seem to be looking out of the bowl, I would see these as more phallus-birds, ready to communicate with the one carried by the woman. As Lewis thoughtfully points out, "in contrast to assumptions about female fear of male sexuality, the imagery centres on affection for the phallus".[32]

Which brings me back to dildos proper. Often juxtaposed to the Aristophanic evidence, though from the rather different context of the Hellenistic period, is Herodas' *Mimiamb* 6, in which two women talk at some length about a "red-stitched *baubon*", apparently an alternative word for *olisbos* (*Mimiamb* 6.17–19 and 65–73):[33]

(ΜΗ.) λίσσομαί [σ]ε, μὴ ψεύσηι,
φίλη Κοριττοῖ, τίς κοτ' ἦν ὅ σοι ῥάψας τὸν κόκκινον
βαυβῶνα;
(ΚΟ.) ἀλλ' ἔργα, κοῖ ἐστ' ἔργα· τῆς Ἀθηναίης αὐτῆς ὁρῆν τὰς χεῖρας, οὐχὶ Κέρδωνος,
δόξεις. ἐ[γὼ] μέν—δύο γὰρ ἦλθ' ἔχων, Μητροῖ—ἰδοῦσ'
ἅμ' ἰδμῆι τὤμματ' ἐξεκύμηνα·
τὰ βαλλί' οὕτως ἄνδρες οὐχὶ ποιεῦσι
—αὐταὶ γάρ εἰμεν—ὀρθά· κοὐ μόνον τοῦτο,
ἀλλ' ἡ μαλακότης ὕπνος, οἱ δ' ἱμαντίσκοι
ἔρι', οὐκ ἱμάν[τες]. εὐνοέστερον σκυτέα
γυναικ[ὶ] διφῶσ' ἄλλον οὐκ ἀνευρ[ή] σ[εις

---

31 Kilmer 1993, 101 R414; Dover 1978, 133 R414. Johns 1982, 66–67 fig. 50 includes this vase in a discussion of the association between the phallus and the Evil Eye, both performing an apotropaic function; the photo used by Johns is no longer available for reproduction, and the vase itself is in too delicate a condition to be re-photographed — hence the drawing for our Figure 6. Cf. the fragmentary tondo of Berlin F2275, in which a crouching naked woman holds a bowl with no fewer than 6 eyed phalluses peeping out (Kilmer 1993, 101 R298; Johns 1982, fig. 26), and the pelike Syracuse inv. 20065, on which a naked woman appears to be climbing into a basket of eyed phalluses, holding one in her oustretched left hand Dover 1978, 102 R1071.

32 Lewis 2002, 127; see 128, fig. 3.28 for a further phallus-bird, with a fully-clothed woman (pelike fragment Athens Agora P27396); and 67 fig. 2.5 for the tondo of Berlin 1966, 21, in which a phallus-bird appears above two fully-clothed women who are grinding grain (= Kilmer 1993, 1192).

33 The term is discussed by Headlam and Knox 2001 [1922], 228–229 (*ad loc.*).

METRO: I beg you, don't lie, Koritto dear, who was it who stitched your red dildo?
KORITTO: But the work, [real Koian] it is; you'd think you were looking at the handiwork of Athene herself, not Kerdon. But I — he brought two with him, Metro — when I saw them I thought my eyes would burst from their sockets. Men never make their phalluses so straight — it's just us here — and not only that, but soft as sleep, and the laces are like wool, not leather. You might look for a shoemaker more friendly to women, but you wouldn't find one!

Specification of the colour red is an innovation here — Aristophanes' Woman A just mentioned the colour as being lifelike — but the material is again leather, and this time we are explicitly told that the maker is a cobbler; indeed, the next poem in Herodas' collection, *Mimiamb 7*, is actually set in Kerdon's shoe-shop.[34] Mention of "little straps" or "laces" (*himantiskoi*), 3 lines up from the bottom, has led some to suggest that we have here the wherewithal for a strap-on device for use between women[35] — but the rest of the dialogue is all about solo use of the dildo, even if it appears to be passed around between friends. I would see the "laces" just as the stitching necessary to construct such an implement out of leather — but once again, this is a poem designed for a male readership, on which we surely should not rely for straightforward historical evidence about women's sexuality.

Similarly problematic is a passage from Lucian's *Dialogues of the Courtesans* 5 (291–292), in which Leaina is reporting her experience with a butch female client Megilla, who sometimes calls herself "Megillus" and refers to her long-term partner Demonassa as her wife:

... καὶ τὸ ἀνδρεῖον ἐκεῖνο ἔχεις καὶ ποιεῖς τὴν Δημώνασσαν ἅπερ οἱ ἄνδρες; Ἐκεῖνο μέν, ἔφη, ὦ Λέαινα, οὐκ ἔχω· δέομαι δὲ οὐδὲ πάνυ αὐτοῦ· ἴδιον δέ τινα τρόπον ἡδίω παρὰ πολὺ ὁμιλοῦντα ὄψει με.
Πάρεχε γοῦν, ὦ Λέαινα, εἰ ἀπιστεῖς, ἔφη, καὶ γνώσῃ οὐδὲν ἐνδέουσάν με τῶν ἀνδρῶν· ἔχω γάρ τι ἀντὶ τοῦ ἀνδρείου. ἀλλὰ πάρεχε, ὄψει γάρ.

"...and you have everything that a man has, and can play the part of a man to Demonassa?" "I haven't got what you mean, Leaina" said she, "I don't need it at all. You'll find I've a much pleasanter method of my own."...
"If you don't believe me Leaina," said she, "just give me a chance, and you'll find I'm as good as any man; I have a substitute of my own. Only give me a chance, and you'll see".

---

34 See Caspers 2018, 123–125 on the artful juxtaposition of "dildo-talk... and shoe-talk" in the two poems.
35 E.g. Fountoulakis in this volume.

Leaina's interlocutor, fellow-*hetaira* Klonarion, presses her for details, but is disappointed — and so the modern scholar, too, is left to speculate. It has been suggested that Megilla's "much pleasanter method... a substitute of my own" might refer to a strap-on dildo, though, as argued elsewhere in this volume by Andreas Fountoulakis, such an interpretation relies on an old-fashioned, phallocentric assumption of women's desire for penetration; a reference to *cunnilingus* seems more likely.[36] While I agree with Fountoulakis about this passage, there is one rather better piece of evidence for the existence of such a device, from Pseudo-Lucian's *Affairs of the Heart* 28. The impassioned speaker Charikles, supporter of heterosexual love, is challenging his opponent Kallikratidas to imagine — horror of horrors — a female counterpart to the male homosexual practices the latter champions (transl. Macleod):

... χάρισαι τὴν ἴσην ἐξουσίαν καὶ γυναιξίν, καὶ ἀλλήλαις ὁμιλησάτωσαν ὡς ἄνδρες· ἀσελγῶν δὲ ὀργάνων ὑποζυγωσάμεναι τέχνασμα, ἀσπόρων τεράστιον αἴνιγμα, κοιμάσθωσαν γυνὴ μετὰ γυναικὸς ὡς ἀνήρ· τὸ δὲ εἰς ἀκοὴν σπανίως ἧκον ὄνομα—αἰσχύνομαι καὶ λέγειν—τῆς τριβακῆς ἀσελγείας ἀνέδην πομπευέτω.

... bestow the same privilege upon women, and let them have intercourse with each other just as men do. Let them strap to themselves cunningly contrived instruments of lechery, those mysterious monstrosities devoid of seed, and let woman lie with woman as does a man. Let wanton Lesbianism—that word seldom heard, which I feel ashamed even to utter—freely parade itself.

These "cunningly contrived instruments of lechery" certainly sound like phalluses that can be attached to a woman — indeed, they need "strapping on" (ὑποζυγωσάμεναι): Charikles evidently cannot imagine women achieving sexual pleasure without such an instrument, unlike Lucian's more sophisticated Megilla.[37]

---

36 As Evangelou notes (p. 363), the term *tribas*, regularly used to refer to those given to female homosexual activity, suggests that the ancient Greeks conceptualised Lesbian sex as involving "rubbing" rather than penetration. Hales 2002 and Bissa 2013 offer interesting discussions of the dialogue in light of modern debates about gender expression and the transgender spectrum; both credit Lucian with a degree of sympathy for female homoeroticism.

37 On this passage see also Fountoulakis (above pp. 126–127). Rabinowitz 2002, 142 fig. 5.22 follows Kilmer 1993, 29–30 and 98–99 R141.3 in identifying a woman wearing a strap-on dildo on the exterior of a cup attributed to Epiktetos. The vase is certainly intriguing, with three women on the reverse apparently each playing with one or more dildos, but unfortunately the vase, once in the Castellani collection, Rome, is now lost, leaving us reliant on drawings.

4 The sandal

The potentially erotic connotations of footwear have recently been explored by contributors to Pickup and Waite (eds. 2018). Of particular relevance here is the substantial first chapter (Waite and Gooch 2018), which surveys a catalogue of 240 examples of the motif of sandals, suspended in the background of scenes in Athenian painted pottery. The authors note its particular prevalence on drinking cups, the shape presupposing a male, sympotic viewer, and conclude that "the suspended sandal, albeit polysemic, relates to a nexus of interrelated themes linked to mobility, transformation, transition and eroticism".[38] Also germane is chapter 3's study of scenes of the (un)tying of sandals, Yael Young's "Donning Footwear: The Invention and Diffusion of an Iconographic Motif in Archaic Athens". The social significance of the motif can be seen for example in the two instances presented by the Ambrosios Painter's cup, c. 510 BC:[39] in the tondo, the lone figure of a youth has his left foot raised on a step, above which hang a sponge and aryballos, as he ties a long strap around his ankle; on the exterior, a seated woman named "Rhodo..." reaches down to tie the sandal on her right foot, while other women work wool or interact with bearded men. Immerwahr reads the vase as a whole as "preparations for a party", the sandal-tying in both cases indicating that the figure is preparing to go out; Fischer sees the exterior as "a glimpse into the life of prostitutes", working wool at home before being taken out by the men.[40] Lee goes further, pointing out that both *hetairai* and boys "are desirable potential partners for the elite male symposiasts, underscoring the erotic connotations of sandal tying".[41]

The actual direct use of the sandal in erotic contexts should be read in light of this broader background of symbolic significance. For many scholars, the raised sandal in explicitly sexual scenes is all about control, usually exercised by high-status men over socially inferior women.[42] Such usage is illustrated in a number of scenes of group sex discussed in Hubbard's chapter in this volume. While reading the sandal as a "tool of command", however, Hubbard sees its function in many cases as symbolic rather than necessary (Hubbard Figures 1 and

---

38 Waite and Gooch 2018, 43.
39 Munich, private collection; Young 2018, 110–111.
40 Immerwahr 1984, 10 pls 2–3; Fischer 2013, 231.
41 Lee 2015, 164.
42 Though see Pickup (2018) on representations of Aphrodite wielding a sandal, in both vase-painting and Hellenistic sculpture: "the sandal is an expression of Aphrodite's power, albeit very much within her sphere of sex and love" (243).

6), and is open to the possibility of an alternative function, in some cases, as a stimulant (Hubbard Figure 2b).[43] I would certainly concur that stimulation, rather than coercion, would seem more likely in the case of the Thalia Painter's tondo (Hubbard Figure 8), where the sandal is wielded by a woman.[44] Nor is patriarchal control obviously in question in the extraordinary image which inspired Shapiro's comment about the possibility of the sandal being the real-life Leagros' "favourite sex-toy", with which I started (**Figure 7**). Here a young man holds up a slipper, reaching out towards a boy who seems to be calmly walking away — with an exceptionally large (for a boy), semi-erect penis and the inscription LEAGROS KALOS. I have argued elsewhere in favour of reading this as punishment for masturbation, but I would not rule out the alternative that the boy's arousal is a response to the raised slipper, as Shapiro suggests.[45]

5 Conclusion

So, to summarise, is there such a category as the sex-toy in ancient Greece? In the end I probably have to conclude that there are sexual *accessories* — olive oil for lubrication, sponges and washing-bowls for cleaning up afterwards — but that none of these is what one might call specialist equipment: everything is susceptible of non-erotic use too.[46] The same can be said of the sandal: it is an item which has come to hand, even if the prevalence of the sandal in erotic contexts gives it some claim to being an implement of choice for coercion or stimulation. The one "specialist" item is the dildo: there can be no doubt that this fits the bill as a "sex toy" in the modern sense — but the degree to which it was a real item used for

---

43 On Hubbard Figure 1 (the Pedieus Painter's *kylix*, Louvre G13), see also Thumiger in this volume; Robson 2013, 134 figs. 24–25; Skinner 2005, 102–103, fig. 3.17; Rabinowitz 2002, 142–145 fig. 5.23; Kilmer 1993, R156; Sutton 1992, 12 fig. 2; Johns 1982, 127, 129, fig. 107. On Hubbard Figure 6 (the Nikosthenes Painter's *kantharos*, Boston 95.61), see also Lear and Cantarella 2008, 117–120 fig. 3.10; Kilmer 1993, R223; Johns 1982, fig. 97; Dover 1978, R223. More generally, cf. e.g. Skinner 2005, 103: "these images leave it unclear whether the sandal is being employed as a weapon or a mild sexual stimulant".
44 Berlin 3251. Stafford 2011, 348–389 fig. 4; Stewart 1997, 165–167 figs. 105–107; Johns 1982, 140–142, fig. 117.
45 Stafford 2011, 249–251, fig. 5; Shapiro 2000, 29–30, fig. 15. See also Lear and Cantarella 2008, 121–123 fig. 3.12; Kilmer 1993, 104–105 R18.
46 Kilmer 1993 adduces various other items being pressed into erotic service, e.g. the pointed bottom of an upturned amphora straddled by a woman (R114), while the narrow neck of another amphora is penetrated by a satyr (R148).

women's sexual pleasure, rather than a figment of men's sexual fantasy, remains open to debate.

Bibliography

Bissa, E. (2013), 'Man, Woman or Myth? Gender-bending in Lucian's *Dialogues of the Courtesans*', in: *Materiali e Discussioni per L'analisi del Testi Classici* 70, 79–100.

Boardman, J. (1992), 'The Phallus-bird in Archaic and Classical Greek Art', in: *Revue Archéologique* 2, 227–242.

Caspers, C. (2018) '*Pantāi krēpides*: shoe-talk from Homer to Herodas', in: Pickup/Waite (2018), 118–130.

Davidson, J. (2007), *The Greeks and Greek Love*, London.

Dover, K.J. (1978), *Greek Homosexuality*, London.

Fischer, M. (2013), 'Ancient Greek Prostitutes and the Textile Industry in Attic Vase-painting ca. 550–450 BCE', in: *Classical World* 106, 219–259.

Fisher, N.R.E. (2008), 'The Bad Boyfriend, the Flatterer and the Sycophant: Related Forms of the "Kakos" in Democratic Athens', in: I. Sluiter/R. Rosen (eds.), *KAKOS: Badness and Anti-value in Classical Antiquity*, Leiden, 185–231.

Garrison, D.H. (2000), *Sexual Culture in Ancient Greece*, Norman.

Hales, S.P. (2002), 'Lucian's "Leaena and Clonarium": voyeurism or a challenge to assumptions', in: N.S. Rabinowitz/L. Auangar (eds.), *Among Women: From Homosocial to the Homoerotic in the Ancient World*, Austin, 286–303.

Headlam, W./Knox, A.D. (2001 [1922]), *Herodas: The Mimes and Fragments*, London.

Henderson, J. (1991 [1975]), *The Maculate Muse: Obscene Language in Attic Comedy*, 2nd ed., Oxford/New York.

Hubbard, T.K. (ed.) (2014), *A Companion to Greek and Roman Sexualities*, Hoboken.

Immerwahr, H. (1984), 'An Inscribed Cup by the Ambrosios Painter', in: *Antike Kunst* 27, 10–13.

Johns, C. (1982), *Sex or Symbol? Erotic Images of Greece and Rome*, London.

Keuls, E.C. (1993 [1985]), *The Reign of the Phallus: Sexual Politics in Ancient Athens*, Berkeley.

Kilmer, M.F. (1993), *Greek Erotica on Attic Red-Figure Vases*, London.

Lear, A./Cantarella, E. (2008), *Images of Ancient Greek Pederasty*, London/New York.

Lee, M.M. (2015a), *Body, Dress and Identity in Ancient Greece,* Cambridge.

Lewis, S. (2002), *The Athenian Woman: An Iconographic Handbook*, London/New York.

Lissarrague, F. (1990), 'The Sexual Life of Satyrs', in: D.M. Halperin/J.J. Winkler/F.I. Zeitlin (eds.), *Before Sexuality: The Construction of Erotic Experience in the Ancient Greek World*, Princeton, 53–81.

Montserrat, D. (1996), *Sex and Society in Græco-Roman Egypt*, London.

Oikonomides, A.N. (1986), 'Κόλλιξ, ὄλισβος, ὀλισβοκόλλιξ', in: *Horos* 4, 168–178.

Osborne, R. (2018), *The Transformation of Athens: Painted Pottery and the Creation of Classical Greece*, Princeton.

Pickup, S. (2018), 'A slip and a slap: Aphrodite and her footwear', in: Pickup and Waite (2018), 229–246.

Pickup, S./Waite, S. (eds.) (2018), *Shoes, Slippers, and Sandals: Feet and Footwear in Classical Antiquity*, London/New York.

Rabinowitz, N.S. (2002), 'Excavating women's homoeroticism in ancient Greece: the evidence from Attic vase-painting', in: N.S. Rabinowitz/L. Auangar (eds.), *Among Women: From Homosocial to the Homoerotic in the Ancient World*, Austin, 106–166.

Robson, J.E. (2013), *Sex and Sexuality in Classical Athens*, Edinburgh.

Robson, J.E. (2006), *Humour, Obscenity and Aristophanes*, Tübingen.

Shapiro, H.A. (1981), 'Courtship scenes in Attic vase-painting', in: *AJA* 85, 133–143.

Shapiro, H.A. (2000), 'Leagros and Euphronios: painting pederasty in Athens', in: T.K. Hubbard (ed.), *Greek Love Reconsidered*, New York, 12–32.

Skinner, M.B. (2005), *Sexuality in Greek and Roman Culture*, Oxford/Malden, MA.

Sparkes, B.A. (1998), 'Sex in Classical Athens', in: B.A. Sparkes (ed.), *Greek Civilization: an Introduction*, Oxford, 248–262.

Stafford, E.J. (2011), 'Clutching the Chickpea: Private Pleasures of the Bad Boyfriend', in: S.D. Lambert (ed.), *Sociable Man. Essays in Greek Social Behaviour in Honour of Nick Fisher*, Swansea, 337–363.

Stewart, A. (1997), *Art, Desire and the Body in Ancient Greece*, Cambridge.

Sutton, R.F. (1992), 'Pornography and Persuasion on Attic Pottery', in: A. Richlin (ed.), *Pornography and Representation in Greece and Rome*, Oxford, 3–35.

Venit, M.S. (1998), 'Women in their Cups', in: *The Classical World* 92, 117–130.

Waite, S./Gooch, E. (2018), 'Sandals on the wall: the symbolism of footwear on Athenian painted pottery', in: Pickup/Waite (2018), 17–89.

Wormhoudt, A. (1950), 'The unconscious bird symbol in literature', in: *American Imago* 7, 173–182.

Young, Y. (2018), 'Donning footwear: the invention and diffusion of an iconographic motif in archaic Athens', in: Pickup/Waite (2018), 105–117.

Figures

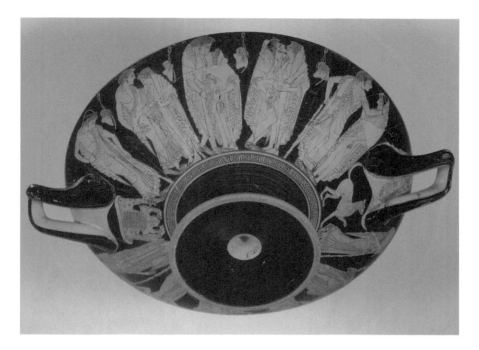

Fig. 28: Aryballoi, strigils and sponges in homosexual courting scene. Exterior of Attic red-figure cup attributed to Peithinos, c. 500 BC (Berlin 2279). Photo: bpk / Antikensammlung, SMB / Johannes Laurentius.

Fig. 29: Homosexual courting scene. Attic red-figure cup attributed to Douris, c. 490 BC (Munich SH 2631). Photo: courtesy of the Staatliche Antikensammlungen, Munich.

Fig. 30 a and b: Gym assemblage in heterosexual, commercial context. Attic red-figure kylix attributed to Makron, signed by potter Hieron, c. 480 BC (Toledo 72.55). Photos: courtesy of Toledo Museum of Art.

Fig. 31: Woman with two dildos. Attic red-figure cup, attributed to the Nikosthenes Painter, c. 520-500 BC (British Museum E815). Photo: © The Trustees of the British Museum.

Fig. 32: Woman / nymph with dildo and satyr. Attic red-figure cup by the Nikosthenes Painter, c. 500 BC (Boston RES.08.30a, Gift of Edward Perry Warren). Photo: © 2021 Museum of Fine Arts, Boston.

Fig. 33: Woman carrying phallus-bird and revealing a basket with two eyed phalluses, one with red-painted head. Attic red-figure amphora attributed to the Flying Angel Painter, c. 490 BC (Paris, Petit Palais ADUT 318). Drawing: Sheila Bewley.

Fig. 34: Young man with slipper and boy: punishment or sex-play? Inscription: LEAGROS KA-LOS. Attic red-figure pelike by Euphronios, c. 510 BC (Rome, Villa Giulia 121109). Photo: courtesy of the Soprintendenza Beni Archeologici Etruria Meridionale, Rome.

Regina Höschele
Statues as Sex Objects

Abstract: This chapter explores the phenomenon of statue-love by considering how ancient texts portray instances of erotic desire for, or even sexual intercourse with, works of art. Offering a taxonomy of agalmatophilia tales, it traces the origins of the motif, identifies typical narrative patterns and investigates how the sexual allure of statuary is conceptualised in Greco-Roman literature. While all anecdotes concerning sexual interaction with existing (as opposed to poetically fabricated) statues involve a male lover (in line with ancient gender stereotypes that assign the active role to men), some texts and visual representations also toy with the idea of female agalmatophiliacs.

Luis Buñuel's 1930 movie *L'âge d'or* contains a wonderfully bizarre, comically dysfunctional love scene. While guests at a party are listening to an orchestral version of Wagner's "Liebestod", the final aria of his *Tristan und Isolde*, which culminates in the death of the heroine sinking into supreme bliss (*höchste Lust*), a man and a woman retreat to the garden so as to have sex. Though yearning for sexual release, the lovers are kept from consummating their desire through constant distractions and disturbances — no sublime union for them, but a perpetual *coitus interruptus*. Shots of the two hungrily sucking each other's fingers give way to the uncanny image of the man's fingerless hand caressing the woman's cheek. Their heads knock into each other as the woman leans in for a kiss; their kiss, in turn, is interrupted as the man's gaze is drawn to the foot of a marble statue. When they have finally made it down to the ground, eager for further action, the man is summoned away by a phone call. Deprived of her lover, the woman clings to the statue's pedestal and starts to suck, longingly and ever more voluptuously, on its big toe.[1]

---

[1] On the use of sculpture in this scene, cf. Felleman 2017, 57–61.

https://doi.org/10.1515/9783110695793-011

Fig. 35: Lya Lys in Luis Buñuel's *L'Age d'or* (1930).

The statue, which becomes the object of this lapidary fellatio, is a replica of the Diana of Gabii, housed in the Louvre and thought by some to be a copy of Praxiteles' Brauronian Artemis.[2] An emblem of virginity, Diana fittingly presides over the lovers' unsuccessful attempts at copulation. In placing their sex scene next to a marble statue and turning the statue itself into an object of displaced desire, Buñuel appropriates an age-old literary (and artistic) motif: that of statue-love. It most famously appears in Ovid's story of Pygmalion (*Met.* 10.243–297), the sculptor who falls in love with the ivory image of a woman he has fashioned with his own hands.[3] Recounting the wondrous transformation of an inanimate statue into a living being, the story has undergone countless transformations of its own, fuelling for millennia the fantasy of writers and artists alike.[4] Though unique in its enduring and multifaceted afterlife, the story of Pygmalion is far from the only tale of statue-love to have come down to us from Antiquity. Indeed, numerous

---

2 This identification, first proposed by Studniczka 1884, 25–34, is nowadays commonly rejected, cf. Kansteiner et al. 2014, 92.
3 Cf. Michalopoulos in this volume.
4 Cf. e.g. Dörrie 1974, Dinter 1979, Blühm 1988, Joshua 2001, Stoichita 2008.

ancient authors mention instances of erotic desire for, or even sexual intercourse with, actual works of art, not just poetic fabrications.

Modern psychology has labelled this kind of desire "agalmatophilia", a form of sexual paraphilia, reports of which, however, seem largely confined to ancient sources and later literary texts. According to Scobie and Taylor, agalmatophilia has been dropped "over a few thousand years" from mankind's "repertoire of pathologies"; or "it might merely have changed its form because the burgeoning plastics industry has rendered obsolete the pathological focus on stone statues *per se*".[5] Accepting only a single documented case of agalmatophilia as genuine, White argues for viewing it as a pornographic fantasy rather than an actual behavioural perversion.[6] Whether or not there is a kernel of historical truth to any of the incidents mentioned in our sources (something impossible to determine), the frequency with which such anecdotes are told in a wide variety of contexts is remarkable. As Bettini has argued, agalmatophilia tales form part of a wider narrative pattern — what he calls "the fundamental story" — surrounding the triad of lover, beloved and portrait.[7] There are many variations on this theme, in which the portrait serves as a substitute for an absent or dead beloved (think, for instance, of Laodamia taking to bed a wax figure of her deceased husband, or of Admetus' plan to do the same with an image of Alkestis, who is about to sacrifice her life for him).[8] In the case of the agalmatophilia narratives that form the subject of my chapter the beloved *qua* referent of the portrait has disappeared and the image itself takes on the role of the beloved.[9]

---

5 Scobie/Taylor 1975, 49. Since the 1970s, the fabrication of sex dolls has become increasingly more sophisticated: fashioned from silicone, so-called RealDolls are designed to resemble the human body in appearance, texture and weight; they are custom-made to fit the sexual preferences of each client. A closer comparison between the erotic desire for ancient statues and modern-day sex dolls would be fascinating, though lies beyond the scope of my paper.
6 White 1978. For the discussion of statue love as a sexual perversion in the 19th century, cf. Janssen 2020, 423–424.
7 Cf. Bettini 1999, with 57–74 on agalmatophilia.
8 For Laodamia, cf. Apollod. 3.30, Hyg. *Fab.* 103–104 with Bettini 1999, 9–14; see also Michalopoulos' discussion of *Heroides* 13 in this volume; for Alkestis, cf. Eur. *Alc.* 348–354 with Bettini 1999, 18–25.
9 Bettini 1999, 66: "In a story of incredible love, the beloved simply *is* the portrait itself; the image supersedes the referent. Our fundamental story (two lovers, and the portrait of one of them) is thus drastically transformed: the beloved and his (or her) portrait *are conflated*, abruptly eliminating one of the pawns from play and producing what we might call a more economical variation on our fundamental story".

I would like to ask how ancient texts envision the sexual interaction between human and statue.[10] Erotic desire could also be elicited by two-dimensional pictures — indeed, love for a painting seems to have been a popular rhetorical *topos*[11] — but my discussion will be limited to cases of statue-love. What physical acts are, I ask, represented, and in what light do they appear? What kind of statues elicit sexual desire? And is such desire ever truly satisfied? My chapter is decidedly not concerned with the question of whether statues actually functioned as sex objects in antiquity, and how common a practice this might have been. I would think that pretty much any object could and was used for sexual purposes at some point in human history, but barring any scientific evidence, such as traces of semen detectable upon the stone (as they could allegedly be seen on Praxiteles' Knidian Aphrodite), we really cannot tell what the ancients did or did not do to their statues. What I am interested in is how they conceptualised the sexual allure of statuary, and how agalmatophilia manifests itself as a literary motif.

I would like to begin my considerations with an example taken not from the world of humans but from the animal realm. According to Pausanias, a bronze mare dedicated by Phormis at Olympia[12] drove stallions so wild that (5.27)

> they rush into the Altis, breaking their fetters or escaping from those who lead them, and they leap upon it with much greater frenzy than if they were mounting the most beautiful mare, living and tame. Their hoofs slip off and nonetheless they do not give up neighing ever more and leaping upon it with yet fiercer passion, until they are dragged away with whips and sheer force. Before that there is no way of separating them from the bronze.

This forceful reaction is all the more surprising as the image could not compete in size or beauty with other equine statues in its vicinity — it was an unremarkable sculpture deformed by a broken tail (might this have been a result of earlier

---

10 On the motif of agalmatophilia, cf. Gourevitch 1982, Olmos 1992, González García 2006, Bossi 2012, Ferrari 2013; Gross 2006 and Hersey 2009 consider the phenomenon within wider studies on animated statues and artificial humans.

11 Onomarchos of Andros (2nd cent. AD) presented a speech in the voice of an image-lover (ἐπὶ τοῦ τῆς εἰκόνος ἐρῶντος); cf. Philostr. VS 2.18. Severus of Alexandria (4th cent. AD) wrote an *ēthopoiía* on the topic τίνας ἂν εἴποι λόγους ζωγράφος γράψας κόρην καὶ ἐρασθεὶς αὐτῆς ("What would a painter say who had painted a girl and fallen in love with her?" Sev. Alex. Ethop. 8 = Ps.-Liban. Ethop. 27). For the motif see also Aristaenet. 2.10 with Höschele 2012, 176–178.

12 Originally from Maenalos, Phormis distinguished himself in the service of the Syracusan tyrant Gelon in the early 5th cent. BC. The statue in question — a work by Simon of Aegina — was accompanied by the image of a groom; it stood next to another horse and groom by Dionysios of Argos, likewise dedicated by Phormis.

assaults by randy stallions? one wonders). The Elians, Pausanias tells us, therefore believed the bronze to be charmed, containing the mysterious aphrodisiac *hippomanes* (a substance "driving horses mad"). As Aelian (*HA* 14.18), who likewise discusses the stallions' curious passion for the image, asserts, "the bronze plays a trick on the living horses through some hidden contrivance of the artist (κρυφίῳ τινὶ μηχανῇ τοῦ τεχνίτου), for the representation could not possess such great accuracy (τοσαύτην ἀκρίβειαν) that horses upon seeing it should be deceived and inflamed to that extent".[13] But could it truly not? Athenaios, after all, recalls a bronze cow mounted by a bull in Peirene (Ath. 13.605f), Valerius Maximus (8.11 ext. 4) knows of another such case in Syracuse;[14] in addition, there seem to have circulated stories about dogs, pigeons, geese and horses excited by *pictures* of their female counterparts (Ath. 13.605f; Val. Max. 8.11 ext. 4; Clem. Al. *Protr.* 4.57.4). That animals could very well exhibit such behaviour is incontrovertibly proven by an amorous moose in Grand Lake, Colorado, which was caught on tape some years ago in the act of mounting the statue of another male moose (according to locals, it started doing so within a week of the statue's erection and would come to mate with the object of its desire every morning).[15]

Aelian's comment, at any rate, touches upon a crucial aspect of agalmatophilia tales: the idea of lifelikeness. Even as he rejects the possibility of such illusory power, ancient *ekphraseis* often praise artworks for deceiving their spectators — be they humans or animals — into thinking they truly are what they purport to be. A case in point are the numerous epigrammatic variations on the cow of Myron, which looks so authentic that it is stung by a gadfly (*AP* 9.739), calves desire to suckle from it (*AP* 9.721, 735) and bulls try to mount it (*AP* 9.730 and 734, Auson. 63.3 and 64, *Ep. Bob.* 12).[16] In this instance, the sex-crazed bull is but one among many (fictional) examples illustrating the stunning lifelikeness of Myron's work. Note, too, that it is precisely the lifelike appearance of the ivory girl that makes Pygmalion fall in love with his own creation: "she has the appearance of a real girl, and you could believe that she's alive and wishes to move, if her modesty did not stand in the way: *ars adeo latet arte sua* ("so much was art hidden by its own art"), as Ovid memorably put it (*Met.* 10.250–252).

---

13 Cf. also Plin. *NH* 28.181.

14 He presumably refers to the incident that Livy records as a prodigy for the year 177 BC: *vaccam aeneam Syracusis ab agresti tauro, qui a pecore aberrasset initam ac semine dispersam* ("a bronze cow in Sicily mounted by a wild bull, which had erred away from his herd, and besprinkled by his semen").

15 Cf. https://www.usatoday.com/videos/news/2013/06/03/2383923.

16 On the epigrams about Myron's cow, cf. Squire 2010.

It surely is no coincidence that tales of agalmatophilia seem to emerge in response to statues of the classical age, at a point, that is, when Greek sculptors were striving for ever greater naturalism in their art. Most frequently such stories are spun around specific statues, including widely celebrated masterpieces. As O'Bryhim has recently argued, cities may have disseminated tales of this kind to attract visitors to the artworks they housed.[17] I would not go so far as to attribute the origin of all agalmatophilia tales to the ancient tourist industry, but it is certainly conceivable that they were exploited for economic purposes. At the same time, the anecdotes became part of the art critical discourse: as Robert observed, they were told not simply for the purpose of amusement, but, like biographical anecdotes taken from an artist's life, they were used to exemplify certain qualities of his work.[18]

The vast majority of references to incidents of statue-love are to be found in writings of the Imperial age, but some texts point us to earlier sources, the eldest of which date to the 4th/3rd century BC. Let me begin with a brief overview of the statues featured in these narratives and the contexts in which we encounter them.[19] Interestingly, the motif is first attested in Middle and New Comedy: Athenaios (13.605f–606a) quotes three lines each from plays by Alexis (41 K.–A.) and Philemon (127 K.–A.), which recall how a man locked himself up in a temple on Samos to sleep with a statue that had caught his fancy. The comedy of Alexis, from which Athenaios draws his quotation, was entitled Γραφή ("The Picture"), and on the basis of this title one may speculate that it featured a young man infatuated with a painting,[20] though this supposition is solely based on the parallel drawn between the statue-loving man in Samos and what seems to have been a similar occurrence in the play (41 K.–A.):

> γεγένηται δ', ὡς λέγουσιν, κἄν Σάμῳ
> τοιοῦθ' ἕτερον. λιθίνης ἐπεθύμησεν κόρης
> ἄνθρωπος ἐγκατέκλεισέ θ' αὑτὸν τῷ νεῷ.

---

17 O'Bryhim 2015.
18 Cf. Robert 1992, 385: "Ces anecdotes, ainsi que celles qui concernent la vie des artistes auxquelles elles sont étroitement liées [...], ne sont pas de simples amusements de rhéteurs, elles fonctionnent comme de véritables *exempla* qui n'illustrent pas simplement, mais traduisent sous forme de récit, un jugement critique en mettant en scène la ou les *virtutes* caractéristiques d'un peintre ou d'un sculpteur, à l'intérieur d'un système d'échelle de valeurs prédéterminé." He argues that periegetes at the court of Pergamon were the first to systematically use such anecdotes.
19 For an overview of all sources, cf. also the Appendix to this article.
20 Thus the hypothesis of Meineke, *FCG* 3.402, who speculates that Aristainetos 2.10 might have been inspired by Alexis' comedy. Arnott 1996, 149 calls the idea "attractive but unverifiable".

Something like this happened, they say, also in Samos: A man was seized by desire for a girl in stone and he locked himself into the temple.

According to Athenaios, Adaios of Mytilene, who wrote a treatise Περὶ Ἀγαλματο-ποιῶν in the second half of the 3rd century BC, identified the image in question as a work by Ktesikles, an otherwise unknown artist.[21] Polemon of Ilion, or "whoever wrote the treatise entitled *Account of Greece*", recorded a similar incident concerning the stone image of a boy, one in a pair of two παῖδες set up in the Treasury of Spina at Delphi.

By far the most famous "victim" of a man's desire was Praxiteles' Knidian Aphrodite. No other sculpture features as often in tales of agalmatophilia (there are 9 references in 7 authors from Valerius Maximus to Tzetzes).[22] And no wonder: Praxiteles' sculpture was celebrated for being the first life-size representation of a female nude.[23] Reportedly modeled on Phryne, the artist's courtesan lover (who also inspired Apelles' *Aphrodite Anadyomene*), this marble image of the goddess of love came to be seen as the epitome of erotic allure. Here is what Pliny the Elder writes (*NH* 36.20):

> But greater than all works, not only of Praxiteles, but indeed in the whole world, is the Venus, for whose sake many have sailed to Knidos just in order to see her. He had made two statues and put them up for sale at the same time. One of them was represented with her body veiled, for which reason the people of Kos, whose choice it was, preferred it, even though he had offered both at the same price, as they judged this representation to be stern and chaste. The people of Knidos bought the rejected one, whose fame has become immeasurably greater. Later on, King Nikomedes wished to buy it from the Knidians, and promised that he would cancel the city's entire debt, which was immense. They, however, rather bore everything, and not without reason. For with that statue Praxiteles rendered Knidos famous. Its shrine is open all around, so that it is possible to behold from every side the image of the goddess, whose fabrication was, it is believed, favoured by Venus herself. Nor indeed is there any side from which the statue would be less admirable. People say that a certain man was once seized by desire for the statue and, after hiding away there at night, he embraced it, leaving behind a stain as a mark of his lust (*eiusque cupiditatis esse indicem maculam*).

---

21 According to the *DNO* 2645, the statue might have been a nude Aphrodite fashioned in the style of Praxiteles' *Knidia* some time after 340 BC. In Alexis' comedy we hear of a κόρη, not a goddess, but one may suppose that he chose this designation to align the *exemplum* with the plot of his play.
22 Posidippus, *Peri Knidou* (as quoted by Clem. Al. *Protr.* 4.57.3, Arnob. *Adv. Gent.* 6.22); Ptolemaios Hephaistion (as quoted by Tzetzes, *Chil.* 8.375); Plin. *NH* 36.21, 7.121; Luc. *Imag.* 4; *Am.* 13-16; Philostr. *VA.* 6.40; Val. Max. 8.11 ext. 4.
23 On the Knidian Aphrodite, cf. Havelock 1995 and Corso 2007, 9–186.

Again, the narrative follows the same basic pattern, centred on a man satisfying his lust, while he is locked up in the temple overnight. As far as we can tell, the occurrence was first recorded in the treatise Περὶ Κνίδου, whose author, Posidippus, is possibly identical with the well-known Hellenistic epigrammatist.[24] Another local history from the Hellenistic age (also 3rd cent. BC), Philostephanos' *Kypriaka* (*FHG* 3.31 F 13 Müller), seems to have preserved an earlier version of the Pygmalion story, in which the latter is a king of Cyprus and has sex with the ivory image of a nude Aphrodite. We owe our knowledge of these Hellenistic treatments of statue-love to two Christian authors, Clement of Alexandria (2nd/3rd cent.) and Arnobius (3rd/4th cent.), who bring up both anecdotes in their railings against pagan idolatry (Clem. Al. *Protr.* 4.57.3; Arnob. *Contr. Gent.* 6.22).[25] Where ancient texts celebrate art's capacity to deceive its spectators, Clement finds this sort of deception highly objectionable. "But", he writes, "it was the eyes of the spectators that were deceived by art (ὑπὸ τῆς τέχνης). For no man sound of mind would have embraced a goddess, entombed himself with a dead body, or loved a demon and stone".[26] Sex with statues is scandalous, no doubt about that – but while Christian authors see in it the peak of immorality, the ancients clearly delighted in the titillating nature of such tales (even if the transgressive desire is, in some cases, presented as leading to the statue-lover's death, the imagined penalty ultimately serves to heighten the drama and with it the reader's narrative pleasure; it is not the basis for a moralising condemnation of the agalmatophiliac's behaviour).

The Knidian Aphrodite was not the only work by Praxiteles to attract a lover: according to Pliny (*NH* 36.22), a nude Eros sculpted by the same artist, which was at display in the Parian colony of Propontis, suffered the same fate. Several further instances of agalmatophilia are recorded in the *Natural History*: Lysippos' *Apoxyomenos*, which had been brought to Rome and set up in the Baths of Agrippa, was desired by none other than Emperor Tiberius (34.61–62). Nero, in turn, was in love with an Amazon by the 5th-century sculptor Strongylion known as "She-of-the-shapely-legs" or Εὔκνημος (34.48; 82), while a bronze statuette of

---

24 According to Jacoby, *FGrH* III b comm 292 n. 2 one can neither prove nor disprove the identity of this author with the homonymous epigrammatist. For further discussion, cf. also Robert 1992, 388 n. 39.

25 On the demonisation of pagan statues, including the evocation of the Knidia in Christian polemics, cf. Hinz 1998, 96–106.

26 Arnobius brings up the examples of Pygmalion and the Knidian Aphrodite in the context of a wider argument against the notion that gods inhabit their images: Why, he asks, would Aphrodite have allowed this violence against her statues? Why did she not punish the men, or bring them back to their senses?

a boy by the same artist was loved by Brutus, the murderer of Caesar, who conferred his own name on the boy (34.82).[27] An otherwise unknown Roman knight, Iunius Pisciculus, became enamoured with one of the Thespian Muses, which had likewise been brought to Rome and erected next to the temple of Felicitas in the Campus Martius (36.39 with reference to Varro). Last but not least, Aelian (*VH* 9.39) tells us of a young man who fell in love with a statue of *Agathē Tychē*, which stood next to the *prytaneion* in Athens.

Before taking a closer look at individual episodes, let me make some general observations. Among the transmitted cases of agalmatophilia, we find 6 female statues as objects of desire vs 4 statues representing boys/male youths. Without exception, the human lover is male. Women could, as we shall see below, also be envisioned in sexual acts with statues, but none of the tales related to actual artworks involve a female lover. Most of the statues are fashioned from marble, but the corpus also contains three works in bronze (Strongylion's two pieces as well as Lysippos' *Apoxyomenos*) and one in ivory. Apart from the ivory image of Aphrodite, loved by Pygmalion, which probably belongs to the realm of legend, all of the statues were or appear to have been real sculptures.

In several instances, the lover is an anonymous figure: τις (Philostr. *VA* 6.40); ἄνθρωπος ... τις (Philem. 127.2 K-A), *quendam* (Plin. *NH* 36.21), νεανίσκος (Ael. *VH* 9.39) etc. Pseudo-Lucian, who offers the most detailed account of a man's one-night stand with the Knidian Aphrodite,[28] even reflects on the anonymity of the protagonist, made nameless by his blasphemous deed: οὐκ ἀσήμου γένους νεανίαν — ἡ δὲ πρᾶξις ἀνώνυμον αὐτὸν ἐσίγησεν ("a young man from a distinguished family — but his act has made his name unspeakable", *Am.* 15). However, a greater number of reports identifies the agalmatophiliac by name, and nearly all of them — with the exception of Tiberius, Nero and Brutus — are otherwise completely obscure to us: from Kleisophos of Selymbria (in love with the Samian *agalma*, Athen. 13.605f), Alketas of Rhodes (passionate for the Parian Eros, Plin. *NH* 36.22) and Makareus of Perinthos (lusting after the Knidian Aphrodite)[29] to the *eques* Iunius Pisciculus (enamoured of a Thespian Muse, Plin. *NH* 36.39). Such specific identifications presumably served to give the accounts a semblance of historicity and a verisimilitude comparable to the emphatic lifelikeness of the statues. Interestingly, only the Romans seem to have ascribed agalmatophiliac

---

27 His passion for the boy is commemorated also in several epigrams by Martial (2.77, 9.50, 14.171).

28 Cf. Haynes 2013.

29 According to Tzetzes, *Chil.* 8 *hist.* 195, this name was given by Ptolemaios Hephaistion, i.e. Ptolemaios Chennos, a grammarian from Alexandria (fl. c. 100 AD).

behaviour to historical figures, though one cannot exclude that similar anecdotes about prominent Greeks have been lost.

In some cases, the reference is extremely brief and does not provide any details about how (and if) the lover acted upon his desire. All we hear about Iunius Pisciculus, for instance, is that he loved (*amavit*) one of the Thespiades. In general, however, we can distinguish between two modes of sexual conquest: first, appropriation of the statue for private purposes, and second, secret copulation with the statue in its sacred precinct. Notably, agalmatophiliacs do not refrain from showing their affection for a statue openly; their public interaction with the image, indeed, resembles that of worshippers, who might offer gifts to an *agalma* or embrace it (in one of his Verrine orations Cicero, for instance, recalls a bronze image of Hercules in Agrigentum, "whose mouth and chin are a little worn away because men, in addressing their prayers and congratulations to him, are accustomed to not simply venerate but even to kiss it").[30] The sexual act itself, however, occurs — if it does occur — in secrecy.

Let us contemplate the examples of (failed or successful) appropriation: the young man in love with *Agathē Tychē* kissed and embraced the statue in public; driven wild by desire he went to the Athenian *boulē* and proposed to purchase the statue for a great sum of money. When they denied his request, he decorated his beloved with bands, garlands and jewellery before killing himself in despair. It is certainly easier to get hold of a statue when you happen to be a Roman emperor: Tiberius had Lysippos' *Apoxyomenos* transferred from the baths to his bedroom, putting another sculpture in its place (Plin. *NH* 34.61–62). His liaison with the *Scraper* was, however, not meant to last: when an outraged public demanded "give us back our *Apoxyomenos*", he grudgingly returned the object of his desire. What he did with the bronze youth in the privacy of his bedchamber is left to our imagination. Attracted by the beautiful legs of Strongylion's Amazon, Nero had the image carried around in his retinue wherever he went (we are not told about any physical interaction with the bronze Amazon; like the boy of Brutus, it may have been a statuette[31] rather than a life-size representation, and one might question its use for sexual purposes). Noteworthy in this context is also a papyrus

---

30 Cic. *Verr.* 2.4.94. On ritual treatment of Greek cult statues, cf. Scheer 2000 54–66 and Steiner 2001, 105–120. On physical interaction with statues in the Roman world, cf. Weddle 2010, with ch. 4.2 on touching and kissing; see also Kiernan 2020, 200–207.

31 The hypothesis that the Amazon was a statuette is based solely on the fact that Nero is said to have brought it along on his travels (*DNO* 1165), though surely it would not have been impossible for a Roman emperor to have a life-size image transported wherever he went.

fragment dating to the 3rd cent. AD from a work containing questions and answers on antiquarian subjects (*P.Oxy.* 2688). It records how Aphrodite herself came to sleep with a man who had stolen an image of her in Paphos.[32] The story seems to have been an *aetion* for a custom in the temple of Paphian Aphrodite involving garlands and roses, but the text is too fragmentary to make out all details. By connecting the theft of the statue with an epiphany of the goddess, it does, at any rate, reflect on the belief that deities were present in their cult images (which, in many cases, makes agalmatophiliac desire all the more transgressive).

Instances of actual copulation with a statue are only reported for Praxiteles' Knidian Aphrodite and his Parian Eros, Ktesikles' *agalma* in Samos, and the image of a boy in Delphi. As we have seen, the narratives follow the same basic pattern, with the man locking himself up with the statue overnight. The agalmatophiliac at Delphi was caught after his tryst with the marble παῖς, but since he had left a garland behind at the site of his crime, the oracle of Apollo declared that he should be released as he had given appropriate payment. Less fortunate was the fate of Aphrodite's lover: after satisfying his lust, he reportedly hurled himself off a cliff and vanished without a trace (Ps.–Luc. *Am.* 16). What he did leave behind was, allegedly, a dark mark on one of Aphrodite's thighs.[33] Taking the stain to be a natural blemish in the stone, Lykinos, the narrator in Pseudo-Lucian's *Erotes*, admires Praxiteles for having hidden "the disfigurement of the stone in the parts that can be less easily examined" (15). It is this comment that inspires the female temple attendant to reveal the "true" origin of the mark. After hearing the story, Lykinos' friend, Kallikratidas, a passionate pederast, is quick to point out that "although the enamoured youth had taken the whole night so as to have the opportunity to completely satisfy his passion, he nevertheless had intercourse with the marble as with a boy, because, I'm sure, he didn't want to face the female parts" (ὁ ἐρασθεὶς νεανίας παννύχου σχολῆς λαβόμενος, ὥσθ' ὅλην τοῦ πάθους ἔχειν ἐξουσίαν κορεσθῆναι, παιδικῶς τῷ λίθῳ προσωμίλησεν βουληθεὶς οἶδ' ὅτι μηδὲν πρόσθεν εἶναι τὸ θῆλυ, *Am.* 17). His is a rather idiosyncratic reading of the "evidence"; a more objective observer might conclude that the statue's posture made frontal sex less practicable (Aphrodite was, after all, covering her *pudenda* with one hand). Also worthy of note is another remark by the pederast: "we don't

32 ἁρπάσας τῆς ἐν Κύπρῳ Ἀφ[ροδίτης |]ιον ἐκ[όμ]ι[σ]εν εἰς τὴν οἰ[κίαν· ἡ μὲν ἤ-| κουσα [καὶ] ἰδοῦσα τὸν νεαν[ίαν ἔχον- | τα αὐτὸ ἐν τῇ χειρὶ εἰς ὁμε[ιλίαν καὶ | πλησιασμὸν ἦλθεν. ("stealing [the image] of the Cyprian Aphrodite, he brought it to his home. When she came and saw the young man holding it in his hand, she approached him for sexual intercourse", *P.Oxy.* 2688.7–11).
33 Cf. also Plin. *NH* 36.20 quoted above.

know yet, Charicles, whether we won't hear many such stories when we come to Thespiae" — a marvellous reflection on the popularity of agalmatophilia tales. While no such report concerning Praxiteles' Thespian Eros survives, Pliny tells us that a similar mark — he calls it a *vestigium amoris* (*NH* 36.22) — could be seen on the sculptor's Parian Eros (his mention of the incident is extremely brief, but it is likely that a more detailed anecdote resembling the ones we just considered was attached to it).

At this point one might ask: what is it like to have sex with a statue? Kleisophos, at least, found the experience rather disappointing. Here is the full account, as given by Athenaios (605f):

> οὗτος γὰρ τοῦ ἐν Σάμῳ Παρίου ἀγάλματος ἐρασθεὶς κατέκλεισεν αὐτὸν ἐν τῷ ναῷ, ὡς πλη-
> σιάσαι δυνησόμενος· καὶ ὡς ἠδυνάτει διά τε τὴν ψυχρότητα καὶ τὸ ἀντίτυπον τοῦ λίθου,
> τηνικαῦτα τῆς ἐπιθυμίας ἀπέστη καὶ προβαλλόμενός τι σαρκίον ἐπλησίασεν.

> Having fallen in love with a statue in Parian marble at Samos, he locked himself into the temple so as to be able to have sex with it. However, when he was unable to perform due to the coolness and resistance of the stone, he desisted from his desire and putting before him a piece of meat he had sex with it instead.

The two men consorting with Praxiteles' statues do not seem to have had the same troubles, but this comical anecdote well captures the drawbacks of using a sculpture for sex: the images may resemble living beings, but in the end, they cannot respond to a lover's touch and their lack of life becomes manifest in the rigidity of the material.[34] In a way, the passivity of the image is in line with the role that the ancient gender discourse ascribed to women, and one can see why the idea of a male agalmatophiliac more readily suggested itself to the ancient imagination than that of a female one attempting to have sex with an immobile statue.[35] The impossibility of such intercourse is evoked in a fascinating comparison in Achilles Tatius' *Leukippe and Kleitophon* (5.22). When the novel's male protagonist adamantly refuses to have sex with Melite, she observes: "I seem to

---

34 The hardness of the stone makes the statue appear in the role of a *dura puella*, the mistress of Latin love elegy. Ovid indeed plays with this topos by casting Pygmalion as an elegiac lover and the ivory statue as his cold and unresponsive beloved; cf. Sharrock 1991.
35 Similarly, Bettini 1999, 72: "Given a culture in which the practice of pleasure was fundamentally based on the stereotype of penetration, and on a polarised contrast of active and passive, the image would thus be able to represent the very prototype of sexual passivity."

love a statue, I get no more than ocular satisfaction from my beloved" (ἔοικα δὲ εἰκόνος ἐρᾶν· μέχρι γὰρ τῶν ὀμμάτων ἔχω τὸν ἐρώμενον).³⁶

Even as the statue in Melite's comparison epitomises the complete unresponsiveness of her beloved and his persistent denial of intercourse, there are texts which envision women using statues as sex objects. That the ancients could conceive of *female* desire for statuary is shown by an observation attributed to the pre-Socratic philosopher Empedokles, who thus explained the existence of children resembling people other than their parents (DK 31A81 = Aetius 5.12.2). According to the Byzantine physician Aetius, Empedokles said "that embryos are shaped by the imagination of the woman at the time of conception: for often women are seized by a passion for statues or images (πολλάκις γὰρ ἀνδριάντων καὶ εἰκόνων ἠράσθησαν γυναῖκες) and they give birth to children resembling them". While the women in this theory of maternal impression³⁷ (as it is commonly known) are filled with sexual desire for a statue or image they have seen, they act on this desire only insofar as they fantasise about it while sleeping with their husband; they do not physically interact with the image. In a world where the movement of women and their contact with men outside of their household was severely restricted, it may not be a coincidence that female fantasies would (or were thought to) focus on statues, i.e. objects located in places they could freely access in the context of cult festivals: the images were available to fantasise about in a way that flesh-and-blood men were not.

As mentioned above, none of the agalmatophilia narratives concerning actual works of art feature a female protagonist.³⁸ A text where we do encounter the idea of women sexually engaging with statues is the anonymous collection of *Carmina Priapea*, in whose centre stands a statue of the ithyphallic garden god.³⁹ This fictional Priapus again and again threatens to punish thieves (of either gender) by penetration, though for the most part his punitive action remains limited to verbal abuse.⁴⁰ The epigrams, at any rate, offer a fascinating variation on tra-

---

36 Note how the use of *erōmenos* with reference to Kleitophon underlines the reversal of the usual gender stereotypes of active (male) lover and passive (female) beloved in this scene.
37 For ancient instances of the maternal impression theory, see Beagon 2005, 213–215 on Plin. *NH* 7.52.
38 Clem. *Protr.* 4.51 contains a vague reference to a girl who reportedly fell in love with an image; the context suggests that it was a painting, not a statue (ἐρασθῆναι κόρην εἰκόνος λέγουσιν).
39 For a more detailed discussion of the examples given below, cf. Michalopoulos in this volume.
40 Altogether, Priapus cuts a rather ridiculous figure, as he becomes increasingly impotent in the course of the collection; cf. Holzberg 2005 and Höschele 2010, 295–307.

ditional agalmatophilia tales by contemplating the idea of sexual relations between human and image *from the statue's perspective*. As far as female agalmatophiliacs are concerned, Priapus claims, for instance, that lascivious girls desire its member (c. 25.3 *quod pathicae petunt puellae*).[41] One epigram speaks of a *puella* giving kisses to his mid-section (c. 43.2), which Priapus interprets as a sign that she wishes to be penetrated by him, while another shows him in a state of complete exhaustion, since "neighbouring women, horny without end" have tired him out all night (c. 26.3–4: *quod totis mihi noctibus fatigant / vicinae sine fine prurientes*). These epigrammatic fantasies are clearly meant for the amusement of the reader. Intercourse with Priapus is presented in a completely different light by Augustine, who evokes with horror a nuptial rite which ordered "the new bride to sit on the god's gigantic and ugly phallus" (*de civ. Dei* 6.9[42]); in other Christian authors, who recall the same rite, the Italic god Mutunus Tutunus appears in the role of Priapus.[43] Notably, we do not have any reports of such a custom on the part of pagan authors, and one may have doubts about its existence. That we hear of it from Christians, who condemn all forms of idolatry, is hardly surprising. As we have seen, to them sexual interaction between humans and statues is the perfect example of ungodly, demonic behaviour — an idea that continues to live on: Nikephoros' Byzantine *Life of St Andrew the Fool*, for instance, tells of a woman possessed by the devil who causes her to dream of embracing the statues in the Hippodrome at Constantinople, "urged by a whorish desire to have intercourse with them".[44]

But let us return once more to the ancient world and a more cheerful vision of sex with statues, as it appears on a Roman sarcophagus from around 150 AD.[45] Its depiction of a Dionysiac feast is framed by two remarkable images: on the left,

---

41 In c. 66 Priapus, moreover, insinuates that a woman who turns her gaze away from his member wishes to have inside her what she fears to look at (*nimirum, nisi quod times videre / intra viscera habere concupiscis*, v. 3–4).

42 *Priapus nimius masculus, super cuius inmanissimum et turpissimum fascinum sedere nova nupta iubebatur* (cf. also *de civ.* 7.24).

43 E.g. Arnob. *Adv. Gent.* 4.7 (*Tutunus, cuius immanibus pudendis horrentique fascino vestras inequitare matronas*); Lact. *Div. inst.* 1.20.36 (*Tutinus, in cuius sinu pudenda nubentes praesident*). For a full collection of references to this god, cf. Herter 1927.

44 Cf. ll. 2491–2494 Rydén (780c): Πάλιν ἐν ἑτέρᾳ νυκτὶ ὁρᾷ ἑαυτὴν ἐν τῷ θεάτρῳ τοῦ ἱπποδρομίου ἑστῶσαν καὶ ἀσπαζομένην τὰ ἐκεῖσε ἑστῶτα ἀγάλματα, νυττομένην ὑπὸ πορνικῆς ἐπιθυμίας τοῦ συγγενέσθαι μετ' αὐτῶν. ("Again, in another night, she sees herself standing in the hippodrome theatre and kissing the statues that stand there, urged by a whorish desire to have intercourse with them.")

45 It forms part of the collection of the Museo Nazionale in Naples (inv. N. 27710). On this Dionysiac sarcophagus, cf. Zanker/Ewald 2012, 139–141 with images; Leveritt 2016, 291–294.

a female faun inserts the erect phallus of a herm into her vagina,[46] on the right, another female faun is about to be penetrated from behind while holding on to the herm of a satyr.

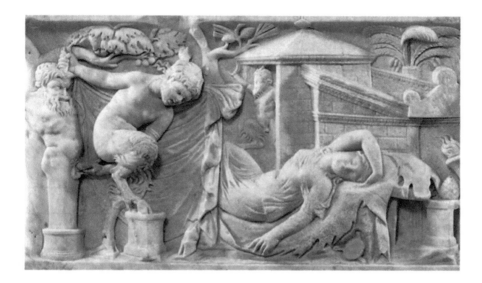

Fig. 36: Scene from a Roman sarcophagus, c. 150 AD (Museo Nazionale, Naples, Inv. no. 27710).

The image is humorous — note, in particular, how the faun is holding on to an erect lock of Priapus' hair so as not to tip over. The herm itself seems to come to

---

46 As Évelyne Prioux points out to me, the same motif can be found on a (lost?) carnelian stone reproduced and described in Pierre François Hugues d'Hancarville's *Monuments du culte secret des dames romaines* (1784), n. 22 (https://gallica.bnf.fr/ark:/12148/bpt6k55160418.texteImage), though this stone might be a modern fake inspired by reproductions of the Naples sarcophagus (cf. e.g. a 16th-century print by Marcantonio in the British Museum, inv. 1868,0808.3181; https://www.britishmuseum.org/collection/object/P_1868-0808-3181). Other erotic interactions (without penetration) can be seen, for instance: on an engraved amethyst (Hancarville, n. 6), where a woman caresses Priapus' member, holding a vase underneath it, presumably to catch his semen; on a jasper which shows two women fondling a statue of Priapus (Bibliothèque Nationale de France inv.58.1678ter; http://medaillesetantiques.bnf.fr/ws/catalogue/app/collec tion/record/23739?vc=ePkH4LF7w6yelGA1iKUSSsKCJuiAoszEglRojUhk2tHHE3wARZQtAA$$); on an engraved gem, where a Maenad embraces an image of Priapus (Gemmenkasten Tav. 11 in the collection of Schloss Wörlitz, https://nat.museum-digital.de/index.php?t=objekt& oges=174 489).

live, tilting its hips forward and happily offering up its member for intercourse, while, in the background, a cult-image of Pan leaps from its shrine, lured out by the action. It strikes me as telling that this representation of agalmatophilia appears in an orgiastic scene populated with mythical creatures, i.e. at a distinct remove from the human realm. The image invites us to picture the moment of actual penetration, but the statue-lover, who is herself formed from stone, is eternally frozen in the act of lifting herself onto the phallus. As in Buñuel's *L'âge d'or*, the consummation of sexual desire is forever suspended.

Appendix

Tab. 1: Overview of agalmatophilia tales.

Work	Artist	Location	Lover	Sources
agalma (Aphrodite?), Parian marble	Ktesikles	Samos	Kleisophos of Selymbria	Alexis (*Γραφή*), Philemon, Adaios of Mytilene (*Περὶ ἀγαλματοποιῶν*), all quoted by Athen. 605f–606a
boy in a pair of two παῖδες λίθινοι		Treasury of Spina, Delphi	anonymous	Polemon of Ilion (or another author) in Ἑλλαδικόν, as quoted by Athen. 606b
Aphrodite (marble)	Praxiteles	Knidos	Anonymous, Makareus of Perinthos (acc. to Tzetzes)	Posidippus, *Περὶ Κνίδου* (Clem. Al. *Protr.* 4.57.3, Arnob. *Adv. Gent.* 6.22); Ptolemaios Hephaistion (Tzetz. *Chil.* 8.375); Plin. *NH* 36.21, 7.121; Luc. *Imag.* 4; *Am.* 13–16; Philostr. *VA.* 6.40; Val. Max. 8.11 ext. 4
Aphrodite (ivory)		Cyprus	Pygmalion	Philostephanos, *Κυπριακά*, as quoted by Clement, *Protr.* 4.57 and Arnob., *Adv. Gent.* 6.22
Eros (marble)	Praxiteles	Parian colony of Propontis	Alketas of Rhodes	Pliny, *NH* 36.22
Apoxyomenos (bronze)	Lysippos	Rome	Tiberius	Pliny, *NH* 34.61–62

Work	Artist	Location	Lover	Sources
Amazon Εὔκνημος (bronze)	Strongylion	Rome	Nero	Pliny, *NH* 34.48; 82
παιδίον (bronze)	Strongylion	Rome	Brutus	Pliny, *NH* 34.82 (Martial 2.77; 9.50; 14.171)
Thespiades (marble)		Rome	Iunius Pisciculus, *eques*	Varro, as quoted by Pliny, *NH* 36.39
Agathē Tychē (presumably marble)		Athens	Anonymous young man	Aelian, *Hist. var.* 9.39

Bibliography

Arnott, G. (1996), *Alexis. The Fragments: A Commentary*, Cambridge.

Beagon, M. (2005), *The Elder Pliny on the Human Animal: Natural History, Book 7*, Oxford.

Bettini, M. (1999), *The Portrait of the Lover*, Transl. by L. Gibbs, Berkeley/Los Angeles/London.

Blühm, A. (1988), *Pygmalion: Die Ikonographie eines Künstler-Mythos zwischen 1500-1900*, Frankfurt am Main.

Bossi, L. (2012), *De l'agalmatophilie ou L'amour des statues*, Paris.

Corso, A. (2007), *The Art of Praxiteles II: The Mature Years*, Rome.

Dinter, A. (1979), *Der Pygmalion-Stoff in der europäischen Literatur: Rezeptionsgeschichte einer Ovid-Fabel*, Heidelberg.

Dörrie, H. (1974), *Pygmalion: Ein Impuls Ovids und seine Wirkungen bis in die Gegenwart*, Düsseldorf.

Felleman, S. (2017), 'The Mystery ... The Blood ... The Age of Gold: Sculpture in Surrealist and Surreal Cinema', in: S. Jacobs/S. Felleman/V. Adriaensens/L. Colpaert (eds.), *Screening Statues: Sculpture and Cinema*, Edinburgh, 46–64.

Ferrari, G. (2013), 'Agalmatofilia. L'amore per le statue nel mondo antico: l'Afrodite di Cnido e il caso di Pigmalione', *Psicoart* 3 (https://psicoart.unibo.it/article/view/3452).

González García, J.L. (2006), 'Por amor al arte. Notas sobre la agalmatofilia y la *Imitatio Creatoris*, de Platón a Winckelmann', in: *Anales de Historia del Arte* 16, 131–150.

Gourevitch, D. (1982), 'Quelques fantasmes érotiques et perversions d'objet dans la littérature gréco-romaine', in: *Mélanges de l'Ecole française de Rome, Antiquité* 94, 823–842.

Gross, K. (2006), *The Dream of the Moving Statue*, University Park, PA.

Havelock, C.M. (1995), *The Aphrodite of Knidos and Her Successors: A Historical Review of the Female Nude in Greek Art*, Ann Arbor.

Haynes, M. (2013), 'Framing a View of the Unviewable: Architecture, Aphrodite, and Erotic Looking in the Lucianic *Erôtes*', in: *Helios* 40, 71–95.

Hersey, G.L. (2009), *Falling in Love with Statues: Artificial Humans from Pygmalion to the Present*, Chicago.

Herter, H. (1927), 'De Mutino Titino', in: *RhM* 76, 418–432.

Hinz, B. (1998), *Aphrodite: Geschichte einer abendländischen Passion*, München/Wien.

Höschele, R. (2010), *Die blütenlesende Muse: Poetik und Textualität antiker Epigrammsammlungen*, Tübingen.

Höschele, R. (2012) 'From Hellas with Love: The Aesthetics of Imitation in Aristaenetus's *Epistles*', in: *TAPA* 142, 157–186.

Holzberg, N. (2005), 'Impotence? It Happened to the Best of Them! A Linear Reading of the *Corpus Priapeorum*', in: *Hermes* 133, 368–381.

Janssen, D. (2020), 'From *Libidines nefandae* to sexual perversions', in: *History of Psychiatry* 31, 421–439.

Joshua, E. (2001), *Pygmalion and Galatea: The History of a Narrative in English Literature*, Aldershot.

Kansteiner, S. et al. (2014), *Der Neue Overbeck. Band III Spätklassik: Bildhauer des 4. Jhs. v.Chr. DNO 1799-2677*, Berlin/Boston.

Kiernan, P. (2020), *Roman Cult Images: The Lives and Worship of Idols from the Iron Age to Late Antiquity*, Cambridge.

Leveritt, W. (2016), *Dionysian Triumph Sarcophagi*, diss. Nottingham (http://eprints.nottingh am.ac.uk/33668/1/Thesis%20-%20images.pdf).

O'Bryhim, S. (2015), 'The Economics of Agalmatophilia', in: *CJ* 110, 419–429.

Olmos, R. (1992), 'El amor del hombre con la estatua: de la Antiguëdad a la Edad Media', in: H. Froning/T. Hölscher/H. Mielsch (eds.), *Kotinos: Festschrift für Erika Simon*, Mainz, 256–266.

Robert, R. (1992), '*Ars regenda amore*. Séduction érotique et plaisir esthétique: de Praxitèle à Ovide', in: *Mélanges de l'Ecole française de Rome*, in: *Antiquités* 104, 373–438.

Scheer, T. (2000), *Die Gottheit und ihr Bild: Untersuchungen zur Funktion griechischer Kultbilder in Religion und Politik*, München.

Scobie, A./Taylor, A.J.W. (1975), 'Perversions Ancient and Modern: I. Agalmatophilia, The Statue Syndrome', in: *Journal of the History of the Behavioral Sciences* 11, 49–54.

Sharrock, A. (1991), 'Womanufacture', in: *JRS* 81, 36–49.

Squire, M. (2010), 'Making Myron's Cow Moo? Ecphrastic Epigram and the Poetics of Simulation', in: *AJPh* 131, 589–634.

Steiner, D. (2001), *Images in Mind: Statues in Archaic and Classical Greek Literature and Thought*, Princeton.

Stoichita, V. (2008), *The Pygmalion Effect from Ovid to Hitchcock*, Chicago/London.

Studniczka, F. (1884), *Vermutungen zur griechischen Kunstgeschichte*, Wien.

Weddle, P. (2010), *Touching the Gods: physical interaction with cult statues in the Roman world*, diss. Durham (http://etheses.dur.ac.uk/555/1/Touching_the_Gods.pdf?DDD3+).

White, M. (1978), 'The Statue Syndrome: Perversion? Fantasy? Anecdote?', in: *The Journal of Sex Research* 14, 246–249.

Zanker, P./Ewald, B. (2012), *Living with Myths: The Imagery of Roman Sarcophagi*. Translated by Julia Slater, Oxford.

Charilaos N. Michalopoulos

Having Sex with Statues: Some Cases of Agalmatophilia in Latin Poetry

Abstract: This chapter discusses the role of agalmatophilia in a selection of passages from Latin poetry. Pygmalion's erotic involvement with his statue, narrated by Ovid in his *Metamorphoses* (*Met.* 10.243–297), serves as a starting point, since it offers a set of motifs with high frequency in agalmatophilia narratives. A close reading of Laodamia's infatuation with the wax effigy of her dead husband (Ovid, *Heroides* 13) reveals the importance of these motifs but also the structural and thematic intricacies behind their contextualisation. The *Priapea*, on the other hand, come with an unexpected twist by focusing not on the human agent but on the statue instead. As it proves, most agalmatophilia motifs are still present; however, they are recalled chiefly to be parodied and ridiculed.

Agalmatophilia in broad terms can be described as the pathological condition in which some people establish exclusive sexual relationships with statues. In real life the phenomenon is only sparingly recorded.[1] Whether a fantasy or a behavioural perversion, agalmatophilia is not unknown to classical literature. In fact, stories in which the protagonist falls in love and/or has sexual relationships with a statue indicate the particular appeal of such stories in antiquity.[2]

Among the most celebrated stories of agalmatophilia is the one concerning Praxiteles' statue of naked Venus exhibited in the city of Knidos. The story is preserved in numerous sources (both Greek and Latin), of which the story in ps.-Lucian's *Amores* 13–16 offers the most piquant details of the sexual assault suffered by the statue.[3] A certain young man overcome with lust for the marble statue of the goddess spent several days in her temple admiring the fine artistry and the beauty of Venus' naked body. One night he secretly locked himself in

---

I am grateful to Andreas Serafim and George Kazantzidis for their pertinent comments on an earlier draft of this paper. I would also like to thank Regina Höschele for very helpful bibliographical suggestions.

---

1 White 1978.

2 For a detailed discussion of the sexual allure of statuary in Greek and Roman literature see Höschele in this volume. Cf. also Scobie/Taylor 1975, 50–53 and O'Bryhim 2015 on the financial aspects of the touristic use of agalmatophilia stories in antiquity.

3 For testimonies see Scobie/Taylor 1978, 50–52.

https://doi.org/10.1515/9783110695793-012

the temple and, as "a new Anchises" (*Am.* 16 ὁ καινὸς Ἀγχίσης), he engaged in sexual activities with the marble statue. The following day a stain on the marble was the proof of his amorous acts.[4]

But the archetypal story of agalmatophilia in Latin literature is beyond doubt the story of Pygmalion narrated by Ovid in his *Metamorphoses* (10.243–297); the story of the Cypriot artist who fell madly in love with his own creation, an ivory statue, and managed to bring it to life. Much ink has been spilt on Ovid's creative transformation of Pygmalion's myth from a story about the love of a statue into a story about the illusionary power of art.[5] Ovid through his ingenious and at times ambiguous blend of poetics with erotics offers a multifocal narrative which resists univocal interpretation by challenging the boundaries between artistic representation and bodily presence, between subjective impression and objective reality. The popularity of the Ovidian version and its unprecedented dissemination across time and artistic media has made it the exemplary story of agalmatophilia.[6] As Anderson notes, "this story existed in antiquity, but it is Ovid's narrative, the only true literary treatment of the myth, that has transmitted it to us and made it one of the richest sources of variation".[7] I have no intention of repeating old knowledge.[8] In this chapter I rather aim to focus on certain elements of Ovid's narrative which constitute an indispensable part of the story, since they are intrinsically related with the sexual character of the liaison between the artist and the statue. I would argue that the presence of these elements is so typical that we are justified in considering them as "motifs of agalmatophilia". I am not arguing that the presence alone of (most of) these motifs in a story turns it necessarily into a story of agalmatophilia. Nevertheless, I am very keen on exploring their function in different stories of sexual relations with statues. Such an approach might seem rather formalistic (perhaps it is to a certain extent). This is why my examination of the implications behind the use of these motifs focuses not only on their relation to the wider context (generic,

---

4 Stansbury-O'Donnell 2014, 38–44 offers an informative discussion of the intersection of vision with erotic desire in ps.-Lucian's account of the Knidian Venus.

5 So Rosati 1983, 64: "[il suo senso autentico] è insomma un'illustrazione della potenza illusionistica del' arte".

6 For sources of Pygmalion's story see Höschele in this volume. Generally, on the reception of Pygmalion see Dörrie 1974; Dinter 1975; Blühm 1988; Miller 1988; Danahay 2004; Joshua 2001; Hersey 2006; Stoichita 2008; James 2011.

7 Anderson 1972, 495.

8 The bibliography on Ovid's Pygmalion is vast. A highly selective list of the most comprehensive discussions includes: Rosati 1983, 51–93; Miller 1988; Elsner 1991; Sharrock 1991b; Hardie 2002, 173–226; Salzman-Mitchell 2008.

narratogical, thematic) of each story, but also on the ways, which facilitate the rhetorical needs at hand. The contextualisation of these motifs is treated mostly as a dynamic process dictated by genre and content, and not as a rigid assemblage of structural units. As case studies, I discuss Ovid's account of Laodamia's infatuation with the wax effigy of her husband (*Heroides* 13), and a selection of epigrams from the *Priapea*.

1 Motifs of agalmatophilia

Here is a list of what I call "the motifs of agalmatophilia", as found in Ovid's version of Pygmalion's story (*Met.* 10.243–297), which serve as a blueprint for my discussion:

a. *The prominence of vision (erotic and/or aesthetic).* Pygmalion is not simply an artist who creates; above all, he is an artist who sees.[9] In fact, Ovid allows little space (less than two lines) to the very act of creation as opposed to the description of the sculpture filtered through the eyes of the artist.[10] Given the essentially elegiac texture of the story,[11] Pygmalion behaves as an elegiac poet-lover who desires, constructs and ultimately controls the love-object through his erotic gaze.[12] The reader through his subtle identification with the artist sees and admires the exceptional beauty of the statue through the eyes of Pygmalion.[13] Consequently, the statue turns into a visual object of aesthetic and erotic value which passively succumbs to the controlling desire of the artist. The use of passive verbs twice in the story to portray the statue as an object of the narrator's gaze is no doubt symptomatic of its passiveness.[14] However, the poet's reference to the agent of the gaze includes the statue as well. The description of her coming to life focuses on her

---

9 For Pygmalion as beholder see Elsner's thorough discussion 1991. On the visual quality of Ovid's story in general see Rosati 1983, 51–93; Solodow 1988, 215–219; Elsner 1991.

10 Ov. *Met.* 10.247–249: *interea niveum mira feliciter arte / sculpsit ebur formamque dedit* ("meanwhile he carved his snow-white ivory / with marvelous triumphant artistry"). All translations of Ovid's *Metamorphoses* are by Melville 1986.

11 So Sharrock 1991a.

12 For the visual quality and the dynamics of the erotic gaze in Roman elegy in general see Greene 1998, 55–58, 77–84; O'Neill 2005; Valladares 2005 and 2012.

13 Elsner 1991, 155 acutely remarks: "If Pygmalion the creator is inevitably suggestive of the writer (whether this be Ovid or Orpheus or both), then Pygmalion as a viewer appears as a myth of the reader".

14 Cf. Ov. *Met.* 10.266 *nec nuda minus formosa* **videtur** ("she seemed in nakedness no whit less beautiful"); 281 **visa** *tepere* **est** ("she seemed warm").

eyes (the poet offers a clever twist on the two meanings of *lumen* — light[15] and to eyes)[16] and it is complete with a special reference to her first ever (erotic) look as a human.[17]

b. *The derangement of the lover* which constitutes a necessary requirement for the sexual intercourse to take place. Pygmalion's skill (which is also the cause of his trouble) lies in his ability to disguise art by art (*Met.* 10.252 *ars adeo latet arte sua*, "such art his art concealed"). The statue he has built "with wondrous art" (*Met.* 10.247 *mira...arte*) is so perfect that it deceives even the artist himself. The artist fails to distinguish between reality and fantasy; he cannot tell truth from a lie.[18] As a result, the metamorphosis of the statue into a human takes place in his mind well before the end of the story. Right from the very beginning Pygmalion "admires" (*Met.* 10.252 *miratur*) and becomes trapped in the fantasy of his desire, for he believes that his kisses to the statue are being returned (*Met.* 10.256 *oscula dat reddique putat*, "kisses he gives and thinks they are returned") and that the statue's limbs yield beneath his fingers (*Met.* 10.257 *et credit tactis digitos insidere membris*, "believes the firm new flesh beneath his fingers yields"). This at first sight might give the impression of cognitive failure; actually, it is the very opposite. The artist's perception is put on hold only to allow himself to be taken in by the fiction of representation. As Elsner nicely puts it, "for a realism of a statue to be true, it must always be based on the falseness of the viewing it evokes".[19] Pygmalion ultimately succumbs to his delusion overcome by his self-confidence as an artist and not by some unrestrained erotic passion.[20]

c. *The stupefaction of the lover*. Pygmalion's initial reaction to the miraculous transformation of the statue is his loss of movement and speech (*Met.* 10.287 *dum stupet et medio gaudet fallique veretur*, "his heart was torn with

---

15 OLD *s.v. lumen* 1–3.

16 OLD *s.v. lumen* 9.

17 Ov. *Met.* 10.293–294 *sensit et erubuit timidumque ad lumina lumen / attollens pariter cum caelo vidit amantem* ("felt every kiss, and blushed, and shyly raised / her eyes to his and saw the world and him").

18 On the lifelikeness of the statue as a crucial aspect of agalmatophilia stories see Höschele in this volume, pp. 249 and 254–255.

19 For Pygmalion's derangement as proof of the realist perfection of his statue see Elsner 1991, 161–162.

20 This perhaps explains the absence of *furor* (in the sense of erotic madness) from Pygmalion's narrative, despite the story's erotic texture. Pygmalion first and foremost is in love with his own art. His derangement results primarily (if not exclusively) from his love for the statue and less from his love for the girl.

wonder and misgiving, delight and terror that it was not true").[21] The artist is dumbfounded by the result of the miraculous transformation. This kind of speechless reaction, which is quite frequent in the *Metamorphoses*, is not uncommon in narratives describing one's encounter with exquisite works of art.[22]

d. *The erotic approach of the lover*. It comprises endearments,[23] kisses,[24] caresses,[25] as well as gift offerings.[26] As expected, the sense of touching is dominant in the description of Pygmalion's physical involvement with the statue.[27] Lost as he is between reality and illusion Pygmalion touches the ivory repeatedly to decipher whether it has turned into flesh or not. It is with his hands that he finally perceives the transformation of the statue into a girl.[28]

e. *The (fragmentary) description of the statue* which is in accordance with the descriptive strategies of the female body in Roman elegy. The reader is offered a description of corporeal vignettes, almost disassociated from each other, which gives rather the impression of a series of dismembered bodily parts (face, body-parts, fingers, neck, ears, bosom, veins, lips, eyes) than a unified whole.[29]

---

21 The verb *stupeo* (and its compounds) is common in narratives of metamorphosis. In book 3 of Ovid's *Metamorphoses* Narcissus has the same reaction, when he sees his reflection on the water for the first time (3.418–419 *adstupet ipse sibi*, "spellbound he saw himself"). The interconnection between the stories of Pygmalion and Narcissus has been well documented, most notably by Rosati 1983, 58–67.

22 Cf. e.g. Aeneas' stupefaction as he gazed on the reliefs of the Trojan War in the Temple of Juno at Carthage in the *Aeneid* (1.494–495 *haec dum Dardanio Aeneae miranda videntur, / dum* **stupet** *obtutuque haeret defixus in uno*, "while Trojan Aeneas gazes on these marvels, / while he stands amazed, rock-still and fixed in a single gaze").

23 Ov. *Met*. 10.256, 259, 268.

24 Ov. *Met*. 10.256, 281, 282, 291–292.

25 Ov. *Met*. 10.254–255, 256–258, 267–269, 281, 282–286, 288–289.

26 Ov. *Met*. 10.259–266. Gift offering is an integral part of elegiac courtship, see Sharrock 1991a, 43–46.

27 See Stoichita 2008, 14–20 on (erotic) touching as symmetrical with the act of sculpting in the story.

28 The description of the actual transformation resounds with terms related to touching; this makes the "newly born" girl look almost like a hand-made doll (cf. Ov. *Met*. 10.282 *manibus... pectora temptat*, 283 *temptatum mollescit ebur*, 284 *subsidit digitis*, 285 *cera...tractataque police*). Cf. Stoichita's 2008, 19 acute comment on the tactile phenomenology of the transformation: "It is the caress that softens the ivory; it is the heat that emanates from Pygmalion's fingers which causes the wax to melt; it is the pressure of his hands that materialises the body; and, finally, it is his thumb that perceives the definitive proof of life: the throbbing of a pulse in her veins".

29 Face: Ov. *Met*. 10.250; body/body-parts (in general): Ov. *Met*. 10.253, 255, 257, 258, 263, 289; fingers: Ov. *Met*. 10.264; neck: Ov. *Met*. 10.264; ears: Ov. *Met*. 10.265; bosom: Ov. *Met*. 265, 282; veins: Ov. *Met*. 10.289; lips: Ov. *Met*. 10.291; eyes: Ov. *Met*. 10.294.

Such bodily details could fit any description; as a result, what potentially makes the ivory statue unique is left to the reader's imagination.

f. *The (semi-)nudity of the statue.* The initially naked statue (*Met.* 10.266 *nec nuda minus formosa videtur,* "in nakedness no whit less beautiful") is later ornamentally dressed by the artist (*Met.* 10.263 *ornat... vestibus artus,* "he decks her limbs with robes").

g. *The religious context.* The question of the statue's divinity remains unresolved (or it is so intended by the poet). The extraordinary beauty of the statue (which was not to be found in any woman),[30] its ornamental dressing and the gift offering are suggestive of a cult-statue.[31] In any case, Ovid's story unfolds during the feast day of Venus and the transformation takes place only after the consent of the goddess (*Met.* 10.270–279).[32]

h. *The material of the statue.* There are six references in total to ivory as the material of the statue.[33] The complementary reference to wax (mentioned in a simile about sculptural softening) should also be noted.[34]

i. *The immobility of the statue.*[35] The inability to move is a constitutional feature of every statue.

j. *The muteness of the statue.* Even when the statue comes to life, the girl remains silent.[36]

---

30 Ov. *Met.* 10.248–249: *formamque dedit, qua femina nasci / nulla potest* ("and gave it perfect shape, more beautiful / than ever woman born").

31 Sharrock 1991b, 169–172. Also see Hardie 2002, 190; Bruzzone 2012, 69–71.

32 I find particularly apt the comment made by Clement of Alexandria, a 2nd century Christian apologist, in connection with Pygmalion's story that all naked women signify Venus (*Protrepticus* 4.50: κἂν γυμνὴν ἴδῃ τις ἀνάγραπτον γυναῖκα, τὴν "χρυσῆν" Ἀφροδίτην νοεῖ, "if one sees a woman represented naked, he understands it is 'golden' Aphrodite").

33 Ov. *Met.* 10.248; 255 [bis]; 275; 276; 283. The literature on the meaning behind the use of ivory is extensive ranging from the dazzling whiteness of the material (Salzman-Mitchel 2008, 308–309) and the verisimilitude of the artistic result (Stoichita 2008, 7–10) to the conventional in Greek and Roman tradition association of ivory with deception (Elsner 1991, 162–163). Stoichita 2008, 10–13 contends that ivory is suggestive of the creation not of a life-size statue, but of an ivory doll which was later magnified in scale and was miraculously transformed into a woman.

34 For the metaliterary and magical implications of wax see Sharrock 1991a, 48 and Stoichita 2008, 18–19 respectively. It is noteworthy that a reference to wax also appears in the story of Narcissus, again in a simile (Ov. *Met.* 3.487 *ut intabescere flavae / igne levi cerae,* "as wax melts before a gentle fire").

35 Ov. *Met.* 10.251 *et, si non obstet reverentia, velle moveri* ("wished to move — but modesty forbade").

k. *The conjugal relationship.* The miraculous transformation is complemented by a wedding (blessed by Venus).[37]

2 Ovid's Laodamia (*Her.* 13)

Let us begin first with Laodamia's story, as narrated by Ovid in his *Heroides*. According to myth, Laodamia was the newlywed bride of Protesilaus, the prince of the Thessalian kingdom of Phylace. Protesilaus immediately after his wedding was forced to leave his wife in order to join the Greeks for the Trojan expedition. An oracle stated that the first Greek to set foot on Trojan soil would also die first (*Her.* 13.93–94). Protesilaus (a *nomen omen*) paid no attention to the oracle and disembarked first; so he was the first to be killed (by Hector). The unfortunate story of the couple which was already known in Homer (*Il.* 2.698–702) and the *Cypria* (p. 19K and fr. 14K) was later treated by Euripides in his *Protesilaus* (649–658 *TGF*) and by Laevius in his *Protesilaudamia* (13–19 Courtney). Despite the fragmentary state of the latter works, their influence on Ovid should not be dismissed.[38] In most surviving versions, Laodamia is visited by her deceased husband who informs her about his fate. Unable to withstand the pain of his loss she commits suicide. There are versions, however, in which Laodamia creates a statue of her dead husband which she keeps in her room, venerates and even has erotic relations with.[39] When her father finds out about this unnatural liaison, he orders the statue to be burnt; Laodamia then throws herself onto the pyre.

Ovid's Laodamia is a woman in despair. In a hopeless attempt to undo the impending doom she writes to her husband, urging him to take good care of himself. Her letter is filled with fear, uncertainty and superstition.[40] Unable to

---

36 Ov. *Met.* 10.293–294 *sensit et erubuit timidumque ad lumina lumen / attollens pariter cum caelo vidit amantem* ("felt every kiss, and blushed, and shyly raised / her eyes to his and saw the world and him").

37 Ov. *Met.* 10.295 *coniugio, quod fecit, adest dea* ("the goddess graced the union she had made").

38 On surviving sources and the literary history of the myth see Palmer 1898, 400–402; Jacobson 1976, 195–198; Lyne 1998, 200–204; Reeson 2001, 115–116; Fulkerson 2005, 110 with n. 10–11. For the (rather improbable) influence from Pacuvius' *Protesilaus* (?) see Filippi 2015, 214–215.

39 Cf. Hyg. *Fab.* 104; ps.-Apollod. *Epit.* 3.30; Tzetzes *Chil.* 2.52.773–777.

40 For Laodamia's propensity for magic and superstition see Jacobson 1976, 208–210; Fulkerson 2005, 110–115.

control herself she ultimately surrenders to magic. This is why she makes a wax effigy of Protesilaus and lies with it in bed (*Her*. 13.149–158):[41]

> nos sumus incertae; nos anxius omnia cogit,
> quae possunt fieri, facta putare timor.
> dum tamen arma geres diverso miles in orbe,
> quae referat vultus est mihi cera tuos;
> illi blanditias, illi tibi debita verba
> dicimus, amplexus accipit illa meos.
> crede mihi, plus est, quam quod videatur, imago;
> adde sonum cerae, Protesilaus erit.
> hanc specto teneoque sinu pro coniuge vero,
> et, tamquam possit verba referre, queror.

> But I know nothing for sure; anxious fear makes me
> think that whatever could happen has happened.
> However, while you're off fighting in a remote region,
> I've got a wax image to remind me of your face.
> I speak coaxing words to it and the loving words that are
> rightfully yours, and it accepts my embraces.
> Believe me, the image is more than you might think:
> give the wax a voice, and it'll be Protesilaus.
> I gaze at it, hold it in my arms instead of my real husband
> and complain to it, as if it could reply.[42]

Laodamia is rather bold in the description of her liaison with the statue. Her vocabulary is sexual.[43] Endearments, affectionate embraces and words exchanged between spouses portray what is essentially a loving, conjugal relationship. It is not unlikely that Ovid is expanding here on Euripides' treatment of the story in his *Protesilaus*, which unfortunately survives only in a few fragments. In any case, the scenario is also very similar with that of Admetus in the Euripidean *Alcestis*.[44] According to Euripides, king Admetus offered a sacrifice at his wedding with Alcestis but failed to make the required offering to Artemis.

---

41 The decision of Laodamia to make her husband's statue while she is still unaware of his fate constitutes in most probability an Ovidian invention. In the rest of the surviving versions Laodamia builds the statue after she is informed about his death, see Jacobson 1976, 211–212; Reeson 2001, 203–204.

42 All translations of Ovid's *Heroides* are from Murgatroyd/Reeves/Parker 2017.

43 For a detailed discussion of the sexual nuance of the vocabulary employed by Laodamia see Michalopoulos 2022, 84.

44 Both Euripidean plays centre on the substitution of an art object for the beloved, see Segal 1993, 38 n. 4 with bibliography. For the unresolved chronological relation of Euripides' *Alcestis* with his *Protesilaus* see Parker 2007 on Eur. *Alc*. 348–354 with bibliography.

Consequently, he was warned with an omen of his impending death. Apollo made the Fates drunk and thus managed to extract from them a promise that, if anyone would want to die instead of Admetus, they would allow it. When everybody denied, Alcestis offered to die in his place. Immediately after Alcestis' announcement of her resolution to die Admetus promises his soon-to-be-dead wife to build a statue of hers and spend his nights with it in bed (Eur. *Alc.* 348–354):

σοφῇ δὲ χειρὶ τεκτόνων δέμας τὸ σὸν
εἰκασθὲν ἐν λέκτροισιν ἐκταθήσεται,
ᾧ προσπεσοῦμαι καὶ περιπτύσσων χέρας
ὄνομα καλῶν σὸν τὴν φίλην ἐν ἀγκάλαις
δόξω γυναῖκα καίπερ οὐκ ἔχων ἔχειν:
ψυχρὰν μέν, οἶμαι, τέρψιν, ἀλλ' ὅμως βάρος
ψυχῆς ἀπαντλοίην ἄν. ἐν δ' ὀνείρασιν
φοιτῶσά μ' εὐφραίνοις ἄν: ἡδὺ γὰρ φίλους
κἄν νυκτὶ λεύσσειν, ὄντιν' ἄν παρῇ χρόνον.

A likeness of your person, fashioned by the skilled hand of a craftsman will be laid out in my bed. On this I'll fall and, as I embrace it and call your name, I'll seem to hold my dear wife in my arms, although I hold her not: a chill delight, I realise, but still I might in this way lighten the burden of my soul. But yet, visiting me in dreams, you might still bring me some cheer: for sweet it is, by night, to look on loved ones, for as long as they may stay.[45]

The statue of Alcestis resembles that of Protesilaus, since they both serve as visual reminders of love-in-absence. The similarity between Ovid and Euripides is close, since they both contain references to erotic embraces,[46] love talk,[47] and, more importantly, to the fallacy of the statue as a substitute for the beloved.[48] Admetus' statue and Laodamia's effigy as mimetic works of art contain effectively "both the plenitude of substitution and its emptiness".[49] However, both statues by giving shape to what once was effectively fix the beloved forever as

---

45 The translation is by Conacher 1988.
46 Cf. Ov. *Her.* 13.154 *amplexus accipit illa meos, hanc...teneoque sinu* ~ Eur. *Alc.* 350 ᾧ προσπεσοῦμαι καὶ περιπτύσσων χέρας, 351 ἐν ἀγκάλαις.
47 Cf. Ov. *Her.* 13.153–154 *illi blanditias, illi tibi debita verba / dicimus* ~ Eur. *Alc.* 351 ὄνομα καλῶν σόν.
48 Cf. Ov. *Her.* 13.155–156 *plus est, quam quod videatur, imago; / adde sonum cerae, Protesilaus erit*, 157 *pro coniuge vero* ~ Eur. *Alc.* 351–352 τὴν φίλην ἐν ἀγκάλαις / δόξω γυναῖκα καίπερ οὐκ ἔχων ἔχειν.
49 Segal 1993, 50.

dead thus validating their absence from the upper world.[50] In addition, Admetus rounds off his reference to the statue with a wish that Alcestis after her death would visit him at night during his sleep (lines 354–356); a wish which is actualised in Laodamia's letter, as she receives the nightly visits of her husband's ghost (*Her.* 13.107–114):

> aucupor in lecto mendaces caelibe somnos;
>> dum careo veris gaudia falsa iuvant.
> sed tua cur nobis **pallens** occurrit **imago**?
>> cur venit a labris multa querela tuis?
> excutior somno **simulacra**que **noctis** adoro;
>> nulla caret fumo Thessalis ara meo;
> tura damus lacrimamque super, qua sparsa relucet,
>> ut solet adfuso surgere flamma mero.

> Alone in bed, I seek sleep with its deceptive dreams,
>> enjoying false pleasure in place of the real thing.
> But why is the image of you that comes to me
>> pale, and why does it complain so much?
> That jolts me awake, and I pray to the phantoms of the night.
>> I make offerings at all the altars in Thessaly.
> I burn incense, which I wet with my tears,
>> so the flames flare up, as if sprinkled with wine.

Pallens...imago (*Her.* 13.109) and *simulacra...noctis* (*Her.* 13.111) are suitable descriptions of phantoms, which interestingly enough maintain their association with statuary. [51] Laodamia in her dream merges the phantom of her deceased husband with the lifelike substitute she keeps in her bed. Trapped in her emotional turmoil she perceives the world in statuary terms because her husband's effigy is the only tangible means she has to connect with him. Laodamia throughout her letter is struggling to reunite with absent Protesilaus (who is dead). She gives the impression that she already knows (or at least she fears) that Protesilaus can be accessible only through mimesis, be it ghostly and/or artistic. In her troubled mind, Protesilaus-the ghost and Protesilaus-the statue are the only versions of her husband available to her.[52]

---

50 For the statue in the Euripidean *Alcestis* as a lifelike artifice caught at the crossfire of art, substitution and death see Segal 1993, 37–39, 44–46.
51 For a detailed discussion of the statuesque implications of Protesilaus' ghostly visits in *Her.* 13.107–114 see Michalopoulos 2022, 81–82.
52 On the parallel relationship between Protesilaus' phantom and the effigy see Bettini 1993, 11–12.

With respect to the motifs of agalmatophilia, the first one we come across here is that of *the erotic approach of the lover* judging from the erotic words and caresses offered by Laodamia to the effigy. Laodamia ultimately gives in to the perverse identification of the wax effigy with her husband, even though she is aware that the effigy is merely a substitute.[53] *The muteness of the statue* is also present; we hear Laodamia complaining that, if it was not for the lack of voice, the effigy would be Protesilaus himself.[54]

The conjugal relationship between the statue and the lover obviously needs no justification in Laodamia's case. Nevertheless, it comes with an interesting twist. For Pygmalion agalmatophilia is related with his *ex nihilo* artistic creation, while for Laodamia agalmatophilia becomes a means of remedy and recovery from a loss. Consequently, in the *Metamorphoses* the ivory statue is brought to life in order to become the wife of Pygmalion (*Met.* 10.275 *sit coniunx, opto*, 10.295 *coniugio, quod fecit, adest dea*) who was a committed bachelor (*Met.* 10.245 *sine coniuge caelebs*). In the *Heroides*, the wax effigy will not become a husband, but will replace the absent husband (*Her.* 13.157 *pro coniuge*). Laodamia already has a conjugal life before the construction of the statue, something which Pygmalion lacks. Ovid, of course, is toying here with the idea of a statue both as a depicted image and a depicting object; a distinction Laodamia's agitated mind fails to maintain.[55]

In view of Protesilaus' imminent death his statue can also be seen as a funerary monument.[56] These morbid implications are further strengthened by the use of *the material of the statue* motif. Laodamia's reference to wax is emphatic: firstly,

---

53 Laodamia's address to the recipient of her letter at line 155 (**crede mihi**) is reminiscent of Ovid's similar address to the reader with respect to the verisimilitude of Pygmalion's statue (*Met.* 10.250 *virginis est verae facies, quam vivere* **credas**).

54 *Her.* 13.154–155 *crede mihi, plus est, quam quod videatur, imago; | adde sonum cerae, Protesilaus erit*, "Believe me, the image is more than you might think: / give the wax a voice, and it'll be Protesilaus." In the final scene of Euripides' *Alcestis* the heroine, after her return from Hades, also remains silent in a very "statuesque" manner (*Alc.* 1143–1146) which echoes Admetus' previous reference to her statue in the farewell scene (*Alc.* 348–354), so Cook 1971, 97.

55 On the dual nature of a statue as artistic representation and physical object see Getsy 2004, 2–3.

56 For the morbid connotation of the statue see Fulkerson 2005, 115. Along the same line of interpretation Bettini 1993, 12–13 discusses the deadly implications of Protesilaus' statue by associating it with the funerary statues of archaic Greece. This type of statuary (the *kolossos*) served as a physical representation of the soul of the deceased and offered at the same time passageway between the world of the dead and that of the living, which is exactly the function performed by the effigy of Protesilaus in Laodamia's letter. For more on the role of the ancient Greek *kolossos* see the useful bibliography compiled by Bettini 1993, 12 n. 32.

as the material of the effigy which renders the features of Protesilaus successful (*Her.* 13.152); secondly as a metonymy for the effigy itself (*Her.* 13.156) which, combined with her use of *imago* in the previous line (*Her.* 13.155),[57] clearly alludes to the *imagines*, the wax masks of dead family members paraded at funerals.[58] But Laodamia's emphasis on wax could also entail the heroine's covert hint to her unfaithfulness. Running the risk of over-interpretation I am tempted to detect a bold sound-play behind *cera* which alludes perhaps to the Greek κέρας. The Greek term being a metaphor for "penis"[59] undoubtedly eroticises the self-depiction of Laodamia fondling and caressing the wax statue in her lap. To take things further the idiom κέρατα ποιεῖν τινί means "to be unfaithful".[60] In this light, Laodamia's relationship with the statue effectively becomes an act of marital infidelity. This does not come as a surprise, since the effigy, in Laodamia's own words, has become someone else in the place of her husband (*Her.* 13.157 *pro coniuge vero*).

A final difference-in-imitation between Laodamia and Pygmalion concerns the motif of the *prominence of (erotic) vision*. In Laodamia's letter the traditional gender roles are reversed, since in the place of the all-powerful male artist we find a woman, an infatuated wife determined to take up action. Now it is Laodamia, a woman, who sees (*Her.* 13.157 *hanc specto*), holds (*Her.* 13.154 *amplexus accipit illa meos*, 157 *hanc ... teneo*) and talks to the statue (*Her.* 13.153–154 *illi blanditias, illi tibi debita verba / dicimus*). She, not her husband, is in control of the erotic game. In turn, the beloved is objectified (both literally and metaphorically); Protesilaus becomes a statue which passively receives Laodamia's loving words, embraces, her erotic gaze above all. Perhaps behind the grammatical gender of *cera* (feminine) lies Laodamia's calculated attempt to

---

57 Earlier in her letter Laodamia refers to Protesilaus' ghostly apparition as *pallens...imago* (*Her.* 13.109). Frightened by nightmares she wakes up at nights and worships the *simulacra noctis* by offering incense and tears to the burning altar (*Her.* 13.111–114 *excutior somno simulacraque noctis adoro; / nulla caret fumo Thessalis ara meo: / tura damus lacrimamque super, qua sparsa relucet, / ut solet adfuso surgere flamma mero*, "That jolts me awake, and I pray to the phantoms of the night. / I make offerings at all the altars in Thessaly. / I burn incense, which I wet with my tears, so / the flames flare up, as if sprinkled with wine." The reference here obviously belongs to the religious context-motif.

58 For the *imagines* and the symbolic, social and political implications in their use see Dupont 1987; Flower 1996; Bettini 2005. It is also worth mentioning the Roman practice of replacing the corpse at the moment of the funeral rites with a wax effigy, cf. e.g. Cassius Dio, *Historia Romana* 56.34; Appian, *Historia Romana* 2.17; Herodianus, *Historiae Imperii post Marcum* 4.2. The wax has additional metaliterary undertones through its association with the writing-tablets, see Michalopoulos 2022, 85–86.

59 Adams 1982, 22.

60 LSJ *s.v.* κέρας VI. and κερασφόρος II.

underline such reversal of gender roles on a linguistic level as well. If this is so, then the grammatical "effeminisation" of Protesilaus becomes the perfect foil for her new, "masculine" self. In this light, Laodamia's erotic attachment to the wax effigy becomes much more than merely a remedy for her loss; it helps her embrace her new role in the relationship with Protesilaus, and challenge at the same time her conventional portrayal as a powerless and submissive wife.

3 Priapea

In the vast majority of surviving stories of agalmatophilia the emphasis is placed primarily, if not exclusively, on the human agent. Everything revolves around and is centered on, the thoughts, feelings and reactions of the humans. There are, however, exceptions to this rule. The *Priapea*, an elegant yet sca-brous collection of eighty epigrams from roughly the 1st century AD, proves to be informative in that respect.[61] The protagonist is the wooden statue of god Priapus, the fearful but most often unsuccessful protector of gardens. Through-out the collection the poet exploits the implications of the dual nature of statu-ary both as "depicted image" and "depicting object", even though at times the boundaries between physical presence and representational absence, between the statue and the god are not that clear-cut. In any case, the speaking statue of the god prompts a different set of questions, like: what happens when the statue is given the chance to voice its desire? Is agalmatophilia perceived by the statue in the same way with the humans? Are the terms any different, and if so, to what extent?

The *prominence of (erotic) vision*, a motif of great importance in narratives of agalmatophilia, as we have already seen, plays a central role in the *Priapea* as well. Right from the very beginning the body of the wooden statue is offered to public display, primarily as an object of sexual/visual pleasure. At the open-ing poem the prospective reader is urged either to boldly proceed with the read-ing of the poems or abort the plan by covering the enormous member of the god whom no cloth can cover (*Priap.* 1):

> Carminis incompti lusus lecture procaces,
>   conveniens Latio pone supercilium.
> non soror hoc habitat Phoebi, non Vesta sacello,

---

61 For a concise discussion of the problematic chronology and paternity of the collection see Michalopoulos 2014, 22–29.

nec quae de patrio vertice nata dea est,
sed ruber hortorum custos, membrosior aequo,
    qui tectum nullis vestibus inguen habet.
aut igitur tunicam parti praetende tegendae,
aut quibus hanc oculis aspicis, ista lege.

Dear reader, though my uncombed verse be queer,
    unfurl at once that supercilious sneer.
Both Vesta and Apollo's twin have fled,
    and she who sprang forth from her father's head.
Here stands instead the openly obscene,
    red garden god, more membered than the mean.
So either draw the tunic down I'm wearing
    or else read on (I notice that you 're staring).[62]

The reference to eyebrows in an idiom denoting severity[63] combined with the use of verbs of "seeing/reading" betray the importance of vision in the poem. Whoever sees can also read and vice versa. Right from the very start and throughout the collection the statue's oversized phallus remains an object of erotic display exciting the desire for sexual intercourse in women and men alike.[64]

Yet, Priapus does not remain always an object of erotic gaze. In poem 19 the god's wooden statue boldly usurps the role of the viewer becoming himself the agent of erotic gaze:

Hic quando Telethusa circulatrix,
quae clunem tunica tegente nulla
extis latius altiusque motat,
crisabit tibi fluctuante lumbo,
haec sic non modo te, Priape, posset,
privignum quoque sed movere Phaedrae.

She the bare-ass pavement-pounder
Telethusa (who can shake it
higher than her guts are churning)
put her bumps and grinds in motion,
her technique would set atremble
not just you, Priapus; she could
even turn on Phaedra's stepson.

---

62 All translations of the *Priapea* follow Hooper 1999.
63 See Goldberg 1992 and Callebat 2012 on *Priap.* 1.2.
64 Cf. *Priap.* 1, 8, 10, 66, 73.

This constitutes an interesting deviation from what seems to be the "norm" in narratives of agalmatophilia, where the statue passively receives the gaze and the erotic approaches of the lover. The motif of *the prominence of vision* is present, but turned upside-down. In this short epigram, Telethusa, a dancer, is praised for her erotic dancing which has the power to arouse not merely Priapus, but even chaste Hippolytus. The statue is no longer being watched, but it becomes actively engaged as beholder in Telethusa's provocative dance.

The poet also wittingly plays with the motif of *the immobility of the statue*. The attribution of verbs denoting motion, such as *motat* (line 3), *crissabit* (line 4), *fluctuante* (line 4) to the dancer is understandable. The use, however, of *movere* in connection with Priapus seems rather peculiar. The verb is used here in the sense "to arouse, to stimulate an erotic passion".[65] But *movere* primarily means "to impart motion to, to move", which in relation to the statue's innate immobility sounds very ironic. [66] This is an exaggeration surely, but a needed one, so that the impact of Telethusa's erotic dance is justified. In this light, the humanness of Priapus' wooden statue seems to result primarily, if not exclusively, from its own usurpation of the erotic gaze. The statue's transformation takes place on its own will and not because of the fervent desire of a lover, as it usually happens. From this perspective, I find the choice of Telethusa, the dancer's name, hardly a fortuitous one. Telethusa, deriving from the Greek τελέθω which means "to come into being",[67] seems to be a suitable etymological marker, which placed at the opening line of the poem foreshadows Priapus' transformation into a human in the end.[68]

The nudity of the statue, a motif of high frequency in agalmatophilia stories, is also found in the poem, but with an unexpected twist. The nudity of the statue as we have already seen it at the opening poem of the collection (*Priap.* 1.6 **qui tectum nullis vestibus** inguen habet) is now being transferred to the human agent (*Priap.* 19.2 **quae** clunem **tunica tegente nulla**). This somewhat unexpected transference is surely meant to strike a humorous note.

The *Priapea* are dotted with references to the wooden origin of the statue; [69] a gesture which apparently mocks the presence of *the material of the statue*-motif in most agalmatophilia narratives. Parody is once again the poet's goal.

---

65 OLD *s.v. movere* 12b. Cf. also Pichon 1902 *s.v. movere*.
66 OLD *s.v. movere* 1.
67 LSJ *s.v.* τελέθω I.
68 The name *Telethusa* also appears in Martial (6.71.5; 8.51.23). For more on the name see Goldberg 1992 and Callebat 2012 on *Priap.* 19.1.
69 *Priap.* 6.1–2, 10.4, 25.1–2, 43.1, 63.9–12, 72.4, 73.3.

The cheapness of wood which stands in stark contrast with, for example, ivory (Pygmalion), marble (Narcissus) or wax (Laodamia) in other agalmatophilia stories is suggestive of the poor artistic quality of the statue.[70] In addition, wood can hardly contribute to a lifelike result. Hence, the artistic deceit of the statue's lifelikeness is unveiled. Moreover, the dazzling white of Pygmalion's statue (Ov. *Met.* 10.247–8 *niveum... ebur*) or of fair-skinned Narcissus (Ov. *Met.* 3.423 *in niveo... candore*, 491 *color est... candor*) are now sarcastically contrasted with the red paint on the phallus of the cheap wooden statue (*Priap.* 1.5 *ruber... custos*, 26.9 *ruber*).[71] The white colour of moral purity and beauty seems to be ridiculed by the red colour of passion. Against such background, the humble wooden origin of the statue essentially undermines its illusionary transformation into a human. This is why in the *Priapea* the motif of *the lover's stupefaction* is nowhere to be found, since there is nothing to admire in the statue's crudeness.

Even so, despite the absence of the statue's corporeal beauty, the expectations of sexual intercourse between the statue and the beholder are not annulled. *The derangement of the lover* motif might be absent, but sex is always on the table. Priapus' wooden statue is involved in sexual acts and it does not spare us the details. In fact, what in most agalmatophilia narratives is left to the reader's imagination, in the *Priapea* is being explicitly told, often with juicy details. At last, we are given the opportunity to listen to the thoughts, fears and desires of the statue itself. Poem 26 is a fine example. Priapus worn out by the insatiable demands of a group of lustful women is issuing a formal appeal to his fellow Romans to cut off his member:

> Porro –nam quis erit modus? – Quirites,
> aut praecidite seminale membrum,
> quod totis mihi noctibus fatigant
> vicinae sine fine prurientes
> vernis passeribus salaciores,
> aut rumpar nec habebitis Priapum.
> ipsi cernitis, effututus ut sim
> confectusque macerque pallidusque,
> qui quondam ruber et valens solebam
> fures caedere quamlibet valentes.

---

70 Cf. Callebat 2012 on *Priap.* 6.2: "L'insistance marquée par Priape à souligner sa matérialité (...) et, partant, l'aporie créée entre ce constat et l'activité physique évoquée relèvent de ce qui pourrait être défini comme un 'merveilleux burlesque'".

71 Callebat 2012 on *Priap.* 1.5. For the apotropaic power of Priapus' red-coloured statues see Herter 1932, 172–174.

defecit latus et periculosam
cum tussi miser expuo salivam.

Fellow Roman citizens, there has to be a limit:
Either slice away my member,
which the local sex-starved females,
hornier than springtime sparrows,
spend the whole night devastating,
or I'll burst—goodbye, Priapus!
You can see yourself how ruptured,
thin, fucked out, and pale they've made me,
I who once, bright red and brawny,
cut down robbers by the dozen.
Now my side hurts and a morbid
spittle is expectorated.

The motif of *the lover's erotic approach* which usually involves erotic looks, sweet words, embraces and gifts is absent. The same applies to *the description of the statue,* which is replaced by a sole reference to the statue's sperm producing organ (2 *seminale membrum*). It becomes clear that the focus here is not on the statue's transformation or the process leading to it; instead, the humanisation of the statue is deduced from its miserable condition. The realism of the description and Priapus' use of medical terminology (2 *seminale membrum,* 8 *pallidus,* 9 *ruber,* 11 *latus,* 12 *expuo*) depict a person suffering from excessive sexual activity.[72] All necessary stages building up to the humanisation of the statue are omitted; all attention is given, instead, to the most piquant details of the relationship between the statue and the erotically insatiable crowd of worshippers.

My examination of the *Priapea* concludes with poems 43 and 70, where the poet through his reference to the kisses received by the statue manipulates the motifs of *the religious context* and *the lover's erotic approach.* Once again the poet's aim is parody and humorous deconstruction. In poem 43 an anonymous girl is kissing the god's statues wishing at the same time to feel inside her Priapus' wooden spear:

Velle quid hanc dicas, quamvis sim ligneus, hastam,
oscula dat medio si qua puella mihi?
augure non opus est: "in me, mihi credite", dixit,
"utetur veris usibus hasta rudis."

---

72 For Priapus' use of his "pretentious" weakness as a ruse to assert his sexual potency see Michalopoulos 2018, 428–429.

You wonder, since I'm wooden front to rear,
why girls who kiss my middle want my spear?
No augur's needed. Honestly, she said it:
"In me a rough-hewn spear will gain full credit!"

The description of the kisses given to the statue's middle (2 *oscula dat medio…mihi*) is essentially a description of fellatio; not to mention that these kisses trigger in the girl's mind the desire for sexual intercourse.[73] The poet cleverly exploits the association of the kiss with both the religious and the erotic domain. We know that the kissing of divine statues as a common ritual practice was included in the worship of Priapus.[74] But here this practice of divine veneration is being downgraded to the vulgarity of an open-air fellatio performed by an infatuated girl (*the derangement of the lover*-motif).

The fellatio motif reaches its climax in poem 70, where we find it combined with bestiality:[75]

Illusit mihi pauper inquilinus:
cum libum dederat molaque fusa,
quorum partibus additis in ignem,
sacro protinus hinc abit peracto.
vicini canis huc subinde venit
nidorem, puto, persecuta fumi,
quae, libamine mentulae comeso,
tota nocte mihi litat rigando.
at vos amplius hoc loco cavete
quicquam ponere, ne famelicorum
ad me turba velit canum venire,
ne, dum me colitis meumque numen,
custodes habeatis irrumatos.

That hick farmer's got my number.
When he'd offered cake and spelt meal,
when the table scraps were burned, the
service finished, he departed.
Then a neighbor's bitch came over,
sniffing out the roasted savor;

---

73 So O'Connor 1989, 135; Callebat 2012 on *Priap.* 43.2. Parker 1988, 135 holds that the poem "recalls the custom, condemned by early Church father, whereby women seated themselves on Priapus' member". For more on this ritual see Goldberg 1992, 224–225. Cf. also *Priap.* 73.
74 See Herter 1932, 263; O'Connor 1988, 171 n. 87. Cf. also *Priap.* 25.5 *cui dant oscula nobiles cinaedi* with Goldberg 1992; Callebat 2012 *ad loc.*
75 Buchheit 1962, 77 considers this epigram as an interesting example of generic cross-over of dedicatory epigram with the motif of fellatio.

cock gifts eaten, she consigned that
evening to erection worship.
So don't use this spot to put out
any more libations, lest the
crowd of hungry bitches come here
and, as thanks for your devotions,
I should blow away your watchdogs.

The statue of the god is complaining about a sacrifice which went terribly wrong. The carelessly applied offering caused the neighbour's dog to approach the statue sniffing out for food. The dog is licking the food from the statue's limb thus effectively performing fellatio (lines 7–8). The motif of *the religious context* offers the poet the perfect opportunity for a sarcastic reversal. The careful juxtaposition of terms belonging to different linguistic registers in two consecutive lines (7 *libamine mentulae* and 8 *litat rigando*) gives away the parodic intent.[76] The usual romantic approach of the statue is nowhere to be found; no sweet words, no embraces. In fact, some of its components, such as kissing and gift offering, are still present, but presented in an obscene and vulgar light. The emphasis once again is placed on intercourse which, however, has been regrettably diminished to the level of bestiality. This is agalmatophilia at its worst, still with a touch of grotesque irony.

To conclude, Latin poetry seems to have had a particular taste for stories of agalmatophilia. The theme is persistent across time and genres (epic, elegy, epigram) offering thus an opportunity for a wide range of tones varying from profound sophistication to playful aesthetic delight. In my examination I have tried to make a case for a set of motifs with high frequency in agalmatophilia narratives. These motifs in most cases help to establish the erotic character of the liaison between the statue and the beholder. But there is more to that. Their employment depends primarily on their dynamic intersection with the narrative and thematic context of each narrative. In addition, these motifs are also in tune with the poet's overall rhetorical intent.

While most agalmatophilia narratives focus on the human agent, the *Priapea* constitute an interesting divergence. The mechanics of agalmatophilia can now be seen from an alternative perspective, that of the statue. My discussion has shown that most motifs of agalmatophilia are still present, but are now manipulated so as to cause laughter and derision; in the majority of cases they are recalled only to be parodied and ridiculed. Nevertheless, the ultimate goal of this subversive but artful (mis)application is not to undo the motifs entirely, but

---

76 See Callebat 2012 on *Priap.* 70.7.

rather to reaffirm their (structural and thematic) importance as indispensable components in agalmatophilia narratives.

Bibliography

Adams, J.N. (1982), *The Latin Sexual Vocabulary*, Baltimore.

Anderson, W.S. (1972), *Ovid's Metamorphoses Books 6-10. Edited with Introduction and Commentary*, Norman.

Bettini, M. (1999), *The Portrait of the Lover* (translated from the Italian by Laura Gibbs), Berkeley/Los Angeles/London.

Bettini, M. (2005), 'Death and its Double. *Imagines*, *Ridiculum* and *Honos* in the Roman Aristocratic Funeral', in: K. Mustakallio/J. Hanska/H.-L. Sainio/V. Vuolanto (eds.), *Hoping for Continuity. Childhood, Education and Death in Antiquity and the Middle Ages*, Rome, 191–202.

Blühm, A. (1988), *Pygmalion. Die Ikonographie eines Künstler-Mythos zwischen 1500 und 1900*, Frankfurt am Main.

Bruzzone, R. (2012), 'Statues, Celibates and Goddesses in Ovid's *Metamorphoses* 10 and Euripides' *Hippolytus*', in: *Classical Journal* 108, 65–85.

Buchheit, V. (1962), *Studien zum Corpus Priapeorum* (Zetemata 28), Munich.

Callebat, L. (2012), *Priapées. Texte établi, traduit et commententé. Étude métrique par J. Soubiran*, Paris.

Conacher, D.J. (1988), *Euripides, Alcestis. Edited with translation and commentary*,Warminster.

Courtney, E. (1993), *The Fragmentary Latin Poets*, Oxford.

Danahay, M.A. (1994), 'Mirrors of Masculine Desire: Narcissus and Pygmalion in Victorian Representation', in: *Victorian Poetry* 32, 35–53.

Dinter, A. (1975), *Der Pygmalion-Stoff in der europäischen Literatur: Rezeptionsgeschichte einer Ovid-Fabel*, Heidelberg.

Dörrie, H. (1974), *Pygmalion. Ein Impuls Ovids und seine Wirkungen bis in die Gegenwart*, Opladen.

Dupont, F. (1987), 'Les Morts et la Mémoire: La Masque Funèbre', in: F. Hinard (ed.), *La Mort, les Morts, et l'Au-Delà dans le Monde Romain*, Caen, 167–172.

Elsner, J. (1991), 'Visual Mimesis and the Myth of the Real: Ovid's Pygmalion as viewer', in: *Ramus* 20, 154–168.

Filippi, M. (2015), 'The Reception of Latin Archaic Tragedy in Ovid's Elegy', in: G.W.M. Harrison (ed.), *Brill's Companion to Roman Tragedy*, Leiden/Boston, 196–215.

Flower, H.I. (1996), *Ancestor Masks and Aristocratic Power in Roman Culture*, Oxford.

Fulkerson, L. (2005), *The Ovidian Heroine as Author: Reading, Writing, and Community in the Heroides*, Cambridge.

Glare, P.G.W. (ed.) (1968–1982), *Oxford Latin Dictionary*, Oxford.

Getsy, D.J. (2014), 'Acts of Stillness: Statues, Performativity and Passive Resistance', in: *Criticism* 56, 1–20.

Goldberg, C. (1992), *Carmina Priapea. Einleitung, Übersetzung, Interpretation und Kommentar*, Heidelberg.

Greene, E. (1998), *The Erotics of Domination. Male Desire and the Mistress in Latin Love Poetry*, Baltimore/London.

Hardie, P. (2002), *Ovid's Poetics of Illusion*, Cambridge.

Hersey, G.L. (2006), *Falling in Love with Statues: Artificial Humans from Pygmalion to the Present*, Chicago.

Herter, H. (1932), *De Priapo*, Giessen.

Hooper, R.W. (1999), *The Priapus Poems: Erotic Epigrams from Ancient Rome; Translated from the Latin with Introduction and Commentary*, Urbana.

Jacobson, H. (1974), *Ovid's Heroides*, Princeton.

James, P. (2011), *Ovid's Myth of Pygmalion on Screen: In Pursuit of the Perfect Woman*, London.

Joshua, E. (2001), *Pygmalion and Galatea: The History of a Narrative in English Literature*, Aldershot.

Liddell, H.J./Scott, R. (1940⁹), *A Greek-English Lexicon* (rev. and augm. throughout by H.S. Jones), Oxford.

Lyne, R.O.A.M. (1998), 'Love and Death: Laodamia and Protesilaos in Catullus, Propertius, and Others', in: *Classical Quarterly* 48, 200–212.

Melville, A.D. (transl.) (1986), *Ovid: Metamorphoses*, With an Introduction and Notes by E.J. Kenney, Oxford.

Michalopoulos, C.N. (2014), *Myth, Language and Gender in the Corpus Priapeorum*, Athens.

Michalopoulos, C.N. (2018), 'Disease, Bodily Malfunction, and Laughter in the *Priapea*', in: *Illinois Classical Studies* 43, 420–437.

Michalopoulos, C.N. (2022), 'Statues and the Statuesque in Ovid's *Heroides*', in: *Illinois Classical Studies* 46, 79–102.

Miller, J.M. (1988), 'Some Versions of Pygmalion', in: C. Martindale (ed.), *Ovid Renewed*, Cambridge, 205–214.

Murgatroyd, P./Reeves, B./Parker, S. (2017), *Ovid's Heroides. A New Translation and Critical Essays*, Abingdon-on-Thames/New York.

O'Bryhim, S. (2015), 'The Economics of Agalmatophilia', in: *Classical Journal* 110, 419–429.

O'Connor, E.M. (1989), *Symbolum Salacitatis: a study of the God Priapus as a literary character*, Frankfurt.

O'Neill, K. (2005), 'The Lover's Gaze and Cynthia's Glance', in: R. Ancona/E. Greene (eds.), *Gendered Dynamics in Latin Love Poetry*, Baltimore, 243–270.

Palmer, A.P. (1898), *P. Ovidi Nasonis Heroides with the Greek Translation of Planudes*. Final editing by L.C. Purser, Oxford.

Parker, W.H. (1988), *Priapea: Poems for a phallic god. Introduced, translated and edited, with notes and commentary*, London/New York.

Reeson, J. (2001), *Ovid Heroides 11, 13 and 14. A Commentary*, Leiden.

Rosati, G. (1983), *Narciso e Pigmalione. Illusione e spettacolo nelle Metamorfosi di Ovidio*, Florence.

Salzman-Mitchell, P. (2008), 'A Whole out of Pieces: Pygmalion's Ivory Statue in Ovid's *Metamorphoses*', in: *Arethusa* 41, 291–311.

Scobie, A./Taylor, A.J.W. (1975), 'Perversions Ancient and Modern: I. Agalmatophilia, the Statue Syndrome', in: *Journal of the History of the Behavioral Sciences* 11, 49–54.

Segal, C. (1993), *Euripides and the poetics of sorrow: art, gender, and commemoration in Alcestis, Hippolytus, and Hecuba*, Durham, N.C./London.

Sharrock, A.R. (1991a), 'Womanfacture', in: *Journal of Roman Studies* 81, 36–49.

Sharrock, A.R. (1991b), 'The Love of Creation', in: *Ramus* 2, 169–182.

Snell, B./Kannicht, R./Radt, S. (eds.) (1971–2004), *Tragicorum Graecorum Fragmenta*, Göttingen.

Solodow, J.B. (1988), *The World of Ovid's Metamorphoses*, Chapel Hill.

Stansbury-O'Donnell, M.D. (2014), 'Desirability and the Body', in: T.K. Hubbard (ed.), *A Companion to Greek and Roman Sexualities*, Chichester, 31–53.

Stoichita, V.I. (2008), *The Pygmalion Effect: From Ovid to Hitchcock* (translated by A. Anderson), Chicago/London.

Valladares, H. (2005), 'The Lover as a Model Viewer: Gendered Dynamics in Propertius 1.3', in: R. Ancona/E. Greene (eds.), *Gendered Dynamics in Latin Love Poetry*, Baltimore, 206–242.

Valladares, H. (2012), 'Elegy, Art and the Viewer', in: B.K. Gold (ed.), *A Companion to Roman Love Elegy*, Chichester, 318–338.

West, M.L. (2003), *Greek Epic Fragments from the seventh to the fifth centuries BC, Edited and translated*, Cambridge, MA.

White, M.J. (1978), 'The Statue Syndrome: Perversion? Fantasy? Anecdote?', in: *Journal of Sex Research* 14, 246–249.

Part IV: **Sexual Liminality**

Jeremy McInerney

Hephaistos Among the Satyrs: Semen, Ejaculation and Autochthony in Greek Culture

Abstract: Satyrs occupy a particular place in Greek imagination: drunk and lustful they are cheerful, rambunctious figures who are also a part of the Greek rumination on male sexuality, notably the power incarnated in the erect *phallos*. Paradoxically, however, they rarely attain the object of their desire, and are just as frequently associated with frustration, sexual denial and the absurdity of the aroused but unsatisfied male. It is surprising, then, to find Hephaistos represented as a kind of divine satyr, frustrated in his attempt to have sex with Athena. It is even more surprising to find that the episode of their failed sexual encounter is central to the myth of Athenian autochthony: the birth of Erichthonios. By placing Hephaistos among the satyrs we come to recognise the paradoxes and contradictions underpinning the Athenian claim to autochthony. The source of their greatest pride was also a matter of disgust and pollution.

In a recent discussion of Russ Meyer's infamous grindhouse film, *Faster Pussycat Kill, Kill*, Dean DeFino analyses the hypersexuality of the film's characters in terms of Greek antecedents.[1] The buxom, sexually aggressive women, known as the Pussycats, are likened to maenads, subject to divine enthusiasm, behaving in ways that flout convention, while the opportunistic, leering, yet frequently ineffectual men are likened to Greek satyrs, those figures who are always ready for sex, even if they do not always get to consummate their desires. Sometimes they do, sometimes they do not, and are left either parading around with massive erections or, in some instances, are found pleasuring themselves to the point of climaxing. A Boiotian tripod *pyxis*, for example, depicts a satyr with a tail and overdeveloped thighs proudly holding a gargantuan penis that is as long as his torso and as thick as his forearm.[2] He brandishes it before a woman, whose outstretched arms appear to express apprehension. The same *pyxis* shows another figure happily masturbating, while in a third scene a beardless figure reaches for another man's pubic region. These images show that, as Cornelia Isler-Kerényi

---

1 DeFino 2014, 60–84.
2 Athens 938: Beazley ABV 30, 4. For discussion see Isler-Kerényi 2007, 37.

https://doi.org/10.1515/9783110695793-013

has shown, in the archaic period, the figures of dancers, revelers, symposiasts and satyrs blend into each other. She notes that the satyr "does not belong to a mythological sphere conceptually separated from the human sphere, but to somewhere between human and mythical".[3]

This raises a question: what exactly is the relationship of the satyr to the human? Alexandre Mitchells' 2004 essay proposes a succinct definition: "a satyr is a hybrid mythological being, half-human and half-animal... He is also identifiable as a satyr from a snub, squashed nose, a bald forehead, a bushy beard and an erect penis. The moral character of satyrs is nothing but a list of foibles. In literature, satyrs are cowards, drunkards and lustful creatures. The satyr is the antithesis of the hero, and is considered less than a man... Satyrs often escort Dionysos at his wedding with Ariadne. They are also often represented at vintages, or escorting Dionysos in The Return of Hephaistos. Satyrs are shown on numerous vases serving and drinking pure unmixed wine from wineskins or amphorae. Finally, satyrs pursue maenads on countless vases".[4] Mitchell also notes that "satyrs destabilise traditional iconography". They were omnipresent in classical Athenian culture not merely because of their ubiquity on vases, but also because of the satyr plays that accompanied all tragic trilogies.[5]

The realm of the satyr is located where some divine and human activities overlap. They serve as a signifier of all the human behaviours that are focused on an erection: drunkenness, arousal and a variety of sexual activities. If any imagery ever existed to underscore the ludicrousness of the sexually aroused male it is the image of the satyr.[6] As Robin Osborne has pointed out, they usually occur in scenes that have little or no narrative point. They are simply frozen in a perpetual frenzy of sexual aggression. They do not father heroes. They do not elicit significant transformations on the part of the objects of their desire. They are just desire, full stop. Building on this observation Osborne has explored using the identification of the satyr with the Athenian male to chart changes in sexual attitudes in the fifth century. He concludes, "the satyr's advantage, that he has no reputation to lose, was once what enabled him to do what was extraordinarily shameful; now it makes him unashamed to be ordinary, able to suggest that the

---

3 Isler-Kerényi 2007, 62.
4 Mitchell 2004, 21. For other useful treatments of satyrs as embodiments of unrestrained human behaviour see Lissarrague 1993, 220; Smith 2007, 168. For the Return of Dionysos see Hedreen 2004. Given the outrageous behaviour of satyrs and the frequency with which they are thwarted it is doubtful that their state of permanent arousal should be closely identified with their status as *daimones*, between men and gods, as argued by Simon 1997, 1120.
5 On satyrs and satyr plays see Griffith 2002 and Shaw 2014.
6 On satyr iconography see Hedreen 1992; Hedreen 2006, 277–283.

exotic should be recognised in the ordinary".[7] Osborne's reading almost amounts
to a dumbing down of the satyr's power to shock, as if the community's response
to the riotous display of the erection is now hardly more than a shrug or a smirk,
reflecting, in Martin Henig's words, "contemporary 'barrack-room' humor".[8] Yet
the satyr's virility is by no means the only visual representation of the phallos,
and other striking images, such as that of the penis bird and the gigantic phalloi
of the *Phallophoria* suggest that the erection may be a contested field of unusually
complicated ideas and anxieties about the male body.[9] (See fig. 37) The anatomy
of desire is not simple. To begin with, as Timothy McNiven has demonstrated, in
Athens the ideal gentleman was characterised by a small, dainty penis, depicted
flaccid. Large sexual organs were associated with foreigners and servile characters.[10]

Fig. 37: White-ground Kyathos. Girl riding a phallos-bird, c. 510 BC. Altes Museum, Staatliche
Museen zu Berlin. ISIL-NO: DE-MUS-814319.

Set against these conventions of modesty, the erection, whether displayed by a
satyr or as a winged phallos, is either disembodied or, as it were, takes control of
the male body. It signals a body at war with itself, in which *sophrosynē* and
himeros are locked in a struggle that manifests itself anatomically. In his survey

---

7 Osborne 2018, 204.
8 Henig 1997, 24.
9 Boardman 1992; Barringer 2001, 93–94; Cotter 2014, 110–111. On birds as a substitute for the
penis see Wormhoudt 1950.
10 McNiven 1995.

of the vases depicting the phallos-bird, Boardman noted: "the idea of isolating a part of the human body and giving it independent life and motive power is uniquely applied to our creature [i.e. the phallos-bird]".[11] This prompts the perhaps obvious observation, that the penis is itself unique in being the only part of the male body that regularly displays independent life and motive power. Satyrs and penis-birds, easy to dismiss because they are funny and crude, may give expression to a universal but rarely discussed conundrum of masculine identity: power and masculinity are emphatically manifested by an erection, but, paradoxically, a man has no control over it; as both Plato and Aristotle understood, an erection is a body part with a mind of its own.[12] In a similar vein, the massive phallos used to celebrate the *Phallophoria* is not associated with a body, and in the fully ludic spirit of Dionysiac performance it is ridden by a giant satyr, itself a hybrid whose erection is integral to his identity.[13]

The disembodied phallos also raises the possibility that both it and the phallos-bird, so often cherished by women, are meant to suggest the dildo. Boardman proposed that the phallos-bird showed that in the Archaic period women's sexual appetites were acknowledged, but hardly explored the significance of the disembodied penis. A further complication concerns the vessels decorated with these images: the *kyathos* in fig. 1 is part of the equipment associated with a men's symposion. Equating images of parasexual activity made by and for men with female sexuality is like equating pornography with actual sex: the one is not a good indicator of the other despite the superficial similarity. In fact, nothing confirms heteronormative masculinity more than the belief that women's sexual appetites should depend on a man's penis or its substitute, the dildo. Furthermore, in a society in which sexual identities were structured in a heavily binary fashion around the act of penetration or being penetrated, the erections of satyrs and phallos-birds are constant reminders of the imminence of penetration. Read in terms of the performance of gender constructed on that binary they can easily be construed as a threat, a conformation of sorts of the reign of the phallus. Unlike the hypersexually saturated environment of modern culture, however, the gleeful irrationality of the satyr and the absurdity of the phallos-bird are also ever present reminders of the fact that male arousal is ludicrous.

---

11 Boardman 1992, 237.
12 An observation made by both Plato and Aristotle. See Pl. *Ti.* 91b, where male genitals are described as disobedient and independent (ἀπειθές τε καὶ αὐτοκρατὲς) and Arist. *De motu anim.* 703b. Plato *Ti.* 91c describes the womb in similar terms, as if it were a separate creature with its own desires, calling it a ζῷον ἐπιθυμητικὸν ἐνὸν τῆς παιδοποιίας. See Dean-Jones 1992.
13 Csapo 1997, pl. 3 and 4.

Fig. 38: Sexually excited Satyr facing the viewer. Detail of an Athenian band cup by the Oakeshott Painter, c. 550 B.C.H. 6 7/16 in. (16.4 cm) diameter 11 3/16 in. (28.4 cm). Metropolitan Museum of Art, 17.230.5.

Ever present, but not unchanging. The sixth century saw the merging of komiastic scenes, in which the cavorting of the satyr is part dance and part drunken stumbling, with symposiastic scenes, where the human participants similarly drink, lurch, and unleash their libido. If the symposium is one of the key cultural institutions of the sixth century, the analogising of satyr to komiasts and symposiasts points to a complicated nexus of cultural values embodied in performances of drinking and fornicating, whose relationship to the more sober public behaviour of citizens, once again characterised by *sōphrosynē* is hard to tease out: a dialectical inversion? A comic subversion? A subaltern resistance mocking aristocratic conventions? Komiasts often have potbellies and are physically the opposite of the ideal athlete.[14] In the komiastic setting, the images of libidinous and grotesque satyrs exist outside the world of normative sexual behaviour with its two principal foci: heterosexual encounters and paederastic episodes, orthodox sexual encounters which will end in penetration by the heterosexual man.

In contrast to these, the sexual scenes in which satyrs act are a pictorial world of frustration, voyeurism, masturbation, ejaculation and sex with objects, in a variety of situations that connect the satyrs either to sexual failure, comic deviance or absurdity (or all of these): they chase women in vain, try to rape them in their sleep, hump each other, have sex with amphorae, prepare to have sex with animals or balance drinking cups on the tip of their penis.[15] (See fig. 38) In so

---

14 Seeburg 1971, 3.
15 See for example, Boeotian tripod-pyxis. Athens, National Museum 938 (satyr masturbating in front of a woman); dinos. Athens, Agora P 334 (hairy, ithyphallic satyr chasing a woman); belly lekythos. Buffalo (NY), Albright-Knox Art Gallery G 600 (hairy, ithyphallic satyr astride a

doing they participate in episodes that riotously run counter to conventional behaviour. A simple reading might interpret these as depictions of drunkenness and venal sex, but these are features of the visual world of the satyr, not explanations for it. The satyr is a creature inhabiting a space in Athenian culture where who does what to whom are all up for grabs. Certainty is as slippery as the greasy wineskin with which so many satyrs wrestle.[16]

Fig. 39: Little Master Cup. Black Figure Kylix, 560-530 BC. Munich 7414.

Not every priapic satyr gets the girl, and the question of desire thwarted and penetration averted is an aspect of Greek sexuality that raises its head every time the satyr's gargantuan erection forces itself into our field of vision.[17] Often too the

---

mule with an erection chasing a woman; exterior of red-figure cup, attributed to Makron, c. 490. *ARV* 461.36, Boston Museum of Fine Arts 01.8072 (two satyrs attempting to rape a sleeping woman); red-figure oinochoe, unattributed, from Athens, c. 420. Boston Museum of Fine Arts 01.8085 (an erect satyr contemplates a sleeping woman while another gestures to stop); exterior of red-figure cup, attributed to the Chelis Painter, from Vulci, c. 500. *ARV* 112.1, Munich Staatliche Antikensammlungen 2589 (an aroused satyr lifts the hem of a fleeing maenad); fragment of a dinos (?) Atlantis Antiquities 1988, 55 fig. 48 (hairy satyr buggering another satyr); Attic red-figure kylix by Nikosthenes Painter. Antikensammlung Berlin (Altes Museum), Inv. 1964.4 (multiple satyrs have sex with each other and a sphinx); Nikosthenes Painter, tondo of a red-figure kylix. Kassel Staatlich Museen ALg 214 (satyr have sex with an amphora); red-figure amphora, Euthymides, c. 520 (satyr penetrating an amphora); Archaic black-figure kylix, attributed to the Oakeshott Painter (satyr preparing to bugger an ithyphallic mule); Red-figure cup, Ambrosios painter, c. 500 (satyr balancing a kantharos on his penis). On the Euthymides amphora see Lissarrague 2014, 78–79, and for satyrs and sex see Lissarrague 1990.

16 On satyrs wrestling with wineskins see Lissarrague 2014, 68–76. For satyrs, masturbation scenes and drinking see Kapparis 349.

17 Other body parts may also be involved when male desire is thwarted. The legs were also thought to swell with procreative fluid, as Polyphemos makes clear when he decides to tell his

ridiculousness of the erection is further emphasised by including an ithyphallic donkey or mule in the scene, analogising the human erection to its even grosser animal counterpart. In one late Archaic Little Master Cup (fig. 39) an aroused donkey pursues a woman even as a young male onlooker watches in frustration, furiously masturbating to the point of climax. Other representations of masturbation and ejaculation suggest the same set of associations.[18] Young or old, satyrs and men ejaculating are either disgusting or ludicrous. (Fig. 40) Nor is it a coincidence that these scenes frequently depict the actor looking directly out from the scene. Frontality is uncommon in vase painting. Gorgons, dying warriors and statues exhibit themselves face on, each one category marked as outside ordinary human action, unsettling to behold.[19] Iconographically, then, the erection is not a simple assertion of male power. The truth is a good deal messier.

Fig. 40: Attic Red-Figure kalpis fragment, depicting a satyr masturbating and ejaculating. Attributed to Kleophrades Painter, 500–480 BC Terracotta. The J. Paul Getty Museum, Los Angeles.

---

mother that his head and both legs are throbbing with desire for Galatea. See Liapis 2009. I thank George Kazantzidis for this reference.

18 See, for example, cup by the Amasis Painter. Boston, Museum of Fine Arts 10.651 (pot-bellied men masturbating next to a defecating dog); aryballos by Nearchos. New York, The Metropolitan Museum of Art 26.49 (three hairy satyrs masturbating). The names of these satyrs are Ψωλᾶς, "Erection", Δοφίος, "Masturbator", and Τερπέκελος, "Pleasure-Urge" (?). For discussion of the names see Curbera 2019, 106. For a discussion of the images and the connection between masturbation scenes and symposia see Stafford 2011.

19 On frontality in vase painting see Korshak 1987. On gorgons and dying warriors see Frontisi-Ducroux 1989. On frontality and narrative disjunction see Mackay 2001.

It is important to establish these connections between satyrs and what we might call the politics of the penis: the web of associations that exist for the Athenians, linking erections, masturbation and the satyr's place at the very edge of heteronormativity. This is for two reasons. The first is that it has become commonplace, following the publication of Eva Keuls' *The Reign of the Phallus* to equate the image world of classical Athens with the domination of women through a constant barrage of images focused on the male organ, and the second is because these elements are integral to a key episode in Athenian myth: the story of the Athenians' autochthony through the conception and birth of Erichthonios.[20] The ludicrousness of satyr imagery, however, reveals that there is more to the phallus than simple intimidation, while the story of Hephaistos' awkward ejaculation injects elements of the ludic and satyric into Athens' birth narrative. If Erichthonios is the progenitor of the Athenians, and is born of the very earth as his name suggests, the manner of his begetting is decidedly odd. In the account that is best known from Apollodoros but can be traced back to Euripides through Eratosthenes, Athena approaches Hephaistos to acquire new arms. The smith god, having been cuckolded by Aphrodite, becomes powerfully attracted to Athena but she, wishing to maintain her virginity, rejects his advances. Either as a result of being jabbed by her spear, or spontaneously in the course of his unsuccessful pursuit of Athena, Hephaistos ejaculates, either directly on to the ground or on to her leg, causing her to wipe the semen off with a tuft of wool or throwing it on the ground. Either way, the divine seed mingles with the earth, Erichthonios is born and the Athenians have a narrative that makes them the children of Athena, but also the children of Hephaistos.[21]

Hephaistos is very much unlike the rest of the Olympians in that he is a cripple, either born that way or rendered so by his ejection from heaven, and as various commentators have noted he is the only Olympian who actually works.[22] Fritz Graf has suggested that the ambiguities surrounding Hephaistos arise from the fact that he is the tutelary deity for the artisanal class, and that he therefore re-

---

20 Keuls 1993 introduced the notion of Athens as a phallocracy. On Erichthonios, in a recent article (McInerney 2019) I attempted to link the location of the Hephaisteion on Kolonos Agoraios to the myth of Erichthonios' birth and dealt with some of the themes explored in more detail here.
21 Apollod., *Biblio*. 3.14.6. Other versions in August., *De civ. D.* 18.12; Eratosthenes, *Catasterisms* (Eur. fr. 925 Nauck); Schol. Eur. *Med.* 825; and Hygin. II.13.
22 On Hephaistos in general see Delcourt 1957, Brommer 1978, Càssola 2002, Bremmer 2010, Barbanera 2013, Shear 2016, 156–160.

sembles them more than the *aristoi* who, like Homeric kings, model their behaviour on Olympian gods.[23] Edith Hall has also suggested that these banausic associations would have appealed to a democratic audience, and that the laughter aroused by Hephaistos amounted to a counterattack on the high and mighty, making him a precursor to comedy.[24] And this is born out in many of the stories told of Hephaistos that undercut Olympian authority. He is cuckolded by Ares, scorned by Aphrodite and detested by Hera, but their prestige is hardly enhanced by their treatment of the crippled god. He is most famous not for exploits but contraptions, the golden net that captures Ares and Aphrodite and the cauldrons that shuttle automatically between the palaces of the gods. These are fantastic, but still mechanical. Other gods go to him for objects, such as the arms of Achilles, and once again, while his manufactured goods are extraordinarily clever and cunning, they are still the work of an artisan. His ejection from heaven leaves him bent and broken, and he has to be nursed back to health by the sea-nymphs or by the Sintians of Lemnos, episodes that draw attention to his wounds and physical disabilities, that is, his least divine characteristics. His attempt to rape Athena, a failure in terms of penetration, but a success in terms of conception, is consistent with the ambiguities always associated with him. He is, after all, περικλυτὸς ἀμφιγυήεις. The entire episode of his attempted rape of Athena inverts the Athenians' self-proclaimed view that *eusebeia* (piety) and *sōphrosynē* (moderation) were the hallmarks of being Athenian. Since at first glance the story of Hephaistos' ejaculation recalls episodes of lustful satyrs and their relentless, immoderate erotic pursuits, how are we to read this peculiar story? Why would fifth century artists frequently show the birth of Erichthonios, as Ge hands the infant to Athena, yet never depict the pursuit of Athena? In other words, is there a disquiet at the heart of the Athenian claim to autochthony? To tackle the complex significance of Hephaistos as satyr, it is necessary to explore some of the deeper cultural associations of semen, masturbation and ejaculation.

First, there is the business of semen. This is a complex substance because even though it is necessary for conception and was understood to be so, it is also a source of anxiety and pollution. Medical writers held that if it remained in a woman's body after sex it could putrify and cause a woman to fall ill.[25] Outside the body semen was usually regarded as unclean. Hesiod, *Op.* 733–734 rebukes

---

23 Graf 2005, 142.
24 Hall 2018.
25 For a discussion of Galen on the danger of semen in the womb see Faraone 2011, 8. For a broader discussion of semen and other bodily fluids inside and outside the body see Petrovic and Petrovic 2016, 14.

the man who sits around having polluted his genitals with semen, while the sacred regulations from Cyrene also penalise both masturbation and wet-dreams.[26] As with most aspects of Greek sexuality biology was invoked to support a narrow range of sanctioned sexual behaviour. But even the transfer of semen in heterosexual sex carried a risk of pollution because the substance itself was problematic. Only inside the body and in the right amount was semen acceptable. Modesty and continence were associated with vigour. As Aretaeus wrote in the first century, "vital semen contributes much to health, strength, courage and generation".[27] Yet, even inside the man's body, semen could grow too abundant, according to Plato's *Tim*. 86c3, creating bursts of pleasure or pain in the man so afflicted, driving him mad. The Hippocratics attributed various diseases to the over-abundance of semen, which softened the marrow throughout the body and could lead to death. The *Epidemics* reports a man named Satyros who started having wet dreams when he was around 25 and whose condition worsened until he was experiencing them during the daytime. He died at 30.[28]

From the point of view of its generative power, the Greeks understood that semen had to be transferred through vaginal sex, for the man to plough the field as Aristotle would have it, if conception was to be accomplished. And even if we now recognise that Greek notions of conception were actually very complex and included such concepts as female seed and the battle between different types of seed within the womb, the *sine qua non* for conception was still the womb.[29] Set against this tightly intersecting set of biological and moral notions, extra-vaginal ejaculation, as in the case of Hephaistos and Athena, would appear to be troubling. In fact, there is very little evidence that literary sources (as distinct from scientific or medical writers) addressed any other episodes of non-penetrative ejaculation.[30] When, however, Artemidoros analyses dreams that include masturbation his remarks betray revealing attitudes. He states, for example, that dreaming of masturbation if you own slaves is actually good because the hand is the

---

26 Dillon 1997, 188. See also Parker 1983, 100–102.

27 Aretaeus, *De causis et signis Acut. Morb*. 2.5 (Adams). On semen, ejaculation, desire and sexual health in later writers, notably Galen, see Ahonen 2017.

28 Hp., *Epid*. 6.8.29. On the dangers of sperm building up, causing wet dreams and possibly driving the man insane see Thumiger 2017, 240–243.

29 Arist. *GA* 4.3 769a15–23. On the battle of the seeds and notions of conception see Hansen 1992, 43 and Dean-Jones 1994, 14–15; Ribera-Martin 2019, 87–88.

30 Henderson 1976, 169 claims, "There is no evidence anywhere in Greek literature of *coitus interruptus*, onanism or ejaculation *ante portas*." The Cologne Epode of Archilochos makes reference to the narrator experiencing an orgasm (λευκὸν ἀφῆκα μένος), which Eckerman 2011 has argued is the result of oral sex. For episodes involving gods ejaculating see below, p. 297.

slave of the sex organ, so that the dream of masturbation foreshadows exploiting your slaves. Leaving aside the troubling analogising of masturbation to slave owning, Artemidoros' explanation only makes sense if the expectation is that masturbation is bad. More revealing is the fact that dreaming of masturbation if you do not own slaves is bad. The dreamer, he says, will suffer a loss due to the release of his sperm to no purpose (διὰ τὴν ἄχρηστον τοῦ σπέρματος ἀπόκρισιν).[31] Similarly, in the section on dreaming of sex with one's mother, which he says is complex and has defied many a dream interpreter, he digresses for a moment to consider the meaning of dreaming about oral sex. One who has fellated a stranger (in a dream) will suffer some sort of loss (one cannot say what exactly), once again, because of an ejaculation of seed that serves no purpose: διὰ τὴν εἰς ἄχρη-στον ἀπόκρισιν τοῦ σπέρματος.[32] Measured against prevailing biological notions and psychological dispositions, Hephaistos' attack on Athena, by resulting in an ejaculation outside the womb, is a failure. It does produce a child, to be sure, because the god's seed is hypervirile, but the human performance on which Hephaistos' actions are modelled is risible.[33] Most notably, it does not rise to the challenge of Winkler's "invasive protocol", for, as Winkler argues, "to penetrate is not all of sex, but it is that aspect of sexual activity which was apt for expressing social relations of honor and shame, aggrandisement and loss, command and obedience...".[34] By these standards Hephaistos does not measure up.

Even prior to spilling his seed and failing to penetrate Athena, Hephaistos' behaviour appears to be a kind of derangement. His desire had been inflamed by Aphrodite's departure, and though he is rejected by Athena, whom Apollodoros describes as σώφρων καὶ παρθένος, he is still aroused and continues to pursue her. Medically he exhibits signs of priapism or satyriasis.[35] It is not clear that ancient medical thinkers distinguished between these two states. The former is a medical condition, a form of erectile dysfunction in which a man suffers from a

---

31 Artem. *Onirocriticus* 1.78

32 Artem. *Onirocriticus* 1.79. The notion of "wasted seed" is the subject of a rich tradition of commentary in rabbinic tradition, which distinguished between self-arousal and non-procreative emission. It does not seem to be the case that Greek sources were as scrupulous. See Satlow 1994.

33 Not only are his actions risible, but the nearest parallel is Aristophanic. At *Eq.* 910 the Paphlagonian abses himself and urges Demos to use his head to wipe himself. The line is usually translated as if the fulid in question is snot but Amy Coker has recently suggested that the language is heavily sexualised and that the Paphlagonian is referring to semen. See Coker 2021, 30. If so, the entire encounter between Athena and Hephaistos revolves around disgust.

34 Winkler 1990, 40.

35 On ancient diagnoses and attitudes to satyriasis see Thumiger 2018.

prolonged erection unrelated to sexual stimulation. The latter is a psychological condition often more broadly categorised as hypersexuality. The two categories, however, seem to have operated in tandem for medical writers such as Aretaeus and Caelius Aurelianus, whose comments illustrate how these conditions were viewed in antiquity. Aretaeus' description of the effects of the medical condition, for example, are an apt description of Hephaistos' behaviour and, more importantly, of how Hephaistos' actions would have been understood in an ancient setting,

ἢν δὲ ὑπερίσχῃ καὶ τὴν αἰδῶ τοῦ ἀνθρώπου τὸ πάθος, ἀκρατέες μὲν γλώσσης ἐς τὸ ἄκοσμον· ἀκρατέες δὲ ἐς τὸ ἄμφαδον καὶ τῆς τοῦ ἔργου πρήξιος, παράφοροι τὴν γνώμην ἐς τὸ ἄσχημον.

But if the affliction overcomes the patient's sense of shame, he will lose all restraint of tongue as regards obscenity and likewise all restraint in regard to open performance of the act, being deranged in understanding as much as in indecency.[36]

For Caelius Aurelianus satyriasis is "a state of strong sexual desire with tension due to a bodily disease".[37] Summarising these and other Greco-Roman medical writers, Chiara Thumiger finds "clear evidence of an association between excessive sexual activity and moral deviation".[38] If, then, we examine the Hephaistos and Athena episode with a view to prevailing attitudes towards semen, ejaculation, and the erection, it is impossible to see Hephaistos' actions as anything other than ludicrous at best or pathological at worst. The significance of reading Hephaistos' actions this way is that it forces us to recognise that the patriarchal structure of Athenian society was more complicated than a simple model of domination, signified by the erect phallos. There is always a suggestion that the swollen satyr, or in this case the crippled god, will fall short of his goal. The mating of Hephaistos and Athena, which operates in a comic and transgressive register, demonstrates that there is a space in Athenian culture for reining in the *phallos*.

The conception of Erichthonios is not the only case of extra-vaginal conception and miraculous birth in Greek myth, but it is not a pronounced trope of the genealogies devised by Greek story-tellers. Hesiod's account of the severed genitals of Kronos causing the birth of Aphrodite is probably the best-known example, but it is quite distinct from the case of Hephaistos and Athena: the episode

---

36 Aret., *SA* 2.12 (Adams); similarly, in his discussion of the treatment of the disease Aretaeus speaks of the afflicted being utterly shameless "in the open performance of the act", (ἐπὶ παρρησίῃ τοῦ πράγματος). Aret., CA2.11.

37 Cael. Aur. (*Acut. Morb.* 3.18.175–176).

38 Thumiger 2017, 243.

draws on Near Eastern motifs of conflict in heaven, and arises in the goddess' entry into the Greek pantheon through Cyprus; nor is it the only account of the goddess' birth. Versions that make Dione the mother of Aphrodite offer a more thoroughly Hellenised version of the goddess' genealogy. A little closer to the story of Hephaistos and Athena is a single, late account in Palaephatos of three male gods, Zeus, Poseidon and Hermes, ejaculating (ἀπεσπέρμηναν) on the hide of a sacrificial animal and causing it to bear Orion after ten months buried in the ground.[39] In this tale the hide serves as a kind of womb. The peculiar story attests to the power of divine male seed but it lacks the theme of lusty pursuit altogether and has none of the parodic element in the story of Hephaistos. Closer to the Hephaistos episode are two stories involving Zeus and Poseidon. In the case of Zeus, the god experienced a nocturnal emission that resulted in the daemon Agdistis being born from the ground.[40] Possibly related to this is a ribald tradition preserved in Ptolemy Chennos that appears to have explained the Leukadian Rocks as the place where Zeus found relief from his sexual desires.[41] Finally, Poseidon also suffered from nocturnal emissions that brought forth life:

ἄλλοιδέ φασιν ὅτι καὶ περὶτοὺς πέτρους τοῦ ἐν Ἀθήνας Κολωνοῦ καθευδήσας ἀπεσπέρμηνε καὶ ἵππος Σκύφος ἐξῆλθεν, ὁ καὶ Σκιρωνίτης λεγόμενος

Other say that after falling asleep by the rocks of Kolonos in Athens he ejaculated and the horse Skyphos came forth, the one also known as the Skironian.

(Schol. Ad Lykoph. 766)[42]

Can it be coincidental that Zeus and Poseidon both have sexual histories anticipating the irregular conception and birth of Erichthonios and which intersect closely with Athena? Zeus has asexually produced hermaphroditic offspring (Ag-

---

39 Palaeph. 51. This description has provoked discussion because of the presence of the verb *ourēsai* in the same passage. Even though the connection between ejaculation and urination is obvious, it is unlikely that the gods are imagined as urinating on the skin that bore Orion, as argued by Oleson 1976, 28. A false etymological link is more likely.
40 Paus. 7.17.10. Agdistis is described as a daemon born with two sets of genitals; Arnob., *Adver. Nat.* 5.5–7.
41 Bednarek 2019, 7 summarises the Photian epitome of Ptolemy neatly: "By combining these elements one comes up with the following sophomoric riddle: what is it –its product is white, males do it repeatedly, sitting alone in secrecy when they want to get rid of desire?"
42 A similar tradition relates Poseidon's actions to Thessaly, where he was worshiped as Petraios after sleeping on a rock and having an emission. According to the scholion to Pindar, *Pythian* 4.246, καὶ τὸν θορὸν δεξαμένη ἡ γῆ ἀνέδωκεν ἵππον πρῶτον, ὃν ἐπεκάλεσαν Σκύφιον ("...and receiving his seed, the earth gave up the first horse, which they named Skyphios").

distis) as well as the virgin goddess, Athena. If Agdistis' biform hints at a breakdown of anatomical boundaries, Athena's peculiar birth only confirms her special status. Depictions of her birth from Zeus' head, cleaved open by Hephaistos, render her something other than a "normal" woman: fully grown at birth, fully armoured like a male warrior, released into the world by a caesarian cut to her father's head. Despite its peculiarity, the scene was embraced by the Athenians, who placed it prominently on the Hephaisteion and the Parthenon, possibly because the story of her birth replaced all the ingredients of human sexuality with something more powerful.[43] Free of the hint of human emotional entanglements she is perfect and invulnerable. Similarly, Poseidon, Athena's rival for sovereignty over the land of Attica, is capable of asexual reproduction, yet again it is a birth with odd associations since he sires the first horse on Attic soil at Kolonos. This episode too evokes a tangled relationship with Athena, since Athena and Poseidon are locked in a complementary rivalry over the horse. Poseidon Hippios doubles as Taraxippos, and so is not simply identified with the wild power of the stallion but also with the power to drive the horse into a frenzy, while Athena Hippia is also Chalinitis, the goddess who domesticates the horse.[44] She does this by means of the bridle, another of Hephaistos' inventions, the product as Detienne observes, of Hephaistos' *metis*.[45]

Neither of the episodes involving Zeus or Poseidon corresponds exactly to the story of Hephaistos, but they do suggest the existence of a discernible class of stories that exploit a bizarre dimension of male gods: as sexual beings they are subject to uncontrollable urges that paradoxically mark them as hypervirile. As with their human counterparts, the very member that most completely attests to their masculine power also exhibits a type of agency independent of the god's volition. And if the male gods are distinguished by the independent action of their members, can Athena, too, be regarded as at war with her womb? Does it compel her towards bearing a child, even though this is at odds with her virgin status? It is as if the strange story of Hephaistos and Athena, by layering paradox upon paradox, creates a narrative space for abnormality. Yet the presence of Athena, while necessary if the story is to have any significance for the Athenians, introduces a further element of transgression, as is clear from Artemidoros' comments on dreaming about sex with a goddess. In his class of erotic dreams that are against nature Artemidoros claims that dreaming of sex with Artemis, Athena,

---

43 For the birth of Athena in the pediment of the Hephaisteion, see Stewart 2018. I thank Andreas Serafim for his insights regarding Athena's birth.
44 Detienne 1971.
45 Detienne 1971, 175.

Hestia, Rhea, Hera or Hekate is never beneficial, even if the dreamer enjoys the dream. The dream prophesies doom for the observer (dreamer) after no long period of time. For these goddesses are hallowed, and those who lay a hand on them, says Artemidoros, will receive nothing good for the attempt.

While the satyric associations endow the story of Hephaistos and Athena with comic overtones, the myth cannot be dismissed as a humorous tale of sexual deviance. This story was fundamental to the Athenian view of their autochthony. At the Hephaisteion above the Agora, Athena and Hephaistos were worshipped as twin progenitors of the Athenian people. The cult statues of the Hephaisteion, carved by Alkamenes of Lemnos in 421 BC, showed Hephaistos and Athena side by side. Furthermore, the statue base portrayed the birth of Erichthonios, as did a number of 5th century red figure vases.[46] However bizarre may have been the story of Erichthonios' conception, it was, nevertheless, inseparable from the Athenian claim of autochthony. Does not Hephaistos' conduct contaminate this claim? One possible explanation is that like every other element involving the gods who contributed to the founding of Athens — Zeus, Poseidon, and Athena — Hephaistos' story divorces the female body from any active role in the original conception of the Athenians. This was suggested by Loraux, who noted pithily that Hephaistos' actions "relieved Athenians, in the nick of time, from the other sex and its reproductive function".[47] It is true that Ge alleviated Athena of the burden of childbearing and allowed the Athenians to remove childbirth from the story of their origins, but it replaced this with something no less messy. We are still left with a story tying the Athenians to the earth. In fact, the story of Hephaistos and Athena speaks to the ambiguity that lay at the very heart of claims of autochthony, or as Nicole Loraux refers to it, the "Dark Side of Autochthony".[48] Tracing the community's ancestry to the very land itself raises the spectre of the transgressions, bloodshed and lust that are at the heart of the community. Poseidon will destroy autochthonous Erechtheus and bury him under the rock of the Acropolis, returning him to the earth, and, as Ann Burnett recognised, reversing the scene of Erichthonios' birth.[49] Poseidon's killing of Erechtheus is to avenge the death of his son Eumolpos, who invaded Attica to assert his claim to the land. The resolution of this internecine conflict necessitates the fusing of the two, in

---

46 On the cult statues and their base see Papaspyridi-Karusu 1954–1955, 67–94; Thompson and Wycherley 1972, 140–149; Palagia 2000. For vase paintings depicting the birth of Erichthonios from Ge see Kron 1976, 55–75; Shapiro 1998.

47 Loraux 2000, 24.

48 Loraux 1994. On autochthony see Rosivach 1987, Saxenhouse 1992: 51–52, 111–112, as well as Loraux 1981, 2000 and 2002.

49 Burnett 1970, 147.

the cult of Poseidon Erechtheus.[50] Later in another episode of the violence at the core of autochthony, the original inhabitants of Attica, the Pelasgians, must be slaughtered, the survivors expelled to Lemnos in a repetition of the recurring pattern: where there is an autochthonous founder, there is an autochthonous challenger. For every Romulus, his Remus. And just as fraternal bloodshed is built into the community's foundations, so too sexual violence also anchors lineage. Without Apollo's rape of Kreousa at the Makrai Petrai below the Acropolis and the symbolic repetition of this in Ion's marriage to her, there can be no Ionian people. These are instances of the need to re-root autochthony repeatedly.[51]

These issues were in the air in the 5th century. From Pericles' Citizenship Law and the debate over who counted as Athenian to dramatic investigations of birth and identity, the Athenians engaged in a wide-ranging exploration of the heroic genealogies and traditions that tied them to the soil of Attica and made them Athenian. In Sophocles' *Ajax* they even found a way of incorporating Salamis into their zone of autochthony, despite the fact that Ajax himself had a completely non-Athenian family tree.[52] The *Oresteia* went even further, giving the Areopagos a pedigree that went back to Athena's intervention into the Erinyes' pursuit of Orestes. Fundamental to the court's founding was the transformation of the earth-born avenging spirits into the Dread Goddesses.[53] Athenian justice was thereby envisaged as an outgrowth of the very earth on which Athens' most venerable court sat. Autochthony was a recurring theme of Athenian discourse, but it was not the same as jingoistic patriotism. At every turn bodily functions and bodily fluids suggested the messiness, the ambiguities and paradoxes that underlay autochthony. A similar formula is at work as Clytemnestra revels in the blood of Agamemnon, likening herself to the sown earth rejoicing in a springtime shower. Blood and semen, male and female, life and death reflect the essential ambiguity of life, so that if autochthony is a source of pride, it is equally a source of disquiet, since it included a recognition of elemental urges driving both men and gods: bloodlust, and in Hephaistos' case just lust. Nearly fifty years ago in a study of Euripides *Ion*, a play devoted to the exploration of the Athenians' claim to autochthony, Donald Mastronarde observed, "in poetic terms we are shown in *Ion* that a primitive element of animality lingers in the blood of the earth-born

---

50 Frame 2009, 412.
51 Lape 2010, 123: "The sexual appropriation of the female body [is] necessary to transmit autochthony conceived specifically as an ancestry or bloodline". See also Loraux 1990.
52 For Ajax and Salamis in Athenian mythmaking see McInerney 2019, 250–251.
53 On the *Ajax* see Scodel 2006. On the Erinyes and Semnai Theai see Lloyd-Jones 1990.

race of humans".[54] This astute reading helps us to understand why the Athenians should place Hephaistos among the satyrs. Ann Burnett suggested that Erichthonios "was received by his 'spiritual' mother, Athena, but she could not, as Zeus' chaste daughter, introduce him as a son of hers among the gods."[55] The shame at the heart of the Athenians' autochthonous origins went deeper than questions over their 'mother's' chastity: the "father" was no better than a satyr, less than fully godlike and not much of a man. In fact, behind the discourse on autochthony, a whole range of complex polarities seems to be at play, undercutting certainty at every step.

The Athenians are autochthonous, but the original deed rooting them to the earth is pollution. Moreover the mechanics of sexual reproduction are highly problematic, with men ruled by their penises and women subject to the desires of the womb. Too much semen is dangerous for the man, too little sexual activity a threat to female sanity. And in the case of the Athenians' progenitor gods, the father, like Polyphemos and his swollen legs, cannot contain his desire or his semen, while the mother remains a perpetual virgin and never gives birth. Set against these complex antitheses, like the satyrs who embody the contradictions of desire and the dangers of immoderation, Hephaistos is a god more remarkable for his shortcomings than his accomplishments. In this respect his ambiguity can be read as a gentle subversion of conventional pieties, but Greek culture was certainly vigorous enough to accommodate at least one drunk in heaven.

Bibliography

Ahonen, M. (2017), 'Galen on Sexual Desire and Sexual Regulation', in: *Apeiron* 50, 449–481.
Barbanera, M. (2013), 'The Lame God: Ambiguities of Hephaistos in the Greek Mythical Realm', in: *Scienze dell'Antichità* 19, 55–74.
Barringer, J.M. (2001), *The Hunt in Ancient Greece*, Baltimore.
Bednarek, B. (2019), 'Zeus on the Leukadic Rock: White Magic of an Obscene Passage in Ptolemy Chennos', in: *Acta Classica* 62, 1–9.
Boardman, J. (1992), 'The Phallos-Bird in Archaic and Classical Greek Art', in: *Revue Archéologique* 2, 227–242.
Bremmer, J. N. (2010), 'Hephaistos Sweats or How to Construct an Ambivalent God', in: R.N. Bremmer/A. Erskine (eds.), *The Gods of Ancient Greece. Identities and Transformations*, Edinburgh, 193–208.
Brommer, F. (1978), *Hephaistos. Der Schmiedegott in der Antiken Kunst*, Mainz.

---

54 Mastronarde 1975, 171.
55 Burnett 1970, 143.

Burnett, A.P. (1970), *Euripides: Ion, a Translation with Commentary*, Upper Saddle River.
Càssola, F. (2002), 'Efesto e le sue opera', in: A. Gumlia-Mair/M. Rubinich (eds.), *Le arti di Efesto: Capolavori in metallodalla Magna Grecia*, Trieste, 14–19.
Coker, A. (2021), 'Fluid Vocabulary. Flux in the Lexicon of Bodily Emissions', in: M. Bradley/V. Leonard/L. Totelin (eds.), *Bodily Fluids in Antiquity*, Milton Park, 17–40.
Cotter, J. (2014), 'Φαληρίς: Coot, Plant, Phallus', in: *Glotta* 90, 105–113.
Csapo, E. (1997), 'Riding the Phallus for Dionysus: Iconology, Ritual, and Gender-Role De/Construction', in: *Phoenix* 51, 253–295.
Cubera, J. (2019), 'An Essay on Satyr Names', in: R. Parker (ed.), *Changing Names. Tradition and Innovation in Ancient Greek Onomastics*, Oxford, 100–137.
Dean-Jones, L. (1992), 'The Politics of Pleasure: Female Sexual Appetite in the Hippocratic Corpus', in: *Helios* 19, 72–91.
Dean-Jones, L. (1994), *Women's Bodies in Classical Greek Science*, Oxford.
DeFino, D. (2014), *Faster, Pussycat! Kill! Kill!*, New York.
Delcourt, M. (1957), *Héphaistos ou la légende du magicien*, Paris.
Detienne, M. (1971), 'Athena and the Mastery of the Horse', in: *History of Religions* 11, 161–184.
Dillon, M. (1997), *Pilgrims and Pilgrimage in Ancient Greece*, New York/London.
Eckerman, C.C. (2011), 'Teasing and Pleasing in Archilochus' "First Cologne Epode"', in: *Zeitschrift für Papyrologie und Epigraphik* 179, 11–19.
Faraone, C.A. (2011), 'Magical and Medical Approaches to the Wandering Womb in the Ancient Greek World', in: *Classical Antiquity* 30, 1–32.
Frame, D. (2009), *Hippota Nestor*. Hellenic Studies Series 37, Washington, DC.
Frontisi-Ducroux, F. (1989), 'In the mirror of the mask', in: C. Bérard (ed.), *A City of Images. Iconography and Society in Ancient Greece*, Princeton, 151–165.
Graf, F. (2005), 'Hephaestus', in: *Brill's New Pauly* 6, 140–143.
Griffith, M. (2002), 'Slaves of Dionysos: Satyrs, Audience, and the Ends of the *Oresteia*', in: *Classical Antiquity* 21, 195–258.
Hall, E. (2018), 'Hephaestus the Hobbling Humorist: The Club-Footed God in the History of Early Greek Comedy', in: *ICS* 43, 366–387.
Hansen, A.E. (1992), 'Conception, Gestation, and the Origin of Female Nature in the *Corpus Hippocraticum*', in: *Helios* 19, 31–71.
Hedreen, G. (1992), *Silens in Attic Black-Figure Vase-Painting: Myth and Performance*, Ann Arbor.
Hedreen, G. (2004), 'The Return of Hephaistos, Dionysiac Processional Ritual, and the Creation of a Visual Narrative', in: *Journal of Hellenic Studies* 124, 38–64.
Hedreen, G. (2006), '"I Let Go My Force Just Touching Her Hair": Male Sexuality in Athenian Vase-Paintings of Silens and Iambic Poetry', in: *Classical Antiquity* 25, 277–325.
Henderson, J. (1976), 'The Cologne Epode and the Conventions of Early Greek Erotic Poetry', in: *Arethusa* 9, 159–179.
Henig, M. (1997), '"Et in Arcadia Ego": Satyrs and Maenads in the Ancient World and Beyond', in: *Studies in the History of Art, 54, Symposium Papers XXXII: Engraved Gems: Survivals and Revivals*, 22–31.
Isler-Kerényi, C. (2007), *Dionysos in Archaic Greece: An Understanding through Images*, Leiden.
Kapparis, K. (2018), *Prostitution in the Ancient Greek World*, Berlin/Boston.
Keuls, E.C. (1993), *The Reign of the Phallus. Sexual Politics in Ancient Athens* (rev. ed.), Berkeley.

Korshak, Y. (1987), *Frontal Faces in Attic Vase-Painting of the Archaic Period*, Chicago.

Kron, U. (1976), *Die zehn attischen Phylenheroen. Mitteilungen des Deutschen Archäologischen Instituts, Athenische Abteilung. Beiheft.* 5, Berlin.

Lape, S. (2010), *Race and Citizen Identity in the Classical Athenian Democracy*, Cambridge.

Liapis, V. (2009), 'Polyphemus' Throbbing πόδες: Theocritus *Idyll* 11.70-71', in: *Phoenix* 63, 156–161.

Lissarrague, F. (1990), 'The Sexual Life of Satyrs', in: D.M. Halperin/J.J. Winkler/F. Zeitlin (eds.), *Before Sexuality*, Princeton, 53–81.

Lissarrague, F. (1993), 'On the Wildness of Satyrs', in: T.H. Carpenter/C. Faraone (eds.), *Masks of Dionysos*, Ithaca, NY, 207–220.

Lissarrague, F. (2014), *The Aesthetics of the Greek Banquet. Images of Wine and Ritual*, Princeton.

Lloyd-Jones, H. (1990), 'Erinyes, Semnai theia, Eumenides', in: E.M. Craik (ed.), *Owls to Athens: Essays on Classical Subjects presented to Sir Kenneth Dover*, Oxford, 203–211.

Loraux, N. (1990), 'Kreousa the Autochthon: a Study of Euripides' *Ion*', in: J.J. Winkler/F.I. Zeitlin (eds.), *Nothing to Do with Dionysos*, Princeton, 168–206.

Loraux, N. (1994), *The Children of Athena: Athenian Ideas about Citizenship and the Division Between the Sexes,* Princeton.

Loraux, N. (2000), *Born of the Earth. Myth and Politics in Athens*, Ithaca, NY.

Loraux, N. (2002), *The Divided City: On Memory and Forgetting in Ancient Athens*, New York.

Mackay, E.A. (2001), 'The Frontal Face and "You". Narrative Disjunction in Early Greek Poetry and Painting', in: *Acta Classica* 44, 5–34.

McInerney, J. (2019), 'The Location of the Hephaisteion', in: *TAPA* 149, 219–260.

McNiven, T.J. (1995), 'The Unheroic Penis. Otherness Exposed', in: *Source: Notes in the History of Art* 15.1 *Special Issue: Representations of the 'Other' in Athenian Art, c. 510-400 B.C.*, 10–16.

Mastronarde, D. (1975), 'Iconography and Imagery in Euripides' *Ion*', in: *Classical Antiquity* 8, 163–176.

Mitchell, A.G. (2004), 'Humour in Greek Vase Painting', in: *Revue Archéologique* 1, 3–32.

Oleson, J.P. (1976), 'A Possible Physiological Basis for the Term urinator, "diver"', in: *American Journal of Philology* 97, 22–29.

Osborne, R. (2018), *The Transformation of Athens: Painted Pottery and the Creation of Classical Greece*, Princeton.

Palagia, O. (2000), 'Meaning and Narrative Techniques in Statue-Bases of the Pheidian Circle', in: N.K. Rutter/B. Sparkes (eds.), *Word and Image in Ancient Greece*, Edinburgh, 53–78.

Papaspyridi-Karusu, S. (1954–1955), 'Alkamenes und das Hephaisteion', in: *Athenische Mitteilungen* 69–70, 67–94.

Parker, R. (1983), *Miasma: Pollution and Purification in Early Greek Religion*, Oxford.

Petrovic, A./Petrovic, I. (2016), *Inner Purity and Pollution in Greek Religion: Volume I: Early Greek Religion*, Oxford.

de Ribera-Martín, I. (2019), 'Seed (*Sperma*) and *Kuêma* in Aristotle's *Generation of Animals*', in: *Journal of the History of Biology* 52, 87–124.

Rosivach, V. (1987), 'Autochthony and the Athenians', in: *Classical Quarterly* 37, 294–306.

Satlow, M. (1994), '"Wasted Seed", The History of a Rabbinic Idea', in: *Hebrew Union College Annual* 65, 137–175.

Saxenhouse, A.W. (1992), *Fear of Diversity. The Birth of Political Science in Ancient Greek Thought*, Chicago.

Scodel, R. (2006), 'Aetiology, Autochthony, and Athenian Identity in *Ajax* and *Oedipus Colo-neus*', in: *Bulletin of the Institute for Classical Studies. Supplement 87, Greek Drama III: Essays in Honour of Kevin Lee*, 65–78.

Seeberg, A. (1971), *Corinthian Komos Vases*, London.

Shapiro, H.A. (1998), 'Autochthony and the Visual Arts in Fifth-Century Athens', in: D. Boede-ker/K. Raaflaub (eds.), *Democracy, Empire and the Arts in Fifth-Century Athens*, Cambridge, MA, 125–151.

Shaw, C.A. (2014), *Satyric Play. The Evolution of Greek Comedy and Satyr Drama*, Oxford.

Shear, Jr., T.L. (2016), *Trophies of Victory. Public Building in Periklean Athens*, Princeton.

Simon, E. (1997), 'Silenoi', in: *LIMC* 8, 1108–1133.

Smith, A. (2007), 'Komos Growing up among Satyrs and Children', in: *Hesperia Supplements, Vol. 41, Constructions of Childhood in Ancient Greece and Italy*, Princeton, 153–171.

Stafford, E. (2011), 'Clutching the Chickpea: Private Pleasures of the Bad Boyfriend,' in: S.D. Lambert (ed.), *Sociable Man. Essays on Ancient Greek Social Behaviour in Honour of Nick Fischer*, Swansea, 337–363.

Stewart, A. (2018), 'Classical Sculpture from the Athenian Agora, Part 1: The Pediments and Ak-roteria of the Hephaisteion', in: *Hesperia* 87, 681–741.

Thompson, H.A./Wycherley, R.E. (1972), *The Athenian Agora, Vol. 14, The Agora of Athens: The History, Shape and Uses of an Ancient City Center*, Princeton.

Thumiger, C. (2017), *A History of the Mind and Mental Health in Classical Greek Medical Thought*, Cambridge.

Thumiger, C. (2018), '"A Most Acute, Disgusting and Indecent Disease": Satyriasis and Sexual Disorders in Ancient Medicine', in: C. Thumiger/P.N. Singer (eds.), *Mental Illness in Ancient Medicine*, Leiden, 269–284.

Winkler, J.J. (1990), *The Constraints of Desire: the Anthropology of Sex and Gender in Ancient Greece*, New York.

Wormhoudt, A. (1950) 'The Unconscious Bird Symbol in Literature', in: *American Imago* 7, 173–182.

José Malheiro Magalhães
Human-animal Sex in Ancient Greece

Abstract: This chapter examines several accounts of human-animal sex and explores the way in which this sexual practice was understood in ancient Greece. It examines the myths of three female figures, i.e. Leda, Europa and Pasiphae, while also discussing episodes of human-animal sex in the works of Herodotus, Theocritus, Plutarch and Artemidorus Daldianus. Overall, it offers an analysis of these sources in an attempt to reconstruct ancient views on human-animal sex.

In this chapter, I explore examples of human-animal sex in several ancient sources,[1] in an attempt to assess the kind of information that these literary accounts yield about the cultural and social views on sex between humans and animals.[2] I start by approaching the mythological traditions of three female figures — Leda, Europa and Pasiphae — explaining the differences between these myths and breaking down the information they provide regarding human-animal sex in ancient Greece. These are three myths for which several references and accounts have survived, which are all in some way connected to Zeus, either as the perpetrator of the sexual act or associated to the families of the other mythological figures involved in the myths. While analysing these three myths, I show how

---

1 I first addressed this topic in my PhD thesis, entitled *Para-philias: Transgressive sex in Ancient Greece* (Magalhães 2019). I am grateful to my supervisors, Professor Mike Edwards, Professor Fiona McHardy and in particular Professor Susan Deacy, whose advice was also crucial during the development of this chapter.

2 The ancient Greeks did not have a specific term for sex between humans and animals as we have today, such as "bestiality" or "zoophilia". This fact has led scholars to adapt modern terms when discussing sex with animals in ancient Greece. The adaptation of modern terms is a common practice among classical scholars when approaching ancient sexual activities that share similarities with sexual activities that today's societies deem as transgressive or abnormal, several of them being punishable by law or identified as mental disorders. Robson 2002, in one of the most relevant pieces of classical scholarship on the subject, refers to sex between humans and animals as "bestiality". White 2004, 152 uses bestiality to refer to sexual intercourse between goatherds and goats in Theocritus' first *Idyll*. Alexandridis 2008 explores how zoophilia was imagined in ancient Greece. Younger 2011, 84–86 uses bestiality to refer to sex between humans and animals in myth and art. Boer 2015, explores the concept of bestiality in the ancient Near East. He defines bestiality as "sexual acts between human beings and animals", although recognising that there are other terms such as zoophilia and zooerasty. To avoid potential anachronisms, I shall use the term "human-animal sex". For an analysis of modern terminology used to discuss sexual activities in the ancient world, see Magalhães 2019.

https://doi.org/10.1515/9783110695793-014

Pasiphae stands out as a unique case, and is potentially more relevant for understanding the ancient social perception of human-animal sex. I will then explore references to sex with animals found in the works of various authors, including Herodotus, the poetry of Theocritus, an epigram authored by Meleager, the works of Plutarch and the dream-interpreting writings of Artemidorus Daldianus. Although most of these sources share similarities with the mythological narratives where sex between animals, or animal shaped gods and humans occur, here I will focus on episodes describing sexual acts between humans — men and women and not animal-shaped gods — and animals. Although we can find references to gods — such as Pan in Herodotus and Priapus in Theocritus — these accounts differ from the myths of Leda, Europa and Pasiphae since the gods are not directly sexually involved, and there is no connection with Zeus.

The corpus of sources that I chose to explore concerns multiple literary styles and covers a wide chronological span, from Homer to imperial literature. I find it relevant to consider sources from different periods and geographies since they reflect ancient knowledge, and they help us to how ethical sexual norms developed through time. This is clear when we consider, for example, Artemidorus' work. I find it important to discuss the *Oneirocritica* in the context of sexual transgressions in general and human-animal sex in particular, since it is the only work on dreams that has survived from the antiquity, and we know that dream interpretation was already discussed centuries before Artemidorus' time. He himself makes a reference to Aristander of Telmessus (1.31), the supposed dream-interpreter of Philip and then Alexander the Great and to ancient interpreters of bath dreams (1.64), possibly relating them to Homeric times.[3] Besides the relevance of dream reading in antiquity, Artemidorus' work is particularly significant because it explores sexual themes without carrying any of the biases that other ancient authors might. Simultaneously, it is a window to the sexual lives of the people of his time, since his sources are the dreams dreamt by the people he found while

---

3 See Harris-McCoy's introduction (p. 34) to his translation of the *Oneirocritica*. For the importance on dream-reading before the time of Artemidorus, see Winkler 1990, 25. The relevance of the interpretation of dreams is already clear in the *Iliad* (1.62), when Achilles asks for a dream-interpreter (ὀνειρόπολος) to find out the reason why Apollo was punishing the Achaeans. Theophrastus (*Char.* 16.11), in the fourth century BC, while naming the characteristics of the superstitious man, says that when such a man has a dream he immediately goes to the dream-interpreter (ὀνειροκρίτης), in order to know to which divinity he needs to pray. In one of Theocritus' *Idylls* (21.33), two fishermen discuss a dream that one of them, named Asphalion, had. In this discussion, Asphalion asks his companion if he ever learned to interpret dreams (ἆρ' ἔμαθες κρίνειν ποκ' ἐνύπνια), to which the companion replies by arguing that his guess is as good as anyone's, and that the best interpreter of dreams (ὀνειροκρίτης) is a man with common sense.

travelling through Greece; and most likely a window to sexual practices of the past, which were conveyed by dream-interpreters who preceded him, but whose texts did not survive.[4]

★★★★★

The myth of Leda is first mentioned in Homer (*Od.* 11.298–304), but there is no reference to the sex episode in the *Odyssey*, which is most likely mentioned for the first time in the *Homeric Hymns* (17; 33), where it is stated that Zeus "secretly forced her" (λάθρη ὑποδμηθεῖσα). The animal sex element seems to have appeared at a later stage, in Euripides. In *Helen* (16–22), the protagonist explains that she supposedly was the daughter of Zeus, who pursued Leda and copulated with her having taken before the form of a swan.[5] The myth of Europa follows a similar structure. There is a brief reference to her in Homer (*Il.* 14.321–322), where Zeus confesses that he has loved the daughter of Phoenix, who bore Rhadamanthys and Minos.[6] Like the myth of Leda, it seems that the oldest version of this myth did not consider an animal element. Apollodorus (2.5.7), when reporting the seventh labour of Herakles, the capture of the Cretan bull, states that Acusilaus (sixth century BC) said that the bull was the one who carried Europa to Zeus, and so Zeus was not the beast itself. When we get to Moschus, in the second century BC, the sexual encounter is clear. In Moschus' text, it is said how Zeus spied on her and her female companions while they were among the flowers in the meadow, how he transformed into a bull so he could escape Hera's attention, how the girls were instantly attracted to the bull, and how Zeus licked Europa's neck (λιχμάζεσκεδέρην) and in return she kissed the bull-shaped god (κύσε ταῦρον).[7] Only then does Zeus abduct her, taking her to Crete where he then reveals himself, returning to his anthropomorphic form, and has sex with her.

In both of these myths there seems to be no punishment for the god nor for the women. There is no reference to any consequence for Leda, for example. She was sexually involved with someone other than her husband and carried the progeny of someone other than her husband's who were raised by Tyndareus as

---

4 As noted by Winkler 1990, 24: "Artemidorus' *Dream Analysis* continually puts of exhibit common social assumptions, shows the operation of androcentric and other sex-gender protocols, and yet itself stands outside them".

5 The same tradition is once again referred to by the chorus in *Iphigenia at Aulis* (794–800). For an alternative version of the birth of Helen, see Apollodorus (3.10.7).

6 Moschus (2) also refers to Europa as the daughter of Phoenix, but in Apollodorus (3.1.1) she is referred to as the daughter of Agenor and Telephassa This seems to be the most common tradition in the time of Ovid (*Met.* 2.833–875).

7 See also Buxton 2009, 130.

his own. Similarly, there is no punishment brought upon Europa for copulating with Zeus. This is partially explained by the fact that the male figure is an animal-shaped god and not an actual animal. As Buxton noted, the most common reason for gods to undergo a process of metamorphosis is erotic passion, the desire to engage in sexual intercourse.[8] Leda is not attracted to the swan because she has a particular fetish for birds, but rather because it is a god that seduces her. Therefore, although these encounters show that the theme of sex between animal and humans was common in Greek mythology, they do not convey the ancient Greek perspective on sex with animals, how it was understood by ancient Greek society or how the Greeks regulated sexual contact between humans and animals. These myths, however, reinforce the divine prominence over humans, and they help to remind us that gods are superior to people and, therefore, a sexual liaison with a god is simply a way of obeying to divine will, as a human should always do. These myths do not convey much information concerning the general Greek behaviour towards human animal sex. But the same cannot be said about the myth of Pasiphae.

The myth of Pasiphae is different from the other myths where the topic of sex between animals and humans is observed. It shows a woman taking the sexual initiative to copulate with an animal, albeit guided by divine intervention.[9] In this myth, Minos, wishing to rule over Crete, proclaimed that the kingdom was a divine gift for him. As proof, he asked Poseidon to send him a magnificent bull that he would then sacrifice to the god of the sea. Poseidon acquiesced to Minos' request, but the latter failed to fulfil his pledge, and, instead of sacrificing the bull, he chose to keep it, sacrificing a different one. Enraged, Poseidon made Pasiphae, Minos' wife, develop a powerful passion for the bull. In order to fulfil this desire Pasiphae asked for the help of Daedalus who constructed a wooden cow, where Pasiphae would hide, and so deceive the bull into penetrating her (Apollod. 3.1.4).[10] From this union Asterius, the Minotaur, was born. Pasiphae's myth is unique among the ones being explored here. Contrary to what happens to Leda or Europa, where the initiative of the sexual act is taken by the male figure, in the myth of Pasiphae it is the female figure that takes the initiative, even though she is forced to do so by Poseidon's divine intervention. By having sex with an animal, Pasiphae is effectively breaking the boundaries between species, and her action is further emphasised by her "transformation" into an animal, through the

---

8 Buxton 2009, 96–108.
9 On this see Alexandridis 2008, 299.
10 As Alexandridis 2008, 300 notes, the cow engine could be the most practical solution for attracting the bull, but it also transforms Pasiphae into a beast.

wooden cow trick. Contrary to Leda or Europa, who were conquered by gods, who are, in turn, at the top of the natural order of the Greek world, Pasiphae was unable to control her lust for an animal, the bottom end of the natural order, and so this transgressive encounter could only result in a transgressive outcome: the Minotaur. The birth of the Minotaur is possibly the best example to show how the myth of Pasiphae was considered in a different light from the other myths with animal sex elements, like the one of Leda. According to the most popular tradition, Helen resulted from the union of Zeus/swan and Leda.[11] Her birth was even animalistic, since she hatched from an egg instead of being born. Therefore, Helen shares animal characteristics, like the Minotaur, but she became the most beautiful woman in the world, while the Minotaur was forever a hybrid, a transgressive being that should be destroyed, as he would be at the hands of Theseus. The uniqueness of Pasiphae's situation is noted by the chorus in Euripides' *Cretans* (472e 1–3):

> οὐ γάρ τιν' ἄλλην φημὶ τολμῆσαι τάδε.
> σὺ †δ' ἐκ κακῶν†, ἄναξ,
> φρόνησον εὖ καλύψαι.

> [...] for I say that no other woman dared this. Now you, my lord—think how to conceal (trouble?) following trouble![12]

The rest of the chorus' speech has not survived, but we can deduce enough from the surviving lines to argue that Pasiphae's situation was unique. These lines refer to Pasiphae as the only woman who tried this, which is most likely a reference to the sexual act with the bull. This is one of the major differences between the myth of Pasiphae and the myths of Leda and Europa. These two myths do not disclose sex between animals and humans, but rather gods in animal shape.[13] It is not a category of living beings that would be considered sub-human, but rather the contrary.[14] These myths do not involve the social reaction to human-animal sex, since gods are not restrained by human laws and customs and a mortal man has no capacity to punish a god. Furthermore, the action in these myths usually occurs in the wild, outside of the city borders, in places where the girl was not

---

11 There was also a tradition according to which Helen was the daughter of Nemesis and Zeus. For this version see Apollod. 3.10.5–7.
12 Transl. Collard and Cropp 1995.
13 See Robson 2002 for other myths where sex between animal-shaped deities and humans is disclosed.
14 Robson 2002, 77 points out that these rapes are only committed by gods who are symbols of civilisation, and that is why Dionysus is never the perpetrator.

supposed to be, since she was not protected by the walls of her house, or by her male guardian. It is not only that gods are not liable to human law, but also that these girls are presented in scenarios outside the reach of the city's law. Therefore, not all myths that convey episodes of sexual intercourse between humans and animals, or animal-like figures, disclose information about the social perception of human-animal sex.[15] They do, however, all reinforce the place of humans in relation to the divine.[16] The myth of Pasiphae, on the other hand, shows that the act of human-animal sex is portrayed with negative overtones when it is a human, and in this case a woman, taking the initiative. Although in this case the animal is not a god in disguise, the action conveyed in the myth only takes place due to divine intervention. Therefore, it can be argued that the transgressive character of human-animal sex in myth is also decided by divine will.

When analysing different literary genres, it becomes clear that despite the change in context, style and content, references to human-animal sex are generally conveyed in a negative light. When discussing the manners and customs of the Egyptians, Herodotus (2.46) narrates a peculiar ritual that takes place in the Mendesian province:

> [...] τὸν Πᾶνα τῶν ὀκτὼ θεῶν λογίζονται εἶναι οἱ Μενδήσιοι, τοὺς δὲ ὀκτὼ θεοὺς τούτους προτέρους τῶν δυώδεκα θεῶν φασι γενέσθαι. γράφουσί τε δὴ καὶ γλύφουσι οἱ ζωγράφοι καὶ οἱ ἀγαλματοποιοὶ τοῦ Πανὸς τὤγαλμα κατά περ Ἕλληνες αἰγοπρόσωπον καὶ τραγοσκελέα, οὔτι τοιοῦτον νομίζοντες εἶναί μιν ἀλλ' ὅμοιον τοῖσι ἄλλοισι θεοῖσι. ὅτευ δὲ εἵνεκα τοιοῦτον γράφουσι αὐτόν, οὔ μοι ἥδιόν ἐστι λέγειν. σέβονται δὲ πάντας τοὺς αἶγας οἱ Μενδήσιοι, καὶ μᾶλλον τοὺς ἔρσενας τῶν θηλέων, καὶ τούτων οἱ αἰπόλοι τιμὰς μέζονας ἔχουσι· ἐκ δὲ τούτων εἷς μάλιστα, ὅστις ἐπεὰν ἀποθάνῃ, πένθος μέγα παντὶ τῷ Μενδησίῳ νομῷ τίθεται. καλέεται δὲ ὅ τε τράγος καὶ ὁ Πὰν αἰγυπτιστὶ Μένδης. ἐγένετο δὲ ἐν τῷ νομῷ τούτῳ ἐπ' ἐμεῦ τοῦτο τὸ τέρας· γυναικὶ τράγος ἐμίσγετο ἀναφανδόν· τοῦτο ἐς ἐπίδεξιν ἀνθρώπων ἀπίκετο.

> [...] the Mendesians reckon Pan among the eight gods, who, they say, were before the twelve gods. Now in their painting and sculpture the image of Pan is made as among the Greeks with the head and the legs of a goat; not that he is deemed to be in truth such, or unlike to other gods; but why they so present him I have no wish to say. The Mendesians hold all goats sacred, the male even more than the female, and goatherds are held in especial honour: one he-goat is most sacred of all; when he dies it is ordained that there should be great mourning in all the Mendesian province. In the Egyptian language Mendes is the name both

---

15 Robson 2002, 67 argues, albeit with caution, that it is possible that these myths might be related with both sexual fantasy and sexual practice in ancient Greece.

16 As Robson 2002, 82 notes, these myths "help to define and uphold both the institutions of the city-state and the Greek world order", namely "[...] (i) men's superiority to women, (ii) women's role in society, and (iii) the place of human in relation to the gods".

for the he-goat and for Pan. In my lifetime a monstrous thing happened in this province, a woman having open intercourse with a he-goat. This came to be publicly known.[17]

Herodotus does not disclose a lot of information, but he seems to provide his own reaction to the act. He states that in the province, the goat, and especially the male goat, was a sacred animal due to its association with the god Pan. Then he proceeds to tell a scandalous story: it was publicly known that there had occurred a ritual in which a woman copulated with a male goat. Herodotus deems this a monstrosity (τέρας), further explaining that it was a recent event that happened in his lifetime, without revealing his source. Conveying tales of sexual behaviour of non-Greek societies, and in particular sexual acts that would contrast with the socially approved Greek sexual behaviour, is a commonplace throughout Herodotus' narrative. Tales such as Gyges and Candaules (1.8), the references to the prostitution of the daughters of Lydians (1.93.4) and the prostitution of Babylonian women in the temple of Aphrodite (1.199) are examples of this.[18] In most of these examples, like the one I explored before, Herodotus avoids making in-depth commentaries but when he does add information it usually reflects negative moral judgements. Gyges' actions were described as "lawless" (ἄνομος) and the prostitution of Babylonian wives was described as the "most shameful" (αἴσχιστος). In his account of the events in Mendes, Herodotus refers to the sexual acts of the Mendesians as a monstrosity (τέρας). This comment would most likely reflect the general perception that Greek audiences would have when hearing the details of this story and further emphasise their notion of Greek superiority over non-Greek societies. As noted by Wenghofer, it "is not unreasonable to read Herodotus' depictions of barbarian sexual libertinism against the backdrop of the growing sense of Hellenic consciousness of superiority over non-Greeks consequent to the Greek victories over Persia in the early fifth century BC, as this was the cultural milieu in which Herodotus lived and worked".[19]

Beyond Herodotus, we also find allusions to human-animal sex in the third century BC idylls of Theocritus. In the song of Thyrsis,[20] in Theocritus' first *Idyll*

---

17 Transl. Godley. This practice among the Mendesians was also mentioned by Pindar, according to Strabo (16.19). See also Aristides *Or.* 36.112 and Clement *Protr.* 2.32.4, which also mention the sexual act with a goat in Mendes. See Asheri et. al. 2007, 270.

18 See also Wenghofer 2014 for more information on Herodotus' account of the sexual activities of non-Greeks.

19 Wenghofer 2014, 522.

20 For the love of Daphnis in this text, see Anagnostou-Laoutides, Konstan 2008.

(1.86), sex between goatherds and their goats seems to be implied.[21] In this text, a shepherd named Thyrsis and an unnamed goatherd meet in the pastures. After extensively complimenting each other on their musical qualities, the goatherd convinces Thyrsis to sing him the song about the death of Daphnis, in exchange for a cup that he describes in detail. In this song, Daphnis, a Sicilian shepherd, supposedly offended Eros and Aphrodite and as punishment he became obsessed with love and consequently died. The reason for angering the gods is not clear in Theocritus' poem, nor the circumstances of Daphnis' death.[22] The song opens with Daphnis, tormented by love, being visited by Hermes and then Priapus. Both question Daphnis, but he refuses to reply. When commenting on this obsession with love, Priapus compares Daphnis to a goatherd, stating that when goatherds see goats being mounted (βατεῦνται), they get sad, wishing to be a goat instead of a man (1.80–91):

ἦνθον τοὶ βοῦται, τοὶ ποιμένες, ᾠπόλοι ἦνθον·
πάντες ἀνηρώτευν, τί πάθοι κακόν. ἦνθ᾽ ὁ Πρίηπος
κῆφα· ᾽Δάφνι τάλαν, τί τὺ τάκεαι, ἁ δέ τε κώρα
πάσας ἀνὰ κράνας, πάντ᾽ ἄλσεα ποσσὶ φορεῖται--
ἄρχετε βουκολικᾶς Μοῖσαι φίλαι ἄρχετ᾽ ἀοιδᾶς--
ζάτεισ᾽; ἁ δύσερώς τις ἄγαν καὶ ἀμήχανος ἐσσί.
βούτας μὰν ἐλέγευ, νῦν δ᾽ αἰπόλῳ ἀνδρὶ ἔοικας.
ᾡπόλος ὅκκ᾽ ἐσορῇ τὰς μηκάδας οἷα βατεῦνται,
τάκεται ὀφθαλμώς, ὅτι οὐ τράγος αὐτὸς ἔγεντο.
ἄρχετε βουκολικᾶς Μοῖσαι φίλαι ἄρχετ᾽ ἀοιδᾶς.
καὶ τὺ δ᾽ ἐπεί κ᾽ ἐσορῇς τὰς παρθένος οἷα γελᾶντι,
τάκεαι ὀφθαλμώς, ὅτι οὐ μετὰ ταῖσι χορεύεις.᾽

The oxherds came, the shepherds and the goatherds came, and they
all asked what was troubling him. Priapus came, and said, "Poor
Daphnis, why are you pining away? The girl is wandering by every
spring and every grove –
Begin, dear Muses, begin the pastoral song –
"searching for you. Ah, you are simply a hopeless lover and quite
at a loss what to do. You used to be called an oxherd, but now you
are acting like a goatherd. When he sees the nanny goats being
mounted, the goatherd weeps his eyes away regretting that he wasn't born a goat.
Begin, dear Muses, begin the pastoral song.

---

21 As Samson 2013, 297 notes: "Bestiality is never overt in Theocritus' *Idylls*; however, his characters are certainly aware of the stereotype that herdsman perform bestial acts with their animals".

22 The myth of Daphnis seems to have been known at least since the time of Stesichorus of Himera (sixth century BC). For the tradition of the myth of Daphnis, see Ogilvie 1962.

"And you, when you see how the girls laugh, weep your eyes away
just because you're not dancing with them".[23]

Priapus' speech seems to be offensive towards Daphnis. He starts by emphasising Daphnis' suffering state (Δάφνι τάλαν), and then informs Daphnis that there is a girl/nymph (κώρα) looking for him. We do not know exactly who this girl is. Ogilvie argues that this *kōra* should be the one that Daphnis is longing for, but, since Theocritus uses this term both for nymphs and maidens, we cannot be sure of the status of Daphnis' beloved.[24] Gutzwiller also argues that this *kōra* is the one that Daphnis loves, and that he is simply resisting the erotic urge.[25] Dover proposes different possibilities for this resistance: Daphnis could have been punished by some god and have become impotent, or he is being threatened by a god with punishment in case he has sex with the girl, or he boasted that he was immune to Eros, and so is now afraid of the consequences if he breaks his vow.[26]

In the face of Daphnis' apathy over the possibility of enjoying the company of the girl, Priapus calls him "obsessed with passion" (δύσερως),[27] making the audience aware that Daphnis longed for someone, and "helpless" (ἀμήχανος), emphasising his incapacity to gratify his passion.[28] Priapus further adds that Daphnis reminds him of the goatherd who sadly looks at his goats being mounted, and wishes that a goat himself. What is Priapus really implying here? Gutzwiller argues that the relationship established between the goatherd and Daphnis is a reference to the sexual freedom of the natural world, which the goatherd sees as preferable to the restraints of human relationships.[29] Samson similarly argues that the goatherd might be "only weeping in envy of their sexual freedom", but, contrary to Gutzwiller and Hunter, she poses another possibility: what if the goatherd is weeping because of an erotic feeling towards the goat?[30] Gow had already noticed that goatherds might have been known for their proclivity to sexual excesses.[31] White notes that Theocritus employed a sexual pun by using

23 Transl. Hopkinson.
24 Ogilvie 1962, 108.
25 Gutzwiller 1991, 97. For more on this, see Gutzwiller 1991, 95–101.
26 Dover 1971, 84.
27 On the meanings of this term, see Ogilvie 1962, 107–108.
28 On this passage, see Gutzwiller 1991, 98. For a parallel with Polyphemos and Galateia established by the use of this term, see Hunter 1999, 92.
29 Gutzwiller 1991, 98.
30 Samson 2013, 297.
31 Gow 1950, 20. For an analysis of Gow's arguments, see Giangrande 1977, 179–180.

the verb *elaunō* (89), which can mean "drive" but also *bīneō*, "illicit intercourse".[32] She argues that Theocritus is actively implying that the goatherd is interested in engaging in sexual intercourse with the goats. This seems to be in line with the scholiast on Theocritus (86), who implies that goatherds are more prone to lust than cowherds because the goats provoke them, while cows do not. Similarly, Hunter argues that Priapus' "point may be that the goatherd is δύσερως because, although having in his (female) goats a ready supply of outlets for desire, he longs for the impossible (transformation into a he-goat) rather than merely doing what a Priapus would do to the nearest available she-goat".[33]

I would argue that a certain erotisation of the animal exists here in this passage. It is not a coincidence that the character that makes the sexual allusion is Priapus, a god that symbolises permanent lust and that is commonly associated with Pan and satyrs, mythological figures that often engage in transgressive sexual behaviour. The god's comment is intended to taunt Daphnis, downgrading Daphnis from cowherd to goatherd, which was considered a lower class of herdsmen, and furthermore comparing him to the goatherds who fantasise about sexual intercourse with their goats.[34] Priapus does seem to imply that it would be common for goatherds to use their animals sexually, and the scholiast on Theocritus further justifies this implication. Theocritus adds to the reputation of the herdsmen's uncontrollable sexual desires. As Giangrande notices, the reason for this reputation is due to the demands of their profession, which "took them away from the opposite sex (they had to spend their lives tending herds on solitary hills) so that their sexual energy was pent-up and explosive".[35] Furthermore, Theocritus' choice of words, as noted by White, can be read as a sexual pun, further implying the sexual connection between man and animal. In this case, it is noted that the kind of herdsman more prone to engage in sexual intercourse with an animal is the one that was considered of lower social status. Goatherds were considered an inferior class of herdsmen, especially in comparison to cowherds, and the transgressive sexual act is associated with the lower social status.

The allusion to sexual desire between man and animal, specifically goats in a rural scenario, is also made in a later epigram by Meleager (*A.P.* 12.41):

---

32 White 2004, 152. Hunter 1999, 112 also notes that *elaunō* is a "not uncommon vulgarism with sexual sense". For more on the meaning of *elaunō*, see White 1986.

33 Hunter 1999, 93.

34 Gow 1950, 20. For a detailed analysis of this passage, see Williams 1969. On the herdsman in ancient Greek culture, see Gutzwiller 2006.

35 Giangrande 1977, 179.

Οὐκέτι μοι Θήρων γράφεται καλός, οὐδ' ὁ πυραυγὴς
πρίν ποτε, νῦν δ' ἤδη δαλός, Ἀπολλόδοτος.
στέργω θῆλυν ἔρωτα· δασυτρώγλων δὲ πίεσμα
λασταύρων μελέτω ποιμέσιν αἰγοβάταις.

I do not count Thero fair any longer, nor Apollodotus,
once gleaming like fire, but now already a burnt-out torch.
I care for the love of women. Let it be for goat-mounting herds
to press in their arms hairy pansy-boys.[36]

Meleager writes that he no longer has interest in boys, such as Thero and Apollodotus, whom he once fancied, and the source for such a lack of interest might be that they are now too old, too hairy. Since these hairy boys are no longer attractive, they should only pique the interest of herdsmen who have sex with goats (αἰγοβάταις), who are more used to hairy partners.[37] There is a clear parallel here with Theocritus.[38] Although Meleager refers to *poimēn*, a "herdsman" who is responsible for both cows and goats (contrary to Theocritus who refers specifically to *aipolos*, a "goatherd"), he specifically mentions herdsmen who mount goats (αἰγοβάταις). Both texts not only allude to the sexual use of animals by men, but specifically to the use of goats by their goatherd. They both reflect a possible social stigma towards goatherds, further emphasised by the comment of the scholiast on Theocritus that highlights how goats provoke their keepers, in contrast with cows which are more controlled creatures.

There is also a comparison to be made with myths where sex between humans and animals is portrayed. As I have already shown, this typology of myths commonly shows a maiden outside the city's boundaries, in the wild, falling outside the realm of social regulations and conventions. The herdsman/shepherd daily delves into the wilds, possibly alone or with a colleague,[39] besides sharing the company of animals for long hours. They most likely spend more time with animals than they do with actual people, having plenty of opportunities to satisfy a sexual desire for an animal without suffering any consequences.[40]

---

36 Transl. Paton.
37 It is also an association between goatherds and the god Pan, who is also called *Aigibatēs* (*A.P.* 6.31).
38 This parallel was also noted by Giangrande 1977, 179–180; White 1986, 148.
39 In the *Iliad* (18.525–526), Hephaestus includes two shepherds on the shield of Achilles.
40 Modern studies also point towards the conclusion that episodes of sex with animals are usually associated with easiness of access. Therefore, it is not surprising that the most common animals involved in sexual activity with humans in rural areas are farm animals. Kinsey 1948, 261–262 argued that sexual contact between humans and animals was almost solely confined to rural areas, and his data revealed that seventeen percent of farm boys have "complete sexual relations

Another source for this theme is Plutarch, who wrote three different treatises solely devoted to animal questions, besides including discussions of animals in other texts.[41] One of them, the *Bruta animalia ratione uti*, also known as *Gryllus*, is a parody of the tenth book of the *Odyssey*, where Odysseus, stuck on Circe's island, asks the sorcerer to transform his comrades back into men. Circe acquiesces to Odysseus' request, with one condition: Odysseus first needs to discuss with his pig-shaped friends if they choose to be men again or rather prefer to remain pigs. For the sake of discussion, one pig, Gryllus, is chosen to convey the group's choice. Gryllus' position is clear throughout the entire text: animals are superior to humans (987b), sharing all the human virtues without partaking in any of their flaws and vices. Among the examples Gryllus uses to support his argument, he mentions the human incapacity to resist their sexual cravings, even unnatural ones such as desire for animals. In his words, "For men have, in fact, attempted to consort with goats and sows and mares, and women have gone mad with lust for male beasts" (990f).[42] On the contrary, animals do not partake in inter-species sex, not do they display any lust for humans. Gryllus' intention is to show how animals respect the natural order of the world and do not transgress the species' boundaries, contrary to humans. Most of the examples of unnatural pairings of humans and animals that Gryllus mentions are mythological, but he starts by emphasising general examples of men who had sex with goats, sows and mares. We cannot, nevertheless, conclude that *Gryllus* is making a reference to real cases of human-animal sex. This text is an intellectual exercise of Plutarch,

---

with other animals, and perhaps as many more have relations which are not carried through climax" (459–463). However, it was also noted that this outcome was particularly associated with easiness of access. After observing that urban boys also show a great sexual interest in animals, the report concluded that the only reason why sex with animals was more common in rural areas than in urban was that there was that in the first case it was easier. The available testimonies of persons that disclose their sexual desires for animals, show that some of the most common targeted animals are horses and cows, both animals more easily found in rural areas. In a study published in 2003 by Williams and Weinberg, 51% of the men in active sexual relationships with an animal had a dog as a partner and 37% an equine, with the remaining animals including goats, pigs, cats, and sheep. Among them 17% expressed that they would prefer an equine as a partner, the impediment being that it was difficult to acquire one (p. 529). The allusions to sex between goatherds and goats in both Theocritus and Meleager point to a similar conclusion. It is likely that in antiquity, like today, sex with animals might have been more common in rural areas of Greece. See also Miletski 2002; Miletski 2017.

41 For a general view of the relevance of animals in Plutarch's writings see the introduction in Newmyer 2006 and Newmyer 2014.

42 Transl. Helmbold.

seeking to depict animals in a better light than humans. The specific sexual examples that he uses are mythological. He specifically mentions Pasiphae instead of other mythological examples such as Europa and Leda. It is a reaffirmation of the transgressive character of the sexual act between animal and human that I have already discussed in detail. *Gryllus* mentions goats, pigs and mares as the animals most commonly ravished by men. All of them are animals that humans use to tame, and so they would be at their disposal. This passage from Plutarch emphasises the notion that there were people who sexually enjoyed animals, similar to the allusions made in older sources.

A more definite assertion of sex with animals as a transgressive act is made by Artemidorus Daldianus, the dream-interpreter, active in the second century AD. At the end of the first book of the *Oneirocritica*, Artemidorus explores what he calls "sex contrary to nature" (παρά φύσιν συνουσίας). Under this category he lists dreams where a person is having oral sex, women penetrating women, having sex with a god or goddess, sex with a dead person or with a wild beast (θηρίῳ μιγῆναι) among others. Although these dreams are listed under the category of sex contrary to nature, they are not taken to mean that something terrible will happen. In fact, dreaming of having sex with an animal might be positive, if the person is the one mounting the animal. Supposedly, this would mean that the dreamer would benefit from a person who is similar to the dreamt beast. However, if the dreamer is the one being penetrated by the animal, this may mean that he will suffer immensely, and possibly die. This text explores the meaning and significance of dreams which people had at the time of Artemidorus. Sex between humans and animals is a theme, however, which we can trace back to the early days of ancient Greek culture and society. It seems, therefore, that Artemidorus conveys a social view, not a specific personal bias against the sexual practice, as it is noticeable throughout his work. By stating that sex with beasts is against nature and that it is against the natural sexual behaviour of humans, Artemidorus provides us with a general perception on human-animal sex, not only of the society of his time but most likely — particularly when considering the information conveyed in older sources — the historical view as well.

Conclusion

In this chapter, I have approached sources where elements of sexual contact between humans and animals/animal-shaped gods are disclosed, showing that in general these sources depict human-animal sex as a sexual act against nature. Although the three myths that have been discussed include animal elements, not all of them shed light on human-animal sex since they portray animal-shaped gods, and not animals *per se*. The myth of Pasiphae, however, deviates from the general structure of this typology of myths, since the animal is not a god in disguise, and also because a woman takes the initiative to copulate with the animal. The bestial sex results in a bestial outcome: the Minotaur, the embodiment of the transgression. The Minotaur simultaneously signifies a transgression of the natural laws of human conception. Human pregnancy, which could only be achieved by divine or human intervention is, in this myth, also possible for animals, which consequently results in a monstrous outcome.

I have also showed how human-animal sex is addressed in other literary sources across a wide chronology, namely in the works of Herodotus, Theocritus, an epigram by Meleager, Plutarch and Artemidorus. Despite the diversity of literary genres approached here, which naturally should be read with caution and should not be taken as historical examples of actual sexual behaviour, these sources could be read as examples of how human-animal sex was part of ancient common knowledge and how it was usually depicted as a sexual transgression, a behaviour against nature. Herodotus — as in other episodes where he explores sexual acts among non-Greeks — appears to be shocked by the Egyptian tradition of women offering themselves to a goat, which is most likely the reaction of Greek audiences when faced with an account of human-animal sex. The sexual appeal of goats is also alluded to in Theocritus, Meleager and Plutarch. References to sex with goats seems to have been something of a commonplace in ancient Greek literature, most likely reflecting a real practice or at least rumours that were circulating. Plutarch's *Gryllus* criticises humans who have sex with animals, branding the action as a crime against nature, a crime that animals never commit, since they do not willingly engage in inter-species sex. Artemidorus lists dreams, in which humans are presented as having sex with animals as an example of sex against nature, and dreaming of being penetrated by an animal indicates suffering and possibly death. Therefore, it seems likely that sex between humans and animals not only occurred in ancient Greece, but that it was also negatively considered, a commonly recognised sexual transgression. All the references that we have to human-animal sex, either in myth, iconography or literature,[43] hint that the action was not socially accepted, that it was against the norm and even against nature.

---

43 For more references, including iconography, see Magalhães 2019.

Bibliography

Alcalde Martin, C. (1998), 'El mito de Leda: Sus Metamorphosis en la Historia del Arte', in: J.L. Calvo Martinez (ed.), *Religión, magia y mitología en la antigüedad clásica*, Granada, 9–37.

Alexandridis, A. (2008), 'Wenn Götter lieben, wenn Götter strafen: Zur Ikonographie der Zoophilie im griechischen Mythos', in: A. Alexandridis/M. Wild/L. Winkler-Horaček (eds.), *Mensch und Tier in der Antike: Grenzziehung und Grenzüberschreitung*, Wiesbaden, 285–311.

Anagnostou-Laoutides, E./Konstan, D. (2008), 'Daphnis and Aphrodite: A Love Affair in Theocritus *Idyll* 1', in: *The American Journal of Philology* 129, 497–527.

Asheri, D./Lloyd, A./Corcella, A. (eds.) (2007), *A Commentary on Herodotus Books I-IV*, Oxford.

Boer, R. (2015), 'From Horse Kissing to Beastly Emissions: Paraphilias in the Ancient NearEast', in: M. Masterson/N.S. Rabinowitz/J. Robson (eds.), *Sex in Antiquity: Exploring gender and sexuality in the Ancient World*, London, 67–79.

Buxton, R.G.A. (2009), *Forms of Astonishment: Greek Myths of Metamorphosis*, Oxford.

Campbell, G.L. (ed.) (2014), *The Oxford Handbook of Animals in Classical Thought and Life*, Oxford.

Collard, C./Cropp, M. (ed.) (1995), *Euripides, Fragments*, Warminster.

Dover, K.J. (transl.) (1971), *Theocritus, Select poems*, London.

Earls, C.M./Lalumière, M.L. (2009), 'A Case Study of Preferential Bestiality', in: *Archives of Sexual Behaviour* 38, 605–609.

Giangrande, G. (1977), 'Aphrodite and the Oak-Trees', in: *Museum Philologum Londiniense* 2, 177–186.

Godley, A.D. (transl.) (1920), *Herodotus, The Persian wars*, Cambridge, MA.

Gow, A.S.F. (transl.) (1950), *Theocritus*, Cambridge.

Gutzwiller, K. (1991), *Theocritus' Pastoral Analogies: The Formation of a Genre*, Madison.

Gutzwiller, K. (2006), 'The Herdsman in Greek Thought', in: M. Fantuzzi/T. Papanghelis (eds.), *Brill's companion to Greek and Latin pastoral*, Leiden, 1–24.

Harris-McCoy, D.E. (transl.) (2012), *Artemidorus, Oneirocritica*, Oxford.

Harden, A. (2013), *Animals in the Classical World: Ethical Perspectives from Greek and Roman texts*, Basingstoke.

Helmbold, W.C. (transl.) (1957) *Plutarch, Beasts are Rational*, Cambridge, MA, 489–536.

Hopkinsonn, N. (transl.) (2015), *Theocritus. Moschus. Bion.*, Cambridge, MA.

Hunter, R. (ed.) (1999), *Theocritus, a selection: Idylls 1, 3, 4, 6, 7, 10, 11 and 13*, Cambridge.

Kinsey, A.C./Pomeroy, W.B./Martin, C.E. (1948), *Sexual Behavior in the Human Male*, Philadelphia.

Magalhães, J.M. (2019), *Para-philias: Transgressive sex in Ancient Greece*, Ph.D. Thesis, University of Roehampton, London.

Masters, R.E.L. (1962), *Forbidden Sexual Behavior & Morality*, New York.

Mayor, A. (2014), 'Animals in Warfare', in: G.L. Campbell (ed.), *The Oxford Handbook of Animals in Classical Thought and Life*, Oxford, 282–293.

Miletski, H. (2002), *Understanding Bestiality and Zoophilia*, Bethesda.

Miletski, H. (2017), 'Zoophilia: Another Sexual Orientation?', in: *Archives of Sexual Behaviour* 46, 39–42.

Newmyer, S.T. (2006), *Animals, Rights and Reason in Plutarch and Modern Ethics*, New York/London.

Newmyer, S.T. (2011), *Animals in Greek and Roman Thought: A Sourcebook*, London.

Ogilvie, R.M. (1962), 'The Song of Thyrsis', in: *Journal Hellenic Studies* 82, 106–110.

Paton, W.R. (transl.) (1918), *The Greek Anthology*, Cambridge, MA.

Robson, J. (2002), 'Bestiality and Bestial Rape in Greek Myth', in: S. Deacy/K.F. Pierce (eds.), *Rape in Antiquity: Sexual Violence in the Greek and Roman Worlds,* London, 65–96.

Samson, L.G. (2013), *The Philosophy of Desire in Theocritus' Idylls*, Ph.D. Thesis, University of Iowa, available at: http://ir.uiowa.edu/etd/5051.

Sorabji, R. (1993), *Animal Minds & Human Morals: The Origins of the Western Debate*, London.

Shelton, J. (2014), 'Spectacles of Animal Abuse', in: G.L. Campbell (ed.), *The Oxford Handbook of Animals in Classical Thought and Life*, Oxford, 461–477.

White, H. (1986), 'A Case of Pastoral Humour in Theocritus', in: *Museum Philologum Londiniense* 7, 147–149.

Wenghofer, R. (2014), 'Sexual Promiscuity of Non-Greeks in Herodotus' *Histories*', in: *The Classical World* 107, 515–534.

White, H. (2004), 'Further Notes on the *Idylls* of Theocritus', in: *VELEIA* 21, 147–157.

Williams, C.J./Weinberg, M.S. (2003), 'Zoophilia in Men: A Study of Sexual Interest in Animals', in: *Archives of Sexual Behavior* 32, 523–535.

Williams, F. (1969), 'Theocritus, *Idyll* I 81–91', in: *The Journal of Hellenic Studies* 89, 121–123.

Younger, J.G. (2011), 'Sexual Peculiarities of the Ancient Greeks and Romans', in: M. Golden/P. Toohey (eds.), *Sexuality in the Classical World*, Oxford, 55–86.

Catalina Popescu
The Womb Inside the Male Member:
A Lucianic Twist

Abstract: This chapter discusses the topic of sexuality in Lucians' *Verae Historiae*, namely the sailors' encounter with the vine-women and the lifestyle of the male-only society of the Moon. Several scholars have showed that Lucian's hybrids clearly mock the fears of his times regarding femininity and the gender dichotomies. Popescu argues that the reader fears sexual encounters resulting in impotence. When male dreams of potency are challenged in the vine-women's episode, Lucian shows that a utopian universe without women will lead to the reemergence of femininity inside the males who struggle to perform both the inseminating and the gestational role, either in sequence or at the same time. Lucian's hybrid anatomies (hermaphrodites or eunuchs), created strictly from the need to overcompensate for the absence of the female "other", only reflect that no eradication of femininity is possible because it permanently returns both in anatomy and physiology, as long as the reader thinks in strictly binary terms.

My chapter discusses the sexuality of Lucian's Vine-women and Selenites in *Verae Historiae I* (8–9 and 22–24). In his article "Sex with Moonmen and Vine-Women" Larmour specifies that *Verae Historiae* deconstructs and ridicules the ancient gender polarities through the creation of hybrids whose bodies are fused to the point of making gender irrelevant. At the same time, Lucianic hybridity "is closely associated with, perhaps even a displacement of, a deep-seated cultural anxiety about women and female sexuality".[1] Hybridity is natural in this whimsical universe where Lucian deconstructs heterosexual and homoerotic relationships. Previous scholarship has already emphasised the androgynous potential of Lucian's human-vegetal hybrids as well as the highly impractical procreation practices in a universe where femininity is absent. For my part, I believe that femininity is not absent but only dormant in the Moonite world, and the expression of masculinity suffers from this fearful suppression of the female "other". Through metaphor and ancient medical and botanical theories, using secondary literature on ancient science and gender not related to Lucian (Taiz, Dover, Winkler, Leitao, Totelin, Salzmann-Mitchell or duBois), I will show that Lucian modifies the anatomies of the protagonists beyond recognition apparently to avoid

---

1 Larmour 1997, 144.

https://doi.org/10.1515/9783110695793-015

the female, only to reconfirm later her relevance. My chapter aims to show that the basis of his humour lies in the fictional castration of the male and the transformation of the male member into a womb, right at the moment of its perceived solitary triumph.

My purpose in this chapter is to precisely address the Lucianic reader's inability to pass the gender dichotomy. I will focus on the specific representation of reproductive organs, either male or female, and their physiology. Thus, I intend to prove that the Selenites struggle to imitate feminine reproductive functions, such as gestation, parturition and nourishment of the young. In some situations, the Moonites simply regenerate the feminine "other" through mimicry of feminine physiology. In others, they underperform while struggling to accomplish "feminine" tasks without specialised feminine organs (vaginal orifices, uterine cavities, etc.). Hermaphroditism and castration lay at the centre of Lucian's hybridity, both problematic for the binary concept of gender and highly intriguing in *Verae Historiae*. While the eunuch might easily appear feminine in binary thinking, due to its absence of testes and (sometimes) penis, the hermaphrodite was either genderless and monstrous (*teras*), or was harbouring a penis in the abdomen, without the possibility of pushing it forward:[2] according to Galen (*De Sem.* 2.1), this was also a characteristic of the female.

1 The female alien

The story begins with a miraculous voyage where Lucian's sailors have a sexual encounter with unusually attractive Vine-women who turn them into impotent vine-human hybrids. The encounter happens at the margins of the civilised world, right at the limits of Heracles' voyage.[3] There, they find Vine-women who try to lure them with inebriating kisses and beautiful hybrid bodies (1.8: εὕρομεν ἀμπέλων χρῆμα τεράστιον· τὸ μὲν γὰρ ἀπὸ τῆς γῆς, ὁ στέλεχος αὐτὸς εὐερνὴς καὶ

---

2 Diodorus Siculus confirmed that certain androgynes appeared as women and even married men, until (in some cases) the penis emerged later, finally reassigning them simply as men: *Frag.* 34. 1–15, *Cod. 244* of Diodorus' *Hist Lib.* in Photius' *Bibl.* 377a29–34. A discussion on the topic of hermaphrodites appears in the article of Pfunter 2020, 170, 171: "In such a context, Diodorus' argument against the existence of true dual-sexuals (i.e. those possessed of both male and female sexual attributes) could help Photius and his readers build a scientific as well as theological basis for confirming that human nature includes a gender binary, thereby affirming traditional gender roles" (170).

3 On the sexual dimension of sailing imagery in Aristophanes, see Kanellakis in this volume.

παχύς, τὸ δὲ ἄνω γυναῖκες ἦσαν, ὅσον ἐκ τῶν λαγόνων ἅπαντα ἔχουσαι τέλεια — τοιαύτην παρ' ἡμῖν τὴν Δάφνην γράφουσι νᾶρ τι τοῦ Ἀπόλλωνος καταλαμβάνοντος ἀποδενδρουμένην, "we discovered the most amazing type of grape-vine: from the earth up the stem was sturdy and thick and above, they were women really exquisite in their upper parts — this way our people paint Daphne turning into a tree when Apollo catches her").[4] The lower part is a powerful *stelechos* on which the delicate female torso is mounted (8).[5] Their hair has tendrils, leaves and grapes and their kisses are inebriating. To make things more tempting they grow next to a river of wine with plenty of fish. Additionally, their ripe bodies bear grapes, a sweet promise of nourishment and replenishment of fluid: they are both fruits and sexual lures. Sex, drink and food form an irresistible combination for the tired, thirsty and hungry sailors — all good reasons to give the encounter a chance. The Greek men enthusiastically pluck the Vine-women's grapes and eat them and some later try to mate with them.[6] This episode offers Lucian a chance to explore what the expectations of manliness are in his fantasy world, both in anatomical and behavioural terms.

At a literary-aesthetic level, Larmour (quoting Keuls) asserted that in Lucian's writings the female and the literary narrative are both ensnaring, cosmeticised and mendacious.[7] In other words, untruthful femininity and fictional narratives have in common the veil of lies over the core of truth. While I agree with this statement for Lucian's literary metaphor, I believe that this episode speaks more about the mesmerising anatomy of the female body than about the deviance of the feminine mind. Here, the female is nude from all points of view, but her inner and outer workings remain confusing. As we can see from this depiction, the feminine body is simply alien to the male. Lucian possibly looks through the lenses of confused medical practitioners who failed to properly understand the functionality of female anatomy. The upper part is recognisable as human (even with the dangling fruit-like appendages, possibly resembling breasts), but the lower part is *teratological (terastiai)*. This echoes the difficulty male anatomists

---

4 For the sources of the primary texts that have been included in the volume and some translations, please see the Bibliography.

5 Georgiadou and Larmour 1997, 87–88, observe that this trunk bears sexual similarities with male reproductive organs, making them not only a hybrid between two species, but also subtly androgynous.

6 The act is painful for the hybrid and stands as a symbol of sexual violence according to Longus (2.4.4, 3.33.3) and Heliodorus (10.32.2). Georgiadou and Larmour 1997, 87 also see in this gesture a symbol of rape and deflowering.

7 Larmour 1997, 142–144.

have in classifying female sexual organs and their physiology.[8] The rest of the body might work like that of a man, the standard "human", according to Aristotle, Galen, and the popular perception,[9] but her lower parts are confusing. It is only emblematic that the Vine-women do not have apparent sexual organs, while the males clearly have *aidoia*: the feminine body "lacks" in terms of anatomy. A female's sexual success is also defined through the reactions of her male counterpart: while the Vine-women offer themselves to the sailors with blandishments, they remain stuck to the ground. It is up to the male to consummate the sexual act. The Vine-woman's trunk might remind one of a *phallus*, but it is an inert penis at best, buried in the ground, comparable to the inverted penis lying inside the women's abdomen, according to Galen.

2 The female body as a plant: Care instructions

While at first sight, this scene might seem to depict the expected response of virile sailors in front of available exotic beauties, there are hints from the beginning that the protagonists are failing in their roles, both as men and as Greek civilisers. Their sexual behaviour translates into agricultural and alimentary metaphors. According to Taiz, ancient botanists thought of plants as feminine or genderless (since neutered ultimately meant female).[10] By inversion, Lucian thinks of women as plants. Mythical thinking depicts males as nature tamers and careful fertilisers of the feminine "other" often described in vegetal terms.[11] When examined in such agricultural terms, sexuality implies that the male must maintain a tight control over the growth and expansion of the feminine other. Both womanhood and the resulting progeny are thus reduced to produce, through metaphors of plant growth, foliage and fruit. Calame argues that, in the conceptual domain of

---

8 From the Hippocratic "wandering uterus", to the Aristotelian obsession with female leakage and male dryness and to the inverted penis Galen thought existed in women, a detailed account of the male erroneous perception of the female "other" is offered by Bonnard, J.-B. 2013, 21–39.

9 Aristotle *GA* 716a26–34 for anatomical differences between male and female, but also *GA* 722b32 for sex differences in abilities (males are deemed better performers in every act that the female is also capable of). Also, Pseudo-Aristotle, *Phys.* 806b 32–35. For the female reproductive organs as male organs inside out, see Galen, *De sem. 2.1*. For vase painting which displays women as males with breasts and without penises, see Dover, 1997, 16. For analysis of visual representations, see Bundrick, 2012, 11–35. Also, for a different interpretation of those drawings see Thomas Hubbard in this volume.

10 Taiz 2014, 244–246.

11 On the sexual and sensual aspects of farming and soil, see also Manousakis in this volume.

Greek metaphors, the woman is a plot of land in need of cultivation and fruitful sexuality is symbolised by ploughing and sowing, not careless gathering of wild fruit like we see in this episode.[12] According to duBois, "the body of the woman is not only the property of her husband but also the space in which he labours, a surface that he breaks open and cultivates [...]".[13]

If duBois might capture the metaphor of the idealised relationship between a man and his wife, one should not forget that this metaphor can only partially apply here: in this relationship between a man and his casual female companion, the man has no other concern than performing and satisfying his virile needs.[14] The image of the female also differs from that of a regular wife (*alochos*): she is not a docile plant, but a climbing vine. A specific similarity between the vine and a rogue female is already obvious in Pliny, both in terms of sexual behaviour and anatomy (*NH* XIV, III, 10–11).[15] In his view, a vine is indeed a female and a cross-breeder by nature: to survive, she "marries" other species (poplars) and embraces them with "her" many "digits", "arms" and "knees". While one can expect vulnerability in this need of the vine to cling to a sturdy support, vines in general can go easily rogue without the guiding hand of an agriculturist. A vine can suffocate its mate and expand its body by incapacitating or tying down other species. It can also kill a careless viticulturist who climbs too high to tend it. According to McMahon, the grape-vine requires careful pruning, tying and grafting, or it will grow wild, since vines were also associated with excessive sexual outburst, or production of flowers with no fruitful outcome (Theophrastus, *H.P.* 8.7.4).[16] The fruitless excess of a wild vine is also visible in the eagerness of Lucian's hybrid women to mate with complete strangers and consummate a union void of any reproductive benefits.

As we can see in the paragraph before, these vines needed the guidance of an agriculturist (just as women supposedly needed the guidance of a firm man).

---

12 Calame 1992, 154–160.
13 duBois 1988, 68.
14 Dover 2002, 23, 26.
15 The text from Pliny reads: *in Campano agro populis nubunt, maritasque conplexae atque per ramos earum procacibus bracchis geniculato cursu scandentes cacumina aequant, in tantum sublimes, ut vindemitor auctoratus rogum ac tumulum excipiat*[...] "In the Campanian field, they marry poplars and, by embracing the husbands with their impudent arms and climbing through their branches with their grasp of joints, they match their tops to such heights, that the contracted vine-tender should receive (as insurance) a funeral pyre and a grave...".
16 See also McMahon 1998, 101–103, for plants as sexually expansive.

Lucian's sailors are anything but skilled care takers in their behaviour. Here, impulsive sexuality and careless agriculture mingle.[17] In Lucian's Vine-women episode, the male, to whom ancient societies entrusted the civilising role, is unsuccessful in pruning the female's uncontrolled growth, or in grafting her wild nature. In response, by taking on the behaviour of the invasive vine, the female recovers the wild nature of the pre-cultivated land and corrupts her cultivator.[18] Moreover, she ties him down, instead of being tied by him (a metaphor which translates male inappropriate psychological attachments in bodily terms), and thus incapacitates him from roaming free, essentially from behaving like a free man.[19] If the vine stands for a casual mate (a foreigner for one-night-stand, a *pornē* or a *pallakē*), then a Greek citizen should perform his virile function without being "attached" to such a stranger. Thus, while Larmour believes that as men, the Greek sailors were supposed to resist intercourse (although women were deemed naturally promiscuous),[20] my view is different in this respect: they were not expected to abstain, but to display "sexual dominance", to perform sexual intercourse without suffering emasculation or dangerous attachment.

---

17 Georgiadou and Larmour 1997, 87 assert that the theme is both one of gender tension as well as an inversion between a pre- and post-civilised state, in terms of the tensions between Heracles and Dionysus. See also Georgiadou 1998, 207: "The drawing of a distinction between the lustful Vine-Women and the rest can be explained by the fact that Heracles has already come to the island of the Vine-Women and, in his capacity as a civilizer, tamed the excesses of Dionysus. [...] It would appear, then that Lucian produced a subtle variation in Dio's parable, by changing a pre-Heraclean scene into a post-Heraclean one." For Anderson in his work on Lucian 1976, 27, the episode sends hints to Aristophanes in Plato's *Symposium, 191C,* where the androgynes used to deposit their seed in the ground, "the next thing to an affair with a plant". Ní Mheallaigh 2014, 214 further sees an act of cultural appropriation in "the men's attempts to harvest the Vine-women's fruit — a phrase which contains a sexual metaphor, and here hints at rape, as the pain with which the Vine-women react signifies the tradition's resistance to such violent appropriation".

18 As explained by duBois 1988, 68 in mythical thinking.

19 For use of prostitutes (slaves or free foreigners) as a way to reassert the manliness of citizens, see Dover 2002, 23–24. He also discusses male citizens being shamed for excessive attachment to working girls and lavish expenditures.

20 Larmour 1997, 140–144. He reads female promiscuity as the norm in Greek misogynistic thinking and quotes Keuls 1985, 82.

3 The mistake of self-insemination

In commentaries on Lucian, scholars point out similarities between the sailor drinking wine and Odysseus' food challenges throughout his voyage.[21] I will briefly investigate one such episode, as it strengthens the connection between food intake and lack of sexual dominance. In the *Odyssey*, Hermes advised Odysseus to respond to Circe's sexual advances (*Od. X.* 290–301). Sex with her is not forbidden, but her food is not to be touched, at least not until he softens her aggressive femininity with an even more aggressive male dominance in bed.[22] As a result of such behaviour, he suffered neither somatic nor mental transformation (unlike his comrades condemned to lose both manhood and human intellect). Not only did he save his manhood and human form, but Circe ended up changing from antagonist to submissive supporter, right after Odysseus sexually intimidated her and joined her in a bedroom for a sexual encounter. Should he have chosen otherwise, her magic would have surely proven emasculating: μή σ' ἀπο-γυμνωθέντα κακὸν καὶ ἀνήνορα θήῃ, "lest she may turn you weak and unmanned, once naked" (*Od.* 10.301).

Unfortunately, Lucian's sailors are not in the same position of success. In this case, the sailors were not supposed to carelessly enjoy the fruits of an unknown land, growing on plants which look nothing like regular vines. They cavalierly pluck wild fruits endowed with psychedelic qualities instead of domesticating the vines first, before turning their grapes into a familiar drink, obtained by the trusted *technē* of fermentation. This readily available and alien wine dulls their senses and alters both their minds and bodies (I, 8).[23] It is in fact the alimentary hybris that ruins their sexual experience because, while sexuality reconfirms traditional manhood, eating is filled with sexual ambiguity. But why is food intake emasculating? By plucking and eating the strange women's undomesticated fruit, the sailors do not only fail in gently taming the feminine "plant", but also

---

21 Polyphemos, Circe, the Sirens, the Lotus Eaters and even Calypso were proposed as bearing similarities to this episode. See Larmour 1997, 140 and Georgiadou and Larmour 1998, 73, 80.
22 Larmour 1997, 140 compares the episode of Circe being threatened with a "phallic" sword with Lucian's episode of taming the Ass-Legged Women. The Greek sailors successfully escape that dangerous encounter because they use their masculinity against the dangerous feminine other. Ní Mheallaigh 2014, 215–216 reads the sexual violence against Ass-Women as metaphor of appropriation of literary tradition, similarly to Larmour.
23 Ní Mheallaigh 2014, 213–216 also reads this experience of inebriation through kiss as sexual inversion and insemination of the male by the female, but she believes it to be a metaphor of the relationship between literary production and tradition where the epigonic text ends up impregnated by the original, unable to differentiate itself as innovative (*mimēsis*).

allow their own bodies to be penetrated by her wild seeds. Thus, the male both neglects his role as inseminator and inadvertently transfers it to the female, as a paradox, right when he should assume the penetrating role.[24] It is through ingestion of food and intake of psychedelic liquids that the male opens himself up to sexual inversion.[25] In Hippocratic tradition (*Gyn.* 2.133, 3.213, *Epid.* 6.8.32), this also means trading his dry manly body for a more fluid, leaky alternative (the female).

While it is tempting to read grafting in this sexual act, with the penis as a live twig inserted in a bark slit to sweeten a wild vine, the reality of sex with Vine-women proves that the sailors end up grafted by the female, after the ingestion of fermented fruits (1.8: καὶ δύο τινὲς τῶν ἑταίρων πλησιάσαντες αὐταῖς οὐκέτι ἀπε-λύοντο, ἀλλ' ἐκ τῶν αἰδοίων ἐδέδεντο· συνεφύοντο γὰρ καὶ συνερριζοῦντο. καὶ ἤδη αὐτοῖς κλάδοι ἐπεφύκεσαν οἱ δάκτυλοι, καὶ ταῖς ἕλιξι περιπλεκόμενοι ὅσον οὐδέπω καὶ αὐτοὶ καρποφορήσειν ἔμελλον, "and two of our companions, mating with them, could not detach themselves, but were tied by their genitals: for they grew together with the vines and caught roots. And their fingers were already growing branches and caught in the tendrils, and they were already about to produce fruits themselves"). Caught inside this strange "vagina", the penis "grows with" it (I 8, *symphuein*) into a vine trunk. *Symphuein* is not a verb of potency or erection (unlike *auxein*);[26] it reduces the male member from a potent inseminator to a growing seedling. Through metaphor, such a member changes from procreative organ to an inert vegetal appendage.[27] While this penis is never amputated, physiologically speaking, the copulation described by Lucian is an actual castration. It is relevant that once the penis ceases to function (is "bound" or even disappears), the rest of the anatomy simply mimics the monstrous Vine-woman. The individual now bears fruits like the female, and does so "together" with her, essentially indistinguishable in anatomy and physiology from the opposite sex. Again, if we read Pliny, we notice that this behaviour is the way of the grape-vine: once "married" to a poplar and other species, the grapevine's embrace can be constrictive. Its joints, tendrils and appendages do not only caress and touch, but

---

24 For men's fear of becoming the penetrated partner: Keuls 1985, 153–187; Winkler 1990, 45; Georgiadou and Larmour 1998, 134; Dover 2002, 25–29; Kelleher 2011, 3–9.

25 Bergren 2008, 166–194, on females in myth and tragedy possessing drugs and drinks with pharmaceutical qualities. In a Roman scientific context, Pliny (*Nat. Hist.* 28.70–82) believes that even the feminine menstrual flow has pharmaceutical powers, as the female body is magical and could be both poisonous and beneficial in pest control.

26 McMahon 1998, 119, for a discussion on this verb in botanical and sexual terms.

27 For vegetables and male sexual organs see Keuls 1985, 76; duBois 1988, 184–185; Calame 1992, 160–165; Totelin 2006, 534–536.

also probe the male other, much like the fingers of the Vine-women who entangle the sailors with their tendrils, penetrate and change their bodies, while technically remaining the passive partners of intercourse. Georgiadou and Larmour made a brief mention that the Lucianic hybrids are reminiscent of Ovid's grafting of Salmacis in the story of Hermaphroditus (*Met. IV*, 317–245).[28] I will investigate the implications of such Ovidian echoes for my argument. Hermaphroditus is not yet a man, but a boy at ephebic age, possibly sexually inexperienced and afraid of Salmacis' advances. He is the opposite of the "manly" hoplite from Winkler's argument regarding the classical Greek dichotomy between active and passive sexual roles.[29] Dover believed that the ephebic stage was in fact a boy's experience of femininity:[30] Hermaphroditus' fear stands for this age-related sexual inversion, and he acts as a *parthenos*, a maiden caught in a forcible embrace. If one follows Taiz's theory regarding ancient perceptions on myth and flora, Salmacis is a goddess and her excessive sexual availability translates as outright sexual predation.[31] She surreptitiously takes up the phallic role while offering herself as the passive partner, until her nature fully permeates Hermaphroditus' body. Her desire to be penetrated combined with his impotence due to age causes in my view the ultimate sexual inversion, in an act of feminine predation which the Vine-women copy. The result of this strange sexual act, where the female adds herself to the male (essentially dissolving into his body), is a paradoxical castration. Instead of benefitting from this addition, the male ends up as a *semi-vir* (IV, 385–386: ... *exeat inde semivir et tactis subito mollescat in undis*! "May he come out a half-man and may he soften in the touched waves!") Ovid describes him as different not in anatomical, but physiological terms. He becomes soft, unnerved, possibly lethargic and impotent, perpetually stuck in boyhood, which in Dover's terms was supposed to be only a transient maidenhood.

---

28 Gerogiadou and Larmour 1998, 79. Georgiadou and Larmour 1998, 129 also compare the resulting vine-human hybrids to Empedocles' androgynes: "Empedocles said that trees were the first living things to grow on earth, and that, because of the matching of elements in their mixture, they combined the formula for male and female (A 70 [D-K]; see Guthrie [1962–1981] 2.208–209). He also made no firm distinction between animal and vegetal life-forms and the cabbage on the backside of the Moonmen (1.23) and ears of wood or plane-leaves below (1.25) may be an allusion to Empedoclean theories."
29 Winkler, 1990, 45.
30 Dover 1997, 16–18; 2002, 70–71.
31 Taiz 2014, 204 also reads vegetal grafting in the mythical story of Hermaphroditus: "Significantly, Salmacis' embrace of Hermaphrodite is compared to the grafting of trees. Salmacis is, in fact, a vegetation deity. Once grafted to Salmacis, Hermaphrodite loses his virility and becomes 'tamed' and 'impotent'".

In *VH* the feminine side ultimately surfaces in anatomical malformations. Once a man has lost his ability to penetrate, the body will exhibit any dormant effeminacy. According to Bardel in her analysis of Greek tragedy, a manly body had to be intact, impenetrable, sexually active and autonomous/unbound.[32] Wrapped in tendrils and caught by roots, the male body is now no longer intact nor unbound. Lucian shows what a reader accustomed to a binary gender system might think of a male who is tied down, has no recognisable penis, and suffers penetration like a maiden or Hermaphroditus. One might notice that Lucian never calls the sailors "women" after their metamorphosis: it is enough for the reader to imagine them behaving as the females around, stuck to the ground and producing fruits, to reassign them subconsciously to the feminine gender.

4 A response to the Vine-women: The exclusive world of Moonmen

Since sexuality with even these charming females-plants had such unfortunate outcomes, Lucian later offers his sailors a chance to contemplate a world where no women are in sight: he also places this utopia as far from the Earth as possible — on the Moon. In contrast to the world of wild females, the Moonites "do not even know the word woman" (1.22: οὐδὲ ὄνομα γυναικὸς ὅλως ἴσασι). Depicting a world without women is a challenge when the medical treaties of the time depicted femininity as the opposite of masculinity both in body and physiology. If femininity can ruin manliness, what would its absence do to manhood? And what would a world without women look like? Would anatomy be changed significantly to remove certain cavities and orifices, thought of as feminine? What happens then with the feminine reproductive tasks such as gestating and parturition? Would male bodies give birth?

Lucian asserts that Moonmen marry each other: one of them is sexually passive until he reaches the 25th year of his life, at which point he switches roles and becomes the penetrator.[33] As Georgiadou and Larmour assert, this arrangement is not only a solution to avoid the predatory behaviour depicted above, but also

---

32 Bardel 2002, 51, 60–61.
33 Ní Mheallaigh 2014, 219–220 stresses out that both the determination of gender by age, and the birth through surgery, show the artificiality of a universe which is essentially a mirror of the Earth with somewhat reversing properties.

a clever reminiscence of the classical Greek pederastic practices/patterns, according to which young boys were passive partners until they grew beards and then switched from *erōmenoi* (the passive beloved) to *erastai* (the active lovers).[34] Thus, the Moonites do not need to put up with women and their obnoxious nature which Hesiod and philosophers deplore. The above-mentioned scholars assert that Lucian has in mind certain Platonic dialogues where male-to-male relationships were depicted as superior to heterosexual bonds.[35] The Selenites have male-to-male intercourse in the back of the leg, followed by gestation of the foetus in the calf (1.22: κύουσι δὲ οὐκ ἐν τῇ νηδύϊ, ἀλλ᾽ ἐν ταῖς γαστροκνημίαις, "they get pregnant not in the womb, but in the calf"). Larmour detects a cultural reason for Lucian's anatomical choice: this depiction plays on the sensitivities of Lucian's time regarding the penetration of males, where sex with young boys of good upbringing did not involve anal, but instead intercrural penetration.[36]

One can notice that instead of the gender-neuter verb *plēsiazein* ("to have intercourse"), Lucian uses the verb *gameitai/gamei* which uses different voices to designate passive and active sexual acts: μέχρι μὲν οὖν πέντε καὶ εἴκοσι ἐτῶν γαμεῖται ἕκαστος, ἀπὸ δὲ τούτων γαμεῖ αὐτός ("until 25 years of age, each of them *is married to*, and after that each *marries*"). This verb is charged with gender assumptions, as for the regular Greek, the roles played in the bedroom were either female (recipient) or male (penetrator). Thus, the female is once more "grafted" upon the male, as the Selenite experiences both roles: only now the male and female side are expressed in age-related sequences rather than at once.[37]

While the Vine-women episode is concentrated on sexuality, in the description of Moonites' practices emphasis is placed on reproduction. To supersede the female, the Moonmen must deal with feminine concerns and lose part of sexual pleasure which consisted precisely in casual intercourse without worrying about

---

34 Despite the traditional identification of the Moon with a feminine principle, Lucian's Selenite society is strictly masculine and eager to substitute the feminine 'other', as Larmour 1997, 139 specifies. Georgiadou and Larmour 1998, 123–125 and Larmour 1998, 138 notice precisely this philosophical approach in the episode of Moonites, besides acknowledging this episode as the counterpart of the encounter with the Vine-women. Cf. Keuls 1985, 14; Calame 1993, 93–110; Dover 2002, 16.

35 Georgiadou and Larmour 1998, 125–126.

36 Larmour 1997, 138. For scholiasts, the passage is a clear reference to the second gestational place of Dionysus in Zeus' thigh, after Semele was both impregnated and burned to ashes by the god's thunderbolt (*Schol.* 9, 12), see also Larmour 1997, 139.

37 This was not unusual in Classical Greece, as we can see in Dover 2002, 28–29 and 52–53. Also, Georgiadou and Larmour 1998, 124, for the differences in meaning between active and passive voice in the verb of copulation (*gamein*).

offspring. Since there are no women in this universe, the problem of progeny is more stringent: men can enjoy each other's company (as in the real Greek world), but unlike the real world, they can no longer have intercourse with women for the birth of children. Because of this complication, the anatomy of the Moonites is specifically designed to accommodate gestation and birth. Nevertheless, the calf is an awkward gestational chamber and Lucian needs to draw a tongue-in-the-cheek etymology in order to equate the unhollowed muscular mass of the calf with the uterine cavity (based solely on its bulging shape, 1.22: δοκεῖ δέ μοι καὶ ἐς τοὺς Ἕλληνας ἐκεῖθεν ἥκειν τῆς γαστροκνημίας τοὔνομα, "I believe that from here came to the Greeks the name '*gastroknēmia*/belly of the calf'"). Lucian tactfully asserts that intercourse takes place in the back of the knee and chooses this place because it resembles an entrance without being one.

5 Avoiding the feminine *pathēmata*: A body without orifices

The following subchapters will show how Lucian scrambles the female anatomy to protect the male image of impenetrability and, in doing so, ends up in my view with dysfunctional organs that need prosthetics and assistance in order to function. If Lucian's scholarship usually looks at the act of copulation, I am particularly interested in discussing the potentially problematic aspect of gestation and parturition in the Lucianic all-male world. Conception and pregnancy, while so crucial for the Selenite society, put the gestating male in the awkward feminine position not only during insemination but also, during gestation and parturition.

If in the case of boys who had intercourse with adult males throughout their teenage years, there was a nagging cultural fear that their temporary "feminine" status might become a permanent condition, Lucian's depiction of male pregnancy could only enhance that fear of permanent feminisation. Additionally, there was a subsequent fear that femininity might surface and become obvious not only in behaviour (which could have been kept away from the public eye), but also in bodily terms, in physiognomy.[38] If playing the role of the passive sexual partner was common for both genders in the Greek world, pregnancy and

---

[38] Gleason 1995 discusses the outside presentation of rhetoricians and philosophers in Roman era, particularly in her chapters "Deportment as Language: Physiognomy and Semiotics of Gender", 55–81, and "Aerating the Flesh: Voice Changes and the Calisthenics of Gender", 82–102. I

birth were intrinsically linked to feminine life. Playing with gestation and parturition puts the Moonites in an even more delicate position than sex with men. For this, we need to look elsewhere, for scholarship on male pregnancy as metaphor in myth, comedy, and philosophy: in his analysis of Platonic dialogues, Daniel Leitao pointed out that male pregnancy is problematic even when it is metaphorical (philosophical), because it is still reminiscent of the penetration of the male.[39]

When it comes to male birth, the examples are rare in Greek literature since the subject bears clear signs of embarrassment for male authors. One example survives in myth, as Zeus gives birth to Athena through his head, but without unsightly birth pangs and with Hephaestus' "medical" help to open his body. Another example of male "birth" exists in Greek literature as a joke, in Aristophanes' *Assembly Women*, where a severely constipated man finally finds relief from his distress after a painful defecation which could only resemble a real birth. There is no need to explain why a birth through the anus might be highly uncomfortable to witness and even more so to experience. The scatological aspect is clear in Leitao's analysis of the episode in Aristophanes. As Leitao points out, "if parturient men take women as their models, their [...] pregnancies ought to conclude, as in women, with the emergence of the new-born from the lower abdomen, from between the legs".[40]

Armed with this new insight from other literary sources, I can read his image of Moonmen's calf pregnancies as an attempt to "seal off" any "embarrassing" orifices that might make the male audience uncomfortable. Lucian specifies that the Moonites do not have an anus, not even when it comes to digestion, and they do not lie together using their "seat", *hedra* (1.23: οὐδὲ τὴν συνουσίαν οἱ παῖδες ἐν ταῖς ἕδραις παρέχουσιν, ἀλλ' ἐν ταῖς ἰγνύαις ὑπὲρ τὴν γαστροκνημίαν, "and the boys do not have sex in their seats, but in the hollow above the belly of the calf"). In fact, as Lucian suggests, the Selenites do not excrete any faeces as they subsist on the purest of substances (smoke and air). Georgiadou and Larmour conclude that it might correspond to some philosophical ideals of independence from the material world and its foods: "Their diet is such, as they do not leave any residue".[41] Thus, the image would betray a certain philosophical discomfort with the idea of alimentary waste. I for my part believe that this anatomical absence also

want to thank the anonymous reader who suggested this author as a reference to the male fear of not being able to project enough masculinity in public.

39 Leitao 2012, 274.
40 Leitao 2012, 174. Through his pregnant calf, Zeus becomes both the dispenser of the seed and the fertilised uterus, both the male and the female in one body.
41 Georgiadou and Larmour 1997, 33. I tend to read a sexual fear in this imagery.

speaks of a clear embarrassment regarding sexuality. The lack of anus circumvents the problem Leitao noticed in Plato's *Symposium,* namely the unpleasant "cloacal associations" between anus and vagina in the allegorical image of philosophy as male pregnancy.[42]

In my view, the choice of sealing up the anus goes even further than the fear of being penetrated: it is a fear of sexual fluids and discharge, usually associated with events of feminine physiology (menstruation, afterbirth, lactation< see *Hippocratic corpus*).[43] Lucian sanitises even that department, which is also completely void of fluid exchanges because the Selenites have prosthetic reproductive organs made of noble ivory and sometimes of wood (1.22: αἰδοῖα μέντοι πρόσθετα ἔχουσιν, οἱ μὲν ἐλεφάντινα, οἱ δὲ πένητες αὐτῶν ξύλινα, "they have prosthetic gentials, some of ivory, others who are poor, of wood").[44]

Also, whenever possible, in my view, Lucian adds phallic appendages to their anatomy. As if the absence of an anus were not enough, the Moonites have a tail-like excrescence growing above their buttocks, made of a cabbage leaf (1.23: ὑπὲρ δὲ τὰς πυγὰς ἑκάστῳ αὐτῶν κράμβη ἐκπέφυκε μακρὰ ὥσπερ οὐρά, θάλλουσα ἐς ἀεὶ καὶ ὑπτίου ἀναπίπτοντος οὐ, "above the buttocks for each of them a cabbage leaf grows long like a tail, always green, which does not break, not even if one falls"). Vegetal appendages are common in the Moonites' anatomy, for they have cabbage ears and toes fused into one digit, much like branches merged into one stem. Yet, the cabbage stem is cleverly named *oura* by Lucian, which is also a euphemism for a penis. There is more to it: this excrescence resembling a cabbage is forever *thallousa,* turgescent and strong, and it does not break, not even when one falls on it. The presence of unyielding and erect *phallus* where humans only have a vulnerable orifice associated with excrements further bolster the manly attributes of this species. The cabbage itself bears resemblances with turnip greens and other plants and vegetables associated with male potency. Moreover, being forever green and impervious to pain is the ultimate phallic dream of sexual endurance.

However virile, the Selenite sturdy tail still has some gender ambivalence which has not previously been pointed out in Lucian's literature. The cabbage

---

42 Leitao 2012, 199, 211–213, for a similar problem with philosophy as metaphorical pregnancy.
43 About the male disgust, fear, or mere discomfort to such feminine bodily events such as menstruation, parturition, lactation, see Bonfante 1997, 184–185 for lactation, Laskaris 2008, 460–461 and n. 30 regarding bleeding; also, Salzman-Mitchell 2012, 148.
44 Larmour 1997, 139 for the use of prosthetic penises and sexual toys in ancient Greece, such as a dildo or *olisbos,* but for their use by women, not men. The scholar points out their social status as organs of "envy" and the ridiculousness of their existence in a world without women. I, however, believe that "womanhood" survives in this text.

bud is similar to another leafy garden plant, the lettuce, a plant most often associated with delicate, boyish Adonis. Contrary to expectation of potency discussed above, lettuce was not allowed to be "forever green", but was ritually left to die in the summer heat as a tribute to Aphrodite's beloved boy and his budding masculinity withered too soon.[45] Also, while the bud of the cabbage might be associated with the *phallus*, the surrounding foliage is rather closer to the image of the clitoris: in lyric poetry, Winkler compares leaves with such feminine anatomy.[46] As we can see, sexual ambivalence and even emasculation still play a part in this strange vegetal tail. The first sign of dysfunction is precisely this confusion between a clitoris and a "sturdy tail" in Lucian's choice of such vegetable metaphors.

6 Deconstructing pregnancy and birth

At first sight, scholars agree that the mythical pregnant male in Greek myth constitutes a dream of power directed at supplanting the female "other": "'giving birth' is culturally enshrined in Greek myth as what men do to resist the assaults of women on paternity".[47] However, Leitao and Keuls point out that the imagery of pregnancy and parturition might be particularly uncomfortable for men even in philosophical metaphors.[48] The act of giving birth is particularly humiliating, as it involves pain, spasms and discharge of humours, not to mention that it is dangerous for both mother and child.

If Lucian altered the Moonite anatomy for a "sanitised" conception, he apparently took similar precautions for parturition. Thus, Lucian first eliminates

---

45 On the rituals devoted to Adonis: Detienne 1972, 68; Keuls 1985, 25; Taiz 2014, 201.
46 According to McMahon 1998, 119, a lot of garden greens were associated with the male member: for example, garlic and onion inflorescences as well as the tubular stems of onions. Winkler 1981, 80 believed that buds, inflorescences, and foliage were associated with feminine anatomy and the clitoris.
47 Leitao 2012, 174.
48 Again, Leitao 2012, 53–54 confirms the embarrassment, when he analyses Aristophanes' *The Assembly Women*, where a heavily constipated man experiences pains similar to those of parturition. Keuls 1985, 51–52 asserts that the phallic Greek society developed a mythology where men appropriated childbirth, and duBois 1988, 174–179 specifies that Plato worked this appropriation for an "eventual 'metonymising' of the female body" and regards it as allusion to philosophies of reincarnation in his metaphoric creation of an androgynous philosopher. Georgiadou and Larmour 1998, 125, for similarity between the Moonites and Zeus who gives birth "from all over his body".

any hole by altering the men's bottom anatomy, and later avoids the uterus and the pubis all together with the creation of a gestational chamber in the calf. Lucian successfully downplays this feminine experience and translates it in male terms: he takes this body part away from its usual place on a woman and "transplants it onto a male" in a place with no sexual connotation (1.23). Thus, Lucian chooses the man's calf for pregnancy over the mythical thigh. This body part resembles the belly/stomach (as the name indicates, *gastēr, gastroknēmia*), a hollowed organ without gender appropriation, which both the male and the female share. In addition, as "a belly of the leg", it is different from both *nēdys* (the feminine spasmodic and unstable uterus), and *gastēr* (belly as stomach). The leg becomes a multifunctional organ charged with multiple tasks, and swells under the pressure of pregnancy. Male and female are united under this idea of growth.

The calf has no natural orifices and surgical procedure takes the place of natural birth (1.22: ἐπειδὰν γὰρ συλλάβῃ τὸ ἔμβρυον, παχύνεται ἡ κνήμη, καὶ χρόνῳ ὕστερον ἀνατεμόντες ἐξ ἄγουσι νεκρά, θέντες δ᾽ αὐτὰ πρὸς τὸν ἄνεμον κεχηνότα ζῳοποιοῦσιν, "after the embryo was conceived, the calf swells and after a while, by cutting it open, they drive out the dead babies, and revitalise them by holding them against the wind with their mouths opened"). The Moonites use caesarean and thus sanitise this delivery by removing all undignified pangs, discharge and afterbirth. The spasmodic and often uncertain event of birth is replaced here with a process controlled by the precise knife of a careful physician. Submitting oneself to a knife is a more "manly" way to bleed (with most of the leg surgeries known to that date being for drainage of wounds, relief of swelling and amputations related to intense outdoor life, dangerous travel, and numerous wars). By using the doctor and his scalpel, the individual in question avoids the feminine bleeding events under the compulsion of her pregnant womb and translates it in acceptable male terms.[49] I will explain further in the next subchapter.

7 The male inadequacy for birth

In contrast, women were not expected to bleed under the knife to give birth. Aristotle, for example, uses *thyrazein* to describe the birth process from the perspective of the female body, an opening of a door which happens when the veins feeding

---

49 DuBois 1988, 184 and Arthur-Katz 1989, 169–170 discuss the ancient perception on feminine bleeding from the point of view of male doctors.

the embryo no longer receive nourishment for its support. Then a "gateway" (*exo-dos*) opens up for birth (*Gen. Anim.* VIII 777a20). According to scholars on ancient midwifery, there is a general agreement that caesarean was not the way for Greeks or Romans to deliver a baby from a live mother. Women did not encounter the scalpel of a male doctor as means of delivery, but rather the gentle hands of another female, in charge of soothing the pregnant womb, using her finger very gently to probe for the child, and gently massage the birth canal with goose grease and perhaps softly enlarge it for a smooth delivery.[50] The caesarian procedure might save male self-image, but it also points out that his idealised anatomy has faults. While females are self-sufficient in expelling the foetus through the birth canal, the Moonmen need the assistance of technology to open their bodies for delivery. Also, once more, the verb *anatemnein* inadvertently raises fear of outside probing, of invasive intervention upon a man's intact body, by cutting and mutilating. The midwife who only assists nature is here replaced by the doctor who must take charge of the whole process at the expense of his patient, who only suffers through the process. Moreover, according to Hippocratic texts, pregnancy is a beneficial bodily event for the female, occurring in a specialised organ that "craves" it and has no other function (Hipp. *Nat. Mul.* 5).[51] Here, pregnancy and swelling occur in an organ already busy with a different role, a role that might be hindered in the process. Carrying a baby in the calf does not seem comfortable when walking. In this sense, the foetus looks more like a parasitic tumour which disables the parent than a beneficial addition for the body.

This miniature gestational chamber appears even more dysfunctional when the foetus is born dead through caesarean and needs reanimation through the intervention of winds (22, 8–10).[52] Thus, Lucian exposes the defective surrogacy of such a womb, which lacks the environment for live birth. The reason why it fails is intriguing. In Lucian, the true life-sustaining ability comes from the air. The idea goes back to philosophical texts where air appears as the greatest inseminator of the universe (Diogenes, in Aetius 5.15.4; Leitao 2012, 30–31 emphasises this particular strength of males in Diogenes). I will go further in recalling medical texts where the relationship between air and masculinity is prominent and will read the episode as a critique of the Moonite inability to inseminate as

---

50 Depierri, 1968, 521–524. Todman, 2007, 83. Soranus *Gyn.* I, 4 for midwifery and the process of delivering a baby. The topic of ancient caesarian is so interesting to modern readers, that there is a Wikipedia chapter on it.
51 See Arthur-Katz 1989, 173–174 for the Hippocratic view that the uterus "craves" pregnancy and birth for its own health.
52 Georgiadou and Larmour 1998, 126 regard it as allusion to philosophies of reincarnation.

males. Heat and air were believed to cause erection in men and contribute that *pneuma* to the embryo, giving it the principle of the soul (Aristotle *GA* 1.18.726a 26–27, *De an.* 405a21–25).[53] According to Aristotle, women cannot bring *pneuma*, but only nourish the foetus by converting the menstrual blood supply into food for the embryo (*G.A.* 1.18.726a 26–27).[54] Here, this airy component is absent from the physiology of the Moonites: the pregnant male body is deprived of his essential life-giving element, which is substituted by the outside wind, as a post-partum aid. As a result, while emulating the female, the parturient Selenites cast out their masculine essence: striving to become a self-sufficient androgyne, they lose their life-giving masculine gift of providing *pneuma*. While one was hoping for an enhancement of male reproductive powers and the obsoletion of womanhood, the Lucian's hermaphrodite ends up in the paradox of being a *semivir*. Once again, more is less for the idealised male body which loses its inseminating abilities once absorbing perceived feminine traits.

8 Casting out the female: Dendritai and artificial insemination

Since piling both genders on one individual somewhat backfired when the foetus did not receive the gift of life from his parent, the next scenario involves the opposite process: castration of the male. If the previous model was a hermaphrodite, this one will be a eunuch. The male does not hope anymore to cumulate the roles of both sexual partners but willingly casts aside his masculinity in his effort to procreate. Lucian now offers a "clean" alternative to both the traditional insemination and gestation. In this reproductive variation, there is no longer a sentient sexual partner: the "womb" used for insemination is completely outside of one's body and fully vegetative. The act is so far from sexual reproduction that it can be considered a form of artificial insemination, an asexual reproduction, or even a mere *technē* without the pleasure and intimacy of intercourse. For this process, the male resorts once more to agriculture, the way he did in the episode of the Vine-women. Only this time, the author takes precautions to control and cast out the problematic passive partner/womb and to use a technic more refined than opportunistic fruit-gathering which proved so problematic in the previous episode. This time, his characters use pruning, sowing, systematic harvesting and shelling.

---

53 See Leitao 2012, 30–31
54 For this point in Aristotle, see Bonnard 2013, 202.

A male from the species of the Dendritai literally cuts off his right testicle and places it in the ground, from which a tree of flesh springs out, resembling a *phallus*. This pillar bears fruits from which the Moonites shell out people (22.13–17: ὄρχιν ἀνθρώπου τὸν δεξιὸν ἀποτεμόντες ἐν γῇφυτεύουσιν, ἐκδὲ αὐτοῦ δένδρον ἀναφύεται μέγιστον, σάρκινον, οἷον φαλλός· ἔχει δὲ καὶ κλάδους καὶ φύλλα· ὁ δὲ καρπός ἐστι βάλανοι πηχυαῖοι τὸ μέγεθος. ἐπειδὰν οὖν πεπανθῶσιν, τρυγήσαντες αὐτὰς ἐκκολάπτουσι τοὺς ἀνθρώπους, "they plant in the earth the excised right testicle of a man, from which a big tree of flesh grows, resembling a *phallus*. It has branches and leaves: its fruit are acorns, a cubit in size. Once they are ripe, they shells out men after picking them up"). Larmour and Georgiadou noticed that this tree bears similarity to the trunk of the Vine-women.[55] In my view, it is a battle of dominance between bodies and species: if in the Vine-women episode, the female plant progressively conquered the human form, here the male flesh has its "revenge" on the vegetal "other" through the reconstruction of a giant *phallus* which compensates for the one lost by men to the plant world in the Vine-women episode.

As I stated above, when burying his severed seed and disguising his penis as vegetation, the Moonman is no longer involved in an act of sexual insemination, but rather becomes an agriculturist.[56] Normally, agriculture itself has sexual connotations, placing the man in the position of the fertiliser or the cultivator of crops/offspring and the female in the position of fertile yet untamed nature, "domesticated" by the cultural touch of technology.[57] Here men are born through something that both contains and denies sexuality.[58] Asexual insemination finally meets advanced farming, as an adequate response to the dangers of sex and fruit-gathering in the episode of the Vine-women (1.8).

It is not the first time Lucian uses this playful vegetal imagery to scramble together both the male and the female anatomy. Nevertheless, this time the feminine principle is buried under the ground. The Dendrites who removes his testicle and places it in the soil is a eunuch, perhaps also an androgyne. Contrary to what we might expect in modern days, the eunuch and the hermaphrodite were often confused with each other and with females, due to their common lack of a

---

55 Georgiadou and Larmour 1997, 75–76, 125 notice similarities between the two episodes, between these trees and the vine trunks of Vine-women.

56 See both duBois 1988, 65; Leitao 2012, 53–54 for theories on agricultural insemination vs. sex.

57 Keuls 1985, 122–123; Taiz 2014, 201–202. DuBois 1988, 46–47 even argues that the woman's body and the vessel of earth are interchangeable.

58 Again, for agriculture and sexuality in metaphors, see Leitao 2012, 199; Taiz 2016, 202.

virile functional member.[59] Thus, a eunuch could be regarded as female (see Nero's use of Sporus in Cassius Dio, *Hist*. LXII, 28 – LXIII, 12–13) and even allowed in female company with impunity. In *De Dea Syria* (traditionally attributed to Lucian), the author goes as far as calling eunuchs *gynaikias*, thus underlining the Greek bias that a male who does not have the physiology (power to penetrate) or the anatomy of a man (penis, testicles) is only a female. Even Hippocrates joins the discussion in describing Phrygian eunuchs as *emarees* and describing their voice tones as womanly (*Aer*. 22). Lucian also uses feminine adjectives to describe them (*Asin*. 36).[60] Nevertheless, unlike the sailors in 1.8 who unwillingly lost their penises during an erotic encounter that was gone wrong, his castration is a conscious act, undergone for the sake of reproduction: it is clinical orchidectomy rather than the result of sexual predation. The "male" womb which earlier roused fears of penetrability, lies now completely outside the male body, inside a more acceptable receptacle, the all-feminine "earth" (because a "birth from the earth is essentially a birth 'from woman alone'").[61] Thus, the problematic womb is finally concealed inside the soil. The surface displays only the reassuring shape of the penis, because, instead of generating a foetus, this chthonian uterus grows a whole *phallus* adorned with floral appendages. It is only appropriate for his testicle to germinate, since *balanos* ("testicle") stands also for "acorn".

---

59 Llewellyn-Jones 2002, 29–42 for eunuchs and harems. Bardel 2002, 53 for eunuchs as female in Aristotle. Lightfoot 2002, 73–74, on Lucian's *De Dea Syria* and his mention of eunuchs as "female". Hales, 2002, 97, regarding the hermaphrodite Attis as female, in sculptural representations in Cybele's inner sanctum: "far from depicting mere castration, the artist has removed any sight of male genitals. In their place he has substituted a smooth pubis, its female characteristics complemented by the curves of the torso. A second Attis from the same sanctuary clearly depicts the hermaphroditic nature of the gods, bereft of male genitalia".

60 See the previous note for Lightfoot's quotation of these texts. Also, in my opinion, the eunuch could be construed as female, the way Lightfoot 2002, 74–76; Halles 2002, 87–103; Bullough 2002, 3, assert in their writing on ancient eunuchs. Georgiadou and Larmour 1997, 125 simply call the Dendrite a eunuch.

61 Quotation from Leitao 2012, 168, on Euripides' autochthony, as birth from "mother".

9 The phallic dream with a secret chamber

I will go a little further with Lucian's clever pun over Moonite "nuts".[62] The "earth" surface appears in the ambiguous position of both sexual partner and agent of emasculation. This statement needs further clarification. Since *balanos* stands both for "testicle" and "penis" the Dendrite performs a sexual act, albeit a symbolic one: in the very act of burying his manhood (*balanos*=removed testicle), the Dendrite inserts a tiny penis in the bosom of the earth. Since his *balanos* becomes a miniature gestational chamber buried in the "womb"-like earth, this eunuch conceives both within himself and "into another".[63] All the more impressive, the Dendrite impregnates the bosom of earth, without even using a penis and, as a paradox, is later rewarded with the ultimate phallic dream when the flesh tree springs out.

Before we celebrate this dream of male power, we need to be reminded though that the tree as a symbol of growth is usually connected with feminine deities of fertility (such as Gaia):[64] here, the erect column questions both the feminine symbolism of the Earth-bound tree and its virility, since it is not attached to a man's body, but grows from the earth like an inert plant (both virgin and impotent). It is an erect, yet immobile organ of reproduction, born pregnant and asexual. Just like certain specimens of the vegetal realm, the flesh-tree itself is sexually ambivalent and as a fruit, it is a passive receptacle of life.

The *phallus*-tree full of homunculi recapitulates the destiny of the foetus (for it is planted in the ground), the procreating male (the testicle contains a seed) and the pregnant female (nursing embryos sheathed in protective chambers). If certain medical theorists, including Aristotle, professed the father as the sole seed-producer and the female as the strict nurse of that seed, the Moonites' reproductive system confounds and coalesces both roles: instead of siring children, the man cuts off his seed and instead of gestating a child, the receptacle of the semen grows a penis. Virility is thus not lost but transferred to an unlikely agent. The image stands also for an unexpected feminine triumph, if one remembers

---

62 Georgiadou and Larmour 1997, 128 noted the metaphorical meaning of *balanos* in Lucian's episode (testicle, acorn, penis). For such acorn puns and metaphors for sexual organs, see also Henderson 1991, 41; Totelin 2007, 535.

63 Leitao 2012, 197 finds this idea appropriate only for the highest form of philosophical "intercourse" and discusses it in Plato.

64 Viarre 1964, 136 for the associations between trees and sexual growth, Simoons 2006, 71 for the associations of trees with Gaia and mother deities. Larmour 1997, 139 for "Earth" mockingly being here the Moon.

that Galen imagined an inverted penis lying at the bottom of any female reproductive system, a latent member unable to protrude, due to feminine inherent weakness (*De sem.* 2.1).[65] Thus, pushing out a giant *phallus* from the depths of the womb is the ultimate triumph of female nature finally overcoming its perceived deficiency.

While the severed testicle transmits to the earth the power to grow a penis, the earth performs a similar exchange and offers that penis the power to produce little wombs. The masculine symbol is both reconfirmed and challenged since this member is only as a vegetative gestational chamber. Miniature acorns recapitulate in their shape, both the male seed and the uterine nursery. They are at the same time, the original and the copy, the father (*balanos*, "testicle") and the offspring (*balanos*, "acorn" or "seed") with the feminine principle living on through a "metonymy".[66] While the Dendritai apparently display the triumph of the *phallus* through their anatomy, in physiology they operate as partial or defective females.

The problem of birth-giving and gender assignment is here solved through vegetal hybridisation, which turns the *phallus* into a mere support for multiple pregnant wombs. The male and the female are patched into this being whose acorn stands both for testicle (through metaphor, *balanos*, *Schol.* 9, 13) and uterus (through physiology). Moonites give birth twice, both "uterine" and "ejaculatory".[67] Technology also intervenes twice, in separating a man from his genitals and in shelling out new men from tree acorns. Thus, the somewhat undignified aspect of birth pangs and after-birth is transferred to this prosthetic gestational chamber that acts as an independent and non-sentient organism. Moreover, the father actively aids his new-born child to break the shells of his gestational cell, unlike the mother for whom natural birth was a painful event, comparable to a war between her body and the emerging foetus.[68] According to Hong in Hippocratic texts (*Nat. Ch.* 30.5–8), the female body was supposed to be the antagonist of the foetus in the process of birth, while in the world of birds, the chick and his mother were allies in the process of breaking the egg shell.[69] Nevertheless, the only way for the Moonmen to get any success in ensuring their progeny is by casting aside the phallic and exploring their nurturing side.

---

65 See also Bonnard 2006, 32.
66 Like the one duBois 1988, 174, 185 sees in Plato's philosophical male pregnancy.
67 Since "men 'give birth' to homunculi in the form of ejaculated semen" in Leitao 2012, 190 (quoting Arist. *GA* 1.20).
68 Vivante 2007, 79.
69 Hong 2012, 81–89.

10 Deconstructing nursing – the Moonites' "pocket" and the full-body breast

To make this father-son cooperation even more evident, Lucian discusses the existence of yet another male organ, a *gastēr* lacking entrails and juices. I took the liberty of investigating its womb-like properties, despite the fact that it has usually been associated in scholarship with fashion and purses. The entrance to this "vault" is not a *vagina* (although it is an entrance to a womb), nor a toothed mouth (even if it leads into a "stomach"). The chamber itself is a shaggy *marsupium* that allows the child to crawl inside for warmth (1.24: τῇ μέντοι γαστρὶ ὅσα πήραχρῶνται τιθέντες ἐν αὐτῇ ὅσων δέονται· ἀνοικτὴ γὰρ αὐτοῖς αὕτη καὶ πάλιν κλειστή ἐστιν· ἐντέρων δὲ οὐδὲν ὑπάρχειν αὐτῇ φαίνεται, ἢ τοῦ τομόνον, ὅτι δασεῖα πᾶσα ἔντοσθε καὶ λάσι ός ἐστιν, ὥστε καὶ τὰ νεογνά, ἐπειδὰν ῥιγώσῃ, ἐς ταύτην ὑποδύεται, "they have bellies like pockets holding in whatever they need; there does not seem to be anything in them, except the fact that they are all shaggy and hairy inside so that new-born crawl inside of them when they are cold"). While birth is problematic for them, the Moonites apparently excel in postpartum nursing abilities. This harmless *gastēr* represents a perfect middle ground between a stomach that selfishly feeds itself and a maternal womb that nourishes a baby at its own expense. While incapable of supporting the early stages of fetal life, this secondary womb plays the role of a tender nurse.

Ní Mheallaigh believes that Lucian's description of the Moonites' insides shows some indiscreet probing of their otherwise no-orifice bodies.[70] In my view, the beauty of this womb is that it has volition: nothing breaks it open, but its own will. While the uterus has no choice but to receive an embryo and to expel it through parturition, this ideal body fold negotiates its nurturing function and limits it to provision of warmth. It is due to higher bounds that the parent physically opens himself up to receive the baby. Through its functionality, the marsupial pocket recapitulates both the extra- and the intra-uterine life.[71] To confirm

---

70 ní Mheallaigh 2014, 219.
71 See Leitao on *Philolaos* 2013, 29: "the womb — is rather warm and similar to it [seed]."), while the male provides heat in his seed, for embryonic "cooking" and growth (Arist. *GA* 1.20.729a 11–13; 2.3.737a 15, 2.4.739b 21–26). Thus, Leitao 2012, 24–29, quoting Anaxagoras and Philolaos of Croton specifies regarding the philosophical views on human reproduction: "according to Aristotle's student Menon, whose history of medicine is reported in the famous papyrus known as the *Anonymus Londinensis*, Philolaus claimed that warmth is the primary constituent of the human body because 'seed (σπέρμα) is warm, and this is what creates the living being

this hypothesis, the pocket is both dry and fully furred. Nevertheless, its role, while comforting a baby, falls somewhat in a secondary position to that of a breast or uterus in providing true development or liquid nurture. Moreover, since it resembles a "pocket" or a "purse", it remains somewhat artificial or even alien to the "true" body of the parent. Once more, as in a ring composition, man-made prosthetics come into play to supplant the deficiencies of an imaginary body part.

As an extreme version of wet-nursing abilities, the Moonites' whole bodies secrete milk instead of sweat and their noses drip with honey (1.24: ἀπομύττονται δὲ μέλι δριμύτατον· κἀπειδὰν ἢ πονῶσιν ἢ γυμνάζωνται, γάλακτι πᾶντὸ σῶμα ἱδροῦσιν, ὥστε καὶ τυροὺς ἀπ’ αὐτοῦ πήγνυνται, "they drip the most fragrant honey and after they work out or exercise, they sweat milk all over the body so that cheese can be made from it"). Thus, although deprived of any feminine organs, the Selenites' entire bodies end up as giant mammary glands in the process of lactation. The image of edible mucus and drinkable sweat is probably both hilarious and nauseating. It is also profoundly useless, particularly since the Selenites feed only on smoke and air squeezed in a cup (*kalyx*), like dew. The *kalyx* also stands for yet another sexual imagery where flower chalices (*kalykes*) and Earth receive moisture (dew) from the potent sky.[72] As a result, since they drink dew provided by the sky, the Moonites ultimately appear as infants, or again as female floral receptacles. This alimentary reality renders their lactating abilities useless and places them in the position of a suckling rather than that of a nourisher. Thus, as plants, they fall once more into the feminine side of the gender spectrum.

11 Conclusions

In this chapter, I analysed a piece of *Verae Historiae* with the help of scholarship on ancient science and sexuality unrelated to Lucian. I used Daniel Leitao's application of Aristotle's medical theories to myth as well as Calame's, Winkler's, duBois', and Taiz' research on sexual metaphors or ancient botany, to further the current scholarship on *VH*.

Early in Greek mythology, according to duBois, the female has the upper hand in the sexual act, "while the male suffers only loss", namely "loss of semen

---

(κατασκευαστικὸν τοῦ ζῴου), and the place (τόπος) into which seed is deposited — this is the womb — is rather warm and similar to it [seed]'".

72 Aesch. *Agam.* 1604–1605; also Leitao 2012, 43 for this sexual metaphor in Aeschylus.

and force, which is thus sacrificed to the earth in order to ensure its continued prosperity".[73] As a result, Lucian apparently constructed a few male-to-male alternatives to eliminate the female. Thus, the male has a chance to undermine feminine fertility through reproduction without a female partner. If mythological Zeus could only be a surrogate womb for his children, but not a parthenogenetic parent (because of the sexual intercourse with Metis and Semele), Lucian found two possibilities to avoid the union between male and female in his story. New organs were developed, but as shown above, they ended in complicating the reproductive process and further disabling the male who suffers "wounding" (caesarean or even orchidectomy) to his impeccable anatomy void of problematic orifices. Moreover, this fictitious male anatomy "caves in" and its phallic extensions teem with uterine life.

If Larmour asserted that Lucian presents the fears of the Greeks regarding the feminine "other", and points out the ridiculousness of their strict gender dichotomies, I believe that it is precisely due to this harsh ancient dichotomy (persistent from Hippocrates and Aristotle time, all the way to Galen) that Lucian manages to reveal the female principle dormant in his androgynes (more-than-men) and eunuchs (less-than-men). Without feminine organs and orifices, the life-giving process becomes difficult: they need caesarean birth to cover for their lack of orifices, and revitalisation of the born-dead foetus through winds. Ultimately, the Selenites need to alter their male anatomy to make their features functional, thus losing what made them male (the ability to inseminate via penis, the ability to offer *pneuma*, the ability to keep their testicles during insemination). In the process of embracing both roles without the presence of females, they become either hermaphrodites (both genders in one) or castrated (genderless). The result is an individual who is either physiologically a female or anatomically (since the feminine spectrum could cover, according to the times, any individuals without functional or visible male appendages). At an aesthetic level, Larmour playfully associated Lucian's men with truthfulness and females with "mendacious narrative".[74] Nevertheless, in a biological sense, the idea of male self-sufficiency proves to be equally mendacious. The female ultimately resurfaces in the reproductive efforts of the Moonites since their fragile phallic anatomy sits over concealed wombs and gestational chambers.

---

73 DuBois 1988, 54.
74 Larmour 1997, 142, particularly referring to Vine-women, the reason for Lucian's depiction of Moonites as solely male.

The attempt of the Greek utopist to eliminate the female by circumventing her physiology is a process that ultimately ends in castrating the male who refuses to acknowledge the "other", whether as an inside principle or as a separate partner. The male body cannot successfully cast the female out without reproductive malfunction, just as the woman cannot completely engulf the man without castrating him and hurting herself. As Loraux argues, "the feminine element is part of the ambivalences of virile strength [...] [and] serves in many ways to amplify that strength". Similarly to the myths about Zeus and Metis, the "absorbed" female inside the Selenites keeps protruding through the surface.[75] In this case, Lucian's skill consists precisely in playing a game which includes the male, the female, as well as the castrated and the androgyny as female alternatives. While originally dismissing the female, he later shows that the avoidance of female anatomy and the transference of its physiology to the male (conception, gestation, parturition, and nursing) can only alter the male. At best, this process modifies his anatomy to such an extent that the male is no longer recognisable.

Bibliography

Anderson, G. (1976), *Studies in Lucian's Comic Fiction*, Leiden.

Arthur-Katz, M. (1989), 'Sexuality and the Body in Ancient Greece', in: *Mètis. Anthropologie des mondes grecs anciens* 4, 155–179.

Bardel, R. (2002), 'Eunuchizing Agamemnon: Agamemnon, Clytemnestra and the *Maschalismos*', in: S. Tougher (ed.), *Eunuchs in Antiquity and Beyond*, London, 51–70.

Bergren, A. (2008), *Weaving Truth: Essays on Language and the Female in Greek Thought*, Washington, DC.

Bonnard, J.-B. (2013), 'Male and Female Bodies According to Ancient Greek Physicians', transl. L.E. Doherty/V.S. Cuchet, in: *Clio* 37, 21–39.

Bonfante, L. (1997), 'Nursing Mothers in Classical Art', in: A.O. Koloski-Ostrow/C.L. Lyons (eds.), *Naked Truths: Women, Sexuality, and Gender in Classical Art and Archaeology*, London/New York, 174–196.

Bundrick, S. (2012), 'Housewives, Hetairai, and the Ambiguity of Genre in Attic Vase Painting', in: *Phoenix* 66, 11–35.

Bullough, V.L. (2002), 'Eunuchs and History and Society', in: S. Tougher (ed.), *Eunuchs in Antiquity and Beyond*, Duckworth/London, 1–18.

Calame, C. (1992), *The Poetics of Eros in Ancient Greece*, transl. Janet Lloyd, Princeton.

Depierri, K.P. (1968), 'One Way of Unearthing the Past', in: *American Journal of Nursing* 68, 521–524.

---

75 Loraux 1989, 55.

Detienne, M. (1994), *The Garden of Adonis: Spices in Greek Mythology*, transl. J. Lloyd, Princeton.

Dover, K.J. (1989), *Greek Homosexuality*, 2nd ed., Cambridge, MA.

Dover, J.J. (2002), 'Classical Greek Attitudes to Sexual Behavior', in: L.K. McClure (ed.), *Sexuality Gender in the Classical World, Readings and Sources*, Oxford, 19–33.

duBois, P. (1988), *Sowing the Body, Psychoanalysis and Ancient Representations of Women*, Chicago/London.

Friedrich, K./Mayhoff, T. (1906), Pliny the Elder, *Naturalis Historia*, Lipsiae. (http://penelope.uchicago.edu/Thayer/L/Roman/Texts/Pliny_the_Elder/14*.html)

Georgiadou, A. (1998), 'Lucians' *Verae Historiae* as Philosophical Parody', in: *Hermes* 126, 310–325.

Georgiadou, A./Larmour, D. (1997), 'Lucian's Vine-Women (*VH 1,6-9*) and Dio's Libyan Women (*Orat. 5*): Variations on a Theme', in: *Mnemosyne* 50, 205–209.

Georgiadou, A./Larmour, D. (1998), *Lucians' Science Fiction Novel: Verae Historiae. Interpretation and Commentary*, Leiden.

Gleason, M. (1995), *Making Men: Sophists and Self-Presentation in Ancient Rome,* Princeton/New Jersey.

Halles, S. (2002), 'Looking for Eunuchs: The *Galli* and Attis in Roman Art', in: S. Tougher (ed.), *Eunuchs in Antiquity and Beyond*, London, 71–86.

Harmon, A.M. (1979), Lucian, *Verae Historiae*, Vol. 1, Cambridge, MA/London.

Henderson, J. (1991), *The Maculate Muse: Obscene Language in Attic Comedy*, 2nd ed., Oxford/New York.

Hong, Y. (2012), 'Collaboration and Conflict: Discourses of Maternity in Hippocratic Gynecology and Embryology', in: L.H. Petersen/P. Salzman-Mitchell (eds.), *Mothering and Motherhood in Ancient Greece and Rome*, Austin, 71–96.

John Bostock, M.D./Riley, F.R.S.H.T. (1855), *Pliny the Elder, The Natural History*, London.

Kelleher, B. (2011), 'Acceptance through Restriction: Male Homosexuality in Ancient Athens', in: *Historical Perspective: Santa Clara University Undergraduate Journal of History* 16, 1–24.

Keuls, E. (1985), *The Reign of Phallus*, New York/Harper.

Larmour, D. (1997), 'Sex with Moonmen and Vinewomen: The Reader as Explorer in Lucian's *Vera Historia*', in: *Intertexts* 1.2, 131–146.

Laskaris, J. (2008), 'Nursing Mothers in Greek and Roman Medicine', in: *American Journal of Archaeology* 112, 459–464.

Leitao, D.D. (2012), *Pregnant Male as Myth and Metaphor in Classical Greek Literature*, Cambridge.

Lightfoot, J.J. (2002), 'Sacred Eunuchism in the Cult of the Syrian Goddess', in: S. Tougher (ed.), *Eunuchs in Antiquity and Beyond*, London, 71–86.

Loraux, N. (1990), 'Herakles: The Super-Male and the Feminine', in: D.M. Halperin/J. Winkler/F.I. Zeitlin (eds.), *Before Sexuality: The Construction of Erotic Experience in the Ancient Greek World*, Princeton, 21–52.

Llewellyn-Jones, L. (2002), 'Eunuchs and the Royal Harem in Achaemenid Persia', in: S. Tougher (ed.), *Eunuchs in Antiquity and Beyond*, London, 19–50.

McMahon, J.M. (1998), *Paralysin Cave, Impotence, Perception and Text in the Satyrica of Petronius*, Leiden/New York/Koln.

Murray, A.T. (tr.) (1919), *Homer, The Odyssey*, Cambridge, MA.

ní Mheallaigh, K. (2014), *Reading Fiction with Lucian: Fakes, Freaks and Hyperreality,* Cambridge.

Pfunter, L. (2020), 'Between Science and Superstition: Photius, Diodorus Siculus, and Hermaphrodites', in: *Dumbarton Oaks Papers* 74, 269–284.

Rabe, H. (1971), *Scholia in Lucianum*, Lipsiae.

Reyhl, K. (1969), *Antonios Diogenes, Untersuchungenzu den Roman-Fragmenten der 'Wunderjenseits von Thule' und zu den ,Wahren Geschichten' des Lukian*, Ph.D. Thesis, Tübingen.

Salzman-Mitchell, P. (2012), 'Breast-feeding Mothers in Greek and Roman Literature', in: L. Hackworth Petersen/P. Salzman-Mitchell (eds.), *Mothering and Motherhood in Ancient Greece and Rome*, Austin, 141–165.

Simoons, F.J. (2006), *Plants of Life, Plants of Death*, Wisconsin.

Stengel, A. (ed.) (1911), *De Luciani Veris Historiis*, Berlin. https://www.sacred-texts.com/cla/luc/true/tru01.htm (Accessed on 08/02/2021)

Taiz, L. (2017), *Flora Unveiled: The Discovery and Denial of Sex in Plants*, Oxford.

Totelin, L.M.V. (2007), 'Sex and Vegetables in Hippocratic Gynaecological Treaties', in: *Studies in History and Philosophy of Biology and Biomedical Science* 38, 531–540.

Todman, D. (2007), 'Childbirth in Ancient Rome: From Traditional Folklore to Obstetrics', in: *Australian & New Zealand Journal of Obstetrics and Gynecology* 83. Online:https://obgyn.onlinelibrary.wiley.com/doi/abs/10.1111/j.1479-828X.2007.00691.x (Last access: June 2021).

Viarre, S. (1964), *L'image et la pensée dans les Métamorphoses d'Ovide*, Paris.

Vivante, B. (2007), *Daughters of Gaia, Women in the Ancient Mediterranean World*, London.

Winkler, J.J. (1981), 'Gardens of Nymphs: Public and Private in Sappho's Lyrics', in: H.B. Foley (ed.), *Reflections on Women in Antiquity*, New York/London/Paris, 63–89.

Winkler, J.J. (1990), 'Laying Down the Law: The Oversight of Men's Sexual Behavior in Classical Athens', in: D.M. Halperin/J.J. Winkler/F. Zeitlin (eds.), *Before Sexuality: The Construction of Erotic Experience in the Ancient Greek*, Princeton, 171–209.

Part V: **Sex and Disgust**

Gabriel Evangelou
Sex and Disgust in Martial's *Epigrams*

Abstract: This chapter explores Martial's elicitation of disgust as a device used seemingly to lambast those portrayed as sexual deviants and the sexually undesirable characters of his epigrams. Evangelou argues that the epigrammatist is not interested so much in correcting the behaviour of his fellow-citizens by criticising their sexual acts and desires, but rather in exploiting stock characters who become easy targets of his invective. The ridicule of these characters provokes the audience's laughter by inviting it to experience a sense of physical and moral superiority to them and thus to laugh at their shortcomings. The discussion focuses primarily on Maximina, Philaenis and Postumus, three morally reprehensible characters who are depicted as laughable chiefly because of the incongruity between what they believe about themselves and how they are actually perceived by society in the 1st century BC Rome.

Martial's epigrams offer a unique insight into the life of the average Roman of the second half of the first century AD. Thanks to his vivid descriptions of everyday activities, the modern reader of the twelve books of epigrams gets a sense of the smells, the sounds and many of the sights of Rome.[1] Despite his tendency to exaggerate for comic effect,[2] his epigrams offer valuable information not only about the difficulties that *clientes* (clients) faced on a daily basis, in order to please their *patroni* (patrons),[3] but also about the genuine bonds of friendship that Martial and his fellow Roman citizens developed with one another.[4] Nevertheless, the epigrammatist is best-known for the obscenity in his satiric epigrams and for his derogatory remarks about different types of people.[5] Almost no one can escape

---

1 Roman 2010, 88.

2 Ascher 1977, 443 makes a similar observation by stressing the difficulty of acquiring biographical information about Martial from his epigrams, because, ultimately, the epigrammatist's goal is to entertain, not to provide accurate information about himself. On exaggerated language in Martial, see also Galán Vioque 2002, esp. 95, 163, 365, 472, 497, 508; Williams 2006, 26, 97, 130; Janka 2007, 289–290; Watson 2019, 46.

3 For example, Mart. 12.18.1–6.

4 See, for example, 6.85, in which Martial honours his deceased dear friend, Rufus Camonius.

5 Mulligan 2019, 117–121 explores obscenity in Martial and argues convincingly that it was not simply used by the poet to attract more attention or to boost the sales of his book collections, but rather an effective way to distinguish Roman epigram and himself from Catullus and Ovid, as

https://doi.org/10.1515/9783110695793-016

his criticism;[6] he mocks primarily anyone whose behaviour is incongruous with perceived common decency,[7] i.e. the drunkard, the adulterer, the boastful, the parsimonious, the nouveau riche, but also people with physical peculiarities,[8] since such groups of people were commonly ridiculed in Martial's time.[9] His indignation intensifies in his descriptions of sexual relations between Romans.[10] The numerous references to genitals,[11] anal intercourse,[12] oral sex[13] and old age are central to the amusement of his readers through the elicitation of disgust and

---

well as from Greek epigrammatists. Watson 2005, 78 provides a different interpretation of obscenity in Martial's Book 3 and 11 by attributing its ubiquity to the epigrammatist's intention to attract new readers, i.e. married women who would be interested in reading matters of sexual nature that they could not practice. Hallet 1996, 323 also underscores the significance of obscenity in Martial and likens removing it to "castrating" Martial's poetry. Martial's constant need to defend the use of obscenity in his poems indicates that he was acutely aware that a large part of his readership would — at least initially — object to the use of such language because it was not as prevalent in epigram or other literary genres. Holzberg 1986, 203–204 notes that only 192 (16 per cent) of Martial's epigrams explore the topic of sex, while Sullivan 1991, 185 argues that a mere 10 per cent of Martial's epigrams would be considered obscene by modern standards. However, Spisak 2007, 25 stresses that although obscenity and references to matters of sexual nature can also be found in other authors, they are considerably more prevalent in Martial's epigrams. Notice, however, the complete absence of obscenity from Book 5 and 8 as a sign of respect to the emperor, Domitian.

6 As Watson and Watson 2003, 100 point out, it was dangerous for anyone to attack prominent Roman men and women (Suet. *Dom.* 8.3, *Aug.* 55, Ulp. *Dig.* 47.10.5.9–10). Martial himself suggests that he was facing such danger in 10.5.1–2. Lorenz 2019, 530–531 provides additional examples of epigrams that explore Martial's fear of other authors using his name and writing slanders against the upper class.

7 It is worth noting, as Verstraete 1980, 228 does, that the views expressed in Martial's epigrams widely reflect the sexual social norms of his time. O'Connor 2019, 548 raises a similar point about the *Carmina Priapea*.

8 1.10, 1.83, 3.8, 3.87, 3.89, 3.93, 8.59, 13.2. As Watson 2004, 318 observes, people with physical deformities were a common target of the sceptic tradition. Davis 1973, 89 also remarks on the "fear and disgust" that Martial elicits through his references to physical defects. Papaioannou and Serafim 2021, 8 note that unsightly external appearance was commonly used in invective, as it was associated with "deceit and wickedness".

9 Watson 1982, 71 states that Martial's mockery of men and women with physical flaws was in line both with epigrammatic tradition and with the tendency of his contemporaries to belittle such groups of people. Richlin 2014, 68 perceives his invective against certain groups, such as people whose sexual life deviated from the norms of their time, slaves, or even women in general, as an attempt to oppress them.

10 Janka 2007, 280 underscores the dominance of sexuality in Martial's epigrams.

11 E.g. 1.90, 7.18, 7.35, 11.21.

12 E.g. 6.37, 6.50, 7.67, 9.47, 9.69, 11.20.

13 E.g. 1.94, 2.10, 2.21, 2.22, 2.28, 2.47, 2.61, 3.96, 7.67, 6.50, 9.92, 12.35.

repulsion.[14] Customarily, women become one of the main targets of his attacks either directly or through his scornful remarks about men who find certain women desirable.[15] Men are also condemned for engaging in sexual relations with other men and women,[16] but mostly because they perform sexual acts which were deemed demeaning for a freeborn Roman male (i.e. being penetrated anally or performing oral sex).[17] The following discussion explores the integral role that the arousal of repulsion and disgust plays in Martial's attempt at providing entertainment to his audience.[18]

Throughout his epigrams Martial does not shy away from discussing his own sexual attractions and preferences, or from commenting on his fellow Romans' sexual proclivities. Based on his self-portrayal in his epigrams, he appears to

---

14 After all, as Richlin 1981a, 42 rightly points out, "Obscene poetry is meant to be funny and shocking at the same time". Watson and Watson 2015 argue for a similar interpretation of Martial's negative reference to female sexuality, by perceiving his attacks as attempts to provoke the laughter of his audience, rather to criticise the sexual mores of his time. Kaster 1974, 149–184 draws a functional distinction between reflexive *fastidium* (disgust/repulsion) as well as deliberative and ranking *fastidium*. He argues that there is a third group of more ambiguous cases that is a combination of both. According to Lateiner and Spatharas 2017, 18 Martial, along with Juvenal and Petronius, does not simply follow Horace whose grotesque descriptions cause *fastidium* to his audience, but rather tries to surpass him by creating even more repulsive characters. It is worth noting that in Marital's epigrams the noun *fastidium* and the verb *fastidire* can be found in only six epigrams (1.3, 2.61, 13.17 and 3.31, 3.76, 5.44 respectively). The elicitation of disgust or repulsion in Martial is achieved through references to defecation (1.37, 1.83, 1.92, 3.44, 3.89, 9.69), saliva and mucus (3.17, 7.37, 7.95), oily hair (2.29, 6.57), filthy bodies (2.42) missing eyes (3.8, 8.59, 12.23), illness (1.78, 2.26), foul breath (1.87, 3.28, 13.18), foul smells (1.92, 3.24, 3.55, 3.93, 4.4, 4.87, 6.93, 14.141), dirty clothes (1.103, 7.33), food (3.60, 3.77, 6.75, 13.17), frugality (9.100, 9.102), flatulence (4.87, 7.18), vomiting (7.67, 2.89, 9.92), boasting (4.37, 4.61, 8.6, 9.102), garrulity (5.52), uncivilised behaviour at dinner (7.20), as well as insects (14.37, 14.83), which, according to Pliny (*Nat.* 11.4, 29.27–28), inevitably caused *fastidium* to the reader.
15 Watson 2019, 99 also views women as Martial's main target.
16 In 3.76 Martial mocks Bassus for being sexually aroused by old women and feeling no attraction towards *puellae* (girls/young women). Thus, his attack is directed both at Bassus for his perverse sexual preference and at *vetulae* who were rejected as sexually undesirable.
17 Bauman 1994, 100, 105 stresses the serious legal implications of sexual laxity in the first century AD, especially with *lex Julia de adulteriis coercendis* making it a punishable crime. Richlin 1981b, 395 notes that even though both men and women were not acting in accordance to the law, it is primarily women who are attacked for it in Martial's epigrams.
18 Wills 2008, 68, 72 also observes the combination of repulsion and entertainment in Martial's epigrams. Roman 2008, 101 and Farland 2014, 192, 199 detect the disgust that Martial attempts to elicit in his epigrams, but do not explore it any further. Similarly, Davis 1973, 8, 15, 26–27, 51, 61, 89 briefly examines isolated cases of repulsive images created in Martial's epigrams without discussing the topic of disgust in detail.

have found young women as well as male teenagers and boys (*pueri*) attractive.[19] And even though in his epigrams he depicts himself as someone who engages in sexual relations with both males and females,[20] he is also shown to have a preference for the former.[21] In fact, in one of his most quoted epigrams (11.43) — perhaps because of its shock value — after his wife[22] discovers him anally penetrating a boy and proposes that he anally penetrate her instead,[23] he categorically rejects her offer by telling her: "and consider, wife, that you have two cunts" (*teque puta cunnos, uxor, habere duos*).[24] His remark thus suggests a preference for anal penetration of males over anal or vaginal penetration of females. However, the language that he uses and the fact that his answer is found in the last line of the poem betrays an intention to arouse laughter by reversing the audience's expectations.[25] His preference for young males over any female[26] is explicitly stated in

---

19 Richlin 1993, 537, n. 34 notes that the majority of boys that feature in Martial's epigrams have Greek names, thereby suggesting that they were slaves and not Roman citizens. Verstraete 1980, 228 makes a similar argument by noting that Martial could not insinuate that he engaged in sexual relations with a freeborn Roman boy without displeasing the emperor. According to MacMullen 1982, 491, sexual relationships with slaves who assumed the receptive role were criticised the least because slaves were perceived "almost as non-beings".

20 Sullivan 1991, 186 points out that while men like Martial could have intercourse with either boys or women without facing criticism, sexual relations between women were scornfully rejected.

21 Watson and Watson 2003, 257 also argue that Martial displays a preference for slave boys over women considering that he writes love poems for boys (e.g. 3.65, 7.87), but not for women. Sullivan 1991, 191 reaches a similar conclusion about Martial's sexual preferences.

22 Howell 1995, 2 asserts that, despite Martial's claims in his epigrams (like 11.104), the poet never truly had a wife. Conversely, Ascher 1977 argues convincingly that the existing evidence on Martial's plausible marital life is inconclusive.

23 Habinek 2005, 388 interprets Martial's frequent depiction of himself as a man penetrating others as an attempt for a "relative newcomer" to establish his position in society and in the circles of the "literary elite".

24 For further analyses of this epigram, see Ascher 1977, 442; Verstraete 1980, 227–228; Sullivan 1991, 188; Richlin 1992, 41–42; 1993, 535 n. 29; Williams 2010, 25; Larson 2012, 110.

25 The final line of 11.43 is a typical example of Martial's tendency to raise laughs through the use of a surprising ending (ἀπροσδόκητον) when he delivers the punchline. His reply to his wife's suggestion to choose her as his sexual partner for anal penetration is so harsh that Butler 1909, 257 considers it "disgusting language" and argues that it shows that Martial never had a wife, because it would be unrealistic to have spoken about her in such terms in one of his epigrams. On Martial's frequent use of the ἀπροσδόκητον, see Sullivan 1990, 161–162; Williams 2004, 58, 214; Mindt 2020, 75–76; Vallat 2020, 165. As Wills 2008, 70 observes, "The point of some epigrams is to get close enough in the early lines to deliver a sudden stab in the last". On the use of ἀπροσδόκητον more generally, see also Galán Vioque 2002, 115.

26 Howell 1995, 2 makes a similar observation.

14.205. In 2.36 he provides a more detailed description of what he considers attractive in a male.[27] Before revealing in the last line that Pannychus is effeminate, he states that he prefers someone who looks after himself but not excessively, and even has a beard (2.36.3–4); this gives the impression that he is more interested in male teenagers right before they reach adulthood.[28]

While his sexual desires become apparent through his references to those whom he regards as attractive, considerably higher emphasis is placed on the groups of people whom he mocks for their appearance or behaviour. Because of his frequent invective against women,[29] Martial has been accused repeatedly of misogyny.[30] While he scorns both men and women, the vast number of references to women in his epigrams are negative. Arguably his most vicious condemnations and ridicules are against old women.[31] He evidently follows the epigrammatic tradition against *vetulae* as salacious women who become slaves to their sexual drive and degrade themselves by pursuing men and by expressing their sexual desires publicly, even though their outer appearance renders them completely undesirable for most men, including Martial.[32] The poet is not content with simply

---

27 For a longer discussion of the epigram and its importance in terms of understanding Roman attitudes towards virility and effeminacy, see Williams 2004, 133–137.

28 In contrast, Watson 2019, 102 observes that in Book 12 of the *Anthologia Palatina* growing a beard signals the end of a boy's attractiveness. Miller and Platter 2005, 19 argue that males between 12 and 18 could be viewed as sexually attractive, whereas females between the age of 12 and 50.

29 Spisak 2007, 108 n. 44 notes that more than half of Martial's epigrams in his 12 Books are written in the form of invective. Richlin 2014, 69 provides a list of Roman authors and their works in which there are invectives against women.

30 Williams 2004, 103 observes that Martial's tone in every single epigram of Book 2 in which he addresses a female character directly is negative. According to Wills 2008, 73, Martial "upholds the classical misogyny". Richlin 2014, 63–64 rejects the notion that Martial and other satirists could not have been misogynists simply because they attack men as well in their works. Conversely, MacLahlan 2013, 181–182 points out that while Martial does tend to attack women in his poems, he also composed epigrams in which he praises women, both Roman and foreign. Watson 2019, 101 raises a similar point by providing several examples of epigrams in which women are portrayed as having some laudable qualities.

31 Papaioannou and Serafim 2021, 13–14 observe that Aristotle's, Cicero's and Quintilian's works suggest that "invective is most effective when it aims at ridiculing one's opponent".

32 Watson 1982, 72 notes that old women were a common target not only in epigram, but also in comedy. An excellent discussion of the invective against women in Latin literature can be found in Richlin 1992, 109–116.

rejecting such women,[33] but rather uses their sexual drive and unattractive appearance as a means of generating laughter.

A prime example of Martial's invective against *vetulae* as an attempt to entertain his audience is epigram 2.41, in which the poet mocks Maximina for her desire to engage in sexual relations with men despite her old age.[34] The epigram begins with an ostensibly positive exhortation; the poet simply encourages an unnamed girl or young woman (*puella*) to smile.[35] However, the reader's expectations about the tone of the epigram are quickly shattered in the following lines.[36] After revealing that he is simply quoting Ovid[37] who was addressing a specific *puella*, he emphatically notes that Maximina[38] is most certainly not a *puella*,[39] thus suggesting that she has reached a certain age that no man could find her sexually desirable and that she is acting as if she were under the delusion that

---

33 An even harsher rejection of a woman in Martial's epigrams can be found in 9.97, in which the poet claims that he would die from disgust if he were in close contact with Telessilla. Richlin 2014, 71, 328 n. 17 points out that similar examples of the author's rejection of women precisely because he considers their appearance repulsive can be found not only in Martial (11.97, 11.23), but also in the *Carmina Priapea* (32, 46).

34 For additional discussions of 2.41, see Williams 2006, 336–338; Janka 2007, 285–292; Hinds 2017, 116–117.

35 Richlin 2014, 72 stresses the vast difference between a *puella*, the sexually desirable female, and an old woman in satire. She notes that both in Martial's epigrams and in the *Carmina Priapea* the *vetula* is not only rejected and scorned for her appearance, but also depicted as a repulsive character.

36 On the variety of Martial's reading audience, see Farland 2014, 206–207.

37 For a list of the numerous references to Ovid in Martial's epigrams, see Williams 2004, 6. Sullivan 1991, 225 considers the possibility that the first line of 2.41 was taken from a non-extant poem that Ovid wrote. Williams 2006, 336, 338 acknowledges the fact that 2.41 is written in hendecasyllable, a meter than Ovid does not use in any of his extant poems, and, while he does not completely reject Sullivan's hypothesis, he argues that the striking similarities between certain passages of Ovid's *Ars amatoria* and 2.41 suggest that Martial was strongly influenced by the former.

38 Moreno Soldevila, Marina Castillo and Fernández Valverde 2019, 385 observe that only in epigram 2.41 does the name "Maximina" occur in Martial and argue that since "*maximus natu*" means 'eldest'", the name that the poet chooses could be a further reference to the woman's old age. Similarly, Hinds 2017, 117 considers the possibility that Maximina's name derives from Ovid's *maxima damna* (*Ars am.* 3.280).

39 The rejection of Maximina as a *vetula* is also stressed in Janka 2007, 288–289. Williams 2004, 152 provides a list of references to Martial's epigrams in which young, desirable girls are contrasted with old and repulsive women. He argues that terms like *vetula* tend to be sexually charged. At the same time, Richlin 2014, 70 notes that Martial depicts many women as repulsive, both old and young.

she is still a *puella*.[40] His intention to mock her becomes clearer in his reference to her teeth. He observes that she has three teeth left and that even those are black and yellow.[41] Thus, Maximina is not simply painted as an unattractive old woman, but as an utterly disgusting character whose mere smile would cause anyone revulsion.[42] Maximina may not be the only character whom Martial mocks for their unsightly teeth,[43] but her uniqueness lies on the fact that she is the sole character for whom an entire — relatively long — epigram[44] revolves around their teeth, or lack thereof.[45]

The epigrammatist's mockery of Maximina does not end after he stresses how repulsive her smile is and why she has no reason to smile as if she were a *puella*. Instead, Martial initially seems to act like a concerned teacher who wants to protect his student from humiliation by attempting to help her snap out of her delusion that she is attractive enough to be seen smiling. He argues that all she has to do to face reality is look in the mirror. However, in the unlikely scenario that she

---

40 Janka 2007, 288 offers an interesting reading of the text. He argues that the reader can imagine Maximina smiling at Martial in an effort to display her interest in him. The rest of the poem can be interpreted as the poet's scornful rejection of the old woman's advances. Lucretius also explores the theme of delusion of the love-struck man who sees his object of desire as exceedingly better than she actually is. He argues that passion can make a man blind to a woman's physical imperfections to such an extent that he may love and respect her (4.1152–1168).
41 Janka 2007, 289 notes that part of the reason that the colour of Maximina's teeth is mentioned is to suggest that she will soon be left with no teeth, as they are all about to fall off. The fact that Maximina is depicted as having specifically three teeth left is not necessarily a matter of import, as there is a reference to a man named Picens who also has three teeth left before spiting them all out (8.57), to Aelia, who has four teeth and spits out two teeth after she coughs and two more after a second cough (1.19) and to Vetustilla, who is mocked for her decaying body, which includes four teeth and three hairs (3.93). A reference to an old woman with only two teeth left can be found in the *Appendix Vergiliana* in a poem entitled *Priapeum «Quid hoc novi est?* in line 26. It appears that the reference to a specific number of teeth that a character has is used simply to elicit disgust at the person described and to suggest that they are so old that they are soon to remain with no teeth at all.
42 Richlin 2014, 70 asserts that both Martial and his readers "must be taking pleasure in examining them and proclaiming their disgust".
43 Notably, even though he mocks both men and women, more attacks are targeted towards the latter (1.19, 1.72, 3.93, 5.43, 9.37, 12.23) than the former (6.74, 8.54). He ridicules these persons mainly for their missing teeth (1.19, 3.93, 6.74, 8.57) or for using some false teeth or dentures (1.72, 5.43, 9.37, 12.23, 14.56). Similarly, in Horace's *Sat.* 1.8.46–50 witches are mocked for their appearance and specifically for their hair and false teeth.
44 In fact, the longest in Book 2.
45 In 1.72, for example, Aegle is mocked for her false teeth, Lycoris for her dark skin and Fidentinus for being under the impression that he is a poet, when, in fact, he simply plagiarises Martial.

is so far removed from reality that she cannot see just how repulsive her smile is, the poet provides an alternative: she can trust the judgment of another person who would have no reason to lie to her, i.e. Martial himself. Thus, if she finally admits to herself that her old age has made her smile hideous to look at, she will join many of their fellow citizens, both male and female, who are aware of their repulsive bodily flaws and attempt to mask or conceal them.[46] The language that Martial uses in the advice that he offers Maximina is indicative of the intensity of his attack against her. Maximina is not simply encouraged to keep her mouth closed, since the poet informs her that she has to be afraid (*debes timere*) of smiling in public. Such a fear would protect her from instinctively smiling or laughing, thus causing revulsion to onlookers. In order to avoid that completely from happening, he discourages her from watching comedies or enjoying dinner in a delightful company. With his statement, Martial gives the impression of someone who is irritated by the public space that old women are occupying on a daily basis. As their beauty has long faded, they have nothing to offer to men like Martial who only see value in their appearance or their fortune.[47]

There is, arguably, another possible interpretation of Martial's expressed repulsion at Maximina's appearance that needs to be explored. The epigrammatist could be using a stock character,[48] i.e. the ridiculous *vetula* who refuses to hide her desire to engage in sexual relations with men, not as a commentary on socially unacceptable behaviour, but chiefly in an attempt to arouse laughter. Such a possibility can be observed in his instruction to Maximina to start mourning, following the example of Hecuba and Andromache.[49] Thus, in addition to using a stock character, Martial inverts a tragic episode into a comic one,[50] by imitating women who had experienced one of the gravest calamities in life and had lost everything in the Trojan War, including Hector, Hecuba's son and Andromache's husband. Maximina is expected to adopt an expression which is *prima facie* polar opposite to a person who is smiling. Through the references to the Trojan

---

46 See, for example, Laelia's attempt to conceal her old age in 12.23.

47 In 7.75 an old woman desires to engage in sexual relations with a man, despite her old age. Martial chastises her for not offering at very least some of kind of payment for a man's services.

48 Watson 2019, 94 notes that, unlike Catullus, Martial refrains from attacking real people and opts to direct his attacks against stock figures.

49 For additional mythological exempla in Martial's Book 2, see Williams 2004, 70. Richlin 2014, 71 provides further examples of "hyperbolic comparisons" between old women and characters from Greek mythology in Martial (10.67, 10.90) and the *Carmina Priapea* (57).

50 Serafim 2020, 25 notes that this was common not only in comedy, but also in judicial orations.

women,[51] to Aeneas in line 20,[52] and through the use of imperatives in the last line, the poet seems to mock Maximina further. Throughout the epigram, there are several sets of opposites: the *puella* (1) and Maximina, the *vetula* (5–7); Andromache (14) and Hecuba (14); fear (9) and relaxation (8); comedy (10) and tragedy (21); laughing (1) and crying (23), with which the poem ends in ring composition;[53] additionally, unlike Aeneas, who is famous for his piety (20), Maximina does not respect herself by acting according to her age. Most importantly, Martial's advice to Maximina to cry instead of smiling would be counterproductive, since, as Ovid himself notes, one can mistake a woman for crying when she is in fact laughing (*Ars am.* 3.288). Therefore, if she takes the satirist's advice literally and attempts to hide her smile in public by crying, she will likely expose her three teeth and cause disgust to anyone who happens to see her and thus achieve the exact opposite result.[54] If Maximina is wise, as the poem would suggest at the beginning § 1, she must see through his deception. The time for her to be a *puella* is past, but she can still be wise. If she wants to protect herself from further ridicule, she needs to understand his underlying message: for a sexually repulsive woman of advanced age smiling should be the last thought on her mind. Maximina absolutely should mourn, but only figuratively, the loss of her youth and the sexual desirability that it provides. Through the use of exaggeration, Martial manages to ridicule Maximina, thereby providing ample entertainment to his audience who would consider such mockery amusing.[55]

Ultimately, Martial's invective appears to be a response not simply to the disgust that he experiences at the repulsive sight of Maximina's smile, but rather at the incongruity[56] between her appearance and her erroneous impression that Ovid's advice could possibly concern an undoubtedly sexually undesirable old

---

51 It follows that Martial changes a sublime genre, as epic is, to a petty, as comedy is considered by Aristotle to be. This incongruity is designed to provoke the audience's laughter.
52 I follow Williams 2004, 154 who interprets the use of the epithet *pius* as a reference to Aeneas.
53 As Williams 2004, 41 observes, this technique is widely associated with Catullus.
54 Whether Maximina laughs or mourns, the result will be the same: she will cause disgust to anyone who looks at her, as according to Ovid, people experience disgust at the sight of people who weep (*Ars am.* 3.517).
55 Spisak 2007, 32, following Martial's defence of the invective in his epigrams, argues that the epigrammatist does not attack specific persons, but rather their vices or types of behaviour that are at variance with the social norms of his time, in an effort to provide entertainment to his audience. Similarly, Richlin 2014, 68 interprets invective as an attempt for the satirist to make both himself and his audience, who share his views, feel better about themselves.
56 For in-depth discussions of humour theories — including the theory of incongruity — and their uses in Greek and Latin texts, see esp. Raskin 1984, 30–41; Attardo 1994, 47–50; Morreall 2009, 4–23; Serafim 2021, 87–91; Paraskeviotis 2021, 229–232, 238–240.

woman such as herself.[57] The poet, thus, decides to imitate Ovid to a certain extent, though, instead of encouraging young women to show their attractive teeth by smiling (*Ars am.* 3.513), he teaches Maximina and every old woman[58] with deteriorating looks, including missing teeth, a valuable lesson: their place in society is not determined by themselves or by their perception of themselves,[59] but corresponds to their age and to the sexual attraction or repulsion of their male fellow citizens when they look at them.[60]

While Martial clearly belittles Maximina for her age, there is a notable absence of references to genitals or any kind of obscenity, which is common in his invectives against old women.[61] He thus demonstrates that he is capable of denigrating anyone and of attacking their sexual life without having to rely on obscene language. Conversely, the author of epigram 12 of the *Carmina Priapea* opts for a distinctively different approach. The similarities between the two epigrams are striking:[62] they both mock an old woman; they exaggerate the woman's old age by comparing her to Hecuba, through a reference to a third person (Priam in 2.41.14 and Hector in *CP* 12.1); they state that the woman has specifically three teeth; both women are expected to remain hidden or to hide part of their body;

---

57 Janka 2007, 290–291 offers a different interpretation of the text by arguing that Maximina is simply a *vetula* who pretends to be a *puella* a notably stronger attack against a female character whose perception of herself clashes with reality in Martial's eyes can be found in 3.93. Unlike Martial, Lucretius states that even an unattractive woman can find a male partner. He argues that scrupulous women can trick men into loving them, if they are persistent (4.1274–1287).

58 It is unclear whether Martial's intention in 2.41 is to castigate one specific person or more generally *vetulae* who cause repulsion to their fellow citizens by smiling and displaying an interest in engaging in sexual relations with them. As Williams 2004, 152 points out, the name "Maximina" can only be found in epigram 2.41, unlike characters like Postumus or Zoilus, whom he reproaches in numerous epigrams.

59 Papaioannou and Serafim 2021, 10 note that lack of self-awareness was common in boasters whose false impression of themselves in combination with their boasting caused laughter and led to their criticism.

60 Watson 2019, 96 notes that, contrary to Latin epigram, in some Greek epigrams older women can still be viewed as attractive.

61 Richlin 2014, 73 observes Martial's tendency to focus on the genitalia of the female characters whom he scorns, especially when they are old. His most infamous attack against an old woman can be found in 3.93 in which he mocks and ridicules Vetustilla for desiring to find a husband despite her advanced age. After evoking disgust to his audience through the detailed description of Vetustilla's decaying body, he delivers one of his harshest attacks by informing her that only a torch could penetrate her vagina, thus suggesting that, as someone approaching death, she should not have the audacity to entertain thoughts of remarrying and of sexual intercourse.

62 O'Connor 2019, 544 stresses the similarities between 14 of Martial's Priapic epigrams and poems from the *Carmina Priapea*.

lastly, both satirists use the verb *timeo* in reference to the fear that each woman is expected to experience (2.41.9, *CP* 12.12). Nevertheless, in *CP* 12 the mockery of the old woman for her sexual laxity and her repellent image is much more pronounced. The unnamed (*quaedam*, "some" *CP* 12.1) *vetula* is supposedly of such advanced age that she is approaching death (*CP* 12.4) and can barely stand on her feet. Her hands are full of wrinkles and she raises them to beg Priapus for sexual gratification through an explicit reference to *mentula*. The poet's mockery of her reaches its peak, when after her plea, it is stated that she spits out one of her three remaining teeth. It appears that the author of *CP* 12 satirises an unnamed old woman more than Martial[63] through the grotesque and arguably hysterical image that he creates of a *vetula* who embarrasses herself publicly because of her insatiable sexual appetite.[64]

His impertinent remarks about Maximina are by no means unique in his epigrams. Women of any age are mocked, whether they are old widows who desire to remarry (3.93) or younger women whose sexual practices deviate from the social norms of their time (7.18, 7.30). One such group of women that Martial scorns vehemently are *tribades*, i.e. women who engage in sexual relations with other women. Philaenis, a character that features prominently in Martial's epigrams, becomes the target of one of the poet's most infamous invectives (7.67).[65] The poet sets the tone of the epigram and the expectations of the audience from the very beginning through the use of the verb *pedicat* ("sodomises") in reference to Philaenis' habit of anally penetrating boys.[66] Philaenis, we are told, is a *tribas* ("lesbian") who penetrates both boys (1) and girls (3). Everything about her is performed in excess apparently in an attempt to outdo every man through her

---

63 The consensus in scholarship is that the *Carmina Priapea* were composed before Martial's epigrams. For a more in-depth discussion of their date, see Richlin 1992, 141–143.

64 Hoffmann 1955–1956, 445 provides a list of references to licentious old women in Martial's epigrams.

65 Philaenis is criticised for being a *tribas* also in 7.70. Martial's view of sexual relations between women is even clearer in his censure of Bassa in 1.90, in which he makes a direct reference to tribadism while expressing his indignation at her. Howell 1980, 297 notes that the topic of lesbianism is explored in a particularly small number of texts in antiquity and stresses that in each case the author expresses his disgust. For an extensive analysis of epigram 7.67, see Watson and Watson 2003, 251–255. Moreno Soldevila, Marina Castillo and Fernández Valverde 2019, 467–468 provide a list of references to Philaenis in Martial and note that she is constantly depicted in a negative light in different sexual contexts. Boehringer 2015, 381–382 expresses a similar view by underlining the revulsion that is caused to the reader through Martial's derogatory depiction of Philaenis in the "character-type" that he creates.

66 Williams 1995, 522 n. 32 notes that the verb *pedicare* refers to anal penetration of both males and females.

actions: she has sexual intercourse more frequently even than a lustful man (2–3), she excels at sports and performs impressive feats with ease, thereby surpassing even male athletes (5–6),[67] she drinks excessive amounts of wine (9–11), she displays an excessive appetite through the amount of meat that she consumes (12) and she chooses to perform oral sex only on women because she considers it more virile than fellatio.

Through his description, Martial portrays Philaenis as a woman who desperately desires to usurp the dominant role in society by trying to surpass each and every man at anything that she deems characteristically male, i.e. sex, athleticism as well as consumption of food and wine. She, nonetheless, fails miserably to achieve her goal because she cannot comprehend that her attempts lead to excess that is both revolting and ridiculous to onlookers. Her elongated clitoris[68] with which she penetrates males and females, her dirty clothes and skin, the fact that she subjects herself to vomiting so that she can publicly show that she can consume large amounts of food and wine paint a picture of a disillusioned woman who does not attract praise for her masculinity, but instead evokes disgust and laughter.[69] Martial seems to invite his reader to laugh with him at Philaenis for her moral shortcomings and thus experience the pleasure of moral superiority.[70] Her insistence on performing oral sex on women is a manifestation of her folly. Because of her fervent zeal to prove herself virile, she goes as far as to "devour girls' middles" (*medias vorat puellas*), supposedly because of her belief that cunnilingus would be viewed as a sexual act manlier than fellatio, an allegation that Martial immediately rejects (16–17).[71]

While modern scholars have rightly pointed that Martial's indignation seems to stem from his disapproval of Philaenis' tendency to act contrary to her nature and to disrupt the status quo in her attempts to establish her virility,[72] one needs

---

67 Boehringer 2015, 384 observes that Philaenis is depicted as a woman who has a repulsive body because of her own wrong choices and practices.

68 Watson and Watson 2003, 251. They also note that such a view is expressed again in Martial (3.72.6) as well as in Cael. Aurel. *Gyn.* 2.112.

69 Boejringer 2015, 387 also detects an intention from Martial to elicit disgust and laughter through Philaenis' various depictions in his epigrams.

70 According to Applauso 2019, 11, the disparagement or superiority theory asserts that "ill-natured laughter at the wrongdoings of other individuals considered morally inferior... bestows a sense of superiority".

71 Watson 2019, 105 argues that the objection to cunnilingus revolved around the notion that a man would demean himself through the performance of oral sex on a woman by "being subservient" to her.

72 According to Hallet 1997, 262, the epigrammatist belittles Philaenis because of her false beliefs about the essence of masculinity. Larson 2012, 135 underlines the poet's scorn of women

to bear in mind the epigrammatist's interest in entertaining his audience. The poem is not simply a censure of a woman's behaviour, but also a mockery of her false belief of what constitutes masculinity and of her ridiculous efforts to convince everyone around her that she is more virile than a man.[73] Through Martial's vivid description, the audience can picture Phialenis' violent performance of cunnilingus, hear her moans at the palaestra and even smell the stench of wine and vomit on her clothes. All these details would only elicit repulsion if it were not for her complete failure at achieving her goal and the way in which she attempts to demonstrate her masculinity, all of which make her a laughable character.[74]

While the vast majority of women in Martial's epigrams are depicted negatively, many men also become objects of the satirist's disgusted scorn for their sexual proclivities.[75] Despite homosexual[76] relations between a freeborn man and a slave boy or teenager not being shunned by Martial,[77] any freeborn man who allowed himself to be penetrated, or who offered oral sex to a man or a woman, was scorned and mocked, as his sex life was at variance with the Roman ideal of manhood in the epigrammatist's time.[78] Perhaps part of the reason that men like

---

like Philaenis for their audacity to behave as if they were men "or to exclude men from their circles". Richlin 2014, 74 makes similar observations, but on old women in satire by arguing that they are scorned because they "represent a side of female behaviour that maliciously threatens males" and through their actions they "undermine male control over women".

73 Boejringer 2014, 156–157 also stresses Martial's attempt to provoke laughter through his emphasis on Philaenis' false beliefs about masculinity.

74 O'Connor 2019, 548 makes a similar remark about the god Priapus who acts like a "dominant … freeborn Roman male", while also being laughable.

75 Wills 2008, 73 points out that Martial's scorn of "deviants" is in line with the condemnation found in the works of other satirists.

76 An interesting debate between Richlin and Fogel on the use of the term homosexuality in reference to sexual relations between men and between women in the ancient world can be found in Miller and Platter 2005, 19–26. Williams 1995, 517 n. 1 stresses how problematic the use of the term "homosexuality" is in discussions of sexual relationships in the ancient world. Williams 2010, 230–231; 2015, 461–462 argues against the use of the terms "passive" and "active" in reference to homosexual relationships in the ancient world. Kamen and Levin-Richardson 2015, 449–453 build on Williams' points and demonstrate how agency should be the main criterion used in determining one's role in a sexual act in the ancient world.

77 Selden 2007, 516 and Verstaete 1980, 229 underscore the potential legal ramifications of sexual penetration of non-slave boys. Nonetheless, Richlin 2015, 368 notes that "free children and fantasy children were also sometimes the target of lust".

78 Hubbard 2014, 146 points out that in three of Martial's epigrams (2.51, 3.71, 6.50) there are references to male prostitutes who were hired by other men who desired to assume the receptive role in anal penetration. However, as Watson 2019, 102 rightly observes, both for Greeks and Romans to play the incertive role in anal or vaginal penetration "was to play the masculine role",

Martial found such sexual acts repulsive was that genitalia were considered unclean. Such a view is expressed repeatedly in Martial's depiction of *mentula* ("penis") as something filthy and disgusting *per se*.[79] As a result, a sexual act that involved a *mentula*, such as oral sex or sodomy,[80] would taint the person who assumed the receptive role.[81] Indeed, the epigrammatist questions why a freeborn man would choose to be anally penetrated (9.47), but also stresses that he, personally, would refuse to sodomise another man if he was in his right mind (11.20). Therefore, sodomy was depicted as a repulsive sexual practise that should be completely avoided, especially because of its association with defecation (9.69).[82]

Despite Martial's explicit ridicule and scorn of his contemporaries' sexual proclivities, in certain epigrams he chooses a more playful and less direct approach in his mockery of people who deviated from the social norm. In the "cycle of Postumus",[83] Martial implicitly attacks a man for habitually performing oral sex on other men and for his unwelcome kisses on him.[84] Martial introduces to his reader a new character, who features frequently in Book 2 and can also be found in Book 4 and 5, though as different characters who share the same name.[85] The cycle begins with epigram 2.10, in which the satirist sets the tone for the rest

---

whereas to play the receptive role "was to play the feminine part", because "to be sodomised (or irrumated) represents a humiliating compromise of their masculinity".

79 For example, 2.61, 2.70. Richlin 2014, 74–75 stresses that there is not even a single positive reference to female genitalia in all extant Latin texts and, more importantly, when they are mentioned, they become part of the author's depiction of the woman as repulsive. Conversely, as Watson 2019, 95 points out, the references to the female body in Greek epigram are significantly more positive.

80 Juvenal also expresses his disgust at the thought of anal penetration in his grotesque reference to the sexual act as the *mentula* "encountering yesterday's dinner" (*hesternae occurrere cenae*, 9.44). Morgan 2005, 187 points out the combination of amusement and repulsion that Juvenal elicits through the grotesque picture that he creates in his reference to anal sex. For an insightful discussion of the passage, see Miller 1998, 400–401.

81 According to Richlin 2014, 79, men who choose to be penetrated are depicted as badly as repulsive women.

82 The aforementioned epigram in which Martial sodomises a slave-boy (11.43) suggests that this attitude towards anal penetration concerned sexual intercourse only between adults.

83 On the view of a series of epigrams as forming a "cycle", see Barwick 1958. For a brilliant discussion of the ways in which Martial forms connections between his epigrams in the same or different Books, see Maltby 2008.

84 Lateiner and Spatharas 2017, 208 n. 18 observe that 60 of Martial's epigrams deal with oral sex. For a list of epigrams that explore the theme of the reluctance or unwillingness of certain persons to be kissed by others, see Galán Vioque 2002, 497 with relevant bibliography.

85 Moreno Soldevila, Marina Castillo and Fernández Valverde 2019, 501–502 provide a list of references to Postumus in Martial and a brief discussion of the context of each epigram.

of the references to Postumus. The information that he provides about his relationship and interaction with this man is limited; he simply states that Postumus prefers to kiss him with half his lips, whereas Martial would prefer to refrain from kissing him entirely. The reason that each person does not desire to be kissed freely by the other man is not explained. The reader is thereby forced to speculate before moving on to the rest of the epigrams of Book 2. Based on the information in 2.10, the reader is given the impression that, on the one hand, Postumus does not consider Martial worthy of his full kisses, plausibly because he sees him as socially inferior, and, on the other hand, Martial wants to avoid close conduct with Postumus because of a bad smell, which is likely coming from his mouth.

The epigram arouses the curiosity of the reader who would likely desire to discover the meaning of the epigrammatist's cryptic remarks about Postumus' kisses. Could his disgust stem from Postumus' poor oral hygiene?[86] Or potentially — and perhaps more interestingly — because Postumus is a fellator or a cunnilinctor?[87] Martial mischievously provides an answer to this question by dropping hints in different epigrams of Book 2, not all of which have Postumus as the addressee. In 2.12 the poet comments on the fact that Postumus' kisses always smell of myrrh, thereby confirming that Postumus' mouth is the source of the poet's repulsion.[88] Nevertheless, it is also revealed that, because of the constant use of myrrh, Postumus always smells nice, which makes Martial suspicious

---

[86] As Galán Vioque 2002, 496 points out, hygiene was a serious concern for Martial and his contemporaries, who would understandably desire to avoid being constantly kissed by their fellow citizens.

[87] Corbeill 2002, 201 refers to "non-standard sexual behaviour" as one of the ten main themes that scholars have identified in invectives. According to Wills 2008, 73, both men and women who perform fellatio or cunnilingus are heavily criticised for their disgraceful act. Richlin 1981a, 44 provides a list of Catullus' and Martial's epigrams in which women are depicted as disreputable for offering oral sex to men. Similarly, Watson 2005, 74 n.48 observes that fellatio was considered degrading and that in Martial it was a sexual act that was performed chiefly by prostitutes. Selden 2007, 516–517 notes that "oral sex is uniformly presented in the culture as polluting". Richlin 1992, 249 n. 18 points out that Catullus expresses revulsion in his references to oral sex and female genitalia. Larson 2012, 135 stresses that men of the elite viewed cunnilingus as utterly repulsive and Parker 1997, 52 refers to cunnilingus as a "monstrosity in the system". Watson 2019, 106 states that cunnilingus was perceived as more effeminate than both fellatio and being anally penetrated. For a more extensive discussion of cunnilingus, see, Williams 2010, 218–230.

[88] Postumus displays unmanly behaviour not only because he performs oral sex, but also because of the use of myrrh. As Edwards 1993, 68 points out, along with excessive bathing and depilation of his legs, "The 'effeminate' man is perfumed". On depilation in Persius, Martial, Juvenal and Lucian, see Richlin 1993, 551 n. 69. The topic of depilation is further explored by

of what exactly he is trying to hide. It follows that the repulsion that the epigrammatist experiences does not stem from a natural reaction to a bad smell, but from the consideration of what Postumus is attempting to conceal.

The mystery around Martial's negative depiction of Postumus and the emphasis on his kisses slowly unfolds in Book 2. Postumus as a character returns in three consecutive epigrams. In 2.21 Martial reiterates that he does not wish to be kissed by Postumus and informs him that he would rather Postumus greeted him with a handclasp.[89] The fact that Postumus offers him a choice between a handshake and a kiss gives the impression that between the composition of epigram 2.10 and 2.21 Postumus' esteem for the poet has increased, whereas Martial's opinion of him has evidently remained the same. This hypothesis is reinforced in the following two epigrams, in which Postumus seems to hold the epigrammatist to such a high esteem that he ignores his request to greet him with a handclasp and kisses him with both his lips. The poet complains to the Muse, who, while inspiring him to compose epigrams, has inadvertently made him so popular that he has to endure Postumus' full kisses (2.22). Martial's effort to arouse the audience's curiosity has been successful: in 2.23 he reveals that his readers keep asking him whom the pseudonym "Postumus" refers to,[90] but he refuses to divulge such information, supposedly because Postumus will react by kissing him even more as payback.

Despite the reader's apparently heightened interest in Postumus, one important question remains unanswered: what causes Martial's repulsion? After 2.23, Postumus disappears from Book 2 until 2.67. The poet seems to play with the audience's expectations, as even when Postumus resurfaces, there is no mention of his annoying habit to greet Martial with a kiss. Instead, he focuses on Postumus being the kind of person who irritates him by asking him what he is doing every time he sees him. The answer is finally revealed in the last epigram of Book 2 with Postumus as the addressee. At first glance, in 2.72 Martial simply presents Postumus as a weak man who allows himself to be struck in the face by someone named Caecilius. Interestingly, Martial argues that his report of the incident is not a rumour or gossip that has been travelling around the city; he clearly states

---

Miller 1998, 399, 405–407. Lucretius also discusses the excessive use of perfume and states that the maids of the repulsive woman who uses it laugh at her secretively (4.1174–1176).

89 Lateiner 2009, 17–18 notes how kissing as a greeting was established as a sign of social deference in Rome by Martial's time.

90 Watson 1982, 72 discusses Martial's tendency to use pseudonyms in order to avoid offending specific persons and argues that he never planned on revealing their identity. Laurens 1965, 315 interprets the epigrammatist's tendency to use pseudonyms and the same name for different characters as an attempt to mock types of people and not individuals.

in the very first line that this is a fact (*factum*).[91] What elevates this story that Martial heard from mere rumour to a fact is the existence of witnesses who can confirm that Postumus was indeed hit by someone supposedly without retaliating. The only part of the story that is contested and thus referred to as a rumour (*rumor*) is the person who caused such offense to Postumus' manliness by degrading him with a slap. Postumus' denial of the event ever taking place fails to convince Martial who trusts the testimony of the witnesses.

As Williams convincingly argues, the double entendre of *os percisum* (2.72.3), *rumor* (2.72.6) and *habet testes* (2.72.8) confirms the hypothesis that Postumus is a fellator.[92] Through sexual puns, Martial insinuates that Postumus has an impure mouth (*os impurum*)[93] because he has been irrumated by another man. His irrumation by Caecilius is further hinted at through the reference to Caecilius being the perpetrator of the injustice inflicted upon Postumus as a rumour (an obvious sound-play with *irrumare*).[94] The poet's invective against Postumus and his scrutiny of men who demean themselves by performing oral sex on other men reach their climax in the very last line of the epigram, which constitutes the final reference to Postumus, the fellator. He delivers the final blow to Postumus by stating that Caecilius has witnesses. The phrase *habet testes* works in multiple levels: first, it contradicts Postumus' claim that Caecilius' version of events was a product of fabrication. Second, it implies that, unlike Postumus, Caecilius "has balls", i.e. is a "real man", a quality that Postumus apparently lacks because of

---

91 Williams 2004, 229 repeatedly refers to it as "gossip" or a "rumor".

92 Williams 2004, 229–231. O'Connor 2019, 548 notes how frequently "word play, puns, and sexual double entendres" are used in epigrams.

93 On *os impurum*, see also Richlin 1981a, 44; Sullivan 1991, 189, 199–203; Viogue 2002, 497–504; Fitzgerald 2007, 128–129; Lateiner 2009, 16–17. Bradley 2014, 136 points out that the accusation of *os impurum* was one of the most common slanders against other men from Cicero's to Martial's time. He argues that Romans of the late Republic until the early Empire believed that "what is ingested permeates the body's boundaries, infects it and is then excreted and in turn becomes infectious". As Watson 2019, 104 shows, in Martial it is evident that men who performed oral sex demeaned themselves more than those who were anally penetrated.

94 Adams 1982, 212–213. However, an argument could be made against such an interpretation of the text. According to Kamen and Levin-Richardson 2015, 450–453, there is a vast difference between *irrumatus* and *fellator*. If Martial uses the word *rumor* to insinuate that Postumus was indeed irrumated by Caecilius, it would follow that he does not choose to perform fellatio on men, but rather, that he is being constantly irrumated by other men, because they see him as a weak man who does not stand up for himself and thus an easy target for irrumation. After all, as Kamen and Levin-Richardson 2015, 453 rightly point out, in 3.82.33 the character Zoilus cannot be punished by being irrumated, since he is a fellator. MacMullen 1982, 492 n. 27 notes that nothing was considered more shameful than being irrumated.

the kind of sexual relations that he engages in with other men. The phrase is also a graphic reminder of the sexual acts that he performs on men with the clear reference to testicles.

A final plausible hint that Martial uses to suggest to his readers that he feels disgust at the thought that Postumus is a fellator comes rather unexpectedly.[95] In 2.33 he addresses Philaenis and repeatedly informs her that he has no intention of ever kissing her. Unlike his epigrams to Postumus, in this particular poem the source of his disgust is revealed. After attacking her for her repulsive appearance through a riddle by likening her to a phallus,[96] he explicitly affirms his disdain for fellatio and states that this is the reason that he rejects her by refraining from kissing her.[97] Therefore, a definite answer to the reader's question about Martial's repulsion at Postumus' kisses can only be accessed through the attentive reading of a series of epigrams, i.e. 2.10, 2.12, 2.21, 2.22, 2.23, 2.33 and 2.72. The reader is thus not only amused by Martial's implicit mockery of a man who is depicted as morally inferior, but can also experience a sense of achievement by confirming his initial suspicion that Martial was appalled by the thought of Postumus as a fellator.[98]

In most epigrams of Book 2 Martial presents Postumus as a man who displays almost complete disregard for his virility.[99] The poet suggests that Postumus continuously performs fellatio,[100] hence the constant use of myrrh. Because of the discrepancy between Postumus' desire to appear as a respectable man in society

---

95 Davis 1973, 63 detects a similar intention in Juv. 6.425–433 from the satirist to elicit the disgust of his readers through repulsive imagery of vomiting.
96 Plass 1985, 198 points out the apparent riddle. Conversely, Watson 1982, 72 offers a literal interpretation of Martial's remarks by noting that the epigram reveals that Philaenis has one eye, red hair and is bald, without considering the possibility that all this information is simply used for the punchline in the very last line, i.e. a build up for the reference to Philaenis' habit of offering oral sex to men.
97 Boehringer 2015, 382 notes that Philaenis is depicted as a repulsive character with a foul smell which suggests "oral defilement".
98 Williams 2006, 337 raises a similar point about Martial's allusion to Ovid in 2.41. He argues that by "discovering an allusion" on their own, the readers would experience an "intellectual pleasure". Janka 2007, 280 also stresses the importance of the interaction between Martial, the poet, and his audience.
99 In stark contrast to Postumus' degradation of his masculinity, Martial wastes no opportunity to underline his own in his epigrams. As Edwards 1993, 94 observes, the epigrammatist "is bristlingly masculine". According to Masterson 2014, 25, Martial's threat to anally rape Carmenion, an effeminate man, in 10.7 constitutes a prime example of his attempts to emphasise his virility.
100 According to Parker 1997, 52, men who offered oral sex to other men were also assumed to be cunnilinctors. Therefore, a reader could be left to make a similar assumption about Postumus.

and the revelation to the audience that he is a sexual deviant, the audience is invited to laugh at him, while also experiencing a sense of superiority.[101] Postumus believes that he can hide his impure activities in the same manner that repulsive men and women try to disguise their physical flaws through the use of make-up. However, this excessive use of myrrh is the very reason that the poet supposedly becomes suspicious in the first place that Postumus has something repulsive to hide. The incident with Caecilius simply confirms his suspicion: Postumus is indeed a fellator and his lips are polluted. Now that his secret has been revealed, not only Martial, but most of their fellow citizens would avoid him.

As this chapter has attempted to demonstrate, the elicitation of disgust constitutes a key component in Martial's success at entertaining his readers by inviting them to laugh at their sexually insatiable fellow citizens. The epigrammatist evidently chooses his targets carefully by focusing on types of people whom his audience can identify in society and whose behaviour they, too, would find reproachable: Maximina, the lustful *vetula*; Philaenis, the aggressive lesbian; and Postumus, the effeminate man. Everything about their appearance and their actions is excessive. Maximina is old and decaying. She has lost most of her teeth and yet she still desires to attract a sexual partner through her smile. Philaenis is at pains to outperform every man at everything that she deems as a test of one's virility, including the frequency of her engagement in sexual relations with both men and women. Postumus continuously offers fellatio to men and has to use excessively large amounts of myrrh to avoid raising suspicion over his sexual acts. The poet does not simply rely on the arousal of repulsion, the emphasis on excess and the use of stock characters to provoke laugher. He also stresses the incongruity between each character's beliefs about themselves and reality as seen through his and the readers' eyes. Maximina is naïve to think that any man would find her sexually attractive and be aroused by her smile. The inversion of the tragic theme into a comic one through the reference to Andromache and Hecuba further highlights the laughable situation in which the desperate *vetula* finds herself. Philaenis' physical peculiarities and particularly her actions evoke revulsion rather than respect. She sodomises boys and girls, she is more promiscuous than a lustful man and, most importantly, she chooses to perform oral sex on women under the impression that such a sexual act would prove her virility, when, in fact, it has the opposite effect. Postumus' use of myrrh as a means of

---

101 Papaioannou and Serafim 2021, 19 argue that, based on the disparagement or superiority theory, comic invective can lead to "communal superiority that contrasts with individual inferiority".

concealment also makes him appear ludicrous because it attracts the attention of Martial who initially had no reason to suspect that he was a fellator.

The epigrammatist proves that he can deliver powerful attacks against different types of people both with obscene language and with implicit references to matters of sexual nature. Ultimately, even though in his epigrams Martial lambastes both women and men, his abusive jests about anyone who deviates from the sexual norms of their time does not appear to be a calculated effort to police behaviour. Instead, the poet seems to be more interested in generating a reaction out of his readers, i.e. first to feel disgust at the disgraceful acts of these highly exaggerated characters, then to experience a sense of moral superiority over them and finally to find them so utterly ridiculous that they instinctively burst out laughing.

Bibliography

Applauso, N. (2019), *Dante's Comedy and the Ethics of Invective in Medieval Italy: Humor and Evil*, Lanham/Boulder/New York/London.

Attardo, S. (1994), *Linguistic Theories of Humor*, Berlin.

Adams, J.N. (1990), *The Latin Sexual Vocabulary*, London.

Ascher, L. (1977), 'Was Martial Really Unmarried?', in: *Classical World* 70, 441–444.

Barwick, K. (1958), 'Zyklen bei Martial und in den kleinen Gedichten des Catull', in: *Philologus* 102, 284–318.

Bauman, R.A. (1994), *Women and Politics in Ancient Rome*, London/New York.

Boehringer, S. (2015), 'What is Named by the Name *Philaenis*? Gender, Function, and Authority of an Antonomastic Figure', in: M. Masterson/N.S. Rabinowitz/J. Robson (eds.), 374–392.

Boejringer, S. (2014), 'Female Homoeroticism', in: T.K. Hubbard (ed.), *A Companion to Greek and Roman Sexualities*, Malden, MA/Oxford/Chichester, 150–163.

Bradley, M. (2014), 'Foul Bodies in Ancient Rome', in: M. Bradley (ed.) *Smell and the Ancient Senses*, London, 133–145.

Butler, H.E. (1909), *Post-Augustan Poetry: From Seneca to Juvenal*, Oxford.

Corbeill, A. (2002), 'Ciceronian Invective', in: J.M. May (ed.), *Brill's Companion to Cicero: Oratory and Rhetoric*, Leiden, 197–218.

Davis, L.P. (1973), [diss.], *Martial's and Juvenal's Attitudes toward Women*, University of Richmond.

Edwards, C. (1993), *The Politics of Immorality in Ancient Rome*, Cambridge.

Farland, H.S.J. (2014), 'Observations on Martial's Imagery of Provincial Spain', in: *Glotta* 90, 192–215.

Fitzgerald, W. (2007), *Martial: The World of the Epigram*, Chicago/London.

Galán Vioque, G. (2002), *Martial, Book VII: A Commentary*, Transl. by J.J. Zoltowski, Boston/Cologne.

Habinek, T. (2005), 'Slavery and Class', in: E. Harrison (ed.), *A Companion to Latin Literature: Blackwell Companions to the Ancient World. Literature and Culture*, Oxford, 385–393.

Hallett, J.P. (1996), '*Nec Castrare Velis Meos Libellos*: Sexual and Poetic *lusus* in Catullus, Martial and the *Carmina Priapea*', in: C. Klodt (ed.), *Satura Lanx: Festschrift für Werner A. Krenkel zum 70. Geburtstag*, Hildesheim, 321–344.

Hallett, J.P./Skinner, M.B. (eds.) (1997), *Roman Sexualities*, Princeton.

Hallett, J.P. (1997), 'Female Homoeroticism and the Denial of Roman Reality in Latin Literature', in: J.P. Hallet/M.B. Skinner (eds.), *Roman Sexualities*, Princeton, 255–273.

Henriksén, C. (ed.) (2019), *A Companion to Ancient Epigram*, Hoboken.

Hinds, S. (2007), 'Martial's Ovid / Ovid's Martial', in: *Journal of Roman Studies* 97, 113–154.

Hoffmann, R. (1955/6), 'Aufgliederung der Themen Martials', in: *Wissenschaftliche Zeitschrift der Universität Leipzig, Gesellschafts- und sprachwis*, Reihe 6, 433–474.

Holzberg, N. (1986), 'Neuansatz zu einer Martial-Interpretation', in: *Würzburger Jahrbücher für die Altertumswissenschaft* 12, 197–215.

Howell, P. (1980), *A Commentary on Book One of the Epigrams of Martial*, London.

Howell, P. (1995), *Martial: Epigrams V. Edited with an Introduction, Translation & Commentary*, Warminster.

Hubbard, T.K. (2014), 'Peer Homosexuality', in: T.K. Hubbard (ed.), *A Companion to Greek and Roman Sexualities*, Malden, MA/Oxford/Chichester, 128–149.

Janka, M. (2007), '*Paelignus, puto, dixerat poeta* (Mart. 2. 41. 2): Martial's Intertextual Dialogue with Ovid's Erotodidactic Poems', in: S. Green (ed.), *The Art of Love: Bimillennial Essays on Ovid's* Ars Amatoria *and* Remedia Amoris, Oxford, 279–297.

Kamen, D./Levin-Richardson, S. (2015), 'Revisiting Roman Sexuality: Agency and the Conceptualization of Penetrated Males', in: M. Masterson/N.S. Rabinowitz/J. Robson (eds.), 449–460.

Kaster, R.A. (1974), 'The Dynamics of *Fastidium* and the Ideology of Disgust', in: *Transactions of the American Philological Association* 131, 143–189.

Larson, J. (2012), *Greek and Roman Sexualities: A Sourcebook*, Huntingdon.

Lateiner, D. (2009), 'Greek and Roman Kissing: Occasions, Protocols, Methods, and Mistakes', in: *Amphora* 8, 17–18.

Lateiner, D./Spatharas, D. (eds.) (2017), *The Ancient Emotion of Disgust*, Oxford.

Lateiner, D. (2017), 'Evoking Disgust in the Latin Novels of Petronius and Apuleius', in: D. Lateiner/D. Spatharas (eds.), *The Ancient Emotion of Disgust*, Oxford, 203–233.

Laurens, P. (1965), 'Martial et l'épigramme grecque du Ier siècle ap. J.-C.', in: *Revue des études latines* 43, 315–341.

Lorenz, S. (2019), 'Micro to Macro: Martial's Twelve Books of Epigrams', in: C. Henriksén (ed.), *A Companion to Ancient Epigram*, Hoboken, 521–539.

MacLachlan, B. (2013), *Women in Ancient Rome: A Sourcebook*, London/New York.

MacMullen, R. (1982), 'Roman Attitudes to Greek Love', in: *Historia: Zeitschrift für Alte Geschichte* 31, 484–502.

Maltby, R. (2008), 'Verbal and Thematic Links Between Poems and Books in Martial', in: *Papers of the Langford Latin Seminar* 13, 255–268.

Masterson, M. (2014), 'Studies of Ancient Masculinity', in: T.K. Hubbard (ed.), *A Companion to Greek and Roman Sexualities*, Malden, MA/Oxford/Chichester, 17–30.

Masterson, M./ Sorkin Rabinowitz, N./Robson, J. (eds.) (2015), *Sex in Antiquity: Exploring Gender and Sexuality in the Ancient World*, London, Routledge.

Miller, P.A. (1998), 'The Bodily Grotesque in Roman Satire: Images of Sterility', in: *Arethusa* 31, 398–418.

Miller, P.A./Platter, C. (eds.) (2005), *History in Dispute, vol. 20. Classical Antiquity and Classical Studies*, Detroit.

Moreno Soldevila, R./Marina Castillo, A./Fernández Valverde, J. (2019), *A Prosopography to Martial's Epigrams*, Berlin/Boston.

Morgan, L. (2005), 'Satire', in: S. Harrison (ed.), *A Companion to Latin Literature: Blackwell Companions to the Ancient World. Literature and Culture*, Oxford, 174–188.

Morreall, J. (2009), *Comic Relief. A Comprehensive Philosophy of Humor*, Oxford.

Mulligan, B. (2019), 'Obscenity in Epigram', in: C. Henriksén (ed.), *A Companion to Ancient Epigram*, Hoboken, 111–126.

Mindt, N. (2020), '*Accumulatio* as a Satirical Tool in Martial's Epigrams', in: D. Vallat (ed.), *Martial et l'épigramme satirique: Approches stylistiques et thématiques*, Hildesheim, 71–102.

O'Connor, E. (2019), '*Carminis incompti lusus*: The *Carmina Priapea*', in: C. Henriksén (ed.), *A Companion to Ancient Epigram*, Hoboken, 541–556.

Papaioannou, S./Serafim, A. (eds.) (2021), *Comic Invective in Ancient Greek and Roman Oratory*, Berlin/Boston.

Paraskeviotis, G.C. (2021), 'Humorous Unity and Disunity in Vergil's *Eclogues* 1 and 2', in: A. Michalopoulos/A. Serafim/F. Beneventano Della Corte/A. Vatri (eds.), *The Rhetoric of Unity and Division in Ancient Literature*, Berlin/Boston, 229–242.

Parker, H.N. (1997), 'The Teratogenic Grid', in: J.P. Hallett/M.B. Skinner (eds.), 47–65.

Plass, P. (1985), 'An Aspect of Epigrammatic wit in Martial and Tacitus', in: *Arethusa* 18, 187–210.

Raskin, V. (1985), *Semantic Mechanisms of Humour*, Dordrecht.

Richlin, A. (1981a), 'The Meaning of *irrumare* in Catullus and Martial', in: *Classical Philology* 76, 40–46.

Richlin, A. (1981b), 'Approaches to the Sources on Adultery at Rome', in: H.P. Foley (ed.), *Reflections of Women in Antiquity*, New York/London/Paris.

Richlin, A. (1992), *The Garden of Priapus: Sexuality and Aggression in Roman Humor*, Oxford.

Richlin, A. (1993), 'Not before Homosexuality: The Materiality of the *cinaedus* and the Roman Law against Love between Men', in: *Journal of the History of Sexuality* 3, 523–773.

Richlin, A. (2014), *Arguments with Silence: Writing the History of Roman Women*, Ann Arbor.

Richlin, A. (2015), 'Reading Boy-Love and Child-Love in the Greco-Roman World', in: M. Masterson/N.S. Rabinowitz/J. Robson (eds.), 352–373.

Roman, L. (2010), 'Martial and the City of Rome', in: *Journal of Roman Studies* 100, 88–117.

Selden, D.L. (2007), '*Ceveat lector*: Catullus and the Rhetoric of Performance', in: J.H. Gaisser (ed.) *Catullus: Oxford Readings in Classical Studies*, Oxford, 490–559.

Serafim, A. (2020), 'Comic Invective in the Public Forensic Speeches of Attic Oratory', in: *Hellenica* 68, 23–42.

Serafim, A. (2021), 'Comic Invective in Attic Forensic Oratory: Private Speeches', in: S. Papaioannou/Serafim, A. (eds.), *Comic Invective in Ancient Greek and Roman Oratory*, Berlin/Boston, 79–95.

Spisak, A.L. (2007), *Martial: A Social Guide*, London/Duckworth.

Sullivan, J.P. (1990), 'Martial and English Poetry', in: *Classical Antiquity* 9, 149–174.

Sullivan, J.P. (1991), *Martial: The Unexpected Classic*, Cambridge.

Vallat, D. (2020), 'Foedius nil est ! Le comparatif, un outil satirique au service de Martial', in: D. Vallat (ed.), *Martial et l'épigramme satirique: Approches stylistiques et thématiques*, Hildesheim, 149–182.

Verstraete, B.C. (2008), 'Slavery and the Social Dynamics of Male Homosexual Relations in Ancient Rome', in: *Journal of Homosexuality* 5, 227–236.

Watson, L.C./Watson, P.A. (2003), *Martial: Select Epigrams*, Cambridge.

Watson, L.C. (2004), 'Martial 12.32: An Indigent Immigrant?', in: *Mnemosyne* 57, 311–324.

Watson, L.C. (2019), 'The Masculine and the Feminine in Epigram', in: C. Henriksén (ed.),
A Companion to Ancient Epigram, Hoboken, 93–109.

Watson, P.A. (2005), *Non tristis torus et tamen pudicus*: The Sexuality of the *matrona* in Martial, in: *Mnemosyne* 58, 62–87.

Watson, L.C./Watson, P.A. (2015), *Martial*, London.

Williams, C.A. (1995), 'Greek Love at Rome', in: *Classical Quarterly* 45, 517–539.

Williams, C.A. (2004), *Martial, Epigrams Book Two: Edited with Introduction, Translation, and
Commentary*, Oxford.

Williams, C.A. (2006), 'Identified Quotations and Literary Models: The Example of Martial 2.41',
in: R.R. Nauta/H.J. van Dam/J.J.L. Smolenaars (eds.), *Flavian Poetry*, Leiden/Boston, 329–
348.

Williams, C.A. (2010), *Roman Homosexuality*, 2nd ed., New York.

Williams, C. (2015), 'The Language of Gender: Lexical Semantics and the Latin Vocabulary of
Unmanly Men', in: M. Masterson/N.S. Rabinowitz/J. Robson (eds.), 461–481.

Wills, G. (2008), 'Rome's Gossip Columnist: When the First-Century Poet Martial Turned his
Stylus on you, you Got the Point', in: *American Scholar* 77, 68–76.

Part VI: **The Scripts of Sexuality: Drama, Novel, Papyri and Later Texts**

Nikos Manousakis

To Voice the Physical: Sex and the Soil in Aeschylus

Abstract: The Aeschylean corpus (of plays and fragments) is the shortest in number of lines, compared to the Sophoclean and Euripidean corpora (taking no account of the most likely interpolated ending of *Seven against Thebes*), and in number of extant dramas (considering the disputed *Prometheus Bound*). Yet in this short corpus there is a clear and impressive pattern connected to sexual imagery. Aeschylus' oeuvre, often sensational in the use of sexual language, includes a series of bold — more or less explicit — references to sexual encounters expressed in terms of agricultural fertilisation: a suggestive orgasmic "vision" of slaughtering and a tale of cosmic "penetration" among them. This chapter discusses these references to sexual activity in Aeschylus, bringing to the fore the — rather neglected — sensuality of his poetry.

The question this chapter poses seems to be simple: how did Aeschylus, describe sexual acts in his poetry? Yet there is no obvious, comprehensive, answer to this question. To begin, I would pose a relevant problem: is it actually surprising for scholarship to address a research issue such as the imagery of sexual acts in Aeschylus' dramas? "[A]n ancient commentator on Apollonius mentions that [Aeschylus'] *Hypsipyle* featured an episode [that was] narrated in the *Argonautica*: the Argonauts were caught in a storm and forced to put in at Lemnos, but the Lemnian women attacked them with weapons and would not allow them to come ashore until they swore an oath to have sex with them. It may seem surprising that such an incident — which almost resembles the plot of *Lysistrata* — should have appeared in a tragedy[, and especially by Aeschylus] [...]. In fact, sexual content is perfectly permissible in tragedy, and a lot would have depended on the exact way in which the theme was handled".[1] The claim that sexual content is perfectly permissible in tragedy is true, but not quite evident. Greek tragedy, mainly Euripidean (for which the evidence for the lost plays is more abundant) but also Sophoclean, features some erotic narratives tied to physical appeal and (ardent) desire.[2] Yet, at first

---

1 Wright 2019, 59. See also Sommerstein 2008c, 250–251.
2 Of the lost tragedies by Sophocles and Euripides, it seems that the following had, or could have had, an erotic-sexual aspect: Soph. *Andromeda, Atreus/Women of Mycenae, Children of Aleus, Euryalus, Oenomaus, Phaedra, Phineus, Procris, Thyestes, Tyro, Women of Colchis*; Eur.

https://doi.org/10.1515/9783110695793-017

blush, the specifics of sexual intercourse, the discussion about coitus (unsurprisingly latent as it is due to the conventions of the genre), seems to be a terrain in which Greek tragedy seldom operates.[3] Still, Aeschylus, a poet often distortedly "solemnised" (a practice that seems to have its origins in classical times),[4] is a remarkable exception to this rule.[5] To examine this exception, in the present study I focus on a series of mostly individual passages, that are interconnected through imagery and symbolism.

Aeolus, Alcmeon in Corinth, Andromeda, Antigone, Auge, Cretan Women, Cretans, Chrysippus, Dictys, Hippolytus I (Καλυπτόμενος), Ino, Ixion, Meleager, Oedipus, Oenomaus, Peleus, Phoenix, Pleisthenes, Protesilaus, Scyrians, Stheneboea, Theseus, Thyestes. For each of these plays see, concisely, Wright 2019, *ad loc.*

3 "In general, there was much more focus on love [sex] in the lost plays [of Aeschylus, Sophocles and Euripides,] than in those which survived — a highly suggestive fact. Even though so much remains unknown about the history of transmission, it is hard to avoid suspecting some form of censorship or bowdlerization. Were the more erotic tragedies deliberately cut out of the canon in an attempt to create, by means of careful selection, a more narrowly defined, morally edifying version of the tragic genre?" See Wright 2019, 140–141.

4 Aeschylus is a long-misunderstood figure in this respect. Although probably the most characteristic quality of his work across the ages, solemn gravitas is only one of its aspects, and it does not render Aeschylus conservative in his art or, as a matter of fact, in his life; still, this is how he was received. Half a century after Aeschylus' death, Aristophanes composed *Fr.* "In the [ἀγών at the centre of this play] Euripides and Aeschylus are proxies for what comedians (as well as tragedians, litigants, historians, and philosophers) depict as an antithesis between [πονηροί] (bad, base, useless, inauthentic), the aesthetically, socially, and morally deviant, and [χρηστοί,] the good, noble, useful, authentic. Aeschylus represents [χρηστοί]. He has few allies in Hades, just as he would have at Athens, for "the good element (τὸ χρηστόν) is few and far between [there], just as it is here" (783). Aeschylus contends that poets should espouse what is fine and noble (τὰ χρηστά) and "conceal what is base and ignoble (τὸ πονηρόν) and not stage it or teach it" as he alleges Euripides did (1053–1054)". See Rosenbloom 2018, 71–72. Nevertheless, the actual Aeschylus seems to have had some less solemn aspects too. Plato (*Rep.* 2.383a–c) accuses him of portraying the gods as being dishonest and deceitful. Furthermore, Athenaeus (10.428f) blames Aeschylus for being the first to bring the spectacle of drunks onto the tragic stage in *Cabeiri*. Aeschylus is also fabled for his humorous, bawdy satyr-plays. In antiquity his satyr-plays, now almost all completely lost, were considered of the finest quality (See Diog. Laert. 2.133.5–8; Paus. 2.13.6.8–9). Notably, almost 19 (no less than 16) of the 75 satyr-plays known today are ascribed to him. In actual fact, one can readily believe this piece of information, since his humour is showcased, *mutatis mutandis*, even in the *Oresteia* (see Sommerstein 2002), which is, admittedly, the summit of his tragic art. For Aeschylus' satyr-plays see, e.g., Podlecki 2005. In the same vein, I will attempt to show in this study of sexual imagery that Aeschylus was anything but prudish.

5 Lost Aeschylean plays which would, probabilistically speaking, have encompassed some, more or less extensive, erotic-sexual touches are the following: *Cabeiri, Callisto, Carians or Europa, Danaids, Egyptians, Glaucus of Potniae, Ixion, Myrmidons, Nereids, Oreithuia, Polydectes, Semele, Toxotides, Women of Lemnos.* For each of these plays see concisely, Wright 2019, *ad loc.*

1 God and the maiden: Reverence for the erotic bodies

"Farming for the Greeks was central to their lives in ways unimaginable to denizens of an urban world[: this] makes agriculture the most powerful image for the relationship of humans to the natural world they must exploit to survive. [...] The metaphor of plowing to describe conjugal sex makes the parallelism of marriage and agriculture explicit[, while t]he plowing image was part of the traditional wedding ceremony. [...] Inherent in [...] this imagery is the idea that the woman is earthlike, a source of natural fertility most productive when subjected to masculine rational control".[6] This symbolism is variously present in the Aeschylean corpus.[7] In the corrupt (second century BC) papyrus fr. 99 Radt[8] from *Carians* or *Europa*,[9] we listen to the elderly protagonist, Europa, narrate how she was abducted by Zeus in the form of a bull,[10] and then,

---

6 See Thorton 1997, 145. Plutarch notes in *Mor.* 144b: πάντων ἱερώτατός ἐστιν ὁ γαμήλιος σπόρος καὶ ἄροτος ἐπὶ παίδων τεκνώσει. καλῶς τὴν Ἀφροδίτην ὁ Σοφοκλῆς "εὔκαρπον Κυθέρειαν" προσηγόρευσε. See further, duBois 1988, 39–85; Braswell 1988, 352; Sealey 1990, 25–26; Stehle 1997, 82–83; Stevens 1999, 113–114; Larson 2012, 23; Van Nortwick 2008, 500–552; and Håland 2017, 47–48. "The chief purpose of women was bearing children, particularly sons, and children were regarded as essential in the Greek world. It was woman as a mother who consistently was praised in the Greek world". See Bullough/Shelton/Slavin 1988, 57. Further, Finglass 2018, 259. In modern socio-anthropological terms, Michel Foucault 1978, 104 notes that in the course of the nineteenth and twentieth centuries sexuality is also deployed through "[a] socialization of procreative behaviour".
7 For the sex-related language and imagery of farming in Attic comedy, specifically Aristophanes, see the chapter by D. Kanellakis in this volume.
8 See Barrett 2007, 356; Keen 2005, 63–64. For the emendations and conjectures see TrGF III, 217–221.
9 On this play see the bibliography by Sommerstein 2008c, 111. West 2000 suggested that *Carians* or *Europa* and *Psychostasia* were composed or adapted by Euphorion, Aeschylus' son, who staged them along with *Memnon*, an authentic Aeschylean play, after his father's death. Yet, even though West has some convincing reasons to suspect the authenticity of *Psychostasia*, his arguments for athetising *Carians* or *Europa* are either too speculative (based on his expectations about the Aeschylean dramaturgy: in fact, Sleep and Death could have readily arrived on stage in *Carians* or *Europa* as Athena does in *Eum.* 403–404), or "merely pointers", as he himself admits (see West 2000, 349) — and some of them strained one might say — pointing towards a (rather problematic) connection with the unknown author of the disputed *Pr.*, often thought to be none other than Euphorion. For the athetesis of *Pr.* see Manousakis 2020c.
10 The piece distinctly resembles Euripides' expositional iambic monologic prologues with only the main character present on stage. If it actually is such a piece, it would be a rare case in the (known today) Aeschylean corpus of fully extant plays and fragments. Cf. the prologue spoken

γυνὴ θεῶι μειχθεῖσα παρθένου σέβας
ἤμειψα, παίδων δ' ἐζύγην ξυνάονι.
καὶ τρὶς γονᾶισι τοὺς γυναικείους πόνους
ἐκαρτέρησ' ἄρουρα, κοὐκ ἐμέμψατο
τοῦ μὴ 'ξενεγκεῖν σπέρμα γενναῖον πατρός[/πατήρ].
ἐκ τῶν μεγίστων δ' ἠρξάμην φυτευμάτων
Μίνων τεκοῦσα...¹¹

In intercourse with a god, a mortal girl myself, I exchanged the reverence of virginity, and I was yoked to a partner through children (in parenthood). And thrice the women's pains my arable soil endured, and it did not (ever) grumble so as not to bring forth Father's noble seed(s) [**or** and Father never accused it of not bringing forth the/his noble seed(s)]. And of those planted inside me, I began by (bringing forth) the greatest (sprouts), giving birth to Minos...¹²

"Generally throughout Greek literature, the act of sexual intercourse that engenders or aims at engendering offspring is called 'work', ['labour', 'toil',] while all other varieties of erotic activity are 'play'".¹³ In Europa's case, often also in real-life contexts, an aspiring lover would first have to face another "labour": getting

---

by the homonymous hero in Aeschylus' *Laius* (see the remnants of the ὑπόθεσις in TrGF III, 231). If Europa's speech does not derive from a monologic prologue, it may have been part of the first epeisodion, following an opening parodos: cf. Atossa expressing her concern about the welfare of Xerxres to the Chorus of Persian elders — just as Europa could be doing about Sarpedon to a Chorus of Carians/Lycians. Cf. also Soph. *Trach.* 1–48. See further Keen 2005, 67. At any rate, it is clear that one should be very careful when discussing (the date/introduction of) "Euripidean" opening monologues.

11 ἤμειψα and ἐζύγην is an emendation by Weil. The papyrus writing is ἤμειψε and ἐζύγη. See TrGF III, *ad loc.* For the male "sowing" the female cf. Pind. *Pyth.* 4.254–255; Aesch. *Eum.* 658–661, on which see further below; Soph. *Ant.* 569, *O.T.* 1497–1499; Eur. *Or.* 552–554, fr. 752g Kannicht 25–27 (from *Hypsipyle*), fr. 774 Kannicht 31–4 (from *Phaethon*). See also Soph. *Trach.* 31–33 (with the n. by Davies 1991 on vv. 31 and 33). Most importantly, see Thgn. 581–582, ἐχθαίρω δὲ γυναῖκα περίδρομον, ἄνδρα τε μάργον, | ὃς τὴν ἀλλοτρίην βούλετ' ἄρουραν ἀροῦν: "And I hate a woman who runs around, and a lecher who wants to plough a field belonging to another". The translation is by Gerber 1999. Notably, the man described here does not want to "plough" a woman to beget children. His objective is sexual enjoyment. This observation allows one to claim that the "ploughing" metaphor was used to imply sex for pleasure and not for procreation already in the mid-sixth century BC. Yet there is no such (verifiable) example in Greek tragedy. For the male partner's "yoke" cf. Soph. fr. 583 Radt 11–12 (from *Tereus*), in which (Procne says that) a single night, the wedding night of course, "yokes" women to a life they are forced to praise and to consider happy — even though it is far from being so. "[T]he common metaphor of yoke = marriage or other sexual union". See Barrett 1964, 263.

12 Unless otherwise acknowledged, the translations in this chapter are my own.

13 See Carson 1990, 149. Cf. Aesch. *Ag.* 1207 with the n. by Fraenkel 1950. See also Plut. *Lyc. et Num. comp.* 4.1.9.

the maiden from her guarding "owner", her father.[14] Yet Zeus is not just any lover. He experiences no difficulty in getting Europa, triggering the procreation of children: τοιόνδε μὲν Ζεὺς κλέμμα πρεσβύτου πατρὸς | αὐτοῦ μένων ἄμοχθον ἤνυσεν λαβεῖν.[15] Sch. AB Hom. *Il.* 12.292 (i 427, iii 506 Dindorf), citing Hesiod's *Catalogue of Women* (fr. 140 M.–W.) and also Bacchylides (fr. 10 Sn.), is an account of how Zeus fell in love with the Tyrian princess, daughter of Phoenix, when he caught sight of her in a meadow. He then descended, and took the form of a bull breathing crocus flowers: οὕτως τε τὴν Εὐρώπην ἀπατήσας ἐβάστασε, καὶ διαπορθμεύσας εἰς Κρήτην ἐμίγη αὐτῆι.[16] μείγνυμι, occurring in both the Hesiodic/Bacchylidean account(s) and Aeschylus' fragment from *Europa*, is regularly used in reference to sexual union.[17] During the (abrupt) act of lovemaking in the Aeschylean piece, Europa "concedes" her παρθένου σέβας, the most intimate possession virgins would have to revere, and would be revered for.[18] Interestingly enough, to

---

14 Cf. how strongly (and elaborately) Danaus advises his daughters to guard their virginity, their honour, in Aesch. *Supp.* 996–1013. On this, see below in detail. In Classical Athens, marriage was a transaction between men (the present "owner" of a maiden, her father (or guardian), and her future "owner", the man who would marry her) for which the girl's consent was not required.

15 "Zeus managed to steal such a loot from my old father *effortlessly*, without even having to move". Europa, in sharp contrast, loses her care-free maidenhood in a split second, and goes through a lot of pain in labour, to carry out this procreation. Typically, the virginity of a girl given in marriage was what the bridegroom got in exchange for his gifts to her and her family. In exchange for her virginity, Aeschylus' Europa gets a "yoke" to parenthood. For the labours of childbirth cf. e.g. Eur. *Med.* 1029–1031, *Suppl.* 918–921 and 1134–1135, *Tr.* 760. See also Aesch. *Ag.* 1417–1418; Soph. *O.C.* 553; Eur. *Phoen.* 30–31.

16 Cf. Hes. fr. 141 M.-W.

17 See, especially, *Il.* 9.275; *Od.* 1.73; Pin. *Pyth.* 3.14; Aesch. *Supp.* 295, fr. 281a Radt 32; Soph. *O.T.* 791, 995; Eur. *Andr.* 174, *Ion* 338, fr. 223 Kannicht 101.

18 The life of Greek παρθένοι "was fraught with anxieties surrounding the proper transition from [κόρη] to [γυνή]: sexual intercourse must not take place before marriage". See Lee 2015, 45. However, "it is not easy to capture the meaning of the [Greek] abstract noun [παρθενεία] with a purely sociological definition. It is something subject to seizure ([λαμβάνειν]), a treasure that one guards ([φυλάσσειν]), a value that must be respected (τηρεῖν). A seducer offers gifts in exchange for this prize, which he unwraps ([λύειν]) with the first embrace". See Sissa 1990a, 77, who, as a matter of fact, indicates that for the Greeks virginity was not wholly tied to the breaking of the hymen, and was not irrevocably lost after sexual intercourse took place. "Penetration by a male organ deflowered a virgin, [... but] the event existed only if it was found out [...] or revealed by its consequences. [...] Only seduction could be verified". See Sissa 1990a, 105. Female virginity, as it is notably suggested from Archil. fr. 196a West, seems to be a quality fading away, a fruit ripening until (sooner or later) it gets overripe (as one becomes more and more engaged into sexual practice?). See also, Fletcher 2007 for Aeschylus' virginal Choruses; Manousakis 2020a for this poet's treatment of an accusation for the loss of virginity.

a certain extent analogous — far more pathetically articulated though — is the kind of σέβας occurring in Aesch. fr. 135 Radt:

σέβας δὲ μηρῶν ἀγνὸν οὐκ ἐπῃδέσω,
ὦ δυσχάριστε τῶν πυκνῶν φιλημάτων

And you felt no shame for (failing (to honour)) my holy reverence for your thighs [, getting yourself killed], you ungrateful for the countless firm kisses[19]

In this fr. from *Myrmidons* we, most likely, hear Achilles "reproaching the dead Patroclus for having disobeyed his instructions not to advance too far towards Troy".[20] The erotic context of the reproach is clear from the allusion to intercrural sex and the reference to the countless firm kisses.[21] Plato (*Symp.* 180a = Aesch. fr.

---

19 Or possibly: "And you felt no shame for (failing (to honour)) the holy reverence in our (united) thighs[, getting yourself killed], you ungrateful for the countless firm kisses". I do favour the translation in the body of the text, mainly due to the obvious significance of specifically the *erōmenos'* thighs in intercrural sex (see n. 21 below), and also due to Achilles' wailing self-absorption in *Myrmidons*. When Patroclus dies, Achilles laments only for himself, for what he has lost, not for the dead; and this makes him very human: a masterfully crafted hero. For the special meaning of σέβας and αἰδώς in this passage see Cairns 1993, 211.
20 See Sommerstein 2008c, 145.
21 Here "the kisses should hardly be imagined as being delivered only on the mouth". See Friis Johansen/Whittle 1980(III), 326. About the homosexual relationship between Achilles and Patroclus in Aeschylus' *Myrmidons* see Dover 1978, 197–198; Moreau 1996, 16–20; Michelakis 2002, 41–53; Fantuzzi 2012, 215–225; and Leitao 2018. The double (as far as we know) reference to the (erotic) thighs in *Myrmidons* (fr. 135 and 136 Radt), seems to point to the practice of intercrural (interfemoral) sex (cf. Solon fr. 25 West; Anacr. 407 and 439 PMG (cf. Anacreontea 17.32–7); Soph. fr. 345 Radt). That is, a means for the *erastēs* in a pederastic relationship to achieve gratification without imposing on the *erōmenos* the potential shame of penetration (the utter feminisation of the beloved). In intercrural sex, the *erastēs* would rub his penis between the thighs of the *erōmenos* to create friction that would lead to ejaculation. A concept mainly derived from picto-rial evidence. "Recent scholarship has tended to follow Dover in emphasising the issue of pene-tration in its view of Greek sexual ethics: in this view, anal sex is a defining element of the crude relations with which idealised pederasty contrasts. The prevalence of intercrural scenes in vase painting has been used as evidence for this proposition, but in fact there are a few scenes in vase painting that indicate acceptance of anal sex—or at least the *erastēs'* desire for it—in respectable pederastic relations". See Lear 2015, 126. Actually, the insistence of vase-painting "upon inter-crural intercourse [could be] a kind of visual euphemism: it is a portrayal of sex, but at the same time, a way of avoiding the portrayal of other[,less admirable,] kinds of sex". See Lear/Cantarella 2008, 106. Intercrural intercourse may have been a "disclosable", "hypotonic and somewhat un-satisfactory avenue of sexual gratification" (see Kapparis 2018, 198), and anal penetration, even in decent pederastic relationships, such as that between the two Myrmidon leaders, may not have been out of the question. The "stylization [in vase-painting] — shielding the *erōmenos* from

134a Radt) informs us that in this play Achilles was Patroclus' older lover, his
erastēs. This is confirmed by Achilles' "obsession" with Patroclus' thighs, and the
erotic bond the *erastēs* and the *erōmenos* created through the latter's thighs. In
Aesch. fr. 136 Radt — in a context similar to that of fr. 135 Radt — Achilles says
how he, by shedding tears, has shown due respect for the loss of Patroclus as an
erotic body; since what he recalls in mourning is his sexual intercourse with his
erōmenos — Patroclus' thighs specifically: μηρῶν τε τῶν σῶν ηὐσεβησ' ὁμιλία |
κλαίων.[22] Patroclus' wretched body, and Achilles' fierce desire to caress it, disregarding the miasma of touching, even kissing, the corpse, is, most likely, what fr.
137 Radt also indicates. σέβας ... μηρῶν ἁγνόν in fr. 135 Radt, "my holy reverence
for your thighs", evokes a striking Aeschylean parallel. In *Eum.* 885–7 Athena
keenly attempts to persuade the Furies to stay in Athens, saying:

> ἀλλ' εἰ μὲν ἁγνόν ἐστί σοι Πειθοῦς σέβας,
> γλώσσης ἐμῆς μείλιγμα καὶ θελκτήριον,
> σὺ δ' οὖν μένοις ἄν·[23]

Yet if, on the one hand, holy reverence for Persuasion — for the soothing effect and the
charm of my words — resides in you, then you will stay.

Thus, in the Aeschylean universe the *erōmenos'* (Patroclus') thighs and divine
Persuasion, can somehow be described in similar terms. A reverential designation such as ἁγνὸν σέβας is rather unsurprising when applied to *Peithō*, a deity[24]

---

the crudity of debasing penetration — should not surprise us" (see Parker 2015, 68), and it is not
unexpected that serious art, such as tragedy, would employ this pattern. Hence, if the concept
of the socially "admissible" intercrural coitus that could be made public, protecting the penetrated from being considered as socially inferior to the penetrator, is sound, Aeschylus might
very well have exploited in tragedy a sexual practice that was favoured by the visual arts, to
shape his homoerotic description/allusion and keep Patroclus socially intact. On intercrural and
penetrative sex see also Thorton 1997, chapter 4 and 8 *passim*; Cohen 2004; Davidson 2004. Besides Achilles and Patroclus in Aeschylus, the only other surviving reference to a homosexual-
pederastic couple in Greek tragedy occurs in Soph. fr. 448 Radt (a dying son of Niobe invokes his
lover).

22 I render here Hermann's and Dobree's conjectures for the εὐσεβής and †καλλίωτ in the codd.
See TrGF III, *ad loc.*

23 I follow the punctuation favoured by Page 1972 and West 1990a. Sommserstein 2008b adopts
a different view.

24 In Aeschylus ἁγνός and its variants are in the main associated with the gods (their tem-
ples/altars/offerings to). See n. 89 below for *Supp.* Also, *Per.* 611, 628, *Sev.* 163, 278, *Ag.* 94, 135,
(220 and 245 on Iphigenia's sacrifice), *Ch.* [986] (on Agamemnon's murder/sacrifice), *Eum.* 287,
326, 716, 885, frr. 44.1 and 155.2 Radt (also fr. 300.6 Radt on the vitalising waters (of the rain, the
snow Helios is melting, and the Nile) in Egypt). *Sev.* 753 (on Oedipus defiling the sacrosanct

closely associated with Aphrodite.[25] In contrast, it is suggestive about the sexual bond between Achilles and Patroclus. Based on this linguistic "concurrence" one may claim that Aeschylus seems to consider a divine personification and a sexual act/connection between two men to be of equal weight.[26] The body of the maiden in fr. 99 Radt, the body of the *erōmenos* in fr. 135 Radt, and the divine Persuasion in *Eum.* 885–887 (a crucial strand of sexual seduction) are all tied to (holy) σέβας. That is because the maiden and the *erōmenos* are revered bodies. The maiden loses her revered status along with her virginity, and the same would apply to the young boy when his beard would begin to grow, and he would stop being an *erōmenos*.

Further, one notices that Aeschylus is far less reserved when it comes to the expression of homosexual as opposed to heterosexual intercourse. That is, although Europas' exchange of παρθένου σέβας in fr. 99 Radt, e.g., is a bold but quasi-allegorical sexual undertone, Achilles' σέβας… μηρῶν in fr. 135 Radt, strengthened by fr. 136 and 137 Radt, is a daring homoerotic narrative. As we will

---

"soil" of his mother by having intercourse with her), and fr. 242 Radt (on virgin girls) offer the only, yet distant, Aeschylean parallels to the erotic context of ἁγνός in fr. 135 Radt. The context of *Eum.* 885–887 is quasi-erotic. On this, see further below. σέβας is used in Aeschylus for the gods (see *Supp.* 85, 396, *Ag.* 515, *Ch.* 644, *Eum.* 885), revered social roles (parents (see *Supp.* 707, *Eum.* 545), unmarried sisters (see *Ch.* 243), (wandering) suppliants (see *Eum.* 92), virgins (see fr. 99 Radt 5)) and entities (land (of the ancestors (see *Supp.* 776)), civic institutions (court of law (see *Eum.* 690, 700)), and the dead (righteous rulers, see *Ch.* 55, 156, 628). σέβας occurs in Aeschylus in a strictly sexual context only in *Myrmidons* (fr. 135 and 136 Radt).

25 *Peithō* "is assistant to Aphrodite in Hesiod's account of the creation of Pandora, and appears in the same capacity in a number of visual narratives, notably at the birth of Aphrodite and in the seduction of Helen. [...] *Peithō* [...] [is] almost always linked with Aphrodite, and the closeness of this association is demonstrated by a number of occurrences of *Peithō* as a cult title of Aphrodite". See Stafford 2000, 111. *Peithō*, Persuasion, is crucial for both the sexual and civic seductions. Both erotic and civic *Peithō* have their seat on the lips/mouth. See Buxton 1982, 190–191 n. 25. See also Ibyc. fr. 288 PMG, where a gentle (soft) look is attributed to *Peithō*, following Aphrodite. The "Athenians associated Aphrodite *Pandēmos* [...] with *Peithō* [...] in both art and cult. When the two were represented together in art and worshipped side by side, unification was generally the main theme. Their powers were sought not only in the obvious arenas of love and marriage, but also in the political realm, to unite groups of people in common political agendas. [...] [T]he power of persuasion was of such great importance in matters of erotic love as well as in matters of rhetoric that the abstract noun was eventually transformed into a [...] goddess [...] [who] is both a deity in her own right and personifies an aspect of Aphrodite's powers". See Rosenzweig 2004, 13 and 19. For *Peithō* specifically in Greek tragedy see, in detail, Buxton 1982 (pp. 109–114 on *Eum.*); also, the discussion below on the "seduction" of the Furies by Athena in *Eum.*

26 See Archil. fr. 196a West 15 for heterosexual coitus referred to as θεῖον χρῆμα.

see, while the single Aeschylean homosexual account preserved clearly points to the actual sexual practice, the mouth and thighs being its focus, Aeschylean accounts of heterosexual intercourse — allusions to penetrative sex — are all variously determined by the concept of fertility and procreation, with no literal focus on coitus itself.

The intercourse between the god and the maiden in Aesch. fr. 99 Radt is expressed in terms of plowing. Europa is "yoked" to Zeus' "plough", who "furrows" her "soil", her vagina, sowing his divine "seed", his semen, inside her.[27] Zeus' "plowing" is very effective, leading to the procreation of great offspring. According to the account(s) of Hesiod and Bacchylides, after having sex with Europa, Zeus arranged for her to live with Asterion, king of Crete, and, as she became pregnant from the god, she gave birth to three boys. It seems rather unclear if Europa's sons, Minos, Rhadamanthys, and Sarpedon, are considered triplets according to this account,[28] yet the language of the Homeric scholiast renders it possible.[29] On the contrary, the language in the Aeschylean piece speaks to the strong probability that Europa's sons resulted from three separate births. If so, one could argue that Zeus "ploughed" Europa not once, but three times.[30]

In having sex with Zeus, Europa exchanges her virginity/maidenhood for parenthood.[31] And that is what an actual Greek bride would do (the rite): a passage from the house of the father to that of the husband, ἐπὶ γνησίων τέκνων σπορᾶι/παίδων ἐπ' ἀρότωι γνησίων.[32] In this piece Europa speaks (proudly) about

---

27 Apart from the idea that men own women as they own their land, the metaphor is also tied to the functional and physiological resemblance between agricultural furrows and female genitalia: a soft, pleating, vertical area, in the centre of which lies a hole, an opening. Some natural matter (seed/semen) is put inside that opening, and after a certain amount of time an offspring comes out.

28 According to the much later account of Nonnus of Panoplis *Dion.* 1.352, Europa became pregnant with twins (διδύμηι σφριγόωσα γονῆι κυμαίνετο γαστήρ: Minos and Rhadamanthys) by Zeus. In his *Europa* (166) Moschos speaks of children in general, without giving a number.

29 Were Europa's children considered sons of Asterion? It is interesting that Pausanias, *Descr.* 2.31.1, refers to the Minotaur as Asterion the son of Minos.

30 In his account Diodorus Siculus, *Library* 5.78.2, says that of the three boys born to Zeus and Europa, Minos became king of Crete (evidently after Asterion's death), since he was the eldest (πρεσβύτατον ὄντα). This could either mean that Europa went through three separate labours, or that in a single labour the first to come out of her womb was Minos, followed by Rhadamanthys and Sarpedon.

31 Cf. Aesch. *Supp.* 578–581: Io ἀποστάζει … αἰδῶ "("sheds", i.e. loses, not "exudes")", see Friis Johansen/Whittle 1980(II), 464, and gives birth to a flawless child.

32 For the ancient Greek marriage ceremony see Oakley/Sinos 1993; Garland 1990, 217–225. See further, Redfield 1982; on the wedding ritual in Greek tragedy see Seaford 1987.

how either her fertile "soil", her womb, never complained about the (triple) pains of labour she had to go through to bring forth Father's (if πατρός is right) seed, or about how the Father (if πατήρ is right) of the gods never complained that her womb, was no apposite — infertile or frail — place for his seed. In any case, Europa's procreative power, the resilience of her womb, are highlighted.[33] The notion of the womb protecting the embryo, making sure that someone's else's "matter" is brought forth in the right way, evokes Apollos' "theory" in *Eum.* 658–661: a woman's share in procreation is only to keep the embryo safe.[34] "[T]he women of the myth are notorious [...] [for proving quite] unreliable as containers [...]; both Zeus and Apollo find it necessary to snatch offspring out of a mother's womb and internalise it for safekeeping (as Zeus takes Dionysos from Semele, Apollo rescues Asklepios from Koronis)".[35] Aeschylus' Europa seems to be saying that her womb more than fulfilled its purpose.[36]

---

33 πατρός occurring in lines two and nine in the same metrical position makes it not impossible that the second time it was introduced by some scribe's mistake. "The text is very uncertain at many points, having been copied carelessly by what is apparently a thirteen- or fourteen-year-old boy". See Keen 2005, 64. However, cf. e.g. *Ch.* 106 and 108 (though in stichomythia). The patient, uncomplaining, womb option for the Aeschylean text may be strengthened by contrasting fr. 932 Radt from an unknown Sophoclean drama: ὅρκοισι γάρ τοι καὶ γυνὴ φεύγει πικρὰν | ὠδῖνα παίδων· ἀλλ' ἐπεὶ λήξῃ κακοῦ, | ἐν τοῖσιν αὐτοῖς δικτύοις ἁλίσκεται | πρὸς τοῦ παρόντος ἱμέρου νικωμένη: "And women, let me tell you, swear to stay away from the bitter labour of childbirth. But as soon as their pains are over, conquered by the arousal of the moment, they are caught in the very same mesh". Cf. Eur. *Phoen.* 355–6. In Soph. fr. 932 Radt, sexual pleasure and the pains of labour are juxtaposed. The latter are so strong, they make women promise (every time) to keep away from the pleasures of penetrative intercourse (note the negative language used to describe these pleasures for women); even if this is not a promise they can keep. In any case, there is no way to tell if Aeschylus wrote πατρός or πατήρ in line nine. For the conjectures see TrGF III, 219.

34 According to the "medical" theory Apollo employs, "[n]ot only is the mother not the genetic parent of the child she bears; she is not even to be honoured with the credit of bringing it safely to birth. The credit belongs to "god" [...], who preserves or destroys the foetus according as he is favourably or unfavourably disposed to the *father*". See Sommerstein 1989, 209.

35 See Carson 1990, 155; n. 39 below. See further, Gottschall 2008 for the significance of the female procreative power in the Homeric society and conflict.

36 Europa's pride about her offspring, how she conceived and brought to light illustrious children, evokes Niobe, the boastful mother who lost all her (many great) children—as did the complaining Europa in the fragment under discussion: Minos is dead, Rhadamanthys is immortal but beyond reach, and Sarpedon will be proven dead soon. Aeschylus treated Niobe's myth in a homonymous tragedy (quite famous in antiquity), which opened with Niobe sitting at her children's tomb. On this play see the bibliography provided by Sommerstein 2008c, 161. Cf. Aesch. fr. 100 Radt: ἀλλ' Ἄρης φιλεῖ | ἀεὶ τὰ λῶιστα πάντ' ἀπανθίζειν στρατοῦ, if — by any chance — it refers to Sarpedon. Yet Aesch. fr. 99 Radt 17–18 shows that it most likely refers to armies in general.

2 A word misunderstood: The parent is he who provides the seed

Apollo's famous male vs. female parent argument in *Eum.* 658–661, tied to the "plowing" sexual metaphor, is also exquisitely interesting as regards explicit (precise) sexual language; and this aspect of the narrative has not been sufficiently stressed. Let us examine the passage more closely:

οὐκ ἔστι μήτηρ ἡ κεκλημένη τέκνου
τοκεύς, τροφὸς δὲ κύματος νεοσπόρου·
τίκτει δ' ὁ θρῴσκων, ἡ δ' ἅπερ ξένῳ ξένη
ἔσωσεν ἔρνος, οἷσι μὴ βλάψῃ θεός.

The so-called "mother" is no parent of the child, but merely the nourisher of the *newly sown foetus*; the begetter is *the one ejaculating* (*the one from whom the semen squirts* (the one providing the seed)) [i.e. the male ejaculating inside the female], and she — as a (friendly) stranger (would do) for a (friendly) stranger — only preserves the *young sprout/offspring*; (and just) for those in whose case god is not to inflict harm.[37]

As Sommerstein observes, "we are a long way here from the divinely ordained marriage-bond of which Apollo spoke so impressively in [*Eum.*] 213–223".[38] In this passage the newly sown embryo is the form the male's semen takes inside the female. The female's responsibility is to protect and nourish the embryo, as the land does for the seed.[39] A child is begotten through the woman by a man's substance and effort, as a plant is begotten by a farmer's effort through the land.

---

37 For this theory of reproduction and Apollo's argument see, concisely, Sommerstein 1989, 206–208.

38 See Sommerstein 1989, 209.

39 "While women's centrality in reproduction is taken for granted in mythical examples of goddesses, such as Gaia and Hera, who manage to reproduce parthenogenically, scientific debates [...] tend to assume the primacy of the father. Some thinkers believed in what is called the one-seed theory (in which foetal material derived only from the father), while others subscribed to the two-seed theory (which attributed foetal material to both parents). The most notorious example of the one-seed theory occurs in [Apollo's speech in *Eum.*]". See Hong 2012, 75. Greeks also "attributed [male surrogate parentage] to their gods, and the metaphor of male pregnancy was an especially productive one in Greek thought. It is as old as our earliest evidence, for Homer knew Zeus as the birthing parent of Athena. Hesiod's account of the tale put it squarely in the context of the maintenance of male control and authority: Zeus, warned that Metis would give birth to a god greater than himself, swallowed her and subsequently gave birth to Athena from his head. Zeus also took over Semele's pregnancy after he blasted her with a thunderbolt when she unwisely asked him to appear to her in his true form; nurturing the infant in his thigh, he

There is a clear inconsistency here, of course, since even though the semen is a substance springing from the male, the seed is a product of the land to which it returns to be "reborn". As regards sexual language, what is striking in the passage is the use of θρώισκω. "[I]n its sexual sense [this verb], and its synonym θόρνυμαι, are at home in satyr-play [...] and in zoology [...]; so the use of θρώισκων here strikes a remarkably bestial note, especially since φύσας [...] or κύσας [...] might have been used".[40] According to the LSJ, θρώισκω means "to leap", "spring", "dart"; and, as a synonym of θόρνυμαι, it can also mean "to mount" or "impregnate". In *Eum.* 660, it is widely taken to mean "to mount". Interestingly enough, the two examples concerning the latter sense of the verb in the LSJ are both derived from Aeschylus. Besides *Eum.* 660, the verb occurs in its sexual sense in fr. 15 Radt from Aeschylus' satyric *Amymone*:[41] θρώισκων κνώδαλα. This fr. is obtained from Hesychius' lexicon θ 814, and is explained as: ἐκθορίζων, καὶ σπερματίζων. γεννῶν. But how did a verb that primarily means "to leap", "spring", etc. end up meaning "mounting/impregnating"? Might the implied "leap" be that onto a sexual partner? Actually, the answer seems to have been lying with Hesychius all along. "Several roots served for "jump" in Proto-Indo-European. [...] Alongside [the Middle Irish] *dar-* "spring", [one finds the Greek] θρώισκω, "spring, attack, assault", and [the Sanskrit] *dhārā* "flood", ["torrent, stream, flow";] Greek [also] contributes θορός "semen", presumably with the emphasis on ejaculation rather than the substance, as part of the cognate set from **dher-* "leap, spring"".[42] Thus, θρώισκω was presumably first associated with performing sexual activities, "mounting" and "impregnating", through the "stream" created when semen squirts, "springs", "leaps" out of the penis — and has probably nothing to do with specifically mounting on a sexual partner. Hesychius' ἐκθορίζων, referring to the semen, and σπερματίζων, are quite accurate. θρώισκω, which at first had this special sense, was at some point synecdochally identified with γεννάω. Yet in *Eum.* 660 (and most likely in Aesch. fr. 15 Radt) it is evidently tied to the "ejaculating" meaning, signifying the procreative sex act

---

gave birth to Dionysus. In both cases, the father of the gods maintained control by usurping the female role of childbearing. These fantasies were facilitated by popular notions of the roles of the sexes in reproduction that reduced the female role to little more than a mere incubator. [...] The idea that the woman supplied only nourishment [to the embryo] was given philosophical sanction when Aristotle assigned to the female the role of supplying only lowly matter, whereas the male provided the vital element of form, thus determining the child's rational (and therefore human) nature". See Demand 1994, 134–135.

40 See Sommerstein 1989, 209.

41 For *Amymone* see, concisely, Sommerstein 2008c, 8–9.

42 See Mallory/Adams 2006, 399.

performed by a man, the partner who provides the semen, on a woman (or even on a wild creature).

Eum. 660 is by no means surprising, since there are various passages in the *Oresteia* in which Aeschylus' language is sexually explicit and/or low. In *Eum.* 644 Apollo addresses the Furies as παντομισῆ κνώδαλα, στύγη θεῶν.[43] "The vulgarity of Apollo's reaction [against his adversaries in the Areopagus] is without parallel [...]. Nowhere else in tragedy are human (let alone divine) characters addressed as 'beasts' [...]: that is the language of satyr-play [...] and comedy [...]".[44] Furthermore, Cilissa, Orestes' nurse, describes in *Ch.* 755–760 how she had to constantly be on guard when Orestes was little, to clean his wrappings, since babies do not let their nurses know when they need to pee, and the same applies to defecation.[45] In *Ag.* 1438–1447 Clytemnestra calls Agamemnon Cassandra's λυμαντήριον,[46] her defiler, deflowerer, panderer, and Χρυσηίδων μείλιγμα τῶν ὑπ' Ἰλίωι, the soother (the tender lover) of many Trojan women like Chryseis. She also refers to Cassandra as ναυτίλων δὲ σελμάτων ἱστοτρίβην.[47] Even though much later, at Strabo 8.6.20, "ἵστος 'mast', [...] is used as slang for an erect penis. [Such] an obscene pun, [Agamemnon's] 'mast-rubber'[48] [in the ship's benches],

---

43 In Aeschylus, κνώδαλα is mainly used literally for the (often vicious) animals-beasts: see *Supp.* 264, 1000; *Ch.* 588, 601. Only in *Supp.* 762 the word is tied to the bestial (sexual?) attitude of men. Cf. Aesch. fr. 47a Radt 775 from *Net-Haulers* for the satyrs (κνώδαλα), who Danae is certain will sexually abuse her.

44 See Sommerstein 1989, 204; *id.* 2002, 162.

45 See *Ch.* 755–760. Cilisssa's "feeling of loss is significantly based on her unique relationship to Orestes' body — even to the liquids of his body — and is substantiated by her strikingly vivid manner of describing it. [...] Her low social status perhaps allows her to speak [...] even (oddly) comically about these matters". See Nooter 2017, 230-231. See also Sommerstein 2002, 159–160.

46 "λυμαντήριος [of the house (of Agamemnon)] is applied [by Cilisssa] to Aegisthus at *Ch.* 764, and its cognates suggest a rapist or seducer (Eur. *Hipp.* 1068, *Bacch.* 354). γυναικὸς τῆσδε therefore refers to Cassandra not Clytemnestra herself, and would have been clarified with a gesture". See Raeburn/Thomas 2011, 220. Cf. how the desperate Danae, evidently terrified that she will be raped by the satyrs, uses λυμανθήσομαι in Aesch. fr. 47a Radt 776.

47 "For the ἱστοτρίβης of the MSS [...] most editions give Pauw's ἱστοτριβής. The usual translation of this is "die mit ihm auf des Schriffes Ruderbänken gelegen war" (Nägelsbach) [...] [However,] the general rule [is] that ἱσο- compounds admit a verbal element in the Hellenistic age and not before [...]. [Therefore, and] since in ἱσοτριβής or ἱσοτρίβης the second element cannot reasonably be derived from τριβή or τρίβος, such a compound cannot be ascribed to fifth-century speech, and [...] the conjecture is wrong". See Fraenkel 1950, 680–681. Page 1972 adopts Pauw's emendation in his text. West 1990 and Sommerstein 2008b follow the MSS.

48 See further Friis Johansen/Whittle 1980(III) on *Supp.* 1042, τρίβοι τ' ἐρώτων: "If τρίβοι denotes "rubbings" (cf. *Ag.* 391), it signifies erogenic friction preparatory to sexual intercourse and its contextual aptness is clear enough. This erotic signification is doubtless more or less what is

[seems] unusual in Greek tragedy and especially shocking from female lips, but fits the sexual context, and the word's position at the climax of a sentence of abuse".[49] In the following lines Clytemnestra addresses Cassandra as a relish, a side-dish Agamemnon attempted to supply to the pleasures of her own bed. That is, Clytemnestra standing over the corpses of her husband and his mistress put side by side, sarcastically comments on Agamemnon's will to "spice up" their sex life, the pleasures she could offer in bed, by bringing home a new "treat".[50]

---

assumed, though euphemistically rendered, by Headlam ("dalliance"), Wecklein ("Kosen") [...]. It is apparently not attested elsewhere for τρίβος, but is common enough for τρίβειν and various compounds of it: cf. [Soph.] fr. 483.2 (a satyr-play)".

49 See Raeburn/Thomas 2011, 221. Also, Bardel 2002, 62. Cf. Aesch. fr. 78a Radt 29–30, with Sommerstein 2008c, 89 n. 7. See further Henderson 1975, 176 for τρίβειν. In the same passage Clytemnestra says that Cassandra is Agamemnon's κοινόλεκτρος, πιστὴ ξύνευνος, and φιλήτωρ ("strikingly applied here not to a man as (in the Greek view) the active participant in sex, but to Cassandra. As in the use of the neuter μείλιγμα in 1439, Clytemnestra [seems to be] presenting Agamemnon as unmanly and passive". See Raeburn/Thomas 2011, 221). Sommerstein 2008b, 175 renders ἱστοτρίβης as "this cheap whore of the ship's benches". See also Sommerstein 2002, 154–6.

50 *Ag.* 1446–1447: ἐμοὶ δ᾽ ἐπήγαγεν | εὐνῆς παροψώνημα τῆς ἐμῆς χλιδῆς. See LSJ *s.v.* παροψώνημα. Page 1972 retains the εὐνῆς of the MSS. Fraenkel 1950, followed by West 1990 and Sommerstein 2008b, holds εὐνῆς to be corrupt. Fraenkel 1950, 686–687 notes that "εὐνῆς may have crept in as an undiscerning gloss on χλιδῆς and displaced the original word. Perhaps this was an adjectival attribute to παροψώνημα; but a word of some quite different kind is also conceivable". Yet the critics who reject it consider εὐνῆς to refer to Clytemnestra's adultery with Aegisthus, and χλιδῆς to refer to Agamemnon's vindictive killing. Further, there has been a rather long discussion concerning the subject of ἐπήγαγεν. See especially Pulleyn 1997, 565. I suggest that the key to the meaning of this passage lies with a piece in Soph. *Trach.* Fraenkel 1950, 686 aptly indicates that "[a]nyone who has studied in detail the manner in which Sophocles draws on Aeschylean material can have no doubt that here the younger poet, dealing with a similar situation, had in mind the crowning line [(*Ag.* 1447)] of Clytemnestra's speech, [in composing *Trah.* 538]". However, Fraenkel — surprisingly — fails to notice how in *Trach.* 536–542 Sophocles thematically elaborates and adapts *Ag.* 1446–1447. Agamemnon supplied (ἐπήγαγεν) Cassandra to Clytemnestra as a side-dish (παροψώνημα) to be added up to the pleasures of (t)he(i)r bed: to add up for himself, of course, something new and special to the sexual pleasures Clytemnestra('s bed) had to offer. This does not mean that the three of them were literally sharing the same bed, but that Agamemnon would have a double source of sexual satisfaction readily available. Similarly, Heracles sent as a repayment (ἀντέπεμψε) to his wife Deianira a (female) "gift" (οἰκούρια (sc. δῶρα)) to "share" their bed of love. See also Sommerstein 2002, 156–157.

3 Reaching sexual climax: Clytemnestra's satisfaction in slaughter

Nowhere in his surviving plays and fragments is Aeschylus as forward in the use of sexual imagery as in *Ag.* 1388–1392 — not surprisingly — spoken by Clytemnestra:

> οὕτω τὸν αὑτοῦ θυμὸν ὁρμαίνει πεσών,
> κἀκφυσιῶν ὀξεῖαν αἵματος σφαγὴν
> βάλλει μ' ἐρεμνῆι ψακάδι φοινίας δρόσου,
> χαίρουσαν οὐδὲν ἧσσον ἢ διοσδότωι
> γάνει σπορητὸς κάλυκος ἐν λοχεύμασιν.

Thus, fallen down, he spews his soul — and breathing out/spouting[51] a jagged gush of the blood of his slaughter, he hits/spatters me with a pitch-black drizzle of the gory dew; at which I was taking no less pleasure than the ripening corn takes at the bright, refreshing, heaven-sent water, when labouring for the bursting of the bud.

The sexual suggestiveness of this passage is quite evident to some scholars, while others negate it.[52] Still, there are various suggestions to be made, some of them crucial, and one could add them to this discussion in an attempt to clear up the question. To begin, it has been overlooked how empirically accurate Aeschylus seems to be, concerning the agricultural "knowledge" he conveys. How Clytemnestra describes the third blow she inflicts on Agamemnon (*Ag.* 1386–1387), distinctly invokes a ritual sacrifice: καὶ πεπτωκότι | τρίτην ἐπενδίδωμι, τοῦ κατὰ χθονός | Διὸς νεκρῶν σωτῆρος εὐκταίαν χάριν.[53] What we hear right after — in this peculiar, personal messenger speech/death narrative — is how the queen felt when she saw her husband conquered, splattering her with his blood: she felt like σπορητὸς κάλυκος ἐν λοχεύμασιν, when receiving the διόσδοτον γάνος. But why did Aeschylus focus here on a very specific moment (κάλυκος ἐν λοχεύμασιν) in the growing process of corn (σπορητός): the bursting of the seed coat? Most likely because "the period after crop emergence is critical for [its] growth, and

---

51 "Although the poet does not go into unnecessary anatomical details, his picture is presumably based on the general idea that at least one of the three πληγαί has damaged Agamemnon's lungs (a typical wound, cf. *Cho.* 639f.): in his desperate struggle for breath he spits blood". See Fraenkel 1950, 655.
52 See Allen-Hornblower 2016, 192 n. 479 for the bibliography.
53 See, in detail, Fraenkel 1950, 652, 658–659; O'Daly 1985, 11–12; Raeburn/Thomas 2011, 214–216; and Allen-Hornblower 2016, 191 (n. 477 for bibliography on corrupted sacrifice in Greek tragedy, to which add Zeitlin 1966). Cf. Aesch. fr. 55 Radt from the *Epigoni* for the third libation to Zeus the Saviour.

prolonged delays in watering influence crop yield negatively [...]. A delay of [one] week in the first post-sowing watering from the appropriate period reduces wheat yields by 78 [kilograms per hectare]".[54]

Hence, the most important time to make sure there is adequate water is when the seeds absorb it to activate the biochemical mechanisms required for germination and growth. After absorbing enough water, the plant embryo eventually bursts the outer shell of the seed and the growing sprout emerges.[55] An additional agricultural note tied to fertilisation one can possibly indicate in the Aeschylean passage under discussion is that blood makes a first-class manure.[56] "The power of dead bodies to fertilise the ground after a battle or execution was known to [...] Archilochus by 700 BC and even earlier to the Jews".[57] Furthermore, a scholion in Lucian's *Dialogi Meretricii*[58] informs us that during the fertility festival of *Thesmophoria* — "the best-attested instantiation of a widespread Greek women's ritual"[59] — women used to mix the seeds together with the matter resulting from

---

54 See Hussain/Sakthivadivel/Amarasinghe 2003, 266; further cf. Michael 2014, 35: "irrigation at the crown root initiation stage (20–25 days after sowing) result[s] in the maximum production per unit of water applied, and therefore this stage [is] considered as the most critical stage for [wheat] irrigation". See also Das 2018, 164: "[t]his period is [...] vital for tiller formation. Irrigation is needed very much during this period". One should add here that Aeschylus' possible medical reference tied to this passage is not — and could not have been — as accurate as his agricultural knowledge. "Unlike today's medical advice that the middle period in a woman's menstrual cycle proves optimal for conception, the ancient Greeks believed that the womb would be closed at that time. Instead, Greek medicine recommended the start of the menstrual cycle, when they believed the womb to be wide open, as the best for conception". See Lovano 2019, 229. Aeschylus could be "merging" the optimal period for agricultural fertilisation and what he thought to be the optimal period for conception.

55 In short, "[w]heat seeds comprise three main parts: a protective seed shell, a small embryo, and a starchy nutrient reservoir". See Dhakar/Sarath Chandran/Nagar/Visha Kumari/Subbarao/Kumar Bal/Kumar 2018, 299. "If a grain seed is exposed to the right amount of moisture and warmth, the seed germinates. The [...] embryo [of the plant] (the germ) feeds off the nutrients stored in the rest of the seed (the endosperm) and starts to grow, first sending a little root through the protective bran layers". See Simpson/McLeod 2013, 132. Cf. Herington's 1986, 30 astute "agricultural" observation about the frequently remarked association of the Aeschylean passage under discussion with *Il.* 23.597–599.

56 Dried animal (typically cow) blood is still to this day used as an organic (commercial) fertiliser (called "blood meal").

57 See Churchill Semple 1928, 131. Cf. Martin/Gershuny 1992, 2. See also, Brockliss 2018, 21.

58 Sch. Luc. *Dial. Mer.* 2.1.

59 See, concisely, Stehle 2012, 192–196 (also 203 for further bibliography) on the Thesmophoria, one of the two (the other was Eleusinia) great festivals held in Attica in honour of Demeter, celebrated shortly before seed-sowing in the fall. "Herodotos (2.171) tells us that the Danaids

decayed, sacrificed pigs to fertilise them for the autumn sowing. Since the word χοῖρος was used in vulgar language for the vulva, pigs may have been substitutes for the women themselves:[60] "a surrogate for the woman's [καθάρματα] — menstrual and lochial blood. The starting-point of the [*Thesmophoria*] festival was the primitive practice of secretly disposing of these [καθάρματα], which were used to fertilise the seed-corn".[61]

The most iconic Greek myth about a bloodshed that led to some kind of fertilisation is, no doubt, Hesiod's narrative of *Ouranos*' castration in *Theog.* 154–206, and one may focus on some similarities with Agamemnon's killing in Aeschylus: the Earth turned on her bedfellow, the Sky, for eliminating their children (as Agamemnon eliminated Iphigenia), and she devised a plan to get back at him by shedding his blood.[62] She armed her son's hand, instructing him on what to do, and sent him off to avenge her. When the Sky attempted to have sex with the Earth, Cronus δεξιτερῆι δὲ πελώριον ἔλλαβεν ἅρπην, | μακρὴν καρχαρόδοντα, φίλου δ' ἀπὸ μήδεα

---

brought the Thesmophoria to Greece from Egypt. [...] The case made by Robertson that [Aeschylus' *Danaids* (and the Danaid trilogy)] ended with the founding of [...] [this fertility festival that was only for married women] can be supplemented. Cult *aitia* may have been not uncommon in Aeschylus. The festival and the trilogy share the same paradoxical combination of an 'emphatic anti-sexual ethos' on the part of women (sexual abstinence, violence against males) with the subsequent association of human sexuality with agricultural fertility. [...] [T]he negative aspect of the ritual is in its etiological narrative explored by being taken to the bloody extreme that cannot be actually enacted in the ritual founded at the end of [*Danaids*]. For instance, [...] the Thesmophoria left women with the power to inflict the violence that the Danaids exercised in the trilogy — but now only as a threat, against male intruders into their celebrations"; Seaford 2012, 306; cf. Seaford 1987, 115–116.

60 See Aristoph. *Ach.* 739–747, 764–803 for the girls presented as pigs (in a scene which plays with the double sense of χοῖρος) to be sold as (μυστικάς/μυστηρικάς) sacrificial victims. "χοῖρος [...] is used routinely in [Aristophanes] as a slang term for the female genitalia ([...] note that the primary evidence offers no explicit support for the claim that the word refers specifically to 'the pink hairless cunt of young girls')". This scene alludes "to events in the second day of the Greater Mysteries of Demeter and Kore, when initiands took a piglet down to the sea, washed it and themselves there, and most likely sacrificed it upon their return to the city". See Olson, 2002, 261 and 263. About the sexual meaning of χοῖρος see also, tentatively, Aesch. fr. 310 Radt with Slenders 2005, 41–42 (yet cf. Aesch. fr. 309 and 311 Radt). See further Golden 1988; also, Walker 1997, 21–22.

61 See Thomson 1965, 222.

62 For birth from bloodshed in Greek myth see the list by West 1966, 220.

πατρὸς ἐσσυμένως ἤμησε.⁶³ Perhaps it is no coincidence that Cronus reaps his father's genitals with a sickle the Earth produced, and that the original meaning of ἀμάω is to "reap corn".⁶⁴ Cronus threw away his father's genitals, and the bloody drops hit the Earth. After a long period of time,⁶⁵ from the drops of blood she received on her, the Earth bore, among other beings, the Furies. In *Ag.* 1431–1437 Clytemnestra declares before the Chorus, with an oath to the Justice due to Iphigenia (which, unlike the maiden herself, is now consummated (τέλειον τῆς ἐμῆς παιδὸς Δίκην)),⁶⁶ to Ἄτη, the goddess of ruin, and to the Fury — the trinity of powers to whom, or through whose agency, she shed her husband's blood (αἷσι τόνδ' ἔσφαξ' ἐγώ) — that for as long as Aegisthus lights the fire of her hearth, she has nothing to fear. There may or may not be a sexual undertone in the "lighting" of Clytemnestra's "hearth";⁶⁷ what is evident is that she features the Fury born by Iphigenia's blood as an essential justification/accomplice for her own deed.⁶⁸ What Clytemnestra is unable to see, is that when Agamemnon's blood spatters her, this is not the only Fury present on the scene anymore. Another Fury — comparable it seems to

---

63 See Hes. *Theog.* 179–181: "with his right hand he grasped the monstrous sickle, long and jagged-toothed, and eagerly he reaped the genitals from his dear father". The translation is by Most 2006.

64 "The scanty remains of actual cult of [Cronus] which have lingered on into historical times [...] suggest that he had been a god of the harvest". See Guthrie 1954, 53.

65 The Fury in the *Oresteia* is ὑστερόποινος (*Ag.* 59, cf. *Ag.* 462–467).

66 Cf. *Ag.* 973: Ζεῦ Ζεῦ τέλειε, τὰς ἐμὰς εὐχὰς τέλει | μέλοι δέ τοι σοὶ τῶνπερ ἂν μέλλῃς τελεῖν, where — while her husband disappears into the palace walking on the purple-dyed clothing— Clytemnestra asks for the fulfillment of her revenge. Zeus τέλειος oversees fulfillment or completion, and is mainly tied to destiny, marriage, initiation, and death. For Zeus τέλειος associated with marriage see further below. The τέλειος Δίκη τῆς παιδὸς implies the final fulfillment of Clytemnestra's plans for retribution, but it also evokes Iphigenia's marital consummation that was displaced by her killing. See *Ag.* 227, 1523–1524. See Raeburn/Thomas 2011, n. on vv. 227, 1523–1524. However, cf. Fraenkel 1950, 719–720. For Zeus τέλειος in *Ag.* see also Salviat 1964.

67 See Pulleyn 1997, 566–567. In support of this, one could argue that a certain tone of perverted eroticism may have been originally intended for the whole passage: *Ag.* 1434–1447. Cf. Soph. *El.* 417–425: Clytemnestra has a dream that Agamemnon came back to life and planted his sceptre (usurped by Aegisthus) in the hearth of the house, and from it then grew a luxuriant shoot. A sexual connotation is neither "impossibly allusive" (see Finglass 2007, 215), nor emphasised in the passage. It is present as a subtle shading. In Aeschylus (see *Ch.* 523–33), Clytemnestra dreamt that she gave birth to a snake, wrapped it in swaddling clothes, and offered it her breast to drink. Yet the snake bit her breast, sucking a clot of blood in the milk. Psychoanalytic readings of both these passages, indicating that "the snake and the sceptre symbolise the sexual potency of the father [...,] the snake also [being] a symbolic allusion to [...] Agamemnon's penis" (see Green 1979, 51–52), strain the text beyond its "intentions".

68 "[T]he blood [...] in [Cytemnestra's] eyes also drips from the eyes of the Furies ([*Ag.*] 1428, [*Ch.*] 1058, [*Eum.*] 54)". See Foley 2001, 205.

those engendered when the Earth received the blood of the Sky's castration[69] — is fertilised from the drops Clytemnestra receives, and will act in due time: this Fury will trigger her own violent death.[70]

The current arguments in favour of the sexual suggestiveness of *Ag.* 1388–92 are in the main two.[71] The first, that γάνος, δρόσος,[72] and ψακάς indicate semen, and thus Clytemnestra's outburst of "agricultural" joy is tied to sexual fecundity. The second argument is that the sexual tone of *Ag.* 1388–92 becomes clear when the passage is read with Aeschylus' fr. 44 Radt from the *Danaids*, on the fertile Hierogamy of the Earth and Sky (more on which below), in mind. Even if one sets both these arguments aside, there is, as I have shown, some noteworthy parallel evidence associating Clytemnestra's words with fertility, and thereby with a procreative union: Clytemnestra sheds the blood of Agamemnon, as the Earth sheds the Sky's blood (through Cronus), because of what he had done to her offspring. The fertilising blood of Agamemnon hits his wife, and she reports feeling like the crops feel, while receiving water precisely at the moment they need it most to develop. Clytemnestra receives her husband's blood as the soil receives the rain, and a Fury, seeking her blood, is born. However, this analogy only indicates that Clytemnestra's words could be pointing to a sexual act through a germination connotation. But is this enough evidence to establish such a connection once and for all? Could it not be that the imagery indicates only how Clytemnestra's will for revenge is "irrigated" by Agamemnon's blood? Could it not be that Aeschylus simply "communicates horror by recalling something friendly and harmless[, such as] the carefully tended sprouting and growth of crops",[73] and the passage is not sexually charged? To answer that, one should have to turn to the visual context: a naked man lying on his back in the bath, breathing heavily, splashes

---

69 See *Ch*. 439–443 where the abominable mutilation of the dead Agamemnon's extremities by Clytemnestra, most likely his genitals included, is blatantly mentioned. See Martin 2020, 126; in detail, Bardel 2002.

70 See Aesch. *Ch*. 400–404: ἀλλὰ νόμος μὲν φονίας σταγόνας | χυμένας ἐς πέδον ἄλλο προσαι- τεῖν | αἷμα· βοᾶι γὰρ λοιγὸς Ἐρινὺν | παρὰ τῶν πρότερον φθιμένων ἄτην | ἑτέραν ἐπάγουσαν ἐπ' ἄτηι. "Well, it is certainly the law that when drops of gore flow to the ground, they demand other blood; for slaughter cries out for a Fury who comes from those who perished before to bring further ruin upon ruin". The translation is by Sommerstein, 2008b. Cf. *Ch*. 283–284, 577–578, 648–652.

71 See n. 52 above.

72 "δρόσος means liquid in the form of drops or a film, including dew and drizzle [...], vaginal secretion [...], and semen, whence, like γόνος, it can mean "offspring"". See Dover 1968, 217. It can also possibly mean pre-cum or boys' athletic sweat. See Henderson 1975, 145 n. 194. See also Boedeker 1984, *passim*.

73 See Fraenkel 1950, 656.

the face of a woman — his wife — with a "jolting", "fertilising" body fluid he secretes, at which she takes vitalising pleasure.[74] The sexual tension applicable to the outline of this incident is hard to miss, even if there were no linguistic or other evidence to support it. Therefore, one may argue with some confidence that *Ag.* 1388–92 is indeed sexually charged. Aeschylus' ultimate intention seems to have been to trigger an orgasmic feeling that derives its magnitude from the natural world; to make the audience mentally instantiate a shocking emotional event of perverted fertilisation and bursting to deliver. And he did so in a single phrase. Agamemnon "breath[es] forth a mighty eruption of blood",[75] and fertilises Clytemnestra's "vengeful soil" with this "ejaculating" gore. Iphigenia's conception, delivery, her violent death, as well as the violent death of Agamemnon, leading to the conception of his avenging Fury, are all simultaneously present in this passage of sadistic satisfaction.[76] Nevertheless, they are conveyed not in a consciously rational manner, but through Aeschylus' unique poetic density.

For those still skeptical about the sexual suggestiveness of *Ag.* 1388–1392, Sophocles' "testimony" may be more convincing. Aeschylus' "lines made a strong impression: Sophocles imitated them in describing Haemon's death at *Ant.* 1238–1239:"[77]

> ἐπενταθεὶς
> ἤρεισε πλευραῖς μέσσον ἔγχος, ἐς δ' ὑγρὸν
> ἀγκῶν' ἔτ' ἔμφρων παρθένωι προσπτύσσεται·
> καὶ φυσιῶν[/κάκφυσιῶν][78] ὀξεῖαν ἐκβάλλει ῥοὴν
> λευκῆι παρειᾶι *φοινίου* σταλάγματος.
> Κεῖται δὲ νεκρὸς περὶ νεκρῶι, τὰ νυμφικὰ
> τέλη λαχὼν δείλαιος ἔν γ' Ἅιδου δόμοις.

---

74 γάνος is something bright, particularly a liquid (see LSJ), and a *mot juste* here because related to γάνυμαι, 'I rejoice'". See Raeburn/Thomas 2011, 215.

75 See Fraenkel 1950, 655.

76 According to Wohl 1998, 108 in *Ag.* 1388–1392 "sadism is not merely expressed by Clytemnestra but enacted by her. [...] [S]he admits openly that violence is a source of sexual arousal". Cf. Eur. *Hec.* 557–70: "[t]he startingly erotic account of the sacrifice of Polyxena [...] invites suspicion of a sado-sexual ingredient, but this may be to put too much weight on Euripides' peculiar way of, from time to time, depicting human behaviour in ways which seem to anticipate modern psychological theories". See Parker 2016, xviii.

77 See Raeburn/Thomas 2011, 215; Sommerstein 2002, 154. The lines are also echoed by the author of ps.-Eur. *Rh.* 790–1, see Fries 2014, 35, 411. For the authorship of *Rh.*, see, most recently, Manousakis/Stamatatos 2018.

78 See Griffith 1999, 339.

Pressing himself over the sword, he infixes it halfway into his side; and while being conscious still, he clasps the maiden in his weak arm. And breathing out, he spurts a jagged gush of the gory drippings onto her white cheek. Now a dead body he lies, curled up around another dead body; and he obtained, wretched man, marital consummation in the dwellings of Hades.

"The likeness of [Sophocles'] *Ant.* 1238f. [...] to *Ag.* 1389f. is obvious [...]. Borrowing born of admiration [for Aeschylus] can more than once be seen in the earliest preserved plays of Sophocles [...]".[79] In this messenger speech addressed to Euridice (1192–1243), we hear how Haimon broke into Antigone's bridal chamber of death (see 1205: νυμφεῖον Ἅιδου), and was embracing the hanging girl round her waist, pressing up against her, bewailing the loss of his marriage bed and of the wretched one who was to be his wife, when Kreon arrived along with his entourage (see 1223–1225: τὸν δ' ἀμφὶ μέσσῃ περιπετῆ προσκείμενον, | εὐνῆς ἀποιμώζοντα τῆς κάτω φθορὰν | ... καὶ τὸ δύστηνον λέχος). The visual rendering of this description would be: Haimon standing, lifting up his head, which would be at about the level of Antigone's waist, pressing against the part of the hanging girl's body where her sexual organs lie. Then, with all the strength he had left after pushing the sword into his side, moments before dying, he clasps Antigone, while breathing out what could have been his last breath, and the blood coming out of his mouth reaches her face. There are two possible scenarios about how this could have been possible: he either tautened his body, looking up, to be in some way face to face with Antigone, or — even though there is no clear mention of such an action in the passage — he cut Antigone's noose and she was laying down when he last embraced her. In any case, κεῖται δὲ νεκρὸς περὶ νεκρῷ in 1240 should be the last image of Haimon and Antigone that the messenger saw before leaving the scene to come report what had happened.

Haimon's last conscious act was to caress Antigone. Then, as he was dying, he spattered her with drops of his blood. He had already pressed up his head against the most sexual part of her body — and the seat of reproduction. That is how Haimon was destined to eventually obtain the (perverted) νυμφικὰ τέλη of his marriage to Antigone. "The sexual associations [in the text] are strong (esp[ecially] after ἐς ... ἀγκῶνα ... παρθένωι), [: through this bloody "intercourse"] the fatal marriage is finally [sexually] consummated".[80] When Sophocles "molded" *Ant.* 1238–1239 with *Ag.* 1389–1390 in mind, notably removing the agricultural imagery, and thus rendering his lines less poetic and more dramatic,

79 See Fraenkel 1950, 655.
80 See Griffith 1999, 339. See also Seaford 2012, 174.

he did not just create a phrase which linguistically evokes its model; he transferred the sexual "charge", the feeling of the *Ag.* passage to his own piece. It seems that Sophocles received the Aeschylean, semantically pregnant bloody "intercourse" between Clytemnestra and Agamemnon exactly as such, employing it for his own ends.[81] Thus, if one is not convinced by the other arguments that *Ag.* 1388–92 is in fact sexually suggestive, s/he should bear in mind that Sophocles would most likely think differently.

4 When the Sky Penetrated the Earth: A Tale as Old as Time

In the (known) Aeschylean oeuvre the concept of sexual intercourse in terms of fecund agricultural consummation (τέλος) finds its utmost expression in fr. 44 Radt. This piece derives from the lost *Danaids*: the third play of a thematically connected tetralogy comprising *Supp.*, in which Aeschylus follows Danaus' daughters arriving in Argos from Egypt, in order to escape marrying their cousins. Then, acting like they accept the union, they slay their bridegrooms on their wedding night — all but one, Hypermestra, who spares her husband, most likely because she fell in love with him.[82] Fr. 44 Radt is spoken by Aphrodite herself:

> ἐρᾷ μὲν ἁγνὸς Οὐρανὸς τρῶσαι χθόνα,
> ἔρως δὲ Γαῖαν λαμβάνει γάμου τυχεῖν·
> ὄμβρος δ' ἀπ' εὐνάεντος οὐρανοῦ πεσὼν
> ἔκυσε Γαῖαν· ἡ δὲ τίκτεται βροτοῖς
> μήλων τε βοσκὰς καὶ βίον Δημήτριον

---

81 Cf. *O.T.* 1276–1281 (if no interpolation is involved, see Finglass 2018, 558–560): φοίνιαι δ' ὁμοῦ | γλῆναι γένει᾽ ἔτεγγον, οὐδ᾽ ἀνίεσαν | φόνου μυδώσας σταγόνας, ἀλλ' ὁμοῦ μέλας | ὄμβρος χαλάζης αἵματός ἐτέγγετο. | τάδ᾽ ἐκ δυοῖν ἔρρωγεν, οὐ μονούμενα, | ἀλλ᾽ ἀνδρὶ καὶ γυναικὶ συμμιγῆ κακά. "At the same time as he was striking, bloody eyeballs were wetting his cheeks, nor did they let up damp drops of gore, but together a black shower of hail of blood was being wetted. These evils broke forth from the pair, not from one, but as evils shared by a man and a woman." The translation is by Finglass 2018, 558–559. See the n. by Dawe 2006, on vv. 1278–1279. "The account of the blood flowing from Oedipus' eyes, with the dead Jokasta lying on the ground, evokes both sexual union and rain — like the boast of [Clytemnestra]. The adjective [συμμιγής] in this passage both describes their sufferings and evokes (fertilising) liquids and incestuous sexual union — the three meanings that the same adjective combines in *Septem*". See Seaford 2012, 332.
82 On the Danaid tetralogy see Friis Johansen/Whittle 1980(I), 40–55; Sommerstein 2019, 10–20. For the sequence of the tragedies see also n. 158 below.

δένδρων τ' ὀπώραν· ἐκ νοτίζοντος γάμου
τέλειός ἐστι· τῶν δ' ἐγὼ παραίτιος.

The holy Sky passionately desires to penetrate the surface of the Earth, and passionate desire also takes hold of the Earth to experience (marital) intercourse. Heavy rain falling from the brimming Sky makes the Earth conceive, and she brings forth for the mortals grazing for their flocks, cereals to sustain their life, and the ripe fruit of trees; through this wet, dribbling intercourse she is consummated. And I am the cause of all this/I have a share in causing all this.[83]

Actually, in *Supp.* there is "ample evidence of a general detestation of men, sex and marriage. [The Danaids] equate marriage with slavery (335–337) and pray that they may never be "subject to the power of males" (392–393). The very phrase "the beds of men" prompts them to a cry of horror (142, 152), they wish for death "before an abominated man touches [their] flesh" (788–790, cf. 796–799, 804–807) and they frequently dwell on the miraculous conception of Epaphus [...]. Such attitudes [though,] were not thought normal in women"[84] or young men.[85] In the *Danaids*, Aphrodite notes how her power over nature is a universal mandate, an absolutely inescapable natural order that all living creatures should honour. Hence, the goddess of desire makes clear how the Danaids (save Hypermestra) are in the wrong to avoid marriage and sex. "A context must be provided for the speech of Aphrodite of which fr. 44 is part. It is not possible [...] to determine from the speech itself whether it comes from a defence of Hypermestra (as being excused and justified, in her defiance of her father, by her having acted under the

---

83 A heavily adapted version of Sommerstein's 2008c translation. For the double rendering of παραίτιος see Garvie 1986, 296 in detail.
84 See Sommerstein 2019, 14–15.
85 For instance, as Barrett 1964, 154–155, 172 notes, Eur. *Hipp.* "is the tragedy of a young man who has set himself against any contact with sexual love, and who in the excess of his intolerant contempt for it will bring himself to ruin". "To [him] σωφροσύνη is the cardinal virtue, and he its paragon [...]; though with him control is exaggerated, in the sexual sphere, into abnegation. [...] One must have complete and innate σωφροσύνη, he says [...]. [T]his by ordinary Greek standards is a quite astonishing claim. [...] [Hippolytus'] requirement of moral purity is alien to the ordinary Greek cult until Hellenistic times [...]; [and] his insistence that the purity must be innate would be extraordinary even then. This intense and intolerant young man has built into his cult of the virgin [Artemis] a strange and exclusive puritanism of his own; the Athenian audience, while they feel the beauty of his ideals [...], will at the same time feel their narrowness, and will find it excessive and unnatural". See also, Sommerstein 2019, 26 for the Danaids and the virgin goddesses. Cf. Sissa 1990b, 340–341 for John Chrysostom's striking "anathema" against the Encratite virgin women, who refuse to listen to Christ's word about the honourable and free from stain status of marriage and conjugal intercourse. These women, he claims, are more corrupt than those given over to licentiousness.

influence of Aphrodite's universal power) or from a denunciation of the other Danaids and their father (as having set that power at naught). Aphrodite may, of course, have done both these things in one speech".[86] At any rate, the piece must derive from the final part of the play, in which the natural order disrupted by what the Danaids have done, was eventually restored by divine intervention, and through a narrative about the sexual union between the Sky and the Earth.[87] Thus, the plot of the trilogy would have reached "equilibrium", and those who detested marriage might have embraced this union.[88]

What is highly interesting about Aesch. fr. 44 Radt is how the focus is on mutual desire for sexual intercourse, displacing the male (sexual) violence, dominant until that point in the trilogy. Under Aphrodite's "spell", ἀγνός[89] Ouranos

---

86 See Sommerstein 2010, 109.

87 For this myth in classical literature see Herington 1986. "A very primitive formula involving this belief appears to be preserved by [...] Proclus (fifth century [CE]), who states that at the Eleusinian rites the Athenians "looked up to the sky and shouted ὕε! ("Rain!"), then down to the earth and shouted κύε! ("Conceive!")". See Guthrie 1954, 54.

88 Sommerstein 2019, 27 suggests that "the contention between the Danaids and the Aegyptiads is in large measure a contest of two wrongs. [...] The Danaids are wrong to reject marriage altogether, but they have every right to reject a marriage that is being brutally forced on them and their father. [...] It is [...] appropriate that the Danaids should win the support of the Argives, and appropriate that the Aegyptiads should perish (all but the one who chose the path of loving persuasion in preference to force) while the Danaids apparently live to make new and better marriages". One should add here that by eventually giving in to marriage, the Danaids back away from their determination to die before they are "tamed" by men. In the Greek mind, they "exchange" this wild determination with a new status, that of married woman, who is "appeased" and in balance with the cosmic order of procreation. Hypermestra's "acceptance of Lynceus as her husband [in the *Danaids*] could have been the model for her sisters' [...] fulfilment of the sexuality attributed to all of them in *Supp.* and exalted as a principle in [fr. 44 Radt], since, on that evidence, her motive for sparing Lynceus cannot have been his abstinence but must have been her own ἵμερος". See Friis Johansen/Whittle 1980(I), 53.

89 It is interesting that in the extant plays of Aeschylus ἀγνός occurs nine times in *Supp.* (103, 214, 223, 228, 254, 364, 653, 696, 1030, cf. 226, 751) and no more than three in any of the other five secure Aeschylean plays, or in *Pr.* ἀγνός in Aeschylus refers (more or less closely) to the holy deities (title), their altars/dwellings, a person/action polluted or free of pollution, or is set within a ritual/sacrificial context. In *Supp.*, there is a "leitmotif" about purity, highlighting a core theme of the drama: the Danaids' determination to remain pure, untouched by males. What is thought-provoking, and telling of Aeschylus' poetic ingenuity, is that the adjective recurs in a passage the theme of which is the *par excellence* sexual intercourse, the cosmic union between the Sky and the Earth in the *Danaids*. One could simply read this as a(n ornamental) title for the Sky. It seems though that it was put there to also signify that even the primal, holy Sky feels an unconquerable desire for sexual intercourse.

feels a strong sexual urge to penetrate the Earth, but the Earth is also over-whelmed by the desire to have intercourse. The sexual tone of τρῶσαι is clear, implying that the Sky wants to pierce the Earth's soil[90] and get inside her, as a man pierces a woman's hymen[91] with his phallus, placing inside her his procrea-tive fluids. It seems then that, in this Aeschylean conception of the cosmic mar-riage, the Earth's virginity is renewed every time she gives birth to the Sky's off-spring. According to Pausanias 2.38.2–3, Hera renewed her own virginity every year by bathing at the Kanathos spring in Nauplion. This association evokes the earliest Greco-roman allusion to the myth of the mating of the Earth and Sky,[92] Il. 14.346–351, where (the deceived) Zeus clasps Hera into his arms, and beneath them the earth makes the sprouting grass, and the dewy lotus, and the crocus, and the thick and soft hyacinth all grow, to keep the lovemaking couple off the ground.[93] They lie covered in a fair golden cloud, from which glistering drops are falling.[94]

The "dewy" connection between Aesch. fr. 44 Radt and the Homeric passage is rather obvious. Yet, unlike what is the case with the epic, in Aeschylus the sin-cere sexual feelings, the sex drive of both lovers, is in the foreground; but the way their urge is described makes the narrative culturally emplaced. The Earth, the female "partner" in intercourse, is (linguistically) passive in her desire to have sex; ἔρως ... λαμβάνει γάμου τυχεῖν: desire takes hold of her to experience sex. The subject here is not the Earth, but the ἔρως which seizes her, as the Sky will do. On the contrary, the Sky, the male "partner" in intercourse, is himself the subject of ἐρᾶι, and his desire to "get inside" the Earth is active. In these two lines Aeschylus makes exquisite use of syntax in shaping his imagery. The same de-vice, *mutatis mutandis*, occurs in an iambic line from *Amymone*, Aeschylus' satyr drama accompanying the Danaid Tetralogy. The line is addressed to the homon-ymous daughter of Danaus by Silenus or Poseidon: σοὶ μὲν γαμεῖσθαι μόρσιμον, γαμεῖν δ' ἐμοί. This can be rendered literally, "it is your destiny to get married (to become my wife), and mine to marry you (to make you my wife)"; or euphemisti-

---

90 In Aesch. fr. 44 Radt the Sky wants to penetrate the χθόνα, the surface of the Earth, but makes Γαῖα "pregnant"; and it is Γαῖα who brings forth his offspring.

91 For this term in antiquity see Sissa 2013.

92 "Originat[ing] where one might have expected it to, in the Vedic hymns; for India, of all the lands of the world, has had most reason to be conscious of the power of rain". See Herington 1986, 27.

93 Cf. *Od.* 5.125–128.

94 Cf. Soph. *Ant.* 950 for Ζηνὸς ... γονὰς χρυσορύτους: Zeus' golden-flowing seed which Danae "treasured" inside her.

cally, "it is your destiny to get fucked (be deflowered), and mine to fuck (deflower) you".[95] The active and passive sexual — conjugal — roles in both passages are artfully depicted through the syntax used for the male and the female respectively.

In Aeschylus' description, the Sky is εὐνάεις. That is, there is an abundant gush of water flowing from the Sky. εὖ (+νάω) in this compound, combined with ὄμβρος, implies abundance, not ease or a moderately high degree of flow. Hence, Sommerstein's 2008c use of "brimming" is more accurate than the "fair-flowing" in the LSJ. In Aeschylus' anthropomorphic image, the Sky's "testicles" are quite full of "sperm"; and he cannot wait to "have sex" with his wife, and to "ejaculate" inside her. Furthermore, εὐνάεντος aurally evokes εὐνασθέντος, and thus εὐνή also comes into the picture.[96] The audience is elaborately called upon to imagine the Sky and the Earth having intercourse on a cosmic bedding; the Sky's fluids falling vehemently upon the Earth, penetrating and fertilising her with an ὄμβρος: a storm.[97] In symbolic terms, the sexual intercourse between the Sky and the Earth seems "turbulent" (anything but gentle or gradual), and considerably "wet". Sky's "waters"[98] impregnate the Earth, and in this act of conception the male is once again the active agent. In "fast-forward", the Earth τίκτεται all that sustains life for mortals.[99] In other words, in this passage the Earth is both the agent and experiencer of only one verbal action: giving birth.

Among other things, in fr. 44 Radt the Earth brings forth (δένδρων τ') ὀπώρα:[100] the ripe fruit of trees. "When used metaphorically of males, ὀπώρα signifies 'the bloom of youth', or 'ripe manhood', and does not exclude the pursuit of sexual fulfillment. But when used of females, ὀπώρα means virginity and is to be withheld from all erotic experimentation".[101] In *Supp.* 996–1006 Danaus warns

---

95 I have elsewhere discussed in detail the sexual suggestiveness of this passage, see Manousakis 2020b.

96 See LSJ s.v. εὐνάζω, II *of sexual intercourse*.

97 ὄμβρος (sc. ἐξ Οὐρανοῦ) πεσών (sc. ἐπὶ Γαῖαν) ἔκυσε([ν αὐτήν]), see LSJ s.v. πίπτω, *special usages* I: "fall violently upon, attack". In Opp. *Cyn.* 4.443 ὄμβρος, used here for Sky's procreative fluids, is tied to urine.

98 Cf. ps-Eur. *Rh.* 351–354.

99 Cf. Aesch. *Ch.* 127–128. Γαῖαν ... ἣ τὰ πάντα τίκτεται | θρέψασά τ' αὖθις τῶνδε κῦμα λαμβάνει: "Earth ... who gives birth to all things, nurtures them, and then receives that fruit of her womb back into herself". The translation is by Sommerstein 2008c. On this see Garvie 1986, 76.

100 The fr. in its entirety derives from Ath. 600b, while lines 1–5 are also provided by Eust. 978–925. In Athenaeus, line six begins with: δένδρων τις ὥρα. δένδρων τ' ὀπώραν is a widely accepted conjecture by Diels. See further TrGF 3, *ad loc.*

101 See Carson 1990, 146. In Aristophanes' *Peace*, Ὀπώρα is a handmaiden of the personified Peace (represented by a statue in the play). She becomes the bride of the protagonist, Trygaeus

his daughters "not to put [him] to shame, having the youthful beauty [(ὥραν)] that [they] have, which makes men turn their heads. Tender fruit [(τέρειν' ὀπώρα)] is not all easy to guard: beasts and men alike devour it [...]. In the case of animals, winged or walking, Cypris advertises the availability of juicy fruits before they ripe, preventing them <from resisting> desire; and likewise with the charms of a maiden fair of form, every passer-by is vanquished by desire and shoots a glance of the eye at her that can melt her heart".[102] In *Supp.* 1015 the Danaids answer back, picking up this image: "so far as my 'fruit' [(ὀπώρας)] is concerned, father, you can have confidence: unless the gods have decided on some new plan, I will not deviate from the track my mind has followed till now".[103] However, it seems that in the last play of the trilogy, the *Danaids*, the gods, Aphrodite in particular, did plan otherwise.[104] ὀπώρα, "used figuratively of youthful [virginal] beauty"[105] in *Supp.*, resumes in a (concluding?) passage of cosmogonic coitus: fr. 44 Radt. This is no direct reference to the sexuality of Danaus' daughters, of course. However, the suggestiveness of ὀπώρα illustrated in *Supp.*, makes it possible that there could be an allusion of this kind to its use in fr. 44.[106]

(see Sells 2019, 140), and her sexuality is constantly on display (see vv. 706–712, 726–728, 842–844, 847–855, 863, 867–870, 1192, 1316, 1329–1356). For instance, 855 suggests that Ὀπώρα could be performing oral sex. Also cf. 884–5 where it is suggested that Ariphrades (cf. *Kn.* 1284–1287) will perform oral sex on Θεωρία, another handmaiden of Peace. See further, Storey 2019, 80–83. Alexis composed a comedy called Ὀπώρα, the homonymous protagonist of which is some harlot who πᾶσι γὰρ χαρίζεται. See Geoffrey Arnott 1996, 496–501. Cf. Aelian's letters 7 and 8, addressed to a harlot named Ὀπώρα by a farmer, Δέρκυλλος, and vice versa. In her letter n. 8 Ὀπώρα notes that: τοῦ γὰρ χρηματίζεσθαι παρὰ τῶν βουλομένων μοι προσιέναι καὶ τὸ ὄνομα αἴτιον· παιδεύει γάρ με ὅτι καὶ τὸ κάλλος τῶν σωμάτων ὀπώραι ἔοικεν. ἕως οὖν ἀκμάζει, καὶ τὴν ὑπὲρ αὐτοῦ χάριν προσῆκόν ἐστιν ἀνταπολαμβάνειν· ἐὰν δὲ ἀπορρεύσῃ, τί ἂν ἄλλο εἴη τὸ ἡμέτερον ἢ δένδρον καρπῶν ἅμα καὶ φύλλων γυμνόν; cf. Aristaenetus *Epist.* 2.1: ἔστι δὲ ἡ σὴ ὀπώρα ἡδίων τῆς ἀπὸ τῶν δένδρων.

102 The translation is by Sommerstein 2008a. κηραίνουσι (rendered as "devour"), "since ἀκή-ρατος can mean virgin [...,] is probably also felt as having a slight sexual tinge". See *id.*, 420 n. 206. On this passage, see further Friis Johansen/Whittle 1980(III), 289–298.

103 The translation is by Sommerstein 2008a.

104 For ὀπώρα and Aphrodite cf. Pindar *Isth.* 2.4–5. ὅστις ἐὼν καλὸς εἶχεν Ἀφροδίτας | εὐθρόνου μνάστειραν ἁδίσταν ὀπώραν: "any boy who was beautiful and has had the sweetest bloom of late summer that woos fair-throned Aphrodite". The translation is by Race 1997.

105 See Friis Johansen/Whittle 1980(III), 292.

106 In Aeschylus ὀπώρα occurs only in the Danaid tetralogy and in fr. 458 Radt. Thus, it is not impossible that the dubious fr. 458 Radt, ἀρτίδροπος ὀπώρα νεάζουσα (?), is part of the Danaid tetralogy. The fr. could be construed as follows: "newly plucked fruit/virginity of a juvenile still", since it seems to be sexually suggestive. The ancient scholiast of *Sev.* 333(f) indicates, ἀρτιδρό-ποις: ἤγουν ταῖς κόραις ταῖς ἄρτι δρεπομέναις τὴν παρθενίαν πρὸ τοῦ ἐλθεῖν εἰς ὥραν γάμου. Cf.

"Zeus [τέλειος] [was, among other things,] a marriage-god [who] yoked man and wife together".[107] According to Plutarch, 'when [Zeus'] union [with Hera] was made public [...,] [she] came to be known as [...] [τελεία], "of the Wedding Rites'".[108] This specific "τέλος [is] the consummation of the marriage ceremony",[109] as in *Eum*. 835: θύη πρὸ παίδων καὶ γαμηλίου τέλους, tied to Zeus and Hera: Ἥρας τελείας καὶ Διὸς πιστώματα (*Eum*. 214, cf. Aesh. fr. 383 Radt).[110] "Th[ese cult epithets] seem to be an allusion to the idea of marriage as a completion or fulfilment; [γάμος] is said to be the [τέλος] and those who are married are called [τέλειοι]".[111] The verb "[τελειόω] implies 'making perfect, completing, coming to maturity, bringing fruit to maturity', suggesting harvest".[112] In *Ag*. occurs a subtle τέλος-imagery of marriage/death, through which Iphigenia's sacrifice, Helen's marriage(s), the fall of Troy, and Agamemnon's slaying are interconnected.[113] Now in the *Danaids* fr. 44 Radt, the Earth becomes τέλειος: she comes to consummation, becomes fulfilled in her role (procreation), getting actually married; and that is achieved through having intercourse with the Sky. With ἐκ νοτίζοντος γάμου, in which γάμος is chiefly the sexual union, the consummation act binding the primeval (but also any regular, mortal) couple,[114] securing fecundity with its wet, dribbling quality — the rainwater that stands for the ejaculating sperm — Aeschylus reaches a poetic peak.

Sev. 333–335: κλαυτὸν δ' ἀρτιτρόφους ὠμοδρόπους | νομίμων προπάροιθεν διαμεῖψαι | δωμάτων στυγερὰν ὁδόν. "It is a lamentable thing that young girls should be plucked unripe and should travel to the end a hateful journey from their homes before the time has come for the customary rites of marriage". The rendition is by Hutchinson 1985, 97. Abduction (enslavement) and rape of young girls underlies the passage. Cf. *Sev*. 357–368.

107 See Cook 1914–1940(III), 609. Zeus Ἐπιτέλειος would [...] be only another form of Zeus Τέλειος". See *id*. (II) 1163 n. 2.

108 See Cook 1914–1940(III), 1042. "The sense of fulfilment in the epithet [τελεία] is both active and passive: Hera is fulfilled or made complete by marriage, and she also has the power to make complete those who get married". See Clark 1998, 16.

109 See Goldhill 1984a, 170.

110 See further Elderkin, 1937. Examined under this light, παρ-αίτιος in fr. 44 Radt 7, rendered as: "I have a share in causing all this", not as: "I am the cause of all this", may be implying the divine trinity closely tied to the union of marriage: Zeus, Hera, and Aphrodite. Cf. *Supp*. 1034–1037 with the nn. by Friis Johansen/Whittle 1980(III) *ad loc*.; *Eum*. 213–226.

111 See Clark 1998, 15–16.

112 See Rehm 2002, 332 n. 30.

113 See Lebeck 1971, 68–73.

114 See Soph. *Trach*. 546: κοινωνοῦσα τῶν αὐτῶν γάμων, which is "not necessarily referring to formal marriage". See Easterling 1982, 142. Cf. *Trach*. 539–540: καὶ νῦν δύ' οὖσαι μίμνομεν μιᾶς ὑπὸ | χλαίνης ὑπαγκάλισμα. "And now — being two — we are awaiting beneath a single blanket to be embraced". Cf. Eur. *Hel*. 242 and *Cycl*. 498 for ὑπαγκάλισμα and ὑπαγκαλίζω.

Aphrodite's speech in Aeschylus' *Danaids* must have made a very strong impression on Euripides, who adapts it in fr. 898 Kannicht:[115]

τὴν Ἀφροδίτην οὐχ ὁρᾶις ὅση θεός;
ἣν οὐδ' ἂν εἴποις οὐδὲ μετρήσειας ἂν
ὅση πέφυκε κἀφ' ὅσον διέρχεται.
αὕτη τρέφει σὲ κἀμὲ καὶ πάντας βροτούς.
τεκμήριον δέ, μὴ λόγωι μόνον μάθηις·
{ἔργωι δὲ δείξω τὸ σθένος τὸ τῆς θεοῦ·}
ἐρᾶι μὲν ὄμβρου γαῖ', ὅταν ξηρὸν πέδον
ἄκαρπον αὐχμῶι νοτίδος ἐνδεῶς ἔχηι,
ἐρᾶι δ' ὁ σεμνὸς οὐρανὸς πληρούμενος
ὄμβρου πεσεῖν εἰς γαῖαν Ἀφροδίτης ὕπο·
ὅταν δὲ συμμιχθῆτον ἐς ταὐτὸν δύο,
φύουσιν ἡμῖν πάντα καὶ τρέφουσ' ἅμα,
δι' ὧν βρότειον ζῆι τε καὶ θάλλει γένος.

Do you not see how great a goddess Aphrodite is? You could neither tell nor measure how great she is, and how far her power extends. She nurtures you and me and all mankind. Here is an indication, so you may learn it not just through words {but I may show you the goddess' power in action}: through Aphrodite's influence the earth desires heavy rain when her parched surface, infertile through drought, stands in need of wetness, and in turn the majestic sky, brimming with heavy rain, desires to fall upon the earth; and when they have intercourse, and the two become one, they put forth and also nurture all things for us through which the human race lives and flourishes.[116]

Fr. 898 Kannicht is attributed by Matthiae 1829, 364–365 and others to Euripides' first *Hippolytus* (*Καλυπτόμενος*).[117] If this attribution is sound, the fr. would date from some point before 428 BC, the year the extant *Hippolytus* (*Στεφανίας/Στεφανηφόρος*) was first produced. Aeschylus should have produced his Danaid tetralogy around 463 BC.[118] Hence, and even though this is a highly speculative suggestion, it is not impossible that Euripides' remodeling of Aeschylus' piece is evidence of a posthumous staging of the Danaid tetralogy. Euripides closely follows Aeschylus, linguistically and conceptually, in many respects.

---

115 On which see Milo 2020 with bibliography.
116 An adapted version of the translation by Collard/Cropp 2008.
117 See TrGF 5.2, 909. An argument (by no means decisive or even close to being so) against this ascription would be that there are two resolutions in the thirteen iambics of this passage — though one of them to fit "Aphrodite" in the line — while in the secure frr. of the lost *Hipp.* there are two resolutions in 32 iambics. See Cropp/Fick 1985, p. 80. On this play see Barrett 1964, 10ff.
118 On the dating of *Supp.* see, concisely, Garvie 2006, pr. ix–xii. A dating in 463 BC is, quite plausibly, favoured by this scholar.

About the linguistic affinity one can indicate the following: Aeschylus' ἀγνὸς Οὐρανός becomes σεμνὸς οὐρανός. Aeschylus' ἐρᾶι μὲν ... τρῶσαι χθόνα for the S/sky becomes ἐρᾶι ... πεσεῖν, which evokes the Aeschylean πεσών. In Euripides' piece not only the S/sky ἐρᾶι, but also ἐρᾶι μὲν ... γαῖα—and even before her "partner" does. In both passages, the E/earth will receive an ὄμβρος, and Euripides' νοτίδος echoes Aeschylus' νοτίζοντος, and βρότειον echoes βροτοῖς. πληρούμενος in Euripides' piece construes Aeschylus' (more poetic) εὐνάεντος, and φύουσιν ... καὶ τρέφουσ' ἅμα substitutes for τίκτεται.

In Euripides' passage the focus moves from the male to the female: the S/sky is no more the syntactic centre of the narrative, as it is in Aeschylus, and the E/earth is more featured in this respect. However, and even though her desire is voiced first, the context makes it clear that the E/earth needs the water from the S/sky to prevent drought and infertility. Thus, the S/sky is once more the fertiliser, the source of fecundity. Euripides, unlike Aeschylus, seems to have primarily conceived the earth and sky not as two divine beings, but as two natural elements set in motion by some divine power. They are perceived as having sexual intercourse, συμμιχθῆτον ἐς ταὐτὸν δύο[119] makes this clear, but the climatic and meteorological nuances Euripides uses bring the actual dry earth and heavy clouds to the foreground, leaving the two cosmic lovers in their Aeschylean poetic shadows. Another point of difference is that while in Aeschylus it is Aphrodite herself who is speaking about her cosmic powers, in Euripides some mortal

---

119 It is interesting that in Eur. fr. 484 Kannicht from *Melanippe Sophē*, procreation is the result not of a union between the sky and the earth, but of their detachment. For *Melanippe Sophē* (also *Melanippe Desmōtis*) and this passage, see Jouan/Van Looy 2002/2, 348–396; Collard/Cropp 2008, 569–611; and Cropp 2009, 40–80 (in Collard/ Cropp/Lee 2009). Cosmic procreation might have been one of Euripides' favourite pieces of imagery, since, apart from frr. 484 and 898 Kannicht, he also makes use of it in fr. 839 Kannicht from *Chrysippus*. In that passage the Earth "mates" not with the Sky, but with (Zeus') Aether, begetter of men and gods. For *Chrysippus*, see Jouan/Van Looy 2002/3, 373–389; Collard/Cropp 2008, 459–471; also Mastronarde 1994, 31–38. Eur. fr. 839 Kannicht may or may not have something to do with renouncing homosexuality in *Chrysippus*, the plot of which focuses on the abduction and rape of a young boy by a grown man, and the boy's suicide. In this passage "the Chorus [could be] advocating fertility and marriage as a higher goal than the sterile and violent passion of Laius [for Chrysippus.] [...] [The] play [may have] contained the earliest example known to us in Greek literature of a debate between exponents of heterosexual and homosexual values". See Poole 1990, 148. Yet, "[t]he shame which Chrysippus felt [...] may [...] be a reflex to the double standard by which the passive partner could be subject to disapproval while the active partner was not". See Mastronarde 1994, 35. The imagery under discussion is also, distortedly, present in Eur. *Cycl.* 576–84, where Cyclops, under the "unmixed" influence of wine, sees heaven and earth "mixed/united", and Silenus as some Ganymede who he wants to take to bed. For the erotic vocabulary in *Cycl.* see Slenders 2005.

is trying to convince another mortal that Aphrodite is no negligible deity.[120] The wording makes this evident: οὐχ ὁρᾶις ... οὐδ' ἂν εἴποις οὐδὲ μετρήσειας ἂν ... κἀφ' ὅσον ... τρέφει σὲ κἀμὲ καὶ πάντας ... τεκμήριον δέ, μὴ λόγωι μόνον μάθηις. This interpretation could in fact support the ascription to the lost *Hippolytus*, since one can readily attribute the fragment to some character such as the old serving-man in the opening of the extant *Hippolytus*. There Euripides makes a servant advise the young hunter in stichomythia about how he should revere not only Artemis, but also Aphrodite. In the lost *Hippolytus*, a corresponding old servant, either male or female, could have addressed such a *rhēsis* concerning Aphrodite's potency to Theseus' son, setting forth his "chaste fallacy".[121] However, this is mere guesswork.[122]

---

120 Cf. Soph. fr. 941 Radt (unassignable to a specific play), addressed from an older person to a group of youths: ὦ παῖδες, ἤ τοι Κύπρις οὐ Κύπρις μόνον, | ἀλλ' ἐστὶ πολλῶν ὀνομάτων ἐπώνυ-μος. | ἔστιν μὲν Ἅιδης, ἔστι δ' ἄφθιτος βίος, | ἔστιν δὲ λύσσα μανιάς, ἔστι δ' ἵμερος | ἄκρατος, ἔστ' οἰμωγμός. ἐν κείνηι τὸ πᾶν | σπουδαῖον, ἡσυχαῖον, ἐς βίαν ἄγον. | ἐντήκεται γὰρ πλευμόνων ὅσοις ἔνι | ψυχή· τίς οὐχὶ τῆσδε τῆς θεοῦ πόρος; | εἰσέρχεται μὲν ἰχθύων πλωτῶι γένει, | ἔνεστι δ' ἐν χέρσου τετρασκελεῖ γονῆι, | νωμᾶι δ' ἐν οἰωνοῖσι τοὐκείνης πτερόν *** ἐν θηρσίν, ἐν βροτοῖσιν, ἐν θεοῖς ἄνω. | τίν' οὐ παλαίουσ' ἐς τρὶς ἐκβάλλει θεῶν; | εἴ μοι θέμις —θέμις δὲ τἀληθῆ λέγειν— | Διὸς τυραννεῖ πλευμόνων, ἄνευ δορός, | ἄνευ σιδήρου· πάντα τοι συντέμνεται | Κύπρις τὰ θνητῶν καὶ θεῶν βουλεύματα. "Children, the Cyprian is not the Cyprian alone, but she is called by many names. She is Hades, she is immortal life, she is wild frenzy, and sheer desire, wailing she is. In her is all activity: all that matters, all tranquility, all that leads to violence. For she sinks into the vitals of all that have life; what passage, what device is unknown to this goddess? She enters into the swimming race of fishes, she is within the four-legged brood upon dry land, and her wing ranges among birds ... among beasts, among mortals, among the race of gods above. Which among the gods does she not wrestle and throw three times? If I may speak out — and I may speak out — to tell the truth, she rules even over the heart of Zeus, without spear, without iron; the Cyprian cuts short all plans of mortals and gods". A slightly adapted version of Lloyd-Jones' 1996 translation. Mind how Sophocles, unlike Aeschylus who associates her power particularly with fecundity, makes Aphrodite possess and govern over every (natural and supernatural) be-ing in existence. Cf. *Trach.* 497–502 (see Easterling 1982, 133–134); *Ant.* 781–800.
121 The nurse has also been a "suspect" speaker for this fr. See Webster 1967, 68 and 71.
122 See Friedrich 1953, 127.

5 Depicting a furious lack of intercourse: The Chorus of monstrous spinsters

Aphrodite's speech in the *Danaids* should have been used to exemplify how marriage, and thus fecund intercourse, is the calling/destiny of the Danaids, as it is of women in general. In his reworking of the passage, Euripides brings to the fore the impact of lacking intercourse, by specifying under what dire conditions the E/earth craves for some wetness from the S/sky. The consequences of the lack of intercourse and fertility — rendering the females "dry", barren, and thus repulsive — are to some degree showcased in the Chorus of Aeschylus' *Eum.* In 67–70 Apollo describes the Furies as follows:

> καὶ νῦν ἁλούσας τάσδε τὰς μάργους ὁρᾶις·
> ὕπνωι πεσοῦσαι δ᾽ αἱ κατάπτυστοι,[123] κόραι
> γραῖαι, παλαιαὶ παῖδες,[124] αἷς οὐ μείγνυται
> θεῶν τις οὐδ᾽ ἄνθρωπος οὐδὲ θήρ ποτε—

> And now conquered you see these raving (creatures); in sleep the abominable have fallen: aged maidens, olden damsels, with whom no god nor man nor beast ever has intercourse[125]—

"Apollo ironically uses the diction of sexuality to highlight the [Furies'] repulsiveness [....], and he marks their absolute exclusion from social intercourse with a verb that regularly has sexual connotations, [μείγνυμι]".[126] Howbeit, this is not the only term that could be sexually charged in the passage. μάργος can signify someone furious, gluttonous, but also lewd, lustful; and the dividing line is not always clear. For instance, in *Supp.* (741, 758) Aegyptus' sons are furious, they have a violent appetite for war, but are also lustful, and they will not keep their hands off the virgin Danaids.[127] Apollo describes the Furies as μάργους, primarily

---

123 For the punctuation see West 1990a, *ad loc.* Page 1972 and Sommerstein 1989 both put the comma after κόραι. However, as the Furies are simply called μάργοι at first, they are also simply called κατάπτυστοι afterwards. κόραι γραῖαι and παλαιαὶ παῖδες are two telling antithetical pairs that should not be "disturbed" by punctuation, see West 1990b, 273.
124 Cf. Eur. *Bacch.* 694, on which see Johnston 2020, 131–132.
125 Cf. *Eum.* 350–351.
126 See Rynearson 2013, 14.
127 See Sommerstein 2019, 290. See also Aesch. *Sev.* 380 for Tydeus craving battle, 475 for wild horse-sounds, and 687 for ἄτη. Cf Aesch. fr. 99 Radt 20, fr. 258 Radt 1; Soph. fr. 842 Radt; Eur. *Elec.* 1027. In Aesch. fr. 281a Radt 31, μάργος is (most likely) used for Ares, who in *Supp.* 636, in a *mutatis mutandis* similar context, is called μάχλος. See also, Tsantsanoglou 2020, who suggests

pointing to their ravening attitude towards Orestes. Even so, it is not improbable that a tone of lustfulness is, secondarily, present in the description.[128] In *Eum.* 155–162[129] the Furies are seen as horses being whipped by some charioteer, who is none other than Apollo.[130] These, though, are no ordinary horses, and they are asked to "make their bloody breath blow hard at [Orestes'] back; [...] whither him with [their] exhalation, with the fire in [their] belly; [... to] shrivel him up with a second pursuit".[131] The association between horses and lustful women[132] — "inordinate in their sexual desires"[133] — to be "tamed" by men, was popular in Greek thought, and a subject that engaged Aeschylus' attention.[134] Hence, it is not impossible that, among other things, the Furies are also abstractly conceived by the

---

that fr. 281a Radt derives from the satyr-play of Aeschylus' Argonautic trilogy. In Thgn. (581, 1271, 1301) μάργος is used for lustful (sexually insatiable, more accurately) but also callous people.

128 Some lines below, in *Eum.* 73, Apollo says that the Furies are μισήματ' ἀνδρῶν καὶ θεῶν Ὀλυμπίων. "Now certainly μισητός, from being a stock condemnation of the sexually immoderate, comes actually to mean "sexually immoderate" (Suid., Phot., Hesych.; the shift in meaning is proved [...] by the existence of the deteriorative masc. μισητίας [Suid.] and by the further shift to denote immoderate desire in general [...])[;] that μίσημα should [also] come to mean 'sexually immoderate person' is not perhaps impossible". See Barrett 1964, 234. μισήματα in *Eum.* 73 certainly carries the full verbal force of μισεῖν; the Furies are creatures hateful to men and gods (Cf. *Eum.* 644). That is how one should render the phrase. Yet, as is the case with μάργους, μισήματα may also carry — within this context — a shading of excess/voracity in any action, best showcased for the Greek mind with female wantonness. Cf. *Sev.* 186 σωφρόνων μισήματα for the Chorus of Theban maidens in excessive fear. For the stereotypical female lustfulness, the inability of women to control their appetites/passions, see, in detail, Thorton 1997, 70–76.

129 Cf. *Eum.* 136.

130 The rare καθιππάζομαι is used to indicate how Apollo and the younger gods have dishonoured them. Confined in this play (150, 731, 779, 809) in the Aeschylean corpus, it never occurs in Sophocles. In Euripides *Phoen.* 732, there is καθιππεύω, used literally in the context of actual battle. See also Manousakis 2019, 234ff. For the Furies' repulsive appearance and abhorrent "manners" see, especially, *Eum.* 48–56, 127, 183–184, 192–195, 244–253, 267, 304–305, 370–371, 644. Cf. *Ch.* 1048–1062. See further, Simas 2020; Sommerstein 2002, 163–164.

131 See *Eum.* 137–139. The translation is by Sommerstein 2008b. Cf. *Eum.* 180-4; see further, Manousakis 2020a, 215 for (the possible attribution of) the relevant Aesch. fr. 372 Radt.

132 Also — sexually — energetic men: "stallions"/"studs" in modern slang terms. See, for instance, how in *Il.* 6 503–511 Paris, returning to the battlefield after visiting Helen at home, is likened to a "stabled horse that has fed his fill at the manger, [and then] breaks his halter and runs stamping over the plain — being accustomed to bathe in the fair-flowing river — and exults; on high does he hold his head, and about his shoulders his mane floats streaming, and as he glories in his splendour his legs nimbly bring him to the haunts and pastures of mares". The translation is by Murray 1999. See further Thorton 1997, 38–39.

133 See Aristotle *Hist. An.* 6.21, 572a 10. The translation is by Peck 1970.

134 See Manousakis 2020a, 217ff. for *Toxotides*. Aeschylus would also have treated the (voracious) "sexuality" of mares in *Glaucus of Potniae*. "Glaucus tried to instill a more competitive

poet (visually and in movement/kinesiology too, one might suspect) as wild, blood-dripping, fire-breathing horse-like females, that have not been "tamed" by sexual (or social) intercourse,[135] and are thus "stuck" in an intermediary status between young girls/maidens and mature women.[136] These creatures are voracious/lusting for Orestes(' destruction).

Later in the play, the Furies are associated with human and agricultural infertility: their avenging power and grim lot is, among other things, the other side of fecundity.[137] Further, the Furies state that παλλεύκων δὲ πέπλων ἄκληρος ἄμοιρος ἐτύχθην (352–353): they were made to have no share in the all-white garments.[138] "[W]hite garments were worn at joyful gatherings such as weddings [...], [whereas] black garments[, such as those the Furies wear,] were a sign of mourning".[139] The daughters of the Night are imagined as having been deprived of even attending joyous events, such as the solemnisation of the marital union, and as being closely tied to annulled fruitfulness. However, the Furies will undergo a major transformation during the drama: they will be changed from wild, sterile, black-clad creatures related to suffering, into fecund "brides" of Athens and the Athenian people.[140] Actually, the Furies are wooed and seduced by Athena's (erotic) language of

---

spirit in his horses by feeding them on human flesh, but this made them insatiable, and so they ate their master when their normal supplies of food ran out. It is also reported that Aphrodite was the ultimate cause of Glaucus' ruin, since she wanted to punish [him] for neglecting her worship and for preventing the mares from mating". See Wright 2019, 25. It is quite interesting that the (highly) lacunose Aesch. fr. 36b.7 Radt from *Glaucus of Potniae* might be a description of Aphrodite's power over the creatures of land, sea, and air, such as the ones discussed here. Cf. especially Soph. fr. 941 Radt.

135 "A herd with no herdsman", see *Eum.* 196.

136 "The presexual or asexual female in Greek thought is part of the wilderness, an untamed animal [...]. [A] woman's life has no prime, but rather a season of unripe virginity followed by a season of overripe maturity, with the single occasion of defloration as the dividing line. [...] [M]arriage is the means whereby a woman can be cleansed of bestiality and complete herself as a human being". See Carson 1990, 144–145.

137 If defeated in court, the Furies will poison the Attic soil, causing plants, animals and women to be barren (785) and spreading deadly pestilence (787). See, in detail, *Eum.* 187–8, 478–479, 711–712 (cf. 719–720), 780–787 (811–17), 800–803, 824–825, 830–831. Cf. Eur. *Hel.* 1327–1329 (Hom. *Hym. Dem.* 310): Demetra "cancelling" the fertility of the fields due to what happened to Persephone.

138 Cf. Admetus' cry in Eur. *Alc.* 922–925.

139 See Sommerstein 1989, 142. Cf. *Eum.* 368–371. "Moreover, clothing which is *leukos* may indicate the proper ritual condition in which mortals should approach a god". See Buxton 2013, 61. See also Lee 2015, 215. For the white "rejoicing" robes see further Cleland/Davies/Llewellyn-Jones 2007, 211.

140 On this transformation and the chthonic nature of the Furies, see also Bakola 2019.

persuasion to forever dwell in her land.[141] When this proposition is eventually accepted, the Furies become the *Semnai*, and change their clothes to red/purple
(φοινικοβάπτοις).[142] The reddish "robes worn by the *Semnai* in the final procession
were explained by W. Headlam [...] as symbolising their status as μέτοικοι".[143] Still,
the poet may have had a further reason for choosing this colour. "Certainly, in ancient Greece, red[dish] was the colour of the clothing worn by those who stood outside society, or those who underwent a transformation from one state of being to
another [...]. [A]s a colour which alludes to social transition [for the Greeks],
red[dish] is particularly appropriate for the bridal veil [and/or the wedding
dress]".[144] The colour of these special garments may also "well allude to [...] the

---

141 See, particularly, Rynearson 2013; Nooter 2017, 280–282. The object of sexual desire for the
Furies, the "body" they would crave for, is the land of Athens. See *Eum.* 852: γῆς τῆσδ' ἐρασθή-
σεσθε. Cf. *Ag.* 540–545 for the mutual "erotic" passion involving the Herald, the people and the
land of Argos (cf. Eur. *Phoen.* 359; adesp. com. 431 Kock). On the desire for actual missing bodies
and the pain of an empty bed in Aeschylus, see *Per.* 12–13 (with the n. by Garvie 2009), 59–64,
133–139, 286–289, 537–545 (with the n. by Garvie 2009 in 537–540); cf. 579–580. See also *Ag.*
408–428: Menelaus at home longing for his (unfaithful) wife. Cf. Clytemnestra's (mendacious)
speech about missing Agamemnon, especially *Ag.* 855–862, 887–894.
142 See *Eum.* 1028.
143 See Sommerstein 1989, 281. Yet, see also Connelly 2007, 92.
144 See Llewellyn-Jones 2003, 226. "While this interpretation is certainly attractive, there is no
evidence that a specific colour was prescribed for the ancient Greek wedding veil [or dress], as it
was for the Roman *flammeum*". See Lee 2015, 311. Llewellyn-Jones' argument is largely based on
the colour of Iphigenia's κροκωτός-raiment — a bridal veil? — in *Ag.* 239. This is a notoriously
thorny passage to decipher (see Medda 2017II, 166–173), and one should be very careful when
constructing any elaborate argument relying on it. Garvie 1986, 332 notes that κρόκου βαφάς in
Ag. 239 "denotes Iphigenia's robes but connotes blood". Still, this is open to much discussion.
The only thing one could say with some confidence is that "[i]f science should establish that the
κρόκος could at times dye more red than yellow, the passag[e] [...] would yield [a] more satisfactory[/multifaceted] interpretatio[n]". See Edgeworth 1988, 182. In fact, "[t]he dye stuff is made
from the dried stigmas of the crocus flower (*crocus sativus*), and is obtained by a very labour-
intensive production process, which must be done by hand. An extract of the dried stigmas in
boiling water will rapidly dye silk, wool, and vegetable fibres yellow or orange even without a
mordant, the intensity depending on the amount of colorants used". See Brøns 2015, 68. It is
interesting that even if Aeschylus meant us to imagine Iphigenia in a yellow garment, this would
also be tied to a female "transition" (from childhood to puberty). See, concisely, Medda 2017II,
169. Howbeit, "nowhere is the yellow colour linked specifically to the [ancient Greek] wedding.
The veil was an indicator of sexual maturity; Greek girls began to cover themselves once they
reached marriageable age, and were covered in public for the rest of their lives". See Oakley/Si-
nos 1993, 133. Yet, "the crocus flower [...] itself is present in a number of myths of abduction
and/or seduction". See Coward 2016, 52. In any case, one should never forget that we do not
know what kind of attire is actually described by Aeschylus, and what exactly is its colour/hue.
On the contrary, one should be sure that (what most likely is) the wedding dress of the Kore from

blood lost during the bride's first sexual intercourse or, more intrinsically, to the colour of the perforated hymen".[145]

At the end of *Eum.*, the deities of the Chorus are escorted to their new chambers with songs, cries of joy, and with the light of blazing torches[146] held by Cranaus' children, i.e. male Athenian citizens, and Athena's own female entourage.[147] This torch-lit procession escorted by both men and women,[148] readily evokes the — accustomed in the Greek wedding — nocturnal procession from the bride's to the groom's house, accompanied by many torches.[149] When the Furies give in to becoming the *Semnai*, their human and agricultural infertility curses against Athens are turned into zealous blessings of fecundity — of which they stay in charge.[150] Thus, their transformation comes full circle: what was barren, is now laden with blessings of fertility. In short, it would not be implausible to suggest that the Furies in *Eum.* were, among other things, conceived and presented as wild, "sere" females, deprived of the marriage "passage" and sexual

---

Merenda (Myrrhinous), c. 540 BC (which originally must have stood on Phrasikleia's tomb) is reddish (deep orange κροκωτός). See Wagner-Hasel 2002, 17; *id*. 2010, 104. "The unmarried girl is buried in her wedding attire; [...] imagined as a bride taken off by Hades; [...] The wedding attire is of course not a mere symbol. It would have been worn in the actual marriage that she has been denied". See Seaford 1987, 107. In the much later (*terminus ante quem* second century CE) novel *Leucippe and Clitophon* by Achilles Tatius, Calligone's wedding dress (2.11.2–4) is red. Furthermore, in Sappho 44 Lobel-Page 8–9, about the wedding of Hector and Andromache, and more specifically about Andromache's arrival in Troy, escorted by her future husband and his friends, red robes are mentioned. See Sch. (Vet. and Rec.) Aristoph. *Plut.* 530. See also Sappho 30 Lobel-Page 4–5 for a purple wedding girdle. On Greek and Roman textiles see, e.g., the volume edited by Mary Harlow and Marie-Louise Nosch in 2104.

145 See Llewellyn-Jones 2003, 227.

146 See *Eum.* 1022, 1041–1042, 1043 (1047).

147 Women "keeping a ritual night-watch (no doubt by terms) as "ladies of the bedchamber", as it were, to "queen" Athena", representing the female citizenry in the procession next to the male Areopagites. See Sommerstein 1989, 279.

148 "The format [of the ancient Greek wedding] was the same as for other symposia, with one important difference; men and women celebrated together in the same room, the men on the one side and the women on the other". See Oakley/Sinos 1993, 22.

149 Cf., e.g., *Il.* 18.492–493; Eur. *Med.* 1027, *Tr.* 308–310, *Ion* 1474, *Hel.* 638–640 and 722–723, *Phoen.* 344–346, *I.A.* 732–734. See, in detail, Oakley/Sinos 1993, 4, 11, 14–16, 20, 22, 24, 26, 28–36.

150 See *Eum.* 834–6: πολλῆς δὲ χώρας τῆσδε τἀκροθίνια, | θύη πρὸ παίδων καὶ γαμηλίου τέλους, | ἔχουσ' ἐς αἰεὶ τόνδ' ἐπαινέσεις λόγον: "From this land, mighty as it shall be, you will for ever receive the first-fruits, sacrifices before childbirth and before the completion of marriage, and you will thank me for these words". The translation is by Sommerstein 2008b. Further, see *Eum.* 895, 907–912 (Athena asks the Furies to become the guarantors of the fecundity of her land and people, while she promises martial glory: see *Eum.* 913–5), 923–926, 938–948, 959–961, 1030, 1040.

consummation: the intercourse that would "elevate" them to the state of "appeased" women who are "put in their place". "Marriage is the means, in the Greek view, whereby man can control the wild eros of women and so impose civilised order on the chaos of nature".[151] The Furies can be seen as a flock of "untamed spinsters"[152] who eventually embrace marriage, and are thus "tamed" and integrated into the civilised world. They are παλαιαὶ παῖδες no more; now they are — and this has, of course, nothing to do with the loss of an actual virginity — παῖδες ἄπαιδες: "damsels no more".[153]

In this respect, the protagonist Chorus in *Eum.* is similar to the protagonist Chorus in *Supp.* Danaus' daughters are likened to the wild Amazons, and throughout the play they show how determined they are to remain "untamed". The fertility of the land they visit is endangered by the miasma that would fall on those who will not respect their status — this is the actual power of the Danaids in imposing their will — and when they achieve what they want, they bless the land to stay safe and fecund.[154] The ruling authority of the land, the king, like

---

151 See Carson 1990, 143. Through "sex, the Greek husband domesticates his wild bride and, just as he does for his land and the beasts on it, brings to fruition what would otherwise remain savage and unproductive." See Carson 1990, 149. Torrance 2019, 58 suggests that *Eum.* "restores patriarchal order by acquitting Orestes of matricide and sending him back to rule in Argos. Traditional gender roles are [also] resolved [in this play] in the divine sphere, since Apollo wins out over the Furies."

152 "[T]here was simply no place in Greek society for the adult woman who remained unmarried: her virgin state would exclude her from the world of wives, her age from the world of maidens, and her family would look on her as a failure. When Lysias, cataloguing the crimes of the Thirty, says that they drove many citizens into exile [...], put many unjustly to death and denied them burial, deprived many of their civic rights, and prevented the daughters of many from being married (Lys. 12.21), the last item can be no anticlimax". See Sommerstein 1990, 184. Cf. Soph. *O.T.* 1502: χέρσους φθαρῆναι κἀγάμους for Oedipus' daughters. The Furies' "non-participation in sexual exchange mark[s] their separation from human society". See Goldhill 1984b, 211. The non-married (legitimately) women referred to here have nothing to do, of course, with the (sexually active) ἑταῖραι or παλλακαί. About these social categories of unmarried women see especially Silver 2018.

153 See *Eum.* 1034. Cf. how Euripides in *Hel.* "constructs" Helen's (of all women) "symbolic status as a [παρθένος] [...] threatened by [Theoclymenus'] sexual desires and severed from her proper status as [Menelaus'] wife' — also her "transition from the status of a [παρθένος] to that of a [γυνή]". See Allan 2008, 178, 305–306 with bibliography. The Furies/*Semnai* being ἄπαιδες may, in addition, imply that they will not any more engender woes (cf. *Ag.* 750–756) to torture mortals like Orestes. See *Eum.* 934–937 with the n. by Sommerstein 1989.

154 See, especially, *Supp.* 143 (153), 149, 154–159, 240, 287–289 (with the n. by Sommerstein 2019, *ad loc.*), 347, 375, 385–386, 392–395, 399–401, 407–416, 457–465, 473, 616–620, 634–638 (where the Danaids wish for the lustful Ares to never harm the land of Argos, but they do so in agricultural terms, cf. 663–666), 659–662, 674–677 (Artemis is asked to watch over women giving

Athena in *Eum.*, is torn between protecting the local people and respecting the suppliant(s). However, as we have seen here in some detail, in the third play of the Danaid tetralogy the virgins of the Chorus are "appeased" by none other than Aphrodite herself, are made to see the crucial cosmic importance of the sexual union between male and female, and, most likely, are guided to follow their disobedient sister Hypermestra in embracing marriage, and their distant mother Io in being set free from the ordeals of constant flight through sexual intercourse.[155] Notably, "[t]here is now something of a consensus that [the] secondary [C]horus [in *Supp.*, singing 1034–1051 and parts of 1052–1062,] is to be identified with the Argive soldiers who escort [Danaus] and his daughters into the city; it has been pointed out by Seaford that the[se] lyric exchanges have some of the features of responsive hymeneal songs which were typically sung by two Choruses of opposite sexes".[156] Thus, as is suggested here for the Furies in *Eum.*, the Danaids at the final scene of *Supp.* are also symbolically escorted (for a brief moment), in terms of textual form, to their own marital chambers.[157] In a word, part of the focus of both these plays, *mutatis mutandis* of course, is a female "band" in transition from "untamed" wilderness to social integration that is achieved through literal or symbolic marriage and sexual intercourse.[158]

---

birth), 689–92 (the wording in καρποτελῆ (a hapax pregnant with all possible connotations of τέλος in such a context) δέ τοι Ζεὺς ἐπικραινέτω (cf. *Eum.* 950, 969) | φέρματι ("that which is borne" in general) γᾶν πανώρωι (another hapax), is telling), 787–790, 796–799, 804–807, 1026–1029 (the Danaids calling upon the fertilising powers of the rivers of Argos), 1030–1033.

155 See, especially, *Supp.* 295–296, 300–301, 313, 315, 531–534, 571–573, 575–581 (in 580 ἕρμα Δῖον, Zeus' ballast (burden in her womb), aurally invokes σπέρμα Δῖον), 586–587, 1064–1067.

156 See Sommerstein 2010, 100–101.

157 Danaus and his daughters are offered accommodation both by the city and Pelasgus. "[I]t remains remarkable and somewhat disturbing that so much is made of th[is] point, yet the decision [about where they should stay] is never made". See Friis Johansen/Whittle 1980(III), 301. The question of accommodation is mentioned for the last time by Danaus in *Supp.* 1009–1011, and is set within the long speech with which he warns his daughters to guard their virginity. The indecisiveness about where to lodge could be associated with the safekeeping of the girls' virginity. See, further, Sommerstein 2019, 345.

158 These rather remarkable similarities in the structure of the plays make one tentatively suggest that the Danaid trilogy could have followed the reverse dramaturgical path of that in the *Oresteia*. That is, if *Supp.* is the first play (for the faint possibility to be the second see Sommerstein 2020), the trilogy would have opened with a drama of a threatening protagonist Chorus, such as *Eum.*, and closed with a drama of dominant characters, such as *Ag.* (Clytemnestra, Agamemnon, etc.); since, besides Danaus, "Lynceus, the surviving Aegyptiad, and Hypermestra, who spared him, are [also highly] likely to have had individual roles" in the *Danaids*. See Sommerstein 2019, 18.

6 Conclusions

In this chapter I have discussed the various facets of sexual imagery in Aeschylus, indicating how closely tied heterosexual intercourse is to the concept of agriculture and fertility in his work. Such sexual references in the surviving post-Aeschylean tragedy are rather rare, passing, and mostly not particularly bold. In Sophocles, and especially in Euripides, the sexual phrasing in agricultural terms is allusive (a form of generic decorum fit for tragedy), as it is in Aeschylus, but, unlike what is the case with Aeschylus, it functions more as a poetically "metabolised", largely decayed metaphor, with no actual agricultural significance.[159] According to duBois, "[i]n Sophocles [...] there is already tension, even crisis, about the equation of earth and body; [and] Euripides uses th[is] [agricultural intercourse] trope to refer to his literary predecessors, ostentatiously alluding to a cultural past and building an overcoded, stratified, self-conscious work".[160] As I have shown here, both Sophocles and Euripides were influenced by Aeschylus' poetic use of sexual imagery in agricultural terms. However, as far as one can know of course, none of them has shown any interest in advancing or expanding this kind of imagery beyond its Aeschylean form(s). This is plausibly due to the civic change in the equation of earth and body, but it is also certainly due to the decisive ground that Aeschylus had covered in treating this equation. Aeschylus, the poet famously "attacked" for having nothing to do with Aphrodite,[161] seems to have known well τὰν Ἀφροδίτας πολύπυρον αἶαν.[162] In the Aeschylean poetics of sexuality the female agricultural body is crucial. In ancient Greek thought γυνή is synonymous to γονή,[163] and an "emulator" of mother Earth.[164] In the Greek (male) mind, female sex drive is (or should be) entirely connected to procreation, male interests, action and control: female lust is an offence. Although this seems a risky generalisation, it can be said that in the modern world sexual intercourse can have two objectives: a direct, which is pleasure, and an indirect, which is

---

159 In fact, in *O.T.* 1208–1209 (see Finglass 2018, 533) Sophocles, along with an agricultural metaphor (see vv. 1210–1212), prominently alludes to sexual intercourse employing nautical imagery — a notion not unknown to Aeschylus though, see fr. 154a Radt 3. Unsurprisingly, nautical images are used in tragedy only for devastating, "wrecked" marriages.

160 duBois 1988, 82.

161 See Ar. *Fr.* 1045.

162 See *Supp.* 554–555. Cf. Soph. fr. 847 Radt.

163 See, e.g., Pl. *Crat.* 414a. "That men took wives mainly for the sake of begetting children [...] is frankly admitted by several Greek authors". See Licht 1932, 33. See also n. 6 above.

164 See, e.g., Pl. *Menex.* 238a.

reproduction. However, applied to the archaic-classical Greek world, and specifically to the Aeschylean universe, this division is misleading. In Aeschylus, heterosexual intercourse, in all its forms — mythologised, distorted, perverted even — is (always allusively expressed) mainly set within a linguistic-thematic (more or less knotty) context of agriculture: engendering new life. This wording, which became a cliché (entrenched in the tragic idiom), is in line with the prospects of a community for physical survival. On the contrary, the one homosexual narrative surviving in the Aeschylean corpus is overt, pointing to the actual pleasures of the body as a sexual object (of wail and woe) — telling of male social role(s) in archaic and classical Athens. In a nutshell, Aeschylus composed influential, though unmatchable, suggestive poetry, exploiting the (conceptual and linguistic) intersection of agriculture and sexual intercourse.

Bibliography

Allan, W. (2008), *Euripides:* Helen, Cambridge.

Allen-Hornblower, E. (2016), *From Agent to Spectator: Witnessing the Aftermath in Ancient Greek Epic and Tragedy* (TCSV 30), Berlin.

Bakola, E. (2019), 'Reconsidering the Chthonic in Aeschylus' *Oresteia*: Erinyes, the Earth's Resources and the Cosmic Order', in: A. Hunt/H. Marlow (eds.), *Ecology and Theology in the Ancient World,* London, 103–118.

Bardel, R. (2002), 'Eunuchizing Agamemnon: Clytemnestra, Agamemnon and Maschalismos, in: S. Tougher (ed.), *Eunuchs in Antiquity and Beyond*, London, 51–70.

Barrett, W.S. (1964), *Euripides:* Hippolytos, Oxford.

Barrett, W.S. (2007), *Greek Lyric, Tragedy, and Textual Criticism: Collected Papers* (Assembled and Edited by M.L. West), Oxford.

Boedeker, D. (1984), *Descent from Heaven: Images of Dew in Greek Poetry and Religion*, Chico, CA.

Braswell, B.K. (1988), *A Commentary on the* Fourth Pythian Ode *of Pindar*, Berlin.

Brockliss, W. (2018), 'Abject landscapes of the *Iliad*', in: D. Felton (ed.), *Landscapes of Dread in Classical Antiquity: Negative Emotion in Natural and Constructed Spaces*, London/New York, NY, 15–37.

Brøns, C. (2015), 'Textiles and Temple Inventories: Detecting an Invisible Votive Tradition in Greek Sanctuaries in the Second Half of the First Millennium BC', in: J. Fejfer/M. Moltesen/ A. Rathje (eds.), *Tradition: Transmission of Culture in the Ancient World* (*Danish Studies in Classical Archaeology, Acta Hyperborea* 14), Copenhagen, 43–83.

Bullough, V.L./Shelton, B./Slavin, S. (1988), *The Subordinated Sex: A History of Attitudes Toward Women*, Athens, GA/London.

Buxton, R.G.A. (1982), *Persuasion in Greek Tragedy: A Study of Peitho*, Cambridge.

Buxton, R.G.A. (2013), *Myths and Tragedies in their Ancient Greek Contexts*, Oxford.

Cairns, D.L. (1993), *Aidōs: The Psychology and Ethics of Honour and Shame in Ancient Greek Literature*, Oxford.

Carson, A. (1990), 'Putting Her in Her Place: Woman, Dirt, and Desire', in: D.M. Halperin/J.J. Winkler/F.I. Zeitlin (eds.), *Before Sexuality: The Construction of Erotic Experience in the Ancient Greek World*, Princeton, NJ, 135–169.

Churchill Semple, E. (1928), 'Ancient Mediterranean Agriculture: Part II. Manuring and Seed Selection', in: *Agricultural History* 2, 129–156.

Clark, I. (1998), 'The Gamos of Hera: Myth and Ritual', in: S. Blundell/M. Williamson (eds.), *The Sacred and the Feminane in Ancient Greece*, London.

Cleland, L./Davies, G./Llewellyn-Jones, L. (2007), *Greek and Roman Dress from A to Z*, London.

Cohen, D. (2004), 'Law, Society and Homosexuality in Classical Athens', in: R. Osborne (ed.), *Studies in Ancient Greek and Roman Society*, Cambridge, 61–77.

Collard, C./Cropp, M.J. (2008), *Euripides: Fragments*, vol. VII: Aegeus-Meleager & VIII: Oedipus-Chrysippus, Cambridge, MA.

Collard, C./Cropp, M.J./Lee, K.H. (2009), *Euripides: Selected Fragmentary Plays*, vol. I, Oxford.

Connelly, J.B. (2007), *Portrait of a Priestess*, Princeton, NJ.

Cook, A.B. (1914–40), *Zeus: A Study in Ancient Religion*, vol. I, II & III, Cambridge.

Cropp, M.J./Fick, G. (1985), *Resolutions and Chronology in Euripides: The Fragmentary Tragedies*, London.

Coward, T.R.P. (2016), 'The Robes of Alcman's and Pindar's *Parthenoi*', in: G. Fanfani/M. Harlow/M.-L. Nosch (eds.), *Spinning Fates and the Song of the Loom: The Use of Textiles, Clothing and Cloth Production as Metaphor, Symbol and Narrative Device in Greek and Latin Literature*, Oxford, 43–60.

Harlow/M.-L. Nosch (eds.) (2014), *Greek and Roman Textiles and Dress: An Interdisciplinary Anthology*, Oxford.

Das, N.R. (2018), *Practical Manual on Basic Agronomy*, Jodhpur.

Davidson, J. (2004), 'Dover, Foucault and Greek Homosexuality: Penetration and the Truth of Sex', in: R. Osborne (ed.), *Studies in Ancient Greek and Roman Society*, Cambridge, 78–118.

Davies, M. (1991), *Sophocles:* Trachiniae, Oxford.

Dawe, R.D. (2006), *Sophocles:* Oedipus Rex, Cambridge.

Demand, N. (1994), *Birth, Death, and Motherhood in Classical Greece*, Baltimore, MD.

Dhakar, R./Sarath Chandran, M.A./Nagar, S./Visha Kumari, V./Subbarao, A.V.M./Kumar Bal, S./ Kumar, P. (2018), 'Field Crop Response to Water Deficit Stress: Assessment Through Crop Models', in: S. Kumar Bal/J. Mukherjee/B. Uddin Choudhury/A. Kumar Dhawan (eds.), *Advances in Crop Environment Interaction*, Singapore, 287–316.

Dover, K.J. (1968), *Aristophanes:* Clouds, Oxford.

Dover, K.J. (1978), *Greek Homosexuality*, Cambridge MA.

duBois, P. (1988), *Sowing the Body: Psychoanalysis and Ancient Representations of Women*, Chicago, IL.

Easterling, P.E. (1982), *Sophocles:* Trachiniae, Cambridge.

Edgeworth, R.J. (1988), '*Saffron-Colored* Terms in Aeschylus', in: *Glotta* 66, 179–182.

Elderkin, G.W. (1937), 'The Marriage of Zeus and Hera and Its Symbol', in: *American Journal of Archaeology* 41, 424–435.

Fantuzzi, M. (2012), *Achilles in Love: Intertextual Studies*, Oxford.

Finglass, P.J. (2007), *Sophocles:* Electra, Cambridge.

Finglass, P.J. (2018), *Sophocles:* Oedipus the King, Cambridge.

Fletcher, J. (2007), 'The Virgin Choruses of Aeschylus', in: B. MacLachlan/J. Fletcher (eds.), *Virginity Revisited: Configurations of the Unpossessed Body*, Toronto, 24–39.

Foley, H.P. (2001), *Female Acts in Greek Tragedy*, Princeton, NJ.

Foucault, M. (1978) (transl. R. Hurley), *The History of Sexuality: An Introduction*, vol. I, New York NY.

Fraenkel, E. (1950), *Aeschylus:* Agamemnon, vol. I, II & III, Oxford.

Friedrich, W.H. (1953), *Euripides und Diphilos: zur Dramaturgie der Spätformen*, Munich.

Fries, A. (2014), *Pseudo-Euripides*, Rhesus, Berlin.

Garland, R. (1990), *The Greek Way of Life—from conception to old age*, London.

Garvie, A.F. (1986), *Aeschylus:* Choephori, Oxford.

Garvie, A.F. (2006), *Aeschylus'* Supplices: *Play and Trilogy*, Bristol.

Garvie, A.F. (2009), *Aeschylus:* Persae, Oxford.

Geoffrey Arnott, W. (1996), *Alexis: The Fragments*, Cambridge.

Gerber, D.E. (1999), *Greek Lyric Poetry from the Seventh to the Fifth Centuries BC*, Cambridge, MA.

Golden, M. (1988), 'Male Chauvinists and Pigs', in: *Echos du Monde Classique/Classical Views* 32, 1–12.

Goldhill, S. (1984a), 'Two Notes on τέλος and Related Words in the *Oresteia*', in: *The Journal of Hellenic Studies* 104, 169–176.

Goldhill, S. (1984b), *Language, Sexuality, Narrative: The* Oresteia, Cambridge.

Gottschall, J. (2008), *The Rape of Troy: Evolution, Violence, and the World of Homer*, Cambridge.

Green, A. (1979) (transl. A. Sheridan), *The Tragic Effect: The Oedipus Complex in Tragedy*, Cambridge.

Griffith, M. (1999), *Sophocles:* Antigone, Cambridge.

Guthrie, W.K.C. (1954), *The Greeks and their Gods*, Boston, MA.

Håland, E.J. (2017), *Greek Festivals, Modern and Ancient: A Comparison of Female and Male Values*, Newcastle-upon-Tyne.

Henderson, J. (1975), *The Maculate Muse: Obscene Language in Attic Comedy*, Oxford.

Herington, J. (1986), 'The Marriage of Earth and Sky in Aeschylus' *Agamemnon* 1388–1392', in: M. Cropp/E. Fantham /S.E. Scully (eds.), *Greek Tragedy and its Legacy: Essays presented to D.J. Conacher*, Calgary, 27–33.

Hong, Y. (2012), 'Collaboration and Conflict: Discourses of Maternity in Hippocratic Gynecology and Embryology', in: L. Hackworth Petersen/P. Salzman-Mitchell (eds.), *Mothering and Motherhood in Ancient Greece and Rome*, Austin TX, 71–96.

Hussain, I./Sakthivadivel, R./Amarasinghe, U. (2003), 'Land and Water Productivity of Wheat in the Western Indo-Gangetic Plains of India and Pakistan: A Comparative Analysis', in: J.W. Kijne/R. Barker/D. Molden (eds.), *Water Productivity in Agriculture: Limits and Opportunities for Improvement*, Oxford/Cambridge, MA, 255–272.

Hutchinson, G.O. (1985), *Aeschylus:* Septem Contra Thebas, Oxford.

Johnston, P.G. (2020), 'The Women of Thebes as Aeschylean Erinyes: The First Messenger Speech of Euripides' *Bacchae*', in: H. Marshall/C.W. Marshall (eds.), *Greek Drama V: Studies in the Theatre of the Fifth and Fourth Centuries BCE*, London, 129–135.

Jouan, F./van Looy, H. (2002), *Euripide: Tragédies*, vol. VIII.2: de Bellérophon à Protésilas & vol. VIII.3: de De Sthénébée à Chrysippos, Paris.

Kapparis, K. (2018), *Prostitution in the Ancient Greek World*, Berlin.

Keen, A.G. (2005), 'Lycians in the *Cares* of Aeschylus', in: F. McHardy/J. Robson/D. Harvey (eds.), *Lost Dramas of Classical Athens: Greek Tragic Fragments*, Exeter.

Larson, J. (2012), *Greek and Roman Sexualities: A Sourcebook*, London/New York, NY.

Lear, A. (2015), 'Was Pederasty Problematized? A Diachronic View', in: M. Masterson/N. Sorkin Rabinowitz/J. Robson (eds.), *Sex in Antiquity: Exploring Gender and Sexuality in the Ancient World*, London/New York, NY, 115–136.

Lear, A./Cantarella, E. (2008), *Images of Ancient Greek Pederasty: Boys Were their Gods*, London/New York, NY.

Lebeck, A. (1971), *The Oresteia: A Study in Language and Structure*, Washington, DC.

Lee, M.M. (2015), *Body, Dress, and Identity in Ancient Greece*, Cambridge.

Leitao, D.D. (2018), 'Achilles in Love: Politics and Desire in Aeschylus' *Myrmidons*', in L. Pratt/ M. Sampson (eds.), *Engaging Classical Texts in the Contemporary World: From Narratology to Reception*, Ann Arbor, MI, 51–70.

Licht, H. (1932), *Sexual Life in Ancient Greece*, London.

Llewellyn-Jones, L. (2003), *Aphrodite's Tortoise: The Veiled Woman of Ancient Greece*, Swansea.

Lloyd-Jones, H. (1996), *Sophocles: Fragments*, Cambridge, MA.

Lovano, M. (2019), *The World of Ancient Greece: A Daily Life Encyclopedia*, vol. I, Santa Barbara, CA.

Mallory, J.P./Adams, D.Q. (2006), *The Oxford Introduction to Proto-Indo-European and the Proto-Indo-European World*, Oxford.

Manousakis, N./Stamatatos, E. (2018), 'Devising *Rhesus*: A strange "Collaboration" Between Aeschylus and Euripides', *Digital Scholarship in the Humanities* 33, 347–361.

Manousakis, N. (2019), 'The stray charioteer: Athletic connotations in the shaping of tragic Orestes', in: J.C. Moretti/P. Valavanis (eds.), *Les hippodromes et les concours hippiques dans la Grèce antique (BCH Supplément 62)*, 233–241.

Manousakis, N. (2020a), 'Aeschylus' Actaeon: A Playboy on the Greek Tragic Stage', in: A. Lamari/F. Montanari/A. Novokhatko (eds.), *Fragmentation in Ancient Greek Drama* (TCSV 84), Berlin, 201–233.

Manousakis, N. (2020b), 'Aesch. fr. 13 Radt: A Sexual Pun?', in: *Logeion* 10, 160–167.

Manousakis, N. (2020c), Prometheus Bound: *A Separate Authorial Trace in the Aeschylean Corpus* (TCSV 98), Berlin.

Martin, B. (2020), *Harmful Interaction Between the Living and the Dead in Greek Tragedy*, Liverpool.

Martin, D.L./Gershuny, G. (1992), *The Rodale Book of Composting: Easy Methods for Every Gardener*, Emmaus, PA.

Mastronarde, D.J. (1994), *Euripides:* Phoenissae, Cambridge.

Matthiae, A. (1829), *Euripides: Tragoediae et Fragmenta*, vol. IX, Leipzig.

Medda, E. (2017), *Eschilo:* Agamennone, vol. I & II, Rome.

Michael, A.M. (2014), 'Irrigation Requirements of Common Crop', in: S. Bihari Verma/A. Kumar Shrivastawa/J. Kumar Jha (eds.), *Irrigation Resources*, New Delhi, 31–57.

Michelakis, P. (2002), *Achilles in Greek Tragedy*, Cambridge.

Milo, D. (2020), 'Euripide, fr. 898 Kn.: la forza generatrice di Afrodite', in: L. Austa (in collaboration with G. Giaccardi/F.P. Bianchi) (ed.), *The Forgotten Theatre II: Mitologia, drammaturgia e tradizione del dramma frammentario greco-romano (Atti del secondo convegno internazionale sul dramma antico frammentario, Università di Torino, 28–30 Nov. 2018)*, Baden-Baden, 77–97.

Moreau, A. (1996), 'Eschyle et les Tranches des Repas d'Homère: La Trilogie d'Achille', in: *Cahiers du GITA 9 (Panorama du Théâtre Antique)*, 3–29.

Most, G.W. (2006), *Hesiod:* Theogony, Works and Days, Testimonia, Cambridge, MA.

Murray, A.T. (1999), *Homer:* Iliad, vol. I & II, Cambridge, MA.

Nooter, S. (2017), *The Mortal Voice in the Tragedies of Aeschylus*, Oxford.

Oakley, J.H./Sinos, R.H. (1993), *The Wedding in Ancient Athens,* Madison, WI.

O'Daly, G.J.P. (1985), 'Clytemnestra and the Elders: Dramatic Technique in Aeschylus, *Agamemnon* 1372–1576', in: *Museum Helveticum* 42, 1–19.

Olson, S.D. (2004), *Aristophanes:* Acharnians, Oxford.

Page, D. (1972), *Aeschyli: Septem Quae Supersunt Tragoedias*, Oxford.

Parker, H.N. (2015), 'Vaseworld: Depiction and Description of Sex at Athens', in: R. Blondell/K. Ormand (eds.), *Ancient Sex: New Essays*, Columbus, OH, 23–142.

Parker, L.P.E. (2016), *Euripides:* Iphigenia in Tauris, Oxford.

Peck, A.L. (1970), *Aristotle:* Historia Animalium, vol. II, Cambridge.

Podlecki, A.J. (2005), 'Aiskhylos Satyrikos', in: G.W.M. Harrison (ed.), *Satyr Drama Tragedy at Play*, Swansea, 1–19.

Pulleyn, S. (1997), 'Erotic Undertones in the Language of Clytemnestra', in: *The Classical Quarterly* 47, 565–567.

Poole, W. (1990), 'Male Homosexuality in Euripides', in: A. Powell (ed.), *Euripides, Women, and Sexuality*, London, 108–150.

Raeburn, D./Thomas, O. (2011), *The* Agamemnon *of Aeschylus*, Oxford.

Race, W.H. (1997), *Pindar: Nemean Odes, Isthmian Odes, Fragments*, Cambridge, MA

Redfield, J. (1982), 'Notes on the Greek Wedding', in: *Arethusa* 15—*Texts & Contexts: American Classical Studies in Honor of J.-P. Vernant*, 181–201.

Rehm, R. (2002), *The Play of Space: Spatial Transformation in Greek Tragedy*, Princeton, NJ.

Rosenbloom, D. (2018), 'The Comedians' Aeschylus', in: R. Futo Kennedy (ed.), *Brill's Companion to the Reception of Aeschylus*, Leiden, 54–87.

Rosenzweig, R. (2004), *Worshipping Aphrodite: Art and Cult in Classical Athens*, Ann Arbor, MI.

Rynearson, N. (2013), 'Courting the Erinyes: Persuasion, Sacrifice, and Seduction in Aeschylus's *Eumenides*', in: *Transactions of the American Philological Association* 143, 1–22.

Salviat, F. (1964), 'Les Théogamies Attiques, Zeus Teleios et l'*Agamemnon* d'Eschyle', in: *Bulletin de Correspondance Hellénique* 88, 647–654.

Seaford, R. (1987), 'The Tragic Wedding', in: *Journal of Hellenic Studies* 107, 106–130 (= Seaford 2018, 257–299).

Seaford, R. (2012), *Cosmology and the Polis: The Social Construction of Space and Time in the Tragedies of Aeschylus*, Cambridge.

Seaford, R. (2018), *Tragedy, Ritual and Money in Ancient Greece: Selected Essays edited with a Foreword by R. Bostock*, Cambridge.

Sealey, R. (1990), *Women and Law in Classical Greece*, Chapel Hill.

Sells, D. (2019), *Parody, Politics and the Populace in Greek Old Comedy*, London.

Silver, M. (2018), *Slave-Wives, Single Women and "Bastards" in the Ancient Greek World: Law and Economics Perspectives*, Oxford/Havertown, PA.

Simas, A. (2020), 'Aeschylus and the Iconography of the Erinyes', in: H. Marshall/C.W. Marshall (eds.), *Greek Drama V: Studies in the Theatre of the Fifth and Fourth Centuries BCE*, London, 145–160.

Simpson, S./McLeod, H. (2013), *Uprisings: A Hands-on Guide to the Community Grain Revolution*, Gabriola Island.

Sissa, G. (1990a) (transl. A. Goldhammer), *Greek Virginity*, Cambridge, MA/London.

Sissa, G. (1990b), 'Maidenhood Without Maidenhead: The Female Body in Ancient Greece', in: D.M. Halperin/J.J. Winkler/F.I. Zeitlin (eds.), *Before Sexuality: The Construction of Erotic Experience in the Ancient Greek World*, Princeton, NJ, 339–364.

Sissa, G. (2013), 'The hymen is a problem, still. Virginity, Imperforation, and Contraception, from Greece to Rome', in: *EuGeStA: Journal of Gender Studies in Antiquity* 3, 67–123.

Slenders, W. (2005), 'Λέξις Ερωτική in Euripides' *Cyclops*', in: G.W.M. Harrison (ed.), *Satyr Drama—Tragedy at Play*, Swansea, 39–52.

Sommerstein, A.H. (1989), *Aeschylus:* Eumenides, Cambridge.

Sommerstein, A.H. (1990), *Aristophanes:* Lysistrata, Warminster.

Sommerstein, A.H. (2002), 'Comic Elements in Tragic Language: The Case of Aeschylus' *Oresteia*', in: A. Willi (ed.), *The Language of Greek Comedy*, Oxford, 151–168.

Sommerstein, A.H. (2008a), *Aeschylus:* Persians, Seven Against Thebes, Suppliants, Prometheus Bound, Cambridge, MA.

Sommerstein, A.H. (2008b), *Aeschylus'* Oresteia: Agamemnon, Libation Bearers, Eumenides, Cambridge, MA.

Sommerstein, A.H. (2008c), *Aeschylus:* Fragments, Cambridge, MA.

Sommerstein, A.H. (2010), *The Tangled Ways of Zeus and other studies in and around Greek Tragedy*, Oxford.

Sommerstein, A.H. (2019), *Aeschylus:* Suppliants, Cambridge.

Sommerstein, A.H. (2020), 'Revisiting the Danaid Trilogy', in: A. Lamari/F. Montanari/A.Novokhatko (eds.), *Fragmentation in Ancient Greek Drama* (TCSV 84), Berlin, 155–164.

Stafford, E. (2000), *Worshipping Virtues: Personification and the Divine in Ancient Greece*, London.

Stehle, E. (1997), *Performance and Gender in Ancient Greece: Nondramatic Poetry in its Setting*, Princeton, NJ.

Stehle, E. (2012), 'Women and Religion in Greece', in: S.L. James/S. Dillon (eds.), *A Companion to Women in the Ancient World*, Oxford, 191–203.

Stevens, J. (1999), *Reproducing the State*, Princeton, NJ.

Storey, I.C. (2019), *Aristophanes:* Peace, London.

Thomson, G. (1965), *Studies in Ancient Greek Society: The Prehistoric Aegean*, New York, NY.

Thorton, B.S. (1997), *Eros: The Myth of Ancient Greek Sexuality*, Boulder.

Torrance, I. (2019), *Euripides:* Iphigenia among the Taurians, London.

Tsantsanoglou, K. (2020), 'παῖς μάργος', in: A. Lamari/F. Montanari/A. Novokhatko (eds.), *Fragmentation in Ancient Greek Drama* (TCSV 84), Berlin, 183–199.

Van Nortwick, T. (2008), *Imagining Men: Ideals of Masculinity in Ancient Greek Culture*, London.

Wagner-Hasel, B. (2002), 'The Graces and Colour Weaving', in: L. Llewellyn-Jones (ed.), *Women's Dress in the Ancient Greek World*, London, 17–32.

Wagner-Hasel, B. (2010), 'The Veil and Other Textiles at Weddings in Ancient Greece', in: L. Larsson Lovén/A. Strömberg (eds.), *Ancient Marriage in Myth and Reality*, Newcastle, 102–121.

Walker, A.E. (1997), *The Menstrual Cycle*, London/New York, NY.

Webster, T.B.L. (1967), *The Tragedies of Euripides*, London.

West, M.L. (1966), *Hesiod:* Theogony, Oxford.

West, M.L. (1990a), *Aeschyli Tragoediae: cum incerti poetae* Prometheo, Stuttgart.

West, M.L. (1990b), *Studies in Aeschylus*, Stuttgart.

West, M.L. (2000), '*Iliad* and *Aethiopis* on the Stage: Aeschylus and Son', in: *The Classical Quarterly* 50, 338–352.

Wohl, V. (1998), *Intimate Commerce: Exchange, Gender, and Subjectivity in Greek Tragedy*, Austin, TX.

Wright, M. (2019), *The Lost Plays of Greek Tragedy: Aeschylus, Sophocles and Euripides,* vol. II, London.

Zeitlin, F.I. (1966), 'Postscript to Sacrificial Imagery in the *Oresteia* (*Ag*. 1235–37)', in: *Transactions and Proceedings of the American Philological Association* 97, 645–653.

Dimitrios Kanellakis
Seminal Figures: Aristophanes and the Tradition of Sexual Imagery

Abstract: This chapter surveys Aristophanes' use of farming and sailing imagery in describing sex and politics, in the light of the literary tradition of such metaphors, and promotes an ironic/pessimistic reading of *Peace*. Agricultural imagery facilitates the fusion of erotic and political meanings because Hesiod had already established such a paradigm, which carried negative connotations. In *Peace* Aristophanes builds on that tradition to warn his audience about the risks of the forthcoming Nician treaty — a warning veiled in cheerful, pornographic comic business. At the same time, naval metaphors are more one-sided in Aristophanes, either sexual or political because there was no literary precedent for combining the two threads. Yet, both with farming and sailing imagery, Aristophanes crosses the limits between mental visualisation (imagining a metaphor) and optical perception (staging a metaphor).

1 Introduction

Visuality in classical literature has gained immense popularity among scholars in the past two decades, from ancient theories of vision to the theme of sight and blindness, and from ancient ophthalmology to the experience of reading and watching drama.[1] This chapter is concerned with the latter aspect, particularly with how Aristophanes exploited the contemporary visual tradition on sex. This tradition, and the visual culture of the ancient Greeks in general, is evidenced not only through the iconography of archaeological artefacts, but also through non-material iconography, that is, through literary imagery. In fact, the latter may be considered a more inclusive testimony of the ancients' visual aesthetics, in the sense that words are a non-restrictive material in contrast to clay or marble.[2] From

---

[1] To restrict myself to monographs and volumes pertinent to drama, see Kampakoglou/Novokhatko 2018, 163–242, Petrides 2014, Harrison/Liapis 2013, Meineck 2011, Kraus/Goldhill/Foley/ Elsner 2007.
[2] This verdict might seem inspired by G.E. Lessing, for whom "painting is inferior: it is hampered by the nature of its signs and their limited syntax. Poetry [on the contrary] relies on an advanced stage of semiosis and is therefore closer to the imagination, which is more central to

https://doi.org/10.1515/9783110695793-018

a linguistic point of view too, literary imagery constitutes part of the visual culture since words are "acoustic images".[3] Based on this premise, I aim to explore sex-related figurative speech and how this is enacted, i.e. performed in front of an audience, in Aristophanes' comedies. Specifically, the focus is on farming and sailing imagery as used to describe sex — a kind of imagery also attested in pottery — and the argument that the dramatist occasionally pursues a connection to the political nuances of such imagery.[4] This chapter is intended as a methodological exercise, tracing the possible intersection of a given metaphor's different meanings in light of its literary tradition, rather than a detailed reading on Aristophanes.

2 *Farmer Wants a Wife* and *The Love Boat*

As the catchy titles of these television shows illustrate, farming and sailing are popular symbols of eros in the industry of entertainment — and so were they in ancient Greece, with special application to sexual intercourse. This kind of imagery had a long literary tradition, which reasonably influenced Greek drama and whose most important traces we shall overview before turning to Aristophanes.

The use of farming imagery to describe sex first appears in Hesiod.[5] "Spreading himself out around Earth in his desire for love, Ouranos lay outstretched in

---

aesthetic appreciation than sensual perception": Grethlein 2017, 30. This classification has received extensive criticism (see Squire 2009, 15–195) but still holds truth as far as my subject matter is concerned: "pictorial representation is itself a visual mode of metaphor [...thus] it is not possible [...] to construct a *particular* metaphor [...whereas] meaning in literary language — indeed language itself — does not have an intrinsically metaphorical structure. Rather, metaphorical expression is *one* use to which language *can be put* [...] which allows particular metaphors [...] to be constructed": Crowther 2003, 90–91.

3 Saussure 2011[=1916], 66–67. In her typology of images in tragedy, Chaston 2010, 17–30 distinguishes between visually perceived and mental/verbal images; on the former category she includes characters and objects on stage; on the latter, references to non-present objects, *ekphrasis,* and "perhaps most importantly" figurative language.

4 Of course, these metaphors also stood for other concepts, e.g. farming for teaching (Pl. *Tht.* 149e2–4; *Phdr.* 276e5–277a4), suing someone (Pl. *Euthph.* 2d–3a) or wining an argument (Ar. *Ves.* 634); sailing for dealing with sorrows (Soph. *El.* 335), joining a fight (Od. *Il.* 422–428), arguing with the appropriate temper (Ar. *Eq.* 756–761, *Ran.* 994–1003), launching a plan (Aesch. *Supp.* 440–442) or suffering a miasma (Soph. *OT* 22–24).

5 Homer only makes implicit analogies: *Il.* 14.346–349, *Od.* 5.125–128; DuBois 1988, 40, 49. See also Manousakis in this volume.

all directions";[6] but their son Kronos reaps his father's genitalia with a monstrous sickle in an act of retribution for Ouranos' suppressing Earth's parturitions (*Theog.* 176–181). Raining, for which Ouranos is a metonymy, is a metaphor for ejaculation while harvesting a means of overthrowing the sexual and political leader. That the son overthrows his father by plot, like Zeus will do later, follows a historically familiar pattern in tyrants' succession. The farming metaphor became particularly popular in tragedy, often denoting patricide like in Hesiod.[7] In *Seven against Thebes*, Oedipus, explicitly called a patricide, is described as someone "who sowed the sacrosanct soil of his mother" (752–756).[8] In *Oedipus Rex*, the chorus in despair asks the protagonist "how could the field your father sowed put up with you so long in silence?" (1210). The field is Jocasta's vagina of course, a "field that has yielded two harvests" (1256).[9] In *Phoenician Women*, Apollo advises Laius: "do not keep sowing the child-begetting furrow against the gods' will; if you sire a son, your own offspring will kill you" (18–19). In *Trachiniae*, Dieaneira says that she and Hercules had "children, whom he, like a farmer who has taken over a remote piece of ploughland, regards only when he sows and when he reaps" (31–33). In all these cases farming stands for procreative sex within marriage, which inevitably implies a sense of ownership over the female body.[10] This sense comes to the foreground in *Antigone*, when Creon is asked how he can kill his son's fiancée and replies "well, there are other furrows that can be ploughed!" (569). Here the implication of bearing children comes second; first and foremost, ploughing is a metaphor for what we may call sex of dominance,

---

6 Unless otherwise specified, the translations are from the Loeb series, slightly adapted.

7 "The metaphor of sowing the female body is active in Pindar's time in the aristocratic, even antidemocratic, circles [...but] one of the most powerful challenges to the earth/body metaphor comes through tragedy, itself a product and a producer of democracy. If the woman's body is like the earth [...] then how can she speak?": DuBois 1988, 63, 68–69.

8 For more Aeschylean examples see Manousakis in this volume, who argues that Aeschylus more or less exhausted the full potential of the agrarian metaphor; Sophocles and Euripides — and Aristophanes, as it will be shown here — did not attempt any radical expansion of it.

9 For Oedipus as sower and Jocasta as furrow, see DuBois 1988, 74–78.

10 "The language of formal Greek betrothal [*engyēsis*] makes it clear that production of children was the purpose of marriage. [...] It was natural to describe the male progenitor as sower in a language where *sperma* could refer to the seed of both plants and animals, and *gone*, 'offspring', was used for children as well as for the fruit of the earth": Cole 2004, 153–154. Cf. Eur. *Or.* 552–553: "My father engendered me, and my mother, ploughland receiving the seed from another, gave me birth"; see Vernant 2006, 171–172. This assimilation exceeded literature; "the same tests used by farmers to measure moisture of the soil were used [by Hippocratic practitioners] to test female moisture. [...] One of the most striking types of recommendations advised both oral and internal application of animal excrement and/or urine": Cole 2004, 162, 169.

like in *Theogony*. Same with a mocking epigram by Sophocles, where the farmer is not the husband but the adulterer: "You're not so clever, Euripides, if you blame Eros for stealing clothes while you're sowing another man's field" (fr. eleg. 4.3–4 West). Despite the cheerful tone here, the nuances of farming *per se* are negative in all examples.[11]

Sailing imagery as a metaphor for eros was already used by Homer, in the scene where Penelope recognises Odysseus. The development of the simile is surprising: like a castaway who finally reaches the coast and rejoices, who has lost his ship in the storm and his skin is crusted with brine, but who eventually is safe and sound... so did Odysseus — we would expect — reach Penelope. And yet, it is Penolope who is compared to the happy castaway who finally finds her harbour, her man (*Od.* 23.233–240). In a homoerotic skolion by Pindar, whoever looks the boy Theoxenus in the eyes is "tossed on the waves of desire" (fr. 123.4 S-M, transl. Hubbard).[12] But for sex *per se* we need turn to Theognis (457–460 and 1361–1362):

> A young wife is not suitable for an old husband.
> For she is like a boat that does not obey the rudder,
> nor do the anchors hold. She breaks her moorings
> and often finds another harbour at night.

> You've lost my love, boy, like a ship that has struck a rock,
> and you've grasped a rotten rope.

In the first passage the harbour represents the man, like in the *Odyssey*, but unlike the *Odyssey* here many men are the harbour of the lascivious wife, who is a ship out of control. In the second passage a boy is the ship — in both cases the ship is the passive partner. For some unspecified reason, the *erastēs* has lost his interest in the *erōmenos* and pays him back (ἀντελάβου) with a rotten rope, that is, with a flaccid penis. Therefore, in contrast to Homer, naval metaphors in Theognis denote anything but a healthy relationship. The same is true, although with

---

11 Cf. Sappho fr. 105a L-P, where a ripe bride is compared to a sweet-apple ignored by the apple reapers, i.e. by suitors. Even though the poem praises the bride, the metaphor itself objectifies the woman who "was expected to play a passive role in marriage": Griffith 1989, 59. I have not included this passage to my main discussion, as it portrays marriage rather than sex *per se*, even though Winkler 1990, 183 maintains that "we can gather this ['clitoral'] sense not only from the general erotic meaning of 'apples' but from the location of the solitary apple high up on the bare branches of a tree, and from its sweetness and colour". For the imagery of sexual ripeness see Carson 1990, 145–148; Segal 1981, 25–26. For physical attraction through farming imagery, cf. Xen. *Symp.* 8.25.

12 The poem also features erotic, not explicitly sexual, farming imagery: "One must pluck loves, my heart, in due season and at the proper age", 1.

a gruesome effect, of the famous choral from *Oedipus Rex*: "Ah famous Oedipus, the same wide harbour served both you son and your father, to lie [πεσεῖν] on your bridal bed!" (1207–1209). The infinitive is momentous, since the verb πίπτω is used for sleeping (*Il.* 23.209), falling in love (Soph. *Ant.* 782), having sex (Eur. fr. 138 *TrGF*), delivering a baby (*Il.* 19.110) and for sea-fight (*Il.* 13.742). In contrast to Homer and Theognis, the woman is the harbour here.[13]

Such imagery also drew on iconographic tradition. On the side of erotic farming, the most famous vase is an Attic pelike which depicts a woman cultivating a garden of *phalloi*; the scene could be a ritual of fertility from the Thesmophoria or the Haloa, or a mere visual joke about women's delight in the *phallus*, equivalent to the jokes of Old Comedy;[14] what is different from most literary treatments is that a woman is the agent here **(Fig. 41)**. The application of farming imagery to both heterosexual *and* pederastic sex is evidenced in an Attic kylix featuring an orgy set at the symposium, which is represented symbolically by vines; the vase is essentially "a dictionary of sexual positions".[15] In a reverse manner, i.e. with agriculture as the literal referent, an Attic amphora depicts a grape-picking scene which alludes to pederasty; the adult man holding the sickle seems to pay attention to the boy's prominent genitals rather than his job **(Fig. 42)**.[16] On the side of erotic sailing, the most characteristic example is an Attic cup showing two similar Dionysian phallic processions; in both scenes a large the *komast* statue and an enormous *phallus* are set on a horizontal base carried by naked porters; that horizontal base is probably a keel representing Dionysus' sacred ship[17] and the *phallus* is swinging on ropes between the legs of *komast*, so as to appear like "the phallus of another and the rite has more than a suggestion of passive homosexuality" **(Fig. 43)**.[18] Two implicitly sexual images are found on a lekythos which depicts Eros holding a boat miniature in front of Aphrodite **(Fig. 44)** and on a stamnos which shows the ship of Odysseus passing the Sirens and, on the other side,

---

13 For an overview of "the sea of love" in both Greek and Latin from archaic to late antiquity, see Murgatroyd 1995; Aristophanes and other comic poets receive special treatment, but tragedy is ignored. A shorter compilation in Kahlmeyer 1934, 22–26 and Thornton 1997, 35–37. For Jocasta as harbour: Campbell 1986, 118.

14 Parker 2005, 289.

15 Lear/Cantarella 2008, 111 on Berlin, Antikensammlung F1798 (www.scalarchives.com/web/dettaglio_immagine_adv.asp?idImmagine=B012378). "The 'orgies' among the vines [...] are showing us not how or where the Greek had sex but what the Greeks thought about sex": Parker 2015, 103.

16 Dover 1978, pl. B470.

17 Boardman 1958, 7.

18 Csapo 1997, 274.

a group of Erotes — the foremost inscribed Ἵμερος — flying over water and bearing courting-gifts **(Fig. 45)**; "As emblems, even embodiments of sexuality, the Erotes offer the comforting fulfilment of [...] temporary satisfaction".[19] These examples demonstrate that material iconography may capture poetic and indeed comic imagery **(Fig. 41)** and relevant performing practices **(Fig. 43)**, hence constituting a useful guide for visualising Aristophanes' stagecraft.

3 In the field of politics

My aim is to argue that the comic dramatist followed these figurative conventions to speak of sex and present it on stage, but also that he employed the political semiology of farming and sailing imagery and occasionally blended it with their sexual semiology. An overview of the political tradition of such imagery is thus necessary.

We may seek the roots of farming metaphors for politics in Herodotus. The historian asserts, for example, that Peisistratus' tyranny was abolished because it was not "well rooted" (1.60). He also tells the story of Thrasybulus tyrant of Miletus who, wanting to show how tyrants should govern their cities, went into a field and cut off the tallest ears of wheat until he destroyed the best and richest part of the crop; the advice is clear: slay the outstanding men (5.92). Euripides repeats the story (*Supp.* 449) and so does Aristotle (*Pol.* 1284a). The latter emphasises that oligarchies and democracies too have their way of discarding prominent men, through ostracism. But even there, farming imagery comes to underline the tyrannical aspect of democracy rather than the democratic aspect of tyranny. On the fine line between democracy and tyranny, Plato says that "when a tyrant flourishes, he sprouts from the roots of leadership [that the people have assigned] and from no other source" (*Res.* 565c–d). Only once, to my knowledge, does farming imagery stand in a positive way: at the end of *Eumenides*, Athena promises to "cherish like a gardener" the Athenian people (911–912); the figure of a female farmer would be radical within this tradition, were Athena not a masculinised goddess.[20] Since autochthony was a constitutional myth for the Athenians, it is no surprise that they used land as metaphor for their state affairs.

---

19 Benson 1995, 418.
20 For the politician-farmer, see Brock 2013, 193 n. 175.

Sailing imagery floods the Homeric epics but is mostly used in a literal way.[21] In a metaphorical way, storm imagery with a political sense is first found in Archilochus (fr. 105W):

> Look, Glaucus! Already waves are disturbing the deep sea
> and a cloud stands straight round about the heights of Gyrae,
> a sign of storm; from the unexpected comes fear.

Heraclitus who cites this poem (*Alleg. Hom.* 5.3) acknowledges that the storm is an allegory for a coming war, presumably the Lelaltine War.[22] Heraclitus next cites Alcaeus' so-called "ship of state" allegory (fr. 326 L-P):

> I fail to understand the direction [στάσιν] of the winds:
> one wave rolls in from this side,
> another from that, and we in the middle
> are carried along in company with our black ship,
> much distressed in the great storm...

The word *stasis*, "the direction of the winds" but also "the uprising", necessitates a political reading. In contrast to Archilochus, the focus is on the ship, i.e. on the city, rather than on the storm, which here symbolises the interior conflicts of Mytelene.[23] Same with fragment 6 L-P, which not only describes the storm but also suggests ways forward, as if Alcaeus is the captain:

> ... Let us strengthen (the ship's sides) as quickly as possible,
> and let us race into a secure harbour;
> and let soft fear not seize any of us;
> for a great (ordeal) stands clear before us.
> Remember the previous (hardship):
> now let every man show himself steadfast...

The storm again is the internal troubles in Lesbos, the tyranny of Melagrus and then of Pittacus. We should not be misled by Alcaeus' use of "we" in this poem: it is not a call for democracy, but for Alcaeus' own aristocratic circle to take over. Challenging the aristocratic *status quo* is catastrophic for Theognis: "they have

---

21 Brock 2013 does not find any traces in epic either (53, 59). In his excellent account of the "ship of state" allegory (53–65), it is suggested that the ship of state is "not a trireme, a warship, but a merchantman", 60.

22 Cf. Archil. fr. 213W: "and this too when we have the city in the embrace of the waves".

23 Metaphors aside, *stasis* is also linked to farming. Thucydides claims that the fertility of the land is a key-cause of *stasis*, as it enables the aggrandisement of individuals, whereas the infertility of the soil prevents it; see Serafim 2020, 688–689.

deposed the noble helmsman who skilfully kept watch...; the porters rule and the base are above the noble. I'm afraid that perhaps a wave will swallow the ship..." (667–682). To avoid such social disorder, Pindar advises Hieron tyrant of Syracuse to guide his people "with a rudder of justice" (*Pyth*. 1.86). In tragedy too the storm stands for war or internal conflicts. In *Seven Against Thebes*, Thebes is said to have survived the storm, i.e. the attack by Polynices whose army "is like a roaring land-wave" (64), without a leak: "the city has let no water into her hull" (795). In *Ajax*, Menelaus condemns Ajax's arrogance and disobedience, behaviours which make a "well-sailing city sink to the bottom" (1083). In Euripides' *Suppliant Women*, Creon warns Theseus that Thebes could raise a heavy storm, i.e. a war against Athens (473–475). In all cases the metaphors create the feeling of a pressing threat and, from an ideological point of view, echo the elitist tradition of archaic lyric. Thus in *Agamemnon*, Aegisthus arrogantly rebukes the chorus: "You talk like that, you sitting down there at the oar, when it is those on the poopdeck who command the ship?" (1617–1618). The most elaborate application of sailing imagery to politics is Plato's *Republic* (6.488–489): the ship's rudder is left in the hands of incompetent commanders while philosophers, the only true captains, are neglected by the uneducated crew. We read nothing about a storm, which suggests that Plato is primarily concerned with a state's everyday function, rather than with individual crises. This innovation aside, Plato aligns himself with the ideology of the imagery: in Alcaeus and in tragedy Plato found very convenient, aristocracy-friendly poetic language to promote his own elitist ideas.[24]

This overview has suggested the similarities between the sexual and the political meanings, that is, the background which allowed Aristophanes to pursue their connection. The way in which Hesiod used farming imagery to speak of sex, and implicitly of the political antagonism between Cronos and Uranus, evidently determined the subsequent uses of such imagery on both sides: whether describing intercourse or politics, farming metaphors remained linked with patricide, revenge, suppression and male dominance. Even the positive and quasi-female case of Athena in *Eumenides* repeats the stereotype of "owning" the land. Sailing imagery, whether referring to sex or to politics, was traditionally linked with the concepts of devotion or lack of it and danger. It was a very flexible narrative system because the harbour and the ship did not have gender-specific values and

---

24 The *Republic* was authored almost ten years after Aristophanes' death, hence not part of the literary tradition known to him. I include it here as an overt example of adopting the inherited ideology of the metaphor. Aristophanes' *Knights* is another example (see below).

the focus could move from the storm to the ship or to the harbour.[25] A key difference is that, whereas Hesiod had offered a popular paradigm for connecting the sexual and the political aspect of farming imagery, on which the tragedians elaborated,[26] there was no such paradigm for sailing imagery by Aristophanes' time — at least, no such paradigm has reached us.[27]

4 Aristophanes: An overview

So how does the playwright employ the "literary lexicography"[28] pertinent to sex (or what I call "seminal figures" in the title of this chapter)?[29] First and foremost, by adopting such metaphorical language in short scenes and passing jokes.[30] For example, in the context of Dicaeopolis' phallic litany in *Acharnians*, the protagonist sings his intention to "catch a budding maid [...] grab her waist, lift her up, throw her down and take her cherry" (272–275), which "is beyond any doubt a rape".[31] We can imagine the large *phallus*-prop of this procession being carried

---

25 Craik 1990, 3; Brock 2013, 61.

26 Another instance of such an elaboration, not included in my previous account since the sexual act is too implicit, is Clytaemnestra's dream in Sophocles' *Electra*. In her dream, Agamemnon comes back to life, takes back his sceptre from Aegisthus, and plants it beside the hearth from where a fruitful bough grows up (*El.* 417–423). "The sexual symbolism [...] is inseparable in this instance from the social symbolism. The *skēptron* is a kind of mobile representation of sovereignty. [...] By re-establishing it in the hearth, Agamemnon wrenches it from the usurpers and [...] the staff set in the hearth [also] symbolises the royal seed (*sperma*) placed earlier by Agamemnon in Clytaemnestra's womb, where it grows: Orestes": Vernant 2006, 166–167.

27 As evidence to the contrary, one could cite Thucydides' description of the Sicilian expedition in erotic terms (6.24.3; see Wohl 2002, 189–194) but sailing, on that case, is a literal reference and the desire for what is craved is constructed more in "romantic" terms (Buis 2012, 209) than explicitly sexual. The only dubious case I can recall is Sappho's *Brothers Song*, "but in the strictly feminine perspective the use of this [naval] imagery applies predominantly to the erotic complex": Bierl 2016, 310, 316–317.

28 Silk 1974, xiii.

29 "Seminal" encapsulates both the erotic semantics and the literary fertility of the imagery under discussion.

30 For a glossary of agricultural and nautical terms for sex and the genitalia in Aristophanes, see Taillardat 1962, 72–73, 75–56, 100–102 and (with some scepticism) Henderson 1991, 161–167. "In his enthusiasm, Henderson overstates his case, and many of his categories and supposedly illustrative examples are dubious. One recalls the story of Freud's patient who indignantly repudiated the interpretation in sexual terms of a particular dream with the retort that when he had a sexual dream he dreamt about sex": Craik 1990, 14 n. 4; cf. Murgatroyd 1995, 12 n. 12.

31 Olson 2002, 150.

around the orchestra in search of a victim. Later on, the chorus express their desire for Reconciliation thus: "Ah but if I got hold of you, I think I could still strike against you three times [or: add three things to my farm].[32] First, I'd shove in a long rank of tender vines, and beside that some fresh fig shoots, and thirdly a well hung vine branch — this oldster would! — and, around the whole plot, a stand of olive trees..." (995–998). Unlike in *Lysistrata*, Reconciliation is not brough on stage here and the chorus probably makes ploughing gestures with their *phalloi* — the "well hung vine branch" should belong to the coryphaeus. Similar gestures are expected from the Athenian delegates in *Lysistrata*, who suffer from endless erection: "Now I'm ready to strip down and start ploughing!" (1173). In *Birds*, Peisetaerus claims that the cuckoo was king of all Egypt and Phoenicia because those peoples would "start reaping the wheat and barley in their fields" at the cuckoo's call (504–506). The line has an obscene interpretation, based on the *double entendres* κριθή=wheat/penis and πεδίον=field/vagina.[33] Thus, the Egyptians and the Phoenicians are said to be in their rut season, as Euelpides' comment comes to confirm: "So that's the real meaning of the saying 'Cuckoo-stripped cocks off to the plain!'" (1174).[34] In terms of comic business, Euelpides perhaps lifts momentarily his chiton to expose his *phallus*, as he reveals the nasty meaning of the expression.

Turning to sailing imagery, in *Birds* we listen to Peisetaerus warn Iris who has just invaded Cloudcuckooland that "she'll be amazed how an old hulk like me can stay aloft for three rammings!" (1256). The parallelism of a trireme's bronze-covered wooden ram to a penis provides a clear threat of rape. In *Lysistrata*, the gender power is reversed: the semichorus of old men are afraid that the old women "will even build frigates and launch naval attacks, cruising against us like Artemisia" (674–675). Since "ναυμαχεῖν and πλεῖν are used of the partner who is on top in sexual intercourse",[35] the men are essentially afraid that the women "will even fuck them" — with emphasis on "even" (ἔτι), for the paradoxicality of such a rape. Similarly, the young man of *Ecclesiazusae* is terrified by the lascivious old hags who chase him (1086–1091):

YOUNG MAN   You two would make rough ferryboat captains.
OLD WOMAN   How's that?

---

32 Olson 2002, 317.
33 Sommerstein 1987, 227; Dunbar 1998, 239.
34 κόκκυ ψωλοὶ πεδίονδε (transl. Dunbar). In Modern Greek we can perfectly translate with the proverb "τους κάνει κούκου" and the orthographic pun "παιδοίο".
35 Henderson 1987, 160.

YOUNG MAN You'd tug your passengers hard enough to wear them out. [...] Yet I am bound [by law] to fuck. But how can I manage to man two boats with a single oar?

Naval metaphors also apply to consensual sex. Thus, in *Frogs* we hear of a homosexual battleship in which Dionysus "was serving topside with Cleisthenes", a man often mocked in comedy for his effeminacy (cf. *Ach.* 116–121, *Lys.* 1092) and possibly a trierarch; the joke is based on the etymological connection between ἐπιβατεύειν, "to serve on board", and ἐπιβαίνειν, "to mount". The two men "sank some enemy ships too, twelve or thirteen of them" (48–50), which indicates the duration of this affair and may also imply the involvement of extra sexual partners.[36] A heterosexual battleship also features in the play, with some Callias (a notorious playboy of his time who squandered much of his riches on mistresses, cf. *Av.* 286) "fighting a naval battle with a cunt, dressed in a lion-skin" (428–430).[37] In *Ecclesiazusae* Aristophanes builds on the ambiguity "violent/consensual sex" of the sailing metaphor; one of the assemblywomen excuses herself for coming late thus: "You know, my dear, the man I live with is from Salamis, and all night long he was sailing me under the sheets!" (37–39). Pragaxora is expected to believe that the wife was indeed forced by her husband, but the audience knows well her willingness, as female lust is a *topos* of Old Comedy. Overall, we note that Aristophanes aligns himself with the literary tradition, i.e. with his audience's horizon of expectations, as he espouses the gender essentialism of farming imagery, the genderfluidity of sailing imagery,[38] and their established sexual meanings (e.g. the notion of devotion in the case of Dionysus and Cleisthenes' battleship, or the notion of farming as rape in *Acharnians*). Reasonably, agrarian metaphors did not apply (nor did Aristophanes attempt to apply them) to homosexual relations, procreation not being a relevant concern.[39]

The same sort of loyalty is evidenced in Aristophanes' use of farming and sailing imagery with reference to politics. Here too the notions of agriculture are always negative: in *Wasps* the old juror Philocleon is asked to explain "what profit [jurors] get from reaping the fruits of Greece" (520) and in *Birds* Euelpides

---

36 For Sommerstein 1996, 160–161, "it is likely that Dionysus is not aware of the *double entendres*, though Heracles and the audience are". In that case, Dionysus' response about the sinking of enemy ships would have a literal referent, i.e. the battleship of Arginousae.

37 What a more appropriate outfit for the champion of sex and a kinky costume for some spice? Sommerstein 1996, 196 (whence the transl.) For an alternative rendering, see Dover 1993, 249.

38 Thus Henderson 1991, 162 distinguishes between "metaphors which involve men sailing women" and those of "women sailing men".

39 As Manousakis, in this volume, demonstrates for the case of Aeschylus.

complains that jurors is "a seed that sprouts" everywhere in Athens (110–111). Later in the play the chorus devotes an entire song to them (1694–1699):

> Over in the land of Extortia, near the Water Cache,
> dwells the wicked race of Thrive-by-Tongues,
> who do their harvesting and sowing and vintaging by tongue,
> and also their culling [συκάζουσί τε].

Not surprisingly, in Aristophanes' imagination the jurors undertake both roles in the farming relationship: a fruit themselves, since the "sycophant" is etymologically linked to "figs", and reapers of others' fruits. In the latter sense, the Sausage Seller in *Knights* accuses Paphlagon, a caricature of Cleon, of "reaping somebody else's harvest [i.e. getting credit for the victory at Pylos]" and of "clamping those ears of corn he brought back with him in the stocks for parching, in hopes of selling them back [i.e. using the Spartan prisoners to bargain for favourable terms]" (391–394).[40] Of course Cleon was a politician, not a juror, but still followed some "sycophantic" practices pertinent to his capacity: "like a fig picker you squeeze [the outgoing] magistrates under review, looking to see which of them is raw, which ripe and unripe" (258–259).

The most elaborate application of sailing imagery to politics is also found in *Knights*;[41] in the parabasis the chorus praises the dramatist for "striding forth against the typhoon and the whirlwind" (511). The kind of the storm is not specified but is obviously Cleon, who is named only once in the play (976). The chorus then explain why Aristophanes had staged his earlier plays under someone else's name: because "one should be an oarsman before handling the tiller, and from there take charge of the bow and watch the weather, and only then become a pilot in one's own right" (542–546). For his decision to do so, the chorus invites the audience to "raise a big wave of applause for him and give him an eleven-oar cheer worthy of the Lenaea". This is the image of a poetic wave going against the political current of Cleon, with Aristophanes at the wheel and the audience as his crew. The naval collectiveness envisioned in this passage echoes and perhaps draws directly on Alcaeus' fr. 6, mentioned earlier ("let us..., any of us..., before us..."): is this a democratic "we" or a populist "we" at the service of the captain's

---

40 The notes are the translator's. On the demagogue-farmer, see Taillardat 1962, 418–421.
41 For other, passing references, see *Vesp.* 29, *Ran.* 361, 704.

aspirations? The very use of sailing imagery, I believe, betrays Aristophanes' conservative disposition, even if chosen unconsciously — not unlike Plato and his "ship of state" in the *Republic*.[42]

Therefore, Aristophanes employed the traditional connotations of both farming and sailing imagery to speak of both sex and politics. The compiled examples also illustrate that, in most cases, there is hardly any political hint in the sexual uses of the imagery (e.g. in Dionysus' gay battleship or in the Phoenicians' eagerness to reap) and vice versa (e.g. in the sprouting of jurors in Athens or in Cleon's storm). The only case so far that presents a nexus between a sexual and a political reading is where the old men in *Lys*istrata are worried that the women might "cruise against them like Artemisia" (674–675), i.e. attempt to rape them/overthrow them. But this joke draws on the legendary masculinity of Artemisia, in particular, and the feminisation of the men around her (Hdt. 8.88), rather than on the tradition of sailing metaphors in general. In principle, Aristophanes did not attempt to mix the sexual and the political nuances of sailing imagery,[43] and this is probably because there was no literary precedent for doing so, as noted above. But there *was* such a precedent regarding farming imagery, in Hesiod and tragedy, and Aristophanes made the most out of it in *Peace*.

5 Aristophanes' *Peace*

There is no doubt Aristophanes pursued the metaphorical assimilation of the political to the erotic, but this was mainly achieved through the figure of the politician-lover, "a figure of speech that came into vogue in Athens during the heyday of her democracy in the later fifth and first half of the fourth centuries BC: the figuration of political emotions and motivations — ambition, patriotism, partisanship and the like — as sexual lust".[44] Thus, for instance, Paphlagon in *Knights*

---

42 This image "arose in aristocratic circles, as a comfortable view of themselves which grounded their claim to authority on a basis of ability and expertise [...] on the other hand, democratic Athens seems to have evolved no maritime imagery to illustrate its [own] ideals": Brock 2013, 56, 59.

43 Not to be confused with Murgatroyd's observation that the figure of erotic sailing "is readily combined with other imagery". What he means is that the "sea of love" can be immediately succeeded, for example, by equestrian erotic imagery (Murgatroyd 1995, 10, 12) whereas my focus is on the semantics of sailing (or farming) metaphor in itself.

44 Scholtz 1977, 1.

is presented as a *kolax-erastēs* of Demos, as an uncontrollable *kinaidos*,[45] and the Reconciliation scene in *Lysistrata* exemplifies how comedy resorts to female figures to portray the "masculinised" aggression of Athens against the "effeminate" weakness of her allied and enemy cities.[46] In *Peace*, farming imagery becomes the "vehicle" for such an assimilation, which in turn is the "tenor" of the metaphor. I wish to propose that the sexual and political connotations of farming imagery, always negative in the literary tradition, provide an interpretative key to the play, promoting an ironic reading. The ironic readings of Aristophanes' comedies have been widely discussed by scholars, as, for example, that in *Knights* Paphlagon is overthrown by the even worse Sausage Seller; that in *Clouds* the comic idea leads to father-beating and arson; that in *Birds* Peisetaerus becomes a demagogue of the kind he used to hate, and so on. It is only *Peace* that scholarship has scarcely ever mentioned a dark side of, which seems reasonable given the self-evidently positive notion of a Panhellenic peace, in contrast to Dicaeopolis' private treaty for example. But if ten of Aristophanes' plays have a (possible) ironic interpretation, it is hard to incontestably accept that *Peace* is merely a nostalgic and fairy-tale-like celebration.[47]

Farming imagery with reference to sex is here more frequent than in any other comedy, thus inviting us to follow its progression throughout the play. We first hear of the chorus' πόθος to go to their fields, a desire which subdues them (584–585: ἐδάμην is a common verb in erotic contexts; cf. *Il.* 14.353). Later on, Hermes passes Opora as a wife to Trygaeus — both names indicate agriculture — "to beget a brood of grapes in the countryside" (706–708). Then Trygaeus tells the chorus that thanks to his plan everyone will be able to "live safely in the fields, screwing and snoozing" (866–867). We start tracing the development of the metaphor: first an almost romantic attraction to peace, then marriage and procreative sex, and now non-procreative sex and leisure, complacency, and stagnancy. The next scene comes to confirm the suspicion that there is a hidden political message;[48] Theoria, a companion to Peace and Opora, is passed on to the members of the Boule, the actual ones who are seated in the *prohedria*, to be gang raped (871–909): "like young lads bang and dig [her] with fist and prick alike!" (898). English translations render Theoria as "Holiday", "Festival-going", or

---

45 Scholtz 1977, 201; Buis 2012, 199–200.
46 Buis 2012, 192–193.
47 Storey 2019, 59, 92–93.
48 For the political nuances of farming imagery, irrespective of sex, cf. 628–629: "[The Spartans] cut down that black fig tree of mine, which I'd planted and nurtured".

"Showtime" and the episode is usually passed over lightly, as a jolly carnivalesque act or even a blessing: "The presiding counsellors [...] are being given custody of a divine handmaiden, symbolic of the freedom to travel without the dangers of wartime".[49] But precisely because θεωρία means, *inter alia*, the sending of state-ambassadors, her rape can be considered a deeply worrying sign which undermines the success of a peace treaty. The implication is rather straightforward: some of the counsellors are abusing/might abuse their power and "fuck up" the negotiations.[50]

A second metatheatrical act follows, with Trygaeus' slave dispensing barley pips to the audience — only its male members, who are invited to also "give barley" to their wives later at night (959–967).[51] Apart from being the most important piece of evidence for the women's spectatorship, probably from the back rows, this passage complements the political message of the previous scene; now it is all citizens (hence men alone) who are given the fruits of peace in their hands, a reminder of *their* civic responsibility. And finally we reach the exodus of the play, where the chorus sings of Opora "We will harvest her! We will deflower her!" (1337), with the verb τρυγήσομεν punning on the hero's name and marking Opora as his property.[52] A happy wedding ceremony *prima facie*, this grotesque call for another gang rape sounds like the foreseeable, unfortunate response of the Athenians to the fruit they were entrusted to protect, led by their lust/greediness.[53] Recalling the traditional, negative nuances of farming imagery since Hesiod and considering its progression throughout the play, at least some in the audience would have their concerns about the ongoing negotiations reinforced. If the hypothesis is correct, then Aristophanes was doubly prophetic: not only was the Peace of Nicias signed just after the staging of the play (421 BC) but it was also

---

49 Storey 2019, 89. An alternative, metatheatrical interpretation is that "Theoria [cf. *theatron, theatai*] becomes instantiated as the participation of the audience in the particular performance of the present comedy" and her handing over to the audience is an invitation "to reflect upon their own experience of the comedy": Sfyroeras 2013, 660–663.
50 Sulprizio 2013, 56–58, who also admits the scene as a rape and challenges the optimistic reading of the play, views Theoria's body as a target receiving "the traumatic reverberations of years of war through its sexual use and abuse", i.e. as a projection of the past — whereas I consider it as a projection of the future.
51 For κριθή as a slang metaphor for penis, see above p. 434; for dispensing food to the audience, *Vesp.* 58–59.
52 Sulprizio 2013, 55.
53 Athens had entered the negotiations "not at all inclined to make a settlement on fair terms" (Thuc. 5.15.2).

reaped, or raped, quite fast; supposed to last fifty years, it only lasted six. Accordingly, the entire mythical structure of the play requires revaluation: while it is an established view that *Peace* replicates the myths of *anodos*,[54] the treatment of Theoria and Opora in the second half suggests a cancellation of the *anodos*, i.e. a re-enactment of Persephone's rape. "Often the poet seems aware of the relations between the various codes united by the metaphors and symbols through which he reinterprets his myths"[55] and here is an exemplary case.

These explicitly pornographic, and implicitly political, farming metaphors are both "acoustic images" and actual images. By performing on stage such sexual imagery — the audience *watches* Theoria's rape and Opora's dragging towards reaping, and *holds* the barley pips — Aristophanes invites his audience to visualise their political future. This is not an abstract kind of visualisation ("to imagine", "to reflect upon" and the like) but a very tangible one, thanks to the personification/objectification of abstract concepts.[56] If poetic metaphors can "set a concept before our eyes" (Arist. *Rhet.* 1411b), theatrical metaphors can literally set a concept before our eyes. And if the possible functions of metaphors are "(1) to make clearer, as in a diagram, (2) to make immediate, as if to the senses, and (3) to exploit associations beyond any limited point of comparison", then Aristophanes' detailed, performable, and polysemous imagery in *Peace* serves all three of them, especially the latter, where metaphor "creates an explosion of suggestions and connections" which *foregrounds* new meanings.[57]

Bibliography

Benson, C. (1995), 'Sirens', in: E. Reeder (ed.), *Pandora: Women in Classical Greece*, Baltimore, 415–418.

Bierl, A. (2016), '"All You Need is Love": Some Thoughts on the Structure, Texture, and Meaning of the *Brothers Song* as well as on Its Relation to the *Kypris Song*', in: A. Bierl/A. Lardinois (eds.), *The Newest Sappho*, Leiden/Boston, 302–336.

Boardman, J. (1958), 'A Greek Vase from Egypt', in: *Journal of Hellenic Studies* 78, 4–12.

Bowie, A. (1993), *Aristophanes: Myth, Ritual, and Comedy*, Cambridge.

Boys-Stones, G.R. (ed.) (2003), *Metaphor, Allegory, and the Classical Tradition*, Oxford.

Brock, R. (2013), *Greek Political Imagery from Homer to Aristotle*, London.

---

54 Olson 1998, xxxvi–xxxviii; Bowie 1993, 142–150.
55 Segal 1981, 19.
56 Lever 1953, 221.
57 Silk 2003, 126, 131.

Buis, E.J. (2012), 'Enemigos íntimos: el imaginario simbólico del matrimonio y las metáforas eróticas de la política internacional en la comedia antigua', in: E. Rodríguez Cidre/E.J. Buis/A.M. Atienza (eds.), *El oikos violentado*, Buenos Aires, 191–228.

Campbell, D.A. (1986), 'Ship Imagery in the *Oedipus Tyrannus*', in: M.J. Cropp/E. Fantham/S.E. Scully (eds.), *Greek Tragedy and Its Legacy*, Calgary, 125–131.

Carson, A. (1990), 'Putting Her in Her Place: Woman, Dirt and Desire', in: D.M. Halperin/J.J. Winkler/F.I. Zeitlin (eds.), *Before Sexuality*, Princeton, 135–169.

Chaston, C. (2010), *Tragic Props and Cognitive Function*, Leiden/Boston.

Cole, S.G. (2004), *Landscapes, Gender, and Ritual Space*, Berkeley.

Craik, E. (1990), 'Sexual Imagery and Innuendo in *Troades*', in: A. Powell (ed.), *Euripides, Women, and Sexuality*, London, 1–15.

Crowther, P. (2003), 'Literary Metaphor and Philosophical Insight: The Significance of Archilochus', in: Boys-Stones 2003, 83–100.

Csapo, E. (1997), 'Riding the Phallus for Dionysus: Iconology, Ritual, and Gender-Role De/Construction', in: *Phoenix* 51, 253–295.

Dover, K.J. (1978), *Greek Homosexuality*, London.

Dover, K.J. (1993), *Aristophanes: Frogs*, Oxford.

DuBois, P. (1988), *Sowing the Body: Psychoanalysis and Ancient Representations of Women*, Chicago.

Dunbar, N. (1998), *Aristophanes: Birds*, Oxford.

Grethlein, J. (2017), *Aesthetic Experiences and Classical Antiquity*, Cambridge.

Griffith, D.R. (1989), 'In Praise of the Bride: Sappho Fr. 105A L-P, Voigt', in: *Transactions of the American Philological Association* 119, 55–61.

Harrison, G./Liapis, V. (eds.) (2013), *Performance in Greek and Roman Theatre*, Leiden/Boston.

Henderson, J. (1987), *Aristophanes: Lysistrata*, Oxford.

Henderson, J. (1991), *The Maculate Muse*, New York.

Kahlmeyer, J. (1934), *Seesturm und Schiffbruch als Bild im antiken Schrifttum*, PhD Thesis, University of Greifswald.

Kampakoglou, A./Novokhatko, A. (eds.) (2018), *Gaze, Vision, and Visuality in Ancient Greek Literature*, Berlin/Boston.

Kraus, C./Goldhill, S./Foley, H./Elsner, J. (eds.) (2007), *Visualizing the Tragic*, Oxford.

Lear, A./Cantarella, E. (2006), *Images of Ancient Greek Pederasty*, New York.

Lever, K. (1953), 'Poetic Metaphor and Dramatic Allegory in Aristophanes', in: *The Classical Weekly* 46, 220–223.

Meineck, P. (2011), *Opsis: The Visuality of Greek Drama*, PhD Thesis, University of Nottingham.

Murgatroyd, P. (1995), 'The Sea of Love', in: *Classical Quarterly* 45, 9–25.

Olson, S.D. (1998), *Aristophanes: Peace*, Oxford.

Olson, S.D. (2002), *Aristophanes: Acharnians*, Oxford.

Parker, H. (2015), 'Vaseworld: Depiction and Description of Sex at Athens', in: R. Blondell/K. Ormand (eds.), *Ancient Sex: New Essays*, Ohio, 23–142.

Parker, R. (2005), *Polytheism and Society at Athens*, Oxford.

Petrides, A. (2014), *Menander, New Comedy and the Visual*, Cambridge.

Saussure, F. (2011), *Course in General Linguistics*, New York.

Scholtz, A. (1977), *Ἐραστὴς τοῦ δήμου: Erotic Imagery in Political Contexts in Thucydides and Aristophanes*, PhD Thesis, Yale University.

Segal, C. (1981), *Tragedy and Civilization: An Interpretation of Sophocles*, Cambridge.

Serafim, A. (2020), 'Sicking Bodies: *Stasis* as Disease in the Human Body and the Body Politic', in: H. Gasti (ed.), *Δόσις ἀμφιλαφής: τιμητικός τόμος για την Κ. Συνοδινού*, Ioannina, 673–695.

Sfyroeras, P. (2013), 'Eirēnē Philheortos and Dionysiac Poetics in Aristophanic Comedy', in: N. Birgalias/K. Buraselis/P. Cartledge/A. Gartziou-Tatti/M. Dimopoulou (eds.), *War, Peace and Panhellenic Games*, Athens, 651–667.

Silk, M.S. (1974), *Interaction in Poetic Imagery*, Cambridge.

Silk, M.S. (2003), 'Metaphor and Metonymy: Aristotle, Jakobson, Ricoeur, and Others', in: Boys-Stones 2003, 115–147.

Sommerstein, A.H. (1987), *The Comedies of Aristophanes: Lysistrata*, Westminster.

Sommerstein, A.H. (1996), *The Comedies of Aristophanes: Frogs*, Westminster.

Squire, M. (2009), *Image and Text in Graeco-Roman Antiquity*, Cambridge.

Storey, I.C. (2019), *Aristophanes: Peace*, London/New York.

Sulprizio, C. (2013), 'You Can't Go Home Again: War, Women and Domesticity in Aristophanes' *Peace*', in: *Ramus* 42, 44–63.

Taillardat, J. (1962), *Les Images d'Aristophane*, Paris.

Thornton, B.S. (1997), *Eros: The Myth of Ancient Greek Sexuality*, Boulder, CO.

Vernant, J.P. (2006), *Myth and Thought among the Greeks*, London.

Winkler, J. (1990), *The Constraints of Desire*, New York.

Wohl, V. (2002), *Love among the Ruins*, Princeton.

Figures

Fig. 41: The Hasselmann Painter, Attic red-figured pelike 440–430 BC, London: British Museum E819. © The Trustees of the British Museum.

Fig. 42: The Antimenes Painter (?), Attic black-figured amphora 540–530 BC, Paris: Musee du Louvre AM1008. Drawing from G. Perrot/C. Chipiez (1914), *Histoire de l'art dans l'antiquité*, vol.10, Paris, 127 (detail).

Fig. 43: Unattributed, Attic black-figured cup 575–525 BC, Florence: Museo Archeologico Etrusco 3897. Su concessione del Museo Archeologico Nazionale di Firenze. © Direzione regionale Musei della Toscana.

Fig. 44: Unattributed, Attic red-figured lekythos 425–375 BC, Berlin: Antikensammlung F2472. Photograph by Johannes Laurentius. © Staatliche Museen zu Berlin, Antikensammlung — Preussischer Kulturbesitz.

Fig. 45: The Siren Painter, Attic red-figured stamnos 500–450 BC, London: British Museum E440. © The Trustees of the British Museum.

Ioannis M. Konstantakos

The Maiden who Knew Nothing about Sex: A Scabrous Theme in Novella and Comedy

Abstract: The ingenuous male or female who has no knowledge of sex is a well-known type of comic personage in the ancient and medieval tradition. The female variant appears in some stories of the Aesopic corpus (*Aesop Romance* 131, fable 386 Perry): an imbecile girl cannot understand the sexual act which a cunning rustic performs on her under the pretext of a beneficial operation. These stories probably derive from an old Ionian novella. In a later collection of fables (410 Perry) the young girl is grotesquely replaced by an ignorant old woman unwittingly raped by a young man. The male counterpart, namely, the foolish man who does not know what to do on his marriage bed, occurs in the humorous Ionian epic *Margites* and in a Hittite apologue. Perhaps the theme passed into Ionian narrative lore from Anatolian sources. Further versions are traced in an Attic mythological comedy by Amphis (fourth century BC) and in the novella of Rustico and Alibech in Boccaccio (*Decameron* 3.10).

1 The ingenuous maiden: Greek fables and novellas

The title of this chapter points to a recurrent character type of the ancient humorous tradition, in its broadest sense; the type may appear in all kinds of facetious literature, narrative and dramatic, and occurs both in Greco-Roman texts and in fictional productions of the ancient Near East. The character in question is the ingenuous personage who has no idea of sex, does not understand the meaning of copulation and cannot even recognise the sexual act when it is performed. The commonest representatives of the type are naive and foolish women, but male characters also feature in this role. Naturally, the inexperienced person is liable to comic misunderstandings and deceptions; she or he may fall victim to shrewd and cunning figures, who take advantage of her/his ignorance for their own self-interested purposes. Around the ingenuous character's ignorance and the tricks of her/his adversaries a funny tale or episode is woven. The misapprehensions committed by the innocent heroine or hero and the frauds perpetrated at her/his

https://doi.org/10.1515/9783110695793-019

expense are usually based on humorous puns and double entendres. These elements form the core of the plot in all the stories of this kind and provide the main source of the comic effect.[1]

A characteristic specimen is the tale of the mentally impaired girl and her mother, who prayed daily to the gods to give her daughter some sense. One of the ancient versions of this story is found, as an inserted parable, in the so-called *Life of Aesop* or *Aesop Romance*, a fictional biography of the legendary fabulist, composed around the first or second century AD.[2] In this novelistic *vita* Aesop appears as a roguish and picaresque hero, undergoes many ridiculous adventures and also recounts several fables and other saucy tales.[3] The ribald story of the stupid maiden is narrated in the last part of the work, while Aesop is incarcerated at Delphi and is awaiting execution on a fabricated charge of sacrilege (ch. 127–128). The fabulist is visited by a friend in gaol and tells a series of comic parables to illustrate his own imprudence and deplore his dire fate (ch. 129–131).[4] This is the text of the story in the earliest and most lively redaction of the *Aesop Romance*, the G, which must be closest to the lost original form of the work (ch. 131):[5]

---

1 Cf. Hansen 2002, 253–254. The type is also common in modern humorous literature and comic lore: see Legman 1968, 113–163. On the worldwide folk tradition of the theme, in particular, see Thompson 1957, 141, 216, 392–393 (motifs J1744–1745.2, J2462, K1363–1363.1.1); Ashliman 1987, 252, 285; Hansen 2002, 251–255; Uther 2004, 217, 282 (tale types 1425, 1542**).

2 See Perry 1936, 24–26; Perry 1952, 1–5, 22; Ferrari 1997, 5, 44; Jouanno 2006, 16–17.

3 On the fables, novellas and other occasional narratives emboxed in the *Aesop Romance* see Perry 1962, 297–302, 329–332; Jedrkiewicz 1989, 186–189; Merkle 1992; van Dijk 1995; van Dijk 1996, 520–521, 530–541; Merkle 1996; Ferrari 1997, 21–36; Adrados 1999–2003, I 654–658; Stramaglia 2000, 307–314; Jouanno 2005, 404–405; Zafiropoulos 2015, 133–146, 166–168.

4 On this final part of the *Aesop Romance* and the tales told by Aesop in its context see Wiechers 1961, 7–42; Jedrkiewicz 1989, 83–107; Holzberg 1992, 69–75; Merkle 1992; van Dijk 1995, 141–150; Merkle 1996, 216, 226–230; Nagy 1999, 279–288; Jouanno 2006, 44–50; Papademetriou 2009, 64–70; Kurke 2011, 53–94, 185–190, 211–217; Zafiropoulos 2015, 130–134, 145–146, 150–172.

5 For the text of the G redaction of the *Aesop Romance* see the editions of Ferrari 1997, 248 and Papathomopoulos 2010, 231–233. In the maiden's final explanatory statement about her experience, I include the supplement <ἀνήρ τις> at the beginning, introduced by Perry (1952, 75) on the basis of the text of the Papyrus Golenischev (see below). The story also occurs in the other extant ancient Greek redaction of the *Aesop Romance*, the W (in both its recensions, MORN and BPThSA). Furthermore, it is preserved in the so-called Papyrus Golenischev (P. Ross.-Georg. I 18, seventh century AD), which transmits ch. 124–132 of the *Aesop Romance*. See Perry 1936, 58–59, 63–64; Papathomopoulos 1999, 137, 201; Karla 2001, 236–237. In these alternative versions the narrative is more abridged and some colourful details and portions of the dialogue are omitted; there are also many minute differences in phrasing by comparison to the G. However, there is nothing new in terms of content, storyline and motifs.

γυνή τις εἶχεν θυγατέρα μωρήν. αὕτη πᾶσι τοῖς θεοῖς ηὔχετο τὴν θυγατέρα νοῦν λαβεῖν, εὐχομένης δὲ αὐτῆς ἡ παρθένος πολλάκις ἤκουσεν. καὶ δή ποτε εἰς ἀγρὸν ἦλθον. ἡ δὲ καταλιποῦσα τὴν μητέρα ἔξω τῆς ἐπαύλεως εἶδεν ὄνον βιαζομένην ὑπὸ ἀνθρώπου, καὶ ἠρώτησεν τὸν ἄνθρωπον· "τί ποιεῖς;" ὁ δέ· "νοῦν ἐντίθημι αὐτῇ." ἀναμνησθεῖσα ἡ μωρὰ τῆς εὐχῆς ἔφη· "ἔνθες καὶ ἐμοὶ νοῦν." ὁ δὲ αὐτὴν οἴφειν ἠρνεῖτο λέγων· "οὐδέν ἐστιν ἀχαριστότερον γυναικός." ἡ δέ· "μὴ λόγον ἔχῃς, κύριε, καὶ ἡ μήτηρ μου εὐχαριστήσει σοι, μισθὸν δοῦσα ὅσον ἂν θέλῃς· εὔχεται γὰρ ἵνα νοῦν ἔχω." ὁ δὲ διεπαρθένευσατο αὐτήν. ἡ δὲ περιχαρὴς πρὸς τὴν μητέρα δραμοῦσα εἶπεν· "νοῦν ἔχω, μῆτερ." ἡ μήτηρ φησίν· "οἱ θεοὶ ἐπήκουσάν μου τῶν εὐχῶν." ἡ κόρη· "ναί, μῆτερ." ἡ δέ· "πῶς ἔσχες νοῦν, τέκνον;" ἡ δὲ μωρὰ ἐξηγήσατο· "<ἀνήρ τις> μακρὸν γὰρ πυρρὸν νευρῶδες ἔξω ἔσω τρέχον ἔσω μοι ἐνέβαλεν." ἀκούσασα δὲ ἡ μήτηρ ἐξηγουμένης τῆς θυγατρὸς αὐτῆς ἔφη· "ὦ τέκνον, ἀπώλεσας καὶ ὃν πρῶτον εἶχες νοῦν."

There was a woman who had a simple-minded daughter. She prayed to all the gods to give her daughter some sense, and the daughter often heard her praying. Then once they went out to the country. The girl left her mother and went outside the farmyard, where she saw a man coupling with a she-ass. She asked the man: "What are you doing?" He said: "I am putting some sense into her". The imbecile girl remembered her mother's prayer and said: "Put some sense in me too". The man, however, refused to screw her and remarked: "Nothing is more thankless than a woman". But the girl said: "Please, sir, do not worry. My mother will thank you for this and will pay you as much money as you want. You see, she prays for me to get some sense". And so the man deflowered her. She was overjoyed and ran to her mother and said: "Mummy, mummy, I have some sense!" Her mother said: "The gods listened to my prayers".[6] The girl: "Of course, mummy!" And the mother asked: "How did you get sense, child?" And the stupid girl told her mother the story: "A man put it inside me with a long, sinewy, red thing that ran in and out". When the mother heard her daughter's explanation, she exclaimed: "Oh, my child, now you have lost what little sense you had".[7]

The tale, as incorporated in the *Aesop Romance*, is loosely paralleled with Aesop's own predicament, while he languishes in gaol. The imbecile girl is unable to recognise the act of copulation and is thus stupidly taken in by a rough rustic, who satisfies his lust upon her. Aesop, it is implied, was equally stupid to ignore the warning signs and let the rascally Delphians deceive and entrap him. Like the

---

6 Probably the mother's statement at this point should be punctuated with a question mark (οἱ θεοὶ ἐπήκουσάν μου τῶν εὐχῶν;), as happens in one of the manuscripts (M) of the W redaction of the romance (εἰσήκουσάν μου τῶν εὐχῶν οἱ θεοί;). See Papathomopoulos 1999, 137; Karla (Forthcoming) *ad loc.* This would better suit narrative logic. The long-suffering mother, hearing her daughter's exclamations, reacts with a puzzled question, rather than a positive assertion; she wonders for a moment whether the gods may have granted her prayers and truly instilled some sense into the silly girl.

7 The translation is based on Daly (1961, 87), with some rephrasing and supplementations.

ingenuous maiden, the thoughtless fabulist also lost at Delphi what sense he possessed.[8]

Perhaps under the influence of the popular biography of Aesop, the story of the stupid maiden also found its way into the corpus of Aesopic fables (fable 386 Perry, 305 Hausrath). It is included in three late Byzantine manuscripts (from the fifteenth and sixteenth century) which belong to a variant branch of the so-called *Vindobonensis* recension of the Greek fabulistic corpus. This compilation was probably put together at the very end of antiquity (fourth or fifth century AD) or in the early Byzantine period (sixth or seventh century AD). Its materials were undoubtedly drawn from earlier collections of fables, ultimately reaching back to much more ancient times.[9] The narrative of the fable is more abridged at certain points than the version of the *Aesop Romance*, but it comprises some additional facetious details, especially with regard to the characters' dialogue and the final twist of the plot.[10]

γυνή τις εἶχε θυγατέρα παρθένον μωράν· πάντοτε οὖν ηὔχετο τῇ θεᾷ νοῦν αὐτῇ χαρίσασθαι. εὐχομένης δὲ αὐτῆς παρρησίᾳ ἡ παρθένος ἤκουσε καὶ τὸν λόγον κατεῖχε. μεθ᾽ ἡμέρας δέ τινας σὺν τῇ μητρὶ εἰς ἀγρὸν ἐξελθοῦσα καὶ τῆς προαυλίου προκύψασα θύρας εἶδεν ὄνον θήλειαν ὑπ᾽ ἀνθρώπου βιαζομένην καὶ προσελθοῦσα τῷ ἀνθρώπῳ εἶπε· "τί ποιεῖς, ἄνθρωπε;" ὁ δέ φησι· "νοῦν αὐτῇ ἐντίθημι." ἀναμνησθεῖσα δὲ ἡ μωρά, ὅτι καθ᾽ ἑκάστην ἡ μήτηρ νοῦν αὐτῇ ηὔχετο, παρεκάλει αὐτὸν λέγουσα· "ἔνθες, ἄνθρωπε, κἀμοὶ νοῦν. καὶ γὰρ ἡ μήτηρ μου πρὸς τοῦτο πολλά σοι εὐχαριστήσει." ὁ δὲ ὑπακούσας κατέλιπεν τὴν ὄνον καὶ διεπαρθένευσε τὴν κόρην φθείρας αὐτήν. ἡ δὲ διεφθαρμένη μετὰ περιχαρείας ἔρχεται πρὸς τὴν μητέρα αὐτῆς λέγουσα· "ἰδού, μῆτερ, κατὰ τὴν εὐχήν σου νοῦν ἔλαβον." ἡ δὲ μήτηρ αὐτῆς φησιν· "εἰσήκουσάν μοι οἱ θεοὶ τῆς εὐχῆς." ἡ δὲ μωρὰ ἔφη· "ναί, μῆτερ." ἡ δέ φησιν· "καὶ ποίῳ τρόπῳ τοῦτο ἔγνως;" ἡ δὲ μωρὰ ἔφη· "ἄνθρωπός τις μακρὸν ποῖρον καὶ δύο στρογγύλα νευρώδη ἔθηκεν ἐν τῇ κοιλίᾳ μου ἔσω βαλὼν καὶ ἔξω ἐντρέχων [ἐνέβαλέ μοι] κἀγὼ ἡδέως εἶχον." ἡ δὲ μήτηρ ἀκούσασα καὶ ἰδοῦσα ἔφη· "ὦ τέκνον, ἀπώλεσας καὶ ὃν πρῶτον εἶχες νοῦν."

A woman had a daughter, a virgin, who was a fool. The woman, therefore, prayed at all times to the goddess to grant her daughter some sense. Since she prayed out loud, the girl heard her and memorised the phrase. After a few days the girl and her mother went out to the countryside. There, as it happened, the girl stuck her head through the door of the stable

---

8 On the thematic connections between the stupid girl's tale and Aesop's fate see van Dijk 1995, 143–144; van Dijk 1996, 535–538; Merkle 1996, 227–228; Hansen 2002, 254; Kurke 2011, 87, 186–187, 213–217; Papademetriou 2009, 65–67.
9 On the textual history of this recension see Chambry 1927, li–lii; Perry 1936, 174–204; Hausrath 1959–1970, I.1 xi–xiii; Adrados 1999–2003, I 90–100, 503–504, II 429–462.
10 On this fable and its textual tradition see Hausrath 1959–1970, I.2 113–114; Adrados 1999–2003, III 370. Hausrath's text is reproduced here; Perry 1952 does not include a separate text of this fable in his edition, because he considers the fable version to be entirely derivative from the *Aesop Romance*. The English translation that follows is mine.

and saw a man who was copulating with a female ass. She approached the man and asked him: "Good sir, what are you doing?" The fellow replied: "I am putting some sense into her". Then the foolish girl remembered her mother's daily prayers, to the effect that she should get some sense. So she implored the man with these words: "Please, sir, put some sense into me as well. You will see, my mother will owe you a great many thanks for this". The man obeyed to the call, left the she-ass aside and deflowered the girl, corrupting her for good. Afterwards, the deflowered girl went to her mother full of joy and exclaimed: "See, mummy, your wish is fulfilled! I got some sense". Her mother said: "Perhaps the gods listened to my prayers". The girl said: "Of course, mummy!" But the mother asked: "And how did you understand this?" The foolish girl replied: "There was a man, and he put into my belly a long long stick and two sinewy little balls, and there he was thrusting in and rushing out all the time. And you know something? I liked it!" When the mother heard this, she had a good look and cried: "Oh, my child, now you have lost what little sense you had earlier!"

In this version the maiden describes her experience with even more graphic physical details than was the case in the *Aesop Romance*. Equally scandalous is the girl's naive final statement that she enjoyed the experience. This particular motif will recur in other specimens of this type of tale, up to the early modern period. The ingenuous woman, even though she does not understand the true meaning and function of the sexual act, is all too appreciative of the pleasure of the process, and in later examples she will also be keen to repeat it. In the end, the mother personally inspects her daughter's crucial anatomical parts (ἰδοῦσα), in order to ascertain the damage — a final piquant detail that also contributes to the stronger focus on bodily aspects which characterises the fable narrative.

These additional details are so well integrated in the storyline, so successful and amusing, that they seem old and authentic. They cannot be the secondary inventions of a late copyist or Byzantine cleric, but must represent genuine ingredients of the original narrative. Apparently, these elements were cut out from the somewhat terse and arid version of the *Aesop Romance*, in which the tale was introduced as an emboxed digression and was therefore liable to curtailment. They must have been included, however, in other variant forms of the story, which presumably circulated in the ancient world, were recorded in different sources or collections and survived up to the late Imperial or early Byzantine period. The tale of the silly maiden was a vibrant piece of popular lore, which went around in oral tradition and existed in parallel versions, with varying degrees of completeness in terms of circumstantial details. The preserved written specimens allow a glimpse into the multiplicity of variants which must have characterised the tale in its raw folk state.

It is not surprising to find a scabrous story of this kind in the collections of didactic Aesopic fables. Next to the familiar animal tales and other allegorical parables, the ancient and medieval corpora of fabulistic literature contain several specimens which properly belong to the narrative genre of the realistic comic novella: that is, tales about amusing incidents of everyday life, mostly revolving around a ribald erotic theme — illicit love affairs, adulterous liaisons or deviant sexual practices. Among other examples, the surviving recensions of ancient Greek fables include the famous novella of the "Widow of Ephesus"[11] and a number of tales of adultery or humorous domesticity[12] comparable to those found later in the great medieval narrative compilations, from Petrus Alphonsi's *Disciplina Clericalis* and the Old French *fabliaux* to the unsurpassable *Decameron* and the *Canterbury Tales*.[13]

The ultimate roots of this genre lie in the ancient Orient. The earliest known specimens of scabrous novella are traced in Sumerian didactic collections and Egyptian cycles of tales from the second millennium BC.[14] In the East this tradition would be continued up to late antiquity and the medieval period, when plenty of such material was included in the large literary compilations of stories, from the Persian *Book of Sindbad* and the *Arabian Nights* to the Indian *Tales of the Parrot* and Somadeva's *Ocean of the Streams of Story*.[15] Possibly the genre was introduced into the Greek world from the Orient. The first Hellenic area in which ribald tales are known to have flourished was Archaic Ionia, the Greek cities of Asia Minor and the eastern Aegean islands. The Ionian people had a flair for novellistic storytelling; their leisurely and jocose temperament favoured especially the development of humorous and piquant stories about amorous affairs, women's guiles and saucy sexual encounters.[16] The rich repertoire of tales, which must have thrived in the oral tradition of Ionia, underlies the satirical creations of Archaic iambic poetry and is reflected in the narratives of Herodotus and the

---

11 See Weinreich 1931, 53–73; Perry 1962, 329–330; Anderson 1984, 161–164; van Dijk 1995, 141–143; Hansen 2002, 266–279; Müller 2006, 336–361; Papademetriou 2009, 67–70.
12 See e.g. fables 350, 379, 381, 386, 388, 410, 419, 420, 421 Perry. In general, on the ribald novellas included in the ancient corpora of fables see Trenkner 1958, 5–13; Perry 1961; Nøjgaard 1964, 92–93, 400–402, 523–525, 533–535; Perry 1966, 296; van Dijk 1995, 141–144, 147–149; Merkle 1996, 216, 226–228; Adrados 1999–2003, I 42, 624–631, II 619–620, 704–705, III 364–371.
13 For grammatological surveys of this rich medieval narrative tradition see Landau 1884; Bolte/Polívka 1913–1932, IV 127–260; Clements/Gibaldi 1977; Gittes 1991; Tolan 1993, 73–94, 132–158; Correale/Hamel 2002–2005; Holm 2013, 9–44.
14 For the Sumerian specimens see Alster 1997, 252–257, 271–272, 442–444, 449; Alster 2005, 368–372; Holm 2013, 73–75. For the Egyptian tradition see Bolte/Polívka 1913–1932, IV 95–101; Quack 2005, 16–80; Burkard/Thissen 2008–2012, I 200–215, II 7–82; Holm 2013, 92–183.
15 On these oriental narrative compilations see e.g. Bolte/Polívka 1913–1932, IV 286–418; Keith 1920, 242–295; Perry 1960; Irwin 1994, 42–102; Holm 2013, 60–69.
16 On the novellistic tradition of Archaic Ionia see Erdmannsdörffer 1870; Hausrath 1914; Aly 1936; Cataudella 1957, 7–8, 41–61; Trenkner 1958, 1–13, 168–177; Aly 1969, 15–30, 208–263.

early logographers.[17] In particular, the tradition of ribald and sensational erotic novella will culminate in Aristides' notorious collection of *Milesian Tales*, published in the ripe Hellenistic age.[18] Ionia, of course, was a close neighbour of the great empires of the East, a longtime subject of the Lydians and then of the Persians, and kept constant contact with the eastern cultures. It is thus likely that the Ionian novellistic tradition grew under the strong influence of oriental story-telling.[19]

The tale of the stupid girl who is ignorant of sex may also stem from the repertoire of early Ionian novella. The central misunderstanding between the maiden and the herdsman, which lies at the core of the plot, is based on an implicit wordplay which best operates not in classical Attic or in the Koine but in the Ionic dialect. The rustic fellow mates with a female ass, called ὄνος in the Greek text. The word ὄνος, if slightly anagrammatised, becomes νόος, the Ionic non-contracted allomorph of νοῦς, "sense"; and νοῦς/νόος is precisely the quality that the imbecile girl lacks, the gift that her mother prays to the gods for. Thus, a prototypical Ionic version of the tale may be reconstructed, in which the misunderstanding is produced very naturally from a linguistic and phonological point of view.[20] The herdsman, when asked what he is doing, would reply "ὄνον ἐντί-θημι", "I am thrusting (my penis) into the she-ass". But he would speak in a lax and rough accent, as country people still do sometimes in rural Greece. As a result, the silly girl would mishear his statement and think that he had answered "νόον ἐντίθημι", "I am putting sense into (her)" — and this latter phrase would make the maiden remember her mother's prayers.

The main canvas of the narrative, therefore, apparently goes back to an older Ionian novella. Perhaps the novella was included in Aristides' *Milesian Tales*, together with the story of the Widow of Ephesus, which closely accompanies the

---

17 On storytelling in iambic poetry see Bowie 2001a; Bowie 2001b; Kantzios 2005, 20–29, 34–74; Carey 2008. On the wealth of novellas in Herodotus and the Ionian logographers see most notably Hausrath 1914, 442–446; Thomson 1935; Cataudella 1957, 39–60; Trenkner 1958, 24–30; Aly 1969; Erbse 1992, 3–117; Tatum 1997; Griffiths 2006; Müller 2006, 6–96, 153–335.
18 See Cataudella 1957, 90, 131–161; Anderson 1976, 108–114; Harrison 1998; Benz 2001; Jensson 2004, 258–301; Bowie 2013.
19 Cf. Erdmannsdörffer 1870, 26–35; Aly 1936, 1176; Cataudella 1957, 15–18, 60–61; Trenkner 1958, 2–3; Aly 1969, 19–24, 252–263.
20 This Ionic wordplay was first detected by Wiechers 1961, 9; see also Winkler 1985, 280–281; Holzberg 1993, 14; Nagy 1999, 283; Stramaglia 2000, 314. Hansen 2002, 254 and van Dijk 1996, 539 express some reservations.

stupid girl's adventure both in the context of the *Aesop Romance* and in the corpus of Aesopic fables.[21] The narrative material *per se* may have been even more ancient.

The Ionian origins of the tale may also account for an intriguing parallel between its plot and an attested idea of early Ionian gynecological medicine, as recorded in the Hippocratic treatise *On the diseases of young girls* (Περὶ παρθενίων). This short text, composed in a language strongly coloured by Ionicisms, must have been written around the end of the fifth or the beginning of the fourth century BC, most probably somewhere in Ionia.[22] As argued by the Hippocratic gynecologist, young girls at menarche, who are ripe for marriage but remain unmarried and have no sexual intercourse with a man (παρανδρούμεναι), are in danger of becoming mentally disturbed and degenerating into insanity, due to the excessive accumulation of menstrual blood in their bodies. The solution, in such cases, is for the girl to marry as quickly as possible and have a child; then the blood finds a proper outlet and the patient's balance is restored. In other words, having sex (within the lawful framework of marriage, of course) is recommended as beneficial for the young woman's mental health.

The scabrous tale of the silly maiden (παρθένος, the same word that is used also for the girls in the Hippocratic treatise) may be read as a crass parody of this concept of Ionian gynecology.[23] The cunning countryman of the story presents the sexual act as beneficial for the girl's mental state, as a process that will instill power of intellect in her. But this time sex is illicit, outside the sanctioned context of marriage, and as a result the girl is considered to have lost even the little mental capacity she possessed — instead of having her mental constitution restored, like the *parthenoi* of the Hippocratic work. The medical notion is comically upturned. Possibly the creator of the original Ionian narrative meant to satirise such ideas of contemporary Ionian medical science, which would have been current in his intellectual environment. The relations between the early Ionian novella and its contemporary rationalistic philosophy and science are a scarcely ploughed field, which may yet yield fruitful hermeneutical crops.

---

21 Cf. Perry 1962, 330, 332; Papathomopoulos 1999, 136; Karla 2009, 18–19, 25.

22 See Demand 1994, 95–99; Flemming/Hanson 1998. See further King 1983, 113–127; Andò 1990; King 1998, 75–88, 194–204.

23 I am grateful to my colleague George Kazantzidis, a renowned expert of ancient medical literature, for drawing my attention to this point.

2 The male booby: Margites and Appu

Indeed, the humorous tradition of early Ionia offers a male counterpart of the character under discussion: not a girl but a foolish man who knows nothing of the sexual act and is therefore prone to ludicrous antics and misapprehensions. This is the famous Margites, the protagonist of a jocular poem probably composed in the seventh or sixth century BC by an Ionian author, who was akin to the poetic idiosyncrasy of Hipponax.[24] As transpires from the extant testimonia, Margites was a silly and ignorant man, who undertook many activities without having the requisite knowledge, and was ridiculed in consequence.[25] Margites is thus one of the earliest embodiments of an archetypical character whom critics usually name "the comic fool" or "the comic failure": this is the comic anti-hero who becomes laughable by constantly failing to live up to the expectations of his role, an incompetent and often buffoonish blunderer who makes a mess of every task he applies himself to. In this respect, Margites is the forerunner and ultimate progenitor of a populous family of amusing figures, which extends from the Dionysus of the *Frogs* to Shakespeare's Master Ford and nowadays includes such illustrious comic losers as Inspector Clouseau, Johnny English and Iznogoud.[26]

One of the major episodes of the poem, as evidenced by the surviving testimonia and papyrus fragments, was Margites' wedding. The foolish hero turned out to be the perfect male analogue to the silly girl of the Ionian novella. He was totally ignorant of the act of sex and did not know what to do with his wife on their wedding night.[27] It is a pity that the side-splitting description of this mismatched couple on their marriage bed has not been preserved in its entirety. A few references in postclassical authors, grammarians and ancient lexica allow a rough glimpse into the ludicrous scene (fr. 4 West, 8a–d Gostoli):

---

24 Cf. Lesky 1971, 111–112; West 2003, 227; Rotstein 2010, 99.
25 On the poem and figure of Margites see most notably Radermacher 1908; Langerbeck 1958; Huxley 1969, 174–176; Bossi 1986; West 2003, 225–228; Gostoli 2007; Rotstein 2010, 98–104; Pralon 2011.
26 See Winkler 1985, 159–165, 289–291; Lazarus 2014, 143–208; Konstantakos 2016. Margites also comes close to the ethological archetype of the *alazōn*, another stock figure of the comic tradition, who pretends to know or achieve more than he can in reality. See Arist. *Eth. Nic.* 1127a13–b32; Konstantakos 2015b, 43–44 with further references.
27 Cf. Radermacher 1908, 445–447; Langerbeck 1958, 53–63; Gostoli 2007, 10, 80–82; West 2008; Pralon 2011, 152–157. On modern humorous lore of the ignorant bridegroom cf. Köhler 1898, 97–100; Bolte/Polívka 1913–1932, I 311–322; Thompson 1957, 141, 216 (motifs J1744.1, J1744.1.1, J2462); Legman 1968, 126–132; Wehse 1979; Ashliman 1987, 285; Uther 2004, 371–372 (tale type 1685).

Dio Chrysostom, *Oration* 67.4: <οὐ> πολύ γ' ἂν εἴη τοῦ Μαργίτου σοφώτερος ἀγνοοῦντος ὅ τι χρὴ γήμαντα χρῆσθαι τῇ γυναικί.

He would not be much smarter than Margites, who did not know what you have to do with a wife when you have got married.

Hesychius, *Lexicon* μ 267: Μαργε<ί>της· μωρός τις ἦν, μὴ εἰδὼς μίξιν γυναικός. καὶ <ἡ> γυνὴ προτρέπεται αὐτόν, εἰποῦσα σκορπίον αὐτὴν δῆξαι καὶ ὑπὸ τῆς ὀχείας <δεῖν> θεραπευθῆναι.

Margites: he was an idiot who did not know about copulation. His wife encouraged him by saying that a scorpion had bitten her and that she had to be healed by means of intercourse.

Eustathius, *Parekbolai in the Odyssey* 1669.48ff.: οὕτως ἔγνωμεν καὶ τὸν ἄφρονα Μαργίτην (...) ὃν ὁ ποιήσας τὸν ἐπιγραφόμενον Ὁμήρου Μαργίτην ὑποτίθεται εὐπόρων μὲν εἰς ὑπερβολὴν γονέων φῦναι, γήμαντα δὲ μὴ συμπεσεῖν τῇ νύμφῃ ἕως ἀναπεισθεῖσα ἐκείνη <ὑπὸ τῆς μητρὸς> τετραυματίσθαι τὰ κάτω ἐσκήψατο, φάρμακόν τε μηδὲν ὠφελήσειν ἔφη πλὴν εἰ τὸ ἀνδρεῖον αἰδοῖον ἐκεῖ ἐφαρμοσθείη· καὶ οὕτω θεραπείας χάριν ἐκεῖνος ἐπλησίασεν.

In the same way we have heard of the foolish Margites (...) whom the author of the *Margites* that bears Homer's name represents as having been born to exceedingly affluent parents, but when he married he did not fall upon his bride until she, at her mother's instigation, pretended to have suffered a wound in her lower parts, and said that no remedy would be of any help except for a male member being fitted to the place: so it was that he made love to her, for therapeutic purposes.[28]

We may imagine the pair of newly-weds lying together, with the unsuspecting Margites in a state of inertia, and the poor lady trying in vain to attract his attention and lure him into performing his marital duty. In the end, as it seems, the wife had recourse to a stratagem; she pretended that she had been bitten by a scorpion in the genital area, and claimed that the only cure for her ailment would be to apply a man's *membrum virile* to her wounded part. Margites was thus persuaded to place his penis into the woman's vagina for therapeutic purposes — and then nature must have taken its course; this is indicated also by some crucial words (]νέον γάμ[ον] βρ[αχ]εῖ ... ἐμίχ[θ]η, "his new marriage in a short time ... he copulated") preserved on an otherwise very damaged papyrus fragment (fr. 9 West, 11 Gostoli, from P. Oxy. 3964).[29] Another papyrus text (fr. 7 West, 9 Gostoli) may also reflect a part of the wedding night, describing further antics of the clumsy bridegroom.[30] Apparently, Margites puts his erect penis into a chamber

---

28 The translations are by West 2003, 247–249.
29 West 2003, 226, 252–253; Gostoli 2007, 62–63, 85–86; cf. Pralon 2011, 156–157.
30 Text from West 2003, 251–252: κ]ύστιν[, χ]ειρὶ δὲ μακρῇι /] τεύχεα, [κ]αί ῥα ἔλασσε / δυοῖσι δ' ἐν π]όνοι[σι]ν εἴχετο /]ν· ἐν δὲ [τ]ῆι ἀμίδι /] ἐξελεῖν δ' ἀμήχανον / κ]αί ῥ' ἐνώμειξεν ταχύ /

pot and is then unable to extricate it. Perhaps the hero thrust his penis into the pot because he misinterpreted some ambiguous instructions given him by the bride (or by another personage beforehand). The author of this poem would have kept good company with Boccaccio.

The type of the sexually ignorant male is already forecast in a Hittite apologue, the so-called *Story of Appu*, preserved on cuneiform tablets from the thirteenth century BC. Although the main part of this work has a didactic character and consists in an allegorical parable about the conflict of good and evil, the introductory episode bears all the marks of a humoristic *Schwank*. Appu, the title hero, is a very rich but childless man, and the narrative makes clear the reason of his lack of heir: Appu is unable to have sex with his wife. Apparently, the two of them do not even know how to go about the task, given that they lie on their bed fully dressed. Appu seems to have no inkling that he should bare his own and his wife's genital parts and utilise them in the process.

> Appu arose, went home and lay on his bed with his shoes on. Appu's wife questioned their servants: "He has never had success before. You don't think he has now had success, do you?" The woman went and lay down with Appu with her clothes on. Appu awoke from his sleep, and his wife questioned him: "You have never had success before. Have you now been successful?" When Appu heard this, he replied: "You are a woman and think like one. You know nothing at all".
>
> Appu rose from his bed, took a white lamb and set out to meet the Sun God. The Sun God looked down from the sky, changed himself into a young man, came to him and questioned him: "What is your problem, that [I may solve] it for you?" When [Appu] heard this, he replied to him: "[The gods] have given me wealth. They have given [me cattle and sheep]. I lack only one thing: I have neither son nor daughter". When the Sun God heard this, he said: "Go get drunk, go home and have good sexual intercourse with your wife. The gods will give you one son".[31]

The verbs used in this passage of the Hittite work indicate Appu's inability to achieve a dynamic sexual performance.[32] As a result, the unfortunate wife falls

---

] κ[αιν]ὴν ἐφράσσατο μῆτι[ν· / ἀνόρουσε] λιπὼν ἄπο δέμνια [θερμά / ὤειξε] θύρας, ἐκ δ' ἔδραμεν ἔξω /]ων διὰ νύκτα μέλα[ιναν /]ύσειε δὲ χεῖρα[[ς]] / δι]ὰ νύκτα μέλαιν[αν /]μεν οὐδὲ φανίο[ν /] δύστηνον κάρ[η /]εδόκεεν λίθ[/]ωι καὶ χειρὶ παχ[είηι / λέπτ' ἔ]θηκεν ὄστρα[κα. Cf. Langerbeck 1958, 59–63; Bossi 1986, 31–34; West 2003, 225–226; Gostoli 2007, 58–60, 82–84.

31 Translated by Hoffner 1998, 82–84. For text and translation of the Hittite narrative see also Siegelová 1971, 1–11, 18–23; Bernabé 1979, 217–223; Pecchioli Daddi/Polvani 1990, 163–169; Haas 2006, 193–197.

32 See Beckman 1983, 2–3; cf. Legman 1968, 126; Bernabé 1979, 222; Pecchioli Daddi/Polvani 1990, 168.

into despair and loudly wonders whether Appu will ever succeed in having intercourse with her. In the end, Appu prays to the Sun God, and the god gives him instructions and grants him the power for a proper performance.

The Hittites inhabited the inland of Anatolia at the time of the acme of the Mycenaean kingdoms and had multifarious contacts with the Achaeans of mainland Greece. Furthermore, the Hittite civilisation was the predecessor of the later Indo-European cultures of Asia Minor, such as the Lydians, Lycians and Carians, the immediate eastern neighbours of the Ionian cities. It is not unlikely that the comic theme of the sexually ignorant man and his ridiculous experiences on the marriage bed was bequeathed to the Ionian *novellistica* from Anatolian sources.

3 Sex and the old girl: a later fabulistic specimen

The later Aesopic tradition produced further variations of the theme. The so-called *Fables of Syntipas the Philosopher* are a group of sixty-two Syriac didactic fables, which were translated into Byzantine Greek by Michael Andreopoulos in the late eleventh century. The Syriac tales themselves had been borrowed and translated from the Greek some time during the late Roman period, a fact that well illustrates the dense network of mutual narrative exchanges between the Hellenic and the oriental world throughout antiquity.[33]

One of the fables of this collection (54 = fable 410 Perry) represents a rewriting of the old Ionian tale of the stupid maiden. This particular fable is transmitted only as part of Andreopoulos' Byzantine Greek version and has no equivalent in the extant manuscripts of the Syriac model. B.E. Perry hypothesised, therefore, that this exceptional story was never included in the Syriac didactic fables but was added to the collection by Andreopoulos himself; the latter must have taken the narrative from an unknown contemporary source, probably a storybook of oriental provenance which contained saucy tales of the novella genre.[34] Be that as it may, it is not necessary to assume that the story itself, in terms of narrative material, was first created in the medieval period, around Andreopoulos' own times. As will transpire immediately below, this fable from the Greek Syntipas collection is closely connected with the old Ionian tale of the ignorant maiden;

---

33 On the *Fables of Syntipas*, their provenance and textual tradition see Perry 1936, 186–190; Perry 1952, 511–528; Perry 1966, 291–296; cf. Hausrath 1959–1970, I.1 xxiv–xxvi; Adrados 1999–2003, I 132–135, 318, II 403–428, 609–616.
34 Perry 1966, 296. On the textual tradition of this story cf. also Perry 1952, 547–548; Adrados 1999–2003, I 133, 534, III 518.

indeed, it seems to have grown out of the plot of the Ionian narrative, as a more grotesque variation. The fable may thus have been fashioned at any period of antiquity, posterior only to the creation and dissemination of the Ionian story of the silly girl.

In this later fable the young girl is replaced by a naive old woman, who is equally clueless about the sexual act and its meaning. Thus, when a young man, who is her travelling companion and helper, experiences wanton desire and rapes her, the elderly maiden cannot understand what she is suffering.

Νεανίσκος τις ὁδοιπορῶν ἐν ἡμέρᾳ καύσωνος ἐντυγχάνει γυναικί τινι γραΐδι, ἥτις καὶ αὐτὴ τὴν αὐτὴν ὁδὸν τῷ νεανίσκῳ συνεπορεύετο. ὁρῶν δὲ αὐτὴν ἐκεῖνος τῷ τε καύσωνι καὶ τῷ τῆς ὁδοιπορίας καμάτῳ δεινῶς ἰλιγγιῶσαν, κατῴκτειρε τῆς ἀσθενείας, καὶ μηκέτι ἐξισχύουσαν ὅλως πορεύεσθαι, ἄρας ταύτην τῆς γῆς ἐπὶ τῶν νώτων αὐτοῦ διεβάσταζε. ταύτην δὲ ἐπιφερόμενος λογισμοῖς τισιν αἰσχροῖς δεινῶς ἐταράττετο, ὑφ' ὧν καὶ πρὸς οἶστρον ἀκολασίας καὶ σφοδρὸν ἔρωτα ὁ αὐτοῦ ἦρτο ἰθύφαλλος. εὐθὺς δὲ τῇ γῇ καταθεὶς τὴν γραΐδα, ταύτῃ ἀκολάστως συνεγένετο. ἡ δὲ πρὸς αὐτὸν ἁπλοϊκῶς ἔλεγε· "τί ἐστιν ὃ ἐπ' ἐμοὶ ἐργάζῃ;" ὁ δὲ αὐτῇ ἔφη ὡς "βαρεῖα πέφυκας, καὶ τούτου χάριν ἀπογλύψαι σου τῆς σαρκὸς διανενόημαι." καὶ ταῦτα εἰπών, καὶ εἰς τέλος αὐτῇ συμφθαρείς, πάλιν τῆς γῆς ταύτην ἐξάρας ἐπὶ τῶν ἑαυτοῦ νώτων ἐπέθετο. καὶ μήκος ὁδοῦ τινος διελάσαντος αὐτοῦ, ἔφη πρὸς αὐτὸν ἡ γραῦς· "εἰ ἔτι βαρεῖά σοι καὶ ἐπαχθὴς πέφυκα, πάλιν με καταγαγὼν πλέον ἐξ ἐμοῦ ἀπόγλυψον."

A young man was walking along on a blazing hot day when he met an old woman who was going the same way. Seeing that she was dreadfully exhausted from the heat of the day and the demands of the journey, he felt sorry for her weakness, and when the woman simply didn't have the strength to go any further, he picked her up off the ground and carried her on his shoulders. While he was carrying her this way, the young man was so strongly aroused by shameful thoughts that he had an erection. Spurred by wanton lust and hot desire, he immediately put the old woman down on the ground and had sex with her. Being simple-minded, the woman asked him, "What are you doing to me?" He answered, "You are too heavy to carry, so I've decided to carve off some of your flesh". The man satisfied himself and then picked the woman up off the ground again and set her on his shoulders. After he had gone some way down the road, the old woman said to him, "If I am still too heavy a burden for you, you can put me down again and carve off some more of me!"[35]

There are obvious similarities between this story and the Ionian tale of the simpleton girl. The protagonist of both narratives is an ingenuous woman who does not understand the meaning of the sexual act performed on her. In both cases a lustful and cunning man takes advantage of the woman's ignorance in order to satisfy his appetites, under the pretext that he is fulfilling a useful task. Like the silly girl in the fable version of the Ionian tale, the old lady of Syntipas' fable discovers that this unfamiliar process brings her pleasure. But while the stupid girl

---

35 The translation is by Gibbs 2002, 265.

expressly states so, the elderly woman displays a more prudish attitude and only indirectly fishes for an opportunity to repeat the enjoyable experience. Clearly, the two stories are variations on the same theme.

The differences between the two tales are also important and significantly alter the logic of the narrative and the humorous result. In the fable of Syntipas the victim's advanced age produces a more grotesque effect. The elderly maid's sudden sexual awakening and her aroused desire for more sex come into crude contrast with her old age and physical decrepitude and generate an even rougher and crueler kind of humour, a mixture of laughter and repulsion, analogous perhaps to the effects created by the scenes of wanton old women in Aristophanic comedy or in Fellini's filmic fantasies.[36] The young man's abrupt lust for an invalid old female is also unmotivated and practically inexplicable — an implausible twist introduced presumably for drawing coarse laughter. For these reasons, it may be suspected that Syntipas' fable is a secondary variation modelled on the earlier, authentic Ionian tale of the stupid girl. The creator of the later narrative replaced the young, silly but nonetheless physically desirable girl of the original story with a decrepit old woman, ridiculously ignorant of the bodily facts in spite of her advanced age, in order to make the story more extreme, more outrageous and grotesque, more perverse in terms of its humour. The Boccaccesque touch of the Ionian novella gives way here to a darker and kinkier, almost oedipal sexuality.

4 A comic mythical archetype: Amphis' Callisto

The theme was also exploited in Attic comedy, which regularly made use of the domestic and piquant subject-matter of the *novellistica*, ever since the women plays of Pherecrates and Aristophanes.[37] Especially mythological burlesque, a popular category of comic plays in the late fifth and the fourth century, often absorbed motifs and storylines of the ribald erotic novella and used them as a canvas on which to comically recast the traditional myths of gods and heroes. For example, the love affairs of Zeus with various female heroines were assimilated to the typical scenarios of scabrous adultery tales. The comic Zeus was portrayed

---

36 On humour — often humour of a grotesque, bizarre and absurd variety — produced by incongruity see Martin 2007, 62–75; Morreall 2009, 9–16, 73–75; Serafim 2020, 23–42 (all providing further references).

37 On the novellistic themes of Attic comedy cf. Trenkner 1958, 79–146; Henderson 2014, 190–195; Höschele 2014.

as an ordinary adulterer and employed a range of cunning tricks in order to approach and seduce his ladylove — e.g. climbing to her window with a ladder at night, attempting to rape her while she was asleep, or playing games with her.[38]

One fourth-century comedy of this latter type, produced by the Middle Comedy poet Amphis, parodied the myth of Callisto, the Arcadian nymph and hunting companion of Artemis, who was raped by Zeus and was left pregnant. According to the myth, Artemis became very angry when she discovered Callisto's pregnancy, because her companion had betrayed her vows of virginity. Therefore, the goddess metamorphosed Callisto into a bear; in the end, Zeus took pity on the unfortunate maiden and transformed her into a constellation, the Ursa Major.[39] The comic poet appears to have turned this mythical story into a ludicrous situation of disguise, errors and misunderstandings.

The title of Amphis' play is not preserved.[40] The only evidence about it is transmitted in a Greek scholion to Aratus' *Phaenomena* (37–44, p. 90 Martin, Amphis fr. 46 Kassel/Austin):

Ἄμφις ὁ τῶν κωμῳδιῶν ποιητὴς περὶ τῆς {τοῦ} μείζονος Ἄρκτου φησὶν ὅτι τὸν Δία ὁμοιωθέντα Ἀρτέμιδι καὶ κυνηγετοῦντα εἰς τὸ ὄρος φθεῖραι αὐτήν. ὕστερον δὲ ἐταζομένην εἰπεῖν μηδένα ἕτερον αἴτιον εἶναι τοῦ συμπτώματος πλὴν Ἄρτεμιν. ἐφ' ᾧ ὀργισθεῖσ<αν τὴν θεὸν> ἐκθηριῶσαι αὐτήν.

The comic poet Amphis, referring to Ursa Major, narrates that Zeus took the form of Artemis and went hunting in the mountain, where he raped Callisto. Later on, while Callisto was being interrogated, she stated that Artemis was the sole responsible for her mishap, and no one else. For this reason the goddess was angered and turned Callisto into a beast.[41]

A similar account is given in the Latin paraphrases of Aratus' *Phaenomena* and the scholia on them, as well as in Hyginus' *Astronomica* (2.1). The ultimate source of all these citations must have been some Hellenistic collection of constellation myths (*Catasterismi*), presumably composed by a well-read Alexandrian scholar who had access to Amphis' comic script.[42] In the ancient citing sources it is not

---

38 See Konstantakos 2002, where several examples are discussed. Cf. Green 2014; Konstantakos 2014a, 173–174; Konstantakos 2014c.

39 On the myth of Callisto and its sources see the overviews of Henrichs 1987, 256–267; Gantz 1993, 725–728; Papachrysostomou 2016, 145–146.

40 It is unknown if the preserved fragment refers to a mythological comedy called, after the central heroine, *Callisto*, as is often assumed by scholars; see Papachrysostomou 2016, 145–146, 267–268.

41 The translation is mine.

42 See Henrichs 1987, 256–262. For a collection of the ancient sources see also Kassel/Austin 1983–2001, II 234; Papachrysostomou 2016, 267.

even made clear whether the summarised comic version of Callisto's adventures was a synopsis of a play's plot (or of a series of dramatised episodes) or simply a narrative told by a character in a speech, in a comedy of an overall different thematic orientation.[43] Nevertheless, given the nature of the erudite mythographical and scholiastic sources and their ultimate provenance from a Hellenistic book of *Catasterismi*, the former possibility may be favoured. This kind of mythographical compilation, when it draws from dramatic texts, is more likely to offer the outline of a play's plot or a summary of dramatic scenes than to paraphrase a character's tirade or another reported passage.[44]

If this assumption is true, part of the plot of the comedy would have revolved around the figure of the ignorant maiden and her ludicrous inexperience in matters of sex. As indicated by the summary, in Amphis' play Zeus took the form of Artemis herself in order to violate Callisto.[45] The latter, in turn, must have been portrayed as an entirely ingenuous maiden, so ignorant of the realities of sex that she did not understand what had happened to her. Apparently, she did not recognise her rapist's male nature but thought that it was actually Artemis who had dallied with her in a hitherto unfamiliar way. This is clearly deduced from Callisto's subsequent reaction towards Artemis, after the goddess discovers the girl's predicament. As indicated in the narrative, when Artemis discovered that her companion had been deflowered, she took Callisto to task for having broken her oath of virginity. However, the simple-minded Callisto had been completely taken in by her attacker's metamorphosis and blamed Artemis herself for her mishap.

One may imagine the side-splitting scene that would have evolved on the comic stage, with the hilarious misunderstandings between the goddess and her

---

43 Cf. Papachrysostomou 2016, 145–146, 267–268.

44 See Henrichs 1987, 254–262; Nesselrath 1990, 234–235; Konstantakos 2015a, 175–176. Cf. e.g. the summary of the storyline of Cratinus' *Nemesis*, transmitted in Pseudo-Eratosthenes' *Catasterismi* and related astrological compilations (test. ii, Kassel/Austin 1983–2001, IV 179). Cf. Bakola 2010, 168–173, 220–224; Henderson 2012.

45 Zeus' artifice is also mentioned in a number of postclassical mythological sources: Ov. *Met.* 2.425–440; Apollod. *Bibl.* 3.8.2; Schol. Callim. *H. Zeus* 41 (II p. 43 Pfeiffer); Nonn. *Dion.* 2.122–123, 33.289–293; Henrichs 1987, 275–276. It is unknown whether Zeus' disguise was a traditional element of the myth or Amphis' own comic invention, which then infiltrated into the later mythographical literature. In any case, the misunderstandings and comic complications, which arise from Callisto's ingenuousness in fr. 46, must have been the product of the comic poet's fertile humorous imagination. As is often the case in Attic mythological comedies, Amphis pursues the marvellous occurrence of the myth (Zeus' metamorphosis) to its most extreme practical and logical consequences and exploits its effects on the ordinary experience of the comic heroes. See Konstantakos 2014b, 91–93; Konstantakos 2015a, 175–177.

ingenuous companion and the outrageous naiveté displayed by Callisto.[46] "Are you reproaching *me*, on top of everything?", the silly maiden might have exclaimed to her divine patroness. "You did this to me yourself, have you forgotten?" Artemis' escalating indignation would have culminated with an outburst of anger, during which the goddess would transform her foolish attendant into a beast, thus bringing the mythical parody to a grotesque finale.

Amphis' play thus offers one more example of this stock theme of humorous erotic novella, this time dramatised on the comic stage. The type of the maiden who knows nothing about sex is projected onto the ludicrously distorted world of the gods and heroes of mythological comedy. It is amalgamated with the figures and the storyline of a traditional myth and serves as the main tool of comic parody, by bringing the mythical episode down to the urban and domestic world of the novella. Amphis must have been active around the middle of the fourth century,[47] and the vogue of mythological burlesques in Attic comic theatre did not persist for long after the 340s or 330s;[48] on this basis, Amphis' comedy about Callisto is likely to have been produced during the earlier phase of Middle Comedy, not later than the 340s. The dating of this play — long before the *Aesop Romance* and the extant collections of fables, even a couple of centuries earlier than Aristides' *Milesian Tales* — provides another indication for the early presence of the "ingenuous maiden" theme in Greek literature.[49]

---

46 Cf. Henrichs 1987, 262; Nesselrath 1990, 234–235; Konstantakos 2014b, 92.

47 See Nesselrath 1990, 197; Papachrysostomou 2016, 11.

48 See Nesselrath 1990, 189–204; Konstantakos 2014a, 161–162.

49 I have been repeatedly asked about the connection between the cycle of tales under discussion and the experiences of Daphnis, the hero of Longus' sophistic novel *Daphnis and Chloe*. The story arc of the novel presents indeed some analogies with the tale type of the ingenuous personage. The teenage herdsman Daphnis is initially ignorant of the procedures of copulation; he lies naked with his beloved Chloe but does not know what to do with her, and the couple cannot consummate their desire (2.9–11, 3.14). The solution to Daphnis' impasse is provided by Lycaenion, a neighbour's pretty wife, who undertakes to initiate the youngster into the act of love. She has sex with Daphnis and demonstrates him what to do, putting an end to his lack of knowledge (3.15–20). Daphnis' main similarity with the protagonists of our cycle of stories is his total ignorance of the procedures of sex. This ignorance causes Daphnis to fruitlessly lie next to his female companion, like Appu with his wife; and his state of inertia is terminated thanks to the ruse of an experienced woman, as in the case of Margites. On the other hand, there are also significant differences, which definitively separate Daphnis' story from the tale type under examination. Daphnis' ignorance is only due to the inexperience and immaturity of his very young age, not to stupidity and mental defectiveness. The tone of Longus' narrative is humorous but with a light touch, and also quite romanticised and emotional, in accordance with the conventions of the bucolic setting and the sophistic novel genre; it is not burlesque and satirical, as in the stories of the imbecile girls and Margites. The failed erotic encounters between Daphnis and Chloe are

5 The incomparable Boccaccio: The final metamorphosis of the Ionian tale

The final literary metamorphosis of this ancient theme takes us forward to Italy in the *trecento*, at the outset of the great surge of Renaissance *novellistica*. A variant of the same type of tale is included in Boccaccio's *Decameron* (3.10), the masterpiece of the western canon in the genre of the novella. Boccaccio's narrative was subsequently reworked by other storytellers, from Sacchetti and Sercambi to La Fontaine.[50]

The simple-minded heroine of Boccaccio's novella is called Alibech and is the daughter of a rich Saracen nobleman at Gafsa, near the North-African coast, in present-day Tunisia. Alibech hears of the admirable religious devotion of the Christian monks who abide in the desert, and decides to go and live with them. After a few days of marching, she arrives exhausted at the desert and is hospitably received by a young hermit called Rustico. The youthful monk offers her shelter but is soon severely tempted by the girl's beauty. Having discovered Alibech's innocence, Rustico devises a scheme so as to have sex with her under the pretext of rendering a religious service to God. For this purpose, the young monk claims that his penis is the devil, that Alibech's vagina is hell, and that the supreme duty of Christian piety is to put the devil back into hell. Under this pretence, Rustico mates with the innocent maiden, who finds out soon enough that this kind of religious service *à deux* brings her considerable pleasure. She therefore keeps pressing the hermit to perform their uplifting and salutary work of putting the devil into hell all too often, until the young man reaches the point of exhaustion.

---

permeated by genuine feelings of love, of which there is no trace in the tales of the silly maidens and their male counterparts. Whatever scabrous elements exist in Longus' scenes, they are kept within the confines of pleasant piquancy and are not pushed to grotesqueness or ridicule. Daphnis is neither a serial blunderer, nor a buffoon, nor a laughing-stock; he is a sympathetic and learning young hero, who experiences some humorously rendered misadventures in the course of his *Bildungsroman*. At most, it might be argued that Longus borrowed some elements from the known narrative type of the "person who knew nothing about sex", but transformed the borrowed material into a far subtler, more moving and sentimental literary creation. I have the strong suspicion, however, that there is no relevance of the former to the latter. Longus' novel is a different and separate fictional structure, which simply happens to share a common thematic concern with the narrative group of the stupid maidens and Margites.

50 On the later reception of Boccaccio's tale see Landau 1884, 162, 318; Lee 1909, 108–109; Legman 1968, 133; Hansen 2002, 251–255; Uther 2004, 217.

In Boccaccio's tale the plot and the setting have been transferred to the monastic milieu, in order to serve the anticlerical satire and the parody of holy Christian discourse, which permeate the whole of the *Decameron*.[51] The central erotic double entendre, on which the deception of the innocent girl relies, is accordingly taken from the religious sphere: "putting the devil into hell",[52] instead of "putting sense into someone" (as was the case in the Ionian and Aesopic tradition). Already in the popular imagination of the ancient Greeks and Romans, the woman's vagina was metaphorically represented as a container of great heat, especially a fiery kitchen implement, such as an oven or brazier.[53] Boccaccio develops and magnifies this traditional metaphor cluster to its utmost conceivable limits; he parallels the vagina with the most burning-hot and fiery site of the western Christian imaginarium, the pit of hell with its eternal flames.

In spite of the differences of setting, however, the main situation in Boccaccio's story is the same as in the old Ionian novella of the stupid maiden: a cunning man exploits the ignorance of the ingenuous girl and copulates with her, making her believe that their act is a salutary and beneficial operation. In both narratives the comic effect is produced through analogous mechanisms of salacious wordplay. It is thus tempting to think that Boccaccio's tale is an ultimate descendant of the early Ionian novella, the one reflected in the *Aesop Romance* and the Aesopic fables.[54]

The heroes' names in the Italian text offer an indication in support of this hypothesis. The young monk is called Rustico, literally "a rustic, a countryman".

---

51 On the parody of theological doctrines and Christian models in Boccaccio's tale see Paolella 1978; Storey 1982; Delcorno 1988; Picone 2008; Grossvogel 2014.

52 On the religious adaptation of the main metaphor cf. Mazzotta 1986, 117–118; Branca 1992, 338–339; Ruggiero 2009; Eisner 2013, 205–206; Branca 2014, 443–445.

53 See e.g. Ar. *Pax* 891–893; *Eq.* 1286; *Thesm.* 912; Herodotus 5.92η; Artemid. *Onir.* 2.10; Catull. 94; Apul. *Met.* 2.7; Auson. *Cent. nupt.* 110–111; Adams 1982, 86–87; duBois 1988, 110–129; Henderson 1991, 142–144. As George Kazantzidis points out to me, such popular, colloquial euphemisms are based on a process of conceptual reconfiguration, through which the sexual act is metaphorically assimilated to a common everyday activity (e.g. baking or cooking), with the purpose of rendering the intensity and inherent violence of the process into something more familiar and palatable. An analogous mechanism operates also in the sexual puns and double entendres that underlie the tales of the silly maiden discussed in this chapter. Only in these latter cases the euphemistic reconfiguration is employed by deceitful agents with the intention of misleading and manipulating the ingenuous personage.

54 Cf. Perry 1960, 14–15; Perry 1962, 332; Hansen 2002, 253–255; Jouanno 2006, 245.

This is exactly the identity of the male hero in the Ionian novella, a coarse countryman who mounts an animal in a farmyard.[55] As for the superficially exotic, Arabic-sounding name of Alibech,[56] this may be an anagram of *blachie*, an acceptable Italian transcription of the Greek word βλακίη, "stupidity"; and stupidity constitutes the maiden's main attribute in the Ionian tale. The form βλακίη, of course, would pertain morphologically to the Ionic dialect (the Attic and Koine allomorph is βλακεία or βλακία). This would suit the linguistic form of the prototypical Ionian narrative, which would have been composed in dialectical Ionic Greek, as indicated also by the underlying wordplay on ὄνος and νόος (see above, section 1).

Boccaccio, at the time he was writing the *Decameron*, in the early 1350s, did not yet know enough Greek to read an extensive Greek text, although he displayed a keen interest in Greek literature and associated with scholars of Greek from early on in his life.[57] He might thus have been acquainted with a now lost intermediary source, perhaps a translation or adaptation of the old Ionian story in Latin. In this putative translation the Greek word βλακίη would have been taken over from the original Ionian version, transcribed in the Latin alphabet and incorporated in the text, either as a characterisation or as a sobriquet of the stupid heroine. Boccaccio would have appropriated this curious appellation from his source text and cleverly anagrammatised it, so as to create an exotically modelled name for his Moorish female protagonist.

In conclusion, the ingenuous personage who has no idea of sex is a recurring figure in the humorous traditions of the ancient and medieval world. This figure lies at the centre of a scabrous comic and novellistic theme, which has a very old literary ancestry but also a distinguished *Nachleben* until modern times. The tale type of "sex and the stupid person", although not profusely attested in extant

---

55 Several scholars propose that the young hermit's name may have been inspired by a letter of St. Jerome (125), addressed to a young monk named Rusticus, in which advice is offered about the difficulties of the monastic life. There may also be an allusion to one or more saints and fathers of the early Latin Church (St. Rusticus of Verona, Narbonne, Lyon, Pisa). See Landau 1884, 318; Branca 2014, 445; Galbi 2014. Porcelli (1995, 69) connects the name with the hermit's typically agrarian herbal diet; Mazzotta (1986, 117) reads a sly reference to the chapter "De amore rusticorum", concerning the desires of the flesh experienced by country folk, in Andreas Capellanus' famous treatise *De amore*. None of these interpretations annuls the connection with the "rustic" of the old Ionian model, which may have operated collaterally as a factor in Boccaccio's choice of name.
56 On the pseudo-oriental morphology of the name and its humoristic, even obscene implications cf. Porcelli 1995, 69; Franceschini 2013, 110–111, 114–120.
57 On Boccaccio's studies of the Greek classics see Pertusi 1964; Wilson 1992, 2–7; Santangelo 2006; Fumagalli 2013; Cursi 2015; Petoletti 2016; Battaglia Ricci 2018.

written sources, yet runs through the literary history of East and West, from the second millennium BC to the Renaissance and beyond. It is a long way from the Hittites to Aristides of Miletus and the *Life of Aesop*, from Archaic Ionia to Boccaccio. Travelling on this way, one may trace the literary history of a sexist, politically incorrect but also hilarious theme.

Bibliography

Adams, J.N. (1982), *The Latin Sexual Vocabulary*, London.
Adrados, F.R. (1999–2003), *History of the Graeco-Latin Fable*, vol. I–III, ed. F.R. Adrados/G.-J. van Dijk, Leiden.
Alster, B. (1997), *Proverbs of Ancient Sumer. The World's Earliest Proverb Collections*, Bethesda.
Alster, B. (2005), *Wisdom of Ancient Sumer*, Bethesda.
Aly, W. (1936), 'Novelle', in: *RE* 17.1, 1171–1179.
Aly, W. (1969), *Volksmärchen, Sage und Novelle bei Herodot und seinen Zeitgenossen*, ed. L. Huber, Göttingen.
Anderson, G. (1976), *Studies in Lucian's Comic Fiction*, Leiden.
Anderson, G. (1984), *Ancient Fiction. The Novel in the Graeco-Roman World*, London/Sydney.
Andò, V. (1990), 'La verginità come follia: il *Peri parthenion* ippocratico', in: *Quaderni Storici* 75, 715–737.
Ashliman, D.L. (1987), *A Guide to Folktales in the English Language Based on the Aarne-Thompson Classification System*, New York.
Bakola, E. (2010), *Cratinus and the Art of Comedy*, Oxford.
Battaglia Ricci, L. (2018), 'L'Omero di Boccaccio', in: A.M. Cabrini/A. D'Agostino (eds.), *Boccaccio: gli antichi e i moderni*, Milan, 7–45.
Beckman, G.M. (1983), *Hittite Birth Rituals*, Wiesbaden.
Benz, L. (2001), 'Die Fabula Milesia und die griechisch-römische Literatur', in: L. Benz (ed.), *ScriptOralia Romana. Die römische Literatur zwischen Mündlichkeit und Schriftlichkeit*, Tübingen, 43–137.
Bernabé, A. (1979), *Textos literarios hetitas*, Madrid.
Bolte, J./Polívka, G. (1913–1932), *Anmerkungen zu den Kinder- und Hausmärchen der Brüder Grimm*, vol. I–V, Leipzig.
Bossi, F. (1986), *Studi sul Margite*, Ferrara.
Bowie, E.L. (2001a), 'Ancestors of Historiography in Early Greek Elegiac and Iambic Poetry?', in: N. Luraghi (ed.), *The Historian's Craft in the Age of Herodotus*, Oxford, 45–66.
Bowie, E.L. (2001b), 'Early Greek Iambic Poetry: The Importance of Narrative', in: A. Cavarzere/ A. Aloni/A. Barchiesi (eds.), *Iambic Ideas. Essays on a Poetic Tradition from Archaic Greece to the Late Roman Empire*, Lanham, 1–27.
Bowie, E.L. (2013), '"Milesian Tales"', in: T. Whitmarsh/S. Thomson (eds.), *The Romance between Greece and the East*, Cambridge, 243–257.
Branca, V. (1992), *Boccaccio medievale e nuovi studi sul Decameron*, Florence.
Branca, V. (2014), *Giovanni Boccaccio, Decameron*, vol. I, Turin.

Burkard, G./Thissen, H.J. (2008–2012), *Einführung in die altägyptische Literaturgeschichte*, vol. I–II, Berlin.

Carey, C. (2008), 'Hipponax Narrator', in: *Acta Antiqua Academiae Scientiarum Hungaricae* 48, 89–102.

Cataudella, Q. (1957), *La novella greca. Prolegomeni e testi in traduzioni originali*, Naples.

Chambry, É. (1927), *Ésope, Fables*, Paris.

Clements, R.J./Gibaldi, J. (1977), *Anatomy of the Novella. The European Tale Collection from Boccaccio and Chaucer to Cervantes*, New York.

Correale, R.M./Hamel, M. (eds.) (2002–2005), *Sources and Analogues of the Canterbury Tales*, vol. I–II, Cambridge.

Cursi, M. (2015), 'Boccaccio lettore di Omero: le postille autografe all'*Odissea*', in: *Studi sul Boccaccio* 43, 5–27.

Daly, L.W. (1961), *Aesop without Morals. The Famous Fables, and a Life of Aesop*, New York.

Delcorno, C. (1988), 'Modelli agiografici e modelli narrativi. Tra Cavalca e Boccaccio', in: *Lettere Italiane* 40, 486–509.

Demand, N. (1994), *Birth, Death, and Motherhood in Classical Greece*, Baltimore.

duBois, P. (1988), *Sowing the Body. Psychoanalysis and Ancient Representations of Women*, Chicago.

Eisner, M. (2013), 'Eroticizing Theology in Day Three and the Poetics of the *Decameron*', in: *Annali d'Italianistica* 41, 198–215.

Erbse, H. (1992), *Studien zum Verständnis Herodots*, Berlin.

Erdmannsdörffer, B. (1870), *Das Zeitalter der Novelle in Hellas*, Berlin.

Ferrari, F. (1997), *Romanzo di Esopo*, introduzione e testo critico a cura di F. Ferrari, traduzione e note di G. Bonelli e G. Sandrolini, Milan.

Flemming, R./Hanson, A.E. (1998), 'Hippocrates' *Peri Parthéniôn* ("Diseases of Young Girls"). Text and Translation', in: *Early Science and Medicine* 3, 241–252.

Franceschini, F. (2013), '*Salabaetto* e i nomi di tipo arabo ed ebraico nel *Decameron*', in: *Italianistica* 42, 107–125.

Fumagalli, E. (2013), 'Giovanni Boccaccio tra Leonzio Pilato e Francesco Petrarca: appunti a proposito della "prima translatio" dell'*Iliade*', in: *Italia Medioevale e Umanistica* 54, 213–284.

Galbi, D. (2014), 'Alibech, Rustico, and the Life of Saint Pelagia', *Purple Motes*, online: https://www.purplemotes.net/2014/03/23/alibech-rustico-pelagia/.

Gantz, T. (1993), *Early Greek Myth. A Guide to Literary and Artistic Sources*, Baltimore.

Gibbs, L. (2002), *Aesop's Fables. Translated with an Introduction and Notes*, Oxford.

Gittes, K.S. (1991), *Framing the Canterbury Tales. Chaucer and the Medieval Frame Narrative Tradition*, New York.

Gostoli, A. (2007), *Omero, Margite. Introduzione, testimonianze, testo critico, traduzione e commento*, Pisa/Rome.

Green, J.R. (2014), 'Zeus on a See-Saw. A Comic Scene from Paestum', in: *Logeion* 4, 1–27.

Griffiths, A. (2006), 'Stories and Storytelling in the *Histories*', in: C. Dewald/J. Marincola (eds.), *The Cambridge Companion to Herodotus*, Cambridge, 130–144.

Grossvogel, S. (2014), 'The Tale of Alibech (III.10)', in: F. Ciabattoni/P.M. Forni (eds.), *The Decameron Third Day in Perspective*, Toronto, 218–234.

Haas, V. (2006), *Die hethitische Literatur. Texte, Stilistik, Motive*, Berlin.

Hansen, W. (2002), *Ariadne's Thread. A Guide to International Tales Found in Classical Literature*, Ithaca.

Harrison, S.J. (1998), 'The Milesian Tales and the Roman Novel', in: *Groningen Colloquia on the Novel 9*, 61–73.

Hausrath, A. (1914), 'Die ionische Novellistik', in: *Neue Jahrbücher für das Klassische Altertum* 33, 441–461.

Hausrath, A. (1959–1970), *Corpus Fabularum Aesopicarum*, ed. H. Hunger, vol. I.1–I.2, Leipzig.

Henderson, J. (1991), *The Maculate Muse. Obscene Language in Attic Comedy*, Oxford/New York.

Henderson, J. (2012), 'Pursuing Nemesis: Cratinus and Mythological Comedy', in: C.W. Marshall/G. Kovacs (eds.), *No Laughing Matter. Studies in Athenian Comedy*, London, 1–12.

Henderson, J. (2014), 'Comedy in the Fourth Century II: Politics and Domesticity', in: M. Fontaine/A.C. Scafuro (eds.), *The Oxford Handbook of Greek and Roman Comedy*, Oxford, 181–198.

Henrichs, A. (1987), 'Three Approaches to Greek Mythography', in: J. Bremmer (ed.), *Interpretations of Greek Mythology*, London, 242–277.

Hoffner, H.A. (1998), *Hittite Myths*, Atlanta.

Holm, T.L. (2013), *Of Courtiers and Kings. The Biblical Daniel Narratives and Ancient Story-Collections*, Winona Lake.

Holzberg, N. (1992), 'Der Äsop-Roman. Eine strukturanalytische Interpretation', in: N. Holzberg/A. Beschorner/S. Merkle (eds.), *Der Äsop-Roman. Motivgeschichte und Erzählstruktur*, Tübingen, 33–75.

Holzberg, N. (1993), 'A Lesser Known "Picaresque" Novel of Greek Origin: The *Aesop Romance* and Its Influence', in: *Groningen Colloquia on the Novel 5*, 1–16.

Höschele, R. (2014), 'Greek Comedy, the Novel, and Epistolography', in: M. Fontaine/A.C. Scafuro (eds.), *The Oxford Handbook of Greek and Roman Comedy*, Oxford, 735–752.

Huxley, G.L. (1969), *Greek Epic Poetry from Eumelos to Panyassis*, London.

Irwin, R. (1994), *The Arabian Nights. A Companion*, London.

Jedrkiewicz, S. (1989), *Sapere e paradosso nell'antichità: Esopo e la favola*, Rome.

Jensson, G. (2004), *The Recollections of Encolpius. The Satyrica of Petronius as Milesian Fiction*, Groningen.

Jouanno, C. (2005), 'La *Vie d'Ésope*: une biographie comique', in: *Revue des Études Grecques* 118, 391–425.

Jouanno, C. (2006), *Vie d'Ésope. Livre du philosophe Xanthos et de son esclave Ésope. Du mode de vie d'Ésope*, Paris.

Kantzios, I. (2005), *The Trajectory of Archaic Greek Trimeters*, Leiden.

Karla, G.A. (2001), *Vita Aesopi. Überlieferung, Sprache und Edition einer frühbyzantinischen Fassung des Äsopromans*, Wiesbaden.

Karla, G.A. (2009), 'Fictional Biography vis-à-vis Romance: Affinity and Differentiation', in: G.A. Karla (ed.), *Fiction on the Fringe. Novelistic Writing in the Post-Classical Age*, Leiden, 13–32.

Karla, G.A. (Forthcoming), *The Life of Aesop. Recension MORN*, Atlanta.

Kassel, R./Austin, C. (1983–2001), *Poetae Comici Graeci*, vol. I–VIII, Berlin/New York.

Keith, A.B. (1920), *A History of Sanskrit Literature*, Oxford.

King, H. (1983), 'Bound to Bleed: Artemis and Greek Women', in: A. Cameron/A. Kuhrt (eds.), *Images of Women in Antiquity*, London, 109–127.

King, H. (1998), *Hippocrates' Woman. Reading the Female Body in Ancient Greece*, London/New York.

Köhler, R. (1898), *Kleinere Schriften*, vol. I: *Zur Märchenforschung*, Weimar.

Konstantakos, I.M. (2002), 'Towards a Literary History of Comic Love', in: *Classica et Mediae-valia* 53, 141–171.

Konstantakos, I.M. (2014a), 'Comedy in the Fourth Century I: Mythological Burlesques', in: M. Fontaine/A.C. Scafuro (eds.), *The Oxford Handbook of Greek and Roman Comedy*, Oxford, 160–180.

Konstantakos, I.M. (2014b), 'Από τον μύθο στο γέλιο: Θαυμαστά μοτίβα και κωμικές στρατηγικές στη μυθολογική κωμωδία', in: M. Tamiolaki (ed.), *Κωμικός στέφανος. Νέες τάσεις στην έρευνα της αρχαίας ελληνικής κωμωδίας*, Rethymno, 75–102.

Konstantakos, I.M. (2014c), 'Zeus on a See-Saw: Additional Remarks on Comic Themes', in: *Logeion* 4, 28–39.

Konstantakos, I.M. (2015a), 'Tendencies and Variety in Middle Comedy', in: S. Chronopoulos/C. Orth (eds.), *Fragmente einer Geschichte der griechischen Komödie — Fragmentary History of Greek Comedy*, Heidelberg, 158–197.

Konstantakos, I.M. (2015b), 'On the Early History of the Braggart Soldier. Part One: Archilochus and Epicharmus', in: *Logeion* 5, 41–84.

Konstantakos, I.M. (2016), Review of Lazarus (2014), in: *Classical Journal Online* 2016.02.05.

Kurke, L. (2011), *Aesopic Conversations. Popular Tradition, Cultural Dialogue, and the Invention of Greek Prose*, Princeton.

Landau, M. (1884), *Die Quellen des Dekameron*, Stuttgart.

Langerbeck, H. (1958), '*Margites*. Versuch einer Beschreibung und Rekonstruktion', in: *Harvard Studies in Classical Philology* 63, 33–63.

Lazarus, B.M. (2014), *Humanist Comic Elements in Aristophanes and the Old Testament*, Piscataway.

Lee, A.C. (1909), *The Decameron. Its Sources and Analogues*, London.

Legman, G. (1968), *Rationale of the Dirty Joke. An Analysis of Sexual Humor. First Series*, New York.

Lesky, A. (1971), *Geschichte der griechischen Literatur*, Munich.

Martin, R.A. (2007), *The Psychology of Humor: An Integrative Approach*, Burlington.

Mazzotta, G. (1986), *The World at Play in Boccaccio's Decameron*, Princeton.

Merkle, S. (1992), 'Die Fabel von Frosch und Maus. Zur Funktion der λόγοι im Delphi-Teil des Äsop-Romans', in: N. Holzberg/A. Beschorner/S. Merkle (eds.), *Der Äsop-Roman. Motivgeschichte und Erzählstruktur*, Tübingen, 110–127.

Merkle, S. (1996), 'Fable, "Anecdote" and "Novella" in the *Vita Aesopi*. The Ingredients of a "Popular Novel"', in: O. Pecere/A. Stramaglia (eds.), *La letteratura di consumo nel mondo greco-latino*, Cassino, 209–234.

Morreall, J. (2009), *Comic Relief. A Comprehensive Philosophy of Humor*, Chichester.

Müller, C.W. (2006), *Legende — Novelle — Roman. Dreizehn Kapitel zur erzählenden Prosaliteratur der Antike*, Göttingen.

Nagy, G. (1999), *The Best of the Achaeans. Concepts of the Hero in Archaic Greek Poetry*, Baltimore.

Nesselrath, H.-G. (1990), *Die attische Mittlere Komödie. Ihre Stellung in der antiken Literaturkritik und Literaturgeschichte*, Berlin/New York.

Nøjgaard, M. (1964), *La Fable antique*, vol. I: *La Fable grecque avant Phèdre*, Copenhagen.

Paolella, A. (1978), 'I livelli narrativi nella novella di Rustico ed Alibech "romita" del Decameron', in: *Revue Romane* 13, 189–205.

Papachrysostomou, A. (2016), *Amphis: Introduction, Translation, Commentary*, Heidelberg.

Papademetriou, J.-T.A. (2009), 'Romance without *Eros*', in: G.A. Karla (ed.), *Fiction on the Fringe. Novelistic Writing in the Post-Classical Age*, Leiden, 49–80.

Papathomopoulos, M. (1999), *Ὁ Βίος τοῦ Αἰσώπου. Ἡ παραλλαγὴ W*, Athens.

Papathomopoulos, M. (2010), *Βίβλος Ξάνθου φιλοσόφου καὶ Αἰσώπου δούλου αὐτοῦ περὶ τῆς ἀναστροφῆς Αἰσώπου. Κριτικὴ ἔκδοση μὲ εἰσαγωγὴ καὶ μετάφραση*, Athens.

Pecchioli Daddi, F./Polvani, A.M. (1990), *La mitologia ittita*, Brescia.

Perry, B.E. (1936), *Studies in the Text History of the Life and Fables of Aesop*, Haverford.

Perry, B.E. (1952), *Aesopica. A Series of Texts Relating to Aesop or Ascribed to Him or Closely Connected with the Literary Tradition that Bears His Name*, Urbana.

Perry, B.E. (1960), 'The Origin of the Book of Sindbad', *Fabula* 3, 1–94.

Perry, B.E. (1961), 'Two Fables Recovered', in: *Byzantinische Zeitschrift* 54, 4–14.

Perry, B.E. (1962), 'Demetrius of Phalerum and the Aesopic Fables', in: *Transactions of the American Philological Association* 93, 287–346.

Perry, B.E. (1966), 'Some Addenda to the Life of Aesop', in: *Byzantinische Zeitschrift* 59, 285–304.

Pertusi, A. (1964), *Leonzio Pilato fra Petrarca e Boccaccio. Le sue versioni omeriche negli autografi di Venezia e la cultura greca del primo Umanesimo*, Venice.

Petoletti, M. (2016), 'Boccaccio e i *Graeca*', in: *Studi Medievali e Umanistici* 14, 223–245.

Picone, M. (2008), *Boccaccio e la codificazione della novella. Letture del Decameron*, Ravenna.

Porcelli, B. (1995), 'I nomi in venti novelle del "Decameron"', in: *Italianistica* 24, 49–72.

Pralon, D. (2011), 'Margitès', in: B. Acosta-Hughes/C. Cusset/Y. Durbec/D. Pralon (eds.), *Homère revisité. Parodie et humour dans les réécritures homériques*, Besançon, 133–158.

Quack, J.F. (2005), *Einführung in die altägyptische Literaturgeschichte*, vol. III, Münster.

Radermacher, L. (1908), 'Motiv und Persönlichkeit. I. Margites', in: *Rheinisches Museum* 63, 445–464.

Rotstein, A. (2010), *The Idea of Iambos*, Oxford.

Ruggiero, G. (2009), 'A Woman as Savior: Alibech and the Last Age of the Flesh in Boccaccio's Decameron', in: *Acta Histriae* 17, 151–162.

Santangelo, E. (2006), 'Per una presenza dell'*Odissea* nel *Decameron*: primi sondaggi e congetture', in: *La letteratura del mare. Atti del Convegno di Napoli, 13–16 settembre 2004*, Rome, 705–722.

Serafim, A. (2020), 'Comic Invective in the Public Forensic Speeches of Attic Oratory', in: *Hellenica* 68, 23–42.

Siegelová, J. (1971), *Appu-Märchen und Ḫedammu-Mythus*, Wiesbaden.

Storey, H.W. (1982), 'Parodic Structure in "Alibech and Rustico": Antecedents and Traditions', in: *Canadian Journal of Italian Studies* 5, 163–176.

Stramaglia, A. (2000), *Ἔρως. Antiche trame greche d'amore*, Bari.

Tatum, J. (1997), 'Herodotus the Fabulist', in: M. Picone/B. Zimmermann (eds.), *Der antike Roman und seine mittelalterliche Rezeption*, Basel, 29–48.

Thomson, J.A.K. (1935), *The Art of the Logos*, London.

Thompson, S. (1957), *Motif-Index of Folk-Literature*, vol. IV, Bloomington.

Tolan, J. (1993), *Petrus Alfonsi and His Medieval Readers*, Gainesville.

Trenkner, S. (1958), *The Greek Novella in the Classical Period*, Cambridge.

Uther, H.-J. (2004), *The Types of International Folktales. A Classification and Bibliography Based on the System of Antti Aarne and Stith Thompson*, vol. II, Helsinki.

van Dijk, G.-J. (1995), 'The Fables in the Greek *Life of Aesop*', in: *Reinardus* 8, 131–150.

van Dijk, J.G.M. (1996), 'The Function of Fables in Graeco-Roman Romance', in: *Mnemosyne* 49, 513–541.

Wehse, R. (1979), 'Bräutigam: Der dümme Bräutigam', in: *Enzyklopädie des Märchens* 2, 738–745.

Weinreich, O. (1931), *Fabel, Aretalogie, Novelle. Beiträge zu Phädrus, Petron, Martial und Apuleius*, Heidelberg.

West, M.L. (2003), *Homeric Hymns, Homeric Apocrypha, Lives of Homer*, Cambridge, MA/London.

West, M.L. (2008), 'A Vagina in Search of an Author', in: *Classical Quarterly* 58, 370–375.

Wiechers, A. (1961), *Aesop in Delphi*, Meisenheim am Glan.

Wilson, N.G. (1992), *From Byzantium to Italy. Greek Studies in the Italian Renaissance*, London.

Winkler, J.J. (1985), *Auctor & Actor. A Narratological Reading of Apuleius's* Golden Ass, Berkeley.

Zafiropoulos, C.A. (2015), *Socrates and Aesop. A Comparative Study of the Introduction of Plato's* Phaedo, Sankt Augustin.

Amphilochios Papathomas and Aikaterini Koroli

Sex and Abuse in Unhappy Marriages in Late Antique Oxyrhynchus: The Case of Two Women's Narratives Preserved on Papyrus

Abstract: Documentary papyri that originate from Greco-Roman Egypt contain plenty of attestations concerning sex in failed marriages, and specifically its use as a form of domestic violence against women. This contribution aims to feed the discussion on this topic through the analysis of two well-preserved narratives from late antique Oxyrhynchus, namely P.Oxy. VI 903 (4th cent. AD), and P.Oxy. L 3581 (4th–5th cent. AD). The particular interest of the documents in question lies in the fact that they were both written by women, who narrate in a rather emotional manner their traumatic experiences as victims of corporal and psychological violence. The recipients of their narratives are asked to restore justice as representatives of the law. Our focus is, first, on the implicit references to the involvement of women in non-consensual sexual contacts, as well as to some aspects of sexual deceit; and second, on the personality traits of both the victimised women and the men-abusers. The two selected narratives are placed in their historical and philological context and are compared to other texts — mostly of documentary nature — that deal with the same topics.

1 Introduction

This chapter deals with sex in unhappy or abusive marriages and its connection to the exercise of physical and psychological violence against women, as attested in documentary papyri,[1] originating from the city of Oxyrhynchus, the capital of the Oxyrhynchite nome in Upper Egypt (Thebaid).[2] Our study focuses, specifically, on two well-preserved late antique narratives, namely P.Oxy. VI 903 (=

---

1 All abbreviations of papyrological editions follow the online-version of the *Checklist*: J.F. Oates, R.S. Bagnall, S.J. Clackson, A.A. O'Brien, J.D. Sosin, T.G. Wilfong, K.A. Worp, *Checklist of Greek, Latin, Demotic and Coptic Papyri, Ostraca and Tablets*, in: https://library.duke.edu/rubenstein/scriptorium/papyrus/texts/clist_papyri.html. All dates mentioned in the article are AD unless otherwise stated.

2 On the use of narrative texts presented on papyrus as sources of information concerning violence in late antique and Byzantine Egypt from the time of Augustus to the time of Justinian, see

https://doi.org/10.1515/9783110695793-020

C.Pap.Jud. III 457d; 4th cent.) and P.Oxy. L 3581 (probably 5th cent.). Both texts were written by victimised women in an effort to redress the injustices committed against them by their abusive husbands and to protect themselves from the latter. The female writers of the narratives in question appear to be trying to recuperate from one or more acts of violence. They present themselves as suffocating, being trapped in unbearable situations, or at least this is what they try to convince the recipients of their texts; and they claim compensation for the damage they have suffered and the restoration of their dignity.

In the selected texts, domestic violence is to some extent sexualised, since sex is used as a means of humiliation of the female writers. Sexualised violence as a sub-category of domestic violence is clearly gendered, in the sense that husbands are undeniably the victimisers and wives the helpless victims, who bear no responsibility as far as their maltreatment is concerned.[3] Another interesting aspect of these narratives is the fact that manhood is not only the protagonist in women's narrations, but also their recipient; in other words, women write about their male tormentors, and address their petitions to male representatives of the law, whom they see as their potential saviours.

As already pointed out in research, eroticism, either in the sense of senti-ments or in the sense of explicit references to sexual life, is underrepresented in

---

Bryen 2008 and 2013; in both works, Bryen cites and discusses plenty of papyrological attesta-tions. Since the two texts under study here date from Late Antiquity, we would like to add to Bryen's long collection of papyrological instances the later petition P.Oxy. LXXXI 5289 also orig-inating from Oxyrhynchus, dated to the seventh century, and written by a woman who fell victim to violence; see especially ll. 10–12: δ ᾽Ενὼχ ὁ μακάριος τ[± 14] ̣ εν | τὰ ἐμὰ πράγματα κ[± 14] | ἐδάρην παρὰ τῆς γυναικὸς αὐτοῦ ("... which the blessed Enoch ... -ed my affairs ... I was thrashed by his wife"; translated by the editor, A. Syrkou; see edition, p. 159). A thorough analysis of the status of women in Late Antiquity and the early Byzantine period, and in particular during the period extending from the fourth to the seventh century on the basis of papyri, as well as of legal, literary, and other kinds of ancient written sources is offered by Beaucamp, 1992, who, among others, cites and discusses plenty of narratives, e.g. petitions, written by women. On the status of women in the legislation system of the Roman Empire, and specifically from 31 BC to 476, on the basis of both legal texts and papyri, see Evans-Grubbs 2002.

3 On gendered domestic violence in the papyri, see Bryen 2013, with nn. 64–66. On domestic violence exercised by men in Late Antiquity, see also Dossey 2008. On the domestic disputes and ruptures in Greco-Roman Egypt as attested in the documentary papyri, see Arnaoutoglou 1995. For a discussion on the concept of female weakness and a list of petitions or similar text types on papyri containing clear references to it, see Beaucamp 1992, 45–49. On the connection of in-tra-marital violence with the concept of "manliness" and the interwoven concept of female weakness, see Dorsey 2008. On women's full submission to men, "weakness" and "modesty" as attested in legal sources and the papyri from 31 BC to 476, see Evans-Grubbs 2002, 48–55.

papyrus letters and documents; this is noteworthy since non-literary papyrological material refers to almost every aspect of everyday life.[4] Crimes related to sex
are no exception.[5] The reasons for which sex is almost absent from the documentary papyri and letters, despite the large amount of published material, is far from
self-evident; it is perhaps related to a generalised mentality regarding the degree
to which this aspect of personal life could be discussed openly.[6]

Both P.Oxy. VI 903 and P.Oxy. L 3581 have been included in the discussion
about violence in Egypt of Late Antiquity.[7] In what follows, we will feed this discussion by focusing on the sexual aspects of violence to which they attest. In doing so, we will initially locate the references to, or rather the implications of, sexualised violence and its psychological impact on the victims that occur in these
emotionally charged documents. The relevant passages will be examined in the
framework of the content and context of the texts. In particular, we will discuss
whether and how sexualised abuse is connected with other forms of either physical and/or verbal violence in the selected examples, trying, at the same time, to
sketch a profile of the male abuser.

Being, among other things, institutional means of defence for those who suffered violence, narrative texts such as petitions, complaints or accusations often
constitute a valuable source of information concerning several aspects of feroc-
ity. This is also the case in private correspondence. Admittedly though, in reality,
these texts present only the petitioners' point of view. Consequently, the line between reality and narrated events should be drawn carefully, given that exaggeration, or even lying, cannot be excluded.[8] Even so, these women's stories are

---

4 For a discussion on the rarity of the relevant papyrological evidence and papyrological attestations, cf. indicatively Whitehorne 1979; Beaucamp 1992, 73–74; Montserrat 1996; Koroli 2018,
119 with n. 19; also Hatzilambrou's contribution to the present volume. Magical and literary papyri offer much more attestations on sexual activities.
5 Cf. Whitehorne 1979, esp. 244–246, where a handful of relevant examples are given, as well as
the remarks of Beaucamp 1992, 74 with n. 20, who also offers a collection of papyrological attestations. More material can be found in literary papyri, such as P.Philammon 2, 4 and 7 (sec. half
of 4th cent.).
6 Cf. Whitehorne 1979.
7 See, e.g., Bryen 2013, 179–182 (with nn. 40–44), who examines both documents together as
characteristic instances of domestic violence in the documentary papyri; see also Thoma 2021;
for more bibliography on the examined papyri, cf. nn. 9 and 20 of the present study.
8 For a discussion on the definition of the concepts of "violence" and "abuse" in Late Antiquity,
as well as the terminology and vocabulary denoting violent acts which are used in the papyri,
see Harries 2006, 85–102; Zimmermann 2006, 343–357; Bryen 2013, 51–85. On the transformation
of violent acts into narratives mainly falling into the legal text type of petitions, and the effort of

worth reading and should be taken into consideration, since they are unique, authentic testimonies from antiquity concerning domestic violence.

2 The selected narratives

2.1 P.Oxy. VI 903 (= C.Pap.Jud. III 457d)[9]

1   Περὶ πάντων ὧν εἶπεν κατ' ἐμοῦ ὕβρεων.
2   ἐνέκλεισεν τοὺς ἑ[α]υτοῦ δούλους καὶ τοὺς
3   ἐμοῦ ἅμα τῶν τροφίμ[ω]ν μου καὶ τὸν προνοητὴν καὶ τὸν
4   υἱὸν αὐτοῦ ἐπὶ ὅλας ἑ[πτ]ὰ ἡμέρας εἰς τὰ κατάγαια αὐτοῦ,
5   τοὺς μὲν δούλους αὐτ[οῦ κ]αὶ τὴν ἐμὴν δούλην Ζωὴν ὑβρίσας
6   ἀποκτίνας αὐτοὺς τῶν π[λ]ηγῶν, καὶ πῦρ προσήνεγκεν ταῖς τρο-
7   φίμαις μου γυμνώσας αὐ[τὰ]ς παντελῶς ἃ οὐ ποιοῦσι οἱ νόμοι, καὶ
8   λέγων τοῖς αὐτοῖς τροφίμοις ὅτι δότε πάντα τὰ αὐτῆς, καὶ εἶπαν
9   ὅτι οὐδὲν ἔχει παρ' ἡμῶν, τοῖς δὲ δούλοις λέγων μαστιγ{γ}ο<υ>μένοι<ς> ὅτι
10 τί ἦρκεν ἐκ τῆς οἰκίας μου; βασανιζόμενοι οὖν εἶπαν ὅτι οὐδὲν
11 τῶν σῶν ἦρκεν ἀλλὰ σῶά ἐστιν πάντα τὰ σά.
12 ἀπήντησεν δὲ αὐτῷ Ζω[ίλ]ος ὅτι καὶ τὸν τρόφιμον αὐτοῦ ἐνέ-
13 κλεισεν, καὶ εἶπεν αὐτῷ ὅτ[ι] διὰ τὸν τρόφιμόν σου ἦλθας ἢ διὰ τὴν
14 τοίαν ἦλθας λαλῆσαι ἐπάνω αὐτῆς;
15 καὶ ὤμοσεν ἐπὶ παρουσίᾳ τῶν ἐπισκόπων καὶ τῶν ἀδελφῶν αὐτοῦ
16 ὅτι ἀπεντεῦθεν οὐ μὴ κρύψω αὐτὴ<ν> πάσας μου τὰς κλεῖς καὶ ἐπέχω ʼκαὶ τοῖς δούλοιςʼ
17 ʼαὐτοῦ ἐπίστευεν κἀμοὶ οὐκ ἐπίστευενʼ οὔτε ὑβρίζω αὐτὴν ἀπεντεῦθεν. καὶ γαμικὸν γέγονεν, καὶ μετὰ
18 τὰς συνθήκας ταύτας καὶ τοὺς ὅρκους ἔκρυψεν πάλιν ἐμὲ τὰς κλεῖς
19 εἰς ἐμέ. καὶ ἀπελθοῦσα [εἰ]ς τὸ κυριακὸν ἐν Σαμβάθῳ, καὶ ἐποίησεν
20 τὰς ἔξω θύρας αὐτοῦ ἐνκλισθῆναι ἐπάνω μου λέγων ὅτι διὰ τί ἀπῆλ-
21 θας εἰς τὸ κυριακόν; καὶ πολλὰ ἀσελγήματα λέγων εἰς πρόσωπόν
22 μου καὶ διὰ τῆς ῥινὸς αὐτο[ῦ], καὶ περὶ σίτου (ἀρτάβας) ρ τοῦ δημοσίου τοῦ
23 ὀνόματός μου μηδὲν δεδωκὼς μηδὲ ἀρτάβ(ην) μίαν. ἐνέκλεισεν δὲ
24 τοὺς τόμους κρατήσας αὐτ[ο]ὺς ὅτι δότε τὴν τιμὴν τῶν (ἀρταβῶν) ρ, μηδὲν
25 δεδω[κὼς] ὡς προεῖπον. καὶ εἶπεν τοῖς δούλοις αὐτοῦ ὅτι δότε συμμά-

---

the victims to compose convincing rhetorical texts, which contain legal terminology and are concurrently intended to move the authorities, see Bryen 2008, esp. 181–182; 185; Bryen 2013, 89–125 and *passim*. As pointed out by Bryen *op. cit.* (2013), one should be skeptical as far as the objectivity of these narrations is concerned.
9 Edition of B.P. Grenfell and A.S. Hunt in P.Oxy. VI (London 1908). On l. 19, see BL III 133. On this papyrus, see Winter 1933, 126–127; Beaucamp 1992, esp. 55 (with nn. 20–22); 92–93; 98; Montserrat 1996, 99–100; Rowlandson 1998, 207–208 (no. 153); Bryen 2013, 105 (with n. 46); 107 (with n. 56); 273–274; see also n. 7 of the present study.

26 χους ἵνα καὶ αὐτὴν ἐνκλείσωσι. καὶ ἐκρατήθη Χωοῦς ὁ βοηθὸς αὐτοῦ
27 εἰς τὸ δημόσιον καὶ παρέσχεν αὐτῷ Εὐθάλαμος ἐνέχυρον καὶ οὐκ ἠρκέσθη
28 ἦρκα κἀγὼ ἄλλο μικρὸν καὶ παρέσχον τῷ αὐτῷ Χωοῦτι. ἀπαντήσας δὲ
29 αὐτῷ εἰς Ἀντινόου ἔχουσα τὸ πρὸς βαλανῖόν μου μεθ᾽ ὧν ἔχω κοσμαρι-
30 δίων, καὶ εἶπέν μοι ὅτι εἴ τι ἔχεις μετ᾽ ἐσοῦ αἴρω αὐτὰ δι᾽ ὃ δέδωκες τῷ
31 βοηθῷ μου Χωοῦτι ἐνέχυρον διὰ τὰ δημόσια αὐτοῦ. μαρτυρῆσαι δὲ
32 περὶ τούτων πάντων ἡ μήτηρ αὐτοῦ. καὶ περὶ Ἀνίλλας τῆς δούλης
33 αὐτοῦ ἔμεινεν θλίβων τὴν ψυχήν μου καὶ ἐν τῇ Ἀντινόου καὶ ἐνταῦθα
34 ὅτι ἔκβαλε τὴν δούλην ταύτην ἐπειδὴ αὐτὴ οἶδεν ὅσα κέκτηται, ἴσως
35 θέλων μοι καταπλέξαι καὶ ταύτῃ τῇ προφάσει ἆραι εἴ τι ἔχω· κἀγὼ οὐκ
36 ἠνεσχόμην ἐκβαλεῖν αὐτήν. καὶ ἔμεινεν λέγων ὅτι μετὰ μῆναν
37 λαμβάνω πολιτικὴν ἐμαυτῷ. ταῦτα δὲ οἶδεν ὁ θ(εός).

3 l. ταῖς 1. τροφίμαις 6 l. ἀποκτείνας 8 l. ταῖς 1. αὐταῖς 1. τροφίμαις 16 l. κλεῖδας 18 l. κλεῖδας 19 l. σαββάτῳ 20 l. ἐγκλεισθῆναι 26 l. ἐγκλείσωσι 28 l. ἀπήντησα 29 l. βαλανεῖον 31 l. μαρτυρήσει 35 l. με 36 l. μῆνα

"Concerning all of the *hybreis* that he said against me: He locked up in his basement his own slaves and my slaves, along with my foster-children and the overseer and his son — for nine whole days. He did violence to his slaves and to my slave, Zoe, (nearly) killing them with beatings. He set fire to my foster children, stripping them completely, which the laws forbid. He said to these same foster children, 'Give me all her things.' But they said, 'She has nothing of ours.' While the slaves were being whipped, he said, 'What has she taken from my house?' They said, while being tortured, 'She took nothing of yours. Your things are safe.' Zoilos went to him, since he had locked up his foster child as well, and he said to him, 'Have you come on account of your foster child, or have you come to talk about this woman?' He swore in the presence of bishops and his brothers that 'From now on, I will not hide all of my keys from her' — he trusted his own slaves, but he didn't trust me — 'and I will even stay away from her, nor will I do violence to her again.' We made a marriage agreement, and after these agreements and the oaths, once again he hid the keys from me. When I went to church on the Sabbath he locked the outside doors, and yelled down at me, 'Why have you gone to the church?' He said many foul things to my face, even speaking through his nose. As for the 100 artabas of grain due in taxes under my name, he has given not the first artaba. He locked up his account books and kept them from me, saying 'Pay the bill of the 100 artabas,' since as I said, he had not paid it. He said to his slaves, 'bring the *symmachoi*, and have them lock her up too.' His assistance, Choous, was locked up in the public prison; Euthalamos paid bail for him, but it was not enough. I had a little money, and gave it to this man, Choous. I met him (my husband) while going to Antinoopolis. I had my bathing bag, in which I keep my jewelry, and he said to me, 'If you have anything with you, I am going to take it on account of the bail you gave for Choous, my assistant, because of his tax problems.' His mother will attest to all of these things. And concerning Anilla, his slave, he continually pressed my soul, both in Antinoopolis and here, (saying), 'Get rid of this slave,' since she knows how much he has. Perhaps he wanted to entangle me, and on this pretense to obtain what I have. But I refused to throw her out. Continually he said to me, 'In a month I'm going to acquire a courtesan.' God only knows".[10]

This long narration, which is preserved in its entirety, offers an instance of repeated domestic violence. The writer accuses her husband of displaying aggressive and abusive behaviour, not only towards herself, but also towards a group of people connected to her household.

The text could be divided into three thematic units. The first (ll. 2–17) refers to the period where the marriage in question was still unwritten (ἄγραφος). In these lines, the writer narrates that her husband incarcerated his own slaves, her slaves and foster daughters, the foster son of a third person, as well as a *pronoētēs* and his son in his basement for nine whole days. During their imprisonment, the aforementioned people were severely tormented due to the rampant brutality and avarice of this man, who wanted to arrogate his wife's property and to be sure that she had not appropriated his. According to his wife's account, he went so far as to beat almost to death some of his male slaves and a female slave belonging to his wife. Furthermore, he scared and humiliated his wife's foster daughters by completely stripping and torturing them with fire. Finally, he whipped the slaves.[11] Throughout this outburst of violence, this man showed that he considered his wife unworthy of trust (cf. her complaint in ll. 16–17), which is why he kept all of the keys away from her. The first part of the text ends with this man's promise, in the presence of bishops and his brothers, that he will neither again hide his keys from his wife nor ever insult her.

The second part (ll. 18–37) begins with the conclusion of a marriage contract. In these lines, a new accusation is added to the already long list of the writer's husband's faults: unreliability and insincerity. The abusive husband shamelessly violates his recently made promises and oaths, as well as his recent marriage contract clauses, since he continues to display mistrust towards his wife. He still targets her financial exploitation and deceit, and continues to use extortion and intimidation as a means of fulfiling his vicious aims. Although he does not exercise extreme physical violence, he clearly and variously expresses his intent to once again humiliate his wife. He takes away the keys from her and even locks her out of their common domicile when she goes to the church, while at the same time using abusive language against her. He refuses to fulfil his financial obligations

---

10 Translated by Bryen 2013, 273–274 (no. 123); English translations are also offered by the editors, B.P. Grenfell and A.S. Hunt; see edition, p. 240; Winter 1933, 126–127; Rowlandson 1998, 273 (no. 153).

11 On papyrological attestations of violence against slaves including the two aforementioned instances, cf. Bryen 2013, 306 n. 25.

and loads them on his wife, although he keeps the account books away from her. Moreover, he purloins his wife's jewelry and orders his slaves to pave the way for her imprisonment. This long list of assaults closes with a threat to his wife because of her refusal to dismiss a slave who knows more than she should about his illegal activities; he warns her that he would be bringing a concubine into their home.

What is noteworthy here is that the petitioner does not speak of one or more isolated assaults or hostilities, but of a systematic degradation of the quality of her life due to her husband's variously humiliating behaviour. The latter causes both corporal and psychological traumas to his wife (cf. θλίβων τὴν ψυχήν μου, l. 33; "continually pressing my soul"), by mistrusting her, by showing no respect for her religious convictions, by trying to turn his closest people against her, by involving her in his illegal activities and, consequently, by embarrassing her and tarnishing her image in the community. The occurrence of sexualised violence does not then come as a surprise, given the broad repertoire of violent behaviour of this man, who is presented not just as an abusive husband, but rather as a sociopath, who does not hesitate to insult the dignity of others and deprive them of their freedom. The writer does her best to convince us that she is not exaggerating, speaking of indisputable witnesses, such as the bishops (l. 15), her husband's brothers (l. 15) and mother (ll. 31–32), and God (l. 37).

The text contains two instances of sexualised violence. In ll. 6–7 of the first part, the writer refers to the stripping of her foster daughters by her husband. Documentary papyri provide us with many instances of this practice. Forced stripping is in any case a means of weakening and humiliating a human being. In some papyri, stripping is merely an act of (public) humiliation that comes from the violation of social rules related to modesty, and is connected to other hostilities such as punching or stealing. In this case, the tearing of clothes is only indirectly related to sexuality, and the victims may belong to both sexes;[12] cf., e.g., the petition P.Cair.Isid. 63 (= SB VI 9185).24–26 (Karanis; after 20 Nov. 297; see BL X 32 and HGV), where a pregnant woman is attacked by a group of women, who, among other indignities, tore her clothes: πλ[ηγα]ῖς ἠκίσαντες (l. αἰκίσαντες) τῶν τριχõν (l. τριχῶν) περι . . . . |τες καὶ τὴν [ἐσ]θῆτα{ν} διαρ<ρ>ήξαντες χαμεριφῆ (l. χαμαιριφῆ) με ἀ|φῖκαν (l. ἀφῆκαν) ("… abused me with blows, pulled out (?) my hair, tore my clothes, and threw me on the floor");[13] the petition P.Kellis I 23.19 (Kellis;

---

12 Cf. the remarks of Bryen 2013, 113.
13 Translated by Bryen 2013, 254 (no. 89); an English translation is also offered by the editors, A.E.R. Boak and H.C. Youtie; see edition, pp. 258–259. For a discussion of the text, see Bryen *op.*

353), where a man is robbed and stripped in public by another man, who also chased him away: ἀλλὰ αὐτὸν τὸν ἄθλιόν μου ἀδελφὸν ἐξέδυσεν τῆς ἐσθῆτος δημοσί[α κ]αὶ ἐφυγάτευσεν (l. -δευ-) ("But he ripped off my poor brother's clothing in public and caused him to flee");[14] cf. also the complaint about violence and robbery P.Lips. I 37.18–22 (Hermopolis; 389; cf. BL I 207), where a shepherd is severely beaten, and his clothes are torn and stolen by a group of villains: οἱ δὲ γυμνώ[σαντες] ε[ὐθ]ὺς μετὰ ῥοπάλων πρ[. . . .]ν . . . | τὴν ἐπικ<ε>ιμένην α[ὐτοῦ ἐ]σθῆτα διαρ<ρ>[ή]ξαντες ἀφ[εί]λαντ[ο], | ἔπειτα κατέκοψα[ν] π̣[ληγ]αῖς αὐτὸν κατά τ[ε] τῶν σκελῶν καὶ | κατὰ τῶν ἄλλων μελῶ[ν] τοῦ σώματος, ἡμιθανῆ{γ} αὐτὸν κατα|στήσαντες ("... but once they stripped him, straightaway with clubs they... they tore apart the clothes he was wearing and stole them, then they pounded him on the legs and on the other parts of his body, leaving him halfdead").[15]

On the other hand, there are attestations where stripping can easily be considered a sexualised violent act, or at least, as Bryen (2013, 113) puts it, a potentially sexualised form of violence; this seems to be the case in the following petitions: P.Oxy. XXXVI 2758.6–13 (Oxyrhynchus; c. 110–112): Ἀπολλῶς Ἡρακλείδου (m. 2) ἀπὸ | τῆς αὐτῆς πόλ(εως) (m. 1) γ{ε}ινόμενος ἐπὶ | τῷ αὐτῷ ἀμφόδῳ ἐπῆλ|θεν τῇ γυναικί μου Τααμόι|τι οὔσῃ πρὸ τῆς θύρας μεθύ|ων καὶ ἐξελυδόρησεν (l. -λοι-) καὶ | ἀνέσ{ο}υρεν αὐτή<ν>, παρόντων | πλείστων ἀξιοχρέων ἀ<ν>δρῶ[ν] ("Apollos, son of Herakleides, [m. 2] from the same city [m. 1] and who lives on the same block attacked my wife Taamois while she was standing in front of our house"),[16] and

---

cit., 102–104 (with n. 33); 179. Bryen considers stripping either as a part of the fight or "as a means of additional degradation and shaming".

14 Translated by Bryen 2013, 265–266 (no. 110); an English translation is also offered by the editor, K.A. Worp; see edition, pp. 70–71. The text is discussed by Bryen 2013, 97–100 (with n. 26); on the topic of stripping, see esp. p. 98; also, *op. cit.*, 266–267. Interestingly, the editor of the petition, K.A. Worp, interprets this stripping as molestation; see p. 71 in the edition.

15 Translated by Bryen 2013, 270 (no. 116). For a discussion of this text, see Bryen 2008, 195–196 with n. 33; idem 2013, 104 (with n. 36); 123–124 (with nn. 93; 94, where parallels are cited). We agree with Bryen's consideration of the stripping as sexualised, only if the word is conceived in its more general meaning. For more papyrological attestations of stripping with no sexual meaning (or with sexual meaning but in a broader sense), see Whitehorne 1979, 244 (n. 2); Bryen 2013, 311 (n. 94); 121–122 (with n. 86). As it is obvious from the papyrological attestations, this kind of stripping is not a gender-based kind of violence, in the sense that the victims can also be men, whereas the victimisers can be women.

16 Translated by Bryen 2013, 227 (no. 35); see also the English translation offered by the editor, A.H. Soliman el-Mosallamy; see edition, p. 38. The text is discussed by Bryen 2013, 113 (with n. 70) as an instance of sexualised stripping; see also, *op. cit.*, 227. However, Whiterhorne 1977, 244 with n. 2 considers this assault as deriving from "drunken malice rather than by any sexual desire". We believe that in this case there is a blurred borderline between sexual desire and the intention of degradation.

P.Flor. I 59.1–7 with BL I 144 (unknown provenance; 225, 241 or 279; see HGV): [- - -] μητρός μου [- - -] | [πληγ]αῖς ἠ[κί]σατο σὺν αὐτοῖς α . . [- - -] | [. . . .]υ καὶ δ[. . . .] . ι κατὰ τῶν πλευ[ρῶν - - -] | ὥστε πληγ[ῆ]ναι μέν με ἔσεσθ[αι - - - κινδυνεύον]|τός μου κα[ὶ] παρ' αὐτοῦ διαφωνῆ[σαι - - -]|δυσας με ἣν εἶχον ἐνδεδυμέν[ην - - -] |σας με ἐβάστασεν ("My mother's... he abused (me) with blows, along with them... and... on my sides... so that, having been beaten, I feel that I am... also in danger of being murdered at his hands... stripping (the garment) I had on... he took (it from me) ...").[17] In cases such as these, sexual harassment or even rape[18] should not be excluded, when a man displays power over a woman. In this context, it should be noted that according to the Christian worldview, even seeing a woman's body naked constitutes a sexualised kind of violence.[19]

In P.Oxy. VI 903, stripping should be seen as a kind of sexual violence, given the circumstances under which it took place. The abuser had imprisoned his victims, so his purpose was obviously not to steal from or humiliate them in public, but rather to shock them, to interrogate them and probably to sexually abuse them; SB VI 9458.16–20 (Tebtynis; 2nd cent.) offers an earlier papyrological parallel, where the stripping of women is combined with extortion: καὶ ὕβριν τὴν ἀνωτάτην ἐποίησεν | ἐπὶ τοσοῦτον ὥστε καὶ παιδ[ί]σκας μου ἐν | μέσῃ πλατείᾳ ἀποδῦσαι τὰς περὶ αὐτὰς | αἰσθῆτας (l. ἐ-). οὐκ ἀρκεσθεὶς ἐπὶ τούτοις ἀλ|λὰ καὶ ἠργολάβησεν αὐτάς ("And committed the most extreme violence, which reached such a point that he even brought my slave girls into the center of the public square and stripped their clothes. Not satisfied with this, he extorted them, too").[20] The

---

17 Translated by Bryen 2013, 249.

18 On the rarity of references to rape in the papyri, see Bryen 2013, 113 (with nn. 67; 68). On explicit references to this crime in Byzantine petitions, see Beaucamp 1992, 71; for legislation on rape, and the mentality regarding this crime in late antique Roman society, see Harries 2007, 88–89.

19 Cf. Testamenta XII Patriarcharum, Testamentum 1, 3: εἰ μὴ γὰρ εἶδον ἐγὼ Βάλλαν λουομένην ἐν σκεπεινῷ τόπῳ, οὐκ ἐνέπιπτον εἰς τὴν ἀνομίαν τὴν μεγάλην. συλλαβοῦσα γὰρ ἡ διάνοιά μου τὴν γυναικείαν γύμνωσιν, οὐκ εἴασέ με ὑπνῶσαι ἕως οὗ ἔπραξα τὸ βδέλυγμα. ἀπόντος γὰρ Ἰακὼβ τοῦ πατρὸς ἡμῶν πρὸς Ἰσαὰκ τὸν πατέρα αὐτοῦ, ὄντων ἡμῶν ἐν Γάδερ, πλησίον Ἐφραθὰ οἴκου Βηθλέεμ, Βάλλα ἦν μεθύουσα καὶ κοιμωμένη ἀκάλυφος κατέκειτο ἐν τῷ κοιτῶνι· κἀγὼ εἰσελθὼν καὶ ἰδὼν τὴν γύμνωσιν αὐτῆς ἔπραξα τὴν ἀσέβειαν, καὶ καταλιπὼν αὐτὴν κοιμωμένην ἐξῆλθον ("If I had not seen Valla wash herself in a secluded place, I would not have fallen into grave sin. Because my mind, having captured the woman's nakedness, did not let me sleep until I committed the abominable act. For when Jacob our father went to visit Isaac his father, while we were in Gader, near the house of Ephratha in Bethleem, Valla got drunk and was lying naked in the bed-chamber. And as soon as I came in and saw her nakedness, I committed the impious act and then went out, leaving her asleep"); translated by the authors of the present contribution.

20 Translated by Bryen 2013, 246; an English translation is also offered by the editor, C.B. Welles, "Complaint from a Priest of Tebtunis Concerning Grain Transportation Charges, of the

phrase ἃ οὐ ποιοῦσι οἱ νόμοι (l. 7 of our text) strengthens the possibility that the abuser did not restrict himself to stripping, but actually proceeded with a more vicious action either in order to elicit information or for his own sadistic pleasure. The abuser's wife is also the target of this sexualised assault, given the close relationship of the tormented women with her.

At the end of the petition (ll. 32–37), the abusive husband hurts and humiliates his already tormented wife by exercising verbal and psychological violence, and specifically, by boldly declaring that he is going to bring home a πολιτική, i.e. a concubine or mistress.[21] This abuse is sexualised in the sense that it concerns the couple's sexual relationship and the writer's sexual dignity, as well as her legal and social status as spouse. For all these reasons, the victim justifiably feels humiliated and deeply hurt. This threat of imminent cheating does not come as a surprise, but rather as a climax of the formerly abuses, both physical and verbal.[22]

2.2 P.Oxy. L 3581[23]

1   [Φλαουίῳ] Μαρκέλλῳ τριβο[ύνῳ ἐπιτεταγμέν]ῳ τῇ εἰρήνῃ vac.
2   [παρὰ Αὐρηλ]ίας Ἀττιένης ἀπὸ [τῆς Ὀξυρυγχειτῶ]ν πόλεως. Παῦλός τις ὁρμώμενος
3   [ἀπὸ τῆς] αὐτῆς πόλεως ῥιψοκινδύ[νως φερόμενο]ς κα[τὰ β]ίαν καὶ κατ᾽ ἀνάγκην ἀφήρπα-
4   [σέν με καὶ] συνῆλθέν μοι πρὸς γάμ[ον . . . .] . δο . . . . . . μ[.] . ἐξ αὐτοῦ θηλυκὸν παιδίον
5   [. . . . . . .] ε[ἰ]σαγαγοῦσα εἰς τὸν ἡμ[έτε]ρ[ον οἶκο]ν μη . [.]νπον . [. .] . [. .] . τὴν ἀνελεύθερον
6   αὐτοῦ προαίρεσιν καὶ πάντα μου τὰ πράγματα κ[.] . ιον . κ [. . .] . [. . .] . σεν καταλείπων με
7   μετὰ καὶ τῆς νηπίας μου θυγατρὸς ἐν καιρ . . [.] . μω συνῆλθεν [ἑ]ταίρᾳ γυναικεὶ καὶ εἴασέν με
8   χηρεύουσα<ν>. καὶ μετὰ χρόνον τινὰ πάλιν ἐξηπά[τησ]εν διὰ πρεσβυτέρων ἄχρις οὗ πάλιν συν-
9   εισενέγκω αὐτὸν εἰς τὸν ἡμέτερον οἶκον γραψάμενός μοι συνπα[ρ]αμεῖναι τὴν συμβίωσιν
10   εἰ δὲ βουληθείη τὰ αὐτὰ ἀνελεύθερα πράγματα διαπράξασθαι ἐκτίσιν αὐτὸν χρυσίου οὐγκίας δύο

Late Second Century"; *Études de Papyrologie* 8, 104–105. Sexualised violence is possibly also implied in P.Ross.Georg. II 20.21–23 (Arsinoite nome?; c. 146); cf. Bryen 2013, 306 n. 25.

21 We adopt the editors' interpretation of the noun πολιτική as prostitute or concubine, and not as a proper name; see edition, n. to l. 37 (p. 241). For a discussion on this question, see also Winter 1933, 147 (with nn. 2; 3); Beaucamp 1992, 55 (with nn. 20–22); Burnet 2003, 84–85 (with nn. 1–5).
22 On verbal abuse in such narratives, often combined with the physical one, as it is the case here, see Bryen 2013, 105–108 (with nn. 45–63).
23 Edition: R.A. Coles in P.Oxy. L (London 1983). On l. 1, see P.Gen. IV 183, n. to l. 1 and BL XI 170. On the dating to the fifth century by J.-L. Fournet and J. Gascou, see BL XIII 163. On this papyrus, see Beaucamp 1992, 52 (with n. 6); 73 (with nn. 13–15); 93–94 (with nn. 57–59); 95; 97 (with n. 75); 98; 111 (with n. 121); 150 (with n. 70); Rowlandson 1998, 208–209 (no. 154); Evans-Grubbs 2002, esp. 216 and 315 (n. 83); Bryen 2008, 194; 112 (with n. 66); 113 (with n. 69); 275; cf. also n. 7 of the present study.

11 καὶ ὁ τούτου πατὴρ ἐνγράφως ἀνεδέξατο αὐτόν. καὶ εἰσαγαγοῦσα αὐτὸν [εἰς] τ[ὸ]ν ἡμέτερον οἶκον χίρο-

12 να τῶν πρώτων αὐτοῦ σφαλμάτων ἐπεχείρησεν διαπράξασθαι καταφρονήσας τῆς ὀρφανίας

13 μου οὐ μόνον ὅτι ἐρήμωσιν εἰργάσατο κατὰ τοῦ οἴκου μου ἀλλὰ καὶ στρατιωτῶν ἐπιξενευσάν-

14 των τῷ οἴκῳ μου ἀπεσύλησεν αὐτοὺς καὶ ἀνεχώρησεν καὶ ὕβρις καὶ ζημίας ὑπέστην ἄχρις

15 οὗ συνχωρήσουσίν μοι τὸ ζῆν. εὐλαβηθεῖσα μὴ κίνδυνον πάλειν ὑπομίνω ὑπὲρ αὐτοῦ ῥεπού-

16 διον διὰ ταβουλαρίου προσέπεμψα αὐτῷ διὰ τοῦ τῆς πόλεως ταβουλαρίου κατὰ τὸν βασιλικὸν

17 νόμον. πάλειν ῥιψοκινδύνως φερόμενος ἔχων τὴν γυναῖκαν αὐτοῦ ἐπὶ τῆς οἰκείας αὐτοῦ

18 συνπαραλαβὼν μεθ’ ἑαυτοῦ πλῆθος ἀνδρῶν ἀτάκτων ἀφήρπασέν με καὶ κατέκλεισεν

19 ἐπὶ τῆς οἰκείας αὐτοῦ ἐπὶ <οὐκ(?)> ὀλίγας ἡμέρας καὶ ὅτε ἐνκύμων ἐγενόμην πάλειν καταλείπων με

20 συνῆλθεν τῇ αὐτῇ λεγομένη αὐτοῦ γυναικεὶ καὶ νῦν ἐπαγγέλλεταί μοι φθόνον τινὰ κεινεῖν

21 κατ’ ἐμοῦ. ὅθεν παρακαλῶ τὴν σὴν τοὐμοῦ στερρότητα κελεῦσαι αὐτὸν παρα[σ]τῆναι

22 καὶ ἀπαιτηθῆναι αὐτὸν κατὰ τὴν ἔνγραφον αὐτοῦ ὁμολογίαν τὰς δύο οὐγκείας τοῦ χρυσοῦ καὶ

23 ὅσα ἐζημιώθην ὑπὲρ αὐτοῦ καὶ ἐπιστραφῆναι αὐτὸν ἐφ’ οἷς τετόλμηκεν κατ’ ἐμοῦ.

24 (m. 2) Αὐρηλία Ἀττίενα ἐπιδέδωκα.

1 P.Gen. IV 183.1 adn. et BL XI 170: [± 10] ς ed. pr. 2 l. Ἀττιαίνης 7 l. ἑτέρᾳ l. γυναικί 8 l. πάλιν l. πάλιν 10 l. ἐκτίσειν 11–12 l. χείρονα 14 l. ὕβρεις 15 l. συγχωρήσωσιν l. πάλιν l. ὑπομείνω 17 l. πάλιν l. γυναῖκα l. οἰκίας 19 l. οἰκίας l. πάλιν 20 l. γυναικί καί κ corr. ex α? l. κινεῖν 21 l. τοῦ ἐμοῦ 22 l. οὐγκίας 23 αὐτόν α corr. ex τ 24 l. Ἀττίαινα

To Flavius Marcellus, tribune overseeing the peace. From Aurelia Attiaina, from the city of the Oxyrhynchites. A certain Paulos, coming from the same city, is a reckless man who by force and compulsion abducted and married me... from him a daughter ... bringing him into our home... his disgusting conduct, and all of my things... leaving me and my infant daughter... he lived with another woman and left me in solitude. After a while he tricked me once again with the help of presbyters, until once again I agreed to bring him back into our home. He made a contract with me in which he stated that the marriage would abide and if he wished to engage in such disgusting practices that he would pay a fine of two ounces of gold. His father provided a written guarantee of this. And so I brought him into our home, where he tried to do things worse than his previous actions. He scorned my orphan state, and not only did he pillage my home, he even robbed the soldiers quartered in the house and fled, whereupon I suffered violence and punishments until they allowed me only to live. Deciding that I wouldn't endanger myself further on his account I sent him a divorce decree through the *tabularius*, according to the imperial decree. Once again he acted recklessly, having his woman in the house, and bringing with him a crowd of disorderly men he snatched me away, locked me up in his house for (not) a few days, and when I became pregnant he left me once again to live with the woman he calls his wife. Now he threatens me, and stirs up envy against me. Therefore I call upon your firmness: order him to appear in court and return the two ounces of gold according to our written agreement, along with compensation for damages for what I suffered, and that he be punished for the things he did to me. (Hand 2) I, Aurelia Attiaina, have submitted this.[24]

This narrative, which falls into the category of petitions,[25] is similar to the previous one in terms of content and expression. Both documents are part of long, sad stories of marriages that collapse due to the extremely abusive behaviour of the husband. Once again, the writer, who is addressing a tribune, narrates in vivid style the sequence of her husband's violent acts, starting with her abduction, which led to a pregnancy. The abduction of a woman who had not given her consent, as seems to be the case here, is clearly related to sexualised violence, namely to non-consensual sex, which directly points to the crime of rape. A marriage concluded on the basis of such a violent act is doomed to be unhappy. The abhorrence and despair caused by such unwanted abductions are vividly presented in another woman's petition, also originating from Oxyrhynchus, namely SB IV 7449 (second half of 5th cent.). According to the female narrator, who is most probably a widow, her nephew, who is a monk, intends to force her younger daughter to marry a relative. When the narrator defends her daughter's opposition to this marriage, her nephew assaults her and tears her clothes making her feel helpless.[26]

---

24 Translated by Bryen, 2013, 275 (no. 125); an English translation is also offered by Rowlandson 1998, 208–209 (no. 154).

25 On Byzantine petitions, see Fournet 2004; Gascou 2004; for a presentation of the relevant bibliography, cf. also Bryen 2008, 181, n. 2. On lists of petitions written by women, see Beaucamp 1992, 239 (n. 102); 394–400; Arnaoutoglou 1995, 14–15; Bagnall 2004; a list of petitions written during the period extending from the fifth to the seventh century is offered by Fournet/Gascou 2004.

26 See esp. ll. 4–15 with BL II.2 136: Ἀλύπιος μονάζων ὁρμώμενος ἀπὸ τῆς ἡμετέρας | κώμης ἀδελ-φιδοῦ[ς] ἡμέτερος τυγχάνων τὴν ἐμὴν | θυγατέρα Μικκὴ<ν> ἠθέλησεν δοῦναι Ἀπαείωνι συγγενεῖ | πά-λιν ἡμετέρῳ. τοῦτο δὲ ποιῆσαι ἐσπούδασαν ἡμέτερα | πράγματα ἔχοντες καὶ μὴ θέλοντες ταῦτά μοι ἀποκαταστῆσαι. | ἐπ<ε>ὶ τοίνυν [οὐ]δὲ αὐτή μου θυγάτηρ ἐκείνῳ <οὐ (?)> βούλεται συνά|πτεσθαι, π[αρὰ] τὸ σχῆμ[α] δὲ διαπραττόμενος ὁ μονάζων | πληγάς μοι ἐπήγαγεν καὶ τὴν ἐσθῆτά μου διέρ<ρ>η-ξεν | καὶ ἀχρ<ε>ίαν ἀπέδ<ε>ιξεν, τούτου [χάρ]ιν παρακαλῶ σου | τὴν ἁγιοσύνην (l. ἁγιωσύνην) κατε-λεῆσαί με καὶ κελεῦσαι αὐτὸν | ἐνεχθῆναι καὶ τύπον με δέχεσθαι τὸν τῇ σῇ ἁγιοσύνῃ (l. ἁγιωσύνῃ) | παριστάμενον, ἁγιώτατε ἐπίσκοπε κύριε ("Alypios a monk, native of our village, who is our nephew, desired to give (in marriage) my little daughter to Apaion, also a relative of ours. And the administrators of our estate, who are unwilling to restore it to me, were eager to do this. Since therefore The[...], my daughter, (does not?) wish to marry him, and acting in defiance of his cloth, the monk beat me and tore my clothing and ruined it, therefore I beg your holiness to have compassion upon me and order him to be brought (before you), and for me to receive whatever decision you shall approve of, my lord, most holy bishop."; translated by Keenan, Manning and Firanko 2014, 527–528 (no. 10.5.4), where a short discussion of the text is also offered; English

Soon after the conclusion of her forced marriage, the petitioner of P.Oxy. L 3581 was abandoned by her husband, who left her alone with their child, in order to live with another woman. After having supposedly regretted his behaviour, he promised that he would change. His commitment that he would pay a fine in case he assaulted his wife again, and a written deed of surety signed by his own father signaled the second phase of this unhealthy marriage. The petitioner accuses him of breaking this promise by behaving even worse than before, and of even robbing the soldiers that lodged at their home leaving her exposed to their rage.

The deed of divorce sent by the petitioner to her husband through a *tabularius* opened the final act of their dramatic marriage. Her brave step did not stop her husband's violent acts; instead, the latter re-abducted her in cooperation with a group of other men, whose names are not mentioned in the document,[27] incarcerated her in his house for some days, again left her pregnant and re-abandoned her, to live possibly as a bigamist with the woman mentioned at the beginning of the document (cf. l. 20: συνῆλθεν τῇ αὐτῇ λεγομένῃ αὐτοῦ γυναικ{ε}ί; "he lived with the woman he called his wife"); cf. l. 7. On top of everything else he threatened that he would incite malice and reproach against her.

This abusive husband's personality and conduct, as presented by the female narrator, bears striking similarities to those of the husband in P.Oxy. VI 903. Both men displayed, in the course of their marital life, their cruelty, lack of ethics and empathy by exercising violence variously and repeatedly. They are both promise-breakers and law violators, they do not hesitate to imprison people both literally and metaphorically. They are unfaithful husbands who unleash threats and aim to humiliate their wives. Acts such as the incarceration of a wife (or, at least, the threat of incarceration, as it is the case in P.Oxy. VI 903), and, in general, her

---

translations are also offered by the editor, H.J. Bell, 'The episcopalis audientia in Byzantine Egypt', *Byzantion* 1 (1924), 142–143; Bryen 2013, 277–278 (no. 130). On this papyrus, see also Beaucamp 1992, 74 (n. 20); 119–120; 122 (with n. 116); 124; 180 (with n. 63); Bryen 2013, 113 (with n. 69); 142 (with n. 55); 277–278. On abduction as a sexual crime, which often leads to the conclusion of a marriage, cf. Baldwin 1963, 261–262; Beaucamp 1992, 71–73; Bryen 2013, 113 with n. 69, where P.Oxy. L 3581 and SB IV 7449 are mentioned as characteristic examples. On the law of Constantine on abduction marriages, enacted in 326, and on the relevant references in the Theodocian code, see Evans-Grubbs 1989; idem 2001, 223–225; idem 2002, 181–184. Baeaucamp (1992, 74) remarks that neither this law nor the Theodosian code seem to be truly respected in Egypt, as is indicated by P.Oxy. VI 903, P.Oxy. L 3581, and SB IV 7449. On the legislation concerning abduction, which was unjust towards women, see Harries 2007, 86.

27 This is often the case when the victim is assaulted by more than one individuals; cf. Bryen 2013, 172–174 (with nn. 17–25).

constant humiliation degrade her status to that of a female slave.[28] The acts of these abusive husbands have long term consequences, not only due to the psychological traumas they cause, but also because they affect the reputation of their wives in the community. These tormented wives live in a state of constant disappointment and bitterness about the past and of fear and anguish for the future. The punishment of the offender and the divorce seem to be the only solution to their problem.

In P.Oxy. L 3581, sexualised abuse is at the core of the story; its occurrence is more intense and much clearer in comparison to P.Oxy. VI 903, since the two abductions and pregnancies of the petitioner point directly to the crime of rape.[29] Moreover, in P.Oxy. L 3581 the husband's infidelity is shown in practice, since the narrator is actually abandoned for another woman. Finally, similar to P.Oxy. VI 903, the writer of P.Oxy. L 3581 tries to move the recipient of the text; the first uses emotionally charged phrases (cf. l. 33: θλίβων τὴν ψυχήν μου; "continually pressing my soul"; l. 37: ταῦτα δὲ οἶδεν ὁ θ(εός); "God only knows"), whereas the latter stresses her solitude and her impotence (cf. ll. 7–8: εἴασέν με | χηρεύουσα<ν>; "left me in solitude"; ll. 12–13: καταφρονήσας τῆς ὀρφανίας | μου; "since he scorned my orphan state").[30]

3 Conclusions

In sum, sexualised violence in the two narratives that are the object of our analysis has the following forms: first, abduction and unwanted marriage, and consequently non-consensual sex; second, stripping, if it is connected to rape; and third, cheating or bigamy. The expressions that the two female writers use when they refer to sexualised abuse are probably aligned with the general tendency mentioned in the introduction, i.e. the lack of explicitness or the lack of references to sexual life altogether. The writers of the selected examples, as well as the above-cited parallels are restricted to implications when it comes to sex. Given the religious tone in P.Oxy. VI 903, and parallels such as SB IV 7449, the possibility that this allusive manner of expression can be attributed to a conservatism, resulting from the predominance of Christian virtues, should not be completely ruled out.

---

28 On the emphatic distinction between free and slave, see Bryen 2008, 188 with n. 17; 192 with n. 29; Bryen 2013, 117–118.

29 Cf. n. 26.

30 Cf. n. 3.

Due to the scarcity of documentation related to sex, we cannot ascertain if the examined texts are unequivocally informative about sexual violence in marital relationships. Similarly, conclusions about the representativeness of these documents that originate from Egypt regarding domestic sexualised violence in the rest of the Greco-Roman world cannot be drawn.[31] Undoubtedly though, sexualised violence, as is testified in the two examined stories of married women living in late antique Oxyrhynchus, should certainly be associated with misogyny and "manly" behaviour, two aspects of a generalised mentality and attitude towards women during late antique and Byzantine periods, and is reflected not only on papyrological documentation, but also on other kinds of social sources.[32] In addition, one could hardly deny that in both narratives women appear as the weak members of society, doomed, so to say, to submit to male power and domination. Forced marriages, non-consensual sex, male adultery and rape that remain unpunished, as well as male control over commonly owned property, leave no space for doubt. However, we should not disregard the fact that the three selected texts are also a proof of these women's efforts, if not to get emancipated, at least to oppose their abusive husbands and to slightly change their fate, which seems to be prescribed. The very writing of these narratives, addressed to the authorities, proves that these women did not hesitate to take matters into their hands. In both instances, the female writers ask for divorce, vindication and their husbands' punishment; they are certainly intimidated by their husbands' repeated violence, but they remain combative.

Though sometimes unclear in terms of content and unable to offer to us but a short glimpse to long-time marital problems and disputes, papyri are informative on unhappy marriages and, to a certain extent, on the role of the spouses' sexual life. The publication of new material and the further analysis of the already published papyri will certainly provide us with more information on this diachronically and interculturally multifaceted topic.

Bibliography

Arnaoutoglou, I. (1995), 'Marital Disputes in Greco-Roman Egypt', in: *The Journal of Juristic Papyrology* 25, 11–28.

Bagnall, R. (2004), 'Women's Petitions in Late Antique Egypt', in: D. Feissel/J. Gascou (eds.), *La petition à Byzance*, Paris, 53–60.

---

31 Cf. the relevant remarks of Beaucamp 1992, 74.

32 Cf. nn. 2 and 3.

Baldwin, B. (1963), 'Crime and Criminals in Greco-Roman Egypt', in: *Aegyptus* 43, 256–263.
Beaucamp, J. (1992), *Le statut de la femme à Byzance, 4ᵉ–7ᵉ siècle, II: 2 : Les pratiques sociales. Travaux et mémoires du centre de recherche d'histoire et civilisation de Byzance, Monographies* 6, Paris.
Bryen, A.Z. (2008), 'Visibility and Violence in Petitions from Roman Egypt', in: *Greek, Roman, and Byzantine Studies* 48, 181–200.
Bryen, A.Z. (2013), *Violence in Roman Egypt. A Study in Legal Interpretation*, Philadelphia, Pennsylvania.
Burnet, R. (2003), *L'Égypte ancienne à travers les papyrus. Vie quotidienne*, Paris.
Dossey, L. (2008), 'Wife Beating and Manliness in Late Antiquity', in: *Past & Present* 199, 3–40.
Evans-Grubbs, J. (1989), 'Abduction Marriage in Antiquity: A Law of Constantine (CTh IX. 24. I) and Its Social Context', in: *Journal of Roman Studies* 79, 59–83.
Evans-Grubbs, J. (2001), 'Virgins and Widows, Show-Girls and Whores: Late Roman Legislation on Women and Christianity', in: R.W. Mathisen (ed.), *Law, Society, and Authority in Late Antiquity*, New York/Oxford.
Evans-Grubbs, J. (2002), *Women and the Law in the Roman Empire. A Sourcebook on Marriage, Divorce and Widowhood*, London/New York.
Fournet, J-L. (2004), 'Entre document et littérature : la pétition dans l'Antiquité tardive', in: D. Feissel/J. Gascou (eds.), *La petition à Byzance*, Paris, 61–74.
Fournet, J-L./Gascou, J. (2004), 'Liste des pétitions sur papyrus des Ve-VIIe siècles', in: D. Feissel/J. Gascou (eds.), *La petition à Byzance*, Paris, 141–196.
Gascou, J. (2004), 'Les pétitions privées', in: D. Feissel/J. Gascou (eds.), *La petition à Byzance*, Paris, 91–113.
Harries, J. (2006), 'Violence, Victims, and the Legal Tradition in Late Antiquity', in: H.A. Drake (ed.), *Violence in Late Antiquity. Perceptions and Practices*, Aldershot et al., 85–102.
Harries, J. (2007), *Law and Crime in the Roman World,* Cambridge.
Keenan, J.G./Manning, J.G./Yiftach-Firanko, U. (2014), *Law and Legal Practice in Egypt from Alexander to the Arab Conquest. A Selection of Papyrological Sources in Translation, with Introductions and Commentary*, Cambridge.
Koroli, A. (2018), 'Verbal Abuse in Ancient Greek Epistolography: The Case Study of an 'Indecent Proposal'', in: *Analecta Papyrologica* 30, 113–135.
Montserrat, D. (1996), *Sex and Society in Graeco-Roman Egypt*, London/New York.
Rowlandson, J. (ed.) (in collaboration with R. Bagnall et al.) (1998), *Women and society in Greek and Roman Egypt. A sourcebook*, Cambridge et al.
Thoma, M. (2021) [forthcoming], 'Dispute Resolution between Husband and Wife in Roman Egypt: Legal Mechanisms and Familial Strategies', in: S. Waebens/K. Vandorpe (eds.), *Seeking Justice in and out of Court: Dispute Resolution in Greco-Roman and Late Antique Egypt* (Studia Hellenistica), Leuven.
Whitehorne, J.E.G. (1979), 'Sex and Society in Greco-Roman Egypt', in: J. Bingen/G. Nachtergael (eds.), *Actes du XVe congrès internationale de papyrologie IV, Bruxelles - Louvain, 29 août-3 septembre 1977*, Brussels, 240–246.
Winter, J.G. (1933), *Life and Letters in the Papyri*, Ann Arbor.
Zimmermann, M. (2006), 'Violence in Late Antiquity Reconsidered', in: H.A. Drake (ed.), *Violence in Late Antiquity. Perceptions and Practices*, Aldershot et al., 343–357.

Rosalia Hatzilambrou
"Asexuality" in the Greek Papyrus Letters

Abstract: This chapter aims to explore the scarcity of love letters among the Greek letters written on papyrus. In the first part, Hatzilambrou briefly presents the extant specimens of Greek love correspondence in post-pharaonic Egypt, while also commenting on points in them that are relevant to her argument. In the second part, she firstly justifies her suggestion that the small number of papyrus love letters appears puzzling, when compared to the emphasis placed on love and sexual desire in other texts of the same period, e.g. in the magical papyri and, secondly, she argues that the reason for the observed "asexuality" in the corpus of the Greek papyrus letters lies in a range of factors, namely the literacy issue, the defective postal system, the moral climate and the deliberate destruction of love letters, which have nothing to do with the sexuality of the Greek speaking inhabitants of post-pharaonic Egypt.

1 Introduction

The letter which expresses love and/or sexual desire is the *rara avis* in the corpus of the c. 8000 papyrus Greek letters which have been published hitherto. Almost half of these letters can be defined as personal, non-official letters. Among them very few can be considered *proper love letters*, in the sense of letters being addressed by a lover to a beloved or intended beloved with the aim of expressing feelings of love and/or sexual desire.[1] Having investigated the corpus of the papyrus Greek letters, I found out five texts only, which have a good chance of qualifying as love letters according to this general definition. Yet, some of these letters differ considerably from each other in terms of scope and content. Four of them are sent by a man to a woman, and one is addressed by a woman to a man. Their dating also varies; it ranges from the first to the sixth century AD. All of them come from the rubbish dumps of the settlement of Oxyrhynchus in Middle Egypt.

In this chapter, my aim is to explore the scarcity of love letters among the Greek letters written on papyrus and similar materials. In the first part of this

---

1 Cf. the only definition of *love letter* coming from antiquity, namely by ps. Libanius (*De forma epistolari* 44, see below p. 496), and the one provided by Hodkinson at https://ahc.leeds.ac.uk/languages-research-innovation/dir-record/research-projects/983/love-letters-and-erotic-letters-antiquity-and-beyond (last retrieved on 20/11/2020).

https://doi.org/10.1515/9783110695793-021

chapter, I briefly present the extant specimens of Greek love correspondence in post-pharaonic Egypt, while also commenting on points in them that are relevant to my argument. In the second part, I argue that the small number of papyrus love letters is inexplicable, when compared to the emphasis placed on love and sexual desire in other texts of the same period, as for instance in the magical papyri. The argument my chapter puts forward is that the reason for the observed "asexuality"[2] in the corpus of the Greek papyrus letters lies in a range of factors, which have nothing to do with the sexuality of the Greek speaking inhabitants of Egypt in the Imperial and Byzantine periods.

The most erotic extant Greek papyrus letter is *P. Wash.* 2 108, dated late in the sixth century, and executed in a practised hand. Despite the bad condition of the manuscript, which has invited much reconstruction, one can read:

[εὔχομαι τὸν] παγελεήμονα θεό[ν], ὅπως [ὑ]γι[α]ίνουσα   1
[ἀπολάβῃς δ]ιὰ γραμμάτων τὴν προσηγορίαν, οἶδεν δὲ
[θεός, ... Ὀ]ξυρύγχου νύκταν καὶ ἡμέρα δι' ὀνείρων σε
[.... παρακαλῶ] δι[ὰ τά]χους ἀποστε[ῖ]λαί μοι γράμματα
[- ca.15 - τὴν] καρδίαν μου ὁ πυρε[τὸς τῆ]ς ἐρ[ωτικῆς]   5
[μανίας ͺͺͺ.λα]μπάσιν ἡ Ἀφροδίτη ἐγ [[α]] βέλος ης ....[-ca.?-]
[- ca.12 -] .. ζητῶν τὸ γλυκύτατόν σου πρόσωπον
[- ca.13 -]θε, ὅτι ἀπὸ Ὀξυρύγχου ἕως τῆς Ἡρακλέους δύο
[- ca.10 -] .ο..ειδι..ταν ζητῶν τὸ δεξιν σου βυζεὶν τὸ
[- ca.10 -]ν παν..... ἥκισεν, οὐχὶ δὲ ἐκ τῆς ἀδυνα-   10
[μίας μου, ἀλλ' ἐ]κ τῆς σοῦ φιλί[ας, π]ολλὰ δὲ ε[ͺͺ.] μητέρα
          σου [-ca.?-]

Back
[-ca.?-]αι τὸν ἀδελφὸ[ν ...]....κ..[.]ν μη ....
[-ca.?-] μετὰ τῶν [σὺ]ν ὑμῖν ἀπάντων †

3. l. νύκτα; l. ἡμέραν   9 l. δεξιόν; l. βυζίν

[I pray to the] all-merciful God, that you [receive] in good health my salutation transmitted by letter. [God] knows [that I . . .] Oxyrhynchos by day and night [seeing] you in dreams. [I beseech you], send me a letter [soon], [for] the fire [of my love and desire consumes] my heart. Aphrodite [burns me] with torches, [Eros] was delighted (?), having taken (?) but one arrow [. . .] seeking your so lovely face [. . .] that from Oxyrhynchos up to Herakleopolis two

---

2 The term "asexuality" is semantically complicated and multifaceted, see Bogaert 2012. In this chapter it is defined as "low or absent interest in or desire for sexual activity", and is used metaphorically to denote the lack of references to love and/or sexuality in the letters that came down to use in the papyri that are under examination.

[. . .] seeking your right breast. [For pain] tormented [me] . . ., not as a result of weakness, [but] because of my love for you. Much [. . .] to (?) your mother [. . .].

Back

[I greet . . .] your brother . . ., your mother (?). . . and everybody with you.[3]

Apart from the Christian health formula at the beginning of the letter and the presence of a cross on the back, reminiscent of the letter's Christian orientation,[4] the literary setting of the rest of the letter is pagan. Aphrodite with torches and Eros with an arrow torture the composer of the letter. *Topoi* of Greek erotic literature, namely the flame of love[5] and the metaphor of love as weakness and sickness, are employed, while the eroticism of the letter reaches a peak in line 9, where reference is made to the longing for the addressee's right breast.[6] Apart from the juxtaposition of Christian and pagan elements, what is also surprising in this erotic letter is the greeting formula at the end and on the back of the letter, which is addressed to the mother, the brother and whoever else is present at the recipient's house. Letters are commonly filled with greetings to everyone in the

---

3 The translation of the papyrus texts which accompany their edition are used, with the exception of *P. Oxy.* 42 3070, see n. 19 below.

4 On the letters written by Christians in Oxyrhynchus see Blumell 2012. See also Naldini 1968; Tibiletti 1979.

5 Cf. also Fournet 2006, 466–467, where the text attested in two ostraca preserving erotic essays (not letters) by the soldier Sosianus at the fortlet Maximianon in the Eastern Desert is published. The ostraca are assigned to the end of the second/beginning of the third century, and bear the inventory number M361 and M359 respectively.

6 The word used for the woman's breast, βυζί(ο)ν, is rare and appears for the first time in the papyri. It is attested in medical texts, see *P. Wash.* 2 108 note on l. 9. On the female breast in Greek erotic literature, often depicted as the greatest source of a woman's beauty, see Gerber 1978. This reference has its importance as a witness to the sexual significance breasts held over time, mostly as objects desired to be caressed, since the archaic period. One may recall, for instance, Hom. *Il.* 14.214–217 (although the main focus of the passage is not on the breasts), Archil. 196a W, l. 32 (if the reconstruction μαζ]ῶν is correct), Hdt. 5.18, all attested in authors whose works were very popular in Greek-speaking Egypt. References to breasts with sexual connotations are more numerous in Hellenistic and post-Hellenistic authors, conspicuously in the work of Nonnus of Panopolis in the fifth century, see, for instance, the long story of Aura at Nonn. *D.* 48.238–978. Interesting, too, is the reference to the right breast of the addressee. It is probably not mere chance that the writer mentioned "the right breast" (and not "breasts"). For parallels in art see *P. Wash.* 2 108 note on l. 9. The reference to the right breast might have been made, because it had a special significance for the two lovers involved in this letter, or might simply have been used as a good-omen (auspicious) word, perhaps expressing promise, good will, and respect.

household, who might be present at the opening of the letter and share its content. But I would not expect the inclusion of such greetings in an explicit love letter addressed to a woman, even to a spouse, which does not appear to be the case here. Additionally, since there is no mention of the father in the greetings, I surmise that the addressee of this letter could be fatherless, that is, an orphan or a bastard. Fatherlessness is a trait of prostitutes, and it could be the case that this letter is addressed to a young prostitute.[7] Another point of interest is that this letter was written and found in Oxyrhynchus, while the addressee probably resided in Heracleopolis (l. 8). This fact suggests that either the letter was never sent, or that it was returned to Oxyrhynchus, perhaps by (or together with) its recipient.

Love and the sorrow of separation are the dominant emotions in the letter attested in *P. Oxy.* 3 528 and assigned to the second century.[8] It was sent by Serenus to his beloved but distant Isidora, possibly, but not certainly, his wife,[9] desiring her return. Serenus recalls their bathing together, an image that appears sexually loaded, and stresses his abstinence from bathing and anointing for some period after Isidora's departure. Isidora had left the house in circumstances that the letter does not clarify. What interests me in particular in this letter with respect to my argument is the reference within the quotation (ll. 18–19) that the woman was made a prostitute. *P. Oxy.* 3 528, written in very bad Greek, reads:

Σερῆνος Εἰσιδώρᾳ [τῇ ἀδελ-]
φῇ καὶ κυρίᾳ πλαῖστ[α χαίρειν].
πρὸ μὲν παντὸς εὔχομ[αί σε ὑγιαι-]
νει καὶ καθ’ ἑκάστης [ἡμέρα]ς κα[ὶ]
ὄψας τὸ προσκύνημά σου πυῶ   5
παρὰ τῇ σε φιλούσῃ Θοῆρι. γινόσκειν
σε θέλω ἀφ’ ὡς ἐκξῆλθες ἀπ’ ἐμοῦ
πένθος ἡγούμην νυκτὸς κλέων
ἡμέρας δὲ πενθῷ. ιβ Φαῶφι ἀφ’ ὅτε
ἐλουσάμην μετ’ ἐσοῦ οὐκ ἐλουσάμην   10
οὐκ ἤλιμε μέχρει ιβ Ἀθύρ, καὶ ἔπεμ-
σάς μυ ἐπιστολὰς δυγαμενου λίθον
σαλεῦσε, οὕτως ὑ λόγυ σου καικίνη-
κάν με. αὐτὴν τῇ ὅρᾳ ἀντέγρα-

---

7 Prostitutes are mentioned in the letters, although these are not addressed to them, attested in *O. Krok.* 267–270. See also Cuvigny 2010.
8 The letter is included in the anthology of letters *Sel. Pap.* I (no. 125), compiled by Hunt/Edgar 1932, and the one compiled by Trapp 2003, 74–75, 219–221 (no. 15).
9 On the use of the term "sister" referring to a wife, sometimes in literal truth in conformity with the marital practice of the Ptolemaic kings, who had taken it over from the pharaohs, see n. 12 below.

ψά συ καὶ ἔδωκα τῇ ιβ μετὰ τῶν   15
σῶν ἐπιστολῶν ἐσσφραγιζμένα.
χωρεὶς δὲ τῶν σῶν λόγων κὲ γρα-
μάτων ὁ Κόλοβος δὲ πόρνην με πεπύ-
ηκεν, ἔλεγε δὲ ὅτι ἔπεμσέ μυ φάσειν
ἡ γυνή σου ὅτι αὐτὸς πέπρακεν τὸ ἀλυ-   20
σίδιον καὶ αὐτὸς κατέστακέ με ε[ἰ]ς τὸ
πλῦν· τούτους τοὺς λόγους λέγεις ἥνα
μηκέτι ⟦φ⟧ πιστευθῶ μου τὴν ἐνβολ[ήν].
ἑδοῦ ποσαρκεις ἔπεμσα ἐπὶ σέ. ἔρχη [εἴτε]
            οὐκ ἔρχη δήλοσόν μυ.[25

Back
    ἀπόδος Εἰσιδόρᾳ π(αρὰ) Σερήνου.

1 l. Ἰσιδώρᾳ   2 l. πλεῖστα   3 παντὸς James : ποντὸς   3–4 l. [ὑγιαί]|νειν   5 l. ὀψίας   5 l.
ποιῶ   6 l. γινώσκειν   7 l. ἐξῆλθες   8 l. κλαίων   9 l. πενθῶν   11 l. ἤλειμμαι; l. μέχρι   11–
12. l. ἔπεμ|ψάς   12 l. μοι; l. δυναμένας   13 l. σαλεῦσαι; l. οἱ; l. λόγοι   13–14 l. κεκίνη|κάν
14 l. αὐτῇ; l. ὥρα   15 l. σοι   16 l. ἐσφραγισμένα   17 l. χωρὶς; l. καὶ   17–18. l. γρα|μμάτων
18–19. l. πεποί|ηκεν   19 l. ἔπεμψέ; l. μοι; l. φάσιν   22 l. πλοῖον; l. ἵνα   24 l. ἰδοῦ, corr. ex
οδου; l. ποσάκις; l. ἔπεμψα   25. l. δήλωσόν; l. μοι   26 l. Ἰσιδώρᾳ

Serenus to his beloved sister Isidora, many greetings. Before all else I pray for your health,
and every day and evening I perform the act of veneration on your behalf to Thoeris who
loves you. I assure you that ever since you left me, I have been in mourning, weeping by
night and lamenting by day. Since we bathed together on Phaophi 12, I never bathed nor
anointed myself until Athur 12. You sent me letters which would have shaken a stone, so
much did your words move me. Instantly I answered you and gave the letter sealed on the
12th, together with letters for you(?). Apart from your saying and writing "Colobus has made
me a prostitute", he said to me "Your woman sent me a message saying "He himself has
sold the chain and himself put me in the boat"". You say this to prevent my being believed
any longer with regard to my embarkation (?). See how many times I have sent to you.
Whether you are coming or not, let me know.

Back
    Deliver to Isidora from Serenus.

Affection is also expressed in *P. Oxy.* 42 3059, a fragmentary letter in a good hand
of the second century, which Didyme sent in all probability to her husband Apollonius.[10] The letter is remarkable for the unique metaphor in the corpus of the
papyrus letters of the addressee of the letter as the sun,[11] which occupies four

---

10 The letter is included in the collection of Bagnall/Cribiore 2006, 275.
11 For the metaphor of the beloved as the sun, cf. *Anthologia Graeca* XII 59.

complete lines (ll. 1–4), and manages to turn the stereotyped beginning epistolary formula to a letter of affection:

Διδύμη Ἀπολλωνίωι τῶι ἀδελφῶι
καὶ ἡλίωι χαίρειν.
γείνωσκέ με μὴ βλέπουσαν τὸν ἥλιον
διὰ τὸ μὴ βλέπεσθαί σε ὑπ' ἐμοῦ.
οὐ γάρ ἔχω ἄλλον ἥλιον εἰ μὴ σέ. εὐ-   5
χαριστῶ δὲ Θεωνᾶτι τῷ ἀδελφῷ σου
[. . .] ̣αι ἃ ἔπεμψα τῷ πατρί σου
[. . .] ̣ο Θέωνος Ἀθηναίου τοῦ φίλου
          . . .

Back
ἀπὸ Διδύ[μης -ca.?-]

3 l. γίγνωσκέ

Didyme to Apollonios, her brother[12] and sun, greetings. You must know that I do not view
the sun because you are out of my view; for I have no other sun but you. I am grateful to
your brother Theonas. [Take delivery of?] What I have sent to your father [...] Theon, son of
Athenaeus, your friend . . .

Back
From Didyme [

This letter is a fine instance of correspondence that seems to express genuine
emotion.[13] However, although this seems to be a love letter, I cannot be absolutely
certain about that: Didyme might have simply been demonstrating her gratitude
to a dear friend or relative, who had supported her.[14]

Sexual desire and longing probably urged an impatient soldier to address a
letter, namely *P. Oxy.* 34 2731, from the fourth or fifth century, perhaps to his

---

12 This is a commonly attested term in women's letters. It might refer to a sibling, a husband, a
sibling who had married his sister, a more distant relative, but even a non-relative, a friend, or
in general, a contemporary person. If the text provides no other evidence, it is often difficult to
define the actual relationship between two people addressed as "brother" and "sister" in the
texts of Ptolemaic and Greek-Roman Egypt. See *inter alia* Bagnall/Cribiore 2006, 85–86; Parsons
2007, 127; see also the interpretation of the brother-sister marriage in Egypt offered by Huebner
2007 and 2013, 189–195, and the criticism of it advanced by Remijsen/Clarysse 2008, and Row-
landson/Takahashi 2009.
13 See Parsons 2007, 134–135; Kotsifou 2012, 66–67.
14 The nearest parallel of the use of this metaphor has been detected by the editor (P.J. Parsons)
in Ps. Galen 19, p. 680, l.3 ("sun of my soul"), where it refers to a friend.

mother-in-law (deduced from ll. 1, 7–8), presumably because his wife was very young. In lines 9–13 he is ordering her to send his wife to him:

ἅπαξ καὶ δὶς
καὶ τρὶς ἐδήλωσά σου τοῦ σε ἀποστεῖλ[αι]   10
τὴν σύμβιόν \μου/ καὶ οὐκ ἐβουλήθης· νῦ[ν δὲ]
μὴ ἀμελήσῃς νυκτὸς καὶ ἡμέρας
τοῦ σε ἀποστεῖλαί με τὴν σύμβιόν μ[ου.]

10 σε corr. ex με

Once, twice, three times I have told you to send my wife and you have refused. Well now exert yourself night and day to send my wife.

However, this letter cannot be *stricto sensu* classified among love letters.[15] Last on my list is a unique text, namely *P. Oxy.* 42 3070, assigned to the first century. It preserves a note which expresses male homosexual desire. It was duly folded and addressed on the back as a letter, and it ends with the common letter greeting formula, but the rest of the text takes the form of an edict. The official form of the text in juxtaposition to the obscene content expressed through τὸ πυγίσαι twice (ll. 4–5, 8),[16] the primitive drawing with the vulgar captions[17] which accompanies the note,[18] and its bad Greek which parodies the language of the edict, reveal the mocking character of the note.[19] The text, taken at face value, consists of a sex proposition by two men to another man:

---

15 According to the definition of love letter provided in n. 1. It was not addressed to a beloved person and it does explicitly express love or sexual desire.

16 On this verb, which explicitly suggests sodomy, see Bain 1991, 67–71; Henderson 1991[2], 202.

17 The words ψωλή and φίκις, denoting the two parts of the male body involved in sodomy, accompany the drawing. On ψωλή, "a thoroughly vulgar" Aristophanic word, see Henderson 1991[2], 110. On the rarely attested φίκις, see Bain 1978, 36; 1983, 56. On the obscene language of the note, see also Koroli 2018, 117–123.

18 For interpretations of the drawing see Gallavotti 1978–1979, 368; Montserrat 1996, 136; 1998, 155; Koroli 2018, 127–128.

19 See also Parsons 2007, 134, who regards it "a joke *billet doux*". Cribiore 2001, 219 further assumes that this letter was composed by two students, who after having learned how to phrase a letter, felt confident enough to write this mock note. I think that the mocking tone is obvious in this text, but Cribiore's assumption that the note originated in the "asphyxiating" educational routine of the grammarian's class cannot be confirmed. For a detailed account of the playful style of the note see Koroli 2018, 124–127.

λέγει Ἀπίων
καὶ Ἐπιμᾶς Ἐπαφροδ(ίτῳ)
τῶι φιλτάτῳι ὅτι
ἡ διδῦς ἡμεῖν τὸ
πυγίσαι κҩὶ καλῶς   5
σοί ἐστι, οὐκέτι οὐ μὴ
δείρομέν σε ἐὰν δώσῃς
ἡμεῖν τὸ ποιγίσαι. ἔρρω(σο).
        ἔρρω(σο).

Ψωλή
(drawing)
καὶ φίκις

Back
    ἀπόδ(ος) Ἐπαφροδ(ίτῳ) τῷ φιλτάτῳ.

4 l. εἰ διδοῖς   8 l. πυγίσαι

Apion and Epimas proclaim to their best beloved Epaphroditos that if you allow us to bugger you, and it is fine with you, we will not thrash you any longer, if you allow us to bugger
you. Farewell.[20]

Penis erected
(drawing)
and buttocks

Back
    Deliver to the best beloved Epaphroditos.

Apart from a mocking tone the note also displays an obvious air of command and
threat. The text consists of an act of verbal abuse, since it proposes to its addressee anal intercourse as an alternative to thrashing, and it attests an insulting
attempt to dominate sexually a socially subordinate man (see below) through the
threat of violence.[21] However, to appreciate the offensive character of the note
with respect to its contemporaries, one has firstly to consider the status of its recipient. It is very likely that the addressee of the letter was a slave or perhaps a
freedman recently manumitted. Epaphroditos, whose name means "charming",

20 For another possibility of translating this text see Gallavotti 1978–1979, 367; Montserrat 1996,
136; 1998, 155; Koroli 2018, 125. My translation agrees with that of Parsons 2007, pl. 27; Koroli
2018, 124.
21 See Montserrat 1996, 136–138; 1998, 156–157; Gallavotti 1978–1979, 366–369; and more emphatically Koroli 2018.

is often a slave's name in Egypt, perhaps given to physically attractive slaves.[22] Additionally, the reference to repeated corporal violence inflicted on Epaphroditos supports this hypothesis because physical abuse against freeborn people was prohibited by law. What is more, if Epaphroditos was a slave, which appears to be the most plausible scenario, he would most likely belong to one (or even to both, if they were brothers) of the senders of the note, since slaves were protected by law and by social structure from abuse by people outside – and even inside – the household they belonged to.[23] If the senders of the note owned Epaphroditos, they would not need to ask for the consent of their slave to their sexual proposal. Sexual exploitation is a common aspect of slavery in every known slave society,[24] and post-pharaonic Egypt would not be an exception. There, as well, within the frame of the vastly asymmetrical power relationship between a master and his slave, the former had ample sexual access to the bodies of his slaves.[25] Thus, if the recipient of this note was indeed a slave, I do not think that its content would be regarded as demeaning within contemporary society. Under such social circumstances what could possibly be the aim of composing and sending such a note? The best answer I could put forward is that this letter might have been composed as part of a practical joke by two probably young men at the expense of one of their slaves. The two senders might have been drunk, and this condition could account for the shaky handwriting. The short letter might never have been sent, but only shown and read to Epaphroditos because I doubt that he would have been able to read it, and perhaps for this reason the crude and obscene drawing had been added; of course, Epaphroditos could ask someone to read it for him. Nonetheless, even if my assumption is correct, the note could still express genuine sexual desire, and it may be an attempt to represent Epimas' and Apion's fantasy of having intercourse with Epaphroditos.[26] For this reason, it is included in my list of the extant letters denoting sexual desire in post-pharaonic Egypt.

---

22 See Montserrat 1996, 137; 1998, 156 and 164 n. 7. Nero also had a freedman called Epaphroditos (Suet. *Ner.* 49.3.10; Tac. *Ann.* 15.55.4).
23 See, among others, Scholl 2014, 446–448; Strauss 2014, 455–456; cf. Fisher 1995; E. Cohen 2014, 185–190.
24 Cf. the sexual exploitation of slaves in the Pre-Civil War United States of America.
25 See, for instance, E. Cohen 2014, 184–198; Harper 2011, 281–285, 291–304.
26 See Montserrat 1996, 137–138; 1998, 155–156.

2 An equivocal situation in post-pharaonic Egypt: Evidenced interest in love but scarcity of love letters

To my knowledge, this is all the published Greek love and/or sexually-oriented correspondence that has been preserved on papyrus from the Ptolemaic times until Late Antiquity. The extremely small number of papyrus love letters is inexplicable, if it is compared to the emphasis placed on love and sexual desire in other texts of the same period, as for instance in the Greek and Demotic magical papyri.[27] A great many of these texts are written as love charms (of various types and names, e.g. ἀγωγαί, φίλτρα etc.), concerned with sexual, heterosexual, but also both female and male homosexual relationships, mostly expressing the need for obtaining sexual gratification for oneself, or denying it to another person.[28] It is noticeable that in the majority of the erotic spells preserved on papyri the user appears to be male and the object and victim female.[29] The study of the magical papyri entices one to suggest that the inhabitants of Egypt of both sexes, at least in the Greek-Roman and Byzantine periods, were highly interested in sexual matters.[30]

This impression is strengthened, if we consider some other evidence unearthed in the sands of Egypt. *P. Oxy.* 39 2891, for instance, a papyrus of the second century, preserves fragments of the sex manual by Philaenis, who flourished in the fourth century BC, concerned with technical aspects of sexual performance.[31] Continuous use of such manuals in Egypt and Palestine is attested by the disapproval of works of this kind by Clement of Alexandria.[32] The interest shown by readers in Egypt in both Greek and Demotic novel, attested by the dozens of papyri of novel excavated in Egypt, should also be taken into account.[33]

---

27 Published in the corpora *PGM, PDM, Suppl. Mag.* I & II.

28 The most important study of this material is Faraone 1999. See also Edmonds III 2014.

29 Faraone 1999, 43 n. 9, *pace* Pachoumi 2013, 298–304.

30 For a survey of the emotion of love and sexual desire in magical papyri, see Montserrat 1996, 180–209.

31 See Perale 2013.

32 Clem. Al. *Protr.* 4.61.2. The sources give the names of nine writers of sexual manuals apart from Astuanassa, the mythological founder of the genre. Philaenis is the most famous and the most frequently attested writer of a sex manual. See also Parker 1992, 94 (in particular); Boehringer 2015.

33 Information on the published papyri preserving fragments of novel could be retrieved by the Leuven Database of Ancient Books (https://www.trismegistos.org/ldab) and the Mertens-Pack³

Mild erotic elements are contained in the novels by Chariton and Achilles Ta-tius,[34] while the salacious sexual narratives encountered in fragments of Lollia-nus *Phoenicica* and "the papyrus of Iolaus" (= *P. Oxy.* 42 3010 from the second half of the second century) suggest that sexual titillation was established as part of the reader's experience, and was indeed appreciated in Greek-Roman and early Byzantine Egypt.

In light of this evidence, one is tempted to postulate a large element of eroti-cism in real life in Greek-Roman and early Byzantine Egypt, and to expect to find additional supporting evidence in the form of love letters, which, however, does not occur. What is more puzzling is that love letters, which seem to be a scarcity in real life, appear frequently in the genre of Greek novel, which was popular in Egypt. Love letters embedded in novels often play a prominent role in their plot, as, for instance, in the novels by Chariton[35] and Achilles Tatius.[36] Additionally, literary products of the Second Sophistic are written in the form of love letters, such as, for instance, the fourth book of the letters of Alciphron supposedly writ-ten by courtesans,[37] as well as scattered letters in each of his first three books,[38] and the seventy-three erotic epistles of Philostratus.[39] However, these last two works have not been attested in papyri, thus they were probably not popular in Egypt. The same is true for the later love letter collection written by Aristaenetus, which is in fact a collection of miniature erotic narratives in a letter form that is dated to the fifth century.[40]

Interestingly enough, the love letter was neglected in the two technical books on letter writing that have survived intact from antiquity. It is not mentioned at

---

online database (http://cip l93.philo.ulg.ac.be/Cedopal/MP3/dbsearch_en.aspx). For an over-view of the papyri of novel published until 2009, see Messeri 2010.

34 On the erotic element in the Greek novel, see Goldhill 1995, *passim*; Whitmarsh 2018, 1–8 in particular.

35 See Rosenmeyer 2001, 137–147.

36 On the function of love letters in the novel of Achilles Tatius see Rosenmeyer 2001, 147–156; Repath 2013, 237–262.

37 On the role of courtesans in Greek letter-books, which accounts for greater directness and explicitness regarding sex, see Hodkinson 2014, 468–469.

38 See again Rosenmeyer 2001, 255–307. Most of Alciphron's love letters do not resemble con-ventional letters with the established epistolary framework, but are rather short essays contain-ing erotic narratives.

39 See Rosenmeyer 2001, 322–338.

40 Hodkinson 2014, 470–472 has asserted that the epistolary form in the works of Alciphron and Aristaenetus functioned as the container for their erotic short stories, since "short story" was not a literary form recognised in antiquity.

all in the earlier one, the *Typi epistolares* (*Epistolary Types*), erroneously trans-mitted under the name of Demetrius of Phalerum,[41] while in the later, *De forma epistolari* (*Epistolary Styles*) ascribed to Proclus or Libanius[42] (known as Ps. Liba-nius), the erotic epistolary type occurs in the last position just before the mixed letter type. The entry includes a brief definition of the type, namely that "the erotic style is that in which we offer amorous words to lovers",[43] and it is followed by an example.[44] Finally, no model of a love letter appears to have been included in the fragmentary manuals with model letters preserved in *P. Bon.* 5 (assigned to the third/fourth century),[45] and the much later *BKT* 9 94 assigned to the sixth cen-tury.[46]

The obvious discrepancy between the scanty evidence of eroticism in the cor-pus of Greek papyrus letters and the strong concern with sexual matters observed in contemporary magical papyri and popular literary readings has been observed by scholars who describe it as problematic, but fail to discuss its reasons. Clarysse is, to the best of my knowledge, the only scholar who has briefly remarked that the absence of love letters in our documentation has to do with a lack of privacy of ancient letters.[47] In the rest of this part of my chapter I, first, explore the factors that violated the private and confidential character of ancient letters, and second, I consider the social reality and moral situation in post-pharaonic Egypt, which should certainly account for the scarcity of papyrus love letters.

The private and personal character of a letter was undermined by the illiter-acy or semi-literacy of the majority of the population in antiquity. In the wake of Harris' influential book on literacy, it is widely accepted that the vast majority of the ancient population was unable to write and read, since no ample and expand-ing school system existed.[48] Nevertheless, it was unthinkable that a wealthy man, unless he was a freedman, or a man who aimed at a kind of distinction in his city life could be illiterate.[49] Women were still less likely to be literate than were

---

41 See Malherbe 1988, 3–4, 30–41.
42 The treatise has been transmitted in two different manuscript traditions; one attributes it to Libanius and the other to Proclus, but neither is correct. See Malherbe 1988, 5, 66–88.
43 Ps. Lib. *De forma epistolari* 44. Translation of the passages of this work is by Malherbe 1988.
44 See below p. 499.
45 Reedited as *C. Gloss. Biling.* 1 16 (Kramer 1983); see also Malherbe 1988, 4–5, 44–57.
46 Luiselli 1997, 643–651.
47 Clarysse 2017, 70.
48 Harris 1989.
49 Harris 1989, 330, phrased as a conclusion, which emerges from Harris 1989, 175–322, regard-ing the Greek-Roman Era and Late Antiquity.

men,[50] however, they are involved as writers or addressees in a remarkable number of letters in the millennium from the death of Alexander to the Arab conquest.[51] As it is expected, the letters came almost entirely from the upper strata of society, namely from members of the upper and the upper middle class, who had better access to schooling and could afford to hire scribes for the writing of their letters.[52] Nevertheless, it has been recently argued that hiring scribes for the writing of *private* letters was uncommon in the Greek-Roman world, and that the vast majority of the private letters that has been preserved was written by the senders themselves.[53] The fact that letter writing concerned people of the upper classes strongly suggests that the cost of the papyrus as writing material was not considered a hindrance to the writing of personal letters, love letters included, by its potential senders. It has been persuasively argued that papyrus was not regarded as expensive in circles above peasants and unskilled laborers.[54] In any case, private letters were normally short and required a moderate quantity of papyrus, and for this reason people could easily obtain writing material for their private letters by cutting an unwritten piece from an old papyrus.[55] In short, the picture that emerges in post-pharaonic Egypt is that there were people who were writing with ease, and certainly people, women included, who could own or hire an amanuensis. It is also plausible that some people with no personal reading and writing ability could find a trustworthy literate relative or friend to help them with their correspondence, even the most personal. Thus, while the lack of literacy may partly explain the extreme scarcity of love letters among the Greek papyri, I do not think that it fully accounts for it.

A second factor that violated the confidential character of letters in antiquity was the system of dispatching them.[56] Safe delivery was problematic in the ab-

---

50 On women's education in Hellenistic and Greek-Roman Egypt see Cribiore 2001, 74–101. Cribiore argues that only a minority of women living in urban environments and belonging to the upper strata of society was able to write and read in Hellenistic and Roman Egypt. The vast majority of women of the lower classes never learned to wield a pen.

51 The collection of letters written by women in post-pharaonic Egypt in Bagnall/Cribiore 2006 amounts to 210 letters (104 were added in the e-book). In this are not included the dozens of letters addressed to women.

52 See Harris 1989; Bagnall/Cribiore 2006, 6–9.

53 Sarri 2018, 192, phrased as a conclusion of the chapter "Authentication" (pp. 125–192).

54 See Skeat 1995; Fournet 2013, 5057–5058.

55 On the reuse of papyrus, see, for instance, Parsons 2007, 123–124.

56 See Llewelyn 1994, 26–43; Parsons 2007, 125–126; Muir 2009, 10–13.

sence of national postal service. The imperial post carried only the official correspondence, and private people could not use it.[57] Some people who owned slaves could employ them, but few could perhaps afford to deliver their letters through their own slaves, if the letter's destination was far away. Thus, letters were normally entrusted for delivery to somebody well known, who happened to be going to the right place. He would most likely be illiterate. In any case, the most personal letters were presumably entrusted for dispatching to somebody in principle trustworthy. As for short distances, people could deliver their correspondence by themselves. Additionally, the private character of correspondence could be protected by the way papyrus letters were rolled and folded. People could exclude others from this communication by tying a string around the letters, sealing them with a clay seal or drawing a saltire pattern or similar design on and around the string that could prevent letters from being opened undetected.[58]

Moreover, there is some evidence that in Greek antiquity the private character of a personal letter was respected. There is a story in Plutarch about a letter sent to Demetrius Poliorcetes, where it is reported that when his wife sent him letters, the Rhodians captured the vessel containing them, and sent it, just as it was, to Ptolemy, i.e. Demetrius' opponent. The Rhodians did not behave like the Athenians, who, having captured Philip's letter carriers when he was making war upon them, read all the letters except the one sent from Olympias, which they sent back to the king with its seal unbroken.[59] Truly, the conditions of dispatching private correspondence in antiquity were far from perfect. However, one is tempted to consider that such conditions existed up until the development of the public postal service, and they do not appear to have had any adverse impact in premodern European societies on the function of the private letter as the means for expressing intimate emotions.[60]

This account would undoubtedly be incomplete, if one does not consider the social realities, moral standards and mentalities that prevailed in the place and at the time discussed.[61] First of all, the meaning of privacy appears to have changed in the post-classical world of vast kingdoms and empires with a diffuse mix of nations and cultures, in the sense that it lost the connotation of exclusion and deprivation, at least for the male citizenry, that it certainly had in classical

---

57 See Llewelyn 1994, 1–25.
58 See Vandorpe 1995.
59 Plu. *Demetr.* 22.
60 See Whitehorne 1979, 243–244.
61 The ambiguity of the extant evidence for the assessment of the sexual morality in post-pharaonic Egypt has been addressed by Whitehorne 1979.

antiquity,[62] and it seemingly started becoming a right, or even a privilege, that one had to defend, as it is considered nowadays. It was perhaps a kind of response on the part of individuals to the pressures of change and the tensions that accompanied it.[63] In any case, the increase of privacy has a connection with shame.[64] In other words, it is shame which requires privacy, since shame is not an individual state of mind, but can be experienced in the face of another. Shame is indeed an emotion named in the context of ancient letter writing. In the brief example of a love letter provided in the aforementioned technical book on letter writing by Ps. Libanius (§40, p. 33 [ed. Weichert]) shame is the *main* theme: "... I am not ashamed for loving (ἐρῶν οὐκ αἰσχύνομαι). For the love of beauty is not shameful (οὐκ αἰσχρόν)". Similarly, in §20 of the *Historia Apollonii regis Tyri*, which in all probability is the translation of a Greek novel, one reads: "If, you are surprised, father, that such a modest girl (*pudica virgo*) has written so immodestly (*impudenter*), I have sent my message by wax, which has no sense of shame (*pudorem*)".[65]

It is understandable that, because of social and legal norms regarding marriage and legitimacy of children, and under the influence of the Greek cultural background of many members of the elite in post-pharaonic Egypt,[66] fear of humiliation was rooted in the possible publicity given via a love letter to a love affair between a man and a woman not married to each other, or to the verbal expression of love. But, why would it be considered shameful to modestly express love and affection to one's spouse or fiancée, especially since in Egypt Greek papyri highlight a laxer legal and moral tradition affecting married women, who did not suffer from the legal and social disabilities of women in classical Greece?[67] Dozens of letters have survived sent from husband to wife and vice versa.[68] As a rule,

---

62 See Carey 2014.

63 On tensions created in the Hellenistic period, and responses to individuals and communities to these, see, for instance, Ager/Faber 2013, 5–15, and all the contributions included in this volume.

64 On the connection between privacy and shame see D. Cohen 1991, 70–97; Rykwert 2001. On shame in Greek antiquity see Konstan 2003.

65 Translation by Archibald 1991.

66 See, for instance, Bagnall 1993, 188–199; Modrzejewski 2005, 348–353. See also Yiftach-Firanko 2003.

67 See Bagnall 1993, 92–99; Arjava 1996, in particular 111–157, 230–254.

68 Dozens of them are included in Bagnall/Cribiore 2006, for instance, *PSI* 3 177 (of the second century) on p. 280, *P. Oxy.* 6 932 (of the late second or early third century) on pp. 297–298; *P. Wash. Univ.* 2 106 (of c. AD 281–280) on p. 322.

they lack both intimate detail and personal sentiment,[69] with their tone being practical and more or less business-like,[70] while emotional language is normally limited to some stock epistolary formulas, in which one cannot be sure whether genuine emotion is always involved.[71] It may be argued that in such cases, people opted for writing within a set epistolary register of limited epistolary phrases, probably taught at schools and incorporated in technical manuals because of deficiency in their own and their scribes' literary skills. Even so, as has been observed in the few love letters that have been preserved, if the writer of a letter wished, he or she could express his or her genuine emotions of affection, even in the clumsy Greek he or she possessed.

The revelation of the exchange of love letters between a man and a woman who are not spouses was apparently a cause of shame; people, therefore, were discouraged from having such correspondence. But as far as homosexual love, in particular male homosexual love and desire, is concerned, one is justified in wondering why its expression would cause shame and would exact secrecy in Egypt in the period from the fourth century BC until the fourth century AD, that is before the spread of Christianity, which had a big impact upon the moral standards of common people.[72] However, it has been shown that in the fourth century, despite the enormous church literature on the body and sexuality that was produced, the impact on the lives of ordinary men and women was probably limited.[73] Nevertheless, apart from the aforementioned erotic note sent by two men (most likely) to a slave (*P. Oxy.* 42 3070), no other homosexual love letter has survived. But this fact should be explored within a broader perspective. In general, oddly enough, homosexual relations did not generate much documentation in post-pharaonic Egypt.[74] Apart from a few homosexual love charms,[75] there is one doubtful reference in *P. Oxy.* 8 1160, a letter of the third or fourth century, where after various statements a father is objecting to his son's stay at Alexandria with his μυχός (presumably to be corrected to μοιχός). This word has been interpreted by the editor

---

69 On reasons for the lack of personal sentiment in the papyrus letters see Whitehorne 1979, 243–244.

70 This is in general the character of the documentary letters; see, for instance, Luiselli 2008, 700–704.

71 On epistolary formulas and the expression of emotion see Kotsifou 2012, 64–68.

72 See, for instance, Brown 1988; Harper 2013.

73 Brown 1988, 320; Bagnall 1993, 198–199; Harper 2013, 2–3.

74 See Bagnall 1993, 195–196; Montserrat 1996, 144–145 and 150–156; cf. Brown 1988, 246.

75 *PGM* XXXII, XXXIIa, LXVI; *Suppl. Mag.* I 42; *Suppl. Mag.* II 54 (probably). See also Montserrat 1996, 156–158, 180–209.

as "paramour". More interesting perhaps is the censure against Maximus the prefect, attested in *P. Oxy.* 3 471 of the second century,[76] in which the prefect's infatuation with a seventeen-year-old boy is denounced, which might suggest that such behaviour was not acceptable, at least among people of high rank. Of course, criticism might have targeted the prefect's obsessive passion rather than the type of relationship, i.e. homosexual or heterosexual.

3 Conclusion

The scarcity of love letters in post-pharaonic Egypt, if considered superficially, gives a distorted image concerning sex and the emotion of erotic love in its cities and villages. There is ample evidence of sex for pleasure (and not for procreation) in the magical papyri, while the popularity in Egypt of some genres with erotic elements, for instance novels, suggests that people were interested in love and sex and that they enjoyed reading about them in their free time. The study of the extant Greek papyrus love letters and the survey of the possible reasons for their scarcity are chiefly important for the determination, understanding and interpretation of interwoven social factors prevalent in the Greek-Roman and early Byzantine world, namely literacy, the defective postal system and the moral environment. All these factors probably shaped a pragmatic attitude towards love letter writing altogether. The risks of violating privacy, the unguaranteed delivery and the delay in receiving a response suggest that the basic aims of love letter writing were not as a rule easily fulfilled in practice. These were the bridging of the spatial gap between people who share feelings of love and sexual desire one for the other, the overcoming of the shyness in the expression of love to the object of this feeling, the reciprocity regarding the pleasure and expectation that personal correspondence, and in particular love correspondence, brings. Thus, people were discouraged from communicating their feelings of love and sexual desire by writing and sending letters. Some impassioned and impatient would-be lovers could always seek assistance from a magician. I believe that such people might have preferred to compromise their privacy in this way because they might have considered it more effective than the sending of a love letter.

---

76 This papyrus is classified among the *Acta Alexandrinorum*, namely the *Acta Maximi*, see Musurillo 1961, 23–28, that is, a collection of texts which narrates confrontations (mostly fictional) in the form of court proceedings, speeches, reports etc. between the Roman government and various Alexandrians. On this text see Whitehorne 1979, 240; Vout 2007, 140–149; Harker 2008, 73–78.

Given these conditions, however, I would still have expected more love letters to have turned up from the sands of Egypt, especially *billets doux,* short love notes, which could be delivered by the senders themselves to their beloved within a relatively short distance. Therefore, I suggest that love letters might have been composed and sent in greater numbers, but were destroyed soon after their delivery for obvious reasons. Bearing this in mind, it is perhaps not a mere coincidence that the majority of the very few extant love letters, which have all been discovered in the rubbish dump of the ancient settlement of Oxyrhynchus, probably involved prostitutes and slaves, i.e. people whose privacy was not considered worthy of respect, while the revelation of their sexual life did not generate much shame. Nonetheless, whether my supposition has some chance of being correct, we will never, I am afraid, be able to find out.[77]

Bibliography

Ager, S.L./Faber, R.A. (2013), 'Introduction: Belonging and Isolation in the Hellenistic World: Themes and Variations', in: S.L. Ager/R.A. Faber (eds.), *Belonging and Isolation in the Hellenistic World,* Toronto/Buffalo/London, 3–16.

Archibald, E. (1991), *Apollonius of Tyre. Medieval and Renaissance Themes and Variations,* Cambridge.

Arjava, A. (1996), *Women and Law in Late Antiquity,* Oxford/New York.

Bagnall, R.S. (1993), *Egypt in Late Antiquity,* Princeton.

Bagnall, R.S./Cribiore, R./Ahtaridis, E. (2006), *Women's Letters from Ancient Egypt,* Ann Arbor.

Bain, D. (1978), 'Another Occurrence of φίκις', in: *ZPE* 30, 36.

Bain, D. (1983), 'φίκις, φικιῶ, *φικιδίζω', in: *ZPE* 52, 56.

Bain, D. (1991), 'Six Verbs of Sexual Congress (βινῶ, κινῶ, πυγίζω, ληκῶ, οἴφω, λαικάζω)', in: *CQ* 41, 51–77.

Blumell, L.H. (2012), *Lettered Christians: Christians, Letters, and Late Antique Oxyrhynchus,* Leiden.

Boehringer, S. (2015), 'What is Philaenis the name of? The Identity, Function and Authority of an Unnamed Figure', in: M. Masterson/N. Sorkin Rabinowitz/J. Robson (eds.), *Sex in Antiquity. Exploring Gender and Sexuality in the Ancient World,* London, 374–391.

Bogaert, A.F. (2012), *Understanding Asexuality,* Lanham.

Brown, P. (1988), *The Body and Society. Men, Women and Sexual Renunciation in Early Christianity,* London/Boston.

---

77 I would like to thank the S.A.R.G. of the National and Kapodistrian University of Athens for the financial support. My thanks are also due to the editors of the volume. I would also like to express my thanks to Professors M.J. Edwards and N. Gonis, to Dr A. Koroli and the librarian at the National and Kapodistrian University of Athens, Mrs A. Frantzi, who helped me in assembling the bibliography.

Carey, C. (2014), 'Μετατοπίσεις των ορίων ανάμεσα στο δημόσιο και το ιδιωτικό στους Αττικούς ρήτορες', in: L. Athanassaki/T. Nikolaidis/D. Spatharas (eds.), *Ιδιωτικός Βίος και Δημόσιος Λόγος στην Ελληνική Αρχαιότητα και στον Διαφωτισμό*, Herakleio, 3–43.

Clarysse, W. (2017), 'Emotions in Greek Private Papyrus Letters', in: *Ancient Society* 47, 63–86.

Cohen, D.J. (1991), *Law, Sexuality, and Society. The Enforcement of Morals in Classical Athens*, Cambridge/New York.

Cohen, E.E. (2014), 'Sexual Abuse and Sexual Rights: Slaves' Erotic Experience at Athens and Rome', in: T.K. Hubbard (ed.), *A Companion to Greek and Roman Sexualities*, Chichester, 184–198.

Cribiore, R. (2001), *Gymnastics of the Mind. Greek Education in Hellenistic and Roman Egypt*, Princeton/Oxford.

Cuvigny, H. (2010), 'Femmes tournantes: Remarques sur la prostitution dans les garnisons romaines du désert de Bérénice', in: *ZPE* 172, 159–166.

Edmonds III, Radcliffe G. (2014), 'Bewitched, Bothered, and Bewildered: Erotic Magic in the Graeco-Roman World', in: T.K. Hubbard, *A Companion to Greek and Roman Sexualities*, Chichester, 282–296.

Faraone, C.A. (1999), *Ancient Greek Love Magic*, Cambridge, MA/London.

Fisher, N. (1995), 'Hybris, Status and Slavery', in: A. Powell (ed.), *The Greek World*, London/New York, 44–84.

Fournet, J.-L. (2006), 'Langues, écritures et culture dans les praesidia', in: H. Cuvigny *et. al.* (eds.), *La route de Myos Hormos. L'armée dans le désert oriental d'Égypte* 1, Caire, 427–500.

Fournet, J.-L. (2013), 'Papyrus, Greco-Roman Period', in: Roger S. Bagnall *et al.* (eds.), *Encyclopedia of Ancient History* IX, 5057–5058.

Gallavotti, C. (1978–1979), '*P. Oxy.* 3070 e un graffito di Stabia', in: *Museum Criticum* 13–14, 363–369.

Gerber, D.E. (1978), 'The Female Breast in Greek Erotic Literature', in: *Arethusa* 11, 203–212.

Goldhill, S. (1995), *Foucault's Virginity. Ancient Erotic Fiction and the History of Sexuality*, Cambridge.

Harker, A. (2008), *Loyalty and Dissidence in Roman Egypt. The Case of the Acta Alexandrinorum*, Cambridge/New York.

Harper, K. (2011), *Slavery in the Late Roman World, AD 275–425*, Cambridge.

Harper, K. (2013), *From Shame to Sin. The Christian Transformation of Sexual Morality in Late Antiquity*, Cambridge, MA/London.

Harris, W.V. (1989), *Ancient Literacy*, Cambridge, MA/London.

Henderson, J. (1991[2]), *The Maculate Muse. Obscene Language in Attic Comedy*, New York/Oxford.

Hodkinson, O. (2014), 'Epistolography', in: T.K. Hubbard (ed.), *A Companion to Greek and Roman Sexualities*, Chichester, 463–478.

Huebner, S.R. (2007), 'Brother-sister Marriages in Roman Egypt: A Curiosity of Humankind or a Widespread Family Strategy?', in: *Journal of Roman Studies* 97, 21–49.

Huebner, S.R. (2013), *The Family in Roman Egypt. A Comparative Approach to Intergenerational Solidarity and Conflict*, Cambridge.

Hunt, A.S./Edgar, C.C. (1932), *Select Papyri, Volume I: Private Documents*, Cambridge, MA.

Konstan, D. (2003), 'Shame in Ancient Greece', in: *Social Research* 70, 1031–1060.

Koroli, A. (2018), 'Verbal Abuse in Ancient Greek Epistolography. The Case Study of an "Indecent Proposal"', in: *Analecta Papyrologica* 30, 113–135.

Kotsifou, C. (2012), 'Emotions and Papyri: Insights into the Theatre of Human Experience in Antiquity', in: A. Chaniotis (ed.), *Unveiling Emotions. Sources and Methods for the Study of Emotions in the Greek World*, Stuttgart, 39–90.

Kramer, J. (1983), *Glossaria bilinguia in papyris et membranis reperta* I, Bonn.

Llewelyn, S.R. (1994), 'The Conveyance of Letters', in: S.R. Llewelyn (ed.), *New Documents Illustrating Early Christianity* 7, 1–57.

Luiselli, R. (1997), 'Un nuovo manuale di epistolografia di epoca bizantina (P. Berol. inv. 21190). Presentazione e considerazioni preliminari', in: B. Kramer/W. Luppe/H. Maehler (eds.), *Akten des 21. Internationalen Papyrologenkongresses, Berlin 13. 19.8.1995*, Stuttgart/Leipzig, 643–651.

Luiselli, R. (2008), 'Greek Letters on Papyrus First to Eighth Centuries: A Survey', in: *Asiatische Studien/Études Asiatiques* 62, 677–737.

Malherbe, A.J. (1988), *Ancient Epistolary Theorists*, Atlanta.

Mélèze-Modrzejewski, J. (2005), 'Greek Law in the Hellenistic Period: Family and Marriage', in: M. Gagarin/D. Cohen (eds.), *The Cambridge Companion to Ancient Greek Law*, Cambridge/New York, 343–354.

Messeri, G. (2010), 'I papiri di narrativa dal 1893 ad oggi', in: G. Bastianini/A. Casanova (eds.), *I papiri del romanzo antico. Atti del convegno internazionale di studi Firenze, 11–12 Giugno 2009*, Firenze, 3–22.

Montserrat, D. (1996), *Sex and Society in Graeco-Roman Egypt*, London/New York.

Montserrat, D. (1998), 'Experiencing the Male Body in Roman Egypt', in: L. Foxhall/J. Salmon (eds.), *When Men Were Men. Masculinity, Power & Identity in Classical Antiquity*, London/New York, 153–164.

Muir, J.V. (2009), *Life and Letters in the Ancient Greek World*, London/New York.

Musurillo, H. (1961), *Acta Alexandrinorum. De mortibus Alexandriae nobelium fragmenta papyracea Graeca*, Lipsiae.

Naldini, M. (1968), *Il christianesimo in Egitto. Lettere private nei papiri dei secoli II–IV*, Firenze.

Pachoumi, E. (2013), 'The Erotic and Separation Spells of the Magical Papyri and *Defixiones*', in: *GRBS* 53, 294–325.

Parker, H.N. (1992), 'Love's Body Anatomised: The Ancient Erotic Handbooks and the Rhetoric of Sexuality', in: A. Richlin (ed.), *Pornography and Representation in Greece and Rome*, Oxford, 90–111.

Parsons, P.J. (2007), *City of the Sharp-Nosed Fish. Greek Papyri Beneath the Sand Reveal a Long-Lost World*, London.

Perale, M. (2013), 'Philaenis und Aristoteles? Zum Philaenis-Papyrus P. Oxy. 2891', in: P. Mauritsch (ed.), *Aspekte antiker Prostitution*, Graz, 127–135.

Remijsen, S./Clarysse, W. (2008), 'Incest or Adoption? Brother-sister Marriage in Roman Egypt revisited', in: *Journal of Roman Studies* 98, 53–61.

Repath, I. (2013), 'Yours Truly? Letters in Achilles Tatius', in: O. Hodkinson/P.A. Rosenmeyer/E. Bracke (eds.), *Epistolary Narratives in Ancient Greek Literature*, Leiden/Boston, 237–262.

Rosenmeyer, P.A. (2001), *Ancient Epistolary Fictions. The Letter in Greek Literature*, Cambridge.

Rowlandson, J./Takahashi, R. (2009), 'Brother-sister Marriage and Inheritance Strategies in Greco-Roman Egypt', in: *Journal of Roman Studies* 99, 104–139.

Rykwert, J. (2009), '*Privacy in Antiquity*', in: *Social Research* 68, 29–40.

Sarri, A. (2018), *Material Aspects of Letter Writing in the Graeco-Roman World 500 BC - AD 300*, Berlin.

Scholl, R. (2014), 'Slaves and Slavery in the Ptolamaic Period', in: J.G. Keenan/J.G. Manning/
    U. Yiftach-Firanko (eds.), *Law and Legal Practice in Egypt from Alexander to the Arab Con-
    quest. A Selection of Papyrological Sources in Translation, with Introduction and Commen-
    tary*, Cambridge, 446–452.
Skeat, T.C. (1995), 'Was Papyrus Regarded as "Cheap" or "Expensive" in the Ancient World?',
    in: *Aegyptus* 75, 75–93.
Strauss, J.A. (2014), 'Slaves and Slavery in the Roman Period', in: J.G. Keenan/J.G. Manning/
    U. Yiftach-Firanko (eds.), *Law and Legal Practice in Egypt from Alexander to the Arab Con-
    quest. A Selection of Papyrological Sources in Translation, with Introduction and Commen-
    tary*, Cambridge, 452–461.
Tibiletti, G. (1979), *Le lettere private nei papiri greci del III e IV secolo d.C. Tra paganesimo e
    christianesimo*, Milano.
Trapp, M. (2003), *Greek and Latin Letters: An Anthology with Translation*, Cambridge.
Vandorpe, K. (1995) *Breaking the Seal of Secrecy. Sealing-practices in Greco-Roman and Byz-
    antine Egypt Based on Greek, Demotic and Latin Papyrological Evidence*, Leiden.
Vout, C. (2007), *Power and Eroticism in Imperial Rome*, Cambridge.
Whitehorne, J.E.G. (1979), 'Sex and Society in Graeco-Roman Egypt', in: J. Bingen/G. Nachtergael
    (eds.), *Actes du XVe Congrès International de Papyrologie* vol. IV, Bruxelles, 240–246.
Whitmarsh, T. (2018), *Dirty Love. The Genealogy of the Ancient Greek Novel*, Oxford.
Yiftach-Firanko, U. (2003), *Marriage and Marital Arrangements. A History of the Greek Marriage
    Document in Egypt, 4th Century BCE – 4th Century CE*, München.

Stephanos Efthymiadis and Charis Messis

From Plato's *Symposium* to Methodius' and Late Antique Hagiography: "Female" Readings of Male Sexuality

Abstract: Diotima's presence among philosophising men in Plato's *Symposium* finds its Christian parallel in three texts from late antiquity that also treat questions of love and sexuality. The *Symposium* attributed to Methodius of Olympus (third-fourth centuries AD) has ten female interlocutors speak in favour of chastity and virginity. In the *Pseudo-Clementines*, an apocryphal text of the New Testament (first half of the third century), a "woman's voice" presents an apologia for chastity and continence. The same ideas about gender and sexuality prevail in a later text, the Christian Martyrdom of Sts Nereus and Achilles, two eunuchs advocating the rejection of marriage and sexuality. With the appearance of Christianity, a novel use of Diotima's paradigm can be noted in literature: female voices become a powerful instrument in the service of male writers, who dispute established social values and denounce the spread of gendered violence.

The indirect presence and speech of Diotima, mediated by Socrates in Plato's *Symposium*, in a convivial gathering of men philosophising about erotic desire, is the culmination and conclusion of a discussion that is purported to have taken place at the home of a wealthy Athenian, Agathon, in c. 416 BC, and been recorded by Plato some thirty years later.[1] The *Symposium* is not a typical Platonic dialogue since the discussion does not result in a precise conclusion nor does it concern a precise philosophical theory; rather, it sets forth seven discourses affirming different theories about *erōs* (love). The woman from Mantinea introduces Eros as the son of Penia (Poverty) and Poros (Resource), meaning that he is always the companion of want and inclined to scheming; as such, he stands midway between wisdom and ignorance or between human beings and divinity. He gives coherence to the universe, longs for beautiful and good things, and his ultimate goal is immortality. In human terms, immortality is achieved through pregnancy and procreation (206c: ἡ κύησις καὶ ἡ γέννησις). Men who are preg-

---

[1] From the vast secondary literature on the subject see Sheffield 2006; Scott/Welton 2008; Cooksey 2010; Lamascus 2016, with earlier bibliography.

https://doi.org/10.1515/9783110695793-022

nant in the body turn to women or heterosexual intercourse and physical procreation, whereas those who are pregnant in the soul turn to people of the same sex in quest of beauty in souls and virtue. Ascending all the rungs of love's mystical ladder, they ultimately contemplate Beauty itself. This is what Plato calls "loving young boys in the right way" (211b: τὸ ὀρθῶς παιδεραστεῖν), that is the search for the substance of Beauty through contact made in terms of virtue and training the bodies and souls of beautiful people. This sums up the Socratic theory of love as pronounced by Diotima.

The fact that it was Diotima who articulated the Platonic manifesto of love has aroused a great deal of controversy, not so much among the Greek and Byzantine readers of the *Symposium* as among the modern scholars who study it. On the very few occasions when Byzantine authors dealt with this question, they did not dispute the authority of Plato's statements but merely expressed their admiration for the fact that Socrates was not averse to learning wise and useful things from women as well as men. As the fifth-century Christian apologist, Theodoret of Cyrus, puts it: "Socrates the son of Sophroniskos and the best of philosophers did not deem it improper of philosophy to learn something useful from women; the thing is that he did not blush, did not refrain from calling Diotima his teacher, while he frequently liked to spend time with Aspasia".[2] In turn, because she possessed all the male qualifications for teaching, Michael Psellos characterises Dosithea, prophetess and friend of patriarch Michael Kerularios, a new Diotima, Eriphylle, Sappho, Aspasia and Theano.[3] Readers in Greco-Roman antiquity and Byzantium alike undoubtedly regarded Diotima as a historical figure.

Modern scholars have put forward various theories interpreting the presence and authority of Diotima's intervention with ideas about gendered roles, masculinity and femininity, all common concepts in the modern and postmodern Western world. Some of them, treading in the footsteps of Byzantine scholars, defend the historicity of the woman from Mantinea, in whose person they recognise a seeress of antiquity, who led the way in spreading knowledge about love. Conversely, other scholars insist on taking her name and person as fictional and a conceit that enabled Plato to reach a variety of contradictory goals: to speak about love in terms of procreation (a concept strictly linked in antiquity to female identity); appropriate the other (woman) and portray her as a disguised version

---

2 Ἑλληνικῶν θεραπευτικὴ παθημάτων, I.17, in: Canivet 2000, 107 (our translation). On the reception of Socrates and Socratism in Early Christianity and Byzantium see Franek 2016; and Trizio 2019.

3 Psellos, *Accusation of patriarch Michael Kerularios*, in Dennis 1994, Or. 1, vv. 1113–1114 and 1147–1154. On this reference see Papaioannou 2013, 218–219.

of man; to conjure up a different idea of masculinity, that of man as a creator and inventor in the matter of love as opposed to a mere pleasure seeker.[4]

Leaving aside this unending and potentially endless discussion, it will suffice here to state that the history of different interpretations of Diotima's presence in the *Symposium* is ultimately the history of certain ideas about sex and gender that are still prevalent among scholars today. Our aim in this chapter is to look at the question of the identity of Diotima and her role in the Platonic narrative through an analysis, on the one hand, of a Christian *Symposium*, that was written, in all likelihood, in the second half of the third century, and, on the other, of two texts about saints (Pseudo-Clementines, *Passio Nerei et Achillei*) which are of a later date and manipulate the female voice on the question of love and its social and spiritual effects.

1 Methodius' *Symposium*

Methodius (d. 311 or 312 AD) is an author of the Roman imperial era about whom very little is known.[5] Choosing to make women the sole discussants in his *Symposium*, which includes a conversation on a topic that touches on erotic desire, is both a literary risk and a programmatic statement. It is a risk because the exclusive presence of women in a philosophical dialogue was almost a *hapax*, a real novelty in Greek and Byzantine literature alike. In his *Dialogues between Courtesans* Lucian is likely to have been providing a satirical response to lost philosophical dialogues that featured women as the main interlocutors on questions of love.[6] The possibility that Methodius knew these dialogues, and that the ten Christian virgins could therefore be regarded as being intended to represent a counterpart to the pagan courtesans, cannot be excluded. Be that as it may, the suggestion that the choice of women for his *Symposium* was also a programmatic statement about the sexual mores of a new society will be addressed in the following lines.

---

4 On the variety of interpretations of Diotima's hidden identity, represented by a vast bibliography, see selectively: Neumann 1965; Halperin 1990; Sier 1997; Rowe 1998; Moisan 2005; Evans 2006; Keime 2014; Nye 2015. On the far-fetched idea of a gay slang used by Plato see Plass 1978.
5 On Methodius and his literary *oeuvre* see Musurillo/Debidour 1963, 9–11; Patterson 1997; and the collective volume by Bracht 2017.
6 See Fountoulakis in this volume.

In his *Symposium* Methodius presents a meeting between ten virgins and their discussion on questions of love and sexuality.[7] Marcella and Theophila, the first two female interlocutors, raise the issue of the propagation of the human species and childbearing by making opposing statements. When the former advances the eschatological proposition that the human race is exempt from the need to multiply, the latter retorts that God has blessed childbearing. The other discussants bring up different subjects, such as chastity and virginity, an interpretation of the *Song of the Songs*, the soul's return to God or an imaginary representation of the Church as a female element corresponding to the male godhead in terms of love. According to the text's editor H. Musurillo, apart from being a paean to chastity and a kind of *summa theologiae*, the *Symposium* must be seen as "an introduction to the Asian technique of allegorical exegesis, thereby becoming a practical guide to psychology, prayer, asceticism and mysticism".[8] Above all, however, it is a manifesto for the Christian way of perceiving and interpreting erotic desire.

Methodius no doubt knew and imitated Plato's *Symposium*; he parodied it in several respects[9] and replaced the notion of Platonic love with what he by and large claims to be its equivalent: Christian virginity.[10] Platonic love and Christian virginity reside in the body and its commitments but, as aspects of the soul, they can be autonomous, resulting in a quest for what is beautiful, perfect and divine. By virtue of the Christian discourse, virginity becomes the means to achieve the Platonic ascension of the soul.

There are many points of convergence and divergence between the two *Symposia*, yet, for reasons of brevity, we shall concentrate on only a few of them. In contrast to the male-dominated world of classical Athens, Methodius put the women of the Later Roman Empire centre stage, in a dimension that, as will be argued, can only be idealised. If in Plato's *Symposium* it is the seeress Diotima who intervenes as a catalyst in a discussion among men about love, in the women's discourse in Methodius' *Symposium* it is Solomon who scatters his verses from the *Song of the Songs* throughout the narrative and chiefly Jesus, as the ideal bridegroom, who is introduced as *Archiparthenos* (Supreme Virgin) and

---

7 On this text and its message see, inter alia, Brown 1988, 183–188; Edwards 2015, 58–60; Fowler 2017; LaValle Norman 2019.

8 Musurillo/Debidour 1963, 13.

9 See introduction, in Musurillo/Debidour, 23–25 and *passim*. Also, König 2008, 102–106, who considers this text "a compendium of Christian views on the sympotic subject of desire" (p. 103).

10 Cf. Dupont 2002, 87, with reference to the transition from pagan banquet to *agapē*, the Christian communal meal.

whom their speeches and endeavours target.[11] This oppositional symmetry that reflects men and women juxtaposes two clashing perceptions of the moral universe. This clash is most clearly delineated in the sections of the two works that deal with what can be termed "the archeology of erotic desire and behaviour". To be more specific, in the Myth of Aristophanes we learn of three protohumans who were cut in two because of their arrogance; ever since this separation, they have been hopelessly longing for their other halves, be it men sought by men, women sought by women, or the androgynous seeking for the opposite sex they are missing.[12] The direction is regressive in that it descends from the golden age of unity to a broken and scattered world.

In opposition to this myth Methodius presents a progressive history of human evolution: he does not pick up the thread of this evolution from the mythical moment of creation but from the time of man's fall, which is for him the real starting point of human history.[13] The evolutionary stages correspond to four different states of sexual conduct: a. incest; b. exogamy-polygamy-erotic disorder; c. monogamy-continence; and d. virginity.[14] Let us turn first to Marcella, the first of the ten virgins, and hear what she has to say, *inter alia*, in praise of virginity in *Discourse I*:

> It was indeed a most extraordinary disposition that the plant of virginity was sent down to mankind from heaven. Hence too, it was not revealed to the first generations: for in those days there were but few men, and it was necessary that their numbers be increased and brought to perfection. Hence men of old did not bring any disgrace upon themselves if they married their own sisters — until the Law came and separated them, forbidding and denouncing as sinful what had previously been thought to be virtuous, and calling him cursed who should uncover the nakedness of his sister. In such wise did God in His goodness bring assistance to the human race in due season as do fathers to their children... But when later it [the world] had become populated from end-to-end overflowing with countless numbers, God did not suffer mankind to continue in its old ways any longer. He took thought how men might make progress and advance further on the road to heaven, until at last they might be perfect by attaining the most sublime goal of all, the science (τὸ μάθημα) of virginity. To begin with, they were to advance from brother-sister unions to marriage with wives from other families. Then they were to give up practising, like brute beasts, multiple marriages (as though men were born merely for intercourse!). The next step was to take them from adultery; and the next, to advance them to continence, and from continence to

---

11 Brown-Hughes 2016, 60–66; and Brown-Hughes 2017.
12 Plato, *Symposium* 189c–193d.
13 For different perceptions of time, see *Le Temps chrétien* 1984; and Saradi/Dellaporta/Kollyropoulou 2018.
14 This fourfold division was very common in Byzantium; see, e.g., Photius, *Letters*, I, 1046–1050, in: Laourdas/Westerink 1983, 34.

> virginity, in which state they train themselves to despise the flesh, and come to anchor un-
> afraid in the peaceful haven of immortality.[15]

This long passage is a narration that aims to explain the development of human mores and remove the obvious contradictions between human physiology and morality. Humanity subject to its physiology is an early stage to be replaced by a humanity defined by morality. In the age of Methodius, humanity was perceived to be in a state of flux, oscillating between a past that had already come full circle and a future in the making. To his mind, the author of the Christian *Symposium* lived at a critical moment in history. In Methodius' view, human evolution follows the path that God himself has laid down. Common human beings represent an acceptable, transitional stage, which leads onto the path to the formation of a "new" human being, as defined by Christianity. To attribute a psychological background to desire and not to consider it simply a mechanism of nature is a higher stage on the path towards deification.

But the superior people, who professed virginity, were far from being a majority in society at the time when Methodius wrote the *Symposium*. The construction of a new human identity was naturally a painful process, requiring much introspection in order to deconstruct someone's social face, transform them into an individual and recreate him or her as a new person in Christ. At the time when Methodius was trying to imitate Plato's *Symposium*, humanity was struggling to reach the third stage, that of monogamy and continence. After the incarnation of Christ, a rapid transition to the fourth stage, i.e. that of virginity, which at least the select few could pursue, was deemed the necessary course. It is at this point that Methodius' argument coincides with the lesson of Diotima: Platonic love of the good and virginity, its Christian counterpart, are confined to the chosen ones, while marriage and reproduction could be permitted to the many.[16] The discourse of Theophila, which follows Marcella's, is pronounced in defence of marriage and procreation as forms of divine invention:

> If then God is still fashioning human beings, would it not be insolent of us to loathe procre-
> ation, which the Almighty Himself is not ashamed to accomplish with His undefiled
> hands?[17]

---

15 Methodius, *Symposium* I. II, in: Musurillo/Debidour 1963, 56–59; transl. Musurillo, p. 43–45.
16 Cf. Zorzi 2003; and Bracht 2017.
17 Methodius, *Symposium* I I. II, in: Musurillo/Debidour 1963, 70–71; transl. Musurillo, p. 50.

It is worth noting that Theophila's discourse goes one step further by adopting medical terminology to describe sexual intercourse in terms of desire and its fulfilment, reproduction and initiation, thereby linking criteria of physiology with social interpretations of carnal love:

> ...this was perhaps the symbolism of that ecstatic sleep into which God put the first man, that it was to be a type of man's enchantment in love, when in his thirst for children he falls into a trance, lulled to sleep by the pleasures of procreation, in order that a new person, as I have said, might be formed in turn from the material that is drawn from his flesh and bone. For under the simulation of intercourse, the body's harmony –so we are told by those who have consummated the rites of marriage- is greatly disturbed, and all the marrow-like generative part of the blood, which is liquid bone, gathers from all parts of the body, curdled and worked into a foam, and then rushes through the generative organs into the living soil of the woman.[18]

As the one who exclusively acts upon a desire linked with the necessity of procreation, the sower in a fiery state deposits his sperm (all the marrow-like and generative part of the blood) into the receptive female earth, who feels no erotic desire but only a thirst for pregnancy. This is a desire of a different order and quality:

> Those who bring the material of clay are the male sex who, desirous of offspring, are brought to deposit their seed in the woman's channels as provided by nature...[19]

The author then goes one to expatiate on the traditional distinction between the male actor and the female receptor, who respond to different kinds of desire. Commenting on an excerpt from the *Apocalypse* (12.1–6), Methodius wonders, in this instance using Thekla as his mouthpiece:

> From whom then did she not fly except, of course, the Dragon, in order that she, the spiritual Sion, might bring forth her *man child*, that is, a people that would return from its feminine passions and immortality to the unity of the Lord, and would be made strong in spiritual endeavour.[20]

He goes on to explain further below:

> Now I think that the Church is here said to bring forth a *man child* simply because the enlightened spiritually received the features and image and manliness of Christ; the likeness

---

18 Methodius, *Symposium* II. II, in: Musurillo/Debidour 1963, 70–73; transl. Musurillo, p. 49–50.
19 Methodius, *Symposium* II. V, in: Musurillo/Debidour 1963, 80–81; transl. Musurillo, p. 54.
20 Methodios, *Symposium* VIII. VII, in: Musurillo/Debidour 1963, 218–219; transl. Musurillo, p. 113.

of Word is stamped on them and is begotten within them by perfect knowledge and faith, and thus Christ is spiritually begotten in each of one.[21]

Or elsewhere:

And thus it is that the Church is said ever to be forming and bringing forth *a man child*, the Word, in those who are sanctified.[22]

His ideas lie somewhere between Origen and Didymos the Blind (first half of the fourth century) and the efforts of the hermeneutic School of Alexandria to treat gender division as a transcendent category, in which male and female, with their stereotyped physiological characteristics, at the same time reflect secular categorisations and acquire a higher theological significance.[23] Based on the concept of the unified human soul shared by men and women, this theological discourse transforms both the male and the female into qualities and spiritual features; males symbolise energetic and spiritual power, whereas females typify passivity and obedience to the power of speech.[24] Men and women alike are postulated to have a female nature in their relationship with God, the eternal bridegroom of the human soul, but, depending on their spiritual maturity and, without any discrimination in terms of gender, can have access to spiritual masculinity and femininity in their relationships with their fellow human beings. No corporeal gender difference plays a role in this redistribution of power. What assigns a role to each male and female is his/her position in the spiritual hierarchy, regardless of gender. By comparison with women men no doubt were thought to have far better skills to achieve spiritual manliness, which is the ultimate goal of human perfection, but women could not be excluded from this endeavor, if their will was strong enough.[25] Be that as it may, spiritual maturity coincides with ideal masculinity. Symbolic femininity functions as the threshold, the first but imperfect stage in

---

21 Methodius, Symposium VIII. VIII, in: Musurillo/Debidour 1963, 220–221; transl. Musurillo, p. 113.

22 Methodius, Symposium VIII. IX, in: Musurillo/Debidour 1963, 222–223; transl. Musurillo, p. 114.

23 Verna Harrison 1998 makes the distinction between moral and psychological allegories, on the one hand, where gender is used to define different identities, virtues and vices in each human person, male or female, and spiritual allegories, on the other, which use the language of genre in order to describe relations between divine and human persons such as Christ, the Church, God and the human soul. On the perception of femininity and masculinity in Philon and Origen and their Byzantine followers see Cline Horovitz 1979.

24 This perception was expanded on in Aristotle's *De generatione animalium* 775a, 787a etc.

25 On certain aspects of the relationships between men and women in the Orthodox tradition see Wesche 1993; Hopko 1993.

spiritual evolution, limited to simply accepting the divine seed. These Early Christian theologians' vision of a new society in Christ points to an almost exclusively "male" society that nevertheless knows how to incorporate features that are symbolically classified as female. In this theological reasoning, the notion of *eros* undergoes the same semantic transformations.[26] Eros between men and women starts to be treated as a natural function, an inevitable natural need, an impersonal force, a mechanism which links two persons for the sole purpose of reproduction or for controlling the channeling of desire.[27] In a similar vein, the term *eros*, as deployed by Plato in his representation of Diotima, points to a deep and sublime feeling that confines its legitimate usage to the intense love that human beings must demonstrate to God.[28] As John Climacus (of the Ladder), an author of the early seventh century AD, writes:

> Physical love can be a paradigm of the longing (*eros*) for God. There is nothing wrong with using opposites for the purposes of finding examples of virtues.[29]

What is symptomatic for carnal love is identical to divine love, but, being opposite to virtue, carnal love must be transfigured to divine love, must become an eloquent metaphorical form in order to describe the relations with the divinity in terms of human language. Still, according to John Climacus:

> There is nothing wrong about offering human analogies for longing, fear, concern, zeal, service and love of God. Lucky the man who loves and longs for God as a smitten lover does for his beloved… Lucky the man who is as passionately concerned with the virtues of a jealous husband watching over his wife.[30]

Whoever is affected by divine love must likewise feel excited by his/her bodily chastity. Whoever participates in *eros* is obliged, according to Christian teaching, to observe sexual renunciation.

---

26 See Bracht 2017.

27 On different perceptions of physical love in Byzantium see Messis/Nilsson 2018.

28 Averil Cameron 1997, 8–10 treats theological and ascetic literature in terms of a literature about eroticism and ends with the reasonable question "If the concept of love is so universally presented in Byzantine discourse in spiritual terms, as a religious term, what does this mean for the actuality of gender relations in Byzantine society?", concluding that: "the Byzantine psyche … was subjected to heavy restrictions laid upon it by language use, and especially by the near-total reservation of "human" erotic language for the religious sphere".

29 John Climacus, *The Ladder of Divine Ascent*, *Patrologia Graeca* 88, 1024B; transl. Luibhead/Russell, 236. On the idea of divine love in John Climacus see Chryssavgis 1985.

30 John Climacus, *The Ladder*, *Patrologia Graeca* 88, 1156BC. See also pseudo-Macarius, *Homélies*, 3.1.2, in: Desprez 1980, 84; transl. Luibhead/Russell, 287.

If we now compare Plato's *Symposium* with that of Methodius, we will discover that "female discourse" is transmitted by women who have overcome the restrictions of their female nature by means of their virginity or their initiation into the mysteries of apocryphal knowledge; women who, once they were illuminated, took up the male role of distributing spiritual seed to an audience who were at a preliminary stage in their spirituality, that of "femininity". It is now apposite to ask why both Plato and his Christian imitator assigned this role to women, the former to Diotima rather than to Socrates himself, the latter to virgins rather than enlightened theologians. We shall attempt to construct a more specific answer, taking Methodius once again as our starting point.

It has been argued that, by selecting women as his discussants, Methodios was addressing a well-educated female audience that was seeking a new dynamic role in the gradually evolving late Roman society. And there may be some truth in this since, at the time when (i.e. late third century) and in the theological milieu where the work was probably written, such a composition was not likely to have been understood as philosophical legacy, nor as a Christian commentary on Plato's *Symposium* and the then prevalent Neoplatonism. Rather it was understood as an exhortation, a text that prefigured the dynamic that the defence of virginity would acquire in the fourth century and in the writings of a succession of later Christian theologians (Athanasios of Alexandria, Basil of Ankyra, Gregory of Nyssa, John Chrysostom, Ambrosius of Milan, etc.).[31]

There are, however, some aspects of this approach that appear to be problematic. To begin with, in the writings on virginity preserved under the names of Methodius' successors this new perception of the female body and sexuality is not fleshed out by women but by a (male) author claiming his authority. By contrast, in the ideal scenery of Methodius' *Symposium* there is no sign of any male presence. Interestingly, in his other philosophical treatises the author introduces himself under the name of Euboulos; in *Symposium*, he adopts the name Euboulion, the feminine form of Euboulos, and it is Euboulion's curiosity that instigates the reproduction of the dialogue in the narrative.[32] Moreover, in all the exhortative texts that we possess today, such as, for instance, the *Passio* to which we shall refer later, what is most conspicuous is polemic about the oppression of women, a feature absent from Methodius' *Symposium*. Everything in this work points to idealisation. The dialogue is not set in the household of a rich Athenian, but is apparently placed in the garden of Eden: food and wine acquire spiritual

---

31 On the treatises on virginity dating from the same period see Introduction in Musurillo/Grillet 1966.
32 See Patterson 1997, 67.

significance, the actors have no historical existence, some of them are given names of personified qualities (Ἀρετή, Θεοφίλα, Θάλεια, Θεοπάτρα, Θάλλουσα, Ἀγάθη), while, for no obvious reason, others have rather Latin names (Μάρκελλα, Πρόκιλλα, Τυσιανή, Δομνίνα), and only one, Thekla, is likely to refer to an eponymous real-life martyr, a disciple of St Paul.[33] Given the allegorical use of manliness and womanhood to which we have already referred, all these elements make us wonder whether Methodius' ten virgins and all the other female figures that turn up in his account are meant to give new meaning to a conversation among philosophising men: in the *Symposium* female characters become an allegory of fallen man himself, whereas the male exemplifies the perfection which mankind is aiming at, that is, *theōsis*, or deification. The female is present throughout the narrative while the male subject of their discussion, Jesus the bridegroom, is what is sought, and what is achieved only through eros and virginity. This is no doubt a plausible explanation. But, on similar grounds, we could reasonably assume that Plato's decision to make Diotima the mouthpiece for Socratic ideas about love and the even more risky choice of Methodius to engage only women in a discussion about love is both a programmatic declaration and a social manifesto. The world of Athenian men, who experienced the limits of their thoughts by formulating conflicting theories about love, and the world of Roman readers, who experienced the limits of their tolerance and endurance before choosing virginity as a path in life, are merely worlds of established values that remain firm or admit slight readjustments, without breaking with the social status quo. Plato and Methodius, using female voices as carriers of philosophical righteousness, were aiming at an epistemological break. The "speech of women" is *par excellence* a groundbreaking reason for establishing not only a new physical and metaphysical idea of love, but also a new society, open in terms of geographic horizons and gender fluidity.[34] On the one hand, Diotima, the priestess woman from Mantinea, would represent Plato's answer to the Athenian rationalism of the city-state, while, on the other, Methodius' ten virgins correspond to the values of the Greco-Roman world in the years when the Empire was experiencing a crisis. The two writers and their protagonists made use of the same dialectical weaponry envisioning a new ethical, philosophical or social order.

---

33 On Thekla and her hagiographies see Dagron 1978; Davis 2001; Jonhson 2006; Narro 2016.

34 We must make a clear distinction between the perception of women in Plato in general and the figure of Diotima who, being the voice of Socrates, epitomises a symbolic femininity. On Platonic ideas about femininity see in general, Buchan 1999; Taylor 2012.

2 The Pseudo-Clementines (BHG 322–341)

Because they interfere with "female discourse", social considerations receive equal or more attention and emphasis in less ambitious texts that, by definition, have no philosophical pretensions and can be reckoned among the first specimens of Christian hagiography. In fact, there are very few texts that put the voice of women centre stage in the narrative. Two of them will be discussed below. The text by the name of *Pseudo-Clementines* is an apocryphal text of the New Testament the Greek version of which is entitled *Homeliai*, while the Latin one is known as *Recognitiones*; its composition has been placed in the first half of the third century, i.e. by and large the same period as Methodius' *Symposium*. It recounts the travels of a young Roman philosopher named Clement who, once he lost his family, departed for Palestine in search of the "good tidings" he had heard about. There he met St Peter and became one of his most faithful companions and the privileged recipient of his theological discourses prior to the apostle's return to Rome. The text thus combines the theological homilies of St Peter and the personal wanderings of Clement, who gradually finds his family again.[35] Among the episodes included in this text we shall single out the hero's encounter in Rome with Appion, a learned man from Alexandria. The assiduous study of Greek philosophy and the longing to deepen his knowledge of the soul caused Clement some depression and, as a result, he confessed to Appion that he had fallen desperately in love with a married and extremely wise lady. Appion promised to help him seduce the woman and to this end he suggested that she be convinced by means of either flattering words or magic. Having chosen this particular weapon of persuasion, Appion prepared an anonymous letter in which he praised adultery:

> Some people consider so-called adultery an evil act although it is good in all respects; for, this act is done at the behest of Eros and for the fecundity of life. In fact, Eros is the most senior of all gods; without him neither intercourse nor the birth of gods, humans, senseless animals, and other beings is possible; as a matter of fact, we are all instruments of Eros.[36]

In what follows Appion denigrates jealousy by recourse to examples drawn from mythology and he prompts the lady to behave like a goddess, in order to take advantage of the benefits enjoyed by heroes and gods and yield to Clement's love.

---

35 Edition of the Greek text by Rehm/Irmscher 1953; Rehm 1992. On this text see also Rehm 1957; Stecker 1981; Edwards 2010; Pouderon 2012.
36 *Homéliai* V.X, in Rehm/Irmscher 1953, 96.

In turn, Clement carries on playing the fool, promises to send the letter to the lady and prepares an appropriate answer, which he submits to Appion as if it had been written by the lady. In this letter the "lady" refutes Appion's argumentation and puts forward her own definition of love:

> Eros does not identify as a God, as he looks to be, but is a desire prompted by the natural disposition of the animal for the continuance of life in accordance with the providence of the One who has made everything so that no species whatsoever will ever become extinct.[37]

Laws and punishments condemn erotic pleasure if it is not for the purpose of procreation. Whereas pagan gods favoured debauchery, even pederasty, the fear that the Christian God inspires becomes the catalyst transforming marriage into a nucleus of virtue.

In the text's reasoning, a female voice defends the values of the new Christian world and presents an apologia for chastity and continence as opposed to the male voice, which defends the values of the old pagan world, in particular sexual promiscuity. The author and the protagonist in the guise of philosophers like Socrates, Plato and Methodius adopt the voice of women in order to speak of new mores relating to eroticism and sexuality. Not unlike in the examples discussed above, in this discourse human *eros* is transformed into a mechanism of nature, provided by God in order to secure procreation, and channel and control desire. Yet in the case of this hagiographical novel and in contrast to what is happening in the two *Symposia* under discussion, women have no influential presence but serve as a mere pretext, a rhetorical device that animates a conversation held between men in which the protagonist adopts a discourse which befits women to establish his own moral identity.

3 The *Passio Nerei et Achillei* (*BHL* 6058–6059, 6061–6064, 6066, *BHG* 1317)

We shall now discuss another hagiographical text, dated to the second half of the fifth century, in which the female voice of philosophical dialogues is associated with a denunciation of men's oppression of women, a feature that we can identify in all fourth-century treatises on virginity. Since its heroes are presented as disci-

---

37 *Homéliai* V.XXIV, in Rehm/Irmscher 1953, 102.

ples of St Peter, it forms, like St Clement's hagiography, part of the so-called Petrine dossier.[38] The originality of this text lies in the fact that the denunciatory "female voice" is put into the mouths of some eunuchs of the *cubiculum*, that is people who were marginal in terms of social status and were regarded as the products of a process of feminisation.[39] We refer to the *Passio* or *Acta of Nereus and Achilles*, a text that must have enjoyed some popularity already in late antiquity, since it has been preserved both in Latin and in Greek. As has been shown, the *Passio* was first written in Latin, most probably in Rome and was soon translated into Greek;[40] moreover, the story of the two saintly eunuchs, Nereus and Achilles, was included in the *Passio* of other martyrs like, for instance, Caesarius (*BHL* 1514). The text is much more than the title *Passio* denotes, as it can be categorised as belonging to what has been called a "cycle hagiographique",[41] which means that it is miscellaneous in character, incorporating as it does the accounts of the martyrdoms of several loosely connected people. All of them are martyred as a result of their rejection of marriage and sexuality. A central role in the narrative is reserved for Domitilla, niece of the Emperor Domitian (81–96). In fact, it is in this emperor's bedchamber that the two eunuchs are said to have served.

In accordance with this first chronological indication, the events narrated in the *Passio* must be placed in the late first-early second century AD. The second chronological indication concerns the two eunuch chamberlains, Nereus and Achilles, who are introduced as having been baptised by St Peter, that is prior to 64/67, the date of the latter's martyrdom in Rome.[42] In that respect the story of the two eunuchs implies that they were among the first to embrace Christianity, the very first being the eunuch of Candace, queen of the Ethiopians, who, according to the *Acts of the Apostles* (8.27), was baptised by the apostle Philip. The *Passio* thus creates a "historical" impression that gives legitimacy to the transmitted message while revisiting the history of Early Christianity and emphasising the events taking place in Rome, the city where their cult will first take root. It was, in fact, Pope Damasus (366–384) who promoted their veneration as two of Rome's

---

38 Lanéry 2010, 115, 121.

39 On the perception of eunuchs as a special category of "women" found in a considerable number of theological treatises see Messis 2014, 85–95.

40 Edition of the Latin versions in *AASS* Mai III, 6e–13b; presentation and English translation of the Latin version, in Lapidge 2018, 201–227. Edition of the Greek text in: Achelis 1893. On its date and the Latin text's chronological priority see Lanéry 2010, 118–119, who does not exclude a sixth-century dating for the text (p. 123).

41 Boulhol 2003, 159 and Lanéry 2010, 113–114. Lapidge 2018, 201, calls it "a conglomerate *Passio*".

42 For a full summary of the *Passio*, see Lanéry 2010, 114–118.

holy martyrs.[43] After a short preamble, the first scene of the *Passio* sets up a "philosophical dialogue" between Domitilla and the two eunuchs. In response to her expressed desire to marry a young aristocrat and give birth to children, the two eunuchs list the perils of marriage, emphasising the loss of freedom that would await the young noblewoman. In Nereus' speech it is the pattern "virginity equals freedom" versus "marriage equals submission" that is highlighted, e.g.:

> You, who never allowed even your parents to exercise authority over your high station, will allow a strange man to be lord of your body, who will abuse you with a kind of base authority, so that anyone's conversation with you will not pass without the risk or danger of a quarrel: neither your neighbours, nor your nurses, nor your slaves brought up at home, will be friendly to you.[44]

When Nereus is interrupted by Domitilla, who vindicates his line of argument by invoking the example of her parents and the jealousy of her father, Achilles takes over the defence of their thesis. He denounces men's supremacy, men's pride, as he calls it at some point (*virilis audacia/superbia* — ἀνδρικὴ αὐθάδεια/ὑπερηφάνεια),[45] and goes on to describe men's behaviour before and after marriage, a progression from hypocrisy to the revelation of truth. Hypocrisy goes with the seduction that precedes a marriage, whereas truth is the behaviour in the marriage, which can develop in two ways. First, the husband may prove an adulterer, who fornicates with his female servants; this can lead to subverting the social order and hierarchy, or it might sometimes end up in socially inferior people being violent towards their social superiors:

> If they (the husbands) are inclined to be wanton, they love slave-girls, and, scorning their wives and treating them as nothing, they defend (their actions) with an arrogant display of rage; and they punish their wives not only with words but with beatings; and when a hurtful word is spoken by a dutiful matron, he can scarcely bear it, and [his] fists, combined with savage kicks of his feet, are inflicted on her.[46]

Achilles, however, has a point to make about what can happen even if the husband proves good and faithful. He highlights the complications that might be involved in a pregnancy as well as the risks of childbirth by listing all the possible cases of children born either with a disability, physical or mental, or stillborn:

---

43 Fasola et al. 1989³; Sághy 2010, 22; Lapidge 2018, 204–205; Maskarinec 2018, 39, 82.
44 Ch. 3 (Latin text: AASS Mai III, 7C; Greek text: Achelis 1893, 215–222); transl. of Latin text: Lapidge 2018, 211.
45 See ch. 7 (AASS Mai III, 8C; and Achelis, 1893, 520 and 67–68).
46 Ch. 3 (Latin text: AASS Mai III, 7C; Greek text: Achelis, 1893, 31–38); transl. of Latin text: Lapidge 2018, 211.

She will carry unwillingly the weight (of the foetus) conceived in her womb; with this weight she becomes ill, swollen, pallid, scarcely able to walk on her own feet; experiencing boredom with nourishing food she delights in harmful food; sometimes the interior of her nose is inflamed with an abundance of blood, or it grows cold with an excess of mucus; or else she is either restricted by skinniness, or is hampered by her body fat; from all these causes diseases spring up in the recesses of the womb once the foetus has been conceived, as a result of which weak or crippled or lame offspring are usually born. And usually, being placed in their own home, they live apart from the normal way (of life). And not only are these feminine problems seen by the eyes of the (pregnant) women themselves, but they are exposed to the medical expertise of unknown men, such that the body of the foetus (the foetus) which often kills its mother before it is born — is customarily extracted by means of an operation. Such a foetus usually turns out deaf or mute or covered with wounds, or is even born possessed by a demon, so that it is necessary to seek an exorcist even before seeking a nurse.[47]

The diatribe on marriage and the denunciation of male behaviour are followed by a eulogy of virginity now delivered by Nereus, who argues for its theological significance. It is rounded off with Achilles' insistence on its social usefulness in terms of women's emancipation:

I wish not to omit the fact that even here in this world virginity does not lose its nobility, does not fear virile audacity, is not subject to man the corrupter, who pollutes the pure (woman), marks her out, destroys her purity, takes away her freedom; and he violently makes a slave to his sexual desire something made noble by God, and dear to God Himself and all His saints. Thereafter he keeps her locked up within the walls of his home as if in a private prison: he does not allow her to be greeted (by anyone), he forbids her to be seen by her parents, he shuts out from her discussion and conversation, her teachers, nurses, and neighbours, as if they were enemies; nor is she allowed to speak freely with children, since he fears that through them their parents will learn of the injuries which he inflicts on his wife.[48]

This emphatic denunciation of male power is the result of an exasperation expressed by socially oppressed "non-men", that is women and eunuchs, who become vehicles for an ideological novelty and social subversion. It is no accident that, in addressing his interlocutor (or a potential female listener), Achilles never calls her "a woman" but uses the generic term *homo*/ἄνθρωπος.[49] In other words, he does not acknowledge the distinction between genders as an essential identity

---

47 Ch. 4 (Latin text: AASS Mai III, 7D; Greek text: Achelis 1893, 311–331); transl. of Latin text: Lapidge 2018, 212.
48 Ch. 7 (Latin text: AASS Mai III, 8B-C; Greek text: Achelis 1893, 518–564); transl. of Latin text: Lapidge 2018, 213.
49 Ch. 8 (Latin text: AASS Mai III, 8C; Greek text: Achelis 1893, 620).

marker. Early Christians aimed to subvert the social order, not to come to terms with its injustices.

4 Conclusion

From Plato's Diotima to the ten virgins of Methodius, the virtuous woman who rejects Appion's vile proposal and the eunuchs of a Roman princess, from Athenian pederasty and its pedagogical function to Christian virginity and its transcendental objective, from the denunciation of adultery to the praise of continence, from philosophical inquiry and intellectual contemplation to the open social denunciation of male domination, *women*'s voices become a powerful instrument in the service of what were, principally, male writers. The "women" who take part in the philosophical dialogues of antiquity and early Byzantium are in effect rhetorical figures of male discourse. The "female" figure in this kind of discourse, whether Diotima or the Christian virgins of Methodius, always expresses an apocryphal knowledge and promotes a metaphysics of love. In the end, "female" erotic discourse stands for the rejection of the physics of love. By contrast, in narrative prose and especially in hagiography, the voices of women are exploited when the authors want to speak of social pathology, to denounce the spread of gendered violence and to express anxiety about their individual and collective future in terms other than those prevailing in the social paradigm and established values. Of this major issue, which involves authors, texts, behaviours and forms of conduct at the point where society and literature intersect and which deserves a longer and more comprehensive analysis, we have offered only a passing glimpse, the inadequate amount that we can grasp from a multifarious past, chained as we are in a Platonic cave of fixed and long-established ideas.

Bibliography

AASS Maii III: 6e–13b.

Achelis, H. (1893), *Acta ss. Nerei et Achillei. Text und Untersuchung*, Leipzig.

Baer, R. (1970), *Philo's Use of the Categories Male and Female*, Leiden.

BHG = *Bibliotheca Hagiographica Graeca*, ed. F. Halkin, Subsidia Hagiographica 8a, Brussels 1957.

BHL = *Bibliotheca Hagiographica Latina*, ed. Socii Bollandiani, Subsidia Hagiographica 6, Brussels 1898–1901.

Börresen, K.E. (1982), 'L'usage patristique de métaphores féminines dans le discours sur Dieu', in: *Revue théologique de Louvain* 13, 205–220.

Boulhol P. (2003), 'Un "Noël des ardents" à Nicomédie: la Passion d'Indès et Domna (*BHG* 822z), modèle d'attraction du sanctoral par le temporal', in: J.-P. Boyer/G. Dorival (eds.), *La Nativité et le temps de Noël. I. Antiquité et Moyen Âge. Colloque international d'Aix-en-Provence, Maison Méditerranéenne des Sciences de l'Homme, 7-9 décembre 2000*, Aix-en-Provence, 157–176.

Bracht, K. (ed.) (2017), *Methodius of Olympus*, Berlin/Boston.

Bracht, K. (2017), 'Eros as Chastity. Transformation of a Myth in the *Symposium* of Methodius of Olympus', in: Bracht, K. (ed.), *Methodius of Olympus*, Berlin/Boston, 38–62.

Bremmer, J. (ed.) (2010), *The Pseudo-Clementines*, Turnhout.

Broudéhoux, J.P. (1970), *Mariage et famille chez Clément d'Alexandrie*, Théologie Historique 11, Paris.

Brown, P. (1988), *The Body and Society. Men, Women and Sexual Renunciation in Early Christianity*, London/Boston.

Brown-Hughes, A. (2016), 'The Legacy of the Feminine in the Christology of Origen of Alexandria, Methodius of Olympus, and Gregory of Nyssa', in: *VC* 70, 51–76.

Brown-Hughes, A. (2017), 'Agency, Restraint, and Desire. Virginity and Christology in Methodius of Olympus', in: K. Bracht (ed.), *Methodius of Olympus*, Berlin/Boston, 85–102.

Buchan, M. (1999), *Women in Plato's Political Theory*, London.

Cameron, A. (1997), 'Sacred and Profane Love: Thoughts on Byzantine Gender', in: L. James (ed.), *Women, Men and Eunuchs. Gender in Byzantium*, London/New York, 1–23.

Canivet, P. (2000), *Théodoret de Cyr Thérapeutique des maladies helléniques, tome I (livres I-VI)*, SC 57/1, Paris.

Carter, R. (2003), 'The Image of God in Man and Woman according to Severian of Gabala and the Antiochene Tradition', in: *Orientalia Christiana Periodica* 69, 163–178.

Chryssavgis, J. (1985), 'The notion of 'divine eros' in the Ladder of St. John Climacus', in: *St. Vladimir's Theological Quarterly* 29, 191–200.

Cline-Horowitz, M. (1979), 'The Image of God in Man – Is Woman included?', in: *The Harvard Theological Review* 72, 175–206.

Cooksey, T.L. (2010), *Plato's 'Symposium': A Reader's Guide*, London/New York.

Dagron, G. (1978), *Vie et Miracles de sainte Thècle. Texte grec, traduction et commentaire*, Subsidia hagiographica, 62, Brussels.

Davis, S.J. (2001), *The Cult of Saint Thecla, A Tradition of Women's Piety in Late Antiquity*, Oxford.

Dennis, G. (1994), *Michaelis Pselli orationes forenses et acta*, Stuttgart/Leipzig.

Desprez, V. (ed.) (1980), *Pseudo-Macaire, Œuvres spirituelles I*, SC 275, Paris.

Dupont, F. (2002), *Le Plaisir et la loi. Du Banquet de Platon au Satiricon*, Paris.

Edwards, M. (1992), 'The Clementina: A Christian Response to the Pagan Novel', in: *ClQ* 42, 459–474.

Edwards, M. (2015), *Religions of the Constantinian Empire*, Oxford.

Evans, N. (2006), 'Diotima and Demeter as Mystagogues in Plato's Symposium', in: *Hypatia* 21.2, 1–27.

Fasola, U.M. et al. (1989³), *Die Domitilla-Katakombe und die Basilika der Märtyrer Nereus et Achilleus*, Vatican City.

Fowler, R. (2017), 'Σωφροσύνη and Self-Knowledge in Methodius' Symposium', in: A.J. Quiroga Puertas (ed.), *Rhetorical Strategies in Late Antique Literature*, Leiden, 26–43.

Franek, J. (2016), '*Omnibus Omnia*: The Reception of Socrates in Ante-Nicene Christian Literature', in: *Graeco-Latina Brunensia* 21, 31–58.

Halperin, D. (1990), 'Why Is Diotima a Woman?', in: D. Halperin, *100 Years of Homosexuality and Other Essays on Greek Love*, London, 113–151.

Halton, Th. (2013), *Theodoret of Cyrus: A Cure of Pagan Maladies*, New York.

Harrison, V. (1998), 'The Maleness of Christ', in: *St. Vladimir's Theological Quarterly* 42, 111–151.

Hopko, T. (1993), 'God and Gender: Articulating the Orthodox View', in: *St. Vladimir's Theological Quarterly* 37, 141–183.

John Climacus, *The Ladder of Divine Ascent*, in: *Patrologia Graeca* 88, 628C–1208A; English transl.: Luibheid, H./Russell, N. (1982), *John Climacus, The Ladder of Divine Ascent*, London.

Johnson, S.F. (2006), *The Life and Miracles of Thekla: A Literary Study*, Washington, DC.

Keime, C. (2014), 'La fonction de Diotime dans le Banquet de Platon (201d1–212c3) : le dialogue et son double', in: *Etudes Platoniciennes* 11, online publication: https://journals.openedition.org/etudesplatoniciennes/535

König, J. (2008), 'Sympotic Dialogue in the First to Fifth Centuries CE', in: S. Goldhill (ed.), *The End of Dialogue in Antiquity*, Cambridge, 98–113.

Lamascus, L. (2016), *The poverty of Eros in Plato's Symposium*, London/New York.

Lanéry, C. (2010), 'Hagiographie d'Italie (300–550). I. Les Passions latines composées en Italie', in: *Hagiographies V*, ed. G. Philippart, Corpus Christianorum, Turnhout, 15–369.

Laourdas, B./Westerink, L. (eds.) (1983), *Photii patriarchae Constantinopolitani Epistulae et Amphilochia*, vol. I, Leipzig.

Lapidge, M. (2018), *The Roman Martyrs. Introduction, Translations, and Commentary*, Oxford.

LaValle Norman, D. (2019), *The Aesthetics of Hope in Late Greek Imperial Literature: Methodius of Olympus' Symposium and the Crisis of the Third Century*, Cambridge.

Maskarinec, M. (2018), *City of Saints. Rebuilding Rome in the Early Middle Ages*, Philadelphia.

Messis, C. (2014), *Les eunuques à Byzance, entre réalité et imaginaire*, Paris.

Messis, C./Nilsson, I. (2018), 'Eros as Passion, Affection and Nature: Gendered Perceptions of Erotic Emotion in Byzantium', in: St. Constantinou/M. Mayer (eds.), *Emotions and Gender in Byzantine Culture*, Palgrave/Macmillan, Cham, 159–190.

Moisan, F. (2005), 'L'étrangère de Mantinée', in: *Analyse Freudienne Presse* 12, 167–177.

Musurillo, H./Debidour, V.-H. (1963), *Méthode d'Olympe. Le Banquet*, SC 95, Paris; English transl.: Musurillo, H. (1958), *St. Methodius. The Symposium: A Treatise on Chastity*, Westminster, Md.

Musurillo, H./Grillet, B. (1966), *Jean Chrysostome La virginité*, SC 125, Paris.

Narro, Á. (2016), 'The influence of the Greek novel on the Life and Miracles of Saint Thecla', in: *Byzantinische Zeitschrift* 109, 71–94.

Nautin, P./Doutreleau, L. (ed.) (1976), *Didyme l'Aveugle Sur la Genèse I-II*, SC 233, 244, Paris.

Neumann, H. (1965), 'Diotima's Concept of Love', in: *The American Journal of Philology* 86, 33–59.

Nye, A. (2015), *Socrates and Diotima. Sexuality, Religion, and the Nature of Divinity*, New York.

Papaioannou, S. (2013), *Michael Psellos. Rhetoric and Authorship in Byzantium*, Cambridge.

Patterson, L. (1997), *Methodius of Olympus. Divine Sovereignty, Human Freedom, and Life in Christ*, Washington, DC.

Plass, P. (1978), 'Plato's 'Pregnant' Lover', in: *SO* 53, 47–55.

Pouderon, B. (2012), *La genèse du Roman pseudo-clémentin. Études littéraires et historiques*, Paris/Louvain/Walpole, MA.

Rehm, B./Irmscher, J. (1953), *Die Pseudoklementinen I. Homilien*, GCS, Berlin.

Rehm, B. (1957), 'Clemens Romanus II (Pseudoclementinen)', in: *Reallexikon für Antikeund Christentum*, III, 197–206.

Rehm, B. (1992), *Die Pseudoklementinen II. Homilien*, GCS, Berlin.

Rowe, C. (1999), 'Socrates and Diotima: Eros, Immortality, and Creativity', in: J. Cleary/G. Gurtler (eds.), Proceedings of the Boston Area Colloquium in Ancient Philosophy 15, Leiden, 239–259.

Sághy, M. (2010), 'Martyr Cult and Collective Identity in Fourth-Century Rome', in: A. Marinkovic/ T. Vedriš (eds.), *Identity and Alterity in Hagiography and the Cult of Saints*, Zagreb, 17–35.

Saradi, H./Dellaporta, E./Kollyropoulou, Th. (eds.) (2018), *Όψεις του βυζαντινού χρόνου*, Athens.

Scott, G.A./Welton, W.A. (2008), *Erotic Wisdom. Philosophy and Intermediacy in Plato's Symposium*, New York.

Sheffield, F. (2006), *Plato's Symposium: The Ethics of Desire*, Oxford.

Sier, K. (1997), *Die Rede der Diotima*, Stuttgart/Leipzig.

Strecker, G. (1981), *Das Judenchristentum in den Pseudoklementinen*, Berlin.

Taylor, W. (2012), 'The Role of Women in Plato's Republic', in: R. Kamtekar (ed.), *Virtue and Happiness: Essays in Honour of Julia Annas (= Oxford Studies in Ancient Philosophy)*, Oxford, 75–87.

Temps chrétien (1984), *Le Temps chrétien de la fin de l'Antiquité au Moyen Age (IIIe-XIIIe siècles)*, Paris.

Trizio, M. (2019), 'Socrates in Byzantium', in: C. Moore (ed.), *Brill's Companion to the Reception of Socrates*, Leiden/Boston, 592–615.

Wesche, K.P. (1993), 'Man and Woman in Orthodox Tradition: The Mystery of Gender', in: *St. Vladimir's Theological Quarterly* 37, 213–251.

Zorzi, M.B. (2003), 'La reinterpretazione dell'eros platonico nel "Simposio" di Metodio d'Olimpio', in: *Adamantius* 9, 102–127.

Notes on Editors and Contributors

Bartłomiej Bednarek is a Postdoctoral Fellow at the Institute of History, University of Warsaw.

Kyriakos Demetriou is Professor of Political Science at the University of Cyprus.

Stephanos Efthymiadis is Professor of Byzantine Studies at the Open University of Cyprus.

Gabriel Evangelou is a Postdoctoral Fellow in Classics at the University of Cyprus.

Andreas Fountoulakis is Associate Professor of Greek Literature and Drama and Director of the Drama and Visual Arts Laboratory of the University of Crete.

Rosalia Hatzilambrou is Assistant Professor of Ancient Greek Literature at the National and Kapodistrian University of Athens.

Regina Höschele is Associate Professor of Classics at the University of Toronto.

Thomas K. Hubbard is the James R. Dougherty, Jr. Centennial Professor of Classics at the University of Texas at Austin.

Dimitrios Kanellakis is Doctor of Philosophy at the University of Oxford.

George Kazantzidis is Assistant Professor of Ancient Greek Literature at the University of the Patras.

Ioannis M. Konstantakos is Professor of Ancient Greek Literature at the National and Kapodistrian University of Athens.

Aikaterini Koroli is Assistant Professor of Ancient Greek Literature at the National and Kapodistrian University of Athens.

José Malheiro Magalhães is Doctor of Philosophy at the University of Roehampton.

Nikos Manousakis is a Researcher at the Research Centre for Greek and Latin Literature of the Academy of Athens.

Charis Messis is Tutor and Researcher at the National and Kapodistrian University of Athens.

Jeremy McInerney is Professor of Classical Studies at the University of Pennsylvania, and chair of the Graduate Group in Ancient History.

Charilaos N. Michalopoulos is Assistant Professor of Latin at the Department of Greek Philology of the Democritus University of Thrace.

Amphilochios Papathomas is Professor of Ancient Greek Literature and Papyrology at the National and Kapodistrian University of Athens.

Catalina Popescu is Lecturer in Classics at the University of Bucharest.

Andreas Serafim is a Researcher at the Research Centre for Greek and Latin Literature of the Academy of Athens.

Manolis Spanakis is a Postdoctoral Fellow in Classics at the University of Crete.

Emma Stafford is Professor of Greek Culture at the University of Leeds.

Chiara Thumiger is a Research Fellow at the Cluster of Excellence Roots at Kiel University.

Index Locorum

https://doi.org/10.1515/9783110695793-024

General Index

https://doi.org/10.1515/9783110695793-025